BLACK DIAMOND QUEENS

REFIGURING AMERICAN MUSIC

A series edited by Ronald Radano, Josh Kun, and Nina Sun Eidsheim

BLACK DIAMOND QUEENS

African American Women and Rock and Roll / **MAUREEN MAHON**

DUKE UNIVERSITY PRESS · DURHAM AND LONDON · 2020

Designed by Matthew Tauch
Typeset in Minion Pro by Westchester Publishing Services

Library of Congress Cataloging-in-Publication Data
Names: Mahon, Maureen, author.
Title: Black diamond queens : African American women and
rock and roll / Maureen Mahon.
Other titles: Refiguring American music.
Description: Durham : Duke University Press, 2020. | Series:
Refiguring american music | Includes bibliographical references
and index.
Identifiers: LCCN 2020014043 (print) | LCCN 2020014044
(ebook) | ISBN 9781478010197 (hardcover) | ISBN 9781478011224
(paperback) | ISBN 9781478012771 (ebook)
Subjects: LCSH: African American women rock musicians—
United States—History—20th century. | Rock music—Social
aspects. | Music and race.
Classification: LCC ML3534.3 .M346 2020 (print) | LCC ML3534.3
(ebook) | DDC 782.421660820973—dc23
LC record available at https://lccn.loc.gov/2020014043
LC ebook record available at https://lccn.loc.gov/2020014044

Cover art: Tina Turner at the hungry i, San Francisco,
October 1967. © Baron Wolman.

For Brian and Callie,

With love and gratitude

CONTENTS

ix   *Illustrations*

xi   *Acknowledgments*

1   Introduction

29   **ONE** Rocking and Rolling with Big Mama Thornton

52   **TWO** LaVern Baker, the Incredible Disappearing Queen of Rock and Roll

76   **THREE** Remembering the Shirelles

105   **FOUR** Call and Response

141   **FIVE** Negotiating "Brown Sugar"

182   **SIX** The Revolutionary Sisterhood of Labelle

213   **SEVEN** The Fearless Funk of Betty Davis

240   **EIGHT** Tina Turner's Turn to Rock

273   Epilogue

285   *Notes*

349   *Bibliography*

375   *Index*

ILLUSTRATIONS

FIGURE 1.1   Big Mama Thornton in San Francisco, 1968   34

FIGURE 2.1   LaVern Baker, publicity photo, 1950s   68

FIGURE 2.2   LaVern Baker in concert at the Lake Glen Country Club, Akron, Ohio, 1950s   70

FIGURE 3.1   The Shirelles, minus the wigs and matching outfits, early 1960s   83

FIGURE 3.2   The Shirelles, publicity photo, 1958   91

FIGURE 4.1   The Blossoms on *Shindig!,* 1965   113

FIGURE 4.2   Merry Clayton in concert at the Bitter End, New York City, 1971   122

FIGURE 4.3   Humble Pie and the Blackberries, publicity photo, early 1970s   125

FIGURE 5.1   Devon Wilson in the June 1970 issue of *Rags*   155

FIGURE 5.2   Marsha Hunt on stage at the 1969 Isle of Wight Festival   168

FIGURE 5.3   Claudia Lennear in *Rolling Stone*, April 1973   175

FIGURE 6.1   Patti LaBelle and the Bluebelles, publicity photo, mid-1960s   186

FIGURE 6.2   Labelle in concert in New York, 1974   196

FIGURE 7.1   Betty Davis, 1970   215

FIGURE 7.2   Betty Davis in concert, 1975   225

FIGURE 8.1   Tina Turner at the hungry i, San Francisco,
October 1967   242

FIGURE 8.2   Ike and Tina Turner with Phil Spector at Gold Star
Studios, 1966   249

FIGURE 8.3   Tina Turner at the Beverly Theatre in Beverly Hills,
California, 1984   266

FIGURE E.1   Brittany Howard of the Alabama Shakes in
concert, 2014   278

ACKNOWLEDGMENTS

The music of the women I discuss in *Black Diamond Queens* and stories about their lives have moved and inspired me over the years of working on this book. Predictably, the project of tracing their creative journeys led me on a journey of my own, one I have taken with the support of institutions, colleagues, friends, and loved ones.

A 2013–14 National Endowment for the Humanities Fellowship and New York University faculty research funding supported the research and writing of this book. A subvention from the Claire and Barry Brook Endowment of the American Musicological Society, funded in part by the National Endowment for the Humanities and the Andrew W. Mellon Foundation, and an NYU Center for the Humanities Book Subvention Grant provided funding that offset expenses associated with publication costs. I am very grateful for this assistance. Portia Maultsby, Guthrie Ramsey, and Mellonee Burnim were early advocates for this project. I thank them for the advice and suggestions they shared when I was starting my research and for writing letters of support for my grant applications.

An earlier version of chapter 1 and material in the epilogue appeared in a different form as "Listening for Willie Mae 'Big Mama' Thornton's Voice: The Sound of Race and Gender Transgressions in Rock and Roll," *Women and Music: A Journal of Gender and Culture* 15 (2011): 1–17. An earlier version of chapter 7 appeared in a different form as "They Say She's Different: Race, Gender, and Genre and the Liberated Black Femininity of Betty Davis," *Journal of Popular Music Studies* 23 no. 2 (June 2011): 146–65. I thank the editorial teams of Suzanne Cusick and Emily Wilbourne at WAM and Gus Stadler and Karen Tongson at JPMS as well as all of the peer reviewers for their help with early iterations of this project.

Throughout the research and writing process my editor Ken Wissoker has been an invaluable interlocutor. I am grateful to him for sharing his intellectual acumen and for his firm commitment to my work. I also thank the peer reviewers for comments and queries that helped me make this a better book.

Finally, thanks to Nina Foster, Susan Albury, and the staff at Duke University Press for production assistance.

For responding with enthusiasm to this project and giving me permission to include their work in this book, I thank photographers Nancy Clendaniel, Bob Gruen, Janet Macoska, Neal Preston, and Baron Wolman. I am also grateful to Helen Ashford at Cache Agency for her assistance in locating and providing photographs. For putting me in touch with the artists, facilitating interviews, and sharing their knowledge, I thank Rudy Calvo, the late Dennis Garvey, Linda Garvey, David Henderson, Juma Sultan, Matt Sullivan, Oliver Wang, and Chris Estey. For sharing memories about the artists and events I discuss in this book, I thank Terry DeRouen, Nat Dove, Kat Dyson, Sherman Fleming, Michael Hill, Emmaretta Marks, Jimmy McCracklin, James Moore, and Chris Strachwitz. I am deeply grateful to Merry Clayton, Sarah Dash, Betty Davis, Gloria Jones, and Beverly Lee for taking time to speak to me about their experiences in rock and roll. I thank them for trusting me with their stories.

Thanks to Nicol Hammond and Siv Lie for careful and exhaustive research assistance and to David A. Johnson, Executive Director of the Alabama Music Hall of Fame; Jessica Lacher-Feldman, Curator of Rare Books and Special Collections at the University of Alabama Library; the staff at the Institute of Jazz Studies at Rutgers University; the staff at the New York Public Library for the Performing Arts; the staff at the Schomburg Center for Research in Black Culture; and Alice Echols and Elijah Wald for help identifying sources.

For inviting me to present my work, providing a warm welcome, and offering help with my research long after my visit, I thank members of the Rock and Roll Hall of Fame staff, especially Jason Hanley, Kathryn Metz, Lauren Onkey, and Ivan Sheehan. Special thanks to Lauren for making it possible for me to meet and conduct a public conversation with Gloria Jones at the Rock Hall in 2012. Thanks also to the Rock and Roll Hall of Fame Library and Archives staff, especially Jennie Thomas and Andy Leach, for research assistance and help locating photos.

I am grateful to my colleagues in the fields of ethnomusicology, musicology, and beyond who have invited me to present my work in public venues. For including me on conference panels, I thank Harry Berger, Mark Burford, Mellonee Burnim, Danny Fisher, Andy Flory, Kristina Jacobson, Meryl Krieger, Kimberly Marshall, Portia Maultsby, Andy McGraw, Honey Meconi, Elliott Powell, Ann Powers, Tim Rice, Jeremy Wallach, Eric Weisbard, and Emily Wilbourne. For inviting me to present lectures at their campuses and for hosting my visits, I thank Marié Abe and Dan Singer at Boston University; Melody Chapin, Michael Deck, Byrd McDaniel, and Dana Gooley at Brown University; Anne Rasmussen, Lauron Kehrer, and Gayle Murchison at the College of William and Mary; Lee Tyson, Judith Peraino, and Catherine Appert at Cornell University; Lei Ouyang Bryant, Gordon Thompson, and Judy Tsou at Skidmore College; Ben Tausig at Stony Brook University; Theo Cateforis at Syracuse University; Nicholas Mathew and Jocelyne Guilbault at UC-Berkeley; Charles Hiroshi Garrett and Mark Clague at the University of Michigan, Ann Arbor; Guthrie Ramsey and Tim Rommen at the University of Pennsylvania; John Covach at the University of Rochester; Patrick Burke and Paige McGinley at the University of Washington, St. Louis; Alexander Rozin and Julian Onderdonk at West Chester University; and Rebekah Ahrendt, Anna Zayaruznaya, and Stefanie Acevedo at Yale University. The opportunity to try out ideas, respond to questions, and receive feedback helped me to sharpen my thinking and improve this manuscript.

I am privileged to work in a fun and stimulating environment. I thank the following faculty and staff of the New York University Department of Music (FAS) for their warm colleagueship, intellectual generosity, and support of my research: Mike Beckerman, Brigid Cohen, Suzanne Cusick, Christine Dang, Martin Daughtry, Elizabeth Hoffman, Deborah Kapchan, Lou Karchin, Yi-Wen Lai-Tremewan, Pauline Lum, Natasha Martinez, Mick Moloney, Jaime Oliver, Margaret Panofsky, David Samuels, Yunior Terry, Alice Teyssier, Kent Underwood, Freeman Williams, and Lawren Young. Special thanks to Mike and David for providing course releases at crucial times, to Suzanne for helping me work through and articulate my ideas at an early stage in this project, and to Martin for commenting on an early draft of my book proposal. Thanks also to the graduate students with whom I have worked over the years; our conversations and exchanges in the seminar room and beyond have been important, energizing resources for me. Finally, I thank my colleagues in NYU's Department of Anthropology, especially Faye Ginsburg, Fred Myers, Bambi Schieffelin, and Rayna Rapp, for their continued support.

I am grateful to work alongside the following scholars whose research has helped me write this book and whose friendship has propelled me over the years: Daphne Brooks, Judith Casselberry, Michelle Habell-Pallán, Eileen Hayes, Alisha Lola Jones, Kyra Gaunt, Matthew Morrison, Sonnet Retman, Gayle Wald, and Richard Yarborough. Special thanks to Judith, Sonnet, and Gayle for reading sections of the manuscript and offering very helpful comments.

For providing impeccable and loving childcare and making it possible for me to leave home on research trips without worrying, I thank Jessica Ayala, Shana Jackson, and Kaegan Sparks.

I owe a huge debt of gratitude to my friends, in Brooklyn and elsewhere, for creating a warm, sustaining community. Thanks to Bob Alotta, Swati Argade, Linda Aro, Lacy Austin, Aisha Bell, Simon Caldwell, Gabri Christa, Marcelle Davies-Lashley, Bridgett Davis, LaRonda Davis, Danielle Downer, Cynthia Edorh, Trevor Exter, Rob Fields, Sherman Fleming, Jared Hassan Foles, Renee Foles, Ruthie Goldberg, Paula Henderson, Neycha Herford, John L. Jackson, Natasha Johnson, Christianne Kapps, Antonio Lauria-Perricelli, Mario Lazzaroni, Wangechi Mutu, Cy Nakpodia, Jairus "Jazz" Odums, Chris Pfaff, Alec Pollack, Queen Godis, Tamar-kali, Bill Toles, Toshi Reagon, Martha Redbone, Vernon Reid, Danny Simmons, Ginny Suss, the late Connie Sutton, Deborah Thomas, Aaron Whitby, and Verushka Wray.

My family has provided limitless support for my endeavors—academic and otherwise. Heartfelt thanks to the late Robert Mahon, Diane Mahon Moody, Lyn Mahon, Alicia Mahon, Shervon Moody Anderson, Mark Anderson, Warren Goolsby, Jordyn Goolsby, the late Florence and Charles Tate, Greg Tate, Geri Augusto, Chinara Tate, and Nile Wood. My mother Mary Mahon (1929–2018) gave me too many gifts to list. For the purposes of these pages, I thank her for her belief that I could accomplish whatever I set out to do and for her unstinting, unconditional love.

My husband Brian Tate and our daughter Callie made the solitary work of writing much less onerous. Their love, understanding, insight, and humor sustain and inspire me.

Callie has been the most understanding of daughters, allowing me time and space to do my work. From the beginning, Brian cared about this project and talked with me for countless hours about its ins and outs. He has suggested writing strategies, helped with editing, and read every word of the manuscript. His loving partnership made this book possible. Brian and Callie are extraordinary people, and I am fortunate to have them in my life. I dedicate this book to them both.

Introduction

Santi White threw down the gauntlet shortly after the 2008 release of her first full-length recording under her moniker Santogold.[1] Some music critics were labeling her as an R&B singer, and she was outraged with what she viewed as inaccurate classification of her music. "It's racist," the singer and songwriter told a reporter. "It's totally racist. Everyone is just so shocked that I don't like R&B. Why does R&B keep coming into my interviews? It's pissing me off. I didn't grow up as a big fan of R&B, and, like, what is the big shocker? It's stupid. In the beginning I thought that was funny. I'm an 'MC,' I'm a 'soul singer,' I'm a 'dance hybrid artist.'"[2] The songs on *Santogold* feature sly and catchy meldings of ska, reggae, and rock rhythms; there are dub echoes and danceable synthesizer effects all with White's laid-back, talk-singing vocals riding over the top. White and her producers had created musical settings that drew on everything from eighties new wave to Jamaican dancehall to electronica, but it was a stretch to hear the album as contemporary R&B. White, an African American woman, argued that commentators assigned her to the genre because of her race, while ignoring her actual sound, and she was not happy about it.

Placing *Santogold* into one of the music genre categories set aside for African American musicians did not make musical sense, but it was part of a long tradition of prioritizing racial identity over musical sound when marketing pop music. Genre categories simplify things for music business professionals, whether at record labels, music venues, or media outlets; they help identify an artist's potential audience and determine how to promote their music. As such, genre labels have a powerful effect on the shape and direction of an artist's career. Concerned with what she viewed as the misrepresentation of her creative work, White resisted the flawed categorization, pointing out that she was being grouped into a style of music for which she had no affinity and to which her genre-blending music was only tenuously connected. Santi White is not the first African American woman to struggle with issues of music genre and professional career. In fact, she is one in a long line of artistically adventurous African American women whose sounds have shaped the musical and cultural terrain, but whose race and gender identities have made their impact difficult to hear and acknowledge. This has been especially true for women participating in the unruly genre of rock and roll. Since the 1950s, when they were among the rhythm and blues artists who created the music that took the name *rock and roll*, African American women have made pivotal contributions to the form as it underwent decades of stylistic and cultural changes. Stories of their involvement in rock and roll, however, have been marginal to the dominant narrative, and, like Santi White, they have been pressed into genres deemed appropriate for African American women or not talked about at all. *Black Diamond Queens: African American Women and Rock and Roll* discusses the careers of a cross-section of black women vocalists, revealing the simultaneous conditions of audibility and inaudibility, of presence and absence, that characterize their careers in order to amplify their musical, creative, and critical voices.

It may seem unusual to foreground black women in a discussion of a genre associated with white youth rebellion, the formation of male identities, and a fair amount of misogyny. Unlike the blues, jazz, or soul, rock and roll is a counterintuitive place to look for African American women. It is precisely this apparent disconnect that compels me. Ideas about what rock and roll music is and who is qualified to perform it—in short, the everyday workings of genre classification—have marginalized African American women in discussions of the history of the genre. This is troubling since black women have influenced the sound, feel, and image of the music from its beginnings. Still, their involvement is often overlooked as assumptions about music genre and social identity combine to create a narrative that is mostly male and predominantly white. In most mainstream histories of rock and roll, black women are mentioned only briefly, if at all, and the particularities of their music and experiences are rarely considered. *Black Diamond Queens* moves black women to the center of the discussion and listens to the voices of African American women in rock and roll from 1953, when blues singer Big Mama Thornton topped the R&B charts with her hit "Hound Dog," to 1984, when the solo career of veteran performer Tina Turner took flight, and she won recognition as the "Queen of Rock and Roll." I examine the race, gender, and genre challenges that Thornton, Turner, and a host of others encountered, and explore the interracial and cross-gender collaborations in which they engaged in order to uncover a hidden history of African American women in rock and roll.

African American Women's Voices
in Rock and Roll

Black Diamond Queens is related to recent work by scholars who reframe music history and criticism to include discussion of professional women musicians and the ways gender and power shaped their experiences. Situating women's music-making in social, historical, and cultural contexts, these authors analyze "how musical activity can be reread through gender and how music likewise helps define what it means to be male or female in a given time or place."[3] Among this work is research that brings black feminist perspectives to bear on contemporary popular music, highlighting the presence and influence of black women in a range of music genres. These studies examine critical discourses embedded in black women's musical practices and consider the impact of race, gender, and class on the creation and circulation of their music.[4] While in many cases their research recovers lost or underacknowledged contributions, these scholars are also concerned with examining the ways power relations, genre categorization, and academic discourses have affected both the professional fortunes and scholarly representation of black women musicians.

The women I discuss in this book have had their singing voices recorded and circulated; yet in spite of their indisputable contributions to American popular music, they have not always been carefully listened to, and they are not always remembered. One reason it has been difficult to hear these "black female voices buried at the bottom of the rock and roll archive," as cultural critic Daphne Brooks puts it, is because vocalists have been undervalued in rock criticism, which prioritizes instrumentalists, songwriters, and producers as the significant creative forces in the field.[5] Possibly because of assumptions that singing is a natural practice, the vocal part of rock music-making receives less sustained attention. In a study that recuperates the artistic and cultural significance of girl group music, a form centered on female vocals, musicologist Jacqueline Warwick critiques the perspective that "belittles the work of singers who breathe life into songs" and adheres to "a code of musical values that regards singing and dancing as activities that 'come naturally' to females and thus deserve scant respect."[6] This viewpoint, which valorizes the work of artists who write the material they perform as "unmediated expressions of pure feeling," devalues the work of vocalists who do not also play an instrument and who do not write the songs they sing.[7] Warwick notes that according to this aesthetic system, which came into being during the 1960s, "mastery of an instrument became a badge of musical truth, while bringing music out from within the body itself was dismissed as facile and 'inauthentic.'"[8] Consequently, as musicologist Laurie Stras observes, "girl singers tend to get short shrift, professionally and critically."[9]

Commenting on a parallel problem in jazz historiography, ethnomusicologist Travis Jackson observes that women singers do not fare well in historical accounts. He suggests that, "because their primary work seems to be interpreting words rather than demonstrating virtuosity, writers with an instrumental bias have difficulty fitting them into the discussion."[10] This is the case even though their work "is generally as intricate as the work of canonized male instrumentalists and composers."[11] He points out, for example, that jazz singers "transform popular songs through choice of key, pronunciation, tempo, phrasing, register, and timbre," in other words, through the use of technical skill and creative thought.[12] Playing an instrument or writing a song, practices associated with the mind, and singing, a practice associated with the body, map on to Western culture's mind/body binary that is in turn linked to the male/female binary that elevates men's pursuits over those of women. Warwick and Jackson challenge these gendered value systems to highlight the contributions of women vocalists and to account for women's marginalization in music studies. Warwick goes a step further and argues, "Voices are the most important elements of a pop song."[13] Sociologist Simon Frith supports this contention, noting that "Voices, not songs, hold the key to our pop pleasures; musicologists may analyze the art of the Gershwins or Cole Porter, but we hear [vocalists] Bryan Ferry or Peggy Lee."[14] In short, the melody, the arrangement, and the instrumentation are in service to the voice.[15] Popular music has been a primary site for the production and dissemination of both voices and ideas about which types of vocal sounds are appropriate for particular racial, classed, and gendered bodies.[16] To explore the sound and significance of African American women's voices in rock and roll, I focus on three distinct aspects of each performer's voice: her vocal quality; her creative voice revealed through choices of material and her public image; and the critical voice through which she analyzed her experiences.[17] As I listen to African American women's voices in rock and roll, I attend to the racial and gendered ideologies of voice, considering their influence on the ways and whether people are able to participate in the form, and the ways and whether that participation is recognized.

There are numerous women whose stories I could have told in this study. I have chosen to focus on Willie Mae "Big Mama" Thornton, LaVern Baker, Betty Davis, and Tina Turner; the vocal groups the Shirelles and Labelle; background vocalists including Merry Clayton, Venetta Fields, Cissy Houston, Gloria Jones, Claudia Lennear, and Darlene Love; and Marsha Hunt and Devon Wilson, women who were denizens of the 1960s counterculture and friends and lovers of rock musicians. Although personal taste and curiosity drew me to some of my subjects, the primary motivation for my choices was a sense that their particular stories would allow me to both discuss women whose formative involvement in rock and roll has been underplayed and to analyze the ways genre serves as a mechanism for policing race, gender, and sexuality in the production and circulation of popular music. In chapters 1, 2, and 3, I discuss Big Mama Thornton, LaVern Baker, and the Shirelles, respectively, important early rock and roll figures whose sound and professional careers are glossed over in rock and roll histories that hurry to talk about the white artists they worked with or influenced: Thornton is a stepping stone to Elvis Presley and Janis Joplin and songwriters Jerry Leiber and Mike Stoller; Baker, without a clear white acolyte, disappears almost completely; and the Shirelles are connected to the Beatles and songwriters Gerry Goffin and Carole King. I foreground Thornton, Baker, and the Shirelles, discussing the musical trends they launched in the 1950s and early 1960s and considering the workings of power and memory that have submerged their voices. In the wake of Bob Dylan and the Beatles in the 1960s, African Americans were increasingly displaced from the center of rock, but in chapters 4 and 5, I demonstrate that African American women had an ongoing presence in the genre. In chapter 4, a focus on the black women who worked as background vocalists on numerous rock recordings in the late 1960s and early 1970s allows me to discuss the extent to which the vocal labor of African American women propelled rock during what is now called the "classic rock era" through cross-racial, cross-gender exchanges that have been little remarked upon in histories of rock. Chapter 5 turns attention toward the racialized erotic element that underwrote these exchanges and that has shaped rock and roll imagery. I discuss the paths taken by Devon Wilson, Marsha Hunt, and Claudia Lennear, African American women who participated in the rock scene as artists and paramours of rock stars during the late 1960s and early 1970s, and examine the ways they both capitalized on and challenged the stereotypical images of black women's sexuality in their personal and professional pursuits. In chapters 6, 7, and 8, I discuss women who self-consciously worked within the rock idiom in the 1970s and 1980s. The trio Labelle, having formed with an explicit goal of being a female version of the Rolling Stones, operated from a women-centered ethos as they navigated the "black" and "white" sides of the popular music industry. Their challenges and successes, like those of singer and songwriter Betty Davis, discussed in chapter 7, are indicative of the ways race, gender, and genre shape African American women's expression in the field of rock. Davis's play with the sonic palette of rock, blues, and funk, and her frank discussion of sexual desire, were confounding to the marketplace. In notable contrast, Tina Turner found a way into rock in spite of the restrictive rules. In chapter 8, I explain how Turner, after years on the rhythm and blues circuit, recast herself as a rocker through musical choices and personal associations and made a successful crossover to the mainstream of rock.

My hope is that by discussing the rock and roll careers of these African American women—the music they made, the successes they achieved, the challenges they faced—*Black Diamond Queens* will encourage a different kind of engagement with the music. I want to invite readers to listen to rock and roll with an awareness of the presence of African American women, because if we listen to and hear the music in a different way, a way that counters the exclusionary work of racialized music genres, it will be easier to include African American women in the grand narrative of rock and roll. The book's title lifts a lyric from "Steppin in Her I. Miller Shoes," a song Betty Davis wrote in honor of her friend Devon Wilson, a black rock and roll woman who was, she sings, "a black diamond queen," a woman who loved and lived rock and roll. The experiences of Wilson, Davis, and the other women I discuss played out in the cultural terrain of rock and roll, and the race, gender, and genre challenges they encountered are instructive. Obviously, there are many other women whose stories could fit into this narrative, and I recognize that some readers might wish that I had chosen different focal figures. I take this as evidence that there is much more work to be done on the subject of African American women and rock and roll.

Genre Cultures

The women I discuss in *Black Diamond Queens* crossed interpersonal, national, and ideological boundaries as they pursued their careers in music in the post–World War II era. At a time when de jure and de facto segregation conditioned social and professional interactions in the United States, these women participated in significant cross-racial collaborations. They worked with white musicians, songwriters, managers, and producers; toured with white artists; and performed for black and white audiences, enacting the desegregation and integration that civil rights movement activists agitated for during the 1950s and 1960s. All of these women traveled internationally, and in some cases they lived outside of the United States, expanding their music's reach and gaining a respite from the race-based limitations of their homeland. These border crossings were artistically and personally liberating, enabling the women to establish a presence in the mainstream public sphere at a time when black women's voices were rarely heard there. Stereotypes of black women's sonority, intellect, and sexuality shaped their experiences in these interracial, intercultural contexts, sometimes opening doors, sometimes restricting access. These dynamics of race and gender played out in a recording industry organized according to another set of boundaries: genre categories. In the American recording industry, music genres facilitate the marketing and promotion of music, identifying artists and their perceived audiences with particular musical sounds and performance styles. Genre categories and the practices and discourses that maintained them created some of the most significant boundaries that these women confronted. One challenge was that their work combined stylistic impulses and performance practices with what were viewed as separate and distinct music genres. This, coupled with their race and gender identities, made their fit within dominant black or white genres imperfect and caused them to stand betwixt and between genres, either in their historical moment or in retrospect.

Discussing "the power as well as the limiting effect of musical labels," musicologist Guthrie Ramsey has observed that stylistic distinctions "tell us much more than which musical qualities constitute a piece of music. They shed light on what listeners value in sound organization. Categorizing also inherently comments on the nature of power relationships in society at large—it tells us who's in charge and running the show."[18] Popular music studies scholars have demonstrated that these social factors influence the formation of music genre categories and the assignment of artists to them.[19] This cultural approach to music genre recognizes that "genres are identified not only with music, but also with certain cultural values, rituals, practices, territories, traditions, and groups of people."[20] Genre categories do cultural work. They place artists and listeners into and outside of meaningful categories of identity and belonging. Through debates over which artists and musical styles are included in or excluded from a given category, recording industry professionals, critics, artists, and audience members bring pop music genres into existence. Over time and through experimentation, these parties define the sound, lyrical content, artist image, instrumentation, and target audience associated with the genre. Growing as they do out of specific cultural contexts and power relations, music genres are not objective, fixed categories; rather, they are flexible and fluid, expanding, contracting, or changing in relation to cultural shifts and the ways struggles over meaning play out. Genre categories organize the sonic world and shape what listeners hear. In his revisionist history of American popular music, Elijah Wald explains that he chose "to avoid the assumptions of genre histories, the divisions of eighty years of evolving popular styles into discrete categories like ragtime, jazz, swing, R&B, and rock . . . because when I step outside them I hear the music differently and understand things about it that I previously missed."[21] Indeed, if we listen beyond the boundaries of genre, it can be easier to identify lines of collaboration, influence, and connection that genre boundaries obscure.

In contemporary popular music, genre is related to commoditization. It is "a way of defining music in its market or, alternatively, the market in its music."[22] The fundamental reality of pop music is that it is produced and sold according to genre categories rooted in "distinctions made by the music industry" that "reflect both musical history and marketing categories."[23] As my opening example of Santi White shows, decisions about how to assign an artist to a genre can underplay an artist's sonic qualities and overemphasize social identity.[24] Most of the existing studies of popular music genres take into account the central role that race plays in genre categorization in the United States. They recognize that a dichotomous view of black and white underpins genre definitions and that this perspective presents challenges for artists whose musical sounds diverge from those associated with their race. Gender is also a crucial category shaping genre categorization. As Jacqueline Warwick shows in her study of girl group music of the 1960s, a process of making gendered distinctions between masculine, authentic rock and feminine, commercial pop has diminished the creative contributions of women and underplayed the commercial motivations of male performers.[25] One consequence of these conditions is the difficulty women have gaining inclusion in the rock canon. In an article about guitarist, singer, and songwriter Joni Mitchell's struggle to win respect as a rock artist, cultural critic Miles Parks Grier observes that "rock's cultural topography [is] one in which race, gender, and genre have served as regions with unequal cultural and economic capital."[26] While Mitchell's whiteness allowed her to fit into the rock community, her gender limited her access to artistic respect and the capital that accompanied it. Similarly, Sonnet Retman's study of the wide-ranging career of African American singer and songwriter Nona Hendryx shows that her race and gender made it difficult for her to claim an identity as a rocker, even though she had been active in the rock scene for years. Hendryx participated in the kinds of musical experimentation and genre-bending practices that critics lauded in male musicians, but that had the effect of rendering a black woman "inscrutable and therefore subject to erasure."[27] Gendered and racialized assumptions about genre have a profound impact on African American women working in rock and roll; they experience a kind of double jeopardy as they navigate terrain in which the body presumed to be appropriate to the genre is white and male.

Genre Histories

A historical overview of the emergence of rock and roll as a genre offers an example of the confluence of musical and cultural factors that contributes to genre formation, while also providing the historical backdrop against which the women I write about pursued their careers. Reviewing this history draws attention to the fact that "genres are constantly changing—as an effect of what's happening in neighboring genres, as a result of musical contradictions, [and] in response to technological and demographic change."[28] Since the 1920s, when record labels began concerted efforts to sell music to African American audiences, race has played a role in the definition of music genre and the marketing of artists. Recordings made by and for African Americans were marketed as "race records" from the 1920s until 1949, when the term *rhythm and blues* came into use.[29] Meanwhile, working-class white southerners were the target market for hillbilly (later country and western), and middle-class whites were the audience for pop. Rock and roll, a new and fluid category that crossed and blurred sonic and racial boundaries, brought together rhythm and blues, country, and pop music. Significantly, rock and roll drew on African American musical practices rooted in West African aesthetics and the "conceptual framework" that Africans brought with them to the New World.[30] Retained, elaborated, and reworked during the centuries that enslaved Africans and their descendants have lived in the United States, many of "the cultural and aesthetic components that uniquely characterize music-making throughout the African diaspora" are present in rock and roll.[31] Ethnomusicologist Portia

Maultsby explains that among these sonic, performance, and stylistic commitments are an emphasis on rhythmic intensity, percussive approaches to singing, the presence of blue notes and syncopation, the conception of music and movement as a single unit, call-and-response, audience participation, and the understanding that "music-making is a participatory group activity."[32] In the early years of rock and roll, these features differentiated the nascent form from the mainstream of European American music and attracted a multiracial, multiclass, teenage audience.

At first, rock and roll was a new name for rhythm and blues. The term was coined by Alan Freed, a white, Cleveland-based radio disc jockey, who had followed the practice of white American radio personalities such as Bill Gordon in Cleveland, Hunter Hancock in Los Angeles, Dewey Phillips in Memphis, and Hoss Allen in Nashville, who played black rhythm and blues on the radio.[33] Although intended for African American listeners, these programs developed white teen audiences, who became fans of what industry insiders called "the big beat." Freed made his mark by repackaging the black-identified genre with the new label. The music was the same, but the linguistic shift tempered the blackness associated with the term *rhythm and blues* and opened the genre up to white teenagers. America's youth gave themselves over to rock and roll and embraced the infectious rhythms and grooves of Fats Domino, Ruth Brown, LaVern Baker, Little Richard, Chuck Berry, and Bo Diddley. Soon, white artists came on board, performing with "the Negro Sound and Negro Feel," to use the language of Sam Phillips, the producer who first recorded Elvis Presley at his Memphis-based Sun Studios in the mid-1950s. A white band, Bill Haley and His Comets, had the fledgling genre's first number one record with "Rock around the Clock" in 1955, and a year later Presley's career took off with "Hound Dog," his jumped-up version of Big Mama Thornton's 1953 rhythm and blues hit. Rock and roll was an only-in-America hybrid rooted in rhythm and blues, country, blues, pop, and Latin music. Along with the abovementioned musicians, rock and roll performers included white artists such as piano-thumping shouter Jerry Lee Lewis; vocal duo the Everly Brothers; and singer-guitarists Carl Perkins, Eddie Cochran, and Buddy Holly; as well as African American vocal harmony groups such as the Platters, Frankie Lymon and the Teenagers, and the Coasters. Teen consumers drove the record industry, supporting musical miscegenation at the same time that civil rights activists were working to desegregate the nation's institutions. Rock and roll was an arena where integration was taking hold. Black and white acts shared space on the industry music charts and concert stages, appearing together in multi-artist rock and roll shows. In the north they performed before integrated audiences; in the south, black and white concertgoers were separated into different sections of the performance spaces or forced to attend white-only or colored-only shows. The moral panic that surrounded rock and roll in its early years—with media outlets, parent groups, and white citizens' councils portraying rock and roll as an insidious threat to the sanctity of mainstream culture—was a response to white youth embracing an African American cultural form and to that form's growing prominence in a culture accustomed to marginalizing African Americans.

By the early 1960s, the sound of rock and roll was changing. The prominent rhythm was still present, but producers were sweetening the music to make it more palatable to a wider audience. Early in the decade, black vocal artists such as the Drifters, the Shirelles, the Crystals, the Marvelettes, the Ronettes, the Miracles, Ben E. King, and Mary Wells catapulted beyond the confines of rhythm and blues and gained a foothold on the pop charts. They used instrumental and vocal arrangements that drew on the same African American musical tropes that had fueled the rise of rock and roll, but sang in a smoother vocal style over musical arrangements featuring orchestral touches. The result was a more racially ambiguous sound that crossed over to non-African American audiences. By late 1963, the artists appearing on the rhythm and blues charts (understood to track black audience taste) and the pop charts (understood to track white audience taste) were so similar that *Billboard* magazine determined that the two charts were redundant and ceased publishing a rhythm and blues chart in November 1963.[34] By January 1965, however, the rhythm and blues chart was back in place. The 1964 arrival of the Beatles upended the short-lived period of racial integration on the charts, as the extraordinary success of the British group ushered in a phalanx of white artists from the United Kingdom. The Detroit-based Motown label, whose owner Berry Gordy made a concerted effort to produce music performed by African Americans with crossover appeal, had a steady stream of hits throughout the decade, but black artists who were not part of the Motown empire were displaced from the pop charts.[35]

The arrival of the British groups and the experiments of musicians in San Francisco, New York, Los Angeles, and London led to changes in rock and roll during the 1960s. Musical blackness was still audible, but it often came from artists who were not black. White artists drew on African American musical practices, shaping their voices, instrumentation, and musical arrangements accordingly. They covered songs originated by African American artists, but they also explored a range of musical styles and lyrical preoccupations. The music they created had a sound, attitude, and identity that distinguished it from the African American styles from which it derived. It also had a new name: *rock*. The abbreviated label marked off the contemporary music from its 1950s progenitor and contributed to the racial delimiting of the genre's boundaries. As it became even more associated with youth (i.e., everyone under thirty years of age) and a youth culture distinct from the mainstream, rock defined itself in opposition to musical others whose sonic practices and musical values distinguished them from rock. Through such processes, rock came to be understood as an art form (not just a commercial product) made by and for those who were young (at least when they first became involved), white, and predominantly male. Accompanying the new name was a new set of aesthetic values. Following the model of Chuck Berry, Buddy Holly, and the Beatles, bands of "self-contained" artists wrote and performed their own songs, supplanting professional songwriters from the central position they had occupied in the recording industry. These artists wrote lyrics that went beyond the dance, romance, and teen themes that animated early rock and roll; following the model of singer and songwriter Bob Dylan, who began his rise to prominence in the early 1960s, rock musicians addressed social, political, and philosophical issues. In an incisive study that examines rock ideology and the processes through which rock music came to be racialized as white during the 1960s, Jack Hamilton observes, "No black-derived musical form in American history has more assiduously moved to erase and blockade black participation than rock music. When rock ideology purged itself of (visible) blackness it was foreclosing not simply African American performers but an entire young tradition of interracial fluidity."[36] The resulting resegregation of popular music practice shaped both reception and perception of African American participation in rock.

While rock established its connection to white youth culture through new media such as *Crawdaddy* and *Rolling Stone* magazines and high-profile concerts such as the Monterey Pop and Woodstock music festivals, soul music emerged as the genre for African Americans. Soul had clear sonic ties to the African American gospel tradition, but artists such as James Brown, Otis Redding, and Aretha Franklin sang about secular rather than sacred subjects. Complementing the rise of black consciousness that manifested in the civil rights, black power, and black arts movements, soul music became the signal sound of African America in the 1960s and early 1970s, and most listeners, black and white, heard it as an authentic black musical expression. Responding to these currents, in 1969 *Billboard* renamed the rhythm and blues chart with the new term of black cultural and musical currency: "soul."[37] Although there were racially separate music charts, musical mixing persisted. African American artists such as Marvin Gaye, Curtis Mayfield, and Stevie Wonder brought the social awareness and expansive musical experimentation present in rock into soul and rhythm and blues. Meanwhile, white rock artists incorporated the sound of black soul into their recordings by working with African American women background vocalists who delivered a secularized gospel sound that provided a layer of audible blackness.

By the beginning of the 1970s, the recording industry was operating with categories of (white) rock and (black) soul/rhythm and blues that separated black people from rock, even as black sound remained integral to it. At this point, the recording industry's racialized practices took a new shape as major record labels formed black music departments and began, for the first time, to work with a critical mass of African American artists performing what was defined as black music. Previously, this music had been the purview of independent labels such as Peacock, Atlantic, Scepter, Motown, and Stax. This new focus meant expanded opportunities for black artists, but it depended on a racially defined approach to marketing popular music: one that likely seemed appropriate to an era of heightened black consciousness and black pride.[38] With few exceptions, black men and women were expected to engage in musical practices perceived to be "black." Still, in spite of the recording industry's insistence on separating black people from rock, the early 1970s saw a new breed of black rock and rollers in self-contained bands that built on the sounds that James Brown, Jimi Hendrix, and Sly and the Family Stone had pioneered in the 1960s. The music was infused with both black cultural pride and the countercultural imperative of expressive freedom. Artists such as Funkadelic, the Ohio Players, Earth, Wind & Fire, Mandrill, War, Labelle, and Betty Davis contributed to this shift in black musical sound, drawing on rhythm and blues, rock, and Latin musical tropes and experimenting with high volume and distortion. Funk, the genre that resulted from this mixture, was not a good match for a segregated marketplace. The music was "too black" to fit on album-oriented rock (AOR) radio and "too rock" for black stations. The blending of "black" and "white" genres that funk bands engaged in did not afford them the mainstream career traction that this process had provided for artists such as Jimi Hendrix, Janis Joplin, and the Rolling Stones in the previous decade.

New Genre Narratives

As this overview indicates, the definition of rock and roll has changed over time, as factors both musical and social have informed how artists, audiences, and recording industry professionals understand the music. Attention to black women's vocal presence in rock and roll highlights the fact that genre labels can underplay common threads across genres, emphasizing points of distinction rather than common ground. Rock and roll and rhythm and blues were the same thing in the 1950s, funk was black rock in the 1970s, and racially mixed audiences and cross-racial musical borrowing existed throughout rock and roll's early decades. However, these facts fade from view when race-based binaries dominate. These binaries drive critical discussions, marketing decisions, and historical representation, entrenching a vision of white versus black and a perception of separate white and black audiences. Understanding the sonic and cultural shifts that have informed the meaning of rock and roll as a music genre is integral to understanding the artists I discuss in *Black Diamond Queens*.

The music and stories of these women have slipped through the cracks of both rock and roll history and African American music studies, and their contributions to American popular culture have not received extensive critical attention. These women do not fit into commonsense notions of who constitutes a rock and roll artist, an identity understood to be white and male. Because of their connections to rock and roll, they fall outside of traditional categories of "black music," a label that embraces rhythm and blues, soul, jazz, gospel, and blues, but not rock and roll. Departing from dominant expectations of the sound and performance style associated with artists of their race and gender, these women engage in "eccentric acts," to use cultural critic Francesca Royster's term for "out of the ordinary or unconventional performances," particularly "those that are ambiguous, uncanny, or difficult to read."[39] These artists and their music can be challenging for the mainstreams from which they deviate to comprehend, and that which is not easily understood is easily overlooked. Still, they have had an impact on contemporary culture, suggesting a dynamic of invisibility and absorption that is similar to the conditions Jayna Brown explores in her study of the early twentieth-century black women theatrical artists whose movement vocabulary seeped into mainstream American popular dance, even as the women were erased.[40] Gayle Wald identifies a similar pattern in her discussion of midcentury gospel artist Sister Rosetta Tharpe, a virtuosic musician "whose charismatic guitar playing and extroverted stage persona helped to establish what today we take for granted as 'rock' convention."[41] Working in the same vein, Kyra Gaunt explores the impact of the handclap and jump rope games that African American girls play on the learning of black musical style in black communities and, by extension, on the sound of commercial black popular music.[42] In all of these cases, the creative work of African American women is an unrecognized source that others incorporate into their work, profiting to a much greater degree than the black female originators. My work shares with these studies a desire to tell unfamiliar stories about the cultural contributions of black women, while accounting for some of the reasons that the women and their stories are so little known.

The history that I present is, like all histories, selective and partial, reflecting the investments of the author. What distinguishes it from mainstream histories of rock is my emphasis on the presence of African American women and my assumption that their voices matter in the formation of the music. Rock history and criticism, as Daphne Brooks has observed, started from a set of cultural and musical assumptions and focused on a set of key figures that "both inscribe a particular kind of historical narrative of past musical innovations that were suffocatingly narrow and establish a lexicon of taste that would perpetuate that narrowness for years to come."[43] For the most part, African American women are marginal in these standard rock histories preoccupied with the musical lineage and contributions of Rock's Great Men. Moving beyond this focus, attending to female lines of descent and to women whose voices reverberate in rock in both subtle and overt ways, is a feminist intervention in the "rock mythologies" that Brooks argues have privileged "the slowhand axe man at the expense of the female virtuosic vocalist and musician."[44] It is, furthermore, an effort to produce "more nuanced, heterogeneous tales" of musical collaborations across lines of race and gender and to explore the ways black women worked with, influenced, and were influenced by white artists.[45]

Reckoning with this history is a challenge. Musicologist Laurie Stras notes that one of the ways feminist scholars have written women into mainstream rock history has been to "point out their influence on more prestigious male artists or repertoires" and to locate them within "the male-centered History of Rock."[46] This is a logical move to make because "in order to have our work taken seriously, we are obliged to site it within the context of that which has gone before," but doing so has the effect of reinscribing the very mythologies feminist scholars hope to trouble.[47] To address this conundrum in her history of women swing band musicians, feminist music historian Sherrie Tucker goes beyond documenting underacknowledged women musicians. She approaches gender as "a field in which power is articulated."[48] Building on the work of feminist historians and music scholars, Tucker considers the ways "notions of gender and race operate within specific musical forms" and writes a history of swing music that deconstructs the genre discourses that omit women instrumentalists.[49] Following the example of these feminist scholars, I attend to the power dynamics present in the music genre cultures in which these women participated and consider the ways the intersection of race, gender, and genre created conditions that made it difficult for African American women to maintain a position within rock.

Black Women and "Brown Sugar"

Santogold was not Santi White's first foray into professional recording. In 2001, she had collaborated with the vocalist Res on her alternative rock and soul album *How I Do*, writing most of the material and serving as one of the project's executive producers.[50] During this period, White also fronted a punk rock band called Stiffed, a name reputed to be a commentary on how she felt after working with a major label on the Res project. Stiffed released two albums: *Sex Sells* (2003) was produced by Darryl Jenifer, bass player for the foundational African American hardcore punk band Bad Brains; *Burned Again* (2005) was coproduced by Jenifer and Stiffed.[51] These recordings departed from mainstream notions of African American women's musical production, and White encountered responses that by the turn of the millennium had become commonplace for African Americans delving into rock. There was the surprise that she was involved in that genre of music, the culling of biographical information to explain her unusual musical digression, and the difficulty of identifying an audience for her music. These were the very issues I had explored in my research on the Black Rock Coalition, a nonprofit organization founded in 1985 to support African American musicians who broke the prevailing rules of race and genre.[52] Once I completed that project, I continued my research by following the work of New York City–based African American women musicians such as Honeychild Coleman, Helga Davis, Neycha, Shelley Nicole, Toshi Reagon, Martha Redbone, Felice Rosser, Simi Stone, Sandra St. Victor, Tamar-kali, and Kamara Thomas, all of whom were independently producing rock, alternative, and otherwise unconventional-for-black-women music. In addition to discussing their creative work, we kept having conversations about the African American women musicians who had come before them and the absence of information about them. I found myself thinking about the dominant rock and roll narrative and how different the story was when I took into account the involvement of African American women.[53] The possibility of learning more about these women and what they had accomplished was hard to resist.

My training as a cultural anthropologist and my teaching position in an ethnomusicology program in a music department inform my perspective on the historical materials with which I am working. I view music as a site of the production of meaning and identity, and as a means through which individuals shape, change, and reproduce their cultural context. I am also concerned with the ways institutions and discourses influence individuals, making it difficult for them to move beyond certain boundaries.[54] As I investigate these issues of power and the construction of meaning in rock and roll, I am doing the classic anthropological maneuver of "making the familiar strange" by revisiting the history of rock from a different point of view, one that centers African American women. This research has allowed me to write a book I wish I had been able to read years ago when I was a teenager dedicating a sizable portion of my time, energy, and cash to rock and roll.[55]

Black feminist scholarship and presuppositions inform my perspective and the archival work on which this research rests. Throughout, I highlight the ways the intersection of race, gender, class, and sexuality shaped the experiences of the women at the center of my study.[56] I also consider how these artists contended with stereotypes that rendered black women as oversexed jezebels or asexual mammies, defining black women by their sexuality or lack of it.[57] These "controlling images," as black feminist theorist Patricia Hill Collins has termed them, communicated that black women were inadequately feminine and lacking in humanity.[58] *Black Diamond Queens* examines the ways African American women negotiated the negative dominant assumptions about black women in the context of rock and roll. But what does the pairing "African American women" and "rock and roll" even bring to mind? Some people might think of Tina Turner and . . . who else? There's one other person who immediately occurs to me: the woman in the song "Brown Sugar." The 1971 Rolling Stones track is a rock and roll classic, a rollicking paean to the sexual wiles of an unnamed, unspeaking black woman. During my teen years of avid rock radio listenership, I heard the song frequently. While I thought the guitar riffs were all right, the lyrics—"Brown Sugar, how come you taste so good? / Brown Sugar, just like a black girl should"—repelled me. As a young black woman I had something in common with the song's focal figure, but I did not want to be mistaken for this racialized and sexualized addressee. I discuss "Brown Sugar" in detail in chapter 5, but mention the song at the outset because its objectifying representation of African American women's sexuality and limited rendering of black womanhood are indicative of the treacherous ground of rock and roll, the terrain on which the women I write about here worked to represent themselves and their subjectivity, sexual and otherwise.

One of the best-known songs in rock, "Brown Sugar" celebrates a black woman's irrepressible desirability and forced sexual availability. Its propulsive musical track features Keith Richards's insistent guitar lines, a pounding roadhouse piano part by Ian Stewart, a sax solo by Bobby Keys, and Mick Jagger's commanding vocals. "Brown Sugar" reached number one on the US pop charts and held the number two spot on the UK singles charts in 1971. Over the years it has become one of the most popular singles in the Rolling Stones' catalogue and is a staple of classic rock radio.[59] Concise and evocative, the song's lyrics refer, in short order, to West Africa's Gold Coast, the Middle Passage, cotton fields, a New Orleans slave market, whips, drums, an English man's cold blood running hot, and a delicious-tasting black girl.[60] The song is rooted in the imagery of the Atlantic slave trade and the sexual exploitation that enslaved women experienced. As scholarship on American slavery has made clear, sexual coercion and sexual violence were part of the everyday lives of enslaved black women.[61] Historian Deborah Gray White explains, "Once slaveholders realized that the reproductive function of the female slave could yield a profit, the manipulation of procreative sexual relations became an integral part of the sexual exploitation of female slaves."[62] Enslaved black women lived with the reality that they could "fall prey to the licentious black and white men on the plantation."[63] Historians Darlene Clark Hine and Kathleen Thompson note the following about the women:

> [They] were subjected to "forcible sexual intercourse," the legal and moral definition of rape. The amount and kind of force used varied. So, too, did the person a woman was forced to give her body to. Sometimes the white master or overseer would force her to the ground in the fields. Sometimes she was locked in a cabin with another slave whose job was to impregnate her. For another woman, the force involved might be less obvious. She was forced to

have sex in the same sense that an enslaved man was forced to plow a field, as a job. Still, it was rape, and black women experienced it every day.[64]

Black feminist scholars have connected this condition of forced sexual labor to the representation of black women's sexuality, tracing the image of a hypersexual, sexually available black woman to antebellum rationalizations of the rape of enslaved black women.[65] The "construction of the black female as the embodiment of sex," which burdened black women with responsibility for the sexual attention they received from white men, developed alongside a similarly flat stereotype of white women as the ideal of femininity, innocent of the taint of the sexual.[66] African American visual artist Lorraine O'Grady has described the binary and interdependent relationship between these constructions of womanhood as follows:

> The female body in the West is not a unitary sign. Rather, like a coin, it has an obverse and a reverse: on the one side, it is white; on the other, not-white or, prototypically, black. The two bodies cannot be separated, nor can one body be understood in isolation from the other in the West's metaphoric construction of "woman." White is what woman is; not-white (and the stereotypes not-white gathers in) is what she had better not be.[67]

These images persisted after slavery and well into the twentieth century, fueling representations of black women like the one the Rolling Stones presented in their hit song. African American women working in rock and roll have wrestled with the sexualized image of black women in different ways. As the authors of a feminist history of women in rock observe, "Some women choose to conform to the sexual stereotypes; some choose to subvert them; others embrace them, flaunt them, and throw them back in the face of the culture that created them."[68] The women of *Black Diamond Queens* weighed these options as they pursued their careers. In the chapters that follow I consider the ways their musical and performance choices responded to the "sexualized mythology" of the Brown Sugar figure that haunts black women.[69]

Black Women, Sexuality, and Rock and Roll

I am aware of the risk of overemphasizing sexuality and physical appearance in a discussion of women performers, but it is essential to examine these issues since they accompany women onto the public stage. Their impact is heightened for black women, whose bodies, as my discussion of "Brown Sugar" demonstrates, are both sexually and racially charged. In fact, rock is "an especially hazardous terrain for women of color who may get caught between racist assumptions about the sexuality of women of color and their own desires to present themselves as sexual agents."[70] But engagement with the sexual is part of the ethos of rock and roll, a sexually liberated space constructed in part through stereotyped ideas about black people, the genre's sonic and symbolic foundation. And, as Santi White proclaimed in her band's first album title, "sex sells." In a book about the convergence of black women and rock and roll, then, there is no way around the sexual. Rock and roll's emphasis on the sensual body is a defining part of the form and grows out of its roots in African American musical practices that included a space for expressions of sexuality. As if to underline the point, the very name *rock and roll* carries a double meaning, describing the bodily movements that respond to great rhythm and serving as a slang term for sex in mid-twentieth century African American communities.[71] Binary ideas about race and sex informed the ways many white listeners understood and experienced the music they were consuming. Black music, black people, and black culture represented a respite from the strictures of white middle-class propriety that prohibited forthright engagement with bodily pleasures. This perspective, which rested on a worldview that separated the mind from the body and reason from emotion, grew from a long-standing notion that blackness was a repository of physical, spiritual, and sexual freedom. One pathway to this freedom was through music.

From nineteenth-century blackface minstrelsy to the white borrowing of black sound that defined rock and roll, a fascination with blackness has fueled white engagement with African American music. These excursions allow white musicians and fans to tap into the perceived hotness and coolness of black musical forms—from ragtime to jazz to rhythm and blues to rap—and to experience "everything but the burden" of actually being black, as cultural critic Greg Tate has put it.[72] They can romanticize blackness and black culture, while their whiteness protects them from experiencing the racism that actual black people routinely confront. Ethnomusicologist Ingrid Monson has noted the gender dimension of these processes. Her discussion of jazz, race, and hipness in the United States in the 1950s and 1980s outlines the ways ideas about masculinity take form through practices of appropriation and projection across racial and class boundaries.[73] Shifting attention to rock and roll reveals a similarly loaded set of raced and gendered images and dynamics, although as musicologist Annie Randall has observed, the ideas that black femininity and sexuality generate in the genre have received little scholarly attention.[74] The vocal sound and symbolic presence of black women, however, are important to the formation of rock and roll's ethos, to the identities of the male rock musicians whose exploits are centered in depictions of rock history and, above all, to the sound of the music. Consequently, throughout the book I attend to the interdependence of music-making, race, gender, sexuality, and power, while also tracking the processes of historical erasure and inscription, of recording industry decision-making, and of genre labeling that foregrounded white men and that involved but marginalized black women who were, in fact, artists with and sonic models for white and black male rockers.

The women I discuss in *Black Diamond Queens* also modeled sound and style for other women. Like most African American women in the post–World War II era, they worked outside of the home, a necessity to support their families.[75] Doing so at a time when the white, middle-class ideal was for women to stay at home raising children, while their breadwinning husbands worked, called their femininity into question. But African American women musicians diverged even further from standards of feminine behavior. They left the confines of their homes and communities, traveling in order to perform and displaying their bodies and voices on stage. Most of the people with whom they worked—musicians, songwriters, producers, agents, and managers—were men. Black feminist scholars have demonstrated that a perception of black women's lack of conventional femininity and sexual difference has been at the crux of the race, gender, and class systems that have marginalized and disempowered black women, historically and in the present day.[76] They further argue that the history of rape and the related image of hypersexuality, the imagery that the Rolling Stones' "Brown Sugar" invokes, have made sexuality a fraught issue for black women. In fact, the prevalent public defamation of the moral character of black women spurred the founding of the first national black women's rights organization, the National Association of Colored Women (NACW), in 1896. As Darlene Clark Hine observes, "At the core of essentially every activity of NACW's individual members was a concern with creating positive images of Black women's sexuality."[77] To counter stereotypes, Hine argues, many African American women—especially those of middle-class status or striving for it—chose to "downplay, even deny, sexual expression."[78] Scholars have labeled these practices as the "politics of respectability" and the "culture of dissemblance," behaviors through which African

American women presented a public face that demonstrated their femininity according to the expectations of European American middle-class culture.[79]

This persistent denial of sexual expression has led African American women to maintain a deep silence around sexuality. As historian of science Evelynn Hammonds notes, "One of the most enduring and problematic aspects of the 'politics of silence' is that in choosing silence black women also lost the ability to articulate any conception of their sexuality."[80] The black lesbian feminist poet and essayist Audre Lorde urged women to embrace the erotic, a concept she deployed to create an expansive space of women's power that includes sexuality and is, she argued, "a considered source of power and information within our lives" that women, to their detriment, have been taught to fear and suppress.[81] Even at the turn of the millennium, it was difficult for many African American women to claim sexuality as a positive and empowered space of expression, pleasurable experience, and exploration.[82] Popular music, however, has been a means through which African American women have expressed sexual subjectivity. Starting in the 1920s with the blues, the art form that black feminist cultural critic Hazel Carby argues is the signal cultural production of working-class black women in the early twentieth century, a critical mass of African American women "constructed themselves as sexual subjects through song."[83] Without the investment in the politics of respectability that dominated middle-class black women's political organizing and social comportment, working-class blues singers, such as Ma Rainey, Bessie Smith, Ida Cox, and Victoria Spivey, expounded upon sexual desire, power relations between men and women, and everyday life; they asserted their personal agency while articulating issues relevant to black women.[84] *Black Diamond Queens* examines the musical productions of later generations of black women vocalists whose work echoes the bold attitude associated with blues women. Spurred by both artistic considerations and economic imperatives, these artists drew on a range of musical styles, crossing and blurring genre boundaries while doing so. Too often, however, the resulting heterogeneity of black women's music is elided.[85] Examining these wider-ranging musical productions, ethnomusicologist Eileen Hayes argues, "has the potential to complicate monolithic notions of Americanness, womanhood, blackness, and black womanhood."[86] I share Hayes's interest in expanding representations of black womanhood, in part because my own musical tastes diverge from those expected of black women. Therefore, before launching my effort, I offer a personal narrative that indicates my musical priorities and encapsulates the dynamics of race, gender, and genre that are the concern of *Black Diamond Queens*.

About the Author

When I was in high school, it never would have occurred to me that I would one day write a book that required me to devote significant attention to the Rolling Stones. Although I liked some of their songs, they were not among my favorite bands. For starters, "Brown Sugar" and the band's protruding tongue logo did not appeal to me. When the Stones came through our town on their 1981 US tour, I had no interest in joining friends who went to the concert. I was more into Queen, David Bowie, and Prince, the theatrical guys who sang wonderfully and, with their gender queerness (as we absolutely did not refer to it back then), were at once unsettling and enticing. Punk, post-punk, and new wave were what I found musically compelling during my teen years in the early 1980s. I was particularly fond of British bands like the Clash, Echo and the Bunnymen, the English Beat, the Gang of Four, the Jam, and the Psychedelic Furs. Over the course of researching this book, I was surprised to learn how prominently British artists figured in the stories of the African American women I was tracing. The Stones, the Beatles, David Bowie, and Humble Pie have a stronger presence in the text than their American counterparts, and I realize that my personal preference for British rock likely led me to focus on these connections—connections that grew out of British musicians' well-documented fascination with African American music. As I write about these transatlantic, cross-gender exchanges, I acknowledge my own fascinated consumption of a musical and cultural Other—the music of (mostly white, mostly male) British artists—and all of the attendant romanticizing, misreading, and mishearing that such sonic encounters can bring. It may be that black or white, male or female, American or British, we think the grass is greener on the other side of the pond.

It wasn't supposed to be this way. As a little kid, my first musical encounters were with the records my African American parents listened to. Pop was a jazz head with a cabinet full of 33⅓ RPM albums by the likes of Miles Davis, the Modern Jazz Quartet, Dave Brubeck, and Count Basie. He supplemented this collection by recording jazz radio programs on his reel-to-reel. Mom liked to hear vocal music, especially opera stars Leontyne Price and Risë Stevens and the soulful sounds of Nina Simone and Ray Charles. Pop played records for me on the living room hi-fi, which I was Not To Touch. Sometimes I asked to hear Mongo Santamaria's version of "Watermelon Man," but mostly I requested Nina Simone's *Silk and Soul* album. I thought she looked like a beautiful queen on the cover, and when I listened to the song "The Turning Point," a musing on school integration that she sang from the point of view of a little girl, I felt like she was speaking directly to me about what I was experiencing in my suburban kindergarten classroom.

I played my own records on my record player, a snappy portable with a solid red bottom, and a red and white candy-striped top. A lever that switched the speed from 33 to 45 to 78 RPMs made it possible for me to listen to *Hopalong Cassidy and the Singing Cowboy*, a set of 78s based on a 1950s TV series that my older brother Bobby, twenty-some years my senior, handed down from his childhood collection. My sister Diane, a couple of years younger than Bobby, gave me *A Christmas Gift for You from Phil Spector*. At first, I was reluctant to accept a "big people" record, as I thought of albums, but it didn't take long for the Ronettes, Darlene Love, and the Crystals to sweep me away with their wall of sound versions of Christmas songs. After my persistent pleading, my father bought me a record by teen dream Bobby Sherman. He was so cute! He wore a choker! I still wonder what went through Pop's mind as he put down his money for *Portrait of Bobby*, an album of middle-of-the-road pop tunes sung by the blue-eyed, longish-haired young man who graced its cover in a velvet jacket and lavender slacks. My brother tried to offset my foray into disposable white pop by giving me *Keeper of the Castle*, an album by Motown's Four Tops that featured "Ain't No Woman Like the One I Got." I liked it, but the more transformative experience was the result of hearing a different Motown act. Diane and my other sister Lyn, who is a few years older than I, played "I Want You Back" by the Jackson Five for me—"You'll probably like this," they said—and set me on a path of Michael Jackson fandom. That's about it for stories about my siblings, who are actually my half-siblings on my father's side, debating or shaping my taste in music. Because of age difference and circumstances, we lived in the same household for only a short time when I was very young. As the years went on, music was not the center of the conversation when we got together, but it was very central to the identity I was forming.

Pop's job in naval research brought the family from New Jersey to the Washington, DC, area when I was three. My parents decided not to live in the Chocolate City in part because of the reputed superiority of the public schools in the suburbs, so I spent my childhood and adolescence in Fairfax, Virginia, one of the middle-class bedroom communities outside of Washington. From kindergarten to high school graduation, I was one of a small number of black kids at the public schools I attended, and most of my friends were white. I didn't see my relationships with my peers in stark racial terms, but I was aware of my black difference. Always present, it was thrown into relief at unexpected moments like when the kids in my third grade class played Confederates and Yankees, or when my mother told me The Truth: "Your hair is not going to lay flat like the white girls' does, Maureen."

Fairfax was where we were living when my father died, and it's where my mother and I stayed on. The only good thing that came out of Pop's death when I was seven years old was unfettered access to his hi-fi. I put my favorites into heavy rotation: Michael Jackson's *Ben*, Earth, Wind & Fire's *Spirit*, and Stevie Wonder's *Songs in the Key of Life* mixed in with *Endless Summer* by the Beach Boys, the soundtrack of the film *The Sound of Music*, and the Carpenters' albums that I bought from the Columbia House mail-order record club when I was in elementary school. Pop's turntable would not play 45s—a format for teenagers, not jazz aficionados—so when I started buying singles in junior high, I played them on the record player in my bedroom or at the homes of friends. We'd work out dance steps to Chic's "Le Freak," listen to the Bee Gees' songs from the *Saturday Night Fever* soundtrack, or memorize the lyrics to Journey's "Lovin', Touchin', Squeezin'." I appropriated Diane's battered copy of *Meet the Beatles* into my growing collection, and friends with older siblings shared the band's later work; we'd play *Sgt. Pepper* and *Abbey Road*, while interpreting the intoxicating Paul Is Dead symbols supposedly embedded in the album covers. On the radio I listened to WPGC, a Top 40 station that carried Casey Kasem's weekly countdown of the nation's hits, and kept track of the chart positions of Stevie Wonder, Chic, Donna Summer, and the Bee Gees, my favorite artists. By sixth or seventh grade, under the influence of older girls in my Girl Scout troop, I started listening to DC-101, a station that played what it dubbed "kick ass rock and roll." The DJs dosed me up with Aerosmith, the Allman Brothers, the Eagles, Journey, Led Zeppelin, Lynyrd Skynyrd, the Rolling Stones, Van Halen, and the Who. I was also watching the smattering of rock and roll available on television. There were the musical guests on the sketch comedy shows *Fridays* and *Saturday Night Live* and the Saturday afternoon trifecta: *American Bandstand* for mainstream rock and pop, *Solid Gold* for disco, and *Soul Train* for the songs topping the black music charts and a connection to the black culture that was absent from my everyday life in the vanilla suburbs.[87]

By the time I graduated from high school, I had formed a habit of listening across genre, race, and gender boundaries and embracing stylistic tendencies that ranged from smooth to rough and from sweet to edgy. The thrashing vocals and guitars of the Sex Pistols and the Clash sounded an exhilarating expression of rage and defiance. Meanwhile, Prince's euphoric celebrations of sex and God were irresistible and his 1999 was indispensable. I adored Michael Jackson's *Off the Wall*, but even before I headed off to college, David Bowie had taken over my turntable. His wide-ranging music—everything from hard rock to shimmering plastic soul to electronic experiments—enthralled me, and I felt a kinship with the alien freak who, with his made-up face and weird-colored hair, looked like he had fallen to earth from outer space, just the way I had been dropped down into white suburbia. The dedication to music continued during my four years at Northwestern. My friends and I were DJs at WNUR-FM, the campus radio station (I did a jazz show), and got on the guest lists for local concerts featuring nationally touring acts. We'd ride the "L" train from Evanston into Chicago to see the next big thing from American indie-rock-land or from the United Kingdom. We'd buy new records, we'd buy used records, we'd borrow records from each other and from WNUR. Records, records, records. The bulk of what I assembled into a record collection was music by white artists, but I was thrilled by the occasional interracial groups like British ska revivalists the English Beat, the Specials, and the Selecter; black British singer-songwriter Joan Armatrading, with her gorgeous, brooding voice, was a revelation. For the most part, though, I did not dwell on the absence of black people in the music that spoke to me. What I am aware of now (but didn't pay attention to then) is the presence of blackness in the rock I listened to, a kind of audio palimpsest in which African diaspora musical practices had been appropriated and twisted around into a new sound, whether by David Bowie, the Clash, Paul Weller in his Style Council period, or the Talking Heads.

In high school and college, I learned that my interest in what was understood as "white music" was not what people, black or white, expected. The perplexed or hostile responses my musical preferences often provoked led me to research race, identity, and music as a professional academic. Still, I cannot report that I spent much time during my teen years wondering why there weren't more women, especially black women, producing the kind of music I liked. The dominant presence of white men in rock was something I took for granted. If the group's maleness was too much to stomach (say, the Red Hot Chili Peppers, naked but for "sox on cox"), it was easy enough to find something more appealing. It was also possible to overlook the egregious. The Specials ranted out "Little Bitch," but their songs were so danceable I didn't want to resist them. It was a relief, though, to discover women artists: Pauline Black, sharp in her narrow suit, slinging herky-jerky vocals against the grooves of her band the Selecter; Poly Styrene of X-Ray Spex haranguing sexist, consumer culture at a fevered pitch; Kate Pierson and Cindy Wilson of the B52s voicing camp quirkiness; and Tina Turner with her haughty cool in the "What's Love Got to Do with It" video. I sought meaningful representations of black women in books much more than in music, reading the usual suspects: Maya Angelou, Gwendolyn Brooks, Nikki Giovanni, Toni Morrison, and Alice Walker. A watershed was *Ain't I a Woman: Black Women and Feminism* by bell hooks, a book of critical analysis that put black women at the center of the discussion of race, gender, and power in the United States. In *Black Diamond Queens* I make a related move and trace the history of the music genre that I have been devoted to through a black feminist lens. Placing black women at the center of a discussion of rock and roll is not simply a self-interested endeavor. It is an effort to counter the erasure black women have experienced in the genre and to talk about the history of rock and roll in a way that marks rather than marginalizes the long-standing presence of black women. It is also a way of recognizing the African American women who paved the way for contemporary artists ranging from Toshi Reagon to Janelle Monáe to Beyoncé to Brittany Howard of the Alabama Shakes to Santi White, whose trials with race, gender, and genre opened this chapter. This is a project of recovery and inclusion, an effort to highlight a submerged history, and a consideration and critique of the workings of power and genre in the recording industry. *Black Diamond Queens* recognizes the artistic contributions of African American women to rock and roll and examines the reasons it is so difficult to hear their voices in the music they were so much a part of creating.

ONE / Rocking and Rolling with Big Mama Thornton

My singing comes from my experience. My own experience. My own feeling. I got my feelin's for everything. I never had no one teach me nothin.' I never went to school for music or nothin.' I taught myself to sing and to blow harmonica and even to play drums by watchin' other people! I can't read music but I know what I'm singing! I don't sing like nobody but myself. / **BIG MAMA THORNTON**

Willie Mae "Big Mama" Thornton's professional story encapsulates the blend of presence and obscurity that is emblematic of black women in rock and roll. At one level, she is an early influence who helped establish the sound of rock and roll through her recording of the original version of "Hound Dog." At another level, she is a one-hit wonder who struggled throughout her career to gain full financial recompense and public recognition for her contribution to American popular music. A biographer's observation that hers is a "rags to rags" story is an astute, if wrenching, characterization of her trajectory.[1] I start my study of African American women and rock and roll with two stories about Thornton because although she precedes rock and roll as a genre category, she helped define what that category became through her role as a resource for two prominent white rock and roll artists: Elvis Presley and Janis Joplin. The arrangement of her 1953 hit single "Hound Dog" anticipates the sound of rock that departed from the horn-centered style of rhythm and blues, and her performance of songs like "Ball and Chain" offered a template for singers seeking ways to express emotional intensity. Thornton operated outside of normative gender behavior, and both Presley and Joplin picked up on her refusals, fashioning rock and roll style for succeeding generations of male and female performers.

A bridge figure between the blues women of the 1920s and the rhythm and blues women of the rock and roll era, Thornton is an important foremother of rock and roll. Her talent helped build the business and creative enterprises of others, but she is not as visible and audible in popular music history as her contribution warrants. In this chapter, I listen for Thornton's musical voice to reveal the ways her vocal sound informed rock and roll in the 1950s and 1960s. I also attend to her analytical voice, drawing on interviews conducted with her in the 1960s, 1970s, and 1980s to reveal the ways she understood her art and interpreted the impact of her race and gender on her career. This approach draws attention to Thornton's critical consciousness, a feature often denied black working-class women.[2] I focus on Thornton's two best-known songs, "Hound Dog" and "Ball and Chain," and the cross-racial exchanges associated with each. In both cases, a young white rock and roller recorded a song that Thornton originated, drawing on her vocal style and transgressive gender presentation as building blocks when fashioning their own musical personae and achieving a level of professional and financial success that Thornton never attained.

Before telling these stories I want to comment on a common assumption about Thornton's sexuality. One of the first things that many colleagues said to me when I mentioned that I was researching Thornton was, "You know she was a lesbian." Actually, having been unable to locate much information about her sexual or romantic relationships, I *don't* know this. My interviews with several people who worked with Thornton yielded stories about men with whom she was involved, but no mentions of female partners. Thornton was a private person, and no one I spoke with claimed that they knew her really well. For the purposes of this chapter, then, and to avoid wrongly closeting or outing Thornton, I defer discussion of her private life and instead focus on her public image. Here, she was a transgressor par excellence. At different times throughout her career, Thornton made a conscious decision to appear on stage in what was understood to be men's clothing, a practice that many thought signaled that she was a lesbian. I find it difficult to imagine that she would have been unaware of this possibility, so what is noteworthy to me is that she was comfortable projecting this image in the years before gay liberation.[3] In this chapter, I treat Thornton's sonic practice as evidence of an unconventional form of black femininity that provided a template for Presley and Joplin as they sought ways to express and liberate themselves through rock and roll. Raised in working-class, African American southern culture and possessing a powerful sense of self, Thornton followed her muse in terms of musical, performance, and sartorial choices. She offers a textbook example of what would later be dubbed rock and roll attitude.

Big Mama Thornton's Life in Music

> **Chris Strachwitz:** Well, why don't we start out with where you were born?
>
> **Big Mama Thornton:** Eleventh of December. An Alabama kid, Montgomery.
>
> **Chris Strachwitz:** What was the year of your birth? Do you mind telling us how old you are?
>
> **Big Mama Thornton:** Well, I—That's a secret. [laughs]
>
> **Chris Strachwitz:** That's a secret. Oh, okay. You mean I'll never find out.
>
> **Big Mama Thornton:** [laughs][4]

Thornton's cagey humor, unveiled at the beginning of a recorded interview with her producer, might indicate why so many of the details of her life have been lost to the ages. In this recording and in published interviews, Thornton provided brief answers to personal questions and kept the focus on her professional life. Still, drawing from interview material and secondary sources, it is possible to outline her trajectory.

Willie Mae Thornton was born on December 11, 1926, in Ariton, Alabama, a small town about seventy miles south of Montgomery, the city she usually claimed as her birthplace.[5] Describing her parents, she said, "Well, my father, he was a minister. My mother, she was a Christian, hard-working woman. She sang Christian songs."[6] Describing her musical background, Thornton told Strachwitz that she didn't remember hearing the blues when she was growing up, and recalled, "I used to go to church a lot but just singing, you know, I didn't do too much singing in church."[7] At some point her family moved to Montgomery; she lived there until she left home to pursue her dream of becoming a professional singer. The recent death of her mother and a job cleaning spittoons at a local tavern gave her little reason to refuse the opportunity to join Sammy Green's Hot Harlem Revue after she successfully auditioned for the troupe. "I started traveling in 1939, when I was fourteen," Thornton told an interviewer in 1975. "I had won first prize on an amateur show, and [Sammy Green] was looking for a singer. So I started traveling with him. I was singing, dancing, doing comedy—I still use a little bit of that now."[8] Billy Wright, a singer who performed with Green's revue, recalled that the company "had a ten-piece band, singers, dancers, comedians. You couldn't repeat. Had to have a new show, new material every week."[9] As a member of this traveling variety show (which originated not in New York City's iconic black neighborhood, but in Atlanta, Georgia), Thornton toured the southern black circuit. "Well, we went [to] Atlanta and Birmingham and back home [to Montgomery] and Columbus, Georgia; Macon, Georgia; North, South Carolina, Florida," she told Strachwitz.[10] Thornton did comedy and sang, burnishing a reputation as an inheritor of Bessie Smith's full-bodied blues style.[11] But unlike Smith and most blues women, Thornton played an instrument, accompanying herself on harmonica.[12] Later, she added drums to her repertoire. She quit Sammy Green's show in 1948 because, she said in an interview, "they owed me quite a bit of money. They wouldn't pay me so I went to Houston, Texas, and got me a job at the Eldorado Club."[13]

Thornton's regular gig at the Eldorado brought her to the attention of local black record mogul Don Robey. He signed her to his Peacock Records label, and she began recording for him in 1951. Thornton continued to tour, winning over audiences with her vocal power, joking repartee, harmonica skills, and personal charisma. "I got the name 'Big Mama Thornton' when I was with the Johnny Otis show, in the fifties," she explained.[14] Frank Schiffman, manager of Harlem's Apollo Theater, christened her with the new moniker after she stole the show from headliner Little Esther. The nickname referenced her physical size—she was a tall, heavyset woman—and the magnitude of her voice. By the time she had installed herself in Houston's music community, her notoriety as a serious drinker matched her growing fame as a masterful blues singer.[15] Describing her habits, Thornton said, "I don't use dope. I just stick with my Old Granddaddy 100 proof and my old moonshine corn liquor. Weeds, pills, needles—I don't need nothing like that jive to get out on the stage and sing. I drink, yeah. It makes me happy. But as for getting drunk, falling around on the streets—never!"[16] The other aspects of her nonmusical reputation that come up most frequently in writing about her are her "vulgarity" and "crudeness," her willingness to get into a physical fight with a man over a slight, and her purported ability to win those battles.[17] This behavior and her onstage appearances in "men's clothes" have contributed to the assumption that she was a lesbian.

In 1953, Thornton scored her first and only number one chart hit with a song Jerry Leiber and Mike Stoller, then fledgling songwriters, had written especially for her. "Hound Dog" spent fourteen weeks on *Billboard*'s R&B charts, seven of them in the number one slot. This was the commercial pinnacle of her recording career. Three years later, Elvis Presley's rendition of "Hound Dog" catapulted him to stardom. In the late 1950s, Thornton became active on the Bay Area blues scene, singing down-home blues in the black clubs of Oakland and Richmond. During the 1960s, Thornton rode the wave of renewed interest in the blues. For Thornton, Muddy Waters, Willie Dixon, and the other African American artists who figured prominently in the blues revival of the 1950s and 1960s, the blues were alive and did not need reviving. Still, they welcomed the interest in their music even if they were surprised by the audience: young, predominantly white Americans and Europeans who had a deeply felt (if romanticized) connection to the African American art form and began drawing on it to create their own music.[18] Thornton's standout performance at the 1964 Monterey Jazz Festival raised her profile and won her sterling media reviews. Ralph Gleason, the dean of San Francisco music writers, declared, with a superfluous reference to her size, that Thornton was "pound for pound the best woman blues singer alive today."[19] She was invited to join the 1965 American Folk Blues Festival, a European tour featuring John Lee Hooker, Mississippi Fred McDowell, and Buddy Guy. Here and in general, she added a female voice to the primarily male contingent associated with the blues revival. Although she toured and recorded with B. B. King, Muddy Waters, Willie Dixon, James Cotton, Otis Spann, and Buddy Guy, her participation in the revival is not always acknowledged. By the mid-1960s, as an interest in the blues expanded among young white scenesters, Thornton found herself performing in San Francisco rock venues such as the Both/And and the Fillmore (see figure 1.1). As a result, she became known to the young blues revivalists and helped to shape the sound of the next phase of rock and roll, most notably through her connection to Janis Joplin, who recorded Thornton's composition "Ball and Chain."

Throughout her career, Thornton expressed herself through a distinctive voice notable for its volume. She once proclaimed, "I can sing louder than any mike . . . and I don't want no mike louder than me!"[20] Vocal power did not compromise Thornton's expressive capacity. She approached her songs with

verve, openness, and flexibility. There are moments of joy and sweetness, such as when she extols the virtues of a generous lover. Sometimes melancholia seeps through as she renders the whipped despair one feels when a love affair goes wrong. Whether she was singing in a low range with a powerful chest voice or reaching up to hit higher notes, Big Mama delivered the blues with feeling. "The blues satisfies the ear," she told Gleason in a 1967 interview. "They can hear what you're sayin' if you sing them fast or slow. In the blues, you got more feelin'. You got to really understand the blues to play the blues."[21] Thornton's deep understanding of the blues was evident to the musicians who worked with her. Guitarist Kat Dyson contrasted her college-level music training to the education she received when her band backed Thornton during a one-week engagement in Montreal in the early 1980s:

> If you really listen to some of the blues, sometimes there's no changes, sometimes they don't move. Sometimes it goes with the flow of the singer. [With Thornton] I learned how to *follow* because she would insist on that. She was like, "Don't move. Where you all going?" She'd stop. [laughs] So I learned the fluidity of the format from someone who shaped it. Not somebody who's imitating somebody else.[22]

Dyson also recalled that Thornton would sing "whatever she was thinking. She didn't always do what the records do. It was not a cookie cutter kind of thing. She might pull a blues from somebody else that nobody knew. We just had to follow."[23]

That improvisatory spirit was in effect decades before when guitarist Terry DeRouen played with Thornton in the early 1960s. "A lot of times Mama would come up and sing some stuff she never sang before. . . . If a line just came to her mind she would fit it in a song somewhere," he told me. "You really had to pay attention to what she was singing. . . . Sometimes she'd be on stage and she would switch to singing gospel and a lot of times you'd watch her and you could see the feeling that she was feeling with some of these songs. Give you that Mahalia Jackson type feel where she would really get into it. And sometimes we would just let her sing by herself."[24] A blues woman and the daughter of a preacher, Thornton loved the blues *and* what she called the "good singing" of gospel artists such as the Dixie Hummingbirds,

---

FIGURE 1.1 (*opposite*) Big Mama Thornton in San Francisco, 1968. © BARON WOLMAN.

the Soul Stirrers, Mahalia Jackson, and the Davis Sisters. "They just knock me out," she said.[25] In 1971 she released an album of sacred music, achieving a goal she had held at least since 1965, when she told Strachwitz, "I've thought about it a great deal and I'd like very much to do spirituals because I feel that I got the voice. I feel like I got the power. I just feel like I could just do them."[26] Chiefly, though, Thornton is known as a blues singer. She played and recorded whenever she could, and over the years she earned the respect of audiences and musicians. She was inducted into the Blues Foundation Hall of Fame in 1984. In her later years, she sat on a chair when on stage, usually sipping what had become her preferred drink, gin and milk, in between songs.[27] Although physically frail, her voice was still strong.[28] A quintessential troubadour, she was frequently on the road, battling the blues until her death in Los Angeles on July 25, 1984.

Big Mama Thornton's "Hound Dog"

August 13, 1952, found Willie Mae Thornton and Johnny Otis at Radio Recorders, a Los Angeles studio, ready for their first recording session together.[29] Otis was a Greek-American bandleader whose immersion in black musical culture was so complete that he was often mistaken for and self-identified as African American.[30] Following the instructions of Peacock label owner Don Robey, he had taken Thornton on the road with his orchestra and was now trying to help her make a hit record. To that end, he had invited two white Jewish songwriters, Jerry Leiber and Mike Stoller, to the studio. Although they were still under twenty years old, Leiber and Stoller were developing a reputation as a good songwriting team in the Los Angeles rhythm and blues scene, and artists such as Jimmy Witherspoon, Charles Brown, and Bull Moose Jackson were recording their compositions.[31] They had worked with Otis a few weeks earlier, writing songs for rhythm and blues singer Little Esther, and were now charged with coming up with material for Thornton.[32] Recalling the session in the 1960s, Thornton told Ralph Gleason, "[Leiber and Stoller] were just a couple of kids then . . . and they had this song written out on the back of a brown paper bag. So I started to sing the words and I put in some of my own. All that talkin' and hollerin,' that's my own."[33] Originally, the song was credited to Leiber, Stoller, and Otis, but following a court case, Leiber and Stoller were credited as sole authors. Otis always maintained that he helped rewrite the song, and Thornton routinely asserted that she added improvised material.[34] Neither Otis nor Thornton was able to establish their claims legally.

Robey waited until early 1953 to release "Hound Dog." In an interview, Thornton recalled that she learned her record was in circulation on her way to a performance in Dayton, Ohio:

> I was going to the theater and I just turned the radio on in the car and the man said, "Here's a record that's going nationwide: 'Hound Dog' by Willie Mae Thornton." I said, "That's me!" [laughs] . . . So when we get to the theater they was blasting it. . . . So I goes up in the operating room, I say, "Do you mind playing that again?" Cause I hadn't heard the record in so long I forgot the words myself. So I stood there while he was playing it, listening to it. So that evening I sang it on the show and everybody went for it. "Hound Dog" just took off like a jet.[35]

"Hound Dog" made such a splash in Houston, Thornton's adopted hometown, that a local haberdasher designed "Hound Dog" shirts with floppy-eared collars.[36] The national R&B press was also enthusiastic. *Billboard* named "Hound Dog" a "New Record to Watch," and its reviewers gave it a rating in the excellent range, noting, with insider slang that turned female singers into birds, "Thrush's vocal is outstanding, and the backing is infectious. This one is mighty potent and could bust thru quickly."[37] *Cash Box* named "Hound Dog" the "Rhythm 'n Blues Sleeper of the Week," and observed, "Willie Mae Thornton gives a frenzied performance. . . . Easy when she should be easy, and driving when she has to bang it home."[38] "Hound Dog" went to number one on *Billboard*'s R&B chart at the end of March and stayed there for seven weeks. Rhythm and blues historian James Salem observes that the song "not only made Big Mama famous in the national blues community but established Peacock Records as a major independent label in black secular music."[39]

Thornton's "Hound Dog" differed from most of the rhythm and blues records of the era.[40] Its spare arrangement lacked the honking saxophone solos and pounding piano flourishes that were signatures of the rhythm and blues sound. Instead, Thornton is supported by guitar, bass, and drums, the instrumental configuration that became the norm for rock by the mid-1960s. Her vocals dominate the foreground, commanding attention from the instant the song begins. "Hound Dog" has no instrumental introduction. Instead, Thornton's voice launches the track with a verbal attack on a trifling lover: "You ain't nothin' but a hound dog," she roars. The instruments join in only after she has stated her position, and they defer to her throughout the track. One of the most notable aspects of Thornton's performance is the way she claims sonic space. During the instrumental break midway through the song, rather than laying back while guitarist Pete Lewis takes his solo, Thornton enters into a call-and-response exchange with him: "Aw, play it, boy, play it," she says. "Aw, you make me feel good.... Now wag your tail. Aw, get it," she improvises, sassy and subversive. Commanding a man to wag his tail marks an upend- ing of gender roles that encapsulates the disruptive form of femininity that Thornton sounds through her assertive vocals. The dressing down is thorough and cathartic. Thornton's confident vocals convey relief at being through with a man who, she has finally allowed herself to realize, has wasted her time and energy. With "Hound Dog," Thornton brought the blues tradition of outspoken women into the rhythm and blues context, putting sexuality and play with gender expectations in the foreground. Both Elvis Presley and Janis Joplin drew on Thornton's disruptive gender presentation when they borrowed her songs.

Thornton's "Hound Dog" was so popular that it spawned ten covers be- fore Elvis Presley recorded his version in 1956, but "Hound Dog" didn't deliver on all of its promise for Thornton.[41] The competition from the covers and R&B singer and disc jockey Rufus Thomas's 1953 answer song, "Bear Cat," coupled with the limited distribution and airplay available to recordings by black artists in the early 1950s, stalled Thornton's reach on the charts.[42] And Thornton always maintained that Peacock did not pay her adequate royalties. "I got one check for $500 and I never seen another," she said.[43] Presley was almost certainly aware of Thornton's "Hound Dog," but the version he recorded borrowed heavily from a Las Vegas lounge act called Freddie Bell and the Bellboys; he had heard them doing the song as part of their set at the Sands Hotel.[44] Presley's "Hound Dog" was released three years after Thornton's and went to number one on *Billboard's* R&B, country, and pop charts, making it the best-known and best-selling ver- sion of "Hound Dog."[45] It sold millions of copies and enjoyed a level of mainstream success that none of Thornton's recordings achieved. "It's just one of those things," Thornton said in a 1972 interview. "I've been singing way before Elvis Presley was born and he jumps up and becomes a mil- lionaire before me . . . off of something that I made popular. They gave him the right . . . now, why do they do that? He makes a million and all this jive because his face is different from mine."[46] Here, Thornton articulates the frustration she felt at being a stepping-stone to a young upstart's success while struggling to sustain a viable career of her own.

The "something" that Thornton says she made popular is much more than the song "Hound Dog." The "something" is the sound, feel, energy, and attitude of rhythm and blues music.[47] In the late 1940s and early 1950s, Thornton and a host of other African American artists were creating a new musical sound that spoke to the urban, postwar experience: heavy, propulsive rhythm; powerful, vernacular vocals; and sometimes raucous lyrics were the building blocks.[48] The burgeoning form's difference from European American musical styles was a major part of its attraction to the white audiences and artists who began to embrace its musical and performance practices. Thornton's comments point out that African Americans had been singing the blues for years without enjoying any white mainstream popularity. Even after young white artists began appropriating and popularizing black musical sound, the majority of African American artists still had minimal access to the charts and radio airplay, limiting their ability to capitalize on the musical trends they had fostered. Thornton also critiques the dynamics of race, gender, and power that parceled out different levels of visibility and mobility to white and black artists and paid more attention to male than female performers. When she laments, "they gave him the right," she might have been recalling that in 1956, Elvis was promoting his records on TV. This kind of access to national television was impossible for black rhythm and blues singers in 1953 when Thornton's "Hound Dog" was released; *no one*, black or white, sang rhythm and blues on US national television until late in 1955 when LaVern Baker, Bo Diddley, and the Five Keys appeared on Ed Sullivan's *Toast of the Town*, a CBS-TV variety show.[49]

Another thing that might have rankled Thornton was the fact that Presley's version of the song didn't make sense. As Thornton sang it, the double entendre–rich "Hound Dog" was a woman's dressing-down of a no-account man. She warns her "dog" that she is going to quit "feeding" him. Thornton's authoritative delivery made "Hound Dog" a powerful statement from a woman confronting the dismal facts of a lousy relationship. None of this survives in the version recorded by Presley, who could not, as a heterosexual man, sing about the same kind of dog as Thornton. Instead, he turns the title character into a literal dog whose failure to capture a rabbit has inspired his master's complaint. In the end, though, Presley's nearly nonsensical lyrics were not a problem for the record-buying public, white or black.

There is no documentation of Thornton and Presley meeting, and I have been unable to learn whether he ever saw her perform.[50] Still, Thornton was one of Presley's teachers. Bob Neal, who managed Presley before "Colonel

Tom" Parker, has said that Presley tried to learn as much as he could about the blues and rhythm and blues. Presley's biographer Peter Guralnick reports, "Whenever Neal went by the house, he found [Presley] with a stack of records—Ray Charles and Big Joe Turner and Big Mama Thornton and Arthur 'Big Boy' Crudup—that he studied with all the avidity that other kids focused on their college exams. He listened over and over seeming to hear something that no one else could hear."[51] He put what he heard into his performances: The snarl in Thornton's voice and the ways she snaps off the words in the song's opening, for example. His faster tempo eradicates some of the confident defiance of Thornton's original, but he imports her swagger and her forceful vocals, following her practice of hollering it out in a deep, husky voice. Ironically, Presley's sexy masculinity comes into being in part as he draws on Thornton's confrontational black femininity.[52] Cultural critic Judith Halberstam characterizes Thornton's vocal style as a product of her "queerly gendered performance" and argues that Thornton's "female masculinity" is "central to the music she produced and the aesthetic style she crafted."[53] Thornton's refusal of conventional femininity led her to assume a transgressive gender presentation—one that Halberstam characterizes as masculine—that was a crucial resource both for Thornton and for Presley.

It is likely that Thornton heard her sound in Presley's sound as he sang what she thought of as her song. Presley's versions of African American rhythm and blues did not erase blackness in the way that the covers recorded by white pop singers such as Pat Boone or Georgia Gibbs did. Instead, he produced a black sound, drawing his predominantly white audiences into a sonic experience whose overt racial mixing was at once enticing and illicit. Recording industry executive and popular music historian Arnold Shaw points out that "To Southern white ears, Elvis sounded so black that [his producer Sam] Phillips had him appear on a local disk jockey show where he identified himself as a student at the local white high school. Both Presley and Phillips felt that without that identification, his record might not be played or sell well in Memphis."[54] Presley could mine blackness, but he could also fall back on his whiteness when the need arose. He did publicly acknowledge the black roots of the music he performed, stating in a 1956 interview, "The colored folks been singing it and playing it just like I'm doin' now, man, for more years than I know. They played it like that in the shanties and in their juke joints."[55] But according to Thornton, Presley never acknowledged her as the originator of "Hound Dog." She described the oversight in a 1971 conversation with vocalist Big Joe Turner and an unidentified interviewer:

Interviewer: What about Elvis? He give you anything for "Hound Dog"?

Big Mama Thornton: I never got a dime.

Interviewer: You mean you didn't even get a box of Geritol?

Big Mama Thornton: I didn't even get a box of nothing.

Big Joe Turner: Did he ever say hello to you at any time?

Interviewer: Did he tip his hat, or something?

Big Mama Thornton: Well, he refused to play with me when he first come out and got famous. They wanted a big thing for Big Mama Thornton and Elvis Presley. He refused. And I'm so glad I can tell the world about it. [laughs]

Interviewer: Well, one thing we're going to do is tell the truth.

Big Mama Thornton: Well, that is the truth.[56]

Assuming Thornton's recollection is accurate, what she tells the interviewer makes sense. Parker was unlikely to have viewed a performance with an African American rhythm and blues singer as helpful to his client just at the point when his star was starting to rise in the American entertainment mainstream. Interestingly, by the late 1960s and 1970s, Presley was performing with the Sweet Inspirations, a black female background vocal group. With these women by his side, Presley acted out his reliance on, regard for, and debt to black women's vocal sound, on stage and on record. In the 1950s, however, he did not publicize his link to the African American woman who was one of the foundational voices of early rock and roll.

Thornton's "Hound Dog" was an important record. It was the first major success for Robey's Peacock Records, an example of a lucrative black-owned label several years ahead of Motown's arrival. It was the first hit song for Leiber and Stoller, two of rock and roll's most celebrated songwriters. Backed with "Don't Be Cruel," "Hound Dog" was Presley's biggest-selling single, establishing him as a dominant force in rock and roll and popular music more generally. The cross-racial exchange that contributed to Presley's version of "Hound

Dog" is an early example of what became a common practice of white male rock and roll artists borrowing from the sound and style of black women. It is also indicative of the ways the vocal and performance practices of African Americans informed those of white rock and roll musicians. To her great frustration, Thornton did not receive any financial compensation for the role she played as originator of what became one of the best-selling records in rock and roll history. Still, she signaled her connection to "Hound Dog" whenever she sang it live or on record. Kat Dyson told me that during her one-week engagement in Montreal in the 1980s, Thornton played two sets a night and sang different songs, depending "on what mood hit her, but 'Hound Dog' was always in there and the story about how it was stolen from her."[57] This laying claim was a well-established practice of Thornton's. Guitarist Terry DeRouen recalled, "She used to make jokes about Elvis doing 'Hound Dog.' She used to tell us, 'You gotta shake your pelvis like Elvis.' [And she'd say], 'Aw that boy's singing my song, messing my song up.'"[58] On a late 1960s album version, Thornton opens the song by singing, "Well, I feel all right this morning. I want everybody to know that I was the one to say, 'You ain't nothing but a hound dog.'"[59] She made it a point to fight the tide that framed "Hound Dog" as Elvis Presley's song.

Big Mama Thornton's "Ball and Chain"

In the summer of 1953, following the chart-topping success of "Hound Dog," Peacock paired Thornton with Johnny Ace, another one of the label's rising stars, and sent them out on the road. Ace was an R&B heartthrob whose smooth, seductive vocals earned him chart hits and headliner status. Thornton, with her brasher, down-home blues style, was the opening act. Sometimes they sang duets. Well-matched as touring partners, the two became friends. On breaks from touring they returned to the studio, recording solo tracks and collaborating on "Yes, Baby" (the song is solely credited to Ace). Their revue toured steadily in 1954, playing throughout New England, New York, Pennsylvania, Ohio, Alabama, the Carolinas, Georgia, Florida, Louisiana, Texas, and New Mexico.[60] The *New York Age Defender* labeled Ace and Thornton "the reigning 'king and queen of the blues,'" and a *Variety* review of an April 1954 show at the Apollo was glowing: "[Thornton] is a heavy rhythm and blues thrush while Ace is a mellow crooner. The contrast is effective and sustains interest and excitement all the way."[61] The Ace–Thornton partnership came to an abrupt and irreversible end on December 25, 1954. They had returned to Houston for a Christmas Day show at the Houston City Auditorium. During the concert's intermission, Ace, who had spent the day playing with a handgun, shot himself dead in what was reported to be a game of Russian roulette gone wrong.[62] Thornton had taken the gun from Ace earlier that day, but he had convinced her to give it back. She was one of several people in the dressing room with Ace when he pulled the trigger. Reflecting on her career in a 1975 interview, Thornton stated, "I worked on his [Johnny Ace's] show up to 1954 when he decided he didn't want to be in the world no more; I *guess* that's what he decided cause he blew his brains out."[63]

Following Ace's death Thornton continued to record, but she was unable to produce another hit single. In 1956, the year Presley covered "Hound Dog," Thornton and Peacock Records parted ways. According to some stories, Robey refused to renew her contract.[64] Thornton claimed that she left over disputes about money: "Peacock cheated me. I didn't get ma [*sic*] money. After they gypped me, I ups and quit, and stayed quit," she said.[65] Thornton decided it was time to leave Houston, and she set her sights on California. She had received a good response when playing there in the early fifties. According to Ace's biographer James Salem, "The *Chicago Defender* reported that 'Big Mama' Thornton 'stopped the show in Tacoma, Oakland and Richmond auditoriums; in Stockton, Sacramento, Bakersfield and at Elks auditorium in Los Angeles.' In San Diego, the paper declared, 'they called out the fire department to cool her off!'"[66] When her friend the rhythm and blues vocalist and songwriter Jimmy McCracklin came through Houston on tour, Thornton enlisted his help. "She said she wasn't doing so good then," McCracklin told me. "She wanted to get out and come out to California. She thought she could improve her condition."[67] In late 1956, McCracklin added Thornton to a tour that ended in Richmond, California, McCracklin's hometown.[68] Once there, she stayed with McCracklin and his family at their home for about nine months while she learned her way around the San Francisco Bay Area and its live music scene.[69] Thornton began playing the nightclubs in Richmond, Oakland, and San Francisco, usually making about $25 a night.[70] Chris Strachwitz, who later recorded her for his Arhoolie label, recalled going to see her in a small bar in Santa Cruz, California, in the late 1950s after a friend told him, "there's this amazing blues singer playing drums and singing and blowing harmonica. You ought to go catch her. . . . So I went there and there she was behind the drums, this ferocious beating of the drums and hollering blues and had her harmonica on the window sill in a glass of water, just accompanied by a piano player."[71] She kept working, kept singing the blues, and, Jimmy McCracklin explained, "Once she got herself going, the people liked her. She was able to maneuver from there on out."[72] By the early 1960s, Thornton was making a name as a formidable blues vocalist and was starting to get the bookings in higher-profile clubs that led to a slot on the 1964 Monterey Jazz Festival and an invitation to join the American Folk Blues Festival that toured Europe in 1965.

From her new home base in the Bay Area, Thornton provided a musical and stylistic template for white rock and rollers in the 1960s San Francisco scene, a process that won her career-saving visibility. Finding Thornton's musicality and attitude concentrated in one woman would have been a revelation for Janis Joplin, who, by the mid-1960s, was immersing herself in folk music and the blues and pursuing her dream of being a musician. Similar to Thornton's other white associates—Otis, Leiber, Stoller, and Presley—Joplin was invested in black musical culture, and she drew on aspects of it as she fashioned her musical identity. Chief among the models that inspired her were African American women musicians. She spent hours with their recordings, memorizing lyrics and imitating their vocal styles, much like Presley had done. Odetta, the African American folk guitarist and vocalist, was a particular favorite of Joplin's, but above all she revered Bessie Smith.[73] Thornton, who had once been billed as "Bessie Smith's younger sister," might have seemed like a direct descendant of her idol and maybe even a way for Joplin to connect to her.[74] In addition to being moved by her musicianship, Joplin might have seen Thornton as a sister in unconventional femininity. Neither woman met the prevailing standards of feminine appearance and behavior. Thornton was nearly six feet tall and, at two hundred or so pounds, she was literally a "big mama." When left to her own devices, she avoided the common practice of glamming up for the stage in gowns and high heels, and by the end of the 1960s was known for an onstage wardrobe of "men's clothes." Radical then and still striking in the twenty-first century, Thornton wore slacks, plaid work shirts, cowboy boots, a stingy brim hat, and, in a spectacular move, a men's suit. The behavior of both women pushed against traditional notions of femininity: They were hard-drinking, hard-living women who rocked and rolled with their fellow musicians, most of whom were men. Above all, they devoted their energy and focus to their music. Thornton's blackness was surely another point of attraction and fascination for Joplin, who, like many white artists of her era, viewed African American people and culture as authentic sources of expression that trumped what they perceived as the emptiness of mainstream European American culture. Thornton was a real life manifestation of the idealized blackness that Joplin sought to reproduce in her own music-making. Perhaps it was inevitable that Joplin would cover one of Thornton's songs.

In the early 1960s, Thornton did some recording with Baytone Records, an independent Oakland label. One of the records she cut was "Ball and Chain," a blues that she wrote and performed regularly in her sets. Baytone never released the record, but when Joplin and Big Brother and the Holding Company guitarist James Gurley heard Thornton sing it live, they thought their band could do something with it. In 1966, the same year that Joplin joined Big Brother, she and Gurley asked Thornton for permission to use the song one night after seeing her perform. Thornton agreed.[75] The band did not copy Thornton's song; indeed, as members of Big Brother have since admitted, their limited musical abilities made it unlikely that they would have been capable of doing so.[76] Explaining that the band was not trying to produce "faithful renditions" of the songs they covered, Big Brother guitarist Peter Albin said, "We used the slash-and-burn method of arranging. The chainsaw method."[77] The slash-and-burn method also applied to Joplin's vocals, which rock critic Robert Christgau described as "two-thirds Willie Mae Thornton and one-third [country vocalist] Kitty Wells."[78] Comparing the two versions, music critic Ellen Willis observed that Thornton's "Ball and Chain" "carefully balances defiance and resignation, toughness and vulnerability. . . . Her singing conveys, above all, her determination to survive abuse. Janis makes the song into one long frenzied, despairing protest. . . . The pain is overwhelming her."[79] Thornton taps into a blues attitude that understands that hard knocks and mean men are an unfair but inevitable part of life. She sings the blues to get through the rough times and, indeed, to cure the blues.

Joplin's vocal style partly grew out of singing against the volume produced by her band. Her biographer Alice Echols points out that she could no longer rely on the "big open notes and very simple phrasing she had used when she was singing like Bessie Smith" in acoustic folk music contexts.[80] The resulting full throttle vocal approach is key to Joplin's self-expression, and it helped set the template for hard rock, metal, punk, and grunge vocals in the seventies, eighties, and nineties. Joplin could sing in a "pretty voice," but she was adamant that she did not want to do so.[81] Studying an artist like Thornton, a blues shouter who sang with considerable volume and did not try to "sound pretty," gave Joplin a viable alternative. Modeling her vocals after Thornton's "rough" delivery enabled Joplin to find her singing voice. She fashioned this different voice and attitude by tapping into the unconventional sound and image of womanhood that Thornton projected.

Joplin's visibility as rock's first female superstar spilled over to Thornton. Higher-profile bookings and a contract with Mercury Records, a major label, resulted from being recognized as the woman who wrote "Ball and Chain," a track on Big Brother's 1968 breakthrough album, *Cheap Thrills*.[82] Both Joplin and Presley recorded songs originated by Thornton, but only Joplin shared the success, inviting Thornton to open for her on a couple of concert dates.[83] Thornton spoke highly of Joplin, who had asked if she could record her song and who publicly acknowledged her. Discussing Joplin in 1972, Thornton said, "I gave her the right and the permission to make 'Ball and Chain.' And she always was my idol before she passed away . . . and I thank her for helping me. I'll always go along the line with that."[84] From the 1960s on, "Ball and Chain" was a crowd-pleasing part of Thornton's repertoire. She would mention Joplin as she introduced the song, calling her "the late and great Janis Joplin" on some occasions.[85] Always, she claimed the song as her own, noting that she would be singing it "in my own way, the way I wrote it." According to Strachwitz, "[Thornton] was really proud of 'Ball and Chain.' It was just one of those things that came to her, you know, because of her love and problems and then [Joplin] made it into a hit and she appreciated Janis helping her get gigs."[86] The creation of the song, ownership of the song, and financial and social recognition of that ownership were all important to Thornton.

As the blues developed a sizable white audience, Thornton found herself playing to enthusiastic white crowds, sometimes backed by integrated bands. A *DownBeat* review of her appearance at the Sky River Rock Festival in Sultan, Washington, in 1968, called her performance "the pinnacle of the festival" and mentioned the musicians playing alongside her: African American blues artist James Cotton on harmonica and European American rock musician Ron "Pigpen" McKernan of the Grateful Dead on organ.[87] In 1969, she was a featured artist at the Ann Arbor Blues Festival, the first major blues festival to be held in the United States.[88] Occurring shortly after Woodstock, the event was organized by University of Michigan students, and most of the twenty thousand people who attended were white.[89] Footage from a 1971 performance at the University of Oregon shows Big Mama Thornton playing harmonica and singing before a youthful, white crowd and backed by a band of black and white musicians.[90] These are scenarios that Thornton probably could not have imagined when she started singing the blues in the 1940s. The cross-racial exchanges that Thornton and numerous others had been involved in during the 1950s and 1960s made this integrated blues-rock scene and sound possible. By the early 1970s, young white fans and musicians played and identified with the blues that Thornton and the other blues revival musicians had taught them and were claiming the blues as their own.

Hearing Big Mama Thornton's Voice

A shift in musical values within rock and roll coupled with the tyranny of conventional race and gender roles have contributed to Thornton's lack of visibility and audibility in rock and roll history. Thornton referred to the music she made as the blues—"Play the blues," she would instruct her band.[91] She did not think of herself as a rock and roll artist, and she considered rock and roll to be "nuthin' [sic] but the blues speeded up."[92] Still, her attitude and artistry contributed to the shape rock and roll took in the 1950s and 1960s. Ironically, the blues revival that helped give Thornton's career a second wind ushered in an aesthetic that contributes to her marginalization. Cultural critic Ulrich Adelt has noted that the blues revival was marked by "the rise of the guitar-as-fetish in the reception of white blues fans with the simultaneous devaluation of vocal blues styles."[93] These are the conditions that shaped and continue to shape rock music writing and canon formation, and they marginalize the influence of black women vocalists. Indeed, under this system, even the significance of a white rock superstar like Janis Joplin is muted because her instrument was her voice and her gender is female. As Echols observes, "[Joplin's] style was absorbed, without credit and in a way that obscured her influence."[94]

The blues revival expanded the audience for blues and precipitated a shift in the sound and aesthetic of rock and roll, which was renamed "rock" by the late 1960s as guitar-virtuosity took center stage. This emphasis facilitated the ascendance of Eric Clapton and Jimi Hendrix—great guitarists lacking traditionally "good" voices—and the celebration of the blues guitarist forebears such as Robert Johnson, John Lee Hooker, and Muddy Waters who influenced them. Rock fans and critics were paying less attention to the kind of vocal mastery that marked Thornton's performances. This situation mirrors what can happen on stage when the guitar is turned up so loud that it blots out the vocals: When rock and roll is constructed as a guitar-centered art form, it becomes hard to hear Big Mama Thornton's voice and, by extension, her influence. If we shift the focus and center the voice instead of the guitar, highlighting vocalists instead of guitarists, we can recognize Big Mama Thornton as one of the sources of the blues-based vocals that generations of rock and rollers have adapted, absorbed, and built on. If we listen, we can hear a line of descent from Thornton to Elvis Presley and Janis Joplin on through to Robert Plant, Axl Rose, Kurt Cobain, Jack White, and Brittany Howard.[95]

Thornton had a reputation for being an exacting taskmaster in live performance; she would not let a song go forward until the musicians were playing the *real* blues. More than once she ordered an ineffective drummer away from the kit so she could play it the way she wanted to hear it. It's a characteristic that indicates her commitment to her craft, but it also represents a breach of conventional gender behavior, and she unnerved some of the men she encountered. Recalling their first impressions of her, Mike Stoller and Jerry Leiber report, "her voice was a force of nature" and describe her as being "absolutely magnificent"; but they also characterize her as being "formidable and a bit frightening. . . . There was something monstrous about Big Mama," they assert.[96] Dick Waterman, who had booked her into the club he was working for, said of Thornton, "It wasn't just that she was strong willed. I figured that she came out of the womb standing up and pissed off."[97] British singer and music writer Ian Whitcomb describes her as having "a reputation as a feisty battle-axe who could drink any man under the table and give as good as she got."[98] In his history of the Summer of Love, music critic Joel Selvin writes that Thornton was "a tough, grizzled blues bitch, quite capable of kicking the woebegone ass of one of her musicians if she didn't like the way he parted his hair."[99] In all of these depictions, the younger white men's discomfort with an assertive black woman is clear. Perhaps it is possible to modulate this tone by turning to other voices belonging to people more able to recognize the fullness of Thornton's humanity. Guitarist Terry DeRouen, who remained on friendly terms with Thornton even after he stopped playing in her band and was a pallbearer at her funeral, told me, "Sometimes she'd get a little ornery. Like most women do. She'd get a little ornery, but it didn't last long."[100] And she was not one to mince words. "Big Mama would tell you what's on her mind," DeRouen explained. "She wouldn't mind her tongue about nothing like that. Not at all. And if she was on stage and you pissed her off, I guess, she'd let you know that you did that. She was a lot of fun to work with. A lot of fun. She was basically good people."[101] Kat Dyson was unfazed by Thornton's demeanor, even as she told me, "I mean she was cantankerous. Demanded respect, but she was real smooth. She was argumentative. She always had that I've-got-a-joke-that-you-don't-know kind of smile. You know how our elders always have an extra something that we don't know."[102] For Dyson, Thornton was an elder artist deserving of respect.

In a 1971 interview, blues and R&B singer Big Joe Turner, who was more than a decade older than Thornton, shared a recollection of his first encounter with Thornton that paints a different picture of a woman who was widely portrayed as a tough, blues broad. This filmed exchange takes place while Turner, Thornton, and Muddy Waters are riding in a car, presumably heading to their next gig. The interviewer asks Turner how he and Thornton met:

Big Joe Turner: Oh, hook up with Willie Mae Thornton? Ohhhh. Been a long time ago. We won't say how long it's been. She was a little girl. Had on a pair of blue jeans.

Big Mama Thornton: '51!

Big Joe Turner: Had on a pair of blue jeans, come into the club. I was working in a little shaggy joint in Houston, Texas. She come in there and said, "Mister, can I sing? Can I sing for you? Can I sing? Can I?" I said, "Go away, girl, you bother me." . . . A while later, I said, 'Well, I'll let her sing. She's going to bug me to death.' Let her sing. . . . She look like a good little ol' girl. Let her sing. . . . I give her the mic and, boy, she cut up there and sung a breeze. Ohhhh, you were singing. Had on little blue jeans. Ohhhh, she was so young and happy. I doubt she—I don't think she even knew nothing about what to drink. In fact, she wasn't due to be in there. They were selling whiskey.

Interviewer: She ordered a Shirley Temple and sang.

Big Joe Turner: Yeah, she was really doing it up good.

Big Mama Thornton: That's a lie. I had a whole fifth in my pocket. [laughs]

Big Joe Turner: That goes to show you, you can't judge a child. But you were a little girl then. A little, bitty girl.[103]

As Turner tells the story, Thornton smiles and responds to his recollections with laughter. This interview clip, featuring Thornton with her friends, reveals another dimension. Appearing to enjoy the brief recollection of the scene in Houston in 1951, she defends herself against what she takes to be an overstatement of her youthful innocence and claims to have been seasoned enough to travel with a personal stash of liquor. While only a few minutes long, this segment rescues Thornton from her stereotyped lot—the scary, angry black woman—and allows her to shine as an individual with a history, community, and a sense of humor. Which is not to say that her professional experiences were always smooth or her demeanor was always sunny. Thornton was out on the road on her own and without a chaperone from the time she was fourteen years old. She had to be tough to survive. Or at least appear to be so. James Moore, who managed her in the 1960s, when the blues revival was buoying her career, suggested as much when I spoke with him:

> **MM:** I was just trying to also get a feel for her personality because first you said she was mean, but then you said she wasn't really. Or was she?
>
> **James Moore:** Well. How can I say this? If she thought she was being taken advantage of, she would, you know, she would be [mean]. But what I'm trying to say is basically she was a nice person. Once you got around that shell, that fence she built around herself. She would put on a Don't Mess With Me [Attitude]. Of course she wasn't to be messed with.[104]

Thornton's gruff exterior might have been a response to the challenges of being a woman in a male-dominated field known for all manner of chicanery. In an interview given toward the end of her life and after years of being one of a handful of women on the scene, Thornton discussed the impact of her gender on her experience. She attributed some of her difficulties to the professional envy of male musicians and her burdensome reputation for being tough. Referring to male musicians, she told a reporter:

> They always have been jealous of me because when I hit that stage, I perform. I give you . . . entertainment. I don't go out on the stage trying to look pretty. I was born pretty. I get out there and crack a few jokes, and sing my song and people love it. That's why they were jealous of me, because the people were giving me recognition and they didn't get the recognition that I had, because I was unique.[105]

Thornton also claimed that some of the male performers (she doesn't give any names) "lied on me, said I would fight the promoters. All I ever did was ask them for my money."[106] Here, her gendered analysis of the meaning of her skill as a performer and her protection of her financial interests acknowledge the ways she challenged the primacy of men in a male-dominated arena, actions that marked her as a dangerous woman. Her comments also undercut explicit and implicit attacks on her physical appearance. "I was born pretty," she proclaims, recognizing her beauty, even if others did not.

In interviews, Thornton confronted the fact that Presley and Joplin achieved greater professional success than she. In 1981, she said, "I deserved it, but I never did cry over somebody else's milk. I always tried to get me a bottle of my own."[107] She hoped to record a song that would match the success of "Hound Dog." In 1965, she quipped, "Right now I wish I could get another dog. Or a cat or something."[108] Giving her the last word in the interview, her producer Chris Strachwitz asked Thornton if there was anything she wanted to tell the world. "Yeah, I need a job," she said before letting out a laugh. She continued:

> I need a job. I need help, help. [laughs] See there are so many youngsters jumping up now, they forget about the old-timers and right now you'd really be surprised that the old timers got more to offer than some of those young-sters. You know, if people would just come out and listen to the old-timers, then they'll realize that they can. Old-timers are still going. Me, all I just need is the break. All I want to do is put something out there that—I mean, just let me sit down and just take my time, put some good background behind it, and let me just show the world what I got. That's all I want.[109]

Thornton outlived both of the white "youngsters" who rose to fame by tapping into her sound and style, and she kept on singing the blues until the end of her life, confident that she had something valuable to share. If we listen beyond the race, gender, and genre assumptions that inform mainstream presentations of rock and roll history, we can hear what she shared. Listen and hear her contribution to the sound, feel, and attitude of rock and roll.

TWO / LaVern Baker, the Incredible Disappearing Queen of Rock and Roll

I always wanted to sing pretty songs and slow blues like "I Cried a Tear," . . . but the people who handled me wanted songs like "Tweedlee Dee," because they wanted a hit— and it worked. / **LAVERN BAKER**

The April 1956 issue of *Ebony* magazine included an article called "The Tweedlee Dee Girl." Replete with the monthly's signature effusive praise for successful African Americans, the article declared LaVern Baker a "high priestess of rock 'n' roll" and, over the course of the five-page feature, depicted "the fruits of her stardom" in words and photos.[1] The article described Baker as "a chunky bundle of musical fire whose husky voice has made her a heroine to millions and is currently earning her an income of $75,000 yearly."[2] A photo caption referring to her performance at the Brooklyn Paramount noted that the "'Rock 'n' Roll Revue' that she headlined there drew a record weekly gross of $148,000."[3] And Baker, the magazine reported, was "deluged with requests for personal appearances."[4]

A vocalist known for what one reporter called her "full-throated, vibrant belting with a sexy tease," LaVern Baker was one of the rhythm and blues artists who popularized "the Big Beat" and modeled the rhythmic vocal approach that was the signature of rock and roll.[5] In the 1950s, Baker made hit records and appeared on television and in film singing the newly christened genre. One of the only women visible in the early rock and roll scene, Baker was a headliner on blockbuster national tours, sharing concert bills with rock and roll luminaries Chuck Berry, Eddie Cochran, Bo Diddley, Fats Domino, the

Everly Brothers, Bill Haley and His Comets, and Buddy Holly and the Crickets. Her November 20, 1955, appearance on Ed Sullivan's variety show *Toast of the Town* with Bo Diddley and the Five Keys marked the first national network television broadcast of rock and roll, paving the way for televised star turns by Chuck Berry, Little Richard, and Elvis Presley.[6]

Baker brought rock and roll into America's living rooms and concert stages, earning critical accolades as she turned teens on to the new sound. Justifying their selection of Baker as *DownBeat*'s Top Female Personality of the Year in 1955, the magazine's editors observed, "She spent 1954 going from good to better performances on record and in-person and was soon head and shoulders above the nearest competition."[7] The African American monthly *Our World* described her as "a mature vocalist gifted with unusual originality. She is the girl most often credited with putting 'rhythm in the blues.'"[8] A 1956 article in *Rock 'n' Roll Jamboree* magazine emphasized her ability to infuse her blues-rooted vocals with propulsive energy: "'She's the rhythm in the Blues' is the title used to describe her as a singer," the reporter explained. "The young fans call her a Rock and Roll Queen."[9]

Baker's contributions to rock and roll have been recognized, perhaps most prominently in 1991, when she became the second woman to be inducted into the Rock and Roll Hall of Fame. She does not, however, receive sustained attention in college textbooks surveying rock and roll from its beginnings in the post–World War II era to the twenty-first century. Reebee Garofalo's *Rockin' Out* acknowledges that Baker was a rare example of a female performer able to "penetrate the weekly best-seller lists with rock 'n' roll material," but John Covach and Andrew Flory's *What's That Sound? An Introduction to Rock and Its History* does not mention her at all.[10] In *Rock: Music, Culture, and Business*, Joseph Schloss, Larry Starr, and Christopher Waterman allow that Baker achieved "modest success on the pop charts during the early years of rock 'n' roll," but distance her and all black women from the form and their textbook's narrative of it:

> Given the tenor of the times, an empowered *black* female rock 'n' roll "idol" would have been even more unlikely—which is why African American women have played no part in this discussion. Only a few female black artists, such as LaVern Baker and Sarah Vaughan, achieved even modest success on the pop charts during the early years of rock 'n' roll.[11]

I wish I could say that I avoided this tendency, but in my first effort to document the participation of African American women in rock and roll, an essay for an edited collection on the history of African American music, I did not discuss Baker.[12] More extensive commentaries on Baker's career appear in studies of the history of rhythm and blues.[13] But, as Fats Domino biographer Rick Coleman has observed, in comparison to other popular music genres, there has been "so little research on *rhythm & blues* that even major figures have disappeared into shadow. . . . The most popular R&B artists of the 1940s and the 1950s, Louis Jordan and Domino, are today little known to most people."[14] LaVern Baker could be added to this list.

It would make sense to assume that women-centered histories of rock and roll would feature Baker as a prominent founding figure, but only Gillian Gaar's revisionist history of the genre, *She's a Rebel*, addresses her career in any detail. In *She Bop*, Lucy O'Brien lists Baker among the Atlantic Records artists who prepared the ground for Aretha Franklin's career at the label, but does not discuss Baker at length.[15] *Trouble Girls: The Rolling Stone Book of Women in Rock*, a volume of essays intended to be "an incisive collection of the histories of these women [in rock] written by women," mentions Baker in a long list of artists "who deserve more attention" but whom the editor was unable to include in the book.[16] Maybe it's better to be left out. In *The Rolling Stone Illustrated History of Rock 'n' Roll*, Baker appears in two group photos (she is partially cut off in one), and, in an essay on Chuck Berry, dean of rock critics Robert Christgau calls her "a second-rate blues and gospel singer who felt like she was selling her soul every time she launched into a first-rate whoop of nonsense like 'Jim Dandy' or 'Bumble Bee.'"[17] In the twenty-first century, Baker's contemporaries Ruth Brown and Etta James are better known than she. During the 1980s, 1990s, and early 2000s, they kept their names before the American public, continuing to record and perform in the United States and reminding audiences of their early contributions to rock and roll through published memoirs.[18] Baker, in contrast, moved overseas in the late 1960s, fading from the collective rock and roll consciousness until her return to the United States in the late 1980s. Her reemergence, helped along by a starring role in the Broadway musical revue *Black and Blue* (she replaced her friend Ruth Brown) and a spate of nightclub concerts, was truncated by poor health. She died in 1997.

While Baker was living abroad in the 1970s and 1980s, Tina Turner became rock and roll's undisputed queen, but what about the first woman to occupy that throne? As I learned more about Baker, I was nagged not only by my mistake in overlooking an artist who had been a key figure at a pivotal phase in the history of music, but also by the fact that overlooking Baker was so common. Baker's presence in the early years of rock and roll is undeniable, yet her significance has been diminished in historical representations. The dynamics of race, gender, and genre shaped Baker's career in the 1950s, and they inform the ways historians and music critics discuss her contribution decades later or whether they discuss her at all. During the mid-1950s, Baker was a well-known singer of rhythm and blues and its newly christened offshoot, rock and roll. In fact, her performances were categorized under both labels. In the fall of 1954, she joined Roy Hamilton, the Drifters, and Faye Adams on the Biggest Rhythm & Blues Revue at the Brooklyn Paramount.[19] A few months later, in the spring of 1955, she was booked on Alan Freed's Rock 'n' Roll Easter Jubilee. The following year, she was second on the bill after headliner Bill Haley and His Comets on the Biggest Rock 'n' Roll Show of 1956, a forty-five-day national tour.[20] In 1955, "Rock around the Clock" by Bill Haley, a white singer and bandleader, became the first rock and roll song to go to number one, and African American artists LaVern Baker, Chuck Berry, Fats Domino, and the Platters appeared on the pop charts with songs that were labeled "rock 'n' roll."[21] By the end of the year, "the pop music business had turned [disc jockey] Alan Freed's pet description of rhythm and blues [i.e., the term *rock and roll*] into a generic classification of the music specifically aimed at America's youth."[22]

In light of Baker's clear connection to rock and roll, it is ironic that popular music histories categorize Baker solely as a rhythm and blues artist; this is a retrospective tidying up of the musically messy 1950s. Observing that such misreadings are a common problem of research on music genres, musicologist Jeffrey Kallberg states, "Later listeners interpret earlier exemplars according to the current precepts."[23] Addressing this problem in his biography of Fats Domino, Rick Coleman notes the following:

> Domino's music, like most early rock 'n' roll, was subversive in its cultural impact, but, following the counterculture of the late 1960s, rock writers demanded music of *overt* rebellion and began dismissing Domino as "harmless" and "nonthreatening." Indeed, judged by the extremes of modern rock, Fats wouldn't register on the outrage radar. He wasn't tortured, violent, or sexually provocative. He didn't scream, take drugs, or trash hotels.[24]

Similarly, Baker's respectable carriage and scream-free vocals do not seem like rock and roll, according to the "current precepts." Baker did not perform in the over-the-top fashion of Little Richard or Elvis Presley, and she does not fit the guitar-centered, white male–dominated style that took hold in the late sixties. Baker's disappearance from the genre is a consequence of both the unstable definition of rock and roll during the 1950s and the redefinition of the form that took place in subsequent years, as "rock and roll" was relabeled "rock." Much of this work involved the realignment of gender and race in relation to musical production and occurred in publications that covered the rock scene. The founding of counterculture music magazines *Crawdaddy* in 1966 and *Rolling Stone* in 1967 and the emergence of serious rock criticism that explored the aesthetics and politics of popular music pushed women and African Americans to the outer limits of rock and roll discourse and representation.[25] Musicologist Norma Coates notes that "in its early years, [*Rolling Stone*] not only covered rock culture, but in large part helped define and characterize it. At the same time, the magazine limned out the boundaries of rock culture and sorted out its insiders and outsiders."[26] In a discussion of the context in which these processes occurred, music historian Bernard Gendron observes, "*Crawdaddy* and *Rolling Stone* were virtual white male fraternities," whose writers denied "cultural accreditation to contemporary black music" through "benign neglect."[27] The resulting marginalization of black music at the end of the 1960s, Gendron argues, "seemed to reflect a deepening division between the marketing and functions of white and black popular music" in which "'album rock' became a code for the art end of the pop spectrum and 'soul' and 'funk' for the entertainment end"; this led to "a disproportionate diversion of the more valuable types of cultural capital toward white rock, leaving the lesser coinage for soul."[28] Commenting on the gender dynamics of these representations, Coates says of *Rolling Stone,* "almost all of its writers were male. . . . Its style, sensibility and subject matter were geared to masculine subjects, readers, and subjectivity."[29] She argues that "masculinity became naturalized in rock in the 1960s, and, as a result, women became marginal and/or subservient to men in rock culture and its discursive formations."[30] Women, Coates explains, were designated as "low Others," and their contributions to rock culture received little attention.[31]

The cultural discourses of the late sixties that "turned rock into a signifier of white masculinity and authenticity" have influenced the ways listeners receive and value popular music created by women and African Americans.[32] As a black woman, Baker did not fit the evolving paradigm of rock and roll and has been subjected to a kind of double exclusion from the genre. Baker's career typifies both the contribution black artists made to rock and roll and the limitations they routinely encountered in the early years of the genre. Following an overview of Baker's emergence as a professional recording artist, I consider the dynamics of gender, race, and genre in three contexts in which she made a mark: the debate over cover records, the circulation of rock and roll though national concert tours, and the films that brought the new sound to a national audience. My intention is to return one of the first rock and roll stars to the genre's history and account for why she was erased in the first place.

Novelty Act

Delores LaVern Baker, born in Chicago on November 11, 1929, established an early bond with a paternal aunt, Merline Johnson, a popular Chicago-based blues singer during the 1930s and 1940s.[33] Some sources identify Baker as a niece of blues guitar great Memphis Minnie (née Lizzie Douglas), while others say Douglas was a close family friend.[34] Whatever the genealogical facts, the two seasoned female musicians exposed the young Baker to the world of professional music-making.[35] She was in her early teens when she cut her first professional record and sought out bookings while she was still attending high school.[36] An early press release explained that Baker launched her professional career in 1946, "as soon as she was old enough to get a permit to work in a cabaret. On her seventeenth birthday LaVern received a present in the form of a contract from [Chicago nightclub owners George and Mable Woods]. The next day Little Miss Sharecropper opened at the Club DeLisa. She was held over for six months."[37] As Little Miss Sharecropper, Baker "kept her hair in pigtails, wore tattered overalls, and carried a basket," evoking an image of the rural south that African American migrants to Chicago from states like Mississippi, Arkansas, and Alabama had left behind.[38] The club owners' decision to present Baker in this costume made sense. A local favorite known as Little Miss Cornshucks who dressed as a backwoods character had recently stopped working at the club, and they wanted to capitalize on her popularity.[39]

Baker developed a wide-ranging club act. "I did comedy, blues, pop, everything," she told music writer Dennis Garvey in a 1991 interview.[40] During the late 1940s and early 1950s, Little Miss Sharecropper performed in Chicago nightspots like the Brookmount Lounge, the Blue Dahlia, the Miramar Ballroom, and the Crown Propeller.[41] Her run at the Club DeLisa brought her to the attention of prominent musicians, including Nat King Cole and Fletcher Henderson, and led to a contract to work at Detroit's Flame Show Bar, a club that booked a predominantly black slate of artists and welcomed both black and white patrons.[42] While at the Flame, Baker met Johnnie Ray, a white singer from Oregon, who was also performing at the club. The two became friends, and she advised him about his approach to vocals, helping him to perfect the highly emotive singing that propelled his 1951 hit "Cry" to number one on both the pop and R&B charts.[43] An early example of both the interracial musical exchanges that shaped rock and roll and black women's influence on the vocal style of white male singers, Ray's debt to Baker became part of the public narrative of both performers. The program notes for the 1957 Biggest Show of Stars tour on which Baker was a featured artist remarked, "[Baker] is the one who taught 'Mr. Emotion, himself,' Johnny [sic] Ray, how to cry the blues," while Ray acknowledged the ways Baker and other African American artists influenced his vocal and performance style in a 1953 Ebony article published under his name.[44]

While touring with bandleader Todd Rhodes in 1952, Baker dropped the Sharecropper costume and character and began to use LaVern Baker as her professional name.[45] Although she had retired her rural persona by the time she signed with Atlantic Records in 1953, it helped her secure the contract. The label's cofounder, Ahmet Ertegun, was a huge fan of Little Miss Cornshucks, whom many artists and fans revered for her vocal power, original phrasing, and creative approaches to ballads. In fact, Cornshucks was the first artist Ertegun recorded; he worked with her in a Washington, DC, studio years before he owned a record company.[46] Within a year of starting Atlantic Records, Ertegun and label cofounder Herb Abramson had used the vocal style of Little Miss Cornshucks as a template for Ruth Brown's first release, "So Long" (1949).[47] Unable to locate Miss Cornshucks and offer her a contract, Ertegun and Abramson signed a woman who, as Little Miss Sharecropper, evoked her vocal style.[48] Contradicting Robert Christgau's characterization of Baker as a "second-rate" talent, Ertegun said of Baker, "Like Cornshucks, she could really sing. For me at that time, Cornshucks, LaVern, Dinah Washington and Little Esther Phillips were the truly great voices."[49] Atlantic label-mates Baker and Brown preferred to sing 1940s style standards in the vein of Cornshucks, but their most successful songs departed from her smooth style. The Atlantic producers insisted that their vocalists accentuate rhythm, a move, Brown recalled, that put them "a step ahead of the accepted sound of the day."[50] Commenting on the situation, Baker noted, "It was a trend and everybody jumped on it. My manager felt that I could better myself if I went that way and then later on go the way I wanted to go, after I was financially fit."[51]

Baker's first record for Atlantic, "Soul on Fire," was a sultry, mid-tempo number that did well enough on the charts to suggest that Ertegun and Abramson had been wise to sign Baker.[52] The next song she recorded, "Tweedlee Dee," gave them solid proof.[53] The first in a string of novelty tunes that Baker placed on the charts, "Tweedlee Dee" featured Baker's rhythmic vocals and a swinging groove. And unlike her first Atlantic release, teenagers were able to hear "Tweedlee Dee" on the radio. It was, rhythm and blues historian Chip Deffaa observes, a safer song than "Soul on Fire," and "some disc jockeys who were afraid to play a record of a sexy black woman frankly singing 'you set my soul on fire' could play a record by that same singer proclaiming the far tamer 'you make my heart go clickety-clack.'"[54] The novelty of the new rhythm and the whimsical lyrics won the record mainstream radio airplay, and the song ascended on both the R&B and pop charts. Describing the song, Deffaa notes, "Some of Baker's sexuality came through. In a vocal fill she sang something that sounded like 'humpy-um-bum-bum' with an overbrimming sensual vitality."[55]

The differences between "Soul on Fire" and "Tweedlee Dee" encapsulate the differences between R&B and rock and roll. The former was music about adult topics; the latter featured youthful attitude, subject matter, and occasional nonsense lyrics (A womp bam a loo bop, a womp bam boom, anyone?). Broadly speaking, rhythm and blues was for adults, specifically black adults, and rock and roll was becoming music for all teenagers. Baker sang using clear diction and "little-girl charm," making her records accessible to a broad audience.[56] Atlantic positioned "Tweedlee Dee" for pop radio airtime by backing Baker with a male vocal quintet, dubbed the Gliders for the session, "who provided a 'sing-along' quality . . . by repeating [the] song's catchiest lines."[57] The background vocalists accentuated the song's hook, a practice producers believed would help cross it over to pop.[58] The strategy worked and the Gliders (actually Atlantic's house background group, the Cues) joined Baker on all of her Atlantic recordings.[59] Sticking to what seemed to work on the charts, Atlantic kept giving Baker material with gimmicky lyrics. Reflecting on her repertoire, Baker said, "I thought they were cute. . . . It seems like every hit I had was a novelty song: 'Bumble Bee,' 'Tra La La,' 'Bop-Ting-a-Ling.' Every novelty song I recorded was a hit, like 'Jim Dandy.' Maybe my voice was good for novelty songs."[60] With its references to Tweedledee and Tweedledum, characters from Lewis Carroll's children's classic *Through the Looking Glass*, and lyrics like "Hubba, hubba, Honey Dew, I'm gonna keep my eyes on you," "Tweedlee Dee" fit with the spate of novelty songs that charted in 1954 and 1955: "Gee" by the Crows (1954), "Sh-Boom" by the Chords (1954), "Ling Ting Tong" by the Charms (1954), and "Ko Ko Mo" by Gene and Eunice (1955).[61] Baker's connection to the youth-oriented sound established her as a rock and roll artist in the genre's early years and propelled her into the mainstream. "Tweedlee Dee" peaked at number 14 and stayed on the pop charts for eleven weeks.[62] This was a rare feat for a black singer in 1955, and Baker was the first Atlantic artist to cross over to pop.[63] She bettered the accomplishments of Ruth Brown, whose 1953 hit "Mama, He Treats Your Daughter Mean" had been voted *DownBeat*'s top Rhythm and Blues record of the year and had peaked at number 23 on the pop charts.[64] Baker's records broke into the pop Top 20, and she maintained a visibility on the rock and roll scene that no other woman, black or white, enjoyed.

Covering a Star

In the mid-1950s, recording industry periodicals *Billboard* and *Cash Box* covered Baker's chart success, and the African American general interest magazines *Our World* and *Ebony* published profiles titled "Tweedlee Dee Girl." Much of Baker's press recounted her criticism of cover records. A closer look at Baker's response to cover records reveals the ways one African American woman navigated the tangle of race and genre that consigned her to a second-class position in a field she had helped to pioneer.

Recognizing Baker as "one of the most imitated girl singers today," the *Our World* article described her situation: "As the original 'Tweedlee Dee' girl she watched her song march right up to the Number One spot on the Hot Parade. But much of LaVern's thunder is stolen from her. Arrangements written for her are duplicated by white pop artists who have hopped aboard the R&B gravy train."[65] By the mid-1950s, the major record labels that had dismissed African American R&B as a fad confronted the fact that it attracted white listeners and sought ways to capitalize on the trend. Rather than signing African American R&B artists, the labels enlisted white artists already under contract with them to record new versions, or "covers," of R&B songs. Commenting on the growing prominence of covers in 1955, *Billboard* reported, "Despite the scarcely-veiled antagonism of many pop publishers and artist and repertoire men to R&B tunes, 13 of the 30 disks on the current best-selling singles chart fall into that category."[66] The practice of covering songs was a long-standing one in the recording industry, encouraged by music publishers who pushed

the songs in their catalogues to multiple parties in order to increase their royalties. In the 1950s, this practice took on a racial dimension. White pop artists
covered R&B songs originated by black artists who had difficulty commanding
airplay on mainstream pop radio, an environment that was as segregated as
the nation it entertained.

The trajectories of Baker's originals and the covers that white pop singer
Georgia Gibbs recorded illustrate the situation. Just two weeks after Baker's
version of "Tweedlee Dee" appeared on the pop charts, Gibbs's version, released on Mercury Records, followed.[67] Gibbs's record outsold Baker's and
reached number two on the pop charts.[68] There is no way to know how far the
original would have gone without this competition, but Baker was outspoken
in her condemnation of covers. She accepted the fact that a singer couldn't
"own" a song in the sense of being the only one to record it. What she took
issue with was the appropriation of the part of the song that *was* hers: the arrangement. "You go to rehearsals with the band and work for hours on just the
right arrangement," Baker recalled in a 1996 interview, "and then someone just
walks in free and easy and copies it—that's sickening."[69] Speaking to a *Chicago
Defender* reporter in 1955 about the artists who covered her recording, she
asked, "Why don't they hire their own arrangers to fit my song to their styles,
instead of fitting their styles to my arrangement for which I paid $1500?"[70]
There's no question that Mercury was trying to duplicate Baker's version. The
label had attempted to hire Tom Dowd, the Atlantic staffer who had engi-
neered Baker's session, promising that they would also hire musicians from
the original session to work with him; Dowd declined the offer.[71]

Many R&B artists suffered from the cover crisis Baker decried. Mercury's
Patti Page hit the *Billboard* Top 40 copying Ruth Brown's "Oh, What a Dream,"
while Brown's version only made it to the R&B charts; to add insult to in-
jury, Page's version crossed over to the R&B charts.[72] Pat Boone covered Little
Richard and Fats Domino and in the process became one of the decade's top-
selling artists, second only to Elvis Presley in the number of charted singles
between 1955 and 1959.[73] Georgia Gibbs built her career performing songs that
black women had originated. In addition to "Tweedlee Dee," she recorded
Baker's "Tra La La," Ruth Brown's "Mambo Baby," and Etta James's "The Wallflower." The *Chicago Defender* reported that James threatened to sue Gibbs
for "revising her own tune of 'Wallflower' and taking the music and adding
new words naming the tune 'Dance with Me Henry.'"[74] James does not seem
to have pursued her case, but she maintained her disgust at what she called
Gibbs's "Suzy Creamcheese version" of her song and the contrasting fates of

the two recordings.[75] "My version went underground and continued to sell while Georgia's whitewash went through the roof," James explained in her autobiography. "Her Henry became a million seller. I was happy to have any success, but I was enraged to see Georgia singing the song on *The Ed Sullivan Show* while I was singing it in some funky dive in Watts."[76] Ruth Brown had a similar lament: "Chuck Willis wrote 'Oh, What a Dream' especially for me, and it was my favorite song, but it was Patti Page, with an identical arrangement, who got to sing it on national television."[77] Little Richard, whose songs "Tutti Frutti" and "Long Tall Sally" were covered by Pat Boone, maintained that racial considerations fueled the covers: "They didn't want the white kids looking up at this big ol' greasy black guy out of Georgia, out of Mississippi, out of Chicago. They wanted their kids to see a little smooth white boy looking pretty and on duty."[78] Covers enabled major labels to profit from black creativity without compensating black performers.

Years later, speaking in her own defense, Gibbs pointed out that, like many vocalists in this era, she did not hear her material until she arrived at the studio to record it.[79] In a 1998 interview she explained,

> Nobody believes I never heard LaVern Baker's recording [of "Tweedlee Dee"]. For the sheer fact that we were living in a very segregated America. Not that we aren't now, but it was terrible then. I couldn't go into a [midtown Manhattan] record store to buy her record, I'd have to go to Harlem to buy it. R&B was only sold up there. So how was I going to hear it? It wasn't played on the radio.[80]

Hearing Gibbs insist on the impossibility of getting access to Baker's release, one might think she was considering a walking trip across an ocean rather than a subway ride uptown to the black neighborhood of Harlem to buy a record. Her comments illustrate the depth of racial segregation, both physical and psychological, during this era; it shaped the experiences of black and white Americans and affected access to popular music, even as the growing popularity of black rhythm and blues was challenging race-based separation.

Performers whose recordings were covered had no legal recourse; they were working within a copyright system that protected written lyrics and music, not recorded performances. Unlike most of the covered artists, Baker sought legal relief for these systemic problems. In 1955, on the heels of "Tweedlee Dee" being covered by Gibbs and two other artists, she took the issue to her congressman. *Billboard* reported that Baker asked Rep. Charles Diggs, Jr. (D-MI) to "Study the possibility of revising the Copyright Act of 1909 in order to protect singers from 'modern-day pirates.'"[81] In her letter, *Billboard* reported, Baker "estimated she lost $15,000 in royalties because purchasers bought other versions of the tune, thinking it was hers."[82] Arguing that the law was "outmoded and should be amended by bringing it into line with present-day conditions," she suggested to Diggs that, "After an investigation of the facts you might see some wisdom in introducing a law to make it illegal for one singer to duplicate another's work. It's not that I mind anyone singing a song that I write, or have written for me by someone, but I bitterly resent their arrogance in thefting my music note for note."[83] Baker spoke out against covers to protect her sound, her primary capital as a performer.

In addition to pushing for legal protection, Baker resorted to humor to deal with the problem. When preparing for a tour of Australia and Japan in early 1957, she purchased insurance for the trip and instructed her manager to send word of the policy to a columnist at the *Chicago Defender*, the nation's preeminent African American newspaper. "LaVern who leaves on Jan. 3 for a personal appearance tour in Australia," the story ran, "sent an air travel life insurance policy to Georgia Gibbs and named Miss Gibbs as the beneficiary."[84] According to the *Defender*, Baker enclosed the following "explanatory note" with the policy:

> Dear Georgia, Inasmuch as I'll be flying over quite a stretch of blue water on my forthcoming Australian tour, I am naturally concerned about making the round trip safely and soundly. My thoughts naturally turn to you at this time, and I am enclosing an insurance policy on my life in the amount of $125,000. This should be at least partial compensation for you if I should be killed or injured, and thereby deprive you of the opportunity of copying my songs and arrangements in the future.[85]

The story of Baker's commentary on industry practices and mockery of Gibbs circulated in the black media and the music industry press; it reemerged years later as an example of Baker's audacity.[86] Baker's criticism of covers became part of her public profile. A week after reporting on her letter to Rep. Diggs, *Billboard* dubbed her "Lavern (Don't Steal My Arrangements) Baker."[87] Humor aside, there were material reasons for her concern. Discussing Baker's situation, Deffaa notes that with covers, in addition to "losing out on sales of a specific record, . . . she was also losing out on publicity and other intangibles that would have boosted her stock as a performer."[88] Eventually, the practice of covers subsided as the record-buying audience developed a preference for the originals. Baker must have been pleased when, in 1956, her version of "Jim

Dandy" became a hit—number one R&B and number 17 pop—outperforming the Georgia Gibbs cover.[89]

The Rock and Roll Highway

Telling images and captions accompany *Ebony*'s 1956 feature on Baker. In one photo she is "Taking stroll near theater, where her name is prominently displayed on marquee."[90] In a backstage shot, "Before show, LaVern adjusts forelock of Bill Haley, whose record 'Rock around the Clock,' sold two million copies."[91] There she is onstage: "Rollicking duet, featuring LaVern and friend Johnny [*sic*] Ray, stops show at Brooklyn Theater."[92] And here she is seated next to a young white man with his arm around her shoulder and her pet poodle on his lap; Baker smiles for the camera of another young white man. The caption reads, "Lionized by students, LaVern is photographed and interviewed in the editorial offices of Long Island University newspaper."[93] Together, the photos and text convey Baker's breakthrough success as a crossover rock and roll star. It is an identity she solidified during the 1950s through her participation in concerts that gave numerous North American teens their first exposure to live rock and roll. As one of the artists who appeared on the most prominent of these shows, Baker was at the forefront of the process of desegregating American popular music.

In April 1955, Baker was one of the headliners on disc jockey Alan Freed's Rock 'n' Roll Easter Jubilee at the Brooklyn Paramount, a week-long concert series featuring four to seven shows a day that broke previous attendance records at the venue.[94] The financial success of the concerts launched a productive professional association between Baker and Freed and prompted others to mount similar events.[95] Baker was a headliner on the largest of the rock and roll tours, Irvin Feld's The Biggest Show of Stars. Consisting of over one hundred musicians and support personnel traveling by bus, the Feld tours played long strings of dates in 1956, 1957, and 1958; the artists played two shows a night and visited as many as twenty-eight states and five Canadian provinces on a single tour.[96] As the 1957 concert program promised, audiences could see "all the foremost artists in the Popular and Rhythm & Blues music world," including Paul Anka, Chuck Berry, Eddie Cochran, the Drifters, the Everly Brothers, Buddy Holly and the Crickets, Frankie Lymon, Clyde McPhatter, and the Platters, for a $2.00 ticket.[97] Listed on many of these bills just below the Biggest Show's biggest star, Fats Domino, Baker usually closed the first half of the show.[98] Her fellow artists remembered her fondly. Phil Everly of the Everly Brothers told an interviewer that Baker "was almost like a [den mother]. When the buttons came off your jackets you knew you could go to LaVern and get them sewed on."[99] The young African American women who were on these tours described the ways she supported them. "I can remember her doing our hair," Beverly Lee of the Shirelles recalled of Baker, "and she helped us with our outfits. We were just crazy about her."[100] Arlene Smith, lead singer of the Chantels, spoke of Baker's kindness and her salty language. "She took us under her wing. I'd never heard so many curse words in my life, but I learned to love her," she recalled. "We used to pal around with her. She liked us, and after a while, she would kind of get the guys to stop doing . . . [laughs] you know, she was protecting these little girls on the show."[101] Breaking the rules of respectability with her vocabulary, while also upholding them by acting as an unofficial chaperone, Baker helped the young women manage one of the risks of touring: predatory men.

Another hazard, one with which all Feld tour artists contended, was Jim Crow. Finding accommodations and restaurants that would serve the interracial group was a challenge, especially in the south, where hotels, restaurants, restrooms, water fountains, and concert venues were segregated. A poster advertising a "Big Midnite Blues Special" featuring LaVern Baker and the Drifters at the Danville Armory (probably in Virginia) notes, "Balcony reserved for white spectators."[102] In smaller venues, a rope would be run down the middle of the room; whites would stand on one side, blacks on the other. Baker recalled the difficulty of adapting her performance to the exigencies of southern segregation: "It was very hard to work with a rope in the middle of the audience. How the heck can you sing with the blacks to your right and the whites to your left? You'd look straight ahead and there's nothing."[103] On some occasions, Baker noted, the audiences "broke the rope because they had what you call musical tantrums."[104] Baker viewed the resulting coming together of the races as "gorgeous," but conservative white southerners reviled the temporary integration and the music that facilitated it.[105]

The jubilant sexuality of rock and roll, its perceptible blackness, and the fact that white people and black people were interacting in its production, performance, and consumption challenged the status quo. Feld's integrated show was unable to run in several southern cities that had laws against black and white performers appearing together on stage.[106] Consequently, the Biggest Show's white acts were dropped from the show when it played Chattanooga and Memphis, Tennessee; Columbus, Georgia; Birmingham, Alabama;

and New Orleans, Louisiana.[107] The black acts were the best-known rock and roll stars and they remained on the bill. Even where the interracial performances were legal, outsiders opposed the music, sometimes threatening violence. By the time of the Feld tours, rock and roll shows had developed a reputation for danger, and Baker braved some of the "riots," usually set off by the antics of inebriated fans or the actions of police officers, that led to rock and roll concerts being banned in some locales.[108]

These rock and roll shows were occurring alongside civil rights movement activism and southern white resistance to desegregation. In 1954, the US Supreme Court had declared the segregation of public schools unconstitutional, and in December 1955, spurred by the refusal of Rosa Parks to obey the rules of municipal bus segregation, black citizens of Montgomery, Alabama, launched a bus boycott that drew national attention to the battle for desegregation. The discourse and demonstrations of African American activists working to overturn segregation coincided with the ascendance of an African American musical form, creating a situation in which the visibility and audibility of African Americans was increasing—both politically and culturally. The fact that white youth were embracing black rock and roll was particularly disturbing to conservative whites adamant about maintaining the racial status quo. The (white) Citizens' Council of Greater New Orleans issued a plea: "Help Save the Youth of America. Don't Buy Negro Records. . . . The screaming idiotic words, and savage music of these records are undermining the morals of our white youth in America."[109] The idea that black music was "pulling the white man down to the level of the Negro," as the Secretary of the North Alabama White Citizens Council put it, fueled the outcry of white segregationists.[110] They had reason to be concerned. Involvement with the music could promote the attitude that white singer, guitarist, and songwriter Buddy Holly revealed to his mother when he returned home to Texas after his first Feld tour. Responding to her question about "how he was getting along with Negroes," he is said to have replied, "Oh, we're Negroes, too! We get to feeling like that's what we are."[111] This was exactly the kind of attitude that encouraged white conservative animus toward rock and roll.

When discussing the tours, Baker downplayed their attack on segregation. "When I was doing these shows, I didn't go there to change anything. I went there to do a show," she said in an interview. "The problems were there when I arrived and they were there after I left. It doesn't pay to say anything because it can't change anything, anyway. My voice is nothing. No voice is."[112] While it is true that these artists might not have intended to work for social change, I would argue that Baker's voice *was* something and that the presence of these predominantly black interracial shows *did* mean something. In working with white artists and in bringing black American music to white and integrated audiences, LaVern Baker and her fellow musicians initiated significant changes in American culture. Within a decade of these tours, a critical mass of young white Americans had embraced music with African American roots as their own and renamed it "rock." In the process, another form of segregation occurred: the presence of African American participants in rock and roll became muted as rock solidified its association with young white people, and a once-prominent figure like Baker receded from view.

Moving Image

Part of the challenge of keeping LaVern Baker in the mainstream of the rock and roll canon has to do with her visual presentation, which, like her sound, does not align with most contemporary conceptualizations of the genre. In her two performances in rock and roll films and in publicity photos from this era, Baker conveys a sophisticated visual image (see figure 2.1). Glamorous in high heels, long gowns, and sleek hairstyles, Baker does not communicate the fevered energy that has come to be associated with rock and roll. Baker was doing a juggling act. She capitalized on her beauty and sex appeal to draw attention, but as an African American woman working in a crossover context, she had to perform in a way that was appropriate for mainstream consumption. Stereotypes of black women's sexuality coupled with the libidinous energy of rock and roll represented an excess of sex that Baker had to manage. There is little archival footage of Baker from the 1950s, but the performances she delivered in two Alan Freed films reveal the choices she made as she developed an onstage style that would fit the 1950s silver screen.

Both *Rock, Rock, Rock* (1956) and *Mr. Rock and Roll* (1957) were low-budget projects, saddled with thin plots, weak acting, and poor production values, but these deficiencies mattered less than performances by the likes of LaVern Baker, Chuck Berry, the Flamingos, and Frankie Lymon and the Teenagers, and the accompanying valorization of rock and roll that were the real point of the films.[113] *Rock, Rock, Rock* features Baker fronting an upright bass, guitar, drum, and saxophone combo during her one song. She strolls to the front of the group and launches into "Tra La La." It's a jaunty, up-tempo number, and Baker maintains a steady motion, swinging her arms from side to side, as she

FIGURE 2.1 The publicity photos that circulated of LaVern Baker in the 1950s highlighted her stylish elegance. Shown here in a sparkling gown, high heels, sleek hair, and wearing a smile, she conveys feminine beauty and respectability rather than the renegade attitude associated with rock and roll. Nevertheless, Baker was one of rock and roll's founding figures and a headliner on the concert tours that brought the fledgling genre to audiences in the United States and Canada during the 1950s. COURTESY RUDY CALVO COLLECTION/ CACHE AGENCY.

sings, "Tra la la, tra la la. You're as sweet as a candy bar." She wears a form-fitting, sleeveless gown, and dangling earrings accent her elegant appearance. Possibly the most important element of her costume, however, is her smile; it reassures white audience members that she is a safe Negro, there to entertain. The poorly matched edits from close-up to mid-shot to profile are disconcerting to contemporary viewers accustomed to more seamless filmic continuity, but her delivery is warm, if low-key. During the sax player's honking solo, she strides over to him and leans in as he plays. Baker gives an exaggerated frown and dismisses him with a wave of her hand, but by the time the camera returns to her after a cutaway to the well-dressed audience of white teenagers, he has won her over; her smile returns and she moves to the beat, reserved but digging his sound. In *Mr. Rock and Roll*, Baker stands before a stage curtain dressed in a shimmering, knee-length gown and sings a proclamation of female desire. As with all of the musical numbers in these films, Baker lip-synchs. Given the production's low budget, she probably had only a few takes to get it right, and she is a bit stiff at first. After a few moments, though, she settles into the performance of "Love Me in the Morning," gently swinging her hips and rocking her arms. She shifts from pouts to smiles, eyebrows arching and her eyes alternately expressing delight and disdain as she sings, "You can use, you can abuse me / If you don't want to lose me, love me, baby / Love me right in the morning." She ends her performance by placing her index finger in her mouth and lowering her eyes. According to *Ebony*, this was a "typical gesture [that Baker] used often near end of numbers."[114]

Baker did not have any speaking lines in either film. Few of the black characters did. Their musical performances provided entertainment, while the plots turned on the words and deeds of the white focal characters. Freed was committed to foregrounding African American artists, but he recognized that he needed to temper rock and roll's dangerous blackness. This became a more urgent project once Elvis Presley's sexy gyrations scandalized cross-sections of the American public in 1956, and rock and roll became associated with violence and juvenile delinquency.[115] Freed wanted to assure parents, the media, and the recording industry that there was no need to be frightened of rock and roll or the black people who were its leading artists. Given this context, it is not surprising that Baker was restrained, but it is worth noting that her film performances toned down the fiery energy that *Ebony* reported was a part of her concerts:

> She has been mobbed, manhandled and assaulted by fans worked into hysteria by her singing. At the Brooklyn Paramount Theater, a male fan,

FIGURE 2.2 LaVern Baker in concert at the Lake Glen Country Club, Akron, Ohio, in the 1950s. Baker strikes a saucy pose that contrasts with the reserve of her publicity photos and hints at the attitude she brought to her concert appearances. The combination of her vocal power and performance energy led *DownBeat* magazine to name her the Top Female R&B Personality of 1956. Jimmy Baynes Collection, Library and Archives, Rock and Roll Hall of Fame. COURTESY ROCK AND ROLL HALL OF FAME.

moved by her rendition of "Tweedlee-Dee," jumped up on stage, screaming. He locked his teeth on her fingers and gnawed away. Comments La-Vern: "He just grabbed my hand and had himself a meal. But I went right on singing 'Tweedlee-Dee.'"[116]

While it is probably prudent to take these descriptions with a grain of salt, the message that Baker was a rock and roll instigator and a recipient of her audience's adulation seems credible based on photos and reports in the press.

When naming Baker Top Female R&B Personality of 1956, *DownBeat* observed that she was, "Perhaps the best on-stage performer of all the girls in R&B."[117] Baker was a seasoned artist who knew how to forge a visceral connection with audiences (see figure 2.2). *Ebony* described her act as follows: "Throwing herself into every performance, she belts out blues with tremendous energy, using sexy gestures and daring body movements that create a unique emotional experience for listeners."[118] The photograph on the profile's opening page captures Baker in a moment of uninhibited motion: her right hand is lifted with palm facing out and she is kicking her high-heeled left foot, while her head tilts back, eyes closed and mouth open in song. This is

Baker rocking and rolling, riding the rhythm, putting on a show. "Throwing self into act," the accompanying caption explains, "LaVern Baker breaks into impromptu dance at the Brooklyn Paramount Theater."[119] A French reporter visiting New York City's music venues in 1960 offered a description of a late-night performance by "the fabulous LaVern Baker" that suggests such outbursts were typical in her live act. When she performed "Jim Dandy," he reported, "a very well-dressed man, very dandy, begins to dance on stage in an enthusiastic fashion; after a few minutes, when LaVern begins to dance with him, a delirious, savage feeling takes hold of the crowd: everyone screams, howls, gesticulates."[120] Little of this effervescence, what we might now think of as rock and roll energy, is present in Baker's "respectable" film appearances, but it was part of her performance arsenal.

Disappearing Act

LaVern Baker continued to perform and record into the 1960s. Her December 1958 release "I Cried a Tear" was her biggest hit, reaching number two on *Billboard's* Rhythm and Blues chart and number six on the pop chart. It stayed on both charts longer than any of Baker's other singles and sold one million copies.[121] Still, by the late 1950s, rock and roll's popularity seemed to have crested. *Variety* and *Billboard* wrote the genre's obituary, as clean-cut white "teen idols" such as Fabian and Ricky Nelson replaced the original rock and rollers. Baker had sung rock and roll because it was the trend, but she had always wanted to perform a wider range of material. She expanded her repertoire in an effort to capture an adult audience, one that would appreciate the sophisticated sound of "I Cried a Tear" or the grown-up blues she offered on her 1958 Atlantic release *LaVern Baker Sings Bessie Smith*. Looking back on this period, Baker said, "I always knew what I wanted and how I wanted to go and how I wanted to sing. But, naturally, during those years your color stopped you. . . . So you had to go the best way you could. You had to be like an 'S.' You had to wiggle your way in and out, in and out, until you got what you wanted."[122] Black women had to "wiggle their way" to sustainable professional music careers, gauging audience expectations and strategizing with producers and managers, while negotiating the race and gender rules that shaped the contexts in which they worked. Baker's career choices, coupled with the changing terrain of rock and roll, caused her to vanish from the genre.

The singles Baker released in the early 1960s charted, but not at the same high positions as her 1950s material. "Saved," a humorous gospel-inflected song about finding religion and leaving rock and roll, was written for her by Jerry Leiber and Mike Stoller, the duo behind "Hound Dog"; it reached number seventeen on the R&B charts and number 37 on the pop charts in 1961.[123] Her 1962 version of "See See Rider," a hit for blues queen Ma Rainey in 1925, went to number 9 on the rhythm and blues chart and 34 on the pop chart.[124] Baker left Atlantic for Brunswick Records in 1965, but it was not a successful move. Only one of her Brunswick releases, a 1966 duet with Jackie Wilson called "Think Twice," charted. Baker was still able to secure lucrative live gigs, but a radio hit was elusive.[125] In a 1991 interview about her career, Baker insisted that gender made a crucial difference in an artist's career. Although she was discussing the Shirelles, a girl group that performed on the same bills with her in the late 1950s, Baker's remarks applied to her own situation:

> [The Shirelles] paid more dues because they were women. They still do, in different jobs, whatever job they're doing. I'll tell you one thing, females don't last as long on the charts as males. You figure two-and-a-half, maybe three years for a female singer to stay up there. But she's got to be very fortunate, like Aretha [Franklin], to really stay up there for a while. Males last a long time, whether they have a record or not. It's just different.[126]

Whether the issue was Baker's race, gender, genre, or some combination of the three, her career was not as stable as she hoped it would be. "When I was here [in the United States] working with my booking agent," Baker said of her situation at the end of the 1960s, "I had no trouble getting jobs. I was just discouraged because I couldn't get a hit at the time. It just seemed like the more I worked, the harder I had to work. It was just one of those things. So I just [she laughs raucously] disappeared."[127] Baker laughed as she made the comment, but she was not joking. She left the United States for twenty years. Taking advantage of an opportunity to work overseas in 1970, she toured Asia and performed for American troops in Vietnam. In Hong Kong, the tour's last stop, she was hospitalized with an enlarged heart and a collapsed lung.[128] Once she had recovered, she began performing at the InterContinental Hotel in Manila; she enjoyed the warm climate, slower pace, and ability to work professionally, so she decided to stay in the Philippines.[129] Baker lived in Manila during the 1970s and 1980s, booking acts and singing at the clubs for military officers and enlisted men on the Subic Bay military base; she had two daughters by a Filipino man and adopted a girl and a boy.[130] Embracing the lower-profile work she did overseas as an administrator and entertainer, Baker stated, "I wasn't making that big money, but I was making an honest, decent living. And I was doing what I wanted to do, what I was brought up doing. I'm the show director for the Marine Corps. I'm still in show business."[131] Baker was proud that she had been able to make a living as a professional entertainer, especially in light of the reality that some of her peers, most notably Ruth Brown, had turned to domestic work in order to earn money.[132] In 1991, when she was going public with the story of her "disappearance," Baker said she valued work, not fame. "I don't particularly care to be a star," she stated. "I prefer to be a performer, because stars fade away. . . . I'd rather be a performer because a performer can always last."[133] Of course, Baker *had* been a star, but her response to the change in her circumstances was to stress what was most important to her as a professional entertainer who was also a parent: "I made money every day, and I supported my children."[134]

As an African American woman who had established her career on the porous genre boundary between R&B and rock and roll, Baker never had the luxury of generic purism, nor did she seem interested in it. What was consistent across her decades-long career was a willingness to adjust her act to meet the demands of her context. In the 1950s, she sang novelty songs pitched to teens; by the 1970s, she had mastered an act that appealed to the varying tastes of American service men and women stationed overseas. As Baker shifted, so too did the genre of rock and roll. Defined as much by its audience as by its sound, rock and roll expanded sonically as the teenagers who had embraced the music of Baker and her peers in the 1950s began to make records in the 1960s. The next generation of rock and rollers introduced changes in instrumentation, subject matter, and attitude that so altered the genre that it took on a new name, "rock," by the end of the decade. Baker's 1950s-era novelty songs seemed out of place in the late 1960s soundscape.

Baker returned to the United States to perform at a celebration of the fortieth anniversary of Atlantic Records in 1989, and again in 1990, to take over Ruth Brown's starring role in the hit Broadway musical *Black and Blue*. In 1991, she became the second woman to be inducted into the Rock and Roll Hall of Fame. "I should have been the first," she pointed out in an interview, "because I was around before Aretha [Franklin, who was the Rock Hall's first female inductee]. But, hey, it's OK. At least I'm in there."[135] In the early 1990s, following her successful run on Broadway, Baker was performing club dates and garnering press that talked of a comeback. Illness caught up with her again, however; she suffered a stroke, and diabetes-related complications led to the amputation of both legs.[136] Still, seated in her wheelchair, she continued to perform. "God gave me a talent and I can still use it," she declared. "I can still go out and sing."[137] Baker performed almost up to the time she died on March 10, 1997.

Baker's story and contribution have slipped from rock and roll memory, partly because she left the country and missed out on two decades of reinforcing her presence in "golden oldies" tours alongside other first wave rock and roll artists such as Fats Domino, Chuck Berry, Little Richard, and Jerry Lee Lewis. Furthermore, her decision not to write an autobiography denied her an opportunity to keep her rock and roll story in the public consciousness in the fashion of black women singers such as Ruth Brown, Etta James, Darlene Love, Ronnie Spector of the Ronettes, and Mary Wilson of the Supremes, who published memoirs in the wake of the success of Tina Turner's 1986 autobiography. These books chronicled the trials and triumphs of their careers and included details about their romances, marriages, divorces, addictions, and experiences of physical and psychological abuse at the hands of spouses and lovers.[138] Sharing these kinds of stories held no appeal for Baker. "My private life is private," she said in a 1991 interview. "I've had some things happen to me that I wouldn't wish on a dog, and I've had some really good times too. Everybody knows about my career; that's in the public domain. The other stuff, I don't want to talk about. I've got secrets that I'll take to the grave with me. I'll keep my privacy."[139] Baker was true to her word. Emphatic in her refusal to disclose personal details and invested in being a performer, Baker wanted the focus to be on the music she made. She had faith, perhaps too much faith, in the ability of her professional record to speak for itself. The vicissitudes of history and the intersection of race, gender, and genre combined to tamp down Baker's audibility and visibility.

Baker's time in the Philippines was a literal and figurative rock and roll exile, and it is a struggle to return her to her rightful place in histories of the genre even though, as I have learned by examining the particulars of her career, LaVern Baker was one of the first rock and roll stars. Her vocal approach to the Big Beat, marked by a gutsy attack that accentuated the propulsive rhythm, offered a template for other vocalists. Baker was one of Elvis Presley's favorite singers, and he performed "Tweedlee Dee," "See See Rider," and "Saved," songs from her repertoire, in concert over the course of his career.[140] An artist who blazed the way for subsequent generations of rock and rollers, Baker was an important influence on Brenda Lee, one of the first white women rock and rollers; and she mentored young women like the Chantels and the Shirelles, the African American teens who spearheaded the girl group movement that brought young women's voices to the center of rock and roll in the late 1950s and early 1960s.[141] Baker made her contribution and then disappeared from view. The fact that she was an African American woman worked against that contribution being fully acknowledged in histories of a genre that had developed a profile as the purview of white men. The irony is that rock and roll's association with white artists and audiences is a result of the success that Baker and other black musicians had promoting their music to white teenagers during the 1950s. The crossing of boundaries is central to the development of rock and roll, with maverick artists and rebellious fans breaking the rules of American segregation. How frustrating, then, to confront the ways race, gender, and genre boundaries persist, sustaining segregation and limiting recognition of a foundational figure like LaVern Baker, the first Queen of Rock and Roll.

THREE / Remembering the Shirelles

> It was 1957. We were neighbors. Beverly and I used to babysit together. We were all schoolmates. Micki was a friend. Doris sang in the choir. We thought she had a terrific voice, so we asked her if she'd sing with us. We were just doing it for fun. In our wildest dreams, we never thought that we'd become recording artists. / **SHIRLEY ALSTON REEVES**

> It's music that people could relate to, especially kids could relate to it because . . . they were going through a lot of what we were singing about. You could listen to it. You could dance to it. It was happy music. / **BEVERLY LEE**

The poster for the 2011 Broadway musical *Baby It's You!* signaled the show's focus. It featured an image of four black women standing on a stage in shimmering silver dresses, their backs turned to the viewer, as they look over glowing footlights and into the audience. Facing the women and the viewer of the poster is the head of a smiling white woman who tilts down her white-framed sunglasses with manicured fingers. The well-lit face is about the same height as the full bodies of the black women, and it looms over them like an otherworldly force. While the white woman's features are visible to the viewer, the black women, smaller and rendered in rear view, are faceless and undifferentiated. Promotional text for the show drove the point home: "The Shirelles made the headlines. . . . She made the Shirelles."[1] *Baby It's You!* was a jukebox musical comprising rock and roll songs from the early 1960s, the majority of which were part of the Scepter Records catalogue. With a book by Floyd Mutrux and Colin Escott, the team that had received Tony Award nominations for their Sun Records jukebox musical *Million Dollar Quartet* the year before, the production was geared to tap the dollars of baby boomers nostalgic for rock and roll classics. The women represented in the poster were the Shirelles, the black female vocal group that recorded for Scepter Records, and Florence Greenberg, the white Jewish woman who was the label's founder. Their professional and personal fates were intertwined, but the musical only tells the improbable story of a housewife with no prior experience in the recording industry starting and running a successful independent record label at a time when a married woman couldn't get a credit card in her own name without her husband's permission.[2]

Equally improbable was the story of four black teenage girls from Passaic, New Jersey, who turned their pastime of singing into a career. The Shirelles were Doris Coley (August 2, 1941–February 4, 2000), Addie "Micki" Harris (January 22, 1940–June 10, 1982), Beverly Lee (b. August 3, 1941), and Shirley Owens (b. June 10, 1941, later Shirley Alston Reeves). The first all-female vocal group to have a number one pop hit in the rock and roll era, the Shirelles ushered in a new musical movement and built a multiracial fan base in the years just prior to the passage of civil rights legislation and the arrival of the Beatles.[3] Called girl groups because the artists themselves were teenagers, the Shirelles and the vocal groups that followed them produced rock and roll with a female voice. Lyrics addressed what were thought to be the chief concerns of female adolescents: parents who didn't understand them, girlfriends who turned on them, and boys, boys, boys. Girl group vocalists harmonized together and, responding to the lead singer's calls, sang in the energetic and often imperfect voices of teenagers. The vocals were passionate and earnest, open and coy, dramatic and intense—very much like teenage girls.

The minimizing of the Shirelles in the musical *Baby It's You!* mirrors the problem of audibility and visibility that girl group artists have faced in popular music history.[4] It's not that girl groups have been ignored. There are overview volumes that provide group-by-group descriptions of both well-known and obscure acts.[5] Histories of women in rock stress their significance as the first critical mass of women artists to participate in the genre.[6] Mainstream rock histories also cover girl groups, but do so in a limited way. As Gillian Gaar observes, rock historians "tend to regard girl groups as interchangeable, easily manipulated puppets, while the ones with the 'real' talent were the managers, songwriters, publishers, and producers who worked behind the group."[7] An example of the dynamic Gaar describes turns up in Greil Marcus's essay on girl groups in the *Rolling Stone Illustrated History of Rock and Roll*. He writes about the girl group sound in laudatory terms, remarking on the continuing freshness of the best songs of the genre, but he spends more time discussing Phil Spector, producer of numerous girl group era hits, than any of the girl groups.[8] The fact that the identities of most girl group artists were subordinated to the overall group sound and image made it difficult for the names and personalities of individual girl group members to emerge. In *Baby It's You!* Shirley, the lead singer, has a few more lines than the other Shirelles, but for the most part, the four characters are, like girl groups in rock and roll history books, barely distinguishable from one another, an undifferentiated group, entering and exiting en masse.

In the weeks after *Baby It's You!* opened, I heard that one audience member—slamming the show for its emphasis on the story of Florence Greenberg—had quipped that the musical should have been called "Baby, It's Me!" Reviews by theater critics shared this critique of the production's handling of the Shirelles. In the *New York Times*, Charles Isherwood observed that the four actresses playing the group members "may actually have more costumes . . . than they do lines of dialogue."[9] He continued, "It seems a small but cruel twist of fate: Knocked from their perch as the reigning girl group by the supersonic advent of the Supremes, decades later the Shirelles are fated to be backup singers in the story of their own career."[10] In *Baby It's You!* Florence Greenberg's is the only story. Side plots about her family and her affair with Luther Dixon, the African American songwriter who produced the Shirelles' hits, take precedence over the Shirelles, the first group Greenberg signed and the group that propelled Scepter's success. In musical theater, as in rock and roll history, the Shirelles were accorded secondary status. Diagnosing the conditions that produce this problem, rock writer Donna Gaines noted, "Like most women in music (and as with black artists, generally), the girl groups' story is a typical one of under-recognition, exploitation, and disappointment."[11] As Gaines suggests, the racial composition of girl groups exacerbates the tendency to overlook their contribution to the sound of rock and roll. Although white girl groups had top-selling songs—both the Angels' "My Boyfriend's Back" (1963) and the Shangri-Las' "Leader of the Pack" (1964) went to number one on the pop charts—it was African American girl groups such as the Shirelles, the Crystals, the Chiffons, the Exciters, the Ronettes, and the Supremes who dominated the pop charts.

Changes in musical values have undermined recognition of the significance of this woman-centered rock and roll movement. The rise of self-contained bands in the late 1960s created an ideal of rock and roll authenticity that depends on the artist's ability to write music and lyrics, play instruments, and perform the material. Girl group artists, who rarely wrote their own songs and did not play instruments on stage, do not meet these requirements. In a context governed by this limiting paradigm, one that uses the aesthetic values of late 1960s rock to evaluate music-making that preceded it, the Shirelles struggle to be heard. But if we shift from a guitar-centered, songwriter-oriented focus to a perspective that centers vocals and considers female lines of descent in rock, we can turn up the volume on the Shirelles.

The first black all-female group to cross over to white audiences, the Shirelles brought young women's voices into the male-centered space of mainstream popular culture. There had been youthful all-female groups prior to the Shirelles: In 1957, the Harlem-based Bobbettes had a number one R&B hit with the propulsive "Mr. Lee." A year later, the beautifully haunting "Maybe" went to number one on the R&B charts, giving the Bronx-based Chantels their first hit. Still, in spite of these successes, the general view of recording industry executives at both major and independent labels was that there was not much of a market for all-female recording groups. The Shirelles' 1960 release "Will You Love Me Tomorrow," in which a teenage girl wonders about the repercussions of giving in to sexual desire, launched a new sound, feel, and attitude in rock and roll. The Shirelles proved that audiences would buy records by women. It is worth noting that it was a woman who signed the group to a recording contract and believed in their professional potential. And the Shirelles were not "just for girls." Among their male fans were members of the Beatles and other British Invasion bands who borrowed their songs and vocal approaches. Once the Shirelles had demonstrated the viability of all-female vocal ensembles, record labels began the fevered process of recording songs featuring young women, creating an avalanche of girl groups on the radio and in the record bins. The Shirelles are second only to Motown's Supremes among girl groups in terms of chart success, but they were not connected with songwriting and producing team Jerry Leiber and Mike Stoller, producer Phil Spector, or Motown label head Berry Gordy, the figures who take precedence in discussions of 1960s era vocal music in histories of rock and roll. As a result, the Shirelles tend to disappear in overviews that celebrate the groundbreaking contributions of these towering behind-the-scenes figures. Yet the Shirelles are the key group. Working with Florence Greenberg and Luther Dixon, who are also given short shrift in these histories, the Shirelles preceded and influenced the girl group projects of Spector and Motown, setting a template for the sound of rock and roll in the early 1960s.

The Shirelles continued breaking down the racial barriers that the black rock and rollers of the 1950s had started to erode, and they helped open doors for women artists. As young black women participating in a male-dominated field increasingly targeted to white teens, they developed a racially ambiguous sound that allowed them to cross over to white audiences. The Shirelles traversed the porous boundary between rhythm and blues and rock and roll, but the sonic style that enabled them to do so makes it difficult to fit them into the narratives that dominate pop music history. The concoction of "feminized" rock and roll and "whitened" rhythm and blues that allowed the Shirelles to reach such a broad audience has compromised their claims to authenticity as either rock and rollers *or* rhythm and blues artists in the ensuing decades. With their elegant gowns and prominent string arrangements, these black women do not conform to contemporary commonsense images of rock and roll; with their integrated, predominantly white audience and pop chart success, they do not read as rhythm and blues artists. More important than any generic categorization, though, is the fact that the Shirelles were a pivotal group. During the late 1950s and early 1960s, they cut numerous records, toured both the black and white concert circuits, made radio and television appearances to promote their music, experienced the exploitation that accompanied these ventures, and influenced numerous artists. The Shirelles changed the sound of rock and roll in the 1960s—and they did so while negotiating the race, gender, and genre barriers that defined the era.

Meet the Shirelles

Beverly Lee, Doris Coley, Micki Harris, and Shirley Owens had become friends in junior high, and they started singing together in their sophomore year of high school.[12] Shirley and Micki sang in the same church choir, and Beverly was on the verge of joining them when the group began to tour. Doris attended the church where her father was a pastor and sang in that choir.[13] Singing sacred music provided an important training ground for the girls, but the doo-wop that was a staple of late 1950s R&B radio was also an influence. "We listened to [New York City radio station] WWRL's Tommy Smalls, [who was known as] Dr. Jive," Beverly Lee recalled when I interviewed her in 2012. "We would come home from school and harmonize with the songs they were playing. We were listening to Little Anthony and the Imperials and the

Chantels and the Flamingos and the Coasters, not knowing that one day we'd be touring with them."[14] Doo-wop singers, whether on record or on the streets, sang close harmonies, supporting a lead with backup vocals, imitating instruments with hums and nonsense syllables like the ones that gave the genre its name, and providing rhythm with hand claps, foot stomps, and finger snaps. By and large, the doo-wop groups that recorded in the 1950s were male, but teenage girls also picked up on the trend. Harmonizing was central to both gospel and doo-wop, and the Shirelles carried that practice into their professional singing.

Performing as the Poquellos, Beverly, Doris, Micki, and Shirley began to make a name for themselves at their integrated high school in Passaic, New Jersey. A desire to avoid punishment for singing instead of paying attention in class put them on a professional path. "We were fooling around in gym," Lee explained, "and Miss Nolan, the guidance counselor, came through and she said, 'There's going to be a show at school. Do the show or fail gym.' So naturally we opted to do the show."[15] While rehearsing for the performance, they wrote their first composition. "We all took a line, one right after another and that's how 'I Met Him on a Sunday' came about," Lee told me.[16] Harmonizing with doo-wop style oohs and doo-ronde-rons and keeping the rhythm with hand claps, the Poquellos performed at the talent show and were a hit. One of the kids in the audience, Mary Jane Greenberg, thought the group would be a good match for the record label her mother was starting. Florence Greenberg (1913–1995) was a music lover who had decided to fight the boredom she felt being a housewife and mother by getting involved in the recording industry. "I was anxious to get out of the house," she told an interviewer in 1992.[17] After immersing herself in the business by spending time at the Manhattan hangouts where songwriters and industry executives gathered, she rented an office near the Brill Building—the Times Square hothouse for pop song creation—and launched Tiara Records.[18] Greenberg loved what she heard when the Poquellos auditioned for her, and she offered the girls a recording contract.[19] When Greenberg suggested a name change for the group, the girls took inspiration from the acts that were already on the charts. "The name evolved from the 'el' sound," Lee told me. "[There were] The Dells, and the Chantels. We liked the 'el' sounds. We just made up different combinations of names and came up with the Shirelles. A lot of people think it came from Shirley's name. It was a name that we made up."[20]

Tiara Records released the first Shirelles single, "I Met Him on a Sunday," in March 1958. It received airplay on local radio stations, and the group promoted it with appearances around northern New Jersey.[21] "Basically we would do record hops and sock hops," Lee explained. In addition to attending these teen-centered dances, the group "would go to radio stations with the disc jockeys. They played the record and talked to us and we started getting on TV shows like *The Rocket Ship Show* with Jocko Henderson."[22] The popularity of the record led to bookings with R&B and rock and roll luminaries such as LaVern Baker, Chuck Berry, Ruth Brown, Louis Jordan, and Big Joe Turner.[23] Decca Records executives took note of the record's success and made a distribution deal with Greenberg that gave "I Met Him on a Sunday" national exposure.[24] The single made it to number 50 on the pop charts, but the label dropped the group after releasing some other less successful singles.[25] "[Decca] gave the Shirelles back to me," Greenberg recalled. "That's when I started Scepter Records."[26] The label's first single was the Shirelles' version of "Dedicated to the One I Love," a "5" Royales song they had heard when both groups played the Howard Theater in Washington, DC.[27]

"Dedicated" and the other initial recordings on Scepter did not sell well, but Greenberg was convinced the Shirelles could top the charts if they had the right material.[28] She forged an alliance with Luther Dixon, a young African American songwriter who had written the doo-wop hit "Sixteen Candles" for the Crests.[29] At first he rejected Greenberg's offer. He was placing his songs with well-known performers such as Pat Boone, the Four Aces, Perry Como, the Platters, and Nat King Cole, and would gain little by having an unknown group record them.[30] Greenberg persisted, however, and she and Dixon worked out an arrangement that gave Dixon considerable creative control. He would be able to produce as well as write, assign his songs to his own Ludix publishing company in order to reap royalties, and gain an ownership stake in Scepter Records if his recordings with the Shirelles were successful.[31] With Dixon on board, the career of the Shirelles took off. "Luther was brilliant," Lee recalled. "He knew how to record us, knew how to get the best out of us, how to choose material for us."[32] In some cases, Dixon suggested harmonies, but, Lee explained, "We had our own way of harmonizing. If somebody sang something, we just automatically came in on our harmony parts. . . . Sometimes he'd give us a demo with the song and we'd rehearse that way and learn it. . . . Luther basically chose our material."[33] He also devised a sonic approach that took the group beyond the boundaries of the rhythm and blues market (see figure 3.1).

FIGURE 3.1 The Shirelles, minus the wigs and matching outfits that were the hallmark of their style, at work in a New York City recording studio in the early 1960s. According to Beverly Lee, "They kept us in the studio a lot. That's why we have so much material released." The Shirelles worked closely with their producer Luther Dixon, who selected their songs and decided on the instrumental arrangements; the women were usually responsible for working out their vocal parts. From left to right: Shirley Owens, Addie "Micki" Harris, Beverly Lee, and Doris Coley. COURTESY CEA/CACHE AGENCY.

The Sound of Crossover

The African American women performing girl group music maintained a balance between presenting an audibly black musical sound and doing so in ways that would not alienate audiences unaccustomed to African American musical performance style. Rhythmically propulsive arrangements were offset with orchestral instruments. Melismatic runs and gospel-infused vocals were minimal; instead, girl groups sang in energetic, teenage voices that were "ethnically ambiguous." In short, girl group music blended "black" and "white" musical sound. "Will You Love Me Tomorrow" was the template. An astute reader of pop music audiences, Luther Dixon determined that the Shirelles'

R&B elements would have to be sweetened to achieve Top 40 success.[34] His first production for the group was "Tonight's the Night," a song he cowrote with Shirley Owens, who sang lead on the track. An up-tempo number, "Tonight's the Night" featured a prominent beat (the key to African American–rooted rock and roll) overlaid with strings (a sonic signifier of sophisticated whiteness). Dixon's arrangement gave the song greater accessibility to Top 40 radio, and the song stayed on the pop charts for three and a half months, laying the groundwork for an even bigger success.[35] The Shirelles' first encounter with "Will You Love Me Tomorrow," a song with music by Carole King and lyrics by Gerry Goffin, was not auspicious.[36] Dixon thought it was a perfect vehicle for the group, but the demo did not impress them. "We didn't want to record 'Will You Love Me Tomorrow' because we didn't like it," Lee told me. "It sounded like a country and western song. It was real twangy. . . . He knew that we didn't care for it."[37] Dixon assured the singers that he would develop a new arrangement and insisted that they give it a try. "You're *gonna* record this song," Lee recalled Dixon telling them.[38] The women were resistant because they heard the song as "too white" and too country for them as black artists, but ultimately they agreed to record it.[39] It is likely that Dixon shared the Shirelles' assessment of the song's aural whiteness, but perceived that as an advantage, recognizing in those twangs the potential for the crossover hit he had been seeking.[40] "He heard what we didn't hear," Lee recalled. "Like I said, he was brilliant. He had a keen ear."[41] Commenting on the new arrangement, Lee stated, "When we heard it in the studio it was awesome."[42] The strings, arranged by Carole King, are a focal point, and they drive the song, heightening the intensity of the lead vocal.[43] Dixon and King might have been thinking of the strings on tracks by the Drifters, a black male vocal group whose songs "Save the Last Dance for Me" and "This Magic Moment" had done well on the pop charts when they were released earlier in the year. In fact, the shared string sound and the similar success on the pop charts led some to call the Shirelles "the female Drifters."[44]

In addition to featuring strings and downplaying the horn sound (an important element in 1950s rock and roll), Dixon made another significant choice in his production: He gave Shirley the lead on "Will You Love Me Tomorrow." When the girls had been singing for fun, they took turns on lead, but this democratic structure vanished once the group began working with Greenberg, who had either Doris or Shirley sing most of the lead parts. Doris's alto, with its rich, warm timbre and her full, sustained notes, was steeped in the gospel tradition and carried an audible blackness typical of 1950s R&B

vocal groups. Doris had sung lead on the group's first Scepter singles, "Dedicated to the One I Love" (1959) and "I Saw a Tear" (1960), but these songs did not fare well on the pop charts.[45] Dixon might have reasoned that tempering some of the up-front vocal blackness would help the group's music win pop radio airplay and a larger mainstream audience. Perhaps "Tonight's the Night," with Shirley on lead, suggested this possibility to him. The song went to number 14 on the R&B chart and number 39 on the pop chart even though it was the record's B-side.[46] Doris sang the A-side, "The Dance is Over," but it was Shirley's track that captured disc jockeys and the record-buying audience.[47] Dixon, with his eye on the marketplace, reasoned that Shirley's voice was worth exploring. Compared with Doris, her style was unembellished and did not have prominent trappings of the black gospel sound. Shirley did not hold notes extensively or build to dramatic finishes. Hers was more of an "every girl's" voice, mixing an innocent tone with a knowing attitude. Girls hearing her on their transistor radios or bedroom record players could sing along without feeling like they were lacking vocal chops. This accessibility, effectively an invitation to be a part of the group, was a hallmark of the girl group sound. It created the impression that the artists were like the members of the audience, even across lines of racial difference.

The racially ambiguous vocal sound of Shirley Owens's teenage voice encouraged audience identification and so did the lyrics. Girl group songs took on topics that were important to teenagers. "Will You Love Me Tomorrow," the first big girl group hit, exemplifies this quality. Its protagonist wrestles with a monumental choice: How far to take things sexually with a boyfriend. "Will You Love Me" lays out what was probably a familiar scenario for many teenagers. The protagonist is addressing a boyfriend, asking him the powerful question that gives the song its title. Owens's delivery of the lyrics leaves the impression that the protagonist is not given to illusions. The strings answer her, alternating with the "sha la la sha" and "ah ah ah" backing vocals of the other Shirelles. Owens's matter-of-fact tone contrasts with the upbeat tempo and urgency of the violins, capturing the complexity of the protagonist's emotions.[48] She understands that the promises the boy is making may be empty ones, and she recognizes her own sexual desire—a bold thing for a young woman to publicly acknowledge in this era. She plans to take responsibility for her actions, but she still wants to know if, from his perspective, there is real substance to their relationship. The quaver in Owens's voice and the fact that she is posing the question at all indicate her vulnerability. She knows that what she does will have an impact on her self-image and reputation. The song does not include the boy's answer because it really doesn't matter. The point is the expression of the young woman's agency and the mature attitude with which she approaches the situation. A situation and set of questions, Lee told me, that "all the young ladies should be aware of."[49]

Without discounting the impact of the song's catchy melody and moving arrangement, it might have been a hunger for some acknowledgment of a dilemma that resonated with teens admonished to "wait until marriage" that fueled the song's rise up the charts. Released in November 1960, "Will You Love Me Tomorrow" held the number one spot on the pop chart for two weeks in December and stayed on the Top 40 for fifteen weeks.[50] The song was the first number one composition for Goffin and King, who went on to become a songwriting powerhouse with tracks like "The Loco-Motion" (1962) for Little Eva, "Up on the Roof" (1962) for the Drifters, and "One Fine Day" (1963) for the Chiffons.[51] The success of "Will You Love Me Tomorrow" generated interest in other music by the Shirelles, and soon the group's 1959 single "Dedicated to the One I Love" was receiving radio airplay and logging significant enough sales to convince Greenberg to re-release it. By February, "Dedicated," a song that had made it only to number 83 on the pop charts when it was originally released, sat in the number 3 slot, enabling the Shirelles to achieve the unusual feat of having two records in the Top 10 at the same time.[52] For an all-female African American group to establish this kind of presence on the pop charts was unprecedented. Suddenly, the sound of four black girls from New Jersey was the sound of the new decade. The Shirelles, the top female group in the country, had become rock and roll stars. Adhering to the black press practice of celebrating the professional success of African Americans in any realm, the *Chicago Defender* followed the fortunes of the Shirelles as the "socksational sepia group" crossed over to white audiences.[53] Reporting on the group's first year on the pop charts, the paper noted that the Shirelles had earned over $300,000, not including royalties, and that in the year-end surveys of *Cash Box*, the recording industry weekly, the group had been rated "as leaders in several divisions . . . three of their records, 'Will You Love Me Tomorrow,' 'Dedicated to the One I Love,' and 'Mama Said' [were] chosen as [being among] the top 100 popular discs of the year."[54] The *Defender* further noted, "Also chosen as '61s top pop and rhythm and blues outfit, the Shirelles have sold more than 9 million records during their five year career."[55]

The successful Dixon/Shirelles collaboration continued into 1962 with the Burt Bacharach/Mack David/Luther Dixon song "Baby, It's You," a Top 10 hit on both the pop and R&B charts.[56] Their second number one pop hit, "Soldier

Boy," followed soon after, staying in the number one spot for three weeks in March.[57] It was the group's biggest-selling record, confirming the wisdom of Dixon's strategy to sweeten the group's sound and seek out material that would be palatable to the mainstream. "Soldier Boy," a string-laden confection, has a singsong quality, and the high range and unison vocals accentuate the girlishness of the women's voices as they declare their affection for a military man. By the end of the year, the Shirelles had six gold records to their name.[58]

Girl group historian John Clemente notes that the Shirelles' records were "the models that other aspiring producers were imitating in 1961."[59] Songwriters and producers consciously fashioned the girl group sound to be amenable to the changing media landscape as the newly instituted Top 40 radio format, with its emphasis on national hits and tightly focused playlists, displaced the more free-wheeling regional radio of the 1950s.[60] Producers smoothed rock and roll's rough edges, replacing shouted vocals and screeching saxophones with young women's voices, often backed by lush string orchestrations, creating heartfelt music with commercial appeal.[61] Luther Dixon's success with the Shirelles showed music producers Phil Spector and Berry Gordy the type of musical arrangements and vocal sound that could cross black female vocalists over to white teen audiences. The compelling, youthful voice of Shirley Owens was a model for Veronica "Ronnie" Bennett of the Ronettes and Diana Ross of the Supremes, icons of the girl group era. Spector believed Bennett to have the ideal teenage girl's voice.[62] Absent from her vocals was the melisma deployed by so many black, gospel-trained women, but her voice possessed enough drama and power to hold its own against Spector's booming instrumental "wall of sound." The Ronettes' first single, "Be My Baby," topped the pop charts in the summer of 1963, adapting the formula of racially ambiguous female vocals, orchestral instrumentation, and rhythmic drive that Dixon had pioneered with the Shirelles. Spector dubbed his results "little symphonies for the kids." At Motown, Gordy recognized that Ross's youthful, clear, and light voice had potential in the pop market. The Supremes started recording in 1961, but it took until 1964 for the group to crack the pop Top 20 with "Where Did Our Love Go." The song was the first in a string of number one hits that consolidated the pop cultural prominence of the Supremes, the only American group to rival the pop chart dominance of the Beatles during the 1960s.

Managing the blackness of these artists was necessary to crossing over in the still segregated United States. In fact, withholding racial information helped the Shirelles in the south, where they developed a white audience through their records, long before they made in-person appearances. "Our albums had drawings on them," Lee told me. "They didn't have our pictures, so [southern fans and concert promoters] didn't know that we were black. And then they wanted us to come and perform, that's when they found out we were black."[63] The cover for the album *Tonight's the Night* (1960), for example, features a box of flowers, a strapless dress propped up on the floor, and a table with a photo of a young white man. Motown executives used a similar tactic when marketing "Please Mr. Postman." Released in the summer of 1961, the banner year for the Shirelles, the single's artwork and the subsequent album cover had a drawing of an open mailbox covered with a spider web; there is no image of the Marvelettes, the young black women who sang the song. "Please Mr. Postman" became Motown's first number one pop single. For both the Shirelles and the Marvelettes, the absence of a visual image of the performers allowed the racially ambiguous music and voices to speak first, facilitating crossover and building an integrated audience at a time when de jure and de facto segregation were the national standard.

Building an Audience

During intermission at the performance of *Baby It's You!* that I attended in 2011, I chatted with the woman sitting next to me.[64] A native New Yorker, she had fond memories of listening to the Shirelles when she was growing up. Her parents felt she was too young to go to the shows they played at the Brooklyn Paramount and the Brooklyn Fox, but she loved hearing them on the radio, and she enjoyed having the chance to hear the songs performed live in the musical. At least on the surface, she seemed typical of the predominantly baby boomer audience members in the theater that evening: white, middle-class, middle-aged, and the type of fan the show's producers hoped to reach. The audience was generous with its applause and even sang along with a few numbers, but it was sedate compared with the crowds that the Shirelles performed for in the early 1960s. According to Dennis Garvey, a music writer who saw the Shirelles at the Brooklyn Fox and the Apollo in Harlem when he was twelve years old, the scene at these concerts was intense.[65] Garvey and I spoke when I was researching this book, and he set the scene for me: Hundreds and hundreds of preteens and teenagers packed into the theaters, carrying on at full throttle as the Shirelles performed. To help me understand the level of screaming and chaos, he likened it to the displays of emotion associated with Beatlemania.[66] In spite of their fame, the group was accessible to fans; Garvey met the Shirelles at one of these shows and established lifelong friendships with each of them. He was especially close to Beverly Lee, and he facilitated my interview with her.[67]

By the time Garvey was seeing the Shirelles in the early 1960s, the audiences were integrated, but the group had started out on the all-black touring circuit in the late 1950s. After they began releasing records in 1958, touring became a central part of their work, a way to earn money and build an audience. In the beginning, they played on multi-artist package shows with black rhythm and blues artists. "We would do what you call the Chitlin Circuit, touring from the Apollo Theater to the Uptown in Philly, the Royal in Baltimore, the Regal in Chicago, and the Howard in Washington, D.C.," Lee recalled. "And they would mix those shows from time to time with different groups and single artists and the comedians. We learned a lot from Pigmeat Markham. We would do little skits with him."[68] Black comedians like Markham, Moms Mabley, Flip Wilson, and Redd Foxx—"his show was a little X-rated," Lee said, "but he was a gentleman"—also appeared on these R&B tours.[69] The Shirelles went from town to town, honing their craft before live audiences at clubs and theaters serving African American clientele.

Once "Will You Love Me Tomorrow" hit the pop charts, the Shirelles broadened the scope of their touring. "We started going out into the colleges and different areas of working," Beverly Lee said.[70] They joined rock and roll package shows that presented a mix of black and white artists to integrated teen audiences. Disc jockeys Alan Freed and Murray the K and television host Clay Cole booked the Shirelles on shows at the Brooklyn Fox and Brooklyn Paramount Theaters. They were also part of Dick Clark's Caravan of Stars summer tours. Launched in 1959 and intended to attract the *American Bandstand* audience, these tours were on the road between Memorial Day and Labor Day and featured as many as seventeen acts.[71] Among the artists that participated in these integrated tours were Paul Anka, Chubby Checker, the Crystals, the Drifters, Duane Eddy, Dee Dee Sharp, and the Supremes.[72] The Shirelles also played on a concert organized as a fundraiser for the 1963 March on Washington. Held in Birmingham, Alabama, in early August, the "Salute to Freedom '63" featured Johnny Mathis, Ray Charles, and Nina Simone, along with the Shirelles, and was the first integrated variety show to play in the stronghold of segregation.[73]

The Shirelles secured their professional foothold through radio airplay and television appearances. Among the Shirelles' numerous supporters was New York City's Murray the K at WINS radio. One of the nation's most prominent rock and roll disc jockeys, Murray the K developed such a close professional association with the leading group of the British Invasion that he began to call himself "the Fifth Beatle." Prior to that band's arrival, though, he secured professional credibility through his association with the Shirelles and later the Ronettes. In fact, according to girl group historian Alan Betrock, Murray the K played the Shirelles "incessantly" on his nightly broadcast.[74] He invited the group to his show for interviews, and his audience responded by voting the Shirelles Most Popular Group "in almost every poll the station had between 1961–1963."[75] The group also appeared on the show of his WABC competitor Cousin Brucie (Bruce Morrow).[76] The Shirelles made their first of several appearances on Dick Clark's *American Bandstand* in the spring of 1958.[77] This was a coup for an African American group at a time when pressure from segregationists in the south caused most television programmers to limit the number of black acts they booked. "We did that [show] so many times," Lee recalled. "Dick became a very good friend of ours, like a big brother to us."[78] The Shirelles were popular enough to get an audition for the *Ed Sullivan Show*, the weekly variety show that was the era's premier venue for exposing entertainers, but they were not booked. "I guess we weren't glamorous enough for him," Lee told me.[79] In a 1987 interview, Shirley Alston Reeves offered a different perspective on Sullivan's decision: "They were afraid the ratings would fall because we were a black rock-and-roll act. We were the number one female vocal group in the country at the time, but they wouldn't let us do it."[80] In 1964, the Supremes became the first black female group to appear on the show, breaking through the racial and genre barriers that had stymied the Shirelles.[81]

Onstage with the Shirelles

The staged performances of the Shirelles and other Scepter artists were the best part of *Baby It's You!* The producers were unable to secure the rights to include "Will You Love Me Tomorrow" in the production, but the renditions of "Soldier Boy" and "Tonight's the Night" allowed the audience to experience a simulated version of the group live in its heyday. The real Shirelles developed a visual image and performance style that enabled them to navigate the contradictory expectations of proper femininity and liberated teenage self-expression. Their race, coupled with their connection to a cultural form whose sexual overtones were never far from the surface, made it necessary for the

FIGURE 3.2 In this 1958 publicity photo, the Shirelles embody propriety in bodily comportment and costuming, fulfilling ideals of femininity and challenging stereotypes of black inferiority. Their respectable appearance helped smooth the women's crossover to white audiences, possibly offsetting concerns about the mature subject matter of their 1960 hit, "Will You Love Me Tomorrow." Clockwise from top: Doris Coley, Addie "Micki" Harris, Shirley Owens, and Beverly Lee. COURTESY RUDY CALVO COLLECTION/CACHE AGENCY.

women to cultivate a public image that afforded them some degree of respectability, particularly once they crossed over to white audiences. The members of the Shirelles were involved in creating this image. "We took care of the clothing ourselves," Lee told me. "We'd go and look together, basically, and try something on to see what we really liked and looked good on everybody."[82] In the early days, they shopped with an understanding that they would wear identical outfits.[83] "At that time we didn't know about style at all," Lee said. "We wanted to look good. We built up to wanting to look a certain way. You know, that comes with maturity. Because we still dressed like young girls."[84] For black women in the early sixties "looking good" was closely related to looking respectable: feminine and not overtly sexual. The result was a wardrobe of sleeveless party dresses or matching dark V-neck sweaters over white blouses (see figure 3.2).

The concern with a "good" appearance extended to onstage movement. "We made up our own [choreography] for a while," Lee explained. Their dancing fit the exuberance of rock and roll and projected feminine attractiveness. "We copied from the guys and just feminized it," Lee said. "We were watching Little Anthony and the Imperials and the Flamingos and, you know, they were suave. We feminized the steps. Then for a while Cholly Atkins taught us."[85] A former vaudeville dancer, Atkins gave the Shirelles a dance vocabulary that he deemed appropriate for young women. "The girl groups had to be more concerned with what I call physical drama," he explained in his autobiography. "Instead of trying to move like the guys, I wanted them to use the kind of body language that was associated with women—using your eyes, hands on the hips, and so forth, but not in a macho way."[86] Together, Atkins and the Shirelles constructed a safe image of black femininity that suited the times. Still, teenage fans of girl group music recognized the sexuality that underpinned these performances. According to Ellie Greenwich, who cowrote a number of girl group era hits, "The boys loved these groups as did the girls . . . there was a lot of 'implied' sex on stage, from short skirts to heavy makeup and appropriate body language."[87] It might have been transgressive for four young black women to sing about sexual desire, but the feminine dance steps, elegant dresses, prominent string section, and sweetly harmonizing voices enabled these black teenagers to smuggle in controversial, female-centered lyrics. After Atkins worked with the Shirelles, he went on to choreograph for the Crystals and then set up shop at Motown where he developed the dances that became the visual signature of the label's most popular artists, including the Supremes.[88]

The Shirelles crossed over to the mainstream by executing the gender-and-race two-step that black women are so often called upon to dance as they manage their black female difference in white arenas. As media studies scholar Susan Douglas notes, "The black teens in girl groups, then, while they sounded orgiastic at times, had to look feminine, innocent, and as white as possible."[89] The Shirelles offset the sexually suggestive nature of their lyrics by conveying propriety in bodily comportment and costuming, at once fulfilling expectations of female respectability and disproving stereotypes of compromised black female sexuality. Commenting on this dynamic, musicologist Laurie Stras observes, "That this work took place behind a veil of respectability, which had the power to include by rendering differences invisible, is surely a major reason for the genre's seemingly contradictory historic importance as a fostering ground for feminine and racial equality."[90] The trappings of respectability that enabled the Shirelles to reach the mainstream also consigned them to looking too proper to be rock and rollers, especially from our perch in the twenty-first century and especially in comparison to the tough-talking Shangri-Las or the self-consciously sexy Ronettes, who according to the group's lead vocalist, deliberately styled themselves in opposition to the country's leading girl group: "When we saw the Shirelles walk onstage with their wide party dresses," Ronnie Bennett Spector reported in her autobiography, "we went in the opposite direction and squeezed our bodies into the tightest skirts we could find."[91] Both the Ronettes and the Shangri-Las more transparently embody the spirit of rock and roll rebellion, but they came onto the scene only after the Shirelles had blazed a path and demonstrated that music performed by and for young women was a financially viable product.

What is extraordinary, given the restrictions placed on women and African Americans at the beginning of the 1960s, is the fact that members of the Shirelles and the other girl groups, most of them black working-class women, were modeling femininity for an integrated audience. They were, Stras argues, "feminine archetypes for millions of adolescent baby-boomers on either side of the Atlantic: what girls were (or thought they should be), and what boys thought that girls were (or that they should be)."[92] Making a case for the cultural significance of girl groups, Susan Douglas argues that as young white women picked up on the songs and dances of these young black women, the rhythm liberated their bodies and the lyrics liberated their minds.[93] She also contends that girl group music, with its public representation of female solidarity, was a starting point for the formation of feminist consciousness and practice.[94] Equally significant is the fact that the Shirelles and other girl groups modeled possibility and primacy for young *black* female fans at a time when young black women were rarely featured in the national media.

Getting Their Due

On April 27, 2011, the same day that *Baby It's You!* was set to open on Broadway, the *New York Daily News* reported that lawyers working on behalf of Beverly Lee and the estates of the two deceased Shirelles, Doris Coley Jackson and Addie Harris Jackson, had filed a lawsuit in New York's Supreme Court against the producers of the show for using the names and likenesses of the artists without their permission.[95] The suit, a public blow to the producers on what should have been a festive day, was joined by former Scepter Records artists Dionne Warwick and Chuck Jackson, who were also depicted in the musical. Shirley Alston Reeves, the other surviving original member of the Shirelles, was not part of the suit. Instead, she participated in the production, giving postshow concerts for four nights during the musical's Broadway run.[96] *Baby It's You*! was a jukebox musical, stacked with popular songs from the early 1960s strung together with a simple plot. The point of the production was the rendition of familiar songs by actors who mimicked the vocal and visual style of the originators. The nostalgic journey would profit the songwriters and those who held publishing rights to the material, but the artists who originated the performances that the actors imitated on stage would not be paid. The artists filing the suit objected to this situation. "It is disappointing," argued their lawyer Oren Warshavsky, "that the producers of the play would simply piggy-back on the careers of these original artists without asking permission at all, let alone without sufficiently compensating the people without whom there would be no Broadway story, original music or iconic styling."[97] The lawsuit highlighted that the music-making of the Shirelles was a form of labor and that the laborers had been exploited. This dynamic of exploitation and appropriation was an integral part of the group's professional experience.

The Shirelles were the first artists signed to Scepter Records, and in the early years, they were the label's best sellers. Florence Greenberg was able to launch the careers of Maxine Brown, the Isley Brothers, Chuck Jackson, the Kingsmen, B. J. Thomas, and Dionne Warwick by capitalizing on the reputation and money that she earned through her association with the New Jersey–based quartet.[98] In fact, it seems reasonable to characterize Scepter Records as "The House That the Shirelles Built." Beyond underwriting a new record label, the Shirelles fueled a new money-making movement in the recording industry. In his comments about the 2011 suit, Warshavsky referenced a grimmer aspect of the group's history by stating, "The Plaintiffs, having been cheated out of their royalties once already when they were young, are being victimized again."[99] He was referring to the Shirelles' circumstances in 1964, when the women, who had recently turned twenty-one, learned that the earnings Greenberg had been holding "in trust" for them were not available.[100] Unable to collect their money, the women entered into a legal battle with their label. The case went to court at the end of 1964, and the group reached a settlement with Scepter in 1965.[101] Years later, Shirley Alston Reeves commented on the situation:

> During the proceedings I found out things that tore me apart. Things I was innocent of. We didn't know we were being treated this way by the people there, because we loved everyone. Our feelings were sincere and theirs evidently weren't. We took to our manager, Florence Greenberg, like a mother. She gave us that mother routine, and being kids, we fell for it completely. We never questioned anything she did. . . . They should have invested the money for us properly. Being the top female group in the country, we should have made a lot of money, and we didn't.[102]

Greenberg's involvement in the Shirelles' career may have seemed like attentive mothering or even a kind of female solidarity as the five women navigated the male-dominated recording industry. In the end, though, the Shirelles did not avoid the kind of exploitation that was rampant in the early years of rock and roll. They had earned money, but they were unable to access it. During the months that they fought their case, they were still bound by the terms of their Scepter contract and could not record for another label. Scepter, meanwhile, focused on other artists, particularly Dionne Warwick, who was emerging as the label's newest star.[103] The suit and the label's shifting attention had a devastating effect on the group's career. The Shirelles did not appear on the Top 40 after 1963.[104]

There were other reasons the group was in a precarious position. They had lost their producer when Luther Dixon left Scepter at the end of 1962.[105] Following his departure, only two of the group's singles reached the pop charts: "Foolish Little Girl" (produced by Dixon before he left the label) and "Don't Say Goodnight and Mean Goodbye," both in 1963.[106] The Shirelles placed their last song on the charts in early 1965, but they continued working together until 1968, when Doris retired from the group; the remaining members continued as a trio, Shirley and the Shirelles.[107] The group recorded new material into the early seventies, but to survive professionally they had to go on tour and sing their early 1960s hits.[108] Thus, the Shirelles became part of a nostalgia craze for early rock and roll even though their songs were barely a decade old.[109] By far the greatest challenge the Shirelles faced was the phenomenon that put them into the oldies category: the arrival of a new rock and roll sound. In 1964, the Beatles and a host of other British bands brought their effervescent take on American rock and roll to the United States. The demand for the sound of the British Invasion pushed almost all of the established American acts to the low end of the pop charts, as rapidly changing pop music tastes rendered them unfashionable. With the notable exception of Motown's artists, black rock and rollers fell to a second tier in terms of sales and visibility. When discussing this phase of rock and roll, many historians treat the Beatles as the saviors of a rock and roll authenticity that the more commercial sound of early sixties vocal groups had supplanted.[110] The continuities between American girl groups and British boy groups, however, are worth noting. "I loved the Beatles," Lee told me, "and they came over and they were talking about how much they loved us."[111] According to Lee, the two quartets missed the opportunity to meet. "We were supposed to get together when they came over," she recalled. "Their office contacted our office immediately, but we were so busy touring we didn't get a chance to hang with them."[112]

By the time the Beatles arrived in the United States in early 1964, they had a deep appreciation both for the Shirelles, the group whose sound was "crucial to the Beatles' development," and for their producer Luther Dixon.[113] Prior to becoming recording artists, the Beatles were a live act, performing in Liverpool, England, and Hamburg, Germany; Shirelles' tracks such as "Will You Love Me Tomorrow," "Mama Said," and "Boys" were among the songs they played in their sets.[114] In his chronicle of the Beatles' professional trajectory, Mark Lewisohn observes that the group closely followed the arrangements of the originals: "Paul bagged 'Mama Said,' using his high register for the lead vocal, John and George on either side of the other microphone for the girl-group backing."[115] When they began to compose their own music, the Beatles continued to follow this model of shared vocal labor. The vocal arrangement for "Please Please Me," an early Lennon/McCartney composition, was "a bit Shirelles," according to Paul McCartney.[116] John Lennon noted that in "P.S. I Love You," McCartney "was trying to write a 'Solider Boy' like the Shirelles."[117] The imprint of the girls from Passaic on the lads from Liverpool was strong; in fact, in one of his early comments about the band, the Beatles' producer George Martin told a reporter that the group "sounded like a male Shirelles."[118] The British invaders recorded some of their covers of Shirelles originals. "Baby, It's You" (with Lennon on lead vocals) and "Boys" (featuring vocals by drummer Ringo Starr) appeared on *Please Please Me*, the group's 1963 debut album.[119] At a time when the idea of a British rock and roll band would have seemed absurd to most Americans, the Beatles asserted their rock and roll credentials by connecting to the music's originators, both in their selection of songs and in their self-representation.[120] A press release anticipating the Beatles' American debut on *The Ed Sullivan Show* included brief group member biographies. The one for John Lennon explained that he liked "steak, chips, jelly, curries, painting, modern jazz, cats, suede and leather clothing, [French actress and singer] Juliette Gréco, The Shirelles and blondes who are intelligent."[121] The Shirelles took pleasure in their link to the band. Years later Shirley Alston Reeves told a reporter, "Whenever anybody interviewed us, we were always proud to say, 'Well, the Beatles said that we're their favorite group.'"[122]

The Rolling Stones also appreciated the girl group sound. In his autobiography, Keith Richards reports that the Shirelles were among the vocal groups that he and Mick Jagger were listening to in the band's early days, and he singles out Shirley Alston Reeves for praise, calling her voice "beautifully balanced with a fragility and simplicity."[123] The Stones' 1964 release "Tell Me" sounds like an answer song to "The Things I Want to Hear," the B-side to the Shirelles' 1962 hit "Baby It's You."[124] "Tell Me" works with a different melody, but it echoes the lyrics, tempo, and feel of the Shirelles' track: a slow and deliberate verse and an upbeat chorus in which the singer intensifies the demands; only the strings are absent. When vocalist Mick Jagger pleads, "You've gotta tell me you're coming back to me" in the chorus, he parallels the lines and mood of the chorus that the Shirelles sing: "You've gotta keep telling me the things I want to hear."[125] "Tell Me" was the first Mick Jagger/Keith Richards composition that the group released as the A-side of a single, and it was the first Rolling Stones record to reach the US Top 40. *Rolling Stone* magazine cofounder Jann Wenner identified "Tell Me" as the first song to have "the seeds of the modern Stones in it."[126] In an interview with Wenner, Mick Jagger acknowledged that the structure of the song established a new sonic approach for the band. "There's a definite feel about it," he told Wenner in 1995. "It's a very pop song, as opposed to all the blues songs and the Motown covers, which everyone did at the time."[127] Following the musical model of the Shirelles helped both the Beatles and the Rolling Stones shift from being bands that covered African American music to becoming artists who created an original rock and roll sound.

Other fledgling male British bands borrowed from the Shirelles. In 1964 Manfred Mann covered "Sha La La," a Luther Dixon production that the Shirelles had released in 1963. Even the Yardbirds, a band famed for launching the careers of virtuoso rock guitarists Jeff Beck, Eric Clapton, and Jimmy Page, covered the Shirelles. Their 1965 release *For Your Love* included "Putty in Your Hands," a track that appeared on the Shirelles' 1962 album *Baby It's You*.[128] Acknowledging these borrowings and their significance, musicologist Jacqueline Warwick argues that "these young male performers were energized by the music of girl groups and female blues singers, and they borrowed the trappings of female sexuality and vulnerability to create versions of masculinity centered around transgressive earthiness or adorable approachability."[129] When I spoke with Beverly Lee about the ways the British rock bands appropriated the sound of the Shirelles and their growing presence on the US pop charts, she maintained a positive attitude:

> **MM:** And what about a group like Manfred Mann doing a song that you had released at around the same time?
>
> **Beverly Lee:** Well, it's always wonderful hearing somebody else's interpretation of your song.
>
> **MM:** What was the impact? Did you feel a change once the British—especially the Beatles—but the other bands, the Animals and Manfred Mann and the rest—once they were in the US? Did you all feel a change?
>
> **Beverly Lee:** Well, we were blessed because we were prepared for a new level. We had a club act that we'd been working on and we started playing clubs.[130]

Lee emphasized that the Shirelles were already shifting away from the teen market focus and were expanding so that they could reach a more upscale audience. Developing an act for adult nightclubs would get them into the venues that were, at the time, the pinnacle for pop music acts. In contrast, when discussing the situation with a reporter in the late 1980s, Shirley Alston Reeves highlighted the negative impact the British Invasion had on her group:

It was a terrible blow to our ego, with everybody dropping our records like hotcakes. . . . Our record, "Sha La La," was starting to make it, and Manfred Mann covered the record. And [they] had the hit. [Disc jockeys] dropped ours like a hotcake as soon as they heard it by an English group. We weren't bitter about it. But they all went nuts at the record company. If you can't get records played on the radio, that's it. Zoom, downhill.[131]

At the point when the Shirelles and Scepter should have been focusing on strategies to address the British challenge—a challenge propelled in part by British artists appropriating the sound of the Shirelles—they were embroiled in a legal battle. By the time the case was resolved, the pop music scene had changed, and the Shirelles were not able to adjust.

Honoring the Shirelles

Toward the end of our 2012 interview, I asked Beverly Lee about the Broadway show.

> **MM:** Do you have any comment about the musical *Baby, It's You!*?
>
> **Beverly Lee:** [pause] God doesn't like ugly.[132]

Maybe there wasn't much else to say. The legal case had been settled in December 2011, and the failure of the production to sustain a long Broadway run—it had closed in September—was a kind of comeuppance for its producers.[133] For me, though, the musical still rankled. Its marginalizing of the Shirelles in a story about how Florence Greenberg built Scepter Records echoed the marginalizing of the Shirelles in the story historians and critics tell about rock and roll. This is not to suggest that the Shirelles and their contribution have gone unrecognized. Passaic High School, where the group started out, now sits on a street named Shirelles Boulevard; inside the building is the Shirelles Auditorium, its lobby decorated with Shirelles photos and memorabilia.[134] In 1994, the Rhythm and Blues Foundation honored the group with a Pioneer Award intended to celebrate "legendary artists whose lifelong contributions have been instrumental in the development of Rhythm and Blues music."[135] Another acknowledgment of the group's influence came in 1996, when the Shirelles were inducted into the Rock and Roll Hall of Fame, but this well-deserved honor came late, a consequence of the race, gender, and genre dynamics that the women had negotiated throughout their careers.

Rolling Stone magazine founder Jann Wenner and Atlantic Records founder Ahmet Ertegun formed the Rock and Roll Hall of Fame Foundation in 1983. Part of the new organization's mission was formalizing the recognition of artists and producers who were central to "the evolution, development and perpetuation of rock and roll."[136] To this end, they began inducting artists into the Rock and Roll Hall of Fame in 1986. The new institution established its legitimacy through the high profile of its founders and the willingness of rock musicians to engage with it. Honorees attend the induction ceremonies, and other artists, perhaps hoping to be inducted at some future point, participate in the proceedings by delivering celebratory remarks about the inductees and performing their music. Punk rock trailblazers the Sex Pistols refused to attend the ceremony the year they were inducted and likened the Rock Hall to "a piss stain," but their response was unusual.[137] Most artists express appreciation for the recognition. The question of which artists receive this recognition, however, has been a fraught issue. The Shirelles had been eligible for induction from the time the Rock and Roll Hall of Fame Foundation began inducting artists, but it was ten years before they were honored.[138] In an article published after the 1996 inductees had been announced, *New York Daily News* music critic David Hinckley addressed the biases that contributed to the delay:

> The Shirelles go into the "Long Overdue" wing of the Rock Hall, which for years has had trouble getting past the idea that rock 'n' roll was defined by guys with guitars. In fact, rock 'n' roll is as wide as the many styles of music from which it was spawned, and early rock 'n' roll radio was shaped just as much by the Shirelles, the Chantels and Brenda Lee . . . as it was by an Eddie Cochran.[139]

For the pioneering African American artists of the music's early decades, this problem of genre definition, sonic preferences, and the resulting exclusion from the Rock and Roll Hall of Fame was an extension of the erasure they experienced during the formative years of their careers, when black artists were tapped as a source and then left to languish while white artists moved into the genre's foreground. I noted this dynamic when I compared the Shirelles with other inductees. Rock acts of the late 1960s and early 1970s who had started their recording careers after the Shirelles and whose impact on rock was arguably less ground-shifting were inducted before them: Creedence Clearwater Revival was inducted in 1993, the Band in 1994, and Elton John in 1994. Even country artist Johnny Cash, inducted in 1992, and reggae icon Bob Marley, inducted in 1994, were deemed more significant to the trajectory of rock and roll than the group of women who brought a new sound to the genre and created a space for women as performers in the process. John Lennon, who publicly acknowledged that the Shirelles had influenced the Beatles, had been inducted twice (as a Beatle in 1988 and as a solo artist in 1994) before the Rock and Roll Hall of Fame recognized the Shirelles.

On the night of the Shirelles' induction, vocalists Merry Clayton, Marianne Faithfull, and Darlene Love did the honors. Speaking in a girl group–style chorus and using a well-placed adverb, they said, "We are very pleased and proud to *finally* be able to induct the Shirelles into the Rock and Roll Hall of Fame."[140] When the three surviving members of the Shirelles took the stage to accept the gold statuettes commemorating their induction, Beverly Lee commented on the delay. Excited and a bit out of breath, she was the first to speak:

> Thank you ever so much. I must say that I thank God in the name of Jesus Christ my Lord the savior for the Shirelles standing here this evening. Nobody knows the trouble that we've seen. Nobody knows but Jesus. And thank God He brought us through it all. [sigh] And I simply have to say, I speak for all of us, I must say that *we deserve this*. [Doris and Shirley laugh and there is a long round of applause.] Can I ask you all a question? What took you so long? [Doris and Shirley laugh again.] No. Please believe me, I'm very, very grateful and we're very, very honored and who would've thought that four teenagers from Passaic High School would write a song called "I Met Him on a Sunday," would have a classmate by the name of Mary Jane Greenberg in the audience whose mother, Florence Greenberg, owned a record company, and would record us and it would lead us to the Hall of Fame and we would have this historical moment?[141]

In a deft balance of gracious acceptance and pointed critique, Lee admonished the institution she was entering for taking so long to admit her group into a space where it clearly belonged. The Rock and Roll Hall of Fame presents itself as an institution that responsibly curates the history of the music form, but Lee's "What took you so long?" questioned the Rock Hall's process and values.

The Rock Hall's website explains that criteria for induction "include the influence and significance of the artists' contribution to the development and perpetuation of rock and roll," but as anyone who has argued with a friend over the merits of a given band knows, the categories "influence" and "significance" are highly subjective.[142] Far from a neutral exercise, the individual tastes and musical investments of the nominating committee and the "body of more than 600 artists, historians and members of the music industry" who select the inductees drive the process.[143] The result has been a tendency to hurry to induct white rock artists of the late 1960s and 1970s, while being slow to induct black rock and roll and rhythm and blues artists of the 1950s and early 1960s who, it seems, do not loom as large in the cultural memory of the selection panel and voters (whose identities are not made public, by the way). The process is also gendered; female artists comprise only 10 percent of the inducted artists, a statistic that led feminist musicologist Laurie Stras to refer to the Rock Hall as "that bastion of the male popular music canon."[144] The Rock Hall has also been slow to induct artists connected to 1970s subgenres of rock such as heavy metal, glam, and progressive rock, commercially successful styles without high levels of critical cachet. Rock fans, critics, and musicians have made a pastime of criticizing the Rock Hall for its decisions about which artists to induct and when to do so.[145] Beverly Lee launched her critique of the process when she stood on the Rock Hall dais at her induction ceremony. During our interview, she told me the reason she spoke as she did:

> Because women were overlooked for a long time and as black women we were definitely overlooked and they seemed to have their picks of who they wanted to put in. David Hinckley had been writing about us and [saying] we should be in, we should be in. And they finally did it. We worked hard and we sold good records, you know, people loved our music. This was our due, that's what I was saying, in essence.[146]

For Lee, the logic behind publicly asking the Rock Hall, "What took you so long?" was simple. "Well, I figured, you have to say what you have to say while you have the opportunity," she explained. "Not wait until fifteen years later and say, 'Why? Why didn't I say what was on my heart?'"[147]

But *why* did the Rock Hall take so long? A desire to elevate rock and roll as an art form seems to inform the voters' decision-making process. Hinckley posited that the Rock Hall had a "deathly fear of opening its doors to artists, from Pat Boone to the Monkees, whose achievements were more commercial than artistic."[148] As music historian Elijah Wald has noted, "Rock historians have routinely dismissed the early 1960s as a dismal period in American pop, and this can to a great extent be traced to the fact that the historians are male and the teen pop market wasn't geared to their tastes."[149] These critics, Wald argues, valorize obscure music and underrate what was most popular. The Shirelles were commercially successful because their music skillfully blended an accessible pop sound and black rhythm and blues energy. In fact, the Shirelles were more successful on the pop charts than on the rhythm and blues charts, placing twenty-six singles on the former and only twenty on the latter; furthermore, the group never had a number one R&B hit.[150] Ironically, the commercial success of the Shirelles, which underwrites the group's claim to pop music significance, compromises the group's image in histories both of rock music *and* of African American music.

The shift in the meaning of rock and roll that occurred during the 1960s also has an impact on the way the Shirelles are remembered. By the end of the decade, their respectable black femininity and sweet sound clashed with the countercultural visual style and high volume distortion that were defining rock. The Shirelles seemed to represent the very status quo that late sixties rock challenged. The Shirelles face spotty inclusion on the African American music side as well. The group's broad appeal to white audiences, the music's teen focus, the hybrid pop/R&B sound, and the resulting commercial success put them outside of the narrative that dominates studies of black popular music in the 1960s. Music writers typically approach this period with a focus on the rise of soul music, a form geared to black audiences that came to index authentic African American expression.[151] The pop orientation of the Shirelles puts them outside of this canon. Their crossover success predates that of the Motown artists, but the Shirelles and their producer Luther Dixon have not received the attention lavished on Berry Gordy's enterprise. As with so many African American women in rock and roll, the Shirelles occupy a betwixt-and-between position in which their race and gender make them outsiders to the center of rock, while their musical sound and association with white audiences make them outsiders to the center of black music.

There is no question, though, that the Shirelles were a groundbreaking group, as Doris Coley and Shirley Alston Reeves asserted in an interview filmed years after the girl group era had ended:

> **Doris Coley:** There did seem to be a blossoming after the Shirelles' opening the doors so that other girl groups could follow. When I think back to it and all of the hard work, when I say that we earned it, we earned it. And I like to think that we were a very intricate part of doing it, opening that door.
>
> **Shirley Alston Reeves:** We kicked those doors—*hard*.[152]

It's easy to remember the Shirelles if you listen to the music that came after them. Their sound is present in the dozens of girl groups that set the rock and roll style of the early 1960s and in the British Invasion acts that followed. The vocal sound of the Shirelles carries through succeeding waves of rock and roll, informing the practices of male and female performers and songwriters who were their contemporaries. Ellie Greenwich credited the group's lead vocalist Shirley Owens with giving her inspiration for her songwriting.[153] Mary Wilson of the Supremes reports that she "loved the Shirelles" and played "Will You Love Me Tomorrow" over and over.[154] Sarah Dash recalled that her group Patti LaBelle and the Bluebelles covered Shirelles songs when they performed in the early 1960s. "We looked up to them," Dash told me, "because they were The Group. *The* female group. And we regarded them as very special people in our lives."[155] Carole King included her version of "Will You Love Me Tomorrow," her signal composition for the group, on *Tapestry* (1971), the blockbuster album that established the seasoned songwriter as a solo singer and recording superstar. The 1971 Laura Nyro and Labelle album *Gonna Take a Miracle*, a suite of girl group and vocal group covers, pays homage to the Shirelles, opening with "I Met Him on a Sunday." Subsequent generations of rockers such as the Ramones, Blondie, Bruce Springsteen, and Billy Joel; latter-day girl groups such as En Vogue and Destiny's Child; and a British contingent represented by vocalists Amy Winehouse and Adele have all borrowed from and built on the girl group sound that the Shirelles, the Chantels, and the Bobbettes set into motion in the late 1950s. And there is another place to listen for the impact of the Shirelles and the girl group sound on rock and roll. By the end of the 1960s, the audible blackness that these groups drew on but tempered in their performances was so valued in the rock mainstream that artists and producers sought out black women singers who could deliver the sound of harmonizing black girl groups on recordings by the era's top rock acts. Echoing the way the Shirelles were depicted in *Baby It's You!* and its promotional poster, these women played supporting roles, working as background vocalists for rock artists. I discuss this phenomenon in the next chapter.

FOUR / Call and Response

The guys in England started gravitating more toward
the American soul singers because they were
beginning to travel, so by having that exposure, they
wanted new sounds. That's how that mixture started
coming in. / **GLORIA JONES**

The special events area of the Tribeca Barnes and Noble in downtown Manhattan was nearly full when I arrived on a summery evening in June 2013. My purchase of the soundtrack to the just-released documentary *Twenty Feet from Stardom* secured a seat at the event: a conversation and performance by the background vocalist and Rock and Roll Hall of Fame inductee Darlene Love. Morgan Neville's film laid claim to the importance of background vocalists, most of them African American women, to the sound of popular music recorded since the early 1960s. The crowd-pleasing movie, which won the 2013 Oscar for best documentary (feature), follows the careers of several of these artists, bringing much-deserved attention to Love and a host of others, some of whom fanned out onto the promotion circuit in the wake of the film's release. Merry Clayton sat for an interview with Terry Gross on the National Public Radio program *Fresh Air*; the online music magazine *Popmatters* published a profile on Claudia Lennear; and Love appeared on the *Late Show with David Letterman* to sing "Lean on Me," one of the songs featured in the film.[1] She performed the song again at the end of the bookstore conversation hosted by songwriter Brian Gari and before posing for pictures with audience members and signing copies of her autobiography, *My Name Is Love*. Finally, Love and the other background vocalists were in the spotlight, decades after they began shaping the sound of rock.

Love was someone I had grown up with. Her voice ringing out on "Christmas, Baby, Please Come Home" each December was a favorite sign that the holidays were upon us when I was a kid. More recently, I looked forward to seeing her sing the song during her annual Christmas-time appearance on David Letterman's late night talk show. During all of those years of listening, though, I was unaware of Love's central role as a background vocalist. I also hadn't given much sustained thought to how common it was to see African American women performing as background vocalists in pop, R&B, and rock settings. As I researched African American women and rock and roll, I began to understand that the prevalence of black women background vocalists and their audibility on record and invisibility in historical accounts of rock and roll history were issues that I needed to address. Background vocalists have received some mention in trade and academic publications. In her history of women in rock, music writer Gerri Hirshey calls the backup singer "the Unknown Stalwart of rock and roll," who, she explains, "is generally paid scale, but is worth ten times her weight in industry platinum. And without her, there would be no rock and roll."[2] Hirshey stresses that background vocalists do important musical work and notes that "the overwhelming majority of backup artistry is female."[3] Musicologists Susan Fast, Annie Randall, and Jacqueline Warwick have analyzed background vocalists in rock from feminist perspectives that highlight interrelated issues of gender, race, power, and social meaning.[4] They view female background singers as occupying a position that is all too typical for women. Warwick asserts that they "provide support to famous performers, in a relationship that can be understood to symbolize the unacknowledged female drudgery behind male success that is critiqued by Marxist feminist writers, and that depends on knee-jerk assumptions about race in order to make sense."[5] Characterizing the lot of background vocalists, Fast observes, "We erase them from the discourse about songs and their musical operations and cultural meanings. We expect them to be there, we may sing along with them, but we rarely stop to reflect on what roles they might be playing."[6]

Although they work in the background, these African American women are an important sonic presence in popular music. Professional vocalists such as Darlene Love, Merry Clayton, Claudia Lennear, P. P. Arnold, Madeline Bell, Ava Cherry, Carolyn Dennis, Venetta Fields, Gloria Jones, Clydie King, and Doris Troy contributed their gospel-trained voices to the sound of rock in the 1960s and 1970s. These singers responded to the call of white rockers who were attracted to African American soul music and wanted to incorporate it into their productions. The women I discuss in this chapter recorded and performed in concert with David Bowie, Joe Cocker, Bob Dylan, George

Harrison, Humble Pie, Carole King, John Lennon, Lynryd Skynyrd, Pink Floyd, the Rolling Stones, the Small Faces, Steely Dan, James Taylor, T. Rex, and Neil Young, among others. The practice of using background vocalists persisted from the sixties until the end of the seventies, becoming so common that it usually went unnoticed. As Susan Fast observes, "It is precisely in such conventions that important ideological work is carried out, and this is why they are worthy of our analytical attention."[7] Similarly, arguing the need to consider the complex roles background vocalists play in rock, Warwick states, "The backup trio as an emblem warrants further examination in feminist and musicological research."[8] Responding to the calls of these feminist scholars, I take seriously the musical and cultural labor that African American women contributed as background vocalists in 1960s and 1970s rock and roll. Of particular interest are the ways the audibly black voices of African American women background vocalists provided sonic authenticity and enabled white artists to maintain a connection to the black roots of rock and roll. Background vocal singing has been the one space where black women's participation in rock is not questioned. Reflecting on her background vocal work with rock artists in the 1970s, Venetta Fields told journalist Kandia Crazy Horse, "That was the time when every act had to have three *black* American singers in the band. They wanted to feel and hear the blackness. They would do anything and pay anything to get it or experience it."[9] To explore the repercussions of this quest for black vocal sound, I examine the dynamics of race, gender, and genre that underwrote black women's participation in the productions of white rock artists and consider the sonic and symbolic work that their voices did.

As background vocalists, black women operated in helpmate roles, shoring up the established rock and roll hierarchies that prioritized male performers. In recording studios in Los Angeles and London, white men and black women collaborated under racially integrated but socially stratified working conditions. The African American women were freelancers hired for the sessions; they were paid union scale for their artistic labor, which often included developing their own arrangements. They were usually (but not always) mentioned in liner notes, sometimes listed with misspelled names or by first name only. Although they were not members of the band, they were an integral part of the sound. The vocals of these women complemented those of the lead singer, filling out the vocal tracks, adding volume, lushness, and warmth, and making up for the limitations of the lead voice without drawing attention away from it. Background vocalists helped provide a stable backdrop against which the lead vocalist could form a unique musical persona. Most rock fans do not know the names of these women, but have been hearing their voices for years. They are part of our musical consciousness, and it is worth discussing their simultaneous audibility and invisibility. In this chapter, I attach names to voices that are a presence in familiar rock songs and consider the reasons that presence was desired. In addition to referring to the recordings, I include comments that these women have made in published interviews and autobiographies. I also draw from interviews I conducted with Merry Clayton and Gloria Jones, two women who were active as professional background vocalists during the period in question. My intention is to listen to the voices of background vocalists in order to expand the ways we hear rock music and understand African American women as cultural producers.

Gospel Meets Rock and Roll

During the 1950s and 1960s, African American political protest and African American popular music propelled a rising tide of blackness into mainstream American culture. Soul music, a secularized form of gospel, and black gospel music itself became signifiers of black musicality and black identity, as musical practices that had been confined to black communities were increasingly audible beyond them.[10] Mahalia Jackson, known as the Queen of Gospel, brought African American sacred music to a broad audience through her radio show, television appearances, and concerts during the 1950s. At roughly the same time, Sam Cooke and Ray Charles followed the example that gospel vocalist and guitarist Sister Rosetta Tharpe had set in the 1940s and used a gospel sound to explore secular themes of romance and longing.[11] By the end of the 1960s, the gospel voice had become *the* authentic black female voice in pop music and musical theater, turning up in Broadway and West End musicals such as *Hair* and *Jesus Christ Superstar* (with background vocalists P. P. Arnold and Madeline Bell on the cast album).[12] These rock musicals incorporated elements associated with gospel, such as rhythm, improvisation, and the call-and-response form, to create an aural sense of community between audience and performers.[13] As Charles Nero observes, these features were compelling to many theatergoers, and black women's gospel voices were used at key moments in musical settings otherwise lacking in the gospel sound.[14] Offering a description that applies to the rock context, Nero suggests that black women's gospel voices in musicals infuse the show with energy and excitement and "provide audiences with enormous pleasure that can propel a show during a slow moment or lift audiences to heights of ecstasy."[15] In the 1960s, as white rock musicians were experimenting with black musical sounds, they began to work with gospel-trained African American women singers who could inject soul into a song with the drop of a melismatic "yeah" or "ooh."

The African American women vocalists who engaged in these collaborations had grown up attending black Protestant churches in which music was a critical part of worship. They sang as members of the congregation, and many participated in church youth choirs. Through church-based music training, they developed knowledge of solo and ensemble singing, arranging vocals, and singing harmony. They learned a large repertoire of songs and internalized a performance style that they carried into the rock and roll arena. "Baptist and Pentecostal choirs were something of a farm system for the pop-music big leagues," Darlene Love quipped in her autobiography. "Aretha [Franklin], Patti LaBelle, Gladys Knight, and Merry Clayton all cut their teeth in the choir loft."[16] Although gospel music was central to their development, these women had access to a range of musical traditions.[17] Merry Clayton listened to plenty of gospel when she was growing up, but she told me that she also recalled hearing "jazz, a lot of Dinah Washington and Billie Holiday and [white pop singer] Gloria Mann and Sarah Vaughan, you know, all the greats: Duke Ellington, Count Basie. And I loved it all. And Ray Charles, of course. . . . I heard Little Richard sing rock and roll."[18] Clayton was a member of her public high school's choir, and she took music theory classes, getting ear training and learning to read music. But she stressed that she really learned harmony, a cornerstone of background singing, through her involvement with gospel singing.[19] Other background vocalists had similarly broad musical exposure. Members of the Blossoms, Darlene Love's vocal group, drew on influences that included "grammar-school music teachers, high-school choirs, talent shows, and glee clubs, formal opera studies . . . and an appreciation for the recordings of light pop ensembles such as the McGuire Sisters."[20]

Still, church music and the church loomed large for these young women, especially for Darlene Love, Merry Clayton, and Gloria Jones, who were preacher's kids. Because of their familial connections, they bore the burden of having to maintain the proper behavior demanded by their respective churches. "It wasn't easy being a PK (preacher's kid)," Love recalled. "There were so many rules—besides the prohibitions on appearance, there was supposed to be no dancing, no real fun of any kind."[21] Above all, as Clayton explained to me, the expectation was that church-trained singers would use their gift to sing only sacred music.[22] After Clayton made her first professional recording, a duet with the white pop vocalist Bobby Darin when she was fourteen years old, the fallout was severe. Her parents supported her, but her minister announced, "Baby Sister [Clayton's nickname] can't be singing in my choir and singing out in the world."[23] Singing "in the world" meant performing secular music in secular arenas, and it was a serious breach. Cissy Houston, who as a member of the Sweet Inspirations sang background on hundreds of pop songs, observed, "Those who the church felt had left gospel, like Dinah Washington, Sam Cooke, and the Staple Singers, were branded 'blues singers,' renegades, apostates, backsliders. They were booed if they ever tried to stand in a church or on a gospel program."[24] In spite of the prohibitions, a number of gospel-trained women got involved in rock and roll. Venetta Fields, for example, had sung with and directed church choirs, but through the accident of being in the right place at the right time, she was invited to join the Ikettes; she toured with the Ike and Tina Turner Revue for five years and then began to work with white rock artists.[25] While still in their teens, Love, Clayton, and Jones made forays into secular music and began recording professionally at the recording studios of Los Angeles, the city where all three women grew up. The primary motivation was financial. "I got tired of the church, and decided to go out and make some money," Clayton told a journalist in a 1970 interview, "so I went to work as a singer."[26] The difference in money was impressive. Cissy Houston reported, "In two full days of sessions in New York, I could earn what it took me a week to earn at RCA [the label where she was signed as a gospel artist]!"[27] According to Merry Clayton, session work was also more lucrative than touring.[28] Perhaps the money made it easier to withstand criticism from their church communities, and the support of their families certainly helped. Clayton's parents, for example, framed their daughter's vocal abilities as a gift from God and accentuated the importance of *using* that gift.[29] Clayton recalled her mother telling her, "You keep on singing, keep on acting, keep on doing what you're doing and God will bless you through it, just don't forget God in all of that. Always remember *who* you are and also remember *whose* you are."[30]

The debate about singing "in the world" was beside the point for the rock musicians who wanted these women to sing on their recordings. Their concern was the full-bodied, resonant vocal sound. Its features, learned "in the choir loft," as Darlene Love put it, include a full-throated vocal timbre, use of vibrato, and displays of vocal agility in which a singer might shift from a head voice to a chest voice when moving across octaves.[31] In gospel singing, departure from the standard text is expected and valued. This can mean adding ascending or descending notes at the end of a musical line; it can also mean improvising with the slurs, slides, and scoops of melisma or adding extra words such as "Yes, Lord" or "Help me, Jesus." These forms of ornamentation, what anthropologist and novelist Zora Neale Hurston labeled a "will to adorn," allow the singer to express her spiritual devotion and place a personal stamp on the song.[32] As professional background vocalists, African American women transported these vocal tropes from the sacred realm of gospel to the worldly context of rock and roll.

Background Beginnings

Overviews of the careers of Darlene Love's Blossoms and Cissy Houston's Sweet Inspirations and some of their key collaborations reveal the growing reliance on African American women's vocals in popular music during the 1960s.[33] The success of both groups rested on assumptions producers, artists, and audiences made about the relationship between race and vocal sound.

By the time producer Phil Spector had christened Darlene Peete (née Wright) "Darlene Love" in 1963, she was a well-established background singer.[34] Her group, the Los Angeles–based Blossoms, had started doing session work in 1958; it soon became a sought-after group for recordings featuring both black and white artists. Los Angeles record producers valued the Blossoms because the women could sing in ways that indexed blackness or a more ambiguous racial identity. "The Blossoms didn't sound white, but we didn't sound black, either," Love states in her autobiography. "The magic of the Blossoms was that we could sound whatever way we wanted."[35] This flexibility, musicologist Jacqueline Warwick notes, and the Blossoms' ability to embody "both white and black stereotypes of femininity in their vocal performances in the recording studio draws our attention to the constructedness of all these roles."[36] In an interview with Warwick, Blossom Fanita James recalled the ways the artists and their producers understood vocal whiteness: "The producers would tell us . . . 'less vibrato, and sound "white."' That's exactly what they would say. That meant smoother . . . we would all breathe together . . . just a softer, and more conservative sound."[37] Describing her group's work with white teen idol James Darren, Love characterized the performance of white vocal sound in a similar way: "There were no whoops, no hollers, no melisma, no shouts," she explained. "All we had to do was echo the lead, with prim wahs and proper whoa-whoas."[38]

The Blossoms could also "sound black," bringing in gospel inflections when recording with African American artists such as Sam Cooke, the Ronettes, or Betty Everett. Using an instrumental metaphor, Love explained, "The Blossoms were like those keyboards that put 162 different rhythms, instruments, and styles at your fingertips. White and black, chaste and loose, church and Broadway and jazz. And because of that, the work started pouring in, from artists as musically and kinetically unrelated as Doris Day and Bobby Day, Roy Rogers and Ray Charles."[39] Their vocal skill won the Blossoms a steady stream of session work and earned them "boatloads of money."[40] A short list of the recordings Love and the Blossoms appeared on indicates the group's range: "Santa's Comin' in a Whirlybird" (1959) by country singer Gene Autry, "Monster Mash" (1962) by pop novelty act Bobby "Boris" Pickett and the Crypt Kickers, "Move over Darling" (1962) by mainstream pop star Doris Day, "In My Room" (1963) by surf rockers the Beach Boys, "The Shoop Shoop Song (It's in His Kiss)" (1964) by R&B singer Betty Everett, "You've Lost That Lovin' Feelin'" (1964) by blue-eyed soul artists the Righteous Brothers, and "River Deep, Mountain High" (1966) by R&B stalwart Tina Turner.[41] The Blossoms also worked with Elvis Presley, singing background (along with the Jordanaires, a white male quartet) on his 1968 comeback television special and joining him in the 1969 film *Change of Habit*.[42]

The ability to cross back and forth between a "white sound" and a "black sound" contributed to the Blossoms—Darlene Love, Fanita James, and Jean King—being hired as background vocalists on *Shindig!*, the first American television program to put rock and roll in an evening time slot (see figure 4.1).[43] Hosted by Jimmy O'Neill, a white disc jockey whose KFWB radio show was popular in southern California, *Shindig!* began its run on September 16, 1964. The clean-cut O'Neill was in the Dick Clark mold, but unlike Clark's *American Bandstand*, where artists lip-synched to their hit records, the acts appearing on *Shindig!* sang live to prerecorded tracks.[44] Quick cuts, nontraditional camera angles, and rapidly changing lighting contributed to the show's frenetic visual style, an effort to mimic rock and roll's youthful energy.[45] The program's most striking visual element, however, was its interracial cast. Each week, the black female Blossoms and their white male counterparts, the Wellingtons, smiled, swayed, and sang background for artists ranging from white acts such as Glen Campbell and the Righteous Brothers to black performers such as Tina Turner and Aretha Franklin.[46] British Invasion acts such as the Beatles, the Animals, the Hollies, the Kinks, and the Who, and American artists including the Beach Boys, Ray Charles, Bo Diddley, Lesley Gore, and Clara Ward appeared on the

FIGURE 4.1 The Blossoms on *Shindig!*, 1965. As background vocalists on *Shindig!*, the first television program to broadcast rock and roll in an evening time slot, the Blossoms sang background vocals with the era's top rock and roll acts at a time when it was unusual to see African Americans on prime-time television. The group's weekly appearances on the program introduced a black female vocal sound that contributed to the increase of audible blackness in popular music during the decade. From left to right: Jean King, Darlene Love, and Fanita James. COURTESY RUDY CALVO COLLECTION/CACHE AGENCY.

program. These performances were noteworthy in an era when it was unusual to see African Americans on prime-time television. With its A-list guests
and eye-catching visuals, *Shindig!* was a televisual success, and the network
extended the program to a full hour.[47] Southern affiliates, however, were not
happy with the show's weekly promotion of rock and roll race-mixing. "Even
after *Shindig!* was a hit," Love states, "[producer Jack Good] continued to get
grief from the network about the 'color' of the show, and the more grief he got,
the more black acts he booked."[48] English by birth, Good was a fan of black
American music and made sure it was represented on his program, flouting
the segregationist practices of American broadcasters. Good quit in late 1965,
and ABC canceled the program in January 1966, but *Shindig!* had already made
an impact on pop culture.[49] *Shindig!* introduced a black female vocal sound
that contributed to the increase of audible blackness in popular music during
the decade, and the Blossoms' weekly presence made a trio of black women as
backing vocalists "a standard trope in popular music."[50]

Another site of the presence of black women's voices in pop was at New
York City–based Atlantic Records. Ray Charles, a foundational figure in soul
music, was on the label's roster, and the vocals of his black female backing
group, the Raelettes, were central to his secularized gospel sound. When working with other artists, Atlantic producers followed this template, often relying
on the Sweet Inspirations.[51] As the unofficial house backing vocalists of Atlantic Records, they sang behind Solomon Burke, the Drifters, Aretha Franklin, Esther Phillips, and Wilson Pickett, among others. Atlantic vice president
and producer Jerry Wexler called the group, "one of the pillars of the Atlantic
Church of Sixties Soul."[52] Sisters Dionne and Dee Dee Warwick and friends
Sylvia Shemwell, Carol Harding, and Myrna Smith began to take their gospel group, the Gospelaires, into the professional studios of New York City in
the early 1960s. In this secular context, they were managed by the Warwicks'
uncle John Houston and eventually became known as the Sweet Inspirations.[53]
When Dionne Warwick was unable to make a recording date, her aunt Cissy
Houston (John's wife and Whitney Houston's mother) filled in and eventually
joined the group. Unlike the Blossoms, who provided racially fluid sounds, the
Sweet Inspirations brought the sound of black Protestant churches into their
recording sessions. Composer and producer Burt Bacharach, who had a long
string of hits during the 1960s, used the Sweet Inspirations' vocals in ways
that took advantage of their audible blackness. Recalling the personnel on
one of his sessions for Dionne Warwick, Bacharach explained the sonic racial
calculus underpinning his arrangement of background vocals on the track:

"Along with Cissy Houston, Dee Dee Warwick, and Myrna Smith, I brought in three white girl singers. . . . On 'Don't Make Me Over,' I had Cissy, Dee Dee, and Myrna singing in the lower register, with the white girls singing on top of them. If you listen to the record, you can hear the soul on the bottom and the altitude coming from the white girls."[54] Here, as with the Blossoms, producers and artists constructed and reproduced essentialized notions of "black sound" and "white sound," with each linked to different aural and emotional qualities.

Known as "Cissy and the girls," Houston's ensemble became the first-call background group for New York City–based producers, including Bacharach, Jerry Leiber and Mike Stoller, Luther Dixon, Clyde Otis, Bert Berns, and the team at Atlantic Records, all of whom were seeking some measure of "black sound" for their recordings.[55] Among the numerous songs that Houston contributed vocals to, working either alone or with the Sweet Inspirations, are "Some Kind of Wonderful" (1961) by the Drifters; "I Say a Little Prayer" (1967) by Dionne Warwick; "Mustang Sally" (1966) by Wilson Pickett; and "Do Right Woman—Do Right Man" (1967), "Chain of Fools" (1967), and "Think" (1968) by Aretha Franklin.[56] The sound of Houston and her group was inescapable in 1963, when they appeared on the following Top 20 hit recordings: "Tell Him" (The Exciters, January 1963), "On Broadway" (The Drifters, April 1963), "If You Need Me" (Solomon Burke, April 1963), "Just One Look" (Doris Troy, July 1963), "Cry Baby" (Garnett Mimms and the Enchanters, September 1963), and "Anyone Who Had a Heart" (Dionne Warwick, November 1963).[57] As the decade wore on, a growing interest in "black sound" created opportunities for black women vocalists beyond the realm of rhythm and blues, and the Sweet Inspirations began to work with white performers, singing on "Brown-Eyed Girl" (1967) by Van Morrison and "Son of a Preacher Man" (1968) by Dusty Springfield.[58] Picking up where the Blossoms left off, they appeared with Elvis Presley during his 1968 comeback performances in Las Vegas and contributed background vocals to his 1969 hit "Suspicious Minds."[59] According to his biographer, Presley believed the sound of the Sweet Inspirations would work well with the white male quartet performing with him and give him access to "the *full spectrum* of American music that he wanted to present onstage."[60] Some configuration of the Sweet Inspirations worked with Presley for the rest of his career as a touring artist, which concluded a few months before his death in August 1977.[61]

At roughly the same time that Presley was establishing ties with the Sweet Inspirations, the executives at Atlantic Records, founded in 1947 as a rhythm and blues label with a roster of African American artists, were turning their attention to white British rock bands that had been inspired by African American musical sound. Atlantic signed Cream, Eric Clapton, and Led Zeppelin and worked out a deal with the Rolling Stones that allowed Atlantic to distribute the band's releases on the newly constituted Rolling Stones Records.[62] These signings implicitly acknowledged what Elvis Presley's producer and Sun Records label owner, Sam Phillips, had recognized more than a decade before: the excellent quality of music performed by African American artists could not offset the fact that in the United States, it was easier and more lucrative to sell white artists playing black music than it was to sell black artists doing so. By the end of the 1960s, many of the white artists who had been performing blues and R&B incorporated black sound in a more literal way, by inviting African American women to work with them as background vocalists on their recordings and in concert.

Audible Authenticity

Starting in the mid-1960s, white rock and roll artists began to collaborate with African American women vocalists, drawing on their distinctive vocal sound to infuse their productions with audible blackness and the authenticity their voices conferred. The popularity of the practice grew and continued into the 1970s, enabling African American women to make a formative contribution to the sound of rock. A reasonable starting point for this discussion is the work of English singer Dusty Springfield, one of the first British artists to work with black American women background vocalists. Springfield began her career as a pop-folk singer, but she developed an interest in incorporating black American sound into her style when she heard the backing vocals of Cissy Houston's Sweet Inspirations on the Exciters' 1963 hit "Tell Him."[63] This "musical conversion," as musicologist Annie Randall calls it, set her on a new path, and she began to record with African American women background vocalists.[64] Her principal collaborator was Madeline Bell, an African American singer who first came to London in 1962 as a cast member in Langston Hughes's gospel play *Black Nativity* and stayed on to pursue a singing career.[65] Charting the musical changes that occurred as Springfield collaborated with Bell, Randall notes that from 1965 to 1968 Springfield "increased the 'gospelisms' in her music," deploying black church-based musical practices.[66] They are on display on her June 1965 release "In the Middle of Nowhere," a Top 10 hit in England.[67] Joining Springfield and Bell are Lesley Duncan, a white English woman, and Doris Troy, an African American R&B singer and songwriter who had moved to London to build a solo career launched by her 1963 Top 10 pop single "Just One Look." "In the Middle of Nowhere" was an upbeat number in which Springfield and her backing vocalists engage in a call-and-response interaction that creates the communal feel associated with gospel and the girl group sound. Liberal use of these tropes made Springfield "sound black" in a context in which such practices were associated with African Americans and established her as a white soul singer.

Springfield was known for her public embrace of African American artists, both through her ongoing collaborations with Bell and through her role as host of *Sounds of Motown,* the 1965 television special that introduced British audiences to the label's music.[68] Randall observes that Springfield's audible and visible connection to African American artists "gave Dusty the stamp of credibility she seemed to crave" and a measure of "authenticity-by-association."[69] Springfield laid the template for British artists to incorporate soulful, gospel-rooted background vocals into their recordings. Assessing the impact of the collaborations between Bell and Springfield, Randall asserts that in the wake of their recordings "an improvised gospel vocal sound began to take root in British pop; it brought the soul solo and backing vocals into affective alignment, which, in turn, gave the records a *soulful* stylistic coherence. This backing sound became *the* desired sound in London's recording studios."[70] British rock and roll artists followed Springfield's example and called on African American women vocalists to help them produce an authentic black sound. This pronounced quest for audible blackness was in keeping with an already established interest in black American music among British artists.

Most of these musicians understood themselves to be making rhythm and blues music, and they studied recordings by African American artists to do so. An interest in the work of African American *women* was part of this process, as evidenced by the number of white male acts who, having listened across race and gender difference, covered songs originated by black American women: The Beatles recorded "Chains" (1963) by the Cookies, "Mr. Postman" (1963) by the Marvelettes, and "Baby It's You" (1963) and "Boys" (1963) by the Shirelles; the Animals recorded "Don't Let Me Be Misunderstood" (1965) by Nina Simone; Manfred Mann recorded "Do Wah Diddy Diddy" (1964) by the Exciters and "Sha La La" (1964) by the Shirelles; the Hollies recorded "Just One Look" and "Whatcha Gonna Do 'bout It" (1964) by Doris Troy; the Moody Blues recorded "Go Now" (1964) by Bessie Banks; and the Mindbenders recorded "Groovy Kind of Love" (1965) by Patti LaBelle and the Bluebelles.

Significantly, many of these covers charted in both the United Kingdom and the United States. In 1964, the Rolling Stones released their version of Irma Thomas's "Time Is on My Side"; it was the group's third US single release, and the first to crack the US Top 10.[71] Stones guitarist Keith Richards mentions African American girl groups when describing the musical tastes he and singer Mick Jagger shared. "We loved the pop records," he explains in his autobiography. "Give me the Ronettes, or the Crystals. I could listen to them all night."[72] According to Mick Jagger's biographer, in the early sixties when the Stones were "still experimenting with their sound and look, the band had thought of using black female backup singers like Ray Charles's Raelettes and Ike and Tina Turner's Ikettes."[73] Within ten years, they were actually doing so. And, as many commentators have noted, the black women's vocal sound that propelled girl group music was so ingrained in the mind of former Beatle George Harrison that he replicated it too faithfully on his 1970 release "My Sweet Lord"; the writers of "He's So Fine," a hit for the Chiffons in 1963, successfully pressed their claim that he had plagiarized their song.[74] These examples of cross-racial and cross-gender influence demonstrate the extent to which black women's voices informed the work of these white male artists and, by extension, the sound of rock and roll in the 1960s.[75] The use of African American background vocalists continued the British artists' interest in black women's vocal sound, but annexed their voices to male bands, centering male voices and concerns.

Emphasizing the vocal instead of the instrumental aspect of British rock reveals black women's influence, but as Randall has noted, "Little has been written about [British rock's] complex vocal element—with strongly avowed roots in the gospel tradition—and the role [black] women played in its creation."[76] Rock music historians have spent far more time discussing the ways white male musicians borrowed from black male musicians, especially blues artists such as Robert Johnson and Muddy Waters, but in the early years of rock and roll, African American women such as Bessie Smith, Ma Rainey, Memphis Minnie, Big Mama Thornton, Ruth Brown, LaVern Baker, Etta James, Tina Turner, Nina Simone, Odetta, the Shirelles, the Crystals, and a host of other girl groups were vocal models for white and black artists, both male and female. White British singers borrowed African American women's phrasing, inflection, and vocal mannerisms, using these features to develop the individual styles that came to be associated with them throughout their careers. With the incorporation of black women as background vocalists, African American women became an actual presence on the recordings of white artists. I now turn to specific examples of these collaborations to illustrate the pervasiveness of the practice, introduce some notable background vocalists, and listen for their presence in the sound of rock.

An early case is a song by Small Faces, an English rock band that was closely associated with the mod subculture. "Tin Soldier," a 1967 release, features lead singer Steve Marriott and background vocalist P. P. Arnold (born Patricia Ann Cole), a former Ikette who had decided to stay in London once the Revue's 1966 tour had ended.[77] Arnold signed to Immediate Records, an independent label that Rolling Stones manager Andrew Loog Oldham had established, and by April 1967, she had become "The First Lady of Immediate." Her singles "The First Cut Is the Deepest" (1967, written by Cat Stevens and produced by Mick Jagger), "Angel of the Morning" (1968) and "(If You Think You're) Groovy" (1968) appeared on the British charts.[78] On "Tin Soldier," Arnold's harmonizing backing vocals lift the energy and intensify the feeling of the song. She provides a response to the call that Marriott issues, fortifying his voice when the two sing together. Here, Arnold executes a background vocalist's typical duties: she joins the lead vocalist on the chorus, underscoring the song's hook, "the most recognizable and appealing musical phrase of the piece."[79] The presence of her voice works to "reinforce the importance of the chorus . . . making it distinct from the verse by changing the vocal timbre."[80] In short, her vocals help sell the song.

Jagger may have had the sound of the intertwining voices of Arnold and Marriott in mind when working on the 1969 Rolling Stones single "Gimme Shelter." Merry Clayton, a Los Angeles–based artist, was called in to the session at the last minute, replacing a flu-ridden Bonnie Bramlett, the soulful white American vocalist originally booked for the recording.[81] This was new territory for Clayton, who told me, "I had never sung rock and roll . . . until I worked with the Stones."[82] In a 1970 interview, she recalled, "[I]t was quite easy. Mick and Keith just stood in front of me and told me where they wanted me to sing. Any way that I felt it."[83] The "Gimme Shelter" session was just another job for Clayton, and she was so little-known to the others involved with the production that her name was misspelled "Mary Clayton" on the album's liner notes. But "Gimme Shelter," it turned out, was special and launched her career in rock.[84] In the song, Clayton starts in traditional background mode, entering after Jagger has sung the first verse. She doubles his voice on the chorus, instantly increasing the song's volume, tension, and sense of foreboding. But, departing from standard practice, she takes a solo, singing the phrase, "Rape! Murder! It's just a kiss away"; her bracing timbre bursts into the foreground of the song. Jagger's voice supports her as he echoes her "kiss away" phrases. Beautifully conceived, the arrangement places one of rock's consummate lead singers in the uncharacteristic position of being a background vocalist, even if only for a few measures.

On "Gimme Shelter," the background singer is unusually prominent. The raw power of Clayton's voice—its volume and finesse—are riveting, and her vocals broaden the sonic palette of the track, a common contribution of background vocalists. Her presence also expands the song's emotional range. Susan Fast argues that Clayton's "immense vocal power and virtuosity are pressed into the service of a kind of catharsis of which Jagger is incapable."[85] Consequently, she fulfills the role typically assigned to African Americans and to women in Western culture: providing emotional expression and emotional support.[86] The power and appeal of the song stem from the juxtaposition of Jagger's cool and Clayton's fire; the contrasting but complementary voices respond to the chaos referenced in the song's lyrics and ride against the brooding instrumental accompaniment. Working without a written part and singing what she felt, Clayton brought the intensity of gospel to the track. Rock critic Greil Marcus singled her out for praise in his *Rolling Stone* magazine review of *Let It Bleed*: "When Mary [*sic*] Clayton sings alone, so loudly and with so much force you think her lungs are bursting, [guitarist Keith] Richards frames her with jolting riffs that blaze past her and take it back to Mick." A few lines later he observes, "She can stand up to Mick and match him, and in fact, she steals the song."[87] The Rolling Stones used African American women background vocalists on several occasions during this period. Madeline Bell and Doris Troy (along with Nanette Newman, a white English actress) sang on the *Let It Bleed* track "You Can't Always Get What You Want," a song that also featured the London Bach Choir. Gloria Jones and Bonnie Bramlett sang on the single-only release "Honky Tonk Women" (1969).[88] *Exile on Main Street* included backing vocals from Clydie King and Venetta Fields on "I Just Want to See His Face," "Let It Loose," "Shine a Light," and "Tumbling Dice," a Top 10 single in the United States and the United Kingdom in 1972.[89] Now hailed as hard rock classics, these recordings relied in part on the sound of soul, delivered by black women, for their sonic force.

Clayton's collaboration with the Stones created performance opportunities for her (see figure 4.2). She was the original Acid Queen in the Who's *Tommy*, singing the role when the rock opera's debut was staged with the 104-piece London Symphony Orchestra and 60-voice Chamber Choir in 1972, and she released three solo albums in the early 1970s.[90] Clayton made her mark, though, as a background vocalist. A partial listing of her credits provides a snapshot of how widespread the use of black women's soulful voices was on the American side of the Atlantic during the early 1970s. Clayton contributed background vocals on recordings by Buffalo Springfield, the Paul Butterfield Blues Band, Delaney & Bonnie, Jerry Garcia, Carole King, Lynyrd Skynyrd, Rare Earth, Linda Ronstadt, Leon Russell, and Neil Young.[91] Merry Clayton also worked extensively with the gravelly voiced English singer Joe Cocker. Given his adulation of Ray Charles, whose vocal inflections he emulated, it is not surprising that he would be eager to work with Clayton, a former Raelette. Cocker and Clayton were label mates at A&M Records. Starting with Cocker's 1969 release *With a Little Help from My Friends,* they collaborated on five of his albums, with Clayton contributing vocals, doing the vocal arrangements for the background singers, and hiring vocalists for recording sessions and for his 1970 *Mad Dogs and Englishmen* tour.[92] Cocker went on to work with Gloria Jones's quartet, the Sanctified Sisters. Church-rooted in name and sound, the four African American women—Jones, Virginia Ayers, Beverly Gardner, and Viola Wills—were featured on the self-titled album Cocker released in 1972.[93] "We took a whole new sound with Joe," Jones told me. "I mean we gave him the real gospel, but still commercial in there . . . We always had good sound and we could go wherever they needed us to go. If they needed us to go pop, we could get them pop or we could get them rock or we could get them gospel."[94] The Sanctified Sisters sang four-part harmony. "So it was strong," Jones recalled. "It was strong and it was different and it was powerful. And that's what he wanted."[95] The gospel sound was still relatively new to non–African American communities, and artists like Cocker were taking a creative leap by tapping into it. "So that was the circuit of the energy of rock," Jones told me. "No color, no pretense or anything, just good creative people making music and making sounds and just making it happen."[96]

As more and more rock artists sought the black gospel sound for recordings and live performances, a network of black women background singers developed. Typically, a producer would call one of the women and assign her the task of hiring the other singers for the session, effectively making her a coproducer of the recording. "There were cliques at that time," Venetta Fields said of the professional terrain. "My first session, I was called by Merry Clayton, and Clydie [King] and Sherlie [Matthews] and Gloria Jones and Edna Wright were there. After that first session I got calls from the other cliques . . . Merry Clayton called me a few times. But I ended up with me, Clydie, and Sherlie."[97] Over time these connections led Fields to jobs singing background

for the Allman Brothers, Tim Buckley, Gene Clark, Delaney & Bonnie, Dr. John, Richie Furay and Poco, Arlo Guthrie, Humble Pie, Pink Floyd, the Rolling Stones, Steely Dan, Barbra Streisand, Tanya Tucker, and Joe Walsh, among others.[98]

The artists with whom the background vocalists collaborated were in some cases aware of the specificity of individual women's voices. Former Small Faces front man Steve Marriott, who named Mavis Staples and Tina Turner as his favorite singers, was familiar with Fields from her work with Ike and Tina Turner and wanted her to sing with Humble Pie, the band he had formed in 1969.[99] Fields recalled Humble Pie's manager "telling me that Steve Marriott had been following my career and admired me a lot and would I get two other girls and come to London to record. I got Clydie King and Billie Barnum. . . . We worked so well recording that Steve asked us to tour North America."[100] Humble Pie's drummer Jerry Shirley has said that he and his bandmates were thrilled to be making music with women who had worked with "our all-time favourite bands and singers," that is, former Ikette Fields with Ike and Tina Turner and former Raelette King with Ray Charles.[101] The arrival of Fields, King, and Barnum, who performed as the Blackberries, was a creative boon to the English band. Discussing the trio's presence on Humble Pie's 1973 release *Eat It*, a critic wrote, "The extra voices add colour and atmosphere to the group's bumping and grinding rock and roll while Steve Marriott sounds as though he's been given an almost superfluous new lease on life."[102]

In the early seventies, psychedelic and progressive rock pioneers Pink Floyd got on board with the trend. "We were already in London with Humble Pie when Dave Gilmour asked Steve [Marriott] if they [Pink Floyd] could borrow us for a few dates in Europe," Fields explained. "They didn't want to send for their girls from America and they had heard about us. Steve said yes, reluctantly."[103] Audible blackness was a property that white artists wanted to

---

FIGURE 4.2 (*opposite*) Merry Clayton's vocals on the 1969 Rolling Stones song "Gimme Shelter" raised her profile in the rock community and paved the way for professional opportunities. She appeared in concert at New York City's Bitter End in 1971 (pictured here) and as the original Acid Queen in the Who's *Tommy*, singing the role when the rock opera's debut was staged with the 104-piece London Symphony Orchestra and 60-voice Chamber Choir in 1972. By 1975 Clayton had released four solo albums, but she made her primary mark as a background vocalist, singing with leading rock artists from both sides of the Atlantic. COURTESY RUDY CALVO COLLECTION/CACHE AGENCY.

possess—to such a degree that the women who carried it could be discussed as property that could be borrowed or reluctantly loaned. Pink Floyd had used a different team of singers on the *Dark Side of the Moon* (1973) sessions. Only one, Doris Troy, was African American; she sang alongside the white British women Liza Strike, Barry St. John, Lesley Duncan, and Clare Torry. But whether the women were black or white, their purpose was to provide a "black sound," which meant a gospel sound, and, Fast argues, they were "sonically marked as black" in the context of the performance.[104] For the purposes of their concerts, however, Pink Floyd seemed to want visible as well as audible blackness—and the associated authenticity.

Affiliation with superstar British rock bands put background vocalists into the upper echelons of the entertainment business. The Blackberries toured with both Pink Floyd and Humble Pie in the early 1970s, and, according to Fields, both bands treated the Blackberries well. Describing her experience with Pink Floyd during the *Dark Side of the Moon* tour, she recalled, "They were so kind and generous. We flew first class, had 5- and 6-star accommodation and limousines. It was the best. They had state-of-the-art equipment and lots of things that I had never seen before . . . I had never sung to such big crowds before."[105] If the members of Pink Floyd were "kind and generous," the guys from Humble Pie were extraordinary. In an unprecedented move, the band made their background vocalists an official part of Humble Pie in 1972.[106] As Marriott's biographers point out, "Many rock acts used black singers on their albums and many insisted on using black artists for support slots, but none invited any black artist to join their ranks, to get equal pay, equal status."[107] Marriott viewed the Blackberries as integral to Humble Pie's sound and live show, and in the fall of 1973, the Blackberries were part of the band's promotional campaign (see figure 4.3). A full-page ad in the English music weekly *Sounds* announced: "Humble Pie on tour with the Blackberries + Heavy Metal Kids."[108] The women were also singled out in press coverage. "[Humble Pie plays] 'Honky Tonk Women,' which ushers in the ladies—the Blackberries, Miss Billie Barnum, Miss Venetta Fields and Miss Carlena Williams [who had replaced Clydie King]," Pete Erskine reported in *Sounds*. "Now, you know they were pretty hot before, but let me tell you that Carlena is quite outrageous. Not only can she sing extraordinarily tastefully, but she's got the power of a vocal Charles Atlas. And the presence."[109] Still, there was resistance to Humble Pie's effort to make black women an official part of the band from both the Humble Pie management team and some of the group's fans.[110] Giving the Blackberries such prominence took them out of the sonic

FIGURE 4.3 In the early 1970s, promotional materials for the English rock band Humble Pie prominently featured the Blackberries, an African American vocal trio who sang background vocals for the band in concert and on record. A&M Records circulated this publicity shot of the two groups, together but still distinct, most likely in support of Humble Pie's *Eat It*, a 1973 double album featuring both groups. From left to right: the Blackberries (Venetta Fields, Billie Barnum, and Clydie King) and Humble Pie (Steve Marriott, Jerry Shirley, Dave "Clem" Clempson, and Greg Ridley). AUTHOR'S COLLECTION.

and social background that the rock community was comfortable with black women occupying. Drummer Jerry Shirley recalled a 1972 performance in Beaumont, Texas, "with a bunch of long-haired white boys" in the crowd.[111] He told a reporter that the show "did not go down well at all. It was very powerful. The audience would stand there staring at us. 'Well, what are those niggers doing on your stage?' It was really weird 'cuz I thought all of that stuff was long gone."[112] The alliance between Humble Pie and the Blackberries lasted for about a year before the expense of the rock and roll high life—planes, limos, drugs—forced it to end.[113]

English rock singer and songwriter David Bowie offers another example of rock's attachment to the sound of American soul. According to his then girlfriend and background singer Ava Cherry, he was "obsessed" with superstar soul singer Aretha Franklin.[114] Bowie had dabbled with the black gospel background sound on his 1973 release *Aladdin Sane*, with black British vocalist Linda Lewis backing him up on "Panic in Detroit," but on *Young Americans* (1975), he went all out.[115] He did the bulk of his recording at Sigma Sound in Philadelphia, the studio where producers Kenny Gamble and Leon Huff had created the Philly soul sound that had become a fixture on the US black music charts in the 1970s. To create what he ultimately dubbed "plastic soul," Bowie hired the Afro-Puerto Rican guitarist and former James Brown sideman Carlos Alomar and brought in Alomar's friend Luther Vandross, a young African American singer, to develop the vocal arrangements.[116] Six of the album's eight tracks featured background vocals by a trio of African American singers: Vandross, Ava Cherry, and Alomar's wife Robin Clark.[117] They lent some authenticity to the proceedings, punctuating Bowie's vocals with cascades of melisma, vibrato, supportive responses to his calls, and resonant "oohs" and "aahs." Here, as in a number of cases, the presence of the background vocalists elicits a new level of performance from the lead singer. It was as if the gospel-rooted voices issued a call that white rockers responded to by mustering more intensity in their own vocals. Bowie's collaboration with Vandross is a rare occasion in which a black male vocalist helped deliver authentic black vocal sound to a white male rocker's performance. Billy Preston also played this role, bringing his church-trained vocals and organ-playing chops to live and recorded performances with the Beatles, George Harrison, and the Rolling Stones.[118] Singer-songwriter Paul Simon drew on male voices, featuring the background vocals of African American gospel quartet the Dixie Hummingbirds on his 1973 single, "Loves Me Like a Rock," and those of the Jessy Dixon Singers on *Still Crazy after All These Years* (1975).[119] The majority of the time, however, background singing was women's work.

For some artists, the addition of background vocalists was a remedy for creative doldrums. Take, for example, glam rock star Marc Bolan, who, after an early 1970s run at the top of the British music charts with his band T. Rex, began working with Gloria Jones, a talented musician with an impressive resumé. Jones had played piano at the church where her father was minister, and when she was fourteen, she began singing with COGIC, a Los Angeles–based gospel group that featured Billy Preston.[120] Shifting to the secular side, she recorded the singles "Tainted Love" in 1964 and "Heartbeat" in 1965; these records made her a leading figure in the Northern Soul scene, a British music subculture built on a passion for lesser-known sixties-era American soul records.[121] In the late 1960s and early 1970s, Jones worked as a staff songwriter at Motown, writing and producing material for Diana Ross, Marvin Gaye, the

Commodores, Junior Walker, Eddie Kendricks, David Ruffin, and the Jackson Five. She was also an accomplished background vocalist. When I interviewed her in 2012, she listed some of the projects that stood out: "I have worked with Elvin Bishop, Van Dyke Parks, and Joe Cocker who is one of my favorite singers. And [I sang on] a lot of the Motown Records, for example, Diana Ross [and the Supremes] 'Someday We'll Be Together.' [I worked in a background group with] Bonnie Bramlett and Merry Clayton. And with Patrice Holloway and Brenda Holloway. We worked with REO Speedwagon, Ry Cooder, Little Feat, and Delaney & Bonnie."[122] Jones, along with Robbie Montgomery, did Ikettes background vocals with Tina Turner on "Proud Mary" and "I Want to Take You Higher."[123] Jones began working with Bolan in 1973, when his chart success was flagging after a string of British Top 10 hits that included "Get It On" (1971), "Jeepster" (1971), and "Telegram Sam" (1972).[124] A 1973 *Melody Maker* profile on Jones offered a tart depiction of the situation: "When white rock gets stale or finds its expressive limitations have been exhausted there are two ways out. One: add horns. Two: Add girl back-up singers, preferably black. Soul and inspiration follows [sic]."[125] Jones contributed backing vocals and clavinet playing to the five T. Rex albums she worked on, starting with *Zinc Alloy and the Hidden Riders of Tomorrow* (1974) and ending with *Dandy in the Underworld* (1977).

Bolan was not alone in turning to black women's voices to help him through a creative impasse. In a period of personal and professional transition, American singer and songwriter Bob Dylan, who was raised Jewish, began a foray into gospel and a conversion to Christianity. During this period, he wrote music that explored his spiritual condition and called on black women vocalists to help him tap into black musical sound. From 1978 to 1987, black women background vocalists were usually part of his on-stage and on-record retinue, but black women's musicianship had influenced Dylan since the 1950s.[126] The haunting sound of African American folk singer and guitarist Odetta had convinced Dylan to relinquish his electric guitar and pick up an acoustic one when he was still in his teens, and he was particularly taken by the voice of gospel singer Mavis Staples of the Staple Singers.[127] He first used background vocalists on his 1970 release *New Morning*, an album that featured a cover photo of Dylan with African American blues singer Victoria Spivey.[128] Critic David Yaffe argues that an engagement with black women as musical models and as subject matter for lyrics has been a constant throughout Dylan's career.[129] He observes that images of African American women "haunt his writing" and lists "Spanish Harlem Incident" (1964), "From a Buick 6" (1965),

"Outlaw Blues" (1965), "I Want You" (1966), and "Brownsville Girl" (1986) as examples of Dylan's "interracial eroticism."[130] By the end of the 1970s, Dylan's embrace of African American sound and fascination with black women led him to gospel.

Dylan scholars identify two African American women, Mary Alice Artes and Helena Springs, as the catalysts for Dylan's turn to Christianity. They encouraged him to pray and to seek solace in Jesus Christ.[131] Dylan's recordings from this period trace his developing commitment to Christian spirituality. "On his way to finding Jesus," Yaffe states, "Dylan worshiped at the shrine of the black female voice."[132] On the albums *Street Legal* (1978), *Slow Train Coming* (1979), *Saved* (1980), *Shot of Love* (1981), *Infidels* (1983), *Empire Burlesque* (1985), and *Knocked Out and Loaded* (1986) and on the related tours, Dylan sang with African American women.[133] Among the women who sang as part of a backing ensemble or in duets with Dylan both live and on record are Louise Bethune, Debra Byrd, Carolyn Dennis, Joanna Harris, Regina Havis (sometimes listed as Regina McCrary), Clydie King, Queen Esther Marrow, Madelyn Quebec, Helena Springs, Elisecia Wright, and Mona Lisa Young.[134] During his 1986 and 1987 tours, he dubbed his backing vocal trio "the Queens of Rhythm," finally bestowing a name on a musical entity that had played a prominent role in his live show for nearly a decade.[135] Was he imagining his own version of the Ikettes with this nod to Ike Turner's Kings of Rhythm? When Dylan toured in 1979 and 1980, the background group opened the shows by performing a set of gospel songs and offering Christian homilies before Dylan came on stage.[136] The music Dylan produced during this period is his idiosyncratic version of gospel; he interweaves his craggy voice with the church-tinged sonorities of his background singers. The content of many of the songs touched on faith, redemption, and mercy, and the voices of the background women amplified these themes through an association with the gospel sound.

African American women vocalists helped Dylan out of a creative and spiritual quandary. In live performance, these women provided vocal support and also, it seems, a not especially tasteful element of sex appeal. Commenting on their skimpy stage costumes, Debi Dye-Gibson, who toured with Dylan during this period, stated, "We looked like hookers. I felt a little stupid singing 'Blowin' in the Wind' with my boobs hanging out."[137] Interpreting the symbolic role of these women, Yaffe suggests that Dylan "appreciated their glitz and decoration, but they were there also to prove something about his artistic and sexual prowess."[138] The fact that they could so easily be called on to serve as eye candy might undercut the important musical role these women and other background vocalists performed, but the examples I have offered—and there are many others—demonstrate how present black women's voices were in music produced during the classic rock era. In fact, they were so ubiquitous in late sixties and early seventies rock that Lou Reed anchored the chorus of his 1972 single "Walk on the Wild Side" with the lyric "and the colored girls go 'do-do-do, do-do, do-do,'" a background vocal sung by the white British backup trio the Thunder Thighs (Karen Friedman, Dari Lalou and Casey Synge). Through the collaborations that Reed's lyrics reference, African American women brought the vocal power, distinctive timbre, and emotional intensity of African American sacred music to rock. They provided a sound that became an inextricable part of the genre until the end of the 1970s, when musical fashion changed, and the prominent use of background vocalists diminished.[139]

Creative Labor

Acknowledging the combination of skill, artistry, and professionalism associated with background singing is key to appreciating the creative labor these women contributed. Background vocalists were proud of the work they did. "To sing background was harder than to sing the lead," Merry Clayton assured me, "because you were singing parts. . . . We had to not overshadow the lead singer. . . . You couldn't sing loud and crazy. You had to complement the lead singer."[140] Because background singing requires the repetition of a limited number of words and is done in the service of someone else's lead vocals, some commentators emphasize the restrictiveness of background singing. In an article explaining the important role background vocalists have played in rock, for example, Susan Fast states that in singing only the chorus, "back-up singers sing the same music and lyrics repeatedly, which restricts their creativity and independence."[141] The notion that background singing is not creative seems to inform Mick Jagger's comment to an interviewer about the practice: "Singing oohs and aahs, you know, it's kind of fun for a minute, but I'm not sure I'd want to do it for a living."[142] Leaving aside the vagaries of power and access that allow Jagger to be a lead singer for a living while talented black women sing in the background, his statement and Fast's observation diminish the inventiveness that underwrote background vocalists' performances and that artists like Jagger required to make their lead vocals shine. In contrast, background vocalists emphasize the creativity and knowledge that animated their work.

The ability to arrange vocals and respond to new material were hallmarks of the valued skills that these vocalists brought to recording sessions. In a discussion of the first days that her group rehearsed with Humble Pie, Venetta Fields recalled, "When we got there Steve [Marriott] and the other Pie members were over the moon that we were there. They couldn't do enough for us. Every time we opened our mouths and sang or made up a part and sang it, they would get so excited."[143] Claudia Lennear described the role she and the other Ikettes played in contributing material that the Revue performed: "[Ike Turner] would pick our brains for ideas. We'd come up with lines for a song and then he would take off. We never got paid for any of that but I think that was the culture at that point."[144] Recalling the way Cissy Houston and the Sweet Inspirations worked, Jerry Wexler said, "They'd come into the studio . . . she'd listen to the tape and they'd gather around the microphone and start working out. It was a collaboration; it was a communal thing. Most of it came from Cissy Houston and the girls, most of the ideas, most of the lines and most of the parts."[145] These comments indicate that background singers were writers and arrangers, developing their parts—often, right on the spot. Blossom Fanita James recalled, "If [the producer] had [written] parts, we'd take them. If not, we would just figure something out real quick."[146] Background vocalists did not receive songwriting credit for the work they did to "figure something out," even though they were often involved in creating parts that helped bring songs together. Producers at the time relied on the ability of background vocalists to fulfill a number of creative roles and to do so under time constraints. The tendency to naturalize black women's ability to sing may be part of the reason that the thought, planning, and labor involved in their singing recedes.

Background work could expand the women's horizons. In a 1973 comment about her experience with Humble Pie, Venetta Fields told a journalist, "It's such a gas to work with all these guys. They have a very distinct English feel to everything they do and it's something that's really fresh. It takes the best out of you and I like that because it's also a challenge."[147] Describing the nature of the collaborations, she said, "You know we sort of laugh about some of the old blues singers like Muddy Waters or Howlin' Wolf, but [the members of Humble Pie] really dig them and [we] learn a lot because of it. We teach them quite a bit, too, I'm sure, so it's like a nice give and take thing."[148] These transatlantic exchanges gave the women a fresh perspective on the music they had grown up with and introduced them to new musical possibilities. Commenting on her time with Pink Floyd, Fields said she experienced "the weirdest music that I soon learned to love and get into. In the beginning, touring with them, I didn't understand the music and laughed about it. But I soon learned and took it seriously and got a great deal out of the experience."[149] Participation in rock also gave these women more vocal latitude than they had in other recording contexts. The artists wanted them to sing with all of their vocal power. "During that time the rock musicians, they embraced the soul singers," Gloria Jones told me. "They weren't frightened of us."[150]

Echoing the idea that background work could be an expansive rather than confining space, Jacqueline Warwick points out that for vocalists such as the Blossoms, the background role "affords surprising freedoms and opportunity to explore different identities—when the Blossoms routinely positioned themselves as adult or teen, white or black, and participated in musical genres ranging from country to funk, there is much to celebrate in the work of the backup singer."[151] Singer Doris Troy viewed session work as a way to stretch creatively. "I don't think I'll ever give up sessions," she told a journalist in 1971. "I'll always do them, there's an outlet for the part of me that needs to do other things."[152] Making a similar observation about the advantages of being a background vocalist, Lynn Mabry, who worked with the Talking Heads on the 1983 *Stop Making Sense* tour, observed, "I can be a chameleon. I never get bored."[153] In their late 1960s and 1970s heyday, the best background vocalists worked with a range of artists and across genres, learning new material and writing musical parts. In contrast, the stars they backed had to perform the same material—that is, their hits—in concert after concert, year after year, to please their fans. Drudgery is in the eyes of the beholder.

Symbolic Labor

The sound of black women's voices alongside those of white male singers expanded the sonic spectrum of rock recordings and concert performances. They added contrast and variety in vocal timbre and style while augmenting the volume of the vocal parts. In addition to this sonic contribution, African American women background vocalists performed important symbolic labor for these artists, carrying into the recordings the energy, emotion, and musicality of audible blackness that indexed authenticity for many listeners. Understanding the meanings associated with black women's vocal presence in rock of this era demands engagement with the ways ideas about race, gender, sexuality, and music-making intersect to construct ideas of musical authenticity and generate "particular social meanings."[154]

An old and resilient set of ideas about racial difference constructed blackness and whiteness in opposition to one another, figuring black people as closer to nature than white people, who were "modern" and "civilized." Minstrelsy, in which white performers put on blackness with burnt cork and acted out what were perceived to be black gestures and voices, is the best-known performance consequence of the dynamic of fascination and repulsion that grew out of this binary system of racial logic.[155] By the 1960s, rock and roll had become the latest iteration of what was by then a long-standing practice of white borrowing of black musical style. White youth on both sides of the Atlantic participated in rock music communities in which a desire for blackness and romanticized notions of black people and black music figured prominently. Whether they were rock and roll fans, blues revivalists, or soul music–loving mods, white youth mined the music created by African Americans, drawing on the seductive, "other" sounds of blues, jazz, gospel, and rhythm and blues as they developed their own music and identities.[156] The belief that black Americans had a special capacity for authentic musical expression and privileged access to emotion, spirituality, and sexuality fueled the attraction to black women's voices; indeed, the very sound of black women's gospel-rooted singing signaled these qualities. In England, the borrowing of black sound and inclusion of black women's voices took place against a peculiar backdrop. While Great Britain's black residents, most of them recent immigrants from Britain's colonies in Africa and the Caribbean, experienced racism and anti-black bias, black Americans occupied a different position and eluded some of these indignities.[157] Largely because of the rising popularity of American music, black Americans were perceived as possessing a special set of gifts. Furthermore, black American singing voices reverberated with the civil rights movement's progressive politics and symbolized resistance to the status quo; white British youth could hear a parallel to their own countercultural critiques of the establishment in the sound of soul music, even if this meant overlooking the struggles with which black British people routinely contended.

The collaborations between black women and white men offered a sonic symbol of racial integration, while the contrasts between male and female voices, and between non-gospel and gospel sound, provided aural pleasure. Venetta Fields stressed that the desire was for the blending of disparate, racially marked sonic practices: "Almost all artists had to have black singers at that time. That is how we seemed to have crossed over. They wanted to meld the two sounds together."[158] Fast points out that for the vocals to have an impact, the distinction between "black" and "white" sound had to remain clear. African American women singing background in the rock context, she explains, "are meant to reference a social world different from that of the band members and, for this, we must be able to hear their otherness."[159] As Bruce Springsteen observed in *Twenty Feet from Stardom*, "These are voices from the church. They bring a world with them."[160] The sonic contrast and the association with that different world make black women's voices "work" in these rock settings. The women understood what they were being asked to represent. Claudia Lennear observed, "I think the motivation of each one of those rock singers who employed singers such as myself, Merry [Clayton], Lisa [Fischer], and others was to give their music some kind of sweetening, to give it that kind of gospel flavor, or a 'blackness.'"[161] Merry Clayton told me that it was "the warm soulfulness and the spirituality" of her voice that made so many artists want to include her on their recordings. And, to make sure I recognized the source, she added, "That's gospel music! That's called the Good News Music. . . . So I guess I have Good News in my voice."[162] Gloria Jones offered a similar assessment. "Our group was what gave them a sound," Jones stated. "They liked the sound. We were really sound givers."[163]

The gospel feeling, that other world of sacred emotion, conferred an almost immediate stamp of authenticity. As a critic for *Sounds* observed of one of these collaborations, "Since being put into the Pie, [the Blackberries] have added a unique flavouring. In a sense they add to the whole credibility of Humble Pie."[164] In some cases, these women helped set the emotional tenor of the songs. Gloria Jones explained that background vocalists often recorded their parts before the lead singer and consequently provided musical inspiration: "When the lead singers would hear that soulful [sound and] those feelings, then they would put their lead vocals on. The background vocals gave them another concept or interpretation of how to do the song."[165] Session vocalists provided cues for developing vocals that would convey the music's message. "The gospel behind the rock and roll gave it that edge," Jones explained; it indexed authentic expression unhindered by white middle-class notions of propriety.[166]

These musical encounters between black women and white men reflected social biases of the era, especially in relation to race, gender, and sexuality. Fast argues that it is possible to hear the women "playing into white male fantasies of black female sexuality, while at the same time reaffirming hegemonic power structures—keeping these women in their place."[167] She observes that along with features such as instrumental virtuosity, high volume, and bodily comportment, the presence of women background vocalists contributed to the "construction of white rock masculinity."[168] African American women were vocal, racial, and gendered Others against which white male rock personae could be thrown into relief. By the early 1970s, black women background vocalists had become another one of the accoutrements of rock artists. Along with state-of-the art quadraphonic sound, phalanxes of expensive guitars, high-powered amps, elaborate light shows, and theatrical sets, background vocalists were a component of the sonic and visual equipment of rock and part of the symbolic capital that superstar rockers accumulated during the years that rock became a big money operation.[169]

According to Venetta Fields, background singers also played another key symbolic and material role: helpmate. "I realized early," she recalled, "that you had to be the band's sister, mother, confidante, dresser, advisor, and singer, etc. . . . It was always fun and interesting about how boys and men never really grow up, and that they had to have a mother figure all the time."[170] The maternal role Fields describes is an extension of the supportive sonic role she and other background vocalists played in the recordings. In a comment about the female background vocals on *Dark Side of the Moon* that could apply to a number of other contexts where black women sing background, Fast notes, "women provide warmth and a link to the social, reinforcing the role that women generally play within culture."[171] Lisa Fischer, who has worked with numerous artists including the Rolling Stones, made a similar observation without using the language of motherhood. When singing background, she said, "You're so into making them [lead singers] happy, making sure they have what they need."[172] Operating in a supporting role, background vocalists shore up the male voices, lending musical aid and comfort. This sonic relation of support calls to mind a familiar, stereotypical role for black women: that of the selfless mammy.[173]

As indexed in the title of the documentary *Twenty Feet from Stardom* and in the very name *background vocalists*, these women occupy a marginal space. This positioning contributed to the difficulty background singers had establishing themselves as solo artists. For a black woman to be front and center was a breach of the race and gender rules of rock in the early 1970s. An exception is Madeline Bell, who, from 1969 to 1974, had success in England as lead vocalist for the rock band Blue Mink.[174] Founded by singer and songwriter Roger Cook, Blue Mink placed eight singles on the British charts, including "Melting Pot," which went to number three in 1969.[175] Most efforts to advance these women, however, were unsuccessful. Merry Clayton's solo career was a pet project of A&M label head Lou Adler, but her solo releases did not take off, a disappointment for a talent of Clayton's caliber.[176] Reflecting on the situation, Adler observed, "She made three really good albums. They sound like she was going to be as big as Aretha Franklin. We did everything possible and it just didn't take."[177] Ex-Beatle George Harrison signed Doris Troy to Apple Records in 1969, giving her three contracts—as writer, producer, and artist.[178] She was an established songwriter—her 1963 single "Just One Look" had been a hit in the United States—and she had sung background with Dusty Springfield, the Rolling Stones, Pink Floyd, and Nick Drake. She coproduced her 1970 release *Doris Troy* with Harrison, who played on the recording alongside Ringo Starr, Eric Clapton, Billy Preston, and Stephen Stills, but the gathering of rock star power did not ignite the charts. Nor did solo releases by Gloria Jones or Claudia Lennear take hold.[179] Other projects never made it to the marketplace. There were plans for a Blackberries album with Humble Pie serving as backing band.[180] They recorded some tracks, but the album was not released. Marriott's biographers claim the album, *Wrap Yourself in My Color*, was "his best work of the '70s."[181] Similarly, David Bowie's effort to produce a solo album for Ava Cherry only got as far as the mixing stage of the recording process.[182] A white male/black female rock collaboration finally clicked in 1984 when Tina Turner, a black woman who had never been in the background, worked with a team of white musicians and producers to launch a remarkably successful solo career.

Although the copresence of black women and white men on rock records and in concert affirmed the connections between rock and soul, it also underscored the differences between their respective sonic and social worlds. Binary thinking that understood black music, people, and culture through a mutually exclusive contrast to white music, people, and culture was at work in both the United States and the United Kingdom, and it underwrote the persistent Otherness of black female voices and bodies in the rock scene. White male and black female artists were bridging difference through their creative interactions, but the borders between black and white, between female and male, remained intact and contributed to the difficulty African American women had establishing themselves as solo artists in the rock milieu. It was fine for black American women to sing background; indeed, they were perceived as necessary to the proceedings. But as African Americans and as women, they did not fit the increasingly widespread notion that a rock artist was a young, white man.

Coda: Liaisons

In their reflections on this period, some background vocalists emphasize the mundane aspects of their rarefied working environment. Commenting on her participation in the sessions for *Exile on Main Street,* one of rock's most celebrated albums, Venetta Fields stated, "We were session singers, and we weren't thinking of the artist's fame at that time. We were working."[183] Gloria Jones told me that although she was meeting a lot of well-known artists including Diana Ross, Marvin Gaye, and the Rolling Stones, she did not do anything to memorialize the encounters. "Because when you work on those sessions, Maureen, it's work," she explained. "So you don't have time to take a picture with anybody, you know, because you're there to do a session."[184] Speaking in a similar vein, Madeline Bell told an interviewer:

> They were just sessions. Seriously, there was nothing personal or anything. We knew [the artists] because we would bump into them, but you would just turn up and there would be a three hour or six hour session. I mean I did sessions with John Lennon, with George Harrison, and Ringo [Starr] and the Stones . . . it was all taken very seriously. There was nothing scandalous or anything going on. They would get down to business in the studio. Time was money.[185]

The black women and white men who collaborated on these recordings also developed creative partnerships such as the one between Madeline Bell and Led Zeppelin's bass player John Paul Jones; the two met when doing sessions in London in the 1960s. Jones and Bell were friends and songwriting partners (and Bell is godmother to three of Jones's children); in 1973, he produced her album *Comin' Atcha.*[186]

Perhaps the emphasis on the businesslike aspects of the collaborations—"nothing scandalous or anything going on"—is intended to counter suspicions that close working relationships between men and women led to sexual relationships. An exchange during Kandia Crazy Horse's interview with Venetta Fields, taking place decades after the sessions occurred, is a case in point:

Kandia Crazy Horse: Any blatant episodes where you felt you or musicians working with you were being objectified due to fantasies about "red-hot mamas" and the like?

Venetta Fields: No! We all loved and respected each other and never got into pettiness. We had music![187]

In the interview, Fields kept the focus on work and used the conversation as an opportunity to shape the representation of background vocalists. At one point she stated, "I'd like to see the story [of black women in the rock world] depicted in a strong positive manner. Especially dwell on the changes we made when they started using black female backing vocals. What an art form we created, and what great singers in our own right we are."[188] The mutual respect, however, did sometimes progress into mutual attraction, but these connections are not easy to trace. In her interview with Fields, Crazy Horse, an African American music journalist, was unable to elicit any details:

Kandia Crazy Horse: Some say you were romantically linked to Mick Jagger in the wake of the *Exile* sessions. Any comments about him?

Venetta Fields: I read that recently on the Internet. That is not true.

Kandia Crazy Horse: Sorry, but on the sister-friend tip, you have worked with some of the finest men in rock, like Kris Kristofferson and Gregg Allman. You got to give it up!

Venetta Fields: That is for my book![189]

Even after invoking a shared connection as black women, Crazy Horse encounters what I interpret as Fields's adherence to the rules of respectability that preclude disclosure about sexuality—and she wants to control and write her own story. Memoirs by Fields or any of the background vocalists I have mentioned in this chapter would likely be a treat to read. They could provide up-close-and-personal perspectives on some of the biggest stars and headiest years of rock through stories that highlight the interracial social interactions—including sexual ones—that accompanied the interracial musical exchanges of the 1960s and 1970s. African American women were not simply an enticing vocal Other, but also an attractive sexual Other, especially in England where black women's bodies, like their voices, seemed to hold special powers. This fascination with an Other ran in both directions. In the 1960s, as segregation was being challenged in the society at large, African American women on the rock and roll scene explored relationships that crossed the boundaries of race. The result is a number of liaisons between black women and white men in rock and roll's historical record.

Addressing these connections, P. P. Arnold, a black woman born and raised in the segregated United States, described her time working in London in terms that highlight England's distinctive musical and social context, contrasting it with the conditions back home in the United States. "Personally, I would not have had the career, the opportunity that I had in the UK, I would never have been integrated so quickly into cosmopolitan white society and be hanging out with whites. We were coming out of the civil rights revolution in America and into the music revolution in the UK, and it was a totally different way of being. They really respected the artistry and the music."[190] The differences also extended to interpersonal connections. Recalling her time as an Ikette on tour with the Rolling Stones in 1966, she said, "Here I was hanging out with these white rock 'n' rollers. And in South Central LA, black girls and white guys definitely did not hang out and party together!"[191] She has acknowledged the bond she developed with her Immediate Records label mate and Small Faces lead singer Steve Marriott: "It was exciting times! Steve Marriott and I really hit it off, we were soul brother, soul sister. . . . He loved the way I sang and I loved the way he sang. He was just hyper in everything he did and we became lovers. He was the first British guy ever to take me home to meet his family."[192] By early 1968, the romance between Arnold and Marriott was over, but their musical collaborations continued. Arnold appears on Humble Pie's *Rock On* (1971) along with Doris Troy and Claudia Lennear and on some of Marriott's solo recordings of the late 1980s.[193] Arnold has also acknowledged liaisons with other prominent London-based rock artists: "Mick and I . . . were an item. But I didn't stay in the UK to be Mick Jagger's girlfriend. Even though I was one of them. Mick was a busy boy."[194] And, responding to a reporter's question about Hendrix, she said, "Jimi? Oh, he's another soul brother and lover!"[195] Here, Arnold flouts the rules of respectability with disclosures that situate her in the thick of Swinging London, following the sexually progressive mores of the rock community: "Everybody had more than one lover back then. We had multiple lovers!" she explained.[196]

Other black women have made public their romantic encounters with white male musicians. Darlene Love does so in her autobiography. Recalling a situation that might have been brought on by a belief in the "red-hot mama syndrome" Crazy Horse referenced, Love states that when working with Elvis Presley on the film *Change of Habit*, he told her, "I've never been with a black woman before. I've never even thought about it. But I'm thinking about it now."[197] Just as Love, who says she was not attracted to Presley, found herself "being drawn into his current," he did an about-face and said, "Hell, what would my people think? My grandma and granddaddy might spin in their graves."[198] Love notes the irony of the fact that "the man who sang and twitched like a black man on stage, who, in fact, presided over the musical miscegenation of the fifties," was afraid to go through with what he proposed. She decided it "was just another threshold he couldn't cross. If he did, he just wouldn't be able to explain it to all the conflicting voices in his head."[199] Love also writes about the relationship she had with Righteous Brother Bill Medley during the 1960s, a time when resistance to interracial couples in the United States convinced them to keep their connection secret.

Secrecy was also in play when Bob Dylan and background vocalist Carolyn Dennis married in June 1986, six months after the birth of their daughter Desiree Gabrielle Dennis-Dylan.[200] The marriage was made public in Howard Sounes's 2001 biography of Dylan, but audience members who had been paying attention to the comments Dylan offered at his concerts during his 1978 tour might not have been surprised.[201] On at least a couple of occasions, Dylan declared from the stage that Carolyn Dennis was "the true love of my life, my fiancée."[202] Dylan's attraction to black women is a well-documented aspect of his elusive personal history.[203] In addition to Dennis, he has been linked to Clydie King, to Mavis Staples ("We courted for about seven years," Staples recalled, "and it was my fault that we didn't go on and get married"), and to some of the women who were his background singers during his gospel period.[204] Because neither Dylan nor most of the women have spoken for the record about these relationships, little is known about them.[205]

A more public marriage was between Ronette Ronnie Bennett and Phil Spector, who had built his reputation as a "genius" producer with the help of her voice. The marriage was not as successful as their recordings, at least according to Ronnie Bennett Spector's memoir.[206] Prior to her marriage to Spector, Bennett made an impression on Keith Richards and figures in his memoir. As he tells it: "We toured with the Ronettes on our second UK tour, and I fell in love with Ronnie Bennett, who was the lead singer. . . . Mick had cottoned to her sister Estelle."[207] The popularity of the Ronettes also put them in proximity to the Beatles, and members of the two groups met during the Beatles' first visit to New York.[208] Ronnie paired off with John Lennon; her cousin Nedra Talley spent time with George Harrison. There are a few other couples from this era worth mentioning. Mick Jagger and Claudia Lennear, who some say inspired the Rolling Stones song "Brown Sugar," were an on-again, off-again pair. (Lennear is also said to have inspired David Bowie's 1973 track "Lady Grinning Soul.")[209] Others suggest Jagger's inspiration was Marsha Hunt, the African American singer and actress who took London by storm in the sixties with her striking looks and her role in the London version of *Hair*. Her only child, Karis, is Mick Jagger's first-born child.[210] Gloria Jones and Marc Bolan lived together openly, and their son, Rolan, was born in 1975. David Bowie met the model and singer Ava Cherry in 1973 during his second US tour; they became lovers and were together, on and off, until 1975, the year he started dating Ola Hudson, the African American clothing designer who made his stage clothes during his *Young Americans* and *Station to Station*/Thin White Duke phase; she also created his costumes for the 1976 film *The Man Who Fell to Earth* in which he had the title role.[211] (Another of Hudson's rock and roll claims to fame: she is the mother of Guns N' Roses guitarist Slash, born Saul Hudson.)

When I started my research, I did not anticipate delving into the love lives of these artists, but doing so was unavoidable, given the ways the realities and fantasies of race, gender, and sexuality animate the sonic and social form rock has taken. Acknowledging these interpersonal connections in tandem with a discussion of black women's vocal and symbolic influence on rock alters the ways we listen to and think about the form and those who participate in it, adding another layer to both the rock and roll narrative and understandings of African American women's history. I continue this effort in the next chapter.

FIVE / Negotiating "Brown Sugar"

> **Maureen Mahon:** I also wanted to ask you about the Rolling Stones song "Brown Sugar." Do you have any thoughts about that song?
>
> **Emmaretta Marks:** That better not be about me! [laughs] Better not be about me.[1]

Prior to starting the research for this book, I had heard the Rolling Stones' "Brown Sugar" countless times, but I had never given much thought to whether the song was about an actual black woman. As it turns out, the identity of the "black girl" to whom the song is addressed has never been confirmed, but there are three women who, over the years, have emerged as plausible candidates. Perhaps lyricist Mick Jagger was thinking about Marsha Hunt, an African American model, actress, and vocalist with whom he'd had a brief affair. Claiming to be his muse in her 1986 memoir *Real Life*, Hunt reports that Jagger "called to say that he'd got an idea to write a song about me called 'Brown Sugar.'"[2] A more common view is that Jagger was motivated by a liaison with Claudia Lennear, a session singer and striving solo artist whom Jagger met in 1969, when she was an Ikette with the Ike and Tina Turner Revue. Or maybe it was Devon Wilson, a beautiful and well-connected rock and roll scenester with whom Jagger had spent a night or two. My goal in this chapter is not to determine which woman or women inspired one of the best-known songs by one of rock's best-known bands.[3] Instead, I want to consider the experiences of Devon Wilson, Marsha Hunt, and Claudia Lennear, African American women who were active in the rock scene of the late 1960s and early 1970s, in relation to the concepts of black women's sexuality that underpin "Brown Sugar" and circulated in the rock scene. These notions had long been part of mainstream American and Western European concepts of black womanhood, and African American women have long negotiated these stereotypes, often working to recuperate their image through group activism and individual comportment that accentuated respectability and moral up-rightness, while downplaying sexuality. Wilson, Hunt, and Lennear took a different approach, choosing to grapple with and capitalize on the pervasive fascination with black women's sexuality.

Wilson, Hunt, and Lennear were young, intelligent, and strikingly attractive, and each embodied the style and energy of the sixties and early seventies; all three confronted simplistic images of black women's sexuality and person-hood in the predominantly white rock scene. In Los Angeles and New York City, Devon Wilson was known for her dalliances with the scene's most prom-inent figures, including Jimi Hendrix and Mick Jagger. As a "super groupie," she occupied one of the only roles available to women on the scene: a fan, caretaker, and lover of musicians. Marsha Hunt moved to England in 1966, where she sang with blues revival bands, performed in the London produc-tion of the rock musical *Hair*, modeled for photographs that communicated with nascent awareness that "Black is Beautiful," recorded a rock album, and had a baby with Mick Jagger. After quitting the Ikettes in 1970, Clau-dia Lennear emerged as one of the era's most visible background vocalists, appearing in popular rock concert films and launching a solo career. Media reports often mentioned her involvement with Jagger, but her friendship with David Bowie received less press attention. The notoriety attached to these three women—much of it rooted in extramusical activities with well-known musicians—speaks volumes about the impact of race, gender, and genre on African American women in the rock scene. This is especially true for Hunt and Lennear, who struggled to establish recording careers. Their personal and professional trajectories also reveal the dizzying highs and lows that come with pushing the limits of established race and gender roles. As I learned about these bold women and the lives they fashioned, I was struck by how underground their stories have remained, how their efforts and adventures have not become part of the canon of African American women's history even though they were active during a critical period of popular music produc-tion. I suspect that their absence is a consequence of their refusal to adhere to respectability politics, their direct and public engagement with sexuality, and their involvement in the rock counterculture, a space that has not occupied the attention of most scholars documenting the experiences of black women.[4] Similarly, their identities as black women place them outside the purview of rock history writing, a field focused on white and male figures, even though, as

I show in this chapter and throughout *Black Diamond Queens*, black women and ideas about black women have done much to shape rock and roll music and culture.

I begin with an overview of the image of black women present in rock music and discourse during the 1960s and early 1970s. Here, I focus on the meanings that emerged as white British musicians encountered black music and black people from the United States. Chief among the material I discuss is the Rolling Stones' 1971 release "Brown Sugar," one of the band's most commercially successful songs. It is also the most widely circulated representation of a black woman in a rock song. Mick Jagger wrote the lyrics and provided the song's catchy musical riff, and it is probably not accidental that he figures in the narratives of all three of the women featured in this chapter. Jagger and many of his contemporaries were invested in stereotypes about sexuality, femininity, and blackness; in a number of cases, they tested these myths through encounters with black women. Their real and imagined interactions with African American women were sources of creative and personal expression, mentioned in memoirs and evoked in song. I discuss some of these references to demonstrate how white British male musicians used imagery that relied on mythologies about the sexual attractiveness and availability of black women and indicate the extent to which certain segments of the rock scene of the late 1960s and early 1970s desired the "brown sugar" that women such as Wilson, Hunt, and Lennear were presumed to possess. In the remainder of the chapter, I sketch the professional and personal lives of the three women in order to consider the ways each of them managed the racialized, sexualized, and nationalized capital of their black American womanhood. I pay particular attention to the limits and possibilities they encountered as they mobilized and negotiated "brown sugar."

"Brown Sugar"

During the 1960s, white British fascination with black musicality coexisted with a fascination with black sexuality. Reflecting on Jimi Hendrix's conquest of the English music scene, guitarist Eric Clapton observed, "You know, English people have a very big thing towards a spade. They really love that magic thing. They all fall for that kind of thing. Everybody and his brother in England still sort of think that spades have big dicks. And Jimi came over and exploited that to the limit . . . and everybody fell for it."[5] Hendrix had tremendous success working the appeal of black musicality and mythologies of black sexuality during the 1960s. The role of black women as participants in these processes and the ideas about black women's sexuality that circulated have received little attention, but they were integral to the rock scene. Representations of black women contributed to the era's ethos and influenced the ways the male rock musicians, whose exploits are centered in depictions of rock history, constructed their identities. The encounters between black American women and white English men were informed by fantasies and stereotypes about race, gender, and sexuality, and these encounters, in turn, shaped the people who engaged with the music. By the mid-1960s, many white musicians and fans were developing a genuine interest in and respect for black women's vocal talents; at the same time, widely circulating stereotypes influenced the perception that black women embodied the sexuality associated with black music. Songs and commentaries written by white English men capture the feelings of desire that black women conjured, while revealing connections between the attraction to blackness and the construction of white masculine prowess and power.

For the most part, these men's long-term relationships and marriages were with white women, but some of the white English musicians who spearheaded the blues revival were sweet on black women. Eric Burdon, vocalist for the Animals, among the first British bands to place songs on the American charts, peppers his memoirs with references to attractive black women. He recalls "staggering out of the Scotch of St. James [nightclub] one night with two beautiful black girls, one on each arm, tripping toward my Corvette. On the street we passed [actor] Sean Connery, in his Savile Row–tailored suit. He looked at me sideways and said, 'Fuck me, I'm in the wrong business.'"[6] Here, Burdon demonstrates his capacity as a ladies' man to the actor known for playing ladies' man James Bond, and he seems delighted to report Connery's response. Elsewhere in his memoirs Burdon talks about an intermittent affair with "Alvenia Bridges, the black beauty,"[7] whom he describes as "stunningly attractive, tall, brown, and beautiful [and] . . . an instant hit with the boys in the band [War],"[8] the all-black Long Beach, California, band that Burdon joined in the late 1960s. Burdon also mentions that "Doreen, my wonderful black girlfriend, was anxious to get engaged,"[9] and devotes a page to sharing fond memories of (and an excess of details about) his sexual exploits with "my new black girlfriend Selina," a Jamaican woman whom he dated in London.[10] Burdon's comments about his sexual attraction to black women intertwine with his descriptions of his social and political views:

The American black experience has always been fascinating to me. On a personal level, I've always found black women among the most alluring. My first serious love affair was with an African girl named Doreen, and I developed an early reputation for having a lot of black friends, particularly displaced Africans in Newcastle [Burdon's hometown], two of whom were members of the first band I was in, the Pagans. I saw what freedom meant to these exiles, and it engendered an even deeper interest in the African experience in America, resulting in a reputation that preceded me to New York. When the Animals set foot in America for the first time, there was graffiti on the wall of our hotel proclaiming "Eric Burdon is a nigger lover." Well, yeah, he is, I thought. And fuck you for not understanding that you should be, too.[11]

Burdon's progressive views coexist with an internalization of long-standing Western European and American practices of sexualizing women of African descent. Granted, it was typical for male rockers of Burdon's generation to objectify women and celebrate sexually libertine ways. Burdon's inclusion of black women among those he pursued could be viewed as a demonstration of open-minded commitment to the equal opportunity that civil rights activists were fighting for as well as a rejection of mainstream habits of discrimination against African Americans. But these declarations, which often expressed an appreciation for African American culture (especially music) and critiqued staid European and European American ways, were also markers of virility. Burdon and his cohort imagined themselves as manly and cool, in part by portraying themselves as men who communed with black people and who slept with black women, actions that registered as renegade in a segregated era and that helped them attain the hypermasculinity associated with black men.

Consider the recollections Keith Richards shares in his 2010 memoir. He describes the pleasure he and the other Rolling Stones took in visiting bars and juke joints "across the tracks" in black neighborhoods when they toured in the southern United States during the 1960s and early 1970s. His memories of musical revelry in black communities mesh with recollections of sexual revelry with black women:

There's food going, everybody's rocking and rolling, everybody's having a good time, and it was such a contrast from the white side of town, it always sticks in my memory. You could hang there with ribs, drink, smoke. And big mamas, for some reasons they always looked upon us as thin and frail people. So they started to mama us, which was all right with me. Shoved into the middle of two enormous breasts . . . "You need a rubdown, boy?" "OK, anything you say, mama." Just the free-and-easiness of it. You wake up in a house full of black people who are being so incredibly kind to you, you can't believe it. . . . You wake up, where am I? And there's a big mama there, and you're in bed with her daughter, but you get breakfast in bed.[12]

Questions about whether Richards, a prodigious imbiber of drugs and alcohol, can remember much of the 1960s and 1970s notwithstanding, the fact that he chooses to present this raced and gendered image as memory is significant. For Richards, all the pleasures—food, drink, music, sex, friendly bonding, and warm mothering—were his for the asking on the black side of town.

Other UK artists shared Burdon's and Richards's fetishizing of black women. Some established romantic liaisons with black women; others celebrated them in song. Van Morrison, a singer-songwriter who hailed from Northern Ireland, wrote "Brown-Skinned Girl" with a Caribbean rhythm, but by the time he recorded it in 1967 (with the African American group the Sweet Inspirations contributing backing vocals), the song had a new title. "I just thought 'Brown-Eyed Girl' sounded better or something," he explained in an interview.[13] "Brown-Eyed Girl," more digestible to the mainstream than the original title, went on to become one of Morrison's best-known songs.[14] David Bowie wrote "Lady Grinning Soul," the four-minute melodrama that closes his 1973 release *Aladdin Sane*, in honor of Claudia Lennear, whom he dated in the early seventies.[15] Guitarist John Mayall's romance with Marsha Hunt inspired him to compose "Brown Sugar" in 1967, a few years before Mick Jagger used the same title for a Rolling Stones track. Mayall was one of the foundational figures of the British blues revival. Born in 1933, he was a decade older than the majority of the British musicians he guided; his involvement in playing the blues and nurturing other musicians earned him the title "Father of British Blues." John McVie and Mick Fleetwood of Fleetwood Mac, Eric Clapton and Jack Bruce of Cream, and Mick Taylor, who joined the Rolling Stones in 1969, are some of the musicians who passed through his band, the Bluesbreakers. Mayall released his 1967 album, *The Blues Alone*, around the time he was living with Marsha Hunt.[16] Their affair inspired three songs: "Brand New Start," an up-tempo celebration of the renewing power of love; "Marsha's Mood," a mid-tempo instrumental; and "Brown Sugar," a traditional blues in which Mayall sings about his newfound preference. True to the blues tradition he studied, Mayall's lyrics are nonlinear and laced with double meanings, starting with the title's reference to something quite different from the sugar used to sweeten food: "I got a taste of brown sugar / Gonna leave white sugar alone," he sings.[17] Mayall's unassuming vocals report on the effects of the woman he has had "a taste of" in a happy blues. He catalogues some of the feelings associated with joyous love and confirms the exotic attractiveness of black women. While the song offers a positive commentary about a specific individual who has captured the narrator's attention, the generic term *Brown Sugar* reduces the woman to her color and racializes her sexuality. It is her blackness that has drawn his interest, and that makes her sweet, desirable, and song-worthy.

The Rolling Stones' "Brown Sugar," recorded two years after Mayall released his version, also traffics in these images, but the song has a different tone, one that helped to burnish the bad boy image the band was cultivating during this period.[18] Jagger's "Brown Sugar" condenses white male interest in and sexualization of black women into three and a half rollicking minutes.[19] Departing from Mayall's adherence to blues form, the Stones' "Brown Sugar," like their other original compositions, pushed their beloved black American music in new directions, helping to establish the hard rock sound. "Brown Sugar" was one of three songs the Stones recorded in the Muscle Shoals Sound Studios in Alabama during a three-day stint in 1969.[20] That storied southern location was revered for being the place where Wilson Pickett and Aretha Franklin had recorded classic soul tracks; this, coupled with the kind of oversimplified feelings about African American culture that Richards expressed in his reverie about life "across the tracks," inspired the men as they recorded. While Jagger's "Brown Sugar" uses the same sugar metaphor as Mayall's, his lyrics are less sweet, offering a narrative of slavery and concubinage in the antebellum South. Set to a seductive riff, the story foregrounds a black woman who is subjected to the sexual whims of her master and a fellow slave, as well as the fantasies of the song's narrator. The raucous excursion into sexual material rendered with an irreverent attitude is in keeping with the Stones' mission to be rock and roll hedonists. Adding a sprinkling of Brown Sugar to the mix allowed them to introduce the controversial subject of interracial sex, while building their reputations for sexual prowess and hinting at their own liaisons with black women.

Is the song about or addressed to a specific woman? By the end of 1969 when the band recorded "Brown Sugar," Jagger had been involved, however briefly, with African American women including Devon Wilson, Marsha Hunt, and two Ikettes: P. P. Arnold and Claudia Lennear. Connecting the song to a specific individual, however, seems less important than attending to the general conception of black women that the song promulgates. Jagger's bandmate

Keith Richards articulates these ideas in comments about his encounters with black women when touring in the United States during the 1960s:

> With English chicks it was you're putting the make on her or she's putting the make on you, yea or nay. I always found with black chicks that wasn't the main issue. It was just comfortable, and if shit happened later, OK. It was just part of life. They were great because they were chicks, but they were much more like guys than English girls were. You didn't mind them being around after the event. I remember being in the Ambassador Hotel with this black chick called Flo, who was my piece at the time. She'd taken care of me. Love, no. Respect, yeah.[21]

Here, Richards's sweeping generalizations and use of colloquialisms for women affirm his virility and experience. He portrays black American women as uninterested in the annoying commitments that concern white English women. They are, he posits, "more like guys," a characterization that echoes stereotypes of black women as inadequately feminine and distinguishes them from white women whose domesticating tendencies drove men to the liberating space of rock and roll in the first place. It may also be that black women served as a proxy for the black masculinity that so many of these musicians fetishized and sought to access. For Richards, black women's difference from the tedium of the more familiar white English women is a sexual spark. "Brown Sugar" celebrates these liaisons, recently savored at the time the band recorded the song.

There is little question that "Brown Sugar" is a song about sex with black women. Its working title was "Black Pussy."[22] The song was a bit of a lark for Jagger, who began writing it while filming *Ned Kelly* in Australia.[23] "At first [the lyrics] made him laugh," Jagger biographer Marc Spitz reports, "but the riff was strong, and soon he was taking the song seriously, writing allegorical lyrics about the slave trade."[24] Obviously no good for airplay, the band traded the raw language for something more allusive. In addition to being less vulgar, the new title permitted a blues-style double entendre, playing on the fact that Brown Sugar "was also the street name of unrefined heroin from Southeast Asia."[25] Still, the sexual explicitness of the original title permeates the song. The New Orleans setting of "Brown Sugar" calls to mind the city's special market for "fancy girls," enslaved women bought to serve as sexual workers at prices that matched or exceeded those paid for skilled, able-bodied enslaved men.[26] The song also depicts the plantation household, referencing the slave master's wife, who frets about the late night goings-on, and the houseboy's possible participation in them. In the final verse, the narrator's voice shifts from describing historical events to addressing a woman he refers to as Brown Sugar and expressing his own excited response. Whether the speaker in the final verse is a modern-day Jagger persona or the antebellum slaver speaking in first person, he is fascinated by black women's sexuality.[27]

One interpretation could be that Jagger is implicating himself in the fraught race, gender, and power dynamics associated with the interracial associations the song depicts. But the tempo and tone of the song evoke celebration rather than criticism of a situation dependent on the coercive power relations signaled by the mention of whipping in the first verse. One commentator observed that Jagger's "'Yeah, Yeah, Yeah, Woah,' at the end [of the song] prompts the ritual raised fist."[28] From the whip at the song's beginning to this chant at the end, the narrator seems to be cheering rape, waiting for his own turn to "taste" some Brown Sugar. True, "Brown Sugar" addresses the violence and power that accompany desire in the white male master/black female slave relationship, but Jagger seems to be both cognizant of and titillated by the uneven power dynamics. And, no big surprise, the black woman's perspective is not part of the song. "Brown Sugar" treats the institution of American slavery as a setting for an edgy bodice-ripper. This much is in keeping with the Stones' mission to be rock and roll bad boys.

The packaging and marketing of "Brown Sugar" annexed the song to a campaign that, together with its music and lyrics, presented the Rolling Stones as aggressive sexual conquerors, shaping the band's identity for the 1970s. The single "Brown Sugar" was the first to be released on the Stones' newly formed label, Rolling Stones Records, and the first to bear the tongue logo that Jagger had developed with graphic designer John Pashe.[29] The picture of a tongue protruding from full lips "slavering in a cunnilingual leer," as one commentator put it, appearing on a record whose lyrics reference tasting a black girl, confirmed the band's sex-centered image.[30] "Brown Sugar" was the first track on *Sticky Fingers*, a title whose meaning should be self-evident in this context. The 1971 album's cover also contained visual sexual references. Designed by pop art instigator Andy Warhol, it featured a close-up of a pair of tight jeans cropped to show the front waist and mid-thigh area, focusing attention on a zipper that, on the first pressings of the album, "opened to reveal well-hung white underwear."[31] And, "in case anyone missed the design's phallic statement," notes one of the band's chroniclers, "the Stones catalogued their first album on their new label as COC 59100."[32] The heavy-handed sexual references shored up the band's image through puerile play with naughty words and pictures. The song helped them consolidate their profile as the ultimate rock and roll band, makers of hard rocking music and revelers in sex, drugs, drink, and mayhem. "Brown Sugar" released the band's collective id and libido into the popular culture atmosphere.

The Rolling Stones have become icons of rock, and "Brown Sugar" is iconic of the band. In a book about his life as a Rolling Stone, bass player Bill Wyman says of the song, "Nasty, rampant and raw, 'Brown Sugar' is everything that's best about the Stones."[33] Wyman recognizes the troubling nature of the lyrics but does not disavow them, remarking, "In recent years, Mick has said that he would probably censor his lyrics of slavery and young black girls if he were writing it now. It's a good job he didn't 30-something years ago. It became the 16th British single release and the 21st in America."[34] Wyman stands by the song's original language and intent. Similarly, when Richards discusses "Brown Sugar" in his autobiography, it is not to wring his hands over the lyrics, but to explain that they almost weren't recorded in their entirety because Jagger kept dropping the line "hear him whip the women just around midnight" and had to be reminded to include it.[35] Jagger's recent performances of the song suggest that he is not as comfortable with the original lyrics as his bandmates, sometimes excising references to tasting and whipping.[36] He has taken a similar approach with the 1978 song "Some Girls," a catalogue of observations about the nature of women.[37] The capsule descriptions of women's qualities, organized by nationality, ethnicity, and race, include the line "Black girls just wanna get fucked all night / I just don't have that much jam." Richards has defended the lyrics stating, "Well, we've been on the road with a lot of black chicks for many years, and there's quite a few that do. It could have been yellow girls or white girls."[38] But, of course, it wasn't. The song's references to Asian women and white women also traffic in stereotypes: "Chinese girls are so gentle / they're really such a tease," and "white girls, they're pretty funny / Sometimes they drive me mad," but these images lack the crudity of the song's assertion about black women.[39]

Richards dismisses the criticism of the "Some Girls" lyrics as the preoccupation of feminists, but in *Shine a Light,* the 2008 Martin Scorsese documentary of the band's 2006 concert at New York's Beacon Theatre, Jagger does not mention black women at all when performing the song.[40] He also drops references to whipping and the "like a black girl should" line from "Brown Sugar" in this performance. I have not found a comment from Jagger explaining the motivation for making these changes, but I can't help but wonder whether he altered his lyrics about black girls not because of a changing cultural climate, but for a more personal reason: in the late 1980s, he reestablished contact with Karis Hunt, the child he had fathered in the 1970s with Marsha Hunt, an African American woman. Did his relationship with this particular black girl, his daughter, encourage him to reassess his public representations of black womanhood?

In her memoir, Hunt does not proffer an opinion of either the Mayall or Rolling Stones version of "Brown Sugar"; instead, she presents a personal narrative that counters the flat images of black women rendered in these songs. In tracing the professional and personal journeys of Wilson, Hunt, and Lennear in the remainder of this chapter, I have a similar goal: to document stories of black rock and roll women in their fascinating complexity. Of course, these women were not simply "black pussy" to be enjoyed in one-night stands or fantasized about in song, but they were caught up in potent racial and sexual mythologies. The coercive power dynamics between white slave masters and black enslaved women referenced in the Stones' "Brown Sugar" had been replaced by an emerging climate of sexual freedom. From their locations in the rock scene, Wilson, Hunt, and Lennear participated in this culture, exercising choices that included seeking sexual pleasure outside of marriage and across racial lines. They confronted and negotiated the dominant ideas associated with black women, capitalizing on them when doing so helped advance their goals, rejecting them when they were a hindrance, and sometimes internalizing them, as they brought their black female bodies and voices into the scene.

Super Groupie

In the late 1960s, Devon Wilson became one of rock's most visible groupies, deriving her notoriety from her public associations with Jimi Hendrix and Mick Jagger. Music critic and Hendrix scholar Charles Shaar Murray describes her as "the New York super-groupie who was the model for Hendrix's song 'Dolly Dagger' and one of the most important women in Hendrix's life."[41] Wilson did not produce recordings, live performances, or song lyrics, nor did she give many interviews. As a groupie, her creativity and contribution were more ephemeral.

The term *groupie* had been coined in the 1960s to name the women who pursued sex with members of rock groups.[42] Groupies achieved their social position through relationships with male rock musicians that at once reinscribed and upended women's traditional roles.[43] They were caretakers who ministered to the domestic needs of male musicians, but did so while pursuing their own sexual pleasure, challenging a sexual double standard that punished women for exercising sexual autonomy.[44] Groupies were a visible and integral part of the rock scene, referenced in songs such as David Bowie's "Suffragette City" (1972), the Rolling Stones' "Star, Star" (1973), and Funkadelic's "No Head, No Backstage Pass" (1975). Rock historian Lillian Roxon called them "the great ladies of rock, the legendary courtesans, the friends, the mistresses, the confidantes."[45] Jimi Hendrix celebrated groupies' commitment to counterculture values. "Instead of saying 'We're part of the love scene,' they're actually doing it," he told *Rolling Stone*. "They take you around, they wash your socks and try to make you feel nice while you're in town because they know they can't have you forever. Used to be the soldiers who were the gallant ones, riding into town, drinking the wine and taking the girls. Now it's the musicians."[46] Guitarist Jimmy Page, whose band Led Zeppelin "gained a reputation for their rampant abuse of groupies," spoke to *Rolling Stone* about his preference for groupies over rank-and-file women.[47] "Groupies are a better ball, by and large, you know," he explained. "They've had more experience and they're willing to try more things."[48] Juma Sultan, an African American percussionist who performed with Jimi Hendrix at Woodstock, assured me that the word *groupie* "was not considered a derogatory term in those days. They were along with the group, you know. They were just there having a good time hanging out."[49]

Pat Hartley, an African American woman who in her own estimation "wasn't a terribly successful groupie," explained the significance of groupies in a 1973 interview: "It used to be that guys could pick and choose. Well, after the first three years it was us choosing, the guys had no choice. There's about four or five sort of famous groupies and Devon [Wilson] was one of them, but she never lasted long with anybody. She didn't want to live with anybody, it was just a real status thing."[50] The women sought out the men, Hartley recalled. "We'd just find out who was in town and what hotel they were in. It's not that difficult, if one decided to put a little bit of effort behind it."[51] The boldness of these actions was noteworthy, and, as feminist music critic Ann Powers observes, "these women made their reputations not simply because they were rock stars' consorts, but because of their sexual independence and bravado."[52] Young and hip, groupies helped male rock musicians consolidate a superstar image, adding sex appeal and glamour to the rock scene.[53] Among the hippest was Devon Wilson, a black woman who, for a few years, enjoyed a charmed existence with access to the highest echelons of the rock and roll scene. Wilson died young and did not leave behind a paper trail. Precise details about her background and her birth date are elusive. The material about Wilson available in the historical record is in biographies of Jimi Hendrix, and I rely on these sources, a 1970 magazine profile, and my conversations with Juma Sultan and Emmaretta Marks—African American musicians who knew Wilson—to consider her negotiation of the Brown Sugar image.

Ida Mae Wilson adopted the name *Devon* when she left her home in Milwaukee at the age of fifteen.[54] Underage and a runaway, Wilson turned to prostitution to make a living.[55] Hendrix biographer David Henderson reports that by age fifteen, Wilson was in Las Vegas, "tricking in the trick capital of the world" and cultivating the street smarts for which she became known.[56] African American composer and producer Quincy Jones met her while she was in Las Vegas and, according to Henderson, "took her under his wing, adopted her as his cousin, and took her on to Los Angeles."[57] Hendrix's biographers do not agree on when and where Wilson met Hendrix. Henderson says the meeting occurred in New Jersey in 1965, when Hendrix was a journeyman R&B sideman playing with the Isley Brothers, and his friend, the drummer Buddy Miles, introduced them.[58] Charles Cross has them meeting in 1967, at a party in Laurel Canyon.[59] Hendrix archivist John McDermott says singer Emmaretta Marks, who knew them both, made the introduction in the summer of 1967.[60] Marks, who sang with Al Kooper's Blues Project and on some late Hendrix tracks, was a friend of Wilson's, but when I spoke with her in 2014, she did not take credit for bringing the two together; she told me she was not sure how they met.[61] Whatever the circumstances of their first encounter, shortly after Hendrix's appearance at the Monterey Pop Festival in June 1967 introduced him to the rock community in the United States, Wilson and Hendrix connected in Los Angeles and started the on-again, off-again relationship that lasted until Hendrix's death in 1970.

Discussions of Devon Wilson highlight her beauty and charisma (see figure 5.1). Henderson rhapsodizes that Wilson was "fine and worldly. . . . The product of an interracial marriage, Devon was half black and half white, light-skinned, tall, vivacious, and voluptuously proportioned."[62] Cross reports, "Devon was exceptionally beautiful, and extremely bright; she looked a bit like a curvier version of Josephine Baker."[63] Juma Sultan told me "she was very attractive . . . a brown-skinned girl. Slim and beautiful."[64] Curtis Knight of Curtis Knight and the Squires, a group Hendrix sometimes played with in the early sixties, noted that Devon "was, above all, magnetic, and she was also attractive, and totally into sex."[65] Arthur Lee, of the band Love and a friend of Hendrix's, asserted, "Devon Wilson was my girlfriend first," that is, before she and Hendrix got together.[66] Al Aronowitz, a journalist at the *New York Post*, recalled, "She was one of the most beautiful and sensuous of the groupies, and one of the most successful, too. I first met her in the '60s when she was hanging out with I forget which superstar, but whenever a rock hero came to New York, the chances were you'd find Devon in his hotel room. They used to recommend her to one another. Her sex was overwhelming."[67] Sexualized and sensationalized as a black woman and a groupie, Devon Wilson developed a reputation as a formidable woman who possessed an authoritative manner, streetwise nature, and an appetite for sexual adventure. Alvenia Bridges, another black woman on the scene who was friends with Hendrix and Eric Burdon, said of Wilson, "She was a pretty wild lady, but she loved Jimi and he loved her and she ran the show."[68] Kathy Etchingham, one of Hendrix's girlfriends, was not impressed by Wilson; according to Cross, she "felt less jealous of Devon than other women, if only because she observed Jimi treating Devon more like an employee than a lover."[69] Pat Hartley attributed Wilson's demeanor to her upbringing, observing, "Devon really needed a lot of love in a peculiar kind of way. I mean someone really didn't love her when she was a kid because she'd behave like a five year old sometimes and she was very bright and very witty but always appealing to people's prurient interests."[70]

The research of Hendrix's biographers and the comments of people in his circle depict a complex relationship between Wilson and Hendrix, one based on strong mutual attraction inflected with jealousy and manipulation. Cross calls the alliance "unusual," noting that "their union bore more similarities to that of two great rivals or two siblings. Devon was constantly informing Jimi of the other A-list stars she had bedded—which occasionally included women, as Devon was bisexual—and Jimi bragged about the other groupies he'd been with."[71] Both Hendrix and Wilson reveled in the sex and drugs that were part of the rock and roll lifestyle. According to McDermott, "Devon had no trouble walking into the Scene [a Manhattan nightclub] and selecting women for an erotic ménage a trois. That was different: relationships with groupies were a diversion, a drug to be enjoyed for a fleeting moment, then forgotten. And when it came to real drugs, Devon possessed a voracious appetite, one that exceeded even Hendrix's."[72] The limited testimony from Wilson herself further contributes to an image of a daring woman. She explained, "I was attracted to Jimmy's [*sic*] flamboyance, even though at the time he wasn't an established star. He had a certain visible flair about him: his hair was longer than any other black musician's that I'd ever seen, and in an original style."[73] Wilson took credit for turning Hendrix on to drugs. "I introduced Jimmy

FIGURE 5.1 This photo of Devon Wilson ran in the June 1970 issue of *Rags*, the counter-culture fashion magazine, alongside an article in which she discussed her relationship with Jimi Hendrix and her recent liaison with Mick Jagger, an occurrence that the magazine hailed as "The Cop of the Year." © BARON WOLMAN.

[*sic*] to his first acid trip, and he liked it a lot," she claimed. "He tried various pills with me and our relationship became one of excitement and exhilaration. He sniffed cocaine, but he had no desire at all to get into heroin at that time, because he knew that this was a one-way street that led to nowhere."[74] Eventually, though, they were both heading down that path. "By 1969," Cross reports, "Devon was increasingly strung out from snorting cocaine and heroin; more and more Jimi was joining her in these vices."[75]

Over time, Wilson became an indispensable member of Hendrix's entourage and his most stalwart champion. Jim Marron, a member of the staff at Hendrix's Electric Lady Studios, observed that she was "intensely into anything she perceived as being good for Jimi."[76] A procurer of everything from apartments to drugs to women, she had ideas about the direction of Hendrix's career; according to Juma Sultan, one goal was "to get him and Quincy Jones together, because [Jones] was a hit maker."[77] By 1968, Wilson had become a right hand to Hendrix, both inside and outside the bedroom. "Early on," McDermott explains, "she adopted the role of protective matron for him, shepherding those Hendrix felt comfortable with while keeping away those she considered undesirable. Most of Jimi's intimate associates were wary of her, yet remained enamored by her electric personality."[78] Wilson was a regular presence at Hendrix's studio and, according to Henderson, "became an unofficial watchdog of the sessions. She would order people out when Jimi wanted the scene cleared. She would say who could stay and who could not. Her attitude was perfectly suited to the task. She seemed to enjoy her power over the scenemakers."[79] As Emmaretta Marks told me, "She liked to be the boss."[80] Soon, reports Henderson, Wilson was on Hendrix's payroll as a Girl Friday, handling "more and more of his affairs."[81] She preferred, however, to identify herself as Hendrix's girlfriend.[82]

Hendrix and Wilson maintained sexual, emotional, and business bonds. Wilson was able to deal with Hendrix's various women, Henderson observes, "often getting rid of the ones he had tired of, or helping him to get new, strange, or exotic ones. Sometimes they did threesomes. They also had a thing with each other, but she and Jimi did as they pleased."[83] For Wilson to do as she pleased sometimes meant displeasing Hendrix. On November 27, 1969, Wilson threw Hendrix's birthday party, inviting a roster of guests that included the Rolling Stones, who had played at Madison Square Garden that evening. In what became a public embarrassment for Hendrix, Wilson left the party with Mick Jagger, to whom she had been linked romantically before.[84] The liaison with Jagger, which happened during his band's 1969 US tour, put

Wilson in the spotlight reserved for the men she pursued. The counterculture fashion magazine *Rags* sent a reporter to talk with her about the occurrence it tagged "The Cop of the Year." In the interview, Wilson offered background about her connection to the English rockers: "I met the Stones a couple of years ago at their press party at the Playboy Club where I was working. I went out with Brian Jones first. I was closer to him than any of the others. He was the true Rolling Stone."[85] Here, she articulates the position of Stones fans who viewed Jones as the band's heart and lamented both his departure from the band and his mysterious July 1969 death. But with Jones gone, Wilson took up with Jagger, describing her time with him in a way that painted an idealized picture of the sexy glamour of groupie life:

> When I heard that the Stones were coming for a tour, I knew I would hear from Mick. He called and asked me to go to Philadelphia for their concert. Then we spent the week together in New York. Six beautiful days and nights. Everyone was really happy for me. Colette [Mimram, a friend who ran a clothing boutique in the East Village] used to help me get dressed before I'd go out with Mick. A lot of chicks were envious. But I'd get calls from my friends who'd congratulate me and say, "Hey, you did it!" Like *heavy* score, right?[86]

Wilson's conquest and her bragging about it were flagrant violations of proper feminine behavior, and she took pleasure in both.

Judging from her tone in the interview, Wilson enjoyed juggling the attention of two of the rock scene's most prominent stars. Heady with her groupie success, she interviewed herself about her "cop": "What did Jimi think? Oh he loved it but he was jealous, too," she said.[87] Accompanying the public pleasure of solidifying her status as a "super groupie" was the private pleasure of sex, which Wilson discussed. "Mick is a very sexually electric person," she told *Rags*. "Especially his mouth and eyes. I think he's had his fair share of sex, don't you? He told me he likes either 14-year-old girls who look like little boys, or 30-year-old women, excepting me of course. I think he's into a heavy spade trip, which had a *little* something to do with us."[88] Here, Wilson shares her insider knowledge of Jagger's tastes and acknowledges that his fascination with blackness helped her seduce him. Wilson is not quoted making a related comment in which she claims an interest in whiteness. Nor does she criticize Jagger for exoticizing black people and black culture. On the contrary, she describes him as a serious and talented student of African Americana. "He understands blues so well because he's into spades," she said. "He digs Tina

Turner, Taj Mahal, Jimi. He wrote a song about me. *Your mother she was a country girl / Where's your father, he done left this world / Every brown girl has to pay a due / Every white boy he just sings the blues.*"[89] These lyrics recognized that black women and white men occupied radically different positions. Wilson's death, just over a year after her liaison with Jagger, was the ultimate payment. Meanwhile, Jagger and a legion of white male rockers carried on singing their versions of the blues, reaping financial rewards and cultural approval in the process.

At the time of the interview, Wilson articulated a vision of her future. Reflecting on her conquest of Jagger, she concluded the interview by asking and answering a question about her plans: "So, what can I do for an encore? I don't know, probably marry Jimi. . . . Will you publish my wedding pictures?"[90] Although her context and behavior are countercultural, Wilson's comments—maybe flip, maybe earnest, definitely quotable—express her ultimate goal as marriage—the same thing the mainstream culture dictated for women. This perspective and the groupie lifestyle it underwrote are indicative of the extent to which traditional gender roles persisted in the rock scene. As music critic Charles Shaar Murray has observed, "Young men wanted to become rock stars themselves, while many young women . . . reacted to the shortage of positive role-models by settling for the next best thing, which was to become starfuckers."[91] Only a handful of women—LaVern Baker, Etta James, Janis Joplin, Grace Slick, and the members of the Shirelles, the Ronettes, and the Shangri-Las—had asserted themselves as rock and roll stars.

Hendrix responded to "The Cop of the Year" with a mix of acceptance and the jealousy Wilson mentioned to the *Rags* reporter. He processed his feelings in "Dolly Dagger," a song written about Wilson; it was one of the first tracks he recorded at his newly opened Electric Lady Studios.[92] For the song's title, Hendrix concocted a name that indexes Wilson's simultaneously enticing and pain-inflicting personality and one that rhymes with the surname of his rival. The lyrics have her drinking blood from a jagged edge, a reference to an incident Hendrix apparently witnessed "in which Mick pricked his finger and Devon, rather than get him a Band-Aid, said she'd suck the wound clean."[93] This image depicts the rapacious side of her personality. Dolly is trouble; nevertheless, Hendrix's protagonist wants in. Wilson's life and death inspired her friend, the African American singer and songwriter Betty Davis, to write about her as well. Davis's 1973 track "Steppin in Her I. Miller Shoes" is, like "Dolly Dagger," critical of Wilson's choices, but for different reasons.[94] "She could have been anything she wanted," Davis sings, "but she chose to be nothing." Set against a propulsive musical track that her rock-loving friend would have appreciated, Davis's song acknowledges Wilson's intelligence, abilities, and the status she enjoyed in the rock scene, while lamenting her decision to take the path of surface glamour and drug-fueled escape. In an interview, Pat Hartley echoed the tenor of Davis's lyrics when reflecting on Wilson: "For some reason she wanted to be nothing and that's what she ended up to be, nothing."[95] Davis rejects the celebratory portrayal of groupie life that Wilson promoted in the *Rags* interview, mentioning the abuse she suffered at the hands of men and suggesting that exploitation coexisted with heady sexual fun in the scene. Wilson devoted herself to pursuing physical pleasure and famous men. What might she have accomplished, Davis's song wonders, if she had developed her other talents? Emmaretta Marks told me that Wilson wanted to sing. "She had a voice. She just needed a little training," Marks said. "And she could carry a tune. She liked to sing, she wanted to sing, but I don't know if she rehearsed enough."[96]

Instead, Wilson followed the path that made sense for a beautiful, intelligent, outgoing woman who enjoyed the excitement of the music scene and the sexual pursuit of attractive men and—according to some reports—women.[97] Her close associations with high-profile musicians such as Jimi Hendrix, Mick Jagger, Brian Jones, Quincy Jones, and Jim Morrison and the rumors that connected her to Duane Allman and Eric Clapton gave her life a sparkle of celebrity.[98] Her death, however, was bleak. The drug use that started as recreational became all-encompassing. Emmaretta Marks witnessed the slide and talked to her friend about the situation: "I told her . . . 'It's not going to take you where you want to go.' . . . I said, 'You need to stop. . . . You know, everybody's worried about you. You need to stop.'"[99] According to Marks, Wilson tried to quit using heroin, but her stints in a rehab program were unsuccessful. Cross reports that the addiction was affecting her appearance: "Her eyelids now drooped, and she was no longer grooming herself. . . . As her heroin addiction had spiraled out of control that summer [i.e., 1970], even Jimi—who hated to say no to anyone—found himself cutting off their friendship."[100] Wilson was distraught when Hendrix died in September 1970; one report claims she attempted to throw herself into his grave at his funeral.[101] Her heroin use escalated after Hendrix's death and, just a few months later, she too was gone, dying at the Chelsea Hotel in February of 1971.[102] Wilson's demise was painful for Betty Davis, but given her friend's activities, it might have also felt inevitable. In "Steppin in Her I. Miller Shoes" she sings, "When they told me that she had died / They didn't have to tell me why or how she'd gone. / I knew!

I knew!" Whether her death was accidental, suicide, or homicide has never been established.[103] Emmaretta Marks told me she did not know the cause of death, but she recalled the grim task of helping Jenni Dean, a young black woman who had been featured in *Rolling Stone*'s groupies issue and was also a friend of Wilson's, pack up Devon's scanty belongings and ship them to her mother in Milwaukee.[104]

Devon Wilson's story encapsulates the contradictions of the community she was a part of. As a groupie, she fulfilled a traditional female role of emotional, domestic, and sexual caretaker, while pursuing her own pleasure in ways that flew in the face of mainstream ideas of female propriety. Wilson established her position in Hendrix's life and in rock and roll history using a mix of intelligence, organizational skills, and feminine wiles. She fit the "Brown Sugar" fantasies associated with black women on an interpersonal level and exploited that connection with the rock stars she encountered. Her rejection of respectability facilitated a high-profile pursuit of pleasure. A daring and unconventional woman, Devon Wilson blazed a rebellious path before flaming out.

Renaissance Woman

In her memoir *Real Life*, Marsha Hunt weaves a tale of personal and professional triumphs and trials in the British rock scene of the sixties and seventies. Hunt's physical appearance provided a desired form of blackness for British youth who were enamored of African American music and culture, but she could not render the vocal blackness expected from African American women during this period. This limitation, in combination with dominant notions of black womanhood, shaped her experiences as a professional recording artist and contributed to her decision to develop a more expansive career. Hunt is not well known in the United States, but this African American actress, model, rock singer, radio talk show host, and author became a recognized public figure in England. Her memoir documents a black American woman's rock and roll odyssey and comes complete with a star-studded array of associates and romantic partners, although its reserved tone will disappoint readers looking for gossipy details about the proclivities of the famous men she has known. Instead, Hunt emphasizes the dynamics of race, gender, and nationality in London's late sixties and early seventies counterculture and their influence on her personal and professional prospects. Hers is a story of a liberated

African American woman who resisted, negotiated, and capitalized on prevailing stereotypes of black women's sexuality and musicality.[105]

Hunt was born in Philadelphia in 1946 to a family of working-class strivers who emphasized self-improvement through education. Her family moved to Oakland when she was a teenager, and she enrolled at UC-Berkeley as the campus's Free Speech movement emerged. A couple of semesters in, she decided that she wanted to travel overseas and identified England as the most compelling, affordable option. What was supposed to be a brief visit to London turned into a long-term stay during which she determined that "music was a strong political force and to sing seemed as romantic and as brazen a departure as my spirit needed."[106] She dropped out of Berkeley and got serious about becoming a professional vocalist. Her timing was good. "I was in London, this Negro kid from Berkeley, when Berkeley was *the* college town at the vanguard of the student movement," Hunt explained. "And, since Motown was the sound of the day, anybody looking and talking vaguely like a Supreme was considered gorgeous."[107] Hunt had arrived in London in 1966, the same year as Jimi Hendrix, and has suggested that her countryman's presence influenced her experiences. "In London, notions and expectations about black sexuality were heightened by Jimi's promotion as leader of the Jimi Hendrix Experience," she observed. "I'd argue that this had nothing to do with me personally, yet it had a lot to do with the attention I got and the opportunities that came my way."[108] Hunt's discussion of race focuses on her own experiences with occasional descriptions of the racial politics of the United States. She does not, however, mention London's black population, comprising immigrants from the Caribbean and sub-Saharan African former colonies, or the racism they routinely experienced.[109] Hunt does describe occasional encounters with British racism, noting, for example, the difficulty she had renting an apartment from white landlords. She finally secured a space by tapping her network of white musician friends; she ended up taking over the lease on Who vocalist Roger Daltrey's flat.[110] Most of what Hunt describes experiencing was a kind of advantageous racializing. Her identity as a Berkeley student and, especially, "a spade chick," as she puts it, gave her cachet in a context where white British youth were enamored of African American culture.[111]

Hunt had little experience singing, but her black American identity made her an attractive addition to bands whose repertoires were rooted in black American blues. "I wasn't gospel trained and wasn't likely to sing like it," she writes, but her race and nationality caused people to assume that she had vocal chops, and they offered her professional opportunities.[112] Hunt got her first work as a vocalist in Free at Last, a band led by guitarist Alexis Korner, who was, along with John Mayall, one of the founding figures of British blues. Hunt left Korner's band to join another English bluesman, vocalist Long John Baldry, in Bluesology. She toured England with these bands, and she enjoyed being on the road. "Immersed in a life style peculiar to the music business," she explained, "I was also a girl playing a boys' game."[113] In addition to breaking gender rules by participating in the itinerant life of a professional musician, she enjoyed short-term romantic attachments, usually with her fellow musicians. In *Real Life* her relationship with Mick Jagger is the primary affair she discusses—it is certainly the one that would convince a publisher to offer a book contract—but she also mentions liaisons with British blues guitarist John Mayall and vocalist Marc Bolan of T. Rex. To alleviate pressures from the British Home Office, she married Michael Ratledge, the keyboard player in the Soft Machine, whom she had met when they were working in London clubs with their respective bands.[114] Hunt also mentions platonic friendships with blues scene musicians such as Mick Fleetwood and John McVie of the blues-rock group Fleetwood Mac.[115]

Hunt's professional break came in 1968, when she was cast in the London production of *Hair: The American Tribal Love-Rock Musical*. A sensation in New York, the show captured the zeitgeist of the counterculture's mélange of free love, anti-war protest, and long tresses. Her role in the musical and the opportunities that issued from it accentuated her black female otherness in a predominantly white context. She was featured on the song "White Boys" with two other black women. "I sang a song about how delicious white boys were," she recalled. "'White boys give me goose bumps, white boys give me chills,' so the lyrics began."[116] The song, which was in dialogue with the show's other race-conscious number, "Black Boys," put Hunt in the position of making a declaration of attraction to white men on a nightly basis. "White Boys" and "Black Boys," like the song "Brown Sugar" sung by Mayall and then by the Stones, aired the taboo subject of interracial desire. Although Hunt was playing a character onstage, the song resonated with the personal path she followed. The affairs she documents in her memoir were with white men. Hunt intimates that her fashionable blackness might have drawn some of her partners to her, commenting on Mick Jagger's "penchant" for African American women, for example.[117] She does not reflect, however, on what seems to be her own penchant for white men and is reticent about the significance of her breaking whatever rules about dating and sex she might have been taught growing up in the segregated United States. Her only comment on the subject is vague: "Six thousand miles from my mother's interference, I was up for almost anything."[118]

Hunt's memoir celebrates her sexual liberation, but her choices intertwined with the sexualized public image of black women. Hunt's introduction to the British public was in an onstage role that foregrounded sexuality in a musical that gained instant notoriety for nightly displays of nudity: the entire cast disrobed just before the curtain fell at the end of the first act. Hunt's attractive face, brown skin, and magnificent Afro were standout features of *Hair*, and her willingness to pose for photos and talk to the press further raised her profile.[119] "I was considered Black and Beautiful," Hunt recalled, "and suddenly my busby [the name she coined for her Afro] and I established a new London fashion."[120] Hunt's black difference from the white British mainstream was intensified by the fact that she did not mind being photographed in the nude. Some of these photographs were taken by one of the investors in the show, Patrick Lichfield, an earl and cousin of Queen Elizabeth who was also a fashion photographer. Explaining the genesis of his first photo shoot with Hunt, Lichfield recalled, "I went to the premiere [of *Hair*, in London] where all the stir about nudity on stage first began. Marsha, of course, appeared nude in the show so when I photographed her the very next morning, for American *Vogue*, she had to be shot this way."[121] The photographs appeared in the January 1969 issue of American *Vogue;* a clothed Hunt also appeared in the December 1968 issue of British *Vogue* in photos taken by Harry Peccinotti, making her one of the pioneering black women to traverse the color bar that dominated fashion magazine photography.[122] The Lichfield photo of Hunt that circulated most widely in England shows her bare-skinned except for bands of bells on an ankle and wrist, seated with her arms and legs folded to cover her breasts and crotch; one hand leans on the floor, the other rests on her knee.[123] Hunt's eyes are heavy with mascara, her lips are pursed, and her pensive face is framed by an abundant Afro. Hunt was comfortable with exposing her body.[124] "Nudity was in and I saw it as positive, an advance on the old mores and a rejection of sexual repression," she explained.[125] Hunt's actions flouted both white middle-class mores and the politics of middle-class black respectability. Hunt's nude body provided striking evidence of the era's popular assertion that "Black Is Beautiful," and celebrated the counterculture's ethos of sexual freedom, but it also fed into stereotypes of the hypersexual black woman, that enticing, erotic figure evoked in "Brown Sugar."[126]

The circulation of Hunt's nude image and her participation in *Hair* augmented her reputation. In March 1969, just months after her West End debut,

Hunt signed a production deal with Track Records, the independent label co-owned by Kit Lambert and Chris Stamp, whose artists included the Jimi Hendrix Experience, the Who, and T. Rex. Hunt was paired with American producer Tony Visconti, best known for his work with T. Rex and David Bowie, and they began recording material for an album.[127] Hunt's first single was a cover of "Walk on Gilded Splinters," a song written by New Orleans pianist Dr. John. It charted in England in May 1969, and won Hunt an invitation to perform on the television program *Top of the Pops*, but a poorly planned outfit garnered more attention than the song itself. According to Hunt, "I appeared wearing a tight bolero top which, unbeknownst to me, allowed my breasts to poke out from the bottom every time I lifted my arms."[128] Hunt was already associated with nudity because of her involvement with *Hair* and the *Vogue* photos. According to Visconti, the mishap had a negative effect. The single "entered the chart at No. 46, but dropped out two weeks later when it stopped getting any radio plays," a change he attributes to the *Top of the Pops* fiasco.[129] In Hunt's telling, the single became "a minor British hit," but the televised snafu "caused me to be seen as being provocatively wayward . . . the incident gave me more exposure [*sic!*], but this time with the slant that I was a bad girl. (My association with the wild boys [i.e., the Who and Jimi Hendrix] signed to Track was further evidence)."[130]

Hunt's bad girl behavior, however inadvertent, and her evident comfort with nudity, captured the attention of Mick Jagger. He asked her to appear in a publicity shot for "Honky Tonk Women," the Stones' upcoming single. "The picture was going to be of a girl dressed like a sleaze bag in a bar with the Stones," Hunt recalled, "and they wanted me to be the girl."[131] Hunt was conscious of the need to protect her own image and that of black women. "The last thing we needed," she observed, "was for me to denigrate us by dressing up like a whore among a band of white renegades."[132] Jagger had not written the lyrics to the song "Brown Sugar" at this point, but the proposed photo Hunt describes was informed by the race, gender, and power dynamics referenced in that song, and she refused to be a part of it. It is telling that while she was comfortable being photographed nude in settings where she appeared alone, she refused to appear clothed in pictures taken with the Stones during a photo shoot that they controlled.

Hunt did not want to vamp with the band, but respectful of its exalted position in the rock community, she telephoned Jagger to decline the offer. During the call, she gave in to his insistence that they meet. He arrived at her home one evening, and, as she tells it, an affair began.[133] Jagger has made few public comments about Hunt, and his biographers rely, as I do, on the account Hunt gives of their relationship in her memoir. She insists that she was not interested in Jagger's fame or status, implicitly distinguishing her motivations from those of groupies. "I have never been a Stones fan," she asserts, "and in spite of my relationship with Mick, I always had a hard time at his concerts getting excited about the music, though I came to appreciate it eventually."[134] This faint praise contrasts with the enthusiasm Devon Wilson expressed for Jagger's facility with black musical culture. Nor was this a physical attraction. She compares Jagger unfavorably to Marc Bolan, another English rocker with whom she had an affair.[135] "He wasn't beautiful or even striking," she writes, "and after Marc's mythical good looks, there was no pretending that Mick was. . . . [He had] lank shoulder-length hair, which was darker than I'd imagined it, making his skin look sallow. . . . His redeeming facial feature was his infectious grin, which was utterly boyish and openly direct and made me less wary."[136] What drew Hunt and Jagger together, she says, was a shared sense of humor, knowledge of one another's cultures, and the feeling that she could talk with him about politics and social issues. She was struck by the fact that Jagger "held no prejudices which he needed to cover up to talk about racial politics, and he was aware of the devices that kept the world in a mess."[137] He was open, expressive, straightforward, decisive, and not "typically white, or English, or rock and roll."[138] In sum, she reports, "He was riveting."[139] Hunt characterizes their attraction as primarily intellectual and summarizes their relationship by saying, "We were not so much lovers as friends."[140]

They saw each other regularly, mostly in the privacy of Hunt's home. According to Hunt, they both had reasons for keeping their liaison secret: Jagger was living with his girlfriend Marianne Faithfull and did not want her (or the press) to know that he was straying. Hunt was concerned about the affair's impact on both her public image and private self: "I always feared that my association with him would crowd out my own identity. I never wanted to be known as Mick Jagger's girlfriend."[141] At this point, Hunt was struggling with professional difficulties. She continued gigging and recording, working with the Who's guitarist Pete Townshend, and Ron Wood, Kenney Jones, and Ian McLagan of Faces, but Track Records label co-owner Kit Lambert had fired Tony Visconti from her project.[142] Hunt says her rocky relationship with Lambert was intensified by the fact that his business partner, Chris Stamp, was unhappy that she had been signed in the first place.[143] In her view, Stamp considered her inauthentic, both as a rocker and as a black person. "Chris acted as if my entrée [into the rock community] via fashion and theatre was a crime that eliminated my right to play," Hunt explained. "My passing up the joint and the snort of coke also made him want to leave me sitting out the play on the bench. He was also one of those chic street people, both Black and white, who thought they had a right to determine who qualified as 'Black' when Black militancy was in vogue."[144] As an artist at Track, Hunt felt "caught in the middle of the power politics, which they seemed to resolve by making me the fall guy," and she argues that being a woman exacerbated her mistreatment.[145] "Kit and Chris used to expect me to eat the rubbish they wouldn't have dared serve up to their male bands," she asserts. "Their juggling of my producers and not being consistent about what direction my album was taking was detrimental to my career."[146]

Hunt was well aware that she was an outsider. "In 1969, the brotherhood of English rock bands was like a drugged soccer league," she states. "I was one of the few girls who had joined it by fronting a hard rock sound and getting out on the road with an aggressive band. This got me into the league in spite of my being a girl."[147] Hunt developed a stage persona intended to resonate in the white male-centered rock scene. She describes herself as being "hard-hitting, boot-grinding, fist-thumping and motor-driven. I learned from the rock boys, and it was a boy's performance I gave, tinted by the pleasure I got from being unmitigatedly female."[148] Hunt, it seems, recognized the performance currency of taking a masculine stance in a male-dominated arena. Doing so would enable her to fit into the codes of the scene. At the same time, however, she also saw the value of exploiting her black feminine difference and using sex appeal to draw the attention of men in the audience. Her tough, sexy persona responded to the dominant image of musical womanhood then circulating in British pop. "One reason I did what I did was because I was tired of English roses," Hunt explained in an interview. "I mean, the sweethearts who sing in front of the microphone and it's all civilized."[149] She took a less refined approach. "I did a peculiar gig in Scotland once and threatened to punch out someone who came up on stage," she recalled in an interview. "And the kids just went mad. I think they were excited by the idea of a chick standing in front of a guy threatening to punch his head in."[150] This was the kind of behavior that led an English reporter writing in 1974 to refer to Hunt as "the same Marsha who had been flung at us as London's wild black lady."[151]

Hunt's onstage behavior might have also raised the specter of the improperly feminine black woman who was at once too sexual and too aggressive. Her one-time producer Tony Visconti commented on Hunt's creative vision and its links to her black female identity; he recalled that she "approached her music very intellectually" and noted that Hunt "was into how we could interpret the material for her album in a very hip, almost psychedelic way. She wanted to make a credible 'guy' record, and not come off as a Black Marilyn Monroe, which is how the record company saw her."[152] Visconti's comment lays out the race and gender assumptions that shaped rock at this time: there were some preferred "hard" sounds associated with men, there were other less desired "soft" sounds associated with women, and a black woman's race and gender difference would be an integral part of her marketing narrative. Hunt was, from the start of her London sojourn, aware that her professional successes were closely connected to her looks and advantageous black difference. "They thought I looked like what black America was all about," she stated in a 1973 interview. "And then I was signed to a record label as basically a publicity hype, which I was."[153]

The challenge of turning the hype into a substantive career was on display in August 1969, when, backed by the Glasgow-based band White Trash, she played the Isle of Wight Festival, taking the stage just before the Who (see figure 5.2).[154] Hunt recalled being "the only girl rocker billed during that three-day outdoor extravaganza."[155] Accustomed to playing small clubs, Hunt and her band were overwhelmed by the vast size of the audience, one of the largest crowds in the short history of outdoor rock concerts, and the challenges of communicating with each other on the enormous stage.[156] At one point, the drummer was playing one song while Hunt and the rest of the band were playing another.[157] Their set was not a musical success and did not introduce Hunt into the countercultural consciousness in the way Lambert might have hoped when he wrangled her the high-profile position on the festival bill. After another single, a cover of a Simon and Garfunkel track called "Keep the Customer Satisfied," missed making the British Top 10, Lambert's interest in working with Hunt waned, and he dropped her from the label.[158]

Hunt's rock career stumbled in part because she had vocal limitations (to which she always admitted), and her efforts to compensate through idiosyncratic style were not enough to put her over. Summarizing her career in a 1974 article, a *Sounds* music critic allowed that Hunt had "some good singles," but ultimately (and somewhat contradictorily) declared, "Speaking as a music critic it wasn't very good. Speaking as a mere man, it was very effective."[159] Penny Valentine, one of the few women to publish regularly in the English music press during the 1970s, resisted getting caught up in Hunt's image when reviewing her 1971 album *Woman Child* and offered her response to Hunt's rock-centered sound:

Her voice has been a very interesting and odd piece of equipment. I can't honestly say she's a great singer in the full meaning of the word but there's something about her weird switches from key to key on various tracks and the sensation you have that you don't quite know what she's going to do next that make this a rather spellbinding album. . . . She soars and falls, hot gospels it, sounds vulnerable, desperate, hard headed and suicidal in equal amounts throughout, often doesn't make it but keeps you interested.[160]

Hunt's now out-of-print UK-only release, *Woman Child* is difficult to find in the United States. I had my first and only encounter with the album in a British Library listening room.[161] What I heard was surprising and, as Valentine posits, idiosyncratic if a bit hit-or-miss. It's an unusual document, as much a performance art piece as a straight-ahead rock album. Comprising covers of rock and soul songs written by Dr. John, Marc Bolan, Steve Winwood, Paul Simon, Bob Dylan, and Holland-Dozier-Holland, it also includes an arch reference to *Hair*. "Let the Sunshine In," one of the most popular songs from the show, appears in the track listing but lasts for fewer than thirty seconds; it features, in rapid succession, an orchestra playing the song's introduction; a piano solo of the same; and then Hunt's faux-operatic vocals, which she abruptly abandons and questions by blurting "Huh?" and laughing. This interlude, sandwiched between the album's first and second full-length songs, acknowledges Hunt's connection to a musical theater production that many rock fans reviled, while allowing her to distance herself from it with a laughing turn to "real rock."

As Valentine suggests, the album's music and Hunt's vocal approach are all over the map, a fevered cutting and pasting of the sounds that fueled the sixties counterculture: sitar-like guitar lines, gospel-styled female background vocalists, a male gospel quartet, psychedelic guitar solos alongside pumping New Orleans trombones, a xylophone and violins, delicate British hippie folk,

---

FIGURE 5.2 (*opposite*) Marsha Hunt on stage at the 1969 Isle of Wight Festival. With her hot pants, high boots, and voluminous Afro, Hunt, the only woman rock artist booked at the festival, embodied the "Black is Beautiful" concept. As an African American woman working in England's predominantly white, predominantly male rock scene, Hunt developed a tough, hard-driving stage persona and gave what she described as "a boy's performance" in order to fit into the male-dominated arena. As evidenced by this photo, she also accentuated her sex appeal. COURTESY HERITAGE IMAGES.

and a cabaret-style piano number. And that's just side one. Hunt's alto voice jumps from head to chest, from whispers to full-throttle blasts; she tends to miss notes and leaves aside the melisma and ornamentation that would impart a black American gospel sound. She takes a theatrical approach to the material, using different vocal styles and inflections to convey different types of characters and emotions: High, sweet, and ultrafeminine on "No Face, No Name, No Number"; off-key to signal a compromised mental state on "My World Is Empty without You"; a southern accent on "You Ain't Going Nowhere"; and insinuating, whispery, energetic, sultry, and laid-back elsewhere. Unfortunately for Hunt, not enough music fans shared Valentine's view that this experimental blend of psychedelic rock and soul warranted exploration. (Hunt did make an impression on Pauline Black, the mixed-race lead singer of the British 2 Tone ska revival band the Selecter; in her memoir, Black describes Hunt as "my teenage crush" and refers to her as "the mighty Marsha Hunt.")[162] It is not clear whether Betty Davis, the provocative African American funk-rock singer who spent some time in London in the early 1970s, was aware of Hunt, but there are interesting parallels between their charged stage personae and their experimental approach to vocals.[163] Hunt was unable to maintain her tenuous place in the boys' club of rock and roll, but her outspoken comments in press interviews paved the way for her to be hired to host a late-night talk show on the recently founded Capital Radio in 1973. The successful show expanded her public profile, and she developed a reputation as a smart woman who conducted compelling interviews.[164]

By the time she was settling into her new job, Hunt was contending with a separate wave of media visibility after filing a paternity suit against Jagger in June 1973.[165] According to Hunt, Jagger introduced the idea that they have a baby.[166] She acknowledges that "Mick was a notorious womanizer" and claims that she thought of herself as "just another of his fancies," but "talking about having his child made me feel that I was special to him," and she took him seriously when he told her he loved her and assured her that she would be a good mother.[167] The two agreed that Jagger would be an "absent father."[168] The conversation, Hunt reports, took place early in 1970; by November of that year, the baby had arrived. Hunt was twenty-three years old; Jagger was twenty-seven. Marriage had not been part of their discussion, and Hunt felt that they were being "modern," talking "about a shared parenthood in a pragmatic way."[169] Once she was pregnant, however, "the notion of a baby became my total reality as it became Mick's passing fancy."[170] Hunt maintains that by the time their daughter Karis was born, Jagger, who had wanted a boy, had lost interest.

Although he made some early efforts at involvement with the baby (who, according to one associate, "looked remarkably like Mick"), he ultimately turned his attention to his new love, Bianca Perez Morena de Macias, whom he married in May 1971.[171]

In the first years of Karis's life, Hunt and Jagger continued a friendship. Over time, though, Jagger distanced himself from them, refusing any involvement with or financial responsibility for Karis. It was under these circumstances that Hunt filed her suit; it was the only legally binding way to secure financial support for a child born outside of marriage under English law.[172] Jagger was reportedly furious that Hunt went public with her allegations: "I'm not upset for myself," he stated. "It's just that my mother didn't know, and she gets so upset about this sort of publicity. Why did Marsha have to be so bloody silly? It wasn't as though I was going to leave her and Karis to starve."[173] While there's something ludicrous about a man who had cultivated a public image as a sexual libertine worrying about his mother's reaction to his exploits, the paternity case was serious business. Unlike the secret affair, the paternity case was public—and unpleasant. "When it hit the newspapers it stank," Hunt recalled. "As no one had been privy to our friendship, the story was reported as though I suddenly appeared with a two-and-a-half-year-old to accuse a pop idol of paternity. . . . There was no doubt that the paternity suit affected how people perceived me."[174] In Hunt's estimation, public opinion was against her. In contrast to groupies whose connections to rock stars conferred an elevated status, Hunt's liaison with Jagger made her a pariah. "I saw no end to the problems that had been created in England through the paternity suit," she recalled. "I went from being tagged 'the girl from *Hair*' to 'the girl who sued Mick Jagger.'"[175] Comments Jagger made to the press at the time called Hunt's integrity into question. When asked about her in 1978, he told a reporter for the Los Angeles–based music news magazine *Soul*, "She's just a hustler, just out for publicity. Everytime [sic] she comes to a low point and she can't be bothered to get any work, she drags me around. She never even gives me a call to say, 'Please Mick, I want some money.' I have no idea if that child is mine or not."[176]

Hunt won her case in January of 1979, when a Los Angeles Superior Court judge ruled that Jagger was the father of Karis and oversaw the "amicable" settlement between the ex-lovers.[177] A few years later, in 1984, Jagger "made a statutory declaration to the Registrar-General in London, where a new birth certificate was entered. By then Jagger, though not having custody, bore sole financial responsibility for the child."[178] In the ensuing years, Jagger grew closer to Karis, legally, financially, and personally. He paid for her education at a private secondary school and at Yale University, and employed her in the Rolling Stones' infrastructure as a researcher on the retrospective video *25×5* in 1990. Karis, in turn, bonded with Jagger's other children.[179] Jade, Jagger's daughter with Bianca, was maid of honor at her wedding, which both Hunt and Jagger attended.[180] Both parents were with Karis at the hospital when she gave birth to her daughter.[181]

Marsha Hunt lived a singular rock and roll life, even though her lack of desired black female vocal style made it difficult for her to sustain a recording career. She turned, instead, to other pursuits that included modeling; acting in film, theater, and television; hosting a radio show; and, in the 1980s, pursuing a career as a writer, starting with the publication of her memoir in 1986. She has since published novels, a family history, and a second memoir chronicling her battle with breast cancer.[182] Hunt turned the cultural capital she accrued as a rock and roll insider into economic capital by publishing *Real Life,* an autobiographical narrative that she could sell. In late 2012, facing financial difficulties, Hunt tapped the material evidence of her relationship with Jagger, putting up for auction ten of the love letters he wrote to her when he was in Australia filming *Ned Kelly* in the summer of 1969.[183] A private collector bought them for approximately $300,000.[184]

Hunt is different from female rock fans and groupies, categories of women who are often trivialized in spite of their centrality to the rock scene, but the position she occupies is similar. Asserting her independent spirit in her memoir, she states, "I never envisioned myself as the sort of girl who would dangle from a man's coat sleeve or find any gratification in being Mr. Somebody's wife."[185] In light of this comment, it is ironic that Hunt is best known for being the mother of a very famous man's child. Still, the sum of her colorful and varied life is greater than that single, notable fact. Aware of this, Hunt took control of her story and represented herself in print, writing herself into rock and roll history on her own terms.

Stellar Gypsy

Mick Jagger has never confirmed whom he had in mind when composing "Brown Sugar," but conventional wisdom has held that Claudia Lennear was the inspiration for the song. She and Jagger met when she was performing as an Ikette during the Ike and Tina Turner Revue's 1969 tour of England. The two began an affair that lasted for a few years. Along with her good looks and her professional connections to high-profile rock musicians such as George Harrison, Joe Cocker, and Leon Russell, Lennear's assumed connection to "Brown Sugar" and her relationship with Jagger received comment in press coverage about her career, competing with discussions of her musical sound and creative vision. The Warner Brothers press release for her album, for example, has seven boldface subheads, one of which is "Brown Sugar."[186] Beyond this, the mythologized sexual enticements of black women that the song "Brown Sugar" extols are embedded in coverage that almost without fail refers to her sex appeal. Substantial professional connections and rock vocal chops allowed Lennear to achieve some success in her career, but as an attractive black woman in the early seventies rock scene, she was confined to a limited professional and cultural space.

Lennear was born in Providence, Rhode Island, and moved to Pomona, California, when she was in her teens.[187] She loved languages and studied Spanish, French, and German in the hope of becoming an interpreter at the United Nations. The plan was derailed as she focused more energy on music and started singing lead in a local R&B cover group called the Superbs.[188] In 1967, Ike and Tina Turner hired her to join their backing vocal group; she was twenty-one years old.[189] Lennear was an Ikette from 1967 to 1969. "It was my first experience with the Army," she quipped about her time with the legendarily demanding outfit.[190] Less than two weeks after departing the Ikettes, she met Joe Cocker and Leon Russell and was brought into their fold, joining the 1970 *Mad Dogs and Englishmen* tour and picking up the nickname *Stellar Gypsy*.[191] For two months of mostly one-nighters, Lennear traveled as a member of this rock version of a soul revue, relishing "the musical and choreographic freedom that the tight steps and written-out singing parts had denied her with the Ikettes."[192] The difference is emblematic of the contrasting aesthetic systems that governed rhythm and blues and rock at the end of the 1960s. Lennear, who had grown up with the former, found herself embracing the latter. Members of the rock scene, in turn, embraced Lennear in part for her ability to bring elements of the rhythm and blues sound—that desired audible blackness—to the rock field. Dave Mason, Delaney & Bonnie, Freddie King, Al Kooper, Humble Pie, Boz Scaggs, Leon Russell, José Feliciano, Taj Mahal, Stephen Stills, and Nigel Olsson invited her to sing background on their recordings.[193] Lennear had a higher profile than most background vocalists, a consequence of her appearances in two rock concert films: *Mad Dogs and Englishmen* (1971), the documentary of Cocker's 1970 tour, and *The Concert for Bangladesh* (1972), a film of the August 1971 concert featuring ex-Beatle George Harrison, Indian sitar maestro Ravi Shankar, and a host of rock luminaries performing to raise awareness about the refugee crisis in the newly established South Asian nation.

By 1972, Lennear had secured a recording contract with Warner Brothers and was preparing her first solo album. Lennear had worked with the Ike and Tina Turner Revue during the time that the Turners started to add rock covers to their repertoire; this, coupled with her connections to key figures in the rock scene, gave her both rock and R&B credibility.[194] The label teamed Lennear with two producers: British songwriter Ian Samwell, who had produced the hit "A Horse with No Name" for the band America, represented rock; while Allen Toussaint, the famed New Orleans–based writer and producer, represented R&B. The goal was to make the most of her strong ties to the two interconnected music genres, but there was a challenge built into the project. By the early 1970s, rock and R&B were marketed as two separate musical fields. Lennear, with one foot in rock and one foot in R&B, occupied a space betwixt and between the genres. She struggled to override the genre, race, and gender rules that dominated the industry, but vocal chops, a seasoned production team, and the kind of It Girl status that garnered a photo spread in the July 1974 issue of *Playboy* and coverage in *Rolling Stone* were not enough to bridge the gap (see figure 5.3). In fact, the format of her 1973 release *Phew!*, with an A-side of rock and a B-side of R&B, reproduced it.[195]

The rock side offers a blast of electrified blues and boogie, and Lennear delivers her vocals with confident cool. She covers two Ron Davies tunes: "Sing with the Children" and "It Ain't Easy," which her sometime boyfriend David Bowie had included on *Ziggy Stardust* the year before. She sings blues man Furry Lewis's song "Casey Jones" with a pronounced southern accent and performs two original numbers, "Not at All," which she cowrote with Ian Samwell, and "Sister Angela," her own composition. "Not at All" gained attention because some commentators heard in it a message to Mick Jagger: "Did you think I'd go around singing the blues because you're on the wanted list and I'm here all alone?" she sings. The song's title is her answer to the question. Here and across the side, the energy level is high with guitar-centered arrangements providing the backdrop for her gritty vocals. Lennear rocks with a heavy measure of swagger, and she makes interesting vocal choices along the way, pushing her voice into a more straining tone, allowing it to break, laying back, hesitating, improvising, and providing her own background fills. "I wanted the raunchy, rock and roll thing," she told *Rolling Stone* reporter Ben Fong-Torres in an interview soon after the album's release.[196] "Sister Angela," Lennear's

FIGURE 5.3 This photo of Claudia Lennear accompanied a one-page *Rolling Stone* profile that ran in April 1973, when she was promoting her debut album *Phew!* © NEAL PRESTON.

song for the black revolutionary activist and intellectual Angela Davis, offers an African American woman's public commentary on Davis's role in the radical politics of the day and a critique of her imprisonment on suspicion of supplying the gun used to shoot a judge and police officer. "Alabama angel deserves freedom's turn and she'll give them hell until they learn," Lennear declares against a mid-tempo musical setting that placed percussion alongside drums and an organ solo.[197] In the only song she wrote on her own, Lennear tackled the politics of black liberation and black women's activism. Clearly, she took seriously the notion that one could address "important" subjects in rock.

In contrast, the second side of her album emphasizes the romance and party lyrics that dominated pop music. Produced and written by Allen Toussaint, it is the "black" side as black music was conceptualized at the time, and features soul showcase instrumentation—a horn section, organ and piano, a wacka-wacka rhythm guitar, background vocals riding over the syncopated funk rhythms—and lyrics about dancing and love.[198] The five tracks aligned with the rhythm and blues/soul/funk templates that African American artists were expected to fill during the early 1970s, even though a number of white rock bands were also deploying these sounds.[199] Lennear's vocals reverberate against a brash, big band sound, but she holds her own as she tries to live up to the declaration of one of her song titles: "Everything I Do Gonna Be Funky." In spite of the attention to the two different album sides in the press, Lennear's vocal approach is consistent across all of the tracks. On *Phew!* she reaches down into a gravelly tone for some low notes and shoots up to reach occasional high head notes, although most of her singing is in the alto range. She lets us hear the breath in her voice as she builds a song, boosting the energy and increasing the sense of excitement. Lennear sings some clear and pretty notes, but most of her vocals have the textured grit associated with rock and soul singing.

Phew! was at once daring and conservative, as if the producers and the label did not quite have the courage of the convictions that led them to put a black woman in a rock setting in the first place. They ended up tempering that interesting move with the more familiar trappings of R&B so that she would make sonic and social sense. The decision to embrace what was perceived as Lennear's musical duality shaped the writing and production of *Phew!* and was the centerpiece of the album's marketing campaign. The one-page Warner Brothers press release for the album included the following text under a section headed "Totally Schizophrenic":

> Although [Lennear] calls it a "totally schizophrenic album," it essentially breaks down into two distinct experimental directions. Side One is reelin' and a rockin' clearly showing the influences of both the Rolling Stones and the Turners. . . . The flip side was written and arranged entirely by Allen Toussaint. It is the album's "black" half and it fairly reeks of wah-wah pedal and a heavy dose of good, old funk.[200]

The press release and the album itself accept the logic that "black" and "white" music are separate entities whose integration has to be explained. Lennear similarly acknowledged and accounted for the unexpected racial mix of her musical sound. "At the beginning I was pretty much into rhythm and blues because that was what I was around the most," Lennear told an interviewer in

1974. "But now if you look at my record collection, it's just one big extreme, just like me. I listen to everything. And my music isn't just rhythm and blues. It's rock, too."[201] Lennear's characterization of her genre-crossing musical taste as "one big extreme" is an indication of how entrenched assumptions about musical segregation were, even in the face of sonic and social evidence of musical integration. Traversing music's racialized boundaries was perceived as unusual when enacted by a black artist, but it was the norm for Duane Allman, Eric Burdon, Joe Cocker, Bob Dylan, John Fogerty, Janis Joplin, and a host of other white artists who built their sound on cross-racial musicality. Try to imagine Mick Jagger or any of his white rock compatriots characterizing their tastes as "extreme" rather than "broad" and "open-minded."

In his review of *Phew!*, *Rolling Stone* writer Stephen Holden emphasized the album's duality: "The daring conception behind *Phew* was that it be a truly 'two-sided' album, directed toward different but overlapping audiences, one rock, the other R&B."[202] Enthusiastic about the experiment, Holden wrote about the album in glowing terms: "*Phew* is a tour de force from start to finish, a truly auspicious debut. Lennear's vocal flexibility and energy are staggering. Her recorded personality, though not intimate, is irrepressibly sexy, her professionalism almost frighteningly intact."[203] But *Phew!* did not catch on with the record-buying public, and the record slipped between the two overlapping contingents, never gaining a significant audience. A year after its release, rock journalist Katherine Orloff, who interviewed Lennear for her 1974 book *Rock 'n' Roll Woman*, outlined what she saw as the album's limitations:

> The problems with the first album were mainly production problems, too much chaotic noise, and not enough direction. It also tried to be all things to all people, one side having a rock orientation, the other rhythm and blues. As a result, Claudia is deprived of a strong musical identity. Confusion naturally exists due to the fact that black women are ordinarily thought of as soul singers, but Claudia has a rock audience.[204]

As Orloff observes, the major issue was the ways race, gender, and genre locked African American women into a limited musical space. By 1974, the black soul/white rock split had become naturalized; a black woman's engagement with rock had to be explained and justified—and even given a pop-psychology diagnosis as schizophrenic! It also had to be tempered by some demonstrated connection to what was understood as appropriate black musical practice. No one seemed to fathom a way to fuse rock and soul (Sly and the Family Stone might have been a good model) or to suggest that Lennear could just be a rocker and aim for that audience. Why did she have to have a "black sound"? Why not acknowledge that rock itself *was* a "black sound"? Lennear was disappointed with *Phew!*, and she expressed her dissatisfaction in public. "I wasn't happy with my first album at all," she said in 1974. "I just knew that I wasn't being guided properly and what I felt about it wasn't being taken into consideration. I was having a hard time being heard."[205] Assessing the album nearly forty years after its release, she observed: "It was too far outside the box for its time. . . . In those days, everything fit a certain square. Warner Bros. had all the right elements in place and the album *should have* taken off but for whatever reason it did not."[206] Lennear is a formidable rock singer, and it is never possible to determine unequivocally the reason a recording does not take off commercially. However, given the white male–dominated context of rock at the time, Lennear's black female vocal presence as lead singer—she was stepping out of the acceptable background role into the authoritative center of attention—might have been disconcerting or unwelcome to some rock listeners invested in the primacy of white men in rock. Similarly, the strong presence of a rock sound—especially the foregrounded, sometimes distorted guitars—might have alienated soul and rhythm and blues fans. There does not seem to have been enough of an audience that was up to the apparent challenge of listening to the entire album, the rock side and the R&B side, in an integrated way, against the segregation that was shaping the recording industry in the 1970s.

The challenges of race and gender that were part of her album's production and promotion also surfaced in Lennear's concert performances. Reviews of Lennear's live shows from this period indicate that she emphasized her sex appeal to spice up the proceedings, changing clothes on stage behind a screen and removing some of them before the eyes of the audience.[207] "Claudia Lennear strong in visual appeal wails up a storm as she delivers blues and rock in a most active set," *Variety* reported. "Miss Lennear puts on a show including sexy dancing and a strip number."[208] A *Billboard* review of a performance soon after her album's release highlighted what the reviewer deemed inadequate attention to musical quality:

> Claudia Lennear is an artist, at this point, better seen than heard. Wearing a transparent green spangled top with few spangles, the black bombshell energetically gyrated her way through tunes from her Warner Bros. album, aptly titled, "Phew!" A bit more discipline and attention to her singing (her vocals for the most part were drowned out by her band) are needed before this situation can be reversed for this obviously talented lady.[209]

Lennear's efforts to establish herself as a solo artist also raised the question of whether background singers could hold the center stage. A reviewer commenting on Claudia Lennear's performance as opening act for Blue Öyster Cult minced no words in diagnosing the problem, calling her "a powerful vocalist who simply lacks the presence and individuality that marks a solid solo performer."[210] Lennear herself discussed the challenge of making the transition from being a member of Cocker's background group to being the headliner: "It's a whole different feeling being in the spotlight instead of hidden in a chorus of nine people. I like it, but I'm just beginning to discover who the real Claudia Lennear is, myself."[211]

As the reviews of her solo performances indicate, Lennear created a sexy persona that met the expectations that audience members who connected her to the song "Brown Sugar" were presumed to have. Highlighting her "black bombshell" qualities by wearing and stripping off revealing outfits, Lennear embodied the sexuality that is at the heart of both rock and roll and stereotypes of black womanhood. Performing Brown Sugar—not the Rolling Stones' song, but the ideas that inform it—was a way for Lennear to capture audience and media attention. Her appearance in the August 1974 issue of *Playboy* was part of this process. In fact, the editors of the magazine approached her after seeing her live act and deciding "that we just had to get some pictures of her into the magazine. With her clothes off naturally."[212] The article is titled "Brown Sugar," naturally; it includes references to her relationship with Mick Jagger and calls her "a rock singer of unbounded spirit and as much pedigree as one could ask for."[213] The five pages she commanded include the requisite nudes (*Playboy*'s standard was for models to be unclothed from the waist up) and an article that lists the high points of her career, reports her misgivings about *Phew!*, outlines her plan for her next album "to convey more of her complex inner self," and notes her foray into acting in the 1974 film *Thunderbolt and Lightfoot*, where she appeared in a scene with Clint Eastwood.[214] The piece concludes with the observation, "Claudia Lennear isn't at all sure who she is. . . . But if her identity is in question—or in flux—she's not going to worry about it."[215] The perception that Lennear lacked self-knowledge developed from the statements she made to the press, but also from the mixed character of the music on her album and the disconnect between her identity as an African American woman and her engagement with rock.

By the time of her 1974 appearance in *Playboy*, Lennear's time in the limelight was just about over. The second album she had started to work on never materialized, and she returned to doing background vocals, a more reliable and less onerous way for her to provide a stable income to support her young daughter than the pursuit of a solo singing career.[216] At the height of the classic rock era, Lennear took advantage of her position as a talented and beautiful black woman vocalist in the rock scene. She seized opportunities, but her career stalled at the intersection of race, gender, and genre. In the early 1980s, when background session work started to dry up, Lennear returned to her first love—languages—and got the training to teach them.[217] When she was interviewed for *Twenty Feet from Stardom*, the 2013 documentary on background vocalists, Lennear was teaching Spanish full-time at Mt. San Antonio College in Walnut, California.[218] Lennear's reinvention differed from that of Marsha Hunt. The Stellar Gypsy did not rely on her prior rock connections and identity to make her way. "I felt that I had just run my course," she said in a 2013 interview.[219] She moved on from the opportunities and limitations that the association with "Brown Sugar" offered and entered an entirely different milieu, one that did not demand a constant reckoning with the mythologies of black women's bodies and voices.

Brown Sugar, Negotiated

In a 1973 reflection on the challenges of establishing a successful recording career, Marsha Hunt observed, "Women in pop are in much the same situation as blacks have been. You've got to slip in through the side door and once you're in, then do your damage. But you're kidding yourself if you think you're going to walk in through the front door on your own terms because the world's been going too long on somebody else's terms."[220] Hunt had been intent on finding a way into rock's mainstream, but in spite of her best efforts, the entrance through even the side door provided only limited opportunities, and the career she dreamed of did not take off. Still, Hunt can claim a set of experiences as a scene-maker, model, performer, and paramour that define her as a rock and roll figure, even though her identity as an African American woman mitigates against that categorization. In fact, her race, gender, and national identity give her rock and roll experience its particular and fascinating shape. Devon Wilson and Claudia Lennear also slipped in through the rock scene's side entrances. Wilson did not live long enough to manage her image in the way that Hunt has done, but the fact that she is still mentioned alongside the names of Hendrix and Jagger is a measure of her impact. Lennear gave up on her efforts to forge a career as a solo artist and ceded her space in the counterculture, but she left behind recordings as a background vocalist and solo artist that encapsulate her experience of the challenges and expressive possibilities of the rock milieu.

In the late 1960s and early 1970s, Devon Wilson, Marsha Hunt, and Claudia Lennear crafted their lives through a compulsory dialogue with "Brown Sugar," a song and a stereotype that black women did not create, but that shadows black women in rock and roll. All three women participated, in public and private ways, with the highest echelons of rock, their brown-skinned beauty conferring both access and notoriety as they negotiated the myth and mystique of Brown Sugar. The stories I have told in this chapter show how three flesh-and-blood African American women engaged this two-dimensional image—capitulating to it, challenging it, and rewriting it—while fashioning their unconventional lives. Their experiences and their stories, shaped by the dynamics of race, gender, and genre that operated in the late 1960s and early 1970s rock scene, are an inextricable if underreported part of the history of African American women and the history of rock and roll.

SIX / The Revolutionary Sisterhood of Labelle

Our music progressed from the pretty love songs to the gutsy hard-hitting love songs with a realistic message. We never sing the same song the same way and nothing that we do onstage is rehearsed. / **SARAH DASH**

We were doing what was considered the best format for black female singers in the Sixties. What we're doing today is like the other side of the moon, as far as the two eras are concerned. We're dealing with today's problems and today's music. / **NONA HENDRYX**

At first I wasn't going for it . . . I loved where we were, and I still do. But I *respect* Labelle more. It says something definite, and there's no other group like Labelle. There were many others like the Bluebelles. / **PATTI LABELLE**

Sitting at a viewing station at the British Film Institute's London offices on a rainy morning in May 2013, I traveled back to March 1975 at the press of a video playback button. The performance, filmed before a live audience for BBC Television and calibrated for a television half-hour, is shorter than a typical concert set, but it offers a glimpse of the energetic artistry of Sarah Dash, Nona Hendryx, and Patti LaBelle, the African American vocal trio known as Labelle.[1] The set is mostly material from their album *Nightbirds*, including "Lady Marmalade," the 1975 single that won them Top 40 success, and songs like "Are You Lonely?," "Space Children," and "(Can I Speak to You before You Go to) Hollywood?" The women are wearing the form-fitting, shiny silver costumes that make them look like they've rocketed down to earth in space-age haute couture, Afro-futuristic long before the term existed. Patti, the lead singer, wears thigh-high silver platform boots and a silver jacket whose high collar frames her head. There are feathers on her shoulders, and a tail hangs down from the jacket's hem. Nona, who sings the low parts and writes many of the group's songs, sports silver tights, silver platforms, and a silver jacket with enormous epaulets. Sarah, who sings the high parts, wears a silver bikini top and a long-sleeved blouse with arm-exposing cutaways, short shorts, and silver platform sandals. All three augment standard eye shadow, blush, and lipstick with costume jewels pasted along their cheekbones and eyebrows. During the musical breaks, the threesome dance nonchoreographed steps as if they were partying at a club, then gather around a single microphone to sing the next phrases. Backed by an all-male band consisting of keyboards, guitar, bass, drums, and percussion, Nona plays tambourine; Sarah shakes sleigh bells; and Patti jumps up and down in place, fluttering her hands and leaning forward to emphasize a lyric.[2] At times, they hold one another's hands. At times, they separate. Even as their bond is clear, each woman comes across as an individual.

Watching the video makes me wish that I could have seen Labelle perform back in the day. The October 6, 1974, concert at New York's Metropolitan Opera House would have been the show to attend, if only for the bragging rights. Two other rock acts—the Who and the singer-songwriter Melanie— had played there, but Labelle was the first African American rock group to appear at the nation's premier classical music venue.[3] For women who had spent the first years of their career traveling by station wagon to gigs at Elks' Lodges, roller rinks, firehouses, and the Chitlin Circuit's network of black theaters, a date at the Metropolitan Opera was a major advance and the culmination of a series of successful, high-profile shows.[4] As Sarah Dash explained to me when I interviewed her in 2014, "We built up such an audience playing Town Hall and then we did Carnegie Hall. We had no hit record, but we had a great following in New York and they were always looking for the next big concert or the next best thing or the next thing to do. And that was the Metropolitan Opera House."[5] The concert was the first of the group's fall tour and was designed to garner attention. Vicki Wickham, Labelle's manager, had ties to the Who's management, and the connection might have given her both the concept and the contacts to mount the sold-out show.[6] The pièce de résistance was the request, included in advertisements for the concert, that concertgoers "wear something silver."[7] Labelle's fans complied, and the Opera House was packed with a sparkling audience, a mix, as one reporter catalogued it, "consisting of gay men in makeup, wigs, and beards sprinkled with glitter, 'golden-oldies' fans who remembered them from their first musical existence, soul freaks, and many, many disco cultists."[8] Describing the scene, Patti LaBelle recalled, "People paraded up the Met's red-carpeted white-marble stairs wearing silver from head to toe. Silver hats, silver skullcaps, silver eyelashes, silver Afros, silver capes, silver jumpsuits, silver body paint, silver Christmas tinsel, silver studs spelling out 'Labelle.' I even saw a silver jockstrap."[9] Thus was the tradition of dressing up when going to see Labelle established.[10]

To entertain this primed audience, the group used stagecraft worthy of an opera. A reporter recounted: "Patti is *lowered* to the stage under hundreds of pounds of black and orange feathers. Nona and Sarah, earthbound, glisten in silvery movements. . . . Their voices penetrate the air like the cries of the Phoenix. The Met is their appropriate launch site."[11] On stage Labelle presented a cocktail of gospel revival intensity, the excess of rock and roll, and funk grooves with a high level of theatricality. The cumulative effect was what one critic called "an all-round musical and visual spectacular."[12] At Labelle's height, the women were tagged as "the most energetic, innovative, and controversial Black females in the music industry."[13] Virtuosic singers and entertainers, Patti LaBelle (b. Patricia Holte, May 24, 1944), Nona Hendryx (b. October 9, 1944), and Sarah Dash (b. August 18, 1945) fomented a musical revolution in the 1970s, bringing a black feminist practice to popular music. An examination of Labelle's music and the responses the group elicited provides an opportunity to consider the ways the intersection of race, gender, and genre shaped the experiences of African American women in rock during the 1970s. The trio communicated in the musical and visual codes of early seventies rock. They did so, according to Patti LaBelle, to signal their desire to be understood as "a female version of the Rolling Stones, the bad girls of rock. Not bad as in evil—bad as in hot, happening, cutting edge."[14] Labelle capitalized on the connections between rhythm and blues, soul, and rock and roll, building on the African American sonic and performance traditions that they had grown up with. In collaboration with their manager Vicki Wickham (b. 1939), the women of Labelle projected themselves into rock, using a musical practice that theorized and responded to their position as black women working in the American recording industry during the 1970s.

LaBelle, Hendryx, and Dash were making music at a time when fascination with the gospel-inspired vocal sound of African American women led a broad cross section of rock artists to include black women vocalists on their recordings as background singers. Labelle took this process to a logical, if unexpected, conclusion by bringing black women's voices and perspectives center stage. The shift marked a return to the early sixties, when black women were at the center of girl group music. But Labelle, veterans of the girl group movement, made conceptual, musical, and business decisions that ensured a level of autonomy that they had been denied when they performed as Patti La-Belle and the Bluebelles. Refusing to be hemmed in by dominant expectations for African American women's musical performance, the women rejected the roles of either producer-reliant girl group artists or background vocal help-mates for rock bands that characterized black women's professional options in the recording industry in the 1960s and 1970s. Instead, Labelle created an artistic agenda organized around self-determination and self-expression. As feminist historian Alice Echols has observed, "Labelle was about nothing less than claiming the same privileged turf—the creative freedom, individuality, sexual forthrightness, and right of reinvention—so effortlessly occupied by male rockers."[15] The response to Labelle's genre-blending musical sound and explosive performance style, chronicled and analyzed in the press the group received, reveals how entrenched the race, gender, and genre codes were in the field of rock, and how audacious the women of Labelle were in disrupting them.

From the Bluebelles to Labelle

In 1959, Patsy Holte and her friend Cindy Birdsong formed a doo-wop group called the Ordettes in their hometown of Philadelphia.[16] Meanwhile, in Trenton, New Jersey, friends Sarah Dash and Nona Hendryx sang in the Del Capris. For these young women, "Singing in church was good," Dash told me, "but some of us who were in the church decided we were going to start a group" in order to sing the secular songs that dominated pop radio.[17] The two vocal groups worked with an artist manager who merged and shifted personnel to come up with a quartet comprising Holte, Birdsong, Dash, and Hendryx. The girls began touring, dropping out of high school to pursue show business careers. Signed to the Philadelphia-based Bluebelle Records Company, the group became the Bluebelles, and Patsy Holte became Patti LaBelle, renamed by the label owner, who thought "the beautiful" in French would be a good name for the group's lead singer (see figure 6.1).[18] Patti LaBelle and the Bluebelles went on *American Bandstand* in support of their hit, "I Sold

FIGURE 6.1 In this mid-1960s publicity photo, Patti LaBelle and the Bluebelles followed the prevailing rules of girl group style: identical gowns, stylish hairdos, and carefully applied make up. Their polished, matching style signaled their group identity and social respectability. Working with their new manager Vicki Wickham in the 1970s, the women abandoned the visual and sonic trappings of the girl group era, blasting into the new decade with a fresh look, sound, and attitude that emphasized the individual voices and personalities of each member of the group. Clockwise from top: Sarah Dash, Patti LaBelle, Nona Hendryx, and Cindy Birdsong. COURTESY RUDY CALVO COLLECTION/CACHE AGENCY.

My Heart to the Junkman" in 1962; made it into the Top 40 with "Down the Aisle" in 1963; and cut versions of "You'll Never Walk Alone" (1964), "Danny Boy" (1964), and "Over the Rainbow" (1965).[19] Excellent live performers, they played the nation's top African American venues and won the title, "the Sweethearts of the Apollo" in recognition of their success at that venerable theater.

The Bluebelles toured with James Brown in 1962, the Rolling Stones in 1965, and Otis Redding in 1966, the same year the group secured a contract with Atlantic Records.[20] Atlantic sent the Bluebelles to England that year, and they made a splash on the youth-oriented pop music program *Ready, Steady, Go.*[21] The show's producer, Vicki Wickham, was so impressed with the women's performance and the audience response to it that she booked them onto the show again the following week, an unprecedented move.[22] Wickham and the Bluebelles became friends, and by the end of the decade, the singers called on her for professional help.[23] Patti LaBelle and the Bluebelles were struggling. Cindy Birdsong had left in 1967 to join the Supremes, following Diana Ross's departure from the group. Atlantic had dropped them from their contract, and they had concerns about the integrity of their manager.[24] Beyond these challenges, they faced a larger problem: soul music and hard rock had supplanted the girl group sound that the Bluebelles were associated with, and they were finding themselves booked onto golden oldies shows, even though they were barely out of their teens.[25] Furthermore, the context of live performance was changing: "People were doing concerts as opposed to working all day in a theater like the Brooklyn Fox or the Apollo," Dash explained to me, and rock acts were presenting their shows at larger and larger venues and in outdoor festivals.[26] They knew Wickham understood the recording industry through her work at both *Ready, Steady, Go* and the rock label Track Records, and, since they trusted her, they asked her to manage them.[27] Hesitant at first, Wickham agreed to come on board on the condition that the Bluebelles undergo a complete reinvention. The foursome set up shop in London and began working out the details of a revamp that linked the group to the rock culture of the new decade through sonic, visual, and lyrical cues.

Wickham's concept was to abandon the trappings of the 1960s girl group era and blast into the 1970s with a fresh look, sound, and attitude. There would be no matching outfits, no wigs, no songs about boys, and no covers of old chestnuts like "Over the Rainbow."[28] The group would emphasize individual voices and personalities in vocals, clothing, and onstage style. Most importantly, they would sing about the things that mattered to liberated young women at the dawn of the new decade. Describing Wickham's concept, LaBelle explained,

"Hers was a vision of women who would never shy away from anything, no matter how controversial."[29] The transformation the women were making was similar to that of other 1960s era artists such as Stevie Wonder, Marvin Gaye, and George Clinton, who each tapped into the experimental ethos of the counterculture as they developed unique creative statements in the 1970s. The changes Wickham proposed grew out of her conviction that Labelle could participate in rock music and rock culture as forward-thinking black women. "Our music would be political, progressive, passionate," LaBelle explained in her autobiography. "Vicki saw us as Labelle, three black women singing about racism, sexism, and eroticism. . . . For Vicki, it wasn't about keeping up with The Supremes. She wanted us to be pacesetters, pioneers. She wanted Sarah, Nona, and me to change the face and future of women in rock music."[30] A rarity as a woman working on the business side of the recording industry, Wickham was a manager in the tradition of the Beatles' Brian Epstein and the Rolling Stones' Andrew Loog Oldham, both of whom shaped the image of the groups they managed. She collaborated with the trio on the changes, and the women had far more say about the direction of their career than during their Bluebelles days. "We were partners with our manager," Dash explained. "It was the four of us."[31] This white British/black American alliance among the four women was unusual for its time and, Dash assured me, advantageous. "It worked in our favor because everyone was coming off the British Invasion," Dash said. "Having a British manager was so unique and different. Her accent worked for us. She was able to open a lot of doors. She had a great Rolodex because she brought groups on to her show, so she had contacts with record companies and what have you."[32]

Wickham secured a Track Records contract for the group and suggested the shorter name that signaled a shift in creative gears.[33] While maintaining a connection to the past, the new name made Dash and Hendryx seem more like equal partners rather than adjuncts to Patti LaBelle, a positioning that was underscored by the fact that in press interviews no one acted as group spokesperson. After careful thought, they decided not to replace Birdsong. "We realized," LaBelle stated, "that there was never a four-part harmony in our group. There was always three-part harmony. Cindy had been doubling up a note so we really didn't need another voice. And we found our own sound with three voices."[34] And, quipped Hendryx, "We got more money as three."[35] The change was also sartorial. Wickham wanted the group to dress in a way that aligned them with the rock culture. "She wanted us to imitate the scruffy, don't-give-a-damn look of white rock groups," Patti

LaBelle explained.[36] They dispensed with the gowns that women wore on the black concert circuit and dressed down in jeans, sweaters, vests, and boots on album covers and on stage.[37] "Vicki always went for the things that people weren't doing to bring us attention," Dash told me. "We were the first females *not* to wear the same gown, not to wear the same wig. You know, we stepped out of that tradition. And that was not an easy thing for record [label] people to deal with."[38]

The most important way the women signaled their connection to rock was through their music. Their first recording as Labelle was with white American singer-songwriter Laura Nyro on *Gonna Take a Miracle* (1971), a loving tribute to the girl group and doo-wop era they were leaving behind. A rare musical collaboration between black and white women, the album "helped heighten awareness among Nyro's own hip cross-cultural audience" of Labelle.[39] On subsequent recordings, Labelle made it clear that they had moved on to a contemporary sound. One way they accomplished this was through the songs they chose to cover. On their first three albums, they featured songs first recorded by the Rolling Stones, the Who, Carole King, and Cat Stevens, linking them to hard rock (the Stones and the Who) and soft rock (King and Stevens, whose "Moonshadow" was the title cut of the group's second album). They also affirmed their connection to progressive black singer-songwriters by featuring songs by Stevie Wonder and Gil Scott-Heron on their early releases; in concert they performed "Four Women" by Nina Simone. The arrangement of the material reflected Labelle's investment in linking British hard rock and adventurous black American popular music. For example, as one critic observed:

> Their apocalyptic reinterpretation of Speedy Keene's "Something in the Air" [a number one single in England in 1969, performed by Thunderclap Newman, a Track Records rock band] extended into a medley via a dramatic chanted poem, "The Revolution Will Not Be Televised" [by Gil Scott-Heron, a Black Arts poet and musician], which would have done even the radically militant Art Ensemble of Chicago proud.[40]

Both songs feature the idea that political change is imminent, establishing Labelle's interest in socially relevant subjects. When performing these covers, the women took ownership of the songs, altering lyrics when necessary. Alice Echols points out that when singing Scott-Heron's composition, they deleted "the demeaning reference to 'hairy-armed women liberationists,'" refusing to fall in with the then-common black nationalist critique of feminism as white women's business; instead, they "gave voice to the varieties of feminism alive at the time."[41]

Covers were fine, but the rock community valued artists who wrote the material they performed. Responding to this climate, Wickham urged the women to take up songwriting.[42] Patti LaBelle cowrote two of the tracks on Labelle's debut album, and Sarah Dash contributed "Peace with Yourself" to *Moon Shadow*, their second release. It was Nona Hendryx, though, who emerged as the group's primary songwriter, providing the words and music for the bulk of the group's recordings. She engaged a wide range of subject matter and wrote songs that referenced environmental issues, personal growth, and the state of the world. One critic observed that the group expressed an ethic that "has something to do with outer space, inner space, political space, and sexual space."[43] Unlike some of her rock contemporaries, Hendryx did not write obscure lyrics. "Hendryx's writing has no use for double entendre or the studied attempt at opacity," one critic noted. "'Goin' on a Holiday,' 'Open Up Your Heart,' and 'Last Dance' seem inspired by rock lyric trends uncharacteristic of black music—boredom, the puzzled acceptance of rejection, the unwillingness to act on any but one's own terms."[44] Hendryx's compositions allowed vocal experimentation, and her "light-beginning-dramatic-crescendo format" became a signature of the group.[45] Much of Labelle's music was danceable, and the women danced when they performed on stage, but their music had a message. Hendryx's lyrics conveyed a progressive politics of gender and sexuality. As one critic pointed out, "Nearly all [Hendryx's] words can be sung outside of any sexist regulation—male or female—and this is what gives her songs both vigor and variable possibilities for personal application."[46] The lyrics of Labelle's sex-positive songs such as "Morning Much Better" (1971), "Touch Me All Over" (1972), "You Turn Me On" (1974), and "Going Down Makes Me Shiver" (1976) celebrated the pleasures of sexuality in forthright terms and could be spoken from any gender position or sexual identity without altering pronouns, offering an open-endedness that surely contributed to the group's appeal among gay men and lesbians.

The inclusion of subject matter that addressed social and political concerns connected the group to the artistic experiments associated with rock and the work of Marvin Gaye, Curtis Mayfield, and Stevie Wonder—African American musicians known for their socially engaged songs. "Most of my material is composed of things that are constantly on my mind," Hendryx stated in a 1975 interview. "I can't get away from them. It all stems from when I was born, where I was reared. I came from a ghetto, a real one—Trenton. I lived hard, and I can't forget it."[47] The song "Sunday's News" (1972), for example, considers the dispiriting effect of reading about current affairs including "crime, race, despair / pollution in the air" and, written at the time of the Vietnam War, "our bombs bursting in air."[48] "What Can I Do for You" (1974) opens with the statement, "People want truth / Or nothing at all / People want sincerity / And nothing false."[49] These lines would have been meaningful at any time, but they took on heightened significance in the era of the Watergate scandal and the federal investigation of President Richard Nixon. "Nightbirds," the title track of Labelle's most successful album, celebrated unconventionality and the risks of celebrity. It was a tribute to Janis Joplin, but also, Hendryx explained, to "people like her such as Billie Holiday, Judy Garland, and Jimi Hendrix, who die tragically and who, to me, are essentially night people."[50] In keeping with the rock scene's emergent emphasis on albums as artistic works, Labelle recorded songs that were not obviously commercial. The title cut of *Moon Shadow* clocked in at over nine minutes, and one of their classics, "(Can I Speak to You before You Go to) Hollywood," was more than six and a half minutes long (and note the length of the title!). They were positioning themselves as rock *artists*. "It's like night and day," Nona Hendryx said of her group's transformation.[51] In interviews, the women expressed the relief they felt at following a different path from the one taken by their girl group–era contemporaries. By the mid-1970s the Supremes, the top girl group of the sixties, toured the oldies circuit without original lead singer Diana Ross and performed their back catalogue. The women of Labelle knew that they could have followed the same path—but that they had fewer well-known hits to propel them. In 1975, Patti LaBelle told a *Rolling Stone* reporter, "We think how lucky we are every day. It might be what [the Supremes] want, but we would not have been happy doing what they're doing, not progressing, just doing the same thing over and over and not really doing music."[52]

On the Border of Rock and Soul

Labelle blended rock's up-front guitars, high volume, and edgy attitude with gospel's vocal harmonies, building on the propulsive rhythms of funk and Latin music to create a unique sound. The group's move "away from the conventional soul format" and the presence of "an English-style hard rock sound" set them apart from other African American women artists of the early 1970s.[53] Critics latched together genre terms to capture the group's unusual synthesis: Labelle offered "the finest visual treat in rock 'n' soul,"[54] "the most satisfying fusions of rock and R&B heard anywhere,"[55] a "unique supercharged blend of rock and R&B,"[56] and were a "contemporary soul-rock unit."[57] They were "in the vanguard of the '70s glitter/glamour rock 'n' soul sound,"[58] playing "discotheque-gospel music,"[59] "glitter gospel,"[60] "godless gospel music,"[61] and "a spangled new black music for the space age."[62] Clearly, the women of Labelle were crossing the racial and sonic boundaries that had solidified in American popular music. Working on the border of "white rock" and "black soul," they incorporated elements from both fields. Labelle's attention to vocal pyrotechnics stood out in a rock context that was more focused on instrumental virtuosity, while the attention to a hard-rocking musical setting sometimes featuring instrumental solos was rare in vocally centered soul and R&B.[63]

Labelle's most notable sonic difference from other black female vocal groups was the individuality of the group members. Each woman conveyed a distinctive personality on stage and a distinctive voice on record. According to Sarah Dash, this was an important part of Wickham's concept. "She wanted everybody to be a lead singer. She was encouraging that we would all use our voices to sing background like we were singing lead. To be a forceful part and not go 'wooo oooo' and just be the lead singer's answer group."[64] Patti LaBelle sang lead most of the time, but not exclusively. This allowed Dash and Hendryx to be in the foreground on some songs, a departure from the girl group model. Commenting on this dynamic, one reviewer noted, "Hendryx and Dash, rather than being restricted to the old formula of injecting that touch of background sweetness to complement the lead, are allowed their own toughness and the resulting interaction is marvelous."[65] In fact, the structure of Labelle's songs relied on and highlighted vocal individuality. *New York Times* critic Clayton Riley celebrated Labelle's voices as "three of the most arresting on the current scene."[66] He rhapsodized that Sarah Dash "is the sound of a deeply sensual human warmth, often fragile but never helpless, a voice that is clear at its center, cream at the edges" and observed that Patti LaBelle "commands respect in every register. Her highs blaze. Extending like flames, they leap up the scale to consume any notes available to the human voice."[67] After more than a decade singing together, the women knew one another's voices, and they used this knowledge to create a vivid and democratic sound.

Rooted in the African American gospel vocal style, the women sang harmonies with an attention-grabbing level of volume and intensity. They often sang at the high end of their ranges, departing from an industry standard that compelled women to sing in the middle range.[68] Some commentators praised the women for their vocal skill, calling them "unique and superlative singers" and noting their capacity for compelling "vocal gymnastics."[69] Others likened them to jazz artists: "Labelle, both the group and the individuals in it, release *and* retain vocal tension continually, keeping the music they make quite unpredictable, in much the same way a more formal black music like jazz achieves this quality."[70] Critics praised the women's vocal skill: "Patti LaBelle doesn't just have a really good voice; she has an incredible voice," a *Melody Maker* writer asserted. "It's the kind of voice you either love or hate: Tough, pliant, everlasting."[71] For some listeners, the "blaring and intense, unstoppable" voices of Labelle, particularly Patti's, were "on the harsh side."[72] Patti LaBelle sang full-throttle with a piercing nasality, her voice cutting through the instrumental backing and rising above the vocalizations of Dash and Hendryx.[73] Even admiring writers acknowledged that LaBelle's vocal quality had the potential to alienate some listeners. Longtime Labelle fan and music critic Vince Aletti observed, "Patti has a strong and daring voice. It's style is rougher, harder, almost strident at times and certainly less graceful than, say, Aretha Franklin's, but she more than makes up for what she lacks in sweet perfection with the robustness and force of her work."[74] The unique vocal sound did not appeal to everyone. In a 1975 article for *Rolling Stone*, James Wolcott stated, "Labelle are terrible singers—raspy, abrasive, as subtle as a battleship hitting a glacier—and possess no sense of lyrical architecture. The only structure Labelle understands is loud, louder, loudest."[75]

Wickham and the women of Labelle might have viewed their hybrid music, with its loud, guitar-based instrumentation and forceful, high-volume vocals, as a logical fit for rock, but some critics took issue with their approach. Russell Gersten, for example, skewered the group's second album, *Moon Shadow,* in his *Rolling Stone* review. Here are three passages:

> The group has gotten good FM airplay and superb notices in the New York press, hailing them as the new liberated black sound. But nothing else about it works. I've seen them bore audiences silly in clubs and big halls, and the new album is as tedious as you'd imagine it to be—energetic and loud, but emotionally barren and musically banal.[76]

> The hard rock guitar emphasis, though voguish, is ill-suited to the kind of singing Labelle does. It leaves everything wobbly; furthermore, it accentuates the occasional harshness of Patti's voice. The result is things getting even more frantic and hysterical than usual.[77]

They substitute noise for interpretation, much as Aretha Franklin did in her dismal version of "The Weight" a few years back. The seven original tunes, with one exception, are horribly pedestrian, filled with that self-conscious straining for Relevance and Art that one finds in a lot of amateur songwriting.[78]

Labelle took on the trappings of the musical sound that had displaced the vocal group music that they had sung in the sixties, but as black female artists, their foray into rock was difficult for some to accept. Who is the "you" that Gersten assumes will share his opinion about the "tedious" show? What is the "usual" that he refers to? There's no crime in a critic disliking an artist's work, but Gersten seems annoyed that these black women had strayed outside of the bounds of sanctioned black female sound. His attack on Aretha Franklin's cover of the Band's single suggests a general discomfort with black women stepping beyond what he deemed to be their proper musical place. This refusal to contain themselves musically is part of what made Labelle so appealing to their fans.

The women of Labelle resisted the racially determined musical boxes that music critics like Gersten, record label executives, and audiences expected black women to occupy. Conscious of these limits, Nona Hendryx told a reporter, "We hate being called a soul group because that's just what we're not."[79] She continued, "We are a rock act . . . we like to think of ourselves as a cross between Tina Turner and the Rolling Stones. That's just the mistake Warner Brothers made with us, trying to get us into the typical, black female group thing."[80] Labelle's musical hybridity also might have disturbed R&B and soul fans. A British critic observed of Labelle, "More than any other soul group of recent years, they've come up with an amalgam of humour, chic and solid musical values. It's the arrangement of these elements that so perplexes soul purists, especially in Britain, who've been known to take a hard line on Labelle."[81] Indeed, Patti LaBelle initially resisted Wickham's new vision because "the changes she proposed were so drastic and so extreme, I was afraid our fans, all the people who had followed us for nearly ten years, would turn away from us."[82] Clearly, Labelle's departures from the rules of rock and soul were challenging. Gersten's *Rolling Stone* review notwithstanding, the early studio recordings earned many positive notices, but the acclaim did not translate into strong record sales or mainstream success. On the fringes, though, Labelle found an audience that appreciated their boundary pushing.

Out There

Paralleling their blending of rock and soul musical sound, the women drew on rock and soul performance aesthetics to create a visual style that signaled their connection to rock without relinquishing their affinity for African American performance. At the same time, the women broke down barriers between artist and audience, celebrated the connections among women, and created an accepting space for gay and lesbian fans. Together, these practices helped the group win a devoted following.

Although Labelle had started the decade in the dressed-down mode then popular on the rock scene, by 1974 the women were dressing way, way up in elaborate stage costumes that distinguished them from every other rock and soul act out there. The mix "of revolutionary tunes and kooky clothing"[83] coupled with the group's vocal delivery and onstage theatrics "turned their concerts into events."[84] The "spacesuit outfits,"[85] as the group's promotional materials called them, came courtesy of Larry LeGaspi, a Puerto Rican clothing designer, who had been a fan of Patti LaBelle and the Bluebelles and was following the 1970s incarnation of the group.[86] "Larry had come down to the [West] Village to the Bitter End and he saw us perform," Dash recalled. "The next week he came back with like ten people and he said, 'I have outfits that I want to make.' He gave us these outfits that he thought suited each one of us. . . . It didn't start with the space outfits. It started with funky strips of fabric and things like that."[87] In the most well-known of LeGaspi's costumes—skin-tight silver lamé, feathered headdresses, aluminum breast plates, bikini tops, shiny platform footwear—the women were an outrageous sight to behold (see figure 6.2). "Looking simultaneously like one of Salvador Dali's dreams, a Yacqui Indian peyote vision and Star Trek extras," one critic explained, "Labelle have the whole theater sex field tied up."[88] Writer Jamaica Kincaid was more succinct: in her estimation, the women looked like "a Puerto Rican's idea of Negroes from Mars."[89]

The new stage costumes connected Labelle with glam rock, the 1970s British rock movement in which male performers, most prominently Marc Bolan of T. Rex and David Bowie, played with the standards of heterosexual male dress and comportment.[90] With their new look, Labelle became "virtually the only all-female group that was as flamboyant as the male glam performers."[91] The members of Labelle were among the first American performers to adopt this style, and they helped set a trend of over-the-top dressing in American

FIGURE 6.2 In concert the women of Labelle offered both vocal and visual excitement. From left to right: Nona Hendryx, Sarah Dash, and Patti LaBelle on stage in New York City in 1974, wearing their signature futuristic stage costumes. © BOB GRUEN/WWW.BOBGRUEN .COM.

popular music. After working with Labelle, LeGaspi went on to design the zany wardrobes of funk master George Clinton's Parliament-Funkadelic and the stage costumes of hard rock band Kiss.[92] LeGaspi's costumes and the exotic feathered ensembles created by Dorian Blakley were among the most commented-upon elements of Labelle's live performances and helped expand the group's audience.[93] With the introduction of the stage costumes, Labelle embraced the black music concert tradition of dressing up when on stage, taking the practice to the extreme 1970s-era conclusions that glam had introduced into rock, and winning praise for "visual excitement."[94] Each woman created characters on stage with "Patti exuding earth-mother warmth, Nona outlining cool, futuristic chic and Sarah radiating a mysterious sensuality."[95] Labelle's embrace of glam's theatricality set the women apart from the mainstream of rock, a context where an "ideology of authenticity mandated that musicians appear on stage as themselves, not as any other persona or character, and discouraged forms of overtly theatrical performance."[96] As one critic explained, "Ambitionwise, Vicki Wickham wants them to be the definitive theatrical group. She means up there with Bowie and Genesis on Broadway, theatrical rock that glows but is not glitter."[97]

The theatricality of Labelle's concerts meshed with a down-home communality that created a palpable bond between artists and their audience and among audience members. Labelle drew the audience into the show through the African American tradition of call-and-response. The most prominent example of this practice was their request that concertgoers "wear something silver" to their performance at the Metropolitan Opera House. The result was a glittering evening during which the artists and audience members were dressed according to a shared theme. The women further broke down the barriers between performer and audience by going out into the crowd to greet their fans and by bringing audience members on stage to dance with them.[98] In addition to forging connections with the audience, the three women solidified the connection among themselves through onstage interactions. "Our act is different," Dash told a reporter, "because we do a lot of touching, which you do not see very many groups do. . . . When we're onstage we touch each other . . . and move through the audience touching the people. It makes them feel closer to us, and there are no barriers when we are performing."[99]

A key barrier Labelle crossed had to do with sexuality. According to *New York Times* writer Ken Emerson, "[Nona Hendryx] and Patti Labelle feign[ed] lesbian love" during at least one performance.[100] Precisely what this entailed is not clear, and the journalists writing the articles that I consulted did not spell out what was happening among the trio on stage (or their editors excised the description). Writing years after the fact, Alice Echols commented on Labelle's "erotically charged display[s] of sisterhood," a wry twist, perhaps, on the female bonding that girl groups had presented in the 1960s.[101] The positive and public staging of erotic desire and sexual self-expression was affirming to fans and especially attractive to gay and lesbian audience members who were grappling with questions of sexuality at both personal and public levels. Nona Hendryx, in particular, projected a renegade sexual difference. Her short hair, preference for leggings rather than skirts, and the occasional presence of a whip as part of her stage ensemble compelled comparison to David Bowie, rock's most visible gender-queer personage.[102] A member of the Atlanta Feminist Lesbian Alliance told *Rolling Stone*, "Lesbians love Labelle. To us, they're very together women who love people and each other. And they have a heavy feminist message."[103] The group's public embodiment of black women loving black women, of the sisterhood that Echols references, was a revelation.[104] In concert, the women enacted their bond through gestures, body language, and "a freedom of touch," as Hendryx put it, that included holding hands, standing close together, leaning into one another when singing, wrapping arms around one another's waists, and singing into the same microphone.[105] And then, of course, there was the sonic intimacy of their harmonizing, intertwining voices. The result was the creation of a black women's space that visualized and sounded out "the power of the erotic," as Audre Lorde might have called it, a space that was occupied and controlled by women who did not seem to require the presence of men for fulfillment.[106]

Labelle's distinctive sound and performance style drew a diverse audience, a fact that press reports highlighted and that the women acknowledged: "We've brought all kinds of people together," Dash observed in a 1975 interview.[107] A *New York Times* critic suggested that Labelle were "Perhaps the first performers to attract simultaneously large numbers of white teenagers, blacks and gays."[108] A *Rolling Stone* writer called their fans "an unusually varied coterie of businessmen, poets, teenagers, freaks, and movie and recording stars."[109] *Melody Maker* catalogued "hordes of black dudes in their best pimp outfit, rock freaks, bizarre faggots and families from uptown and the West side."[110] Most reporters commented on the visible presence of gay men and lesbians at Labelle concerts: "Showtime at the Civic Center in Atlanta brought out an 80/20 black/white mix of friendly bizarre, tinseled gays, lesbians, hip middle class. At least half the 3,500-person crowd were highly adorned black gays who heeded Labelle's standard request 'to wear something silver.'"[111] In interviews, the women of Labelle helped reporters account for the pronounced gay presence at their concerts: "Sarah says their songs—especially the standards—did it; Nona says it was the group's 'intensity and emotion on stage.'"[112] When I spoke with Dash in 2014, she noted that Patti LaBelle and the Bluebelles had a gay fan base in the years before Stonewall. "That was a time when people were not 'out of the closet,'" Dash recalled. "On Wednesday nights, there was a certain spot in the Apollo where all the men who were cross dressers would be. Wednesday nights were their nights to come there and you knew you *better* sing—or else. But they loved us."[113] The trio's return to New York following their London revamp coincided with the emergence of a more public queer presence. Dash explained, "We started playing the Village Gate on Monday nights, and there was a large gay contingent. With word of mouth, they began to follow us."[114] Coupled with the genuine attitude of acceptance that the women of Labelle conveyed, these factors solidified the group's strong gay following.

"They can be themselves at our shows," Dash told a *Melody Maker* reporter in 1975. "We appeal to them all and don't put anyone down."[115] Furthermore, as Patti LaBelle explained, there was important common ground between Labelle and gays: "We played gay clubs and we loved it because gays are into theater. And now we're breaking big because we've learned how to put on a show. Our audiences are a spectacle themselves. And we give them a spectacle in return!"[116]

In his book on African American women vocalists, music writer David Nathan observed, "Labelle was the darling of the proud-to-be-black-and-gay crowd and the group can do no wrong in its eyes."[117] For the straight, white, and male members of the rock press, this black female group's large black and gay audience was a point of fascination and, as the tone of some of their reporting suggests, discomfort:

> **The New York Times:** If one wanted to be catty about it, one could suggest that Sunday's crowd was the Met's opera audience come out of the closet: there can rarely have been so many bearded gentlemen in dresses, razzle-dazzle sequins and arched eyebrows at a Met performance before.[118]

> **Melody Maker:** Labelle opening in New York is different from concerts elsewhere; their followers parade and prune [sic] themselves in theater lobbies with exclamations of divine horror should they be outstaged [sic] by another in still more glittering finery.[119]

> **Rolling Stone:** After a 20-minute intermission that gave the audience a chance to resume parading around the lobby, Labelle came back with the *Phoenix* segment of the show."[120]

In the twenty-first century, an era when gay marriage is a legal right upheld by the US Supreme Court, and public conversations about the rights of gay, lesbian, bisexual, and transgender people are commonplace, it may be difficult to appreciate how bold Labelle's embrace of its queer fans was. In the early 1970s, gay men and lesbians were mobilizing for political, social, and cultural rights, but this was still a time when engaging in homosexual sex was illegal in many states, New York City had only recently decriminalized same-sex public dancing, and the idea that homosexuality was not a mental disorder was new.[121] Gay men and lesbians were still on the social margins, but Labelle embraced them—a move that distinguished the women from most other participants in the rock scene they were striving to enter.

In the Mainstream

The hope was that the 1973 album *Pressure Cookin',* Labelle's first release on RCA, would propel the group into the mainstream, but in spite of strong reviews in *Rolling Stone* and *Crawdaddy*, the album did not catch fire, and the women left RCA to sign with Epic.[122] They arrived at the new label in a precarious position: Labelle had released three critically praised albums and had developed a strong New York City following, but had not scored a national hit. Labelle was at risk of becoming a regional act, unable to appeal to mainstream audiences; the goal for the group's first outing on Epic was to create a commercially successful album.[123] To that end, Epic suggested that the group work with Allen Toussaint, a New Orleans–based producer, songwriter, and pianist with a knack for making hits. Toussaint brought in the Meters, a noted New Orleans funk band, to serve as the backing group; he shortened the songs and coached Patti LaBelle to moderate her vocals, helping her to manage what she admitted was "a tendency to oversing."[124] The result was a more accessible album and a number one pop hit with "Lady Marmalade," the group's first Top 30 single in more than a decade.[125] With their arrival in the mainstream, the women of Labelle encountered challenges as they navigated a media context that they did not control, but had to work within to circulate their music.

For starters, some critics voiced only a grudging acceptance of the calculated effort to produce a hit: "Toussaint has tried to modify and streamline Labelle, with mixed rewards," stated a reviewer in *Crawdaddy*, who also complained that *Nightbirds* was "somewhat of an artistic retreat, the album is 'designed to sell.'"[126] Another reporter noted the gender dynamics of the album's production, especially in light of the group's commitment to empowering women: "Vicki Wickham, along with Labelle, had a strong hand in the first three post-1970 albums. Success came with a male producer."[127] It was true that Toussaint was in charge of selecting the musicians and developing arrangements, but the trio brought "Lady Marmalade" to the project. The members of Labelle first heard the song when songwriter Bob Crewe played the version he and his writing partner Kenny Nolan had produced for the Eleventh Hour, a male group, earlier that year. "We immediately liked the way it sounded, the flavor of it, the funkiness," Patti LaBelle recalled.[128] In the hands of Toussaint and Labelle, the song is bright and upbeat, carried by the propulsive energy of the women's vocals. A tale of a New Orleans prostitute and the client she mesmerized with her sexual wiles, "Lady Marmalade" is a study of sexual obsession with a danceable groove.[129] While LaBelle incorporates a few bracing high notes at strategic moments, she sings most of the song in a radio-friendly middle range. "Lady Marmalade" was a departure from the songs of social engagement and self-determination that the group performed. Hendryx explained that they included the track to balance *Nightbirds*: "We just felt it was a good song to do because most of the songs on the album were very politically oriented. . . . We needed something to lighten the album up a bit."[130] The song first took hold in discos and was soon picked up for the radio airplay that led to pop chart success.[131] Critics, radio programmers, and audience members were enthusiastic. *Rolling Stone* critic Jon Landau wrote: "'Lady Marmalade' is a perfect record—the right song, sung by the right group, produced and played by the right musicians and released at the right time."[132] Riding the tide of the song's success in the clubs, the women of Labelle were "among the earliest stars of disco."[133]

The lyrics of "Lady Marmalade" were not unproblematic. The women of Labelle had a profile as artists who conveyed substantive messages, and here they were getting famous singing about a prostitute and her smitten john. But they also took ownership of the song. At Toussaint's suggestion, the women started the track with the chant, "Hey Sister, Go Sister, Hey Sister, Soul Sister."[134] Uttered in an era when women's liberation and black power had become part of public discourse, the singsong phrase framed the song with a nod to women's solidarity. Labelle seemed to be cheering on Creole Lady Marmalade, and their rendition positions the woman as the one who is in control. Echols argues, "Ostensibly the song is about male pleasure, but from the beginning it's Marmalade, not the john, who has the upper hand. She's blasé whereas he's overcome with desire, driven to crying, 'more, more, more.'" To her ears, Labelle "turned the song into a taunt, thereby underscoring the song's reversal of predictable power relations."[135] Still, Patti LaBelle indicated to *Rolling Stone* that she did not think much of the song:

It's really weird after singing "Sunday's News" and "[The] Revolution [Will Not Be Televised]" and other songs that were just as good or better than "Lady M." It's sad. We believed in the other stuff more than "Lady M"; the lyrical content was just more relevant. But "[Are You] Lonely" could never get to be Number One.... I don't see how a *hooker* got to be Number One, though, because people are afraid of that too. ... I mean, it's kind of a tacky song.[136]

Lady Marmalade was kin to Brown Sugar, the sexually available black woman. Tacky, perhaps, but also a familiar, digestible figure. Hendryx was also dismissive, calling it "just a silly, dumb song that made me laugh."[137] She told *Rolling Stone* that the record was "sweet and sour. I find it sour when people think that 'Lady M' is all Labelle is about."[138] The sweet part was that the song's popularity led to broad public exposure; the group performed on the *Cher* show, the *Dinah Shore* show, and two episodes of *The Midnight Special*.[139] In an era when there were only three national television networks, an appearance on these nationally broadcast programs meant a high degree of pop culture visibility.

Commenting on the reception of her group in the wake of "Lady Marmalade," LaBelle stated, "When we were Patti LaBelle and the Bluebells [*sic*] we were trying to sell sex and we wasn't sellin' nothin'. Now we're selling sex and the songs too. Very good."[140] Labelle enjoyed their status as sex symbols who were representative of liberated black womanhood. Still, their sexual forthrightness could be interpreted as a confirmation of the Brown Sugar and Jezebel stereotypes that constructed African American women as sexually loose. This dynamic played out in some of the press Labelle received. A *Rolling Stone* cover story that ran a few months after "Lady Marmalade" had occupied the number one slot on the pop charts positioned Labelle as sexual revolutionaries who fit the rock scene's ethos of rebellion. Photographed in their silver stage finery, LaBelle, Hendryx, and Dash joined the handful of African American women—Tina Turner, Diana Ross, and Rose Stone and Cynthia Robinson of Sly and the Family Stone—who had appeared on the cover of the magazine up to that point.[141] In the interview, the women spoke about the pleasure they took in singing before an audience, linking onstage and sexual performances. *Rolling Stone* picked up and amplified the talk of sex that was part of the interview. On the magazine's cover, alongside type listing stories on "Drugs!" and "Violence!," was the promise of "Sex! LABELLE Comin' Comin' Comin' to Getcha."[142] The repetition of "comin'," a not-too-subtle double entendre, and the word "getcha" played on images of sexually insatiable black women and used idiosyncratic spelling to render African American English. Inside, the profile highlighted the sex angle, starting with the embellishment of the article title with visual effects: black bubble letters spelled out "Mmmm Unnh Aaah Oh God Oooh It's So Good Oh Baby It's Labelle" in type whose increasing point size and positioning on an undulating line represented a moan of sexual pleasure across two pages.[143]

If the typeface was graphic, so, too, were the juicy interview comments. Only two years earlier, LaBelle had admitted to being conflicted about singing explicit material in public.[144] By the time of the *Rolling Stone* interview, she was comfortable talking about sex to a journalist. "I have great sexual drives and rushes," LaBelle told reporter Art Harris, "but my body is not a sexy body and I don't have a sexy face and voice. But I love sex and my husband considers me a sex maniac."[145] In addition to this liberated statement about sexual pleasure, she likened the sensation of performing before an audience to feelings she associated with making love to a partner: "It's like I'm married to a million men and women when I'm out there. And when I'm married to a person, I give all I have. It's like a climax, and when the audience does it like they did it last night in Atlanta, I come."[146] Dash continued the music/sex connection: "It's like letting a million people see you in bed with whomever you love . . . and being naked and having sex with your music. . . . Having orgasms with something that is so real and that you love."[147] The open discussion of the twin pleasures of musical performance and sexual activity was radical and revelatory. Hendryx even addressed the question of sexual unconventionality: "I like appealing to both men and women. I have no preferences. I don't limit myself. I'm all sexes. I don't know what a heterosexual or a bisexual or a homosexual or a monosexual is. I don't understand the differences."[148] And, she confided, "I like whips—I use one, but not the one I wear onstage."[149] Hendryx's matter-of-fact embrace of nonnormative sexuality was another example of Labelle's liberated spirit. These comments allowed the three women to claim ownership of their sexual desires and subjectivity in a media space where women, especially black women, were usually objectified and voiceless. Along with a handful of other African American women including Betty Davis (whom I discuss in the next chapter), Chaka Khan, and Millie Jackson, the women of Labelle were working in the tradition of 1920s blues women such as Ma Rainey, Bessie Smith, and Alberta Hunter, exploring and affirming their desires.[150] Their willingness to discuss sexuality in *Rolling Stone*, a magazine without much of a presumed black readership, is indicative of how boundary-pushing the women of Labelle were.[151]

There were, however, reprisals for their openness and efforts to police the group. "Lady Marmalade," a song with a direct sexual come-on that was masked by its translation into French, concerned some media gatekeepers. In one instance, the producers of the *Mike Douglas Show*, an afternoon talk show, insisted that the group change the lyric *"Voulez-vous coucher avec moi?"* (Would you like to sleep with me?) to *"Voulez-vous danser avec moi?"* (Would you like to dance with me?).[152] The original language, the producers insisted, was "too strong."[153] Another attack came from other black women. Following the chart success of "Lady Marmalade," a Seattle woman organized a group of concerned parents to protest against Labelle. *Rolling Stone* reported:

> Mrs. Marvin Branham denounced "Lady Marmalade" as a song that "flaunts prostitution and is offensive to blacks." She led an irate group of black mothers from St. Theresa's Catholic Church in hounding radio stations to drop the song. Her key objection lay in the French line, "Voulez-vous coucher avec moi?" . . . The women bought ads in the city's papers and urged parents to tie up radio station switchboards with complaints. Most of the stations did not knuckle under.[154]

Mrs. Branham's actions are rooted in the politics of black respectability, an approach that developed out of black middle-class women's recognition that the lack of sexual morality many perceived in working-class black women reflected on them.[155] Along with comporting themselves in ultrarespectable ways, they tried to modify the behaviors of working-class women, including those aiming for rock stardom. African American women, middle-class or working-class, were always at risk of being taken for prostitutes. The women of Labelle did not escape this condition, which was likely intensified by the fact that they were performing artists (always suspect) who sang a song about a prostitute. A *Melody Maker* reporter presented his meeting with Dash and Hendryx at a New York restaurant (Patti LaBelle was at home in Philadelphia) in terms that echo the scenario of "Lady Marmalade." After his opening line, "My—these girls look good!" he explained, "both girls have chosen to wear outfits that, er . . . display their charms to best advantage. They're so damn foxy that here in the middle I feel like a dealer out on the town showing off the rewards of a profitable day."[156] The attractiveness of the women of Labelle was part of their profile, but it is arresting how, in a few sentences, the writer reduces these veteran musicians to "pros" of a different kind. Documents of male fantasies about the sexual availability of black women (Hello, Brown Sugar), both the *Melody Maker* article and the *Rolling Stone* profile attest to the narrowness of the media space within which Labelle operated. As I detail in the next section, such limited views of African American women shaped the ways the women of Labelle were able to circulate their music and influenced its reception among critics and audiences.

Betwixt and Between

Labelle's progressive sound and politics placed them betwixt and between rock and soul. Their position created marketing challenges, and they worked with their manager Vicki Wickham to develop strategies that would enable Labelle to reach audiences while remaining true to their creative vision. The four women discussed these factors in interviews, offering race-, gender-, and genre-sensitive analyses of the situation.

Labelle's music does not sit comfortably in any one genre. "Lady Marmalade" was classified as disco because of its success with that genre's DJs and fans, and the song now enjoys status as a disco anthem. Generally, though, the group's music is not easy to categorize. This generic slipperiness coupled with the disco affiliation may be one reason Labelle does not appear in historical accounts of rock or funk, most of which are guided by gendered genre discourses that cast disco as "artificial, feminine, and/or queer and suspected of selling out," while funk and rock represent artistic innovation and masculine authenticity.[157] Dash told me that at their record labels, the group would be put in different genre categories depending on who was making the decisions. "There were some areas of the record company that said, 'We should only promote them as R&B.' There were some saying we could do pop. We said, 'Promote us where you can.'"[158] Labelle's expansive sound disrupted the genre boundaries that guided record industry decision making, creating a "crisis of categories," to use cultural critic Sonnet Retman's term, that made the group difficult to fit into accounts built on straightforward genre labels.[159] Labelle's songs featured the electric guitars associated with rock and the sinuous bass lines of funk alongside Latin grooves propelled by congas, maracas, and other percussion. The sound quality of Labelle's vocals—particularly the close harmonies and the use of melisma—reflected the members' gospel training, but the musical arrangements and subject matter associated the women with rock and the output of socially engaged African American singer-songwriters such as Nina Simone, Curtis Mayfield, Marvin Gaye, and Stevie Wonder.

This musical fluidity shaped the women's experiences as performing artists in the 1970s and the group's profile in popular music history. Labelle, whose first national tour was as the opening act for the Who, had enjoyed access to the rock audience, a fact further signaled by the women's appearance on the cover of *Rolling Stone*, the most widely circulated rock magazine in the United States. Still, it was a challenge for the group to traverse the racial, gender, and genre boundaries that cordoned off rock as the purview of white males. Wickham made it her mission to bring Labelle into that field. She has acknowledged that her lack of experience with US racial politics made embarking on the whole Labelle enterprise possible. "I had no concept of the problems a black act had in America," she told *Rolling Stone* in 1975. "English acts, if they were any good, played at [Royal] Festival Hall, and I couldn't understand why a black act, if it was good, couldn't play the same circuit the Who played. My naiveté probably made it work because when the girls would say, 'We can't do that,' I'd say, 'I don't see why not.'"[160] Wickham proceeded with bookings that highlighted Labelle's connections to both black and white music cultures, sites of musical production that by the 1970s were widely viewed as separate. Labelle did shows with African American artists—blues guitarist Albert King, Motown icons Smokey Robinson and the Miracles, R&B chanteuse Roberta Flack, and the singer and songwriter Nina Simone. The group also did shows with rock stalwarts the Who, the English progressive rock band Yes, American rock and roll nostalgia act Sha Na Na, and downtown New York City experimentalists the Velvet Underground.[161] In an update to the executives at Warner Brothers, the group's label during this period, Wickham highlighted the fact that Labelle played at both a "black" and a "white" music venue in the same week: "They are the only group ever to play consecutively Uptown and then Downtown," she wrote, "and, in fact, the only act I can think of to play the Apollo and the Bitter End except Curtis Mayfield."[162]

To counter industry common sense about black artists, Wickham stressed that Labelle appealed to rock audiences, noting, "the girls have done incredibly well so far—they have totally held their own and even drawn encores and ovations despite playing to a totally Who audience, being the opening act (which is pretty unenviable at the best of times) and particularly in huge stadiums which take time to fill and everyone's still coming in."[163] As she became more attuned to the racial dynamics of the American popular music scene, Wickham sounded a persistent theme in her correspondence with Warner Brothers: They needed to promote the group in both black and white markets.[164] Wickham's badgering is probably similar to that of any hardworking artist manager trying to get the attention of busy label executives (and she commented on her persistence in the letters: "Here comes the hassler!" begins one of her missives), but she recognized that the act she was working with presented special challenges.[165]

Labelle's itinerant status in the early seventies was a consequence of the marketing difficulties caused by the intersection of the group's race, gender, sound, and image. After Kit Lambert at Track Records lost interest in working with the group—"They didn't know what to do with us," Dash observed— Labelle went to Warner Brothers.[166] There, they recorded their first two albums, *Labelle* (1971) and *Moon Shadow* (1972); then, they went to RCA for *Pressure Cookin'* (1973), before moving to Epic for *Nightbirds* (1974), *Phoenix* (1975), and *Chameleon* (1976).[167] With their signing to Epic Records, they believed that they had finally made it to a sympathetic home. "At Epic," Sarah Dash told a reporter, "they understand what we're doing and what we want to be."[168] The women of Labelle did not shy away from discussing the problems that the relationship between their race and their sound created. Nona Hendryx stated:

> I think a lot of people dealing in the music industry as far as relating to us as a group, don't see us as black artists and they don't see our music as being black. And they tend to shut us out of certain areas and certain things because our music is what it is. But I don't understand it because we are three black people and whatever comes out of our mouths has to be black. And I don't think you should color our music—our music is what it *is*. And I don't understand when some people say, "Your music sounds white." It's *impossible*.[169]

The racialization of music genres in the 1970s linked African American Labelle to white rock, thereby precluding the women, in some minds, from being black. It was a perspective that ignored the fact that white rock was indebted to African American musical and performance practices, treating "black" and "white" music as isolated fields. Because of this binary way of thinking, the perception was that Labelle's musical sound conflicted with the women's racial identity. *Village Voice* critic Vince Aletti took these contradictory dynamics of race and music genre into account when outlining the factors that prevented Labelle from achieving extensive pop chart success: "The sound was a soul-rock fusion . . . at a time when no one knew just how to respond to such a hybrid. (It was ok for a white group to sound 'black' but for a black group, especially a 'girl group,' to sound 'white,' well—it just wasn't done.)" Furthermore, he continued, "many of the songs were, and remain, aggressively 'relevant'" at a time when "political peace and power songs [were] decidedly out of favor among whites."[170]

This type of commentary about the group's fraught experience in the industry context was part of Labelle's public narrative. "Bewildered record companies still didn't know how to cope," one reporter observed in 1975.[171] Another, writing in 1974, explained, "To date, Labelle has not attracted a really large audience. . . . Much of the problem, Labelle feels, is due to the limited amount of exposure and promotion given to the group by RCA, the label for whom they record."[172] These trials even became part of the group's self-representation. A 1975 press release explained:

> Over the past year, Labelle has slowly but surely worked towards breaking down the barriers which have beset them in the past. Their steadfast white audience, gained primarily through their historic tour with The Who and an album they recorded with Laura Nyro (*Gonna Take a Miracle*), has been growing as work-of-mouth [*sic*] spreads. Black audiences have begun to pick up on some of the ideas that Labelle expresses through their music and Black disc-jockeys have begun to find that, in addition to all their flash, Labelle also makes downright funky, danceable music.[173]

While this dispatch frames the problem as a racial one, Labelle also contended with challenges associated with gender. As a trio of black women, Labelle were doubly outside a genre associated with white male musicians. Consequently, the group faced *gendered* race and genre challenges. As Patti LaBelle explained to a reporter, "We have had record companies and promoters who wanted to put us in a box by telling us that we must be a certain way because we are females . . . we lost many jobs because of our persistence in singing revolutionary tunes."[174] Labelle's assertive black femininity was more than the mainstream was ready for. Reflecting on the impact of their race, gender, and message on their careers, Patti LaBelle told a reporter, "It's hard being black and female and out there saying what we do."[175] The group's decisions to work with a female manager and a female lawyer (Ina Meibach) and to establish their own publishing company are examples of women taking control of their professional destiny.

Looking back on her group's business and music choices, Dash talked about Labelle in relation to second-wave feminist activism. "We were in the women's movement. Just what we did in terms of our evolution into how we presented ourselves. That was totally the women's movement," she explained when we spoke in 2014. "We were a musical movement which said we were women and we have freedom of speech to talk about things and sing about things that most females wouldn't dream of saying. 'Like it in the morning much better.'

What? We didn't march with Gloria Steinem, but we were a movement."[176] Significantly, it was a movement that upset the traditional gender rules of the recording industry. Commenting on this dynamic in 1974, Hendryx said, "There are still some doors and we're gonna kick 'em down. Like the business of promotion and selling records, those guys don't particularly care to deal with a female direct unless you're the prize at the end of the party, know what I mean? They're looking for the mister to back up the missus. There is no mister."[177] Navigating the male-dominated recording industry with "no mister" in their camp, Labelle's backstage female autonomy echoed that of their onstage performances. The group's self-sufficiency evoked the "strong black woman," capable of taking care of herself and her family in a society that devalued her because of her race and gender.[178] Although admired in black communities, some reporters suggested that the strength and independence that Labelle projected frightened white men in the recording industry and alienated some audience members. Writing in the *New York Times*, Clayton Riley made the following observations about Labelle:

> They are, as a friend puts it, "the power." Understanding this means digging on the fact that women in American popular music frequently are forced into one of two simple categories: camp followers for the male stars or sex vessels turning symbolic tricks on stage. Labelle rises light years above either category.[179]

> Quite possibly, the men who run music in all its phases in the Western world are afraid of them. Because they are strong, and because they are black—but calm about these facts in their lives. . . . Perhaps it is simply that they are too much the sound of tomorrow. But I tend to think that any group of women to whom the description "the power" can accurately be assigned, as it can be to Labelle, will experience trouble gaining a large public acceptance.[180]

The confident black female presence of Labelle challenged mainstream imagery and expectations. One reporter observed that their material "is highly-charged, politically and sensually revolutionary, and chilling in performance. Some of it might just be too hot for the conservative industry network of station managers, record companies and TV talk shows."[181] The British music journalist Penny Valentine, who reported on Labelle's tour of the West Coast of the United States for *Sounds*, devoted some of her column inches to unpacking the reasons the group received negative reviews. She cited the assessment of an unnamed friend—not the same friend as Riley's, surely—who connected the tepid response to the unexamined fears of some of the white male reporters covering the group: "They're not used to that much energy, they've seen too many white shows. That's what's wrong with white music today. And I really think they were scared—all that male screw up because they don't like it when girls get aggressive, it scares them."[182]

These commentaries suggest that part of the problem of "the power" of Labelle was a problem of displacing whiteness, maleness, and white maleness from the center. Unlike the black women background vocalists who had become a fixture in rock by this point, Dash, Hendryx, and LaBelle were black women up-front and in charge. Furthermore, their musical style, lyrical content, and visual presentation diverged from what was perceived to be appropriate practice for black women vocalists. As Vince Aletti observed, Labelle departed from "the usual high-gloss stylization of black singing groups—synchronized choreography, precise, dramatic gestures, matching or at least coordinated outfits. . . . Labelle is off somewhere on its own."[183] The group's artistic practice upset dominant rules of race, gender, and genre. That Labelle achieved any mainstream success is a testament to the women's talent and persistence.

Moving On

Labelle followed up *Nightbirds* with *Phoenix* (1975) and *Chameleon* (1976), albums that prioritized artistic growth and experimentation.[184] The women toned down their costuming and developed arrangements in which Hendryx and Dash had a stronger vocal presence.[185] "Labelle is like a chameleon right now," Hendryx told a reporter in 1976. "We're changing because of the conditions and the places that we're in. A lot of other acts are doing the silver and glitter thing, and if you stay there, you become just another act."[186] Their singles "Messin' with My Mind" (1975) and "Get You Somebody New" (1976) reached the R&B chart, but pop chart success was elusive.[187] As Alice Echols observed, "'What Can I Do for You,' the group's fiery 1975 follow-up to 'Lady Marmalade,' reached number seven on the disco charts, but barely made a ripple on the pop and R&B charts. But, then, the song was unapologetically political, demanding peace and power at a time when popular music was moving away from overtly political themes."[188] The process of making the post-*Nightbirds* albums brought into relief artistic differences that had always bubbled within the group and, feeling "rocked out and rolled out," as Patti LaBelle put it, Labelle broke up at the end of 1976.[189]

The women went in different musical directions as they pursued solo careers. Sarah Dash's cover of Nina Simone's "Sinner Man" was a Top 10 disco chart track in 1978, and a clothing line associated with disco fashion picked up her song "Oh La La, Too Soon" for the "Oh, la, la, Sassoon" television ad campaign for designer jeans.[190] Nona Hendryx pursued her interest in hard rock, dance, and experimental music; her biggest chart success was "Busting Out," a dance-oriented collaboration with the No Wave group Material that stayed on the disco chart for twenty weeks in 1981.[191] Patti LaBelle recorded the R&B ballads she loved and that Wickham had dissuaded the group from performing; she broke through as a solo artist in 1986, when her album *The Winner in You* went platinum, buoyed by its number one pop and R&B single, "On My Own," a duet with Michael McDonald, the blue-eyed soul singer who had been the lead vocalist for the Doobie Brothers.[192] The women sustained their careers by working on multiple fronts; they turned, like so many professional black women vocalists, to the stage (LaBelle) and background vocal gigs (Dash and Hendryx) when the solo work was not lucrative enough. Patti LaBelle appeared on Broadway in the gospel musical *Your Arms Too Short to Box with God* with soul singer Al Green in 1982.[193] Nona Hendryx worked with the Talking Heads on their African funk experiment *Remain in Light* (1980), and Sarah Dash joined Rolling Stones guitarist Keith Richards on two of his solo projects, *Talk Is Cheap* (1988) and *Main Offender* (1992); she also sang background on the Rolling Stones' *Steel Wheels* album and tour in 1989. The women collaborated on one another's projects—Dash and Hendryx appeared on LaBelle's 1991 album *Burnin'*, which included the song "Release Yourself," cowritten by Hendryx; LaBelle sang background on "Design for Living," a song Hendryx recorded in 1983. In 2008, reunited as Labelle, they released *Back to Now* and launched a successful national tour.

Labelle's rebellious performance stances, frank engagement with sexuality, and adventurous, high-energy music positioned the group to take a place on the rock stage, but its footing there was not secure. The women of Labelle confronted the assumption that their musical sound did not match their race and gender identities. Eventually, as one reporter characterized the situation, "The burden of being trail-blazers within their own industry became too great."[194] Considering the group's fortunes, Echols stated, "Labelle's disbanding proved that three very talented but uncompromising black women could go only so far in the music industry. Race ruled, if somewhat less so in discos than on the radio. . . . Conceived transatlantically, sustained by their audacious pursuit of the unattainable, Labelle slammed up against the realities of the American music industry."[195] But while they were out there, Labelle advanced black women's presence, voices, and perspectives into the white and male-centered realm of 1970s rock. They crossed and melded music genres; engaged the discourses of women's rights, black power, and gay liberation; and pursued a radical vision of self-determination. And they managed to circulate their work in a context in which narrow concepts of appropriate creative work for black women prevailed. Labelle's theory and practice responded to the particularity of black women's experiences and the still revolutionary idea that, as the Combahee River Collective put it, "Black women are inherently valuable."[196] At once grounded and aspirational, Labelle explored the political and entertainment possibilities of popular music. "We are futuristic," Patti LaBelle explained in 1975, "but we are not outer space or spaced out. . . . We are about space right here on earth, and our music is not just rock. We are about inner space . . . space for everybody to live decently with respect and dignity."[197] Reflecting on Labelle years after the group disbanded, Sarah Dash told me, "We were innovators and change makers in our approach to the whole music industry. We liberated the old way of coming on stage. . . . We showed people that you can be who you want to be and you don't have to follow anybody's patterns."[198] Offering a new pattern, Labelle executed a stunning experiment in the expression of black feminism, black womanhood, and black women's creativity. It was a revolution people could dance to.

SEVEN / The Fearless Funk of Betty Davis

I don't think I was ahead of my time, I think I was just testing the time. / **BETTY DAVIS**

In June 2007, I interviewed Betty Davis. A creative maverick, Davis pushed the limits of musical and lyrical orthodoxies in the 1970s and then vanished from public view at the end of the decade. Light in the Attic Records was reissuing Davis's long out-of-print albums, *Betty Davis* and *They Say I'm Different*, on compact disc and was looking for press coverage. I proposed doing a story about Davis for *EbonyJet.com*, *Ebony* magazine's online platform, where a friend, Eric Easter, was editor-in-chief. Eric was keen to have the piece, and Light in the Attic confirmed that Ms. Davis would be available for an interview. I began preparing my questions and entertained myself with visions of a pilgrimage to western Pennsylvania, where she was rumored to live, to meet the reclusive black rock legend. No such luck. Ms. Davis was only doing phone interviews. At the designated time, I would phone the label's publicist, who would connect me with Davis on a conference call. No need to get on a plane or even get her phone number.

When I was setting up the interview, both Oliver Wang, who had interviewed Davis when he was preparing the liner notes for the reissues, and Chris Estey, the publicist who arranged my conversation with her, warned me that she was not very talkative. Still, I was thrown off by an interlocutor who dealt in short answers with little exposition. Davis was succinct, and in the fifty minutes during which our conversation unfolded, she did not fill in pauses with further comments (so much for that interview strategy; in fact, I had to suppress the urge to fill in the silences myself). Rare and fascinating in an era of celebrity overexposure, Davis did not seem interested in being in the spotlight again. When describing the process of putting together the reissues, Light in the Attic founder and co-owner Matt Sullivan told me that Davis refused an invitation for an on-camera interview with a midwestern television station. And she had managed all of the business related to the reissues by phone and fax. No one from the industry side had seen her in years, and even Sullivan had never met her in person.[1] Being a recluse only added to Davis's mystique. But why all the fuss about her?

Betty Davis wrote her lyrics and music, created musical arrangements, and produced many of the tracks on the albums she released between 1973 and 1976. She tapped into the sounds and energies of the late 1960s and early 1970s, developing a musical aesthetic that foregrounded a voice that was dangerous—in terms of both how it sounded and what it said. She drew on rock, blues, and funk, and built songs around her raw vocal style, high-volume guitars, funky rhythm lines, and occasional horn arrangements. Songs like "If I'm in Luck I Might Get Picked Up," "Don't Call Her No Tramp," and "Nasty Gal" celebrated independent black women who were not afraid to explore their sexual desires. A former model, Davis was a stylish all-American beauty with an enormous Afro (see figure 7.1). Onstage she danced energetically, highlighting her physicality and, to use the language of her era, her sex appeal. As a black woman with a commitment to sonic, lyrical, and performance experimentation, Davis shared many of the goals and challenges of the African American vocal trio Labelle, which had released a self-titled debut in 1971, two years before the arrival of *Betty Davis*. There were, however, significant differences between these artists. Lyrically, Davis operated with a more singular focus on sexuality and relationships, mostly eschewing broader social and political issues. Furthermore, Davis came out of and drew from different musical traditions than Labelle. Absent from Davis's vocals was the gospel sound that had come to signal authenticity in African American singers, particularly in women. Instead, Davis drew on the blues, singing in a raw style against her rock band's guitar-centered arrangements. Her vocal and musical sound did not seem to match her black female body.

The liberated black femininity that Davis modeled grew out of a quest for a form of expression that would allow her to present feelings and experiences using music, lyrics, and a vocal style that resonated with her. For Davis this self-expression included a frank exploration of sexual pleasure and desire, private concerns that had become increasingly public as the sexual revolution took hold during the 1970s. Davis explored these conditions from a black woman's perspective in a cultural context where women were publicly demanding

FIGURE 7.1 Betty Davis, 1970. © BARON WOLMAN.

equal rights and an end to gender-based double standards. Davis's embrace
of the sexuality that had always percolated in rock and roll was dangerous
because it trafficked in imagery that had been used so long and so effectively
to dehumanize black women. Undaunted, Davis wrote songs that celebrated
sexual independence. In grappling with sexuality, Davis offered a release from
dominant images of black women, such as the desexualized mammy, the tragic
mulatto, and the vindictive sapphire.[2] Instead, she confronted and engaged the
image of the black woman as a sexually available object by presenting herself
and the women she sang about as being comfortable with and in control of
their sexuality. The decision to assert a black woman's sexual agency was bold
and risky. In the early 1970s, many African American women, particularly
middle-class women, were still wary of publicly speaking about sexual matters

for fear of confirming stereotypes.[3] Davis addressed the question of black women's sexual subjectivity in a context that offered limited opportunities for black female–centered expressions. In fact, her music can be understood as a response to the aesthetics and politics of male-centered rock and funk music. Davis brought a black woman's voice and concerns into these arenas.

Davis was not the only black woman delving into the politics of sexuality in her music and performance during the 1970s. As I showed in the previous chapter, Labelle also discussed sexuality from a black feminist viewpoint, and singers such as Chaka Khan, Millie Jackson, Roberta Flack, and Aretha Franklin embodied an empowered black femininity. I focus on Davis's exploration of sexual terrain because her significant difference from expected African American musical sound affected the progress of her career in ways that speak directly to the issues of gender, race, and genre that concern me. Davis's vocals and musical arrangements diverged from what was marketed as music for African Americans. Her deliberate genre-bending and the cultural politics that underwrote her aesthetic choices challenged record label personnel, music marketers, radio programmers, journalists, and audiences accustomed to black female vocal artists deploying the subject matter, modes of self-presentation, and gospel-influenced style that produced a soulful sound and image. Betty Davis was not a soul singer. Betty Davis rocked. A friend of Jimi Hendrix, she had been active in the late sixties hard rock scenes of Los Angeles and New York, and she brought rock attitude to her music, conflating categories and crossing boundaries. Drawing from press coverage, her recordings, and the interview I conducted with her, I discuss Davis's trajectory and consider the consequences of her choices. Davis's career is an object lesson in the perils faced by black women artists whose musical productions fall outside the limited parameters of expected and accepted music by black women. She made a valiant effort to give voice to an aesthetic that centered black women's sexual politics; an analysis of her work and its reception show how restrictive notions of race, gender, and genre nearly rendered an unconventional black woman musician inaudible.

Becoming Betty Davis

Betty Davis was born Elizabeth Mabry in Durham, North Carolina, on July 26, 1945.[4] When she was twelve, her family moved from Durham to Pittsburgh, where her father took a job as foreman at a steel mill. At age sixteen, she left home for New York City to attend the Fashion Institute of Technology. Once there, she established herself as a hip young woman about town who moved in fashion and music circles with her friends Jenni Dean, Emmaretta Marks, Winona Williams, and Devon Wilson. She cofounded and managed a dance club called the Cellar and was a friend and early muse of groundbreaking African American fashion designer Stephen Burrows.[5] Davis signed with the Wilhelmina modeling agency and appeared in magazines such as *Seventeen, Ebony,* and *Glamour.* During a period when she lived in Los Angeles, she was a contestant on the television show *The Dating Game* and was also a *Jet* magazine pinup.[6] In the *Jet* photo, a two-page spread in the digest-sized magazine, she posed beachside in a crocheted bikini, her hair blowing in the breeze. The accompanying text, running under the title "Net Gain," reads, "Caught in a net of her own weaving is pretty Betty Mabry of Los Angeles, who designed her own swim outfit of fishnet and spangles. Betty's own design is 32-22-34, and she likes clothes 'that make me feel free and able to move.'"[7]

In addition to pursuing an interest in fashion design, Davis was involved in music. She did some background vocal work for South African trumpeter Hugh Masekela and cut the singles "Get Ready for Betty" (1964) and "Live, Love, Learn"/"It's My Life" (1968).[8] She was also writing songs, placing one with the Chambers Brothers, then an up-and-coming rock and soul band. Her recollection of her encounter with the group reveals her confidence and ambition:

> **Betty Davis:** Well, there was a club in New York called the Electric Circus and they were appearing at the club and on their break I went to them and I introduced myself and I told them I had written a really good song for them. So they wanted to hear it then. So I sang some of it for them and they told me to get in contact with their producer at the time, because they were getting ready to record an album called "Time Has Come." And so I did and they recorded the song.

> **MM:** And you just assumed that you could approach a band with a song even though you hadn't had your . songs recorded before? That seemed like a reasonable assumption?

> **Betty Davis:** Yeah . . . I mean. Anybody could do that. If you have a song and you feel that it's good for a certain

person or a certain group, you can meet them and tell them about the song. And if they're interested—because all artists are open for suggestions.[9]

The Chambers Brothers' recording of her song "Uptown to Harlem" appeared on the band's 1967 debut album, *The Time Has Come*, as "Uptown" and secured Betty Mabry her first songwriting credit.[10] She was twenty-two years old.

During this period she met and, in 1968, married jazz trumpeter Miles Davis, who, at forty-two, was about twenty years her senior.[11] *DownBeat* reported on the whirlwind romance:

> The couple was married in Gary, Ind. on the last day of September, following Davis' engagement at Chicago's Plugged Nickel. Only the trumpeter's closest friends knew of his plans, but Davis was obviously in excellent spirits throughout his stay at the Nickel. The new Mrs. Davis, a 5'7" beauty from Homestead, Pa., first saw Miles two years ago at a concert in New York. She says, "We were introduced, but nothing came of it until six months ago." Engaged five days before the marriage, she said: "He called me from Chicago and said, 'Sweetcakes, get your stuff together and come to Chicago, we're getting married.'"

In her comments to *DownBeat*, the new Mrs. Davis was a devoted wife:

> Obviously happy in her new role, Mrs. Davis said, "One of the sexiest men alive is Miles Dewey Davis. We're going to be married forever, because I'm in love, and Mr. Davis can do no wrong as far as I'm concerned. He's experienced all facets of life, has terrific taste in everything, loves only the best, and has taught me many things." Mrs. Davis added that she has "never really been a jazz fan, because I lean mostly to R&B and pop, but Miles' *Sketches of Spain* and *Kind of Blue* really sock it to me. But Miles is the teacher, so I'm going to be cool, stay in the background, and back up my man."[12]

The reality was more complex. In spite of her assertions to the reporter, she did not "stay in the background" after they married, a point that might have contributed to the dissolution of the union. While they were a couple, though, Betty's influence on Miles was significant. She was the guiding force behind the sharp musical turn that Miles Davis took at the end of the 1960s and that culminated in the 1969 release *Bitches Brew*, a recording *DownBeat* magazine called "the most revolutionary jazz album in history."[13] Betty introduced Miles to her friend Jimi Hendrix, turning him on to the young guitarist's music as well as that of Sly Stone. She helped him update his wardrobe and took him to New York City discos and rock clubs, where music was played at a high, body-shaking volume, helping him find an electric solution to sonic issues that had been nagging him.[14] Miles acknowledged her effect on him, stating, "Betty was a big influence on my personal life as well as my musical life. . . . The marriage only lasted about a year, but that year was full of new things and surprises and helped point the way I was to go, both in my music and, in some ways, my lifestyle."[15] Miles put Betty's photo on the cover of his 1968 release *Filles de Kilimanjaro* and the song "Mademoiselle Mabry," named for her, is a reworking of Hendrix's "The Wind Cries Mary."[16] Miles Davis biographer John Szwed reports that the song "Bitches Brew" was "a roiling, lurching piece that opened with Miles playing off of one of Betty's own songs . . . while he looked at her."[17] She also helped name the album. He was considering "Witches Brew" until Betty suggested alliteration would make a better title.[18]

Davis made music while serving as a muse and midwife for her husband's work. As Miles was recording *Bitches Brew*, Betty was cutting an album for Columbia Records, featuring personnel affiliated with Miles Davis and Jimi Hendrix. Wayne Shorter wrote the charts, Tony Williams and Mitch Mitchell took turns at the drums, and Billy Cox played bass.[19] Teo Macero was the producer, and Miles directed the proceedings, but in the end, the project was shelved. In 2007 Betty told a reporter, "Miles was afraid that if the record came out, I'd leave him. He thought I'd become a star. He wanted to hold me back in a way. He was very old-fashioned."[20] In interviews, Betty references her ex-husband's positive influence on her career, but she has also said that his jealousy and temper made it impossible to stay with him. In his autobiography, Miles confessed that he had made an error in marrying her: "See, Betty was too young and wild for the things I expected from a woman."[21] The couple divorced after roughly a year of marriage.

Newly single, Davis wrote several songs for Lionel Richie's group, the Commodores, then a fledgling funk band that needed material for a demo. They submitted their versions of Davis's songs to Motown and received a recording contract.[22] The label offered Davis a songwriting deal, but she refused to sign the contract because it required her to give up her publishing.[23] She continued writing and took a break from the States with a visit to London. When we spoke she was not specific about the reason for going to England—"I just started to go there, that's all," she told me.[24] Journalist John Balloon, who has chronicled her career, speculates that it had something to do with the fact that at the time she was dating English guitarist Eric Clapton, whom he calls "her post-Miles rebound."[25] While in London she met some of the leading figures of the rock scene.[26]

> **MM:** I wanted to ask you about Marc Bolan because I understand that he had some role in the development of your career. You knew him?
>
> **Betty Davis:** Yeah, before I did my first album. . . . That's when I was having the back and forth with the Commodores. I was living in England at the time and Marc was rehearsing in a studio of a friend of mine and they introduced us. He set me up an appointment with Essex Records.
>
> **MM:** Did he encourage you to continue writing?
>
> **Betty Davis:** He told me I should do my own songs.
>
> **MM:** Had anyone else suggested that?
>
> **Betty Davis:** No.[27]

Before long, Davis had moved to the San Francisco Bay area and signed a deal with Just Sunshine Records, a label started by Michael Lang, one of the organizers of the Woodstock Music and Art Festival.[28] On the strength of her being Miles's ex and a recommendation from a mutual friend, former Sly and the Family Stone drummer Gregg Errico agreed to produce Davis's first album, assembling a band that he has referred to as a "Bay Area who's who."[29] Ex-Family Stone bassist Larry Graham, one of the architects of funk, played on most of the tracks; Carlos Santana's bass player Doug Rauch showed up on the rest. They were joined by Neal Schon, a guitarist who had played with Santana and went on to play in Journey; horn players from the Tower of Power; and the Pointer Sisters and future disco star Sylvester on background vocals. Davis wrote the music and lyrics and created the arrangements for all of the songs. She brought these arrangements into the studio, where the musicians riffed on the structures she had outlined, listened to her hum and verbally describe the parts, and adjusted their approach until they achieved the sound and feel she wanted.[30]

Betty Davis was released in 1973 and garnered media attention because of the singer-songwriter's connection to a jazz great. (Her decision to keep her married name may have been strategic.) A conversation with her ex-husband after her debut release convinced her that she could produce herself, and she went on to produce her subsequent albums.[31] Davis released her follow-up, *They Say I'm Different*, in 1974 and began to tour, mostly on the East Coast and in California. By virtue of her hands-on involvement in songwriting, arranging, singing, producing, and performing, Davis offers a rare example of a woman musician in the pop context who was in charge of conceptualizing an artistic vision and bringing it to fruition. Davis remained on the independent Just Sunshine label for her first two recordings and then moved to Chris Blackwell's Island Records, a label with a more extensive marketing and distribution network and a reputation as a home for cutting-edge music. Blackwell bought Davis's contract with the hope that Island would be able to generate more sales for her work, but her 1975 release *Nasty Gal* disappointed in terms of units sold, and it was not a critical success. Davis continued to tour, and in 1976 recorded her fourth album, *Crashin' from Passion*. Mediocre sales figures and the death of her father weighed on Davis, and by the end of the decade, she had ceased to record, perform in concert, or speak to the press.[32] Her disappearance from the scene was so complete that many of her fans assumed she had died.

Betty Davis on Record

The songs on Davis's first release are sung from the perspective of a woman with few illusions about romantic relationships. In "Anti-Love Song," for example, Davis voices her decision to avoid commitment, a counterintuitive stance, given the fact that pop culture typically encourages women to seek monogamous unions.[33] Davis's narrator acknowledges her paramour's ability to "have me shaking" and "climbing the walls," but she coyly predicts that he would fall even harder for her: "I'd have you eating your ego," she warns. "I'd make you pocket your pride." "Anti-Love Song" is a declaration of independence, a refusal to succumb to the physical enticements of a relationship that would ultimately falter as each of the two lovers struggled to be the one in control. The song expresses a coolheaded reasoning in an arrangement that features Davis's voice singing in an intimate purr against a pulsing musical background. Piano chords punctuate the ends of verses, but rather than build to a climax, the music returns to a steady vamp that underpins the lyrics and shows off Davis's seductive, teasing side.

Davis did not consider herself a vocalist and characterized becoming a front woman as an accident. In a 1974 interview, she said, "I was never really a singer. . . . My main thing is writing. When I went to the record company, I told them that I wasn't a singer. But they liked the way I sounded and said, 'Wow, we have an artist here,' but I didn't come to them as an artist."[34] She thought of herself as a musician who used her voice to convey her musical ideas. Significantly, it was a voice that defied mainstream expectations of how a black woman should sound. Unlike many of her African American contemporaries, Davis's sound was not rooted in the black church; instead, she drew on the blues. When I spoke to her she recalled pleasurable childhood hours spent in rural North Carolina listening to records from her grandmother's "huge blues collection" and learning the music of blues artists John Lee Hooker, Lightnin' Hopkins, Jimmy Reed, Muddy Waters, Big Mama Thornton, and Koko Taylor; she identified this time as central to her musical development.[35] Speaking to an interviewer in 1975 she explained, "Aretha Franklin is a singer. I consider myself more of a projector. I'm into sound. Like I'll work my voice a thousand different ways. I'm into making my voice work with the rhythm track. Whatever feel I'm getting from the rhythm track I'll do it with my voice."[36] An acrobatic stretching and squeezing marks Davis's vocal style. She would sing in an insinuating whisper or a throaty growl, while manipulating words, yelps, squeals, "whoos," and "ooows." Commenting on her sound, writer and musician Vivien Goldman observes, "You can hear courage in the way Davis worked her vocal register—ratcheting her pretty alto into a drilling, grating vibrato and an off-the-meter soprano screech—suggesting a woman pushing herself to extremes, testing her mental and physical endurance, refusing to accept limits."[37]

Her vocals on "Game Is My Middle Name," a song on her first album, exemplify Davis's "singer-as-projector" approach.[38] Midway through the song, she and her background singers engage in a series of vocalizations that anticipate the raw-throated experiments of punk. Repeating the lines, "Whatever you want to play, I said I'll play it with you / Game is my middle name," they rupture the song's groove in order to explore vocal sound. First, Sylvester sings the line in a low voice. Next, the Pointer Sisters take the vocals up an octave, repeating the line and increasing the volume and intensity.[39] Finally, Davis enters, holding notes almost to her voice's breaking point, shifting from singing to wailing to an untethered scream. All the while, the vocals intertwine with a twisting guitar solo. This song, like a number of Betty Davis compositions, breaks "the generic contract" of funk; that is to say, you can't easily dance to

"Games"'s midtune vocal exhibition and guitar solo.[40] Here and elsewhere, Davis used a form of vocalizing that was not associated with black women.

Arguably, she was following the impulse to experiment that characterized the work of Miles Davis, Sly Stone, and Jimi Hendrix, the artists whom she names as her primary influences. She admired Stone's arrangements, and she appreciated Hendrix's approach to his instrument, especially "the amount of bottom that he put on his guitar."[41] Like Hendrix, she had an idiosyncratic singing voice and a love for the blues. Davis's debt to the blues was evident in her lyrical content and performance attitude and, by her second and third albums, in the structure of some of her songs. In "They Say I'm Different," the title cut of her second album, Davis celebrates her southern roots and blues music.[42] With its rhythm and instrumentation, the song would fit on a southern rock playlist. Davis's southern accent augments the song's down-home feel as she recalls waking up early to slop the hogs, sings about a great-grandmother who spit snuff, describes a great-grandfather who would "be rockin' his moonshine to B. B. King and Jimmy Reed," and affirms her love of chitlins. Her connection to southern rural life is the thing that leads others—presumably the northern city dwellers she encountered after her family left North Carolina—to say she is "different" and "strange," as she puts it in the lyrics. With a twanging blues guitar responding to her calls throughout the tune, Davis acknowledges the musicians who shaped her sound. Among the names she calls are Muddy Waters, Sonny Terry, Big Mama Thornton, Albert King, Howlin' Wolf, Lightnin' Hopkins, Bessie Smith, Robert Johnson, Bo Diddley, and Chuck Berry. By 1974 when she recorded the track, it was unusual for young, urban African-Americans to profess an interest in the blues, but this musical love was central to who Davis was as an individual and as a musician. "They Say I'm Different," with its blues-based sonics and list of blues artists, both explained Davis's difference and situated her in an African American musical lineage.

Davis's melding of rock, blues, and funk was very much a product of her era, but Davis and her music were difficult to sell. Racialized practices of music marketing coupled with her identity as a black woman pushed her outside the presumed white and male arena of rock, which was, ironically, populated in part by fans sharing Davis's love of the blues. Instead, she was assigned to the black genre of funk. But the rock and blues that melded with Davis's funky bass lines were not in fashion for the majority of the black record-buyers who were funk's target audience. Add to this a vocal and lyrical approach that refused to be confined to the sounds and subjects deemed appropriate for black women, and you have the Betty Davis package: a musician who confounded audiences—black and white.

Betty Davis Live

Betty Davis put on a good live show, and her onstage performances are central to the Betty Davis legend. Here are some excerpts from contemporary accounts—all written by men.[43] From the *New York Times* in 1974: "She moans, groans, hollers, hisses, begs and demands when she sings one of her own songs. She struts, shakes, twists, turns and sticks her tongue out lecherously when she performs."[44] From *Melody Maker* in 1975: "Her stage shows . . . even more so than her albums, are raucous, raunchy, grinding affairs"; and "She cultivates the image of a mean, foxy, lascivious, outspoken, musically funky lady."[45] And this from a *Billboard* reporter writing in 1976: "Opening the show was Betty Davis, a performer with questionable taste and even more questionable talent."[46] He just wasn't buying it.

To date, I have been unable to locate footage of Betty Davis performing live. Matt Sullivan of Light in the Attic Records told me that in spite of extensive searching, he and his staff did not find anything—a promotional clip, a recording of a European television appearance, a concert video—that they could add to the reissued CD package.[47] The absence of a moving image of Davis is striking, given the availability of footage of artists who were her contemporaries, and it speaks to the ways her sound and performance persona, coupled with her status as an artist on an independent label, limited her access to mainstream airwaves. Without the experience of seeing a Betty Davis concert and without a filmed image of her to study, I turned to people who saw her perform in the 1970s to get a sense of her live show (see figure 7.2). Bearing in mind that a great deal of time had passed since they saw these concerts, that memories may be faulty, and that recollections of the past are often shaped by information available in the present, I still find it useful to draw on these descriptions. Davis made a favorable impression on Sarah Dash, whose group Labelle was pushing sartorial and performance boundaries at the same time as Davis. When I interviewed Dash for this book, she commented briefly on her response to Davis's act: "I saw her in the [West] Village many, many years ago. I loved it. I thought she was just wonderfully out there. She was out there. And it was great because you'd never seen anybody do that. It was different."[48] The two men I spoke with about Davis shared vivid memories of seeing her.

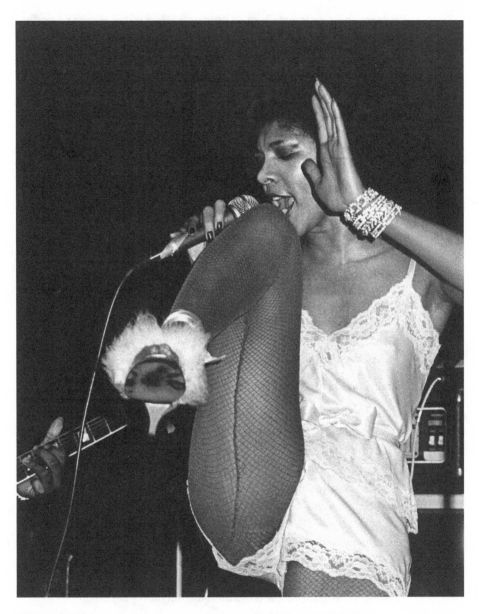

FIGURE 7.2 When performing in support of her 1975 album *Nasty Gal*, Betty Davis made an entrance wearing a long raincoat, but she performed most of her set in lingerie. Pictured here in a teddy, tap pants, fishnet stockings, and high-heeled boudoir slippers, Davis displayed a strong physicality while on stage. Her raised leg and hand are evidence of the "aggressive" style for which her live performances were known. COURTESY RUDY CALVO COLLECTION/CACHE AGENCY.

I present their comments here to provide a sense of her show and performance style. Sherman Fleming, an African American visual and performance artist, saw Davis perform when he was attending college at Virginia Commonwealth University in Richmond, Virginia. The school's black student union had booked her. Fleming decided to go to the concert because he thought the ex-wife of Miles Davis, a highly revered figure, would be worth seeing. He was probably not the only ticket buyer who followed this logic. Indeed, her ex-husband's validation was part of the millennial marketing of Betty Davis. The print ad for the Light in the Attic reissues featured this Miles Davis quote: "If Betty were singing today she would be something like Madonna, something like Prince only as a woman."[49] Recalling the show, Fleming said:

> It was the first time I'd seen a radical black woman performer who wasn't all gussied up the way most black women were back then. Her whole persona ran counter to every other black woman out there. Her music had hints of jazz, R&B, fusion, and soul, but you really couldn't pin down what she was doing. She'd probably fit in now, but in 1973 when I saw her she really didn't fit anywhere. I kind of saw her as a rocker. If she had been a white woman, there would've been no question about where she fit, but as a black woman she was hard to place.[50]

Fleming recalled Davis's powerful visual impact:

> First of all, she was a knockout. She wore high, high boots and she was poured into her outfit and she had this enormous Afro. She kind of made me think of Angela Davis. She had a sexual thing in her performance and there was a cacophony of music. It was a high-energy performance and she really commanded the whole stage. And the way she held the microphone and leaned on the stand accented her body, different parts at different times. She exuded this power. Shimmying, moving, dancing, she was in motion a lot. She was really slinky. She did a lot of kicking and she was wearing these high platforms, but she moved like she was just wearing sandals. The performance was inspiring because she showed that a black woman and black people could do something really different.[51]

Davis's sonic and visual difference also made an impression on Michael Hill, an African American guitarist, singer, and songwriter, who leads the band Michael Hill's Blues Mob; he saw Betty Davis perform in New York in 1975 in support of her third album, *Nasty Gal*. The show was at the Bottom Line, and she opened for blues guitarist Freddie King. An aspiring musician at the time,

Hill and two of his male friends attended the show; he was already familiar with her work. Here's how he described the evening:

> At the beginning of the show she came in wearing a long raincoat, completely covered up. I don't remember whether the band played a fanfare or not. Then she took off the coat to reveal that she was just wearing a slip. A white slip. She was very aggressive on stage. When she came out, there was no chatting with the audience. She wasn't trying to be ingratiating. It was just, here it is, off we go. She was very sensual. As the show went on and she sweated, the slip became see-through. Let's just say my friends and I were very pleased.[52]

Hill enjoyed the visual part of the performance, what he described as "Betty's beauty and sensuality," but he was also taken by the music and the individuality it expressed:

> At that time in music, there weren't that many black women coming with their own sexuality right out there in front. This was her stuff—her songs, her lyrics, her thing. We were seriously excited about her. When she played, most of the audience was kind of stunned. They weren't hostile, but shocked. My group of friends and I were sitting down in front and we were really into it and cheering, but that wasn't the way the rest of the audience was responding. This was a blues audience there for Freddie King. Betty Davis was such a surprise. She was playing intense rock-based funk. . . . Her voice wasn't gospel-R&B derived. It was much more singular, much more of a performance art thing.[53]

The descriptions from Hill and Fleming encapsulate what was compelling about Davis. Discussing her performance style in 1974, Davis told *Jet* magazine, "I'm very aggressive on stage and men don't usually like aggressive women because . . . the whole direction of man is to be strong. They usually like submissive women, or women that pretend to be submissive."[54] Davis's performance persona, an independent woman comfortable with her sexuality and not at all submissive, was unorthodox. Like the best rock and rollers, she was a little dangerous.

Sound and Vision

Betty Davis never made it onto any of the charts in question—R&B, pop, or disco. She did not produce a sound sought by those programming music at black radio stations or at taste-making discotheques, and her race and gender made her automatically off-limits to programmers at rock stations. Davis did not possess the big-voiced vocal power of Aretha Franklin, Tina Turner, the women of Labelle, or Gloria Gaynor; nor did she dabble in the whispery sultriness of Diana Ross or Donna Summer. Soul, R&B, and disco, the musical slots available for black women, were not viable ones for Betty Davis. Funk, the black rock category and an overwhelmingly male arena, was the most likely fit, and that genre was not mainstream.

The visual image that Davis presented compounded the challenges created by her sound. On her album covers, as in her live performances, Davis broke with the long-standing black performance tradition of dressing up. Instead, like Labelle on the group's early album covers, she followed the looser rules of the rock scene. On her first album, she adapted street fashion, appearing in a low-cut, midriff-baring blouse, denim shorts, and thigh-high silver platform boots. Her second album showed her wearing a high-collared, sleeveless leotard with a design that was one part futuristic, one part tribal. For *Nasty Gal*, she took inspiration from the boudoir and wore a black teddy, fishnet tights, and high heels. Complementing her striking attire was her voluminous Afro. This hairstyle had increased in popularity during the 1960s, but it still signaled a level of positive identification with blackness that mainstream whites and blacks who were accustomed to straightened hairstyles for African American women often perceived as confrontational. In a 1976 interview, Davis speculated about the impact of her look on her career:

> One thing I found out about this business, they have to be able to categorize you. If they can't bag you, you're fucked. And aesthetically they couldn't categorize me. I'm not Tina Turner. I don't wear a wig and I don't have three girls shaking it up behind me. The acts that have made it wore straight hair, earrings, and long gowns.[55]

Davis's weariness with the sonic and sartorial expectations for black women and her awareness of the price she paid for departing from them are evident in this quote. She was breaking so many rules on so many levels, it is no wonder that she faced challenges. Some of her white female contemporaries such as Carole King, Joni Mitchell, Laura Nyro, and Carly Simon were establishing creative autonomy by writing their own lyrics and music, and they addressed issues of intimacy and desire from women's perspectives. But none of them fused these lyrical articulations of sexual subjectivity with embodied performances that centered and celebrated sexuality to the degree that Davis did.[56] Furthermore, their vocal sound and instrumental arrangements aligned with soft rock, a gentler style that seemed appropriately feminine. In contrast, every facet of Davis's performance was on the edge. Still, when I spoke with Davis decades after her retirement, she had little to say about the impact of her gender and race on her fortunes in the business, for example:

> **MM:** Did you feel you faced challenges as a songwriter and an arranger because you were a woman? Because it seems like there are very few women doing that kind of work.
>
> **Betty Davis:** No.
>
> **MM:** The guys were willing to listen? Because most of the musicians you were working with were men.
>
> **Betty Davis:** Mmm-hmm. [affirmative]
>
> **MM:** And they didn't—they behaved?
>
> **Betty Davis:** Yeah. I had problems with a couple of them, but not all of them. On the whole, they were very—I had a respect for them and they had a respect for me.

And, a bit later:

> **MM:** So, did you—I kind of asked you this before, but because it's still so unusual for a woman to write and produce the material that she performs—did you think of yourself as doing something unusual when you were writing your own music and eventually producing it?
>
> **Betty Davis:** No, I was just interested in keeping the sound pure.
>
> **MM:** Keeping the sound pure?
>
> **Betty Davis:** Yeah.
>
> **MM:** And you felt that you needed to be in charge of it to make sure your vision was realized? Is that what you mean?
>
> **Betty Davis:** Yeah.

And, one more try:

> **MM:** Do you feel like you faced any particular chal-
> lenges because you were a black woman?
>
> **Betty Davis:** No.

Obviously, my efforts to squeeze an articulated black feminist critique from Davis
fell flat. Coupled with the fact that Davis is not a loquacious interview subject—it
was difficult to get her to speak extensively on most of the topics I raised—is the
possibility that she simply had a mindset that did not view what she was doing as
extraordinary. Maybe anything other than a determined, matter-of-fact attitude
would have impeded her ability to gain control of her music.

Artistic Autonomy

The musical sound, performance style, and public demeanor that Davis put
forward grew out of a commitment to artistic self-determination. She used
her music to construct and convey an image of who she was as a young black
woman, and took control of her music: writing and, after her first album, producing the material herself. Her live performances celebrated black women's
beauty and desirability, while directly confronting the tangled question of
sexual desire and personal autonomy from a black woman's perspective. By
the early seventies, Davis had broken off from a powerful older man in the
recording industry, her ex-husband Miles Davis, and was establishing herself
as an independent professional. Her decision to reject a songwriting contract
offer from Motown because it required her to relinquish songwriting rights
indicates her desire to maintain autonomy and chart her trajectory on her
own terms. Davis was aware that onstage and off she was breaching mainstream ideals of proper femininity. Her performance persona, an independent
woman forthright about her sexuality, was unorthodox as was her insistence
on placing "black female desire and pleasure in the forefront" in spite of "society's stigmas against female sexual agency and desire."[57] Davis's performances
attacked male-centered standards that called on women to highlight their
physical attractiveness and sexual desirability, while repressing their sexual
subjectivity. Direct engagement with sexuality and desire from a woman's perspective was central to Davis's project.

Davis's provocative style led to some of her concerts being canceled because of protests by religious and civic groups, and *Melody Maker* reported that "Women's Lib organizations" had protested against her lyrics.[58] In interviews, Davis focused on her trouble with black middle-class gatekeepers. Her lyrics and imagery broke the rules of black middle-class respectability that throughout the twentieth century sought integration through "proper" behavior.[59] The title of the first track on her first album, "If I'm in Luck I Might Get Picked Up," set the alarming tone. Here, Davis takes on the persona of a woman searching for a sexual good time and details her actions: "I'm wiggling my fanny / I'm raunchy dancing." Davis's narrator joyously names her "vamping, tramping" and describes herself as "crazy," "wild," and "nasty." Some listeners were so uncomfortable with this unvarnished representation of female desire that they complained when a Detroit radio station played the song, leading the local National Association for the Advancement of Colored People (NAACP) to join in the protests.[60] Commenting in 1976, Davis said the following:

> Bourgeois blacks find me very offensive. They've been programmed to think that black women who shake their asses are whorey. The NAACP called up the record company. I have to be honest. I didn't even know what they stood for. . . . What are they? Who are they? I thought about it. They're not trying to advance me. They're trying to stop me from making a living. They stopped all my airplay in Detroit.[61]

Here, Davis offers a gender and class analysis, explaining that going against the rules of black middle-class propriety cost her radio exposure. Her songs and her quip about the meaning of "advancement" can be understood as the kinds of "counternarratives to a black political vision largely defined and maintained by a middle-class Christian patriarchy" that cultural critic Mark Anthony Neal identifies as central to black feminist discourse of the early 1970s.[62]

Both black middle-class activists and the white middle-class press disdained Davis's style, and, by the time of *Nasty Gal*, Davis responded to the attacks in song. She launches "Dedicated to the Press" with the cry, "Hey, now! Extra! Extra! Have you read about me?" and proceeds to recount media critiques and defend her position.[63] She quotes from the negative reviews I have cited here and addresses her detractors directly, pitying their inability to get into her, but claiming not to care. But the very existence of the song suggests that she *did* care, that the criticism was getting under her skin; she even asks, "Why do they blame me for what I am?" Lamenting that this need to respond led Davis to become "obsessed with stating and reasserting her position," Vivien Goldman observes that, "It was as if she had succumbed and adopted tabloid values, agreeing that by virtue of being exuberant, sexual, and confrontational, she was not just lusty, but 'shocking,' 'outrageous,' and that her success depended on it."[64] If Davis's self-conscious responses distracted her from her central themes and creative focus, they were also a way of grappling with the problem facing so many African American women—artists and otherwise. "Do you understand me?" she sings to her critics. "Well, if you don't, how can you like me?" To be understood, to be "legible," black women had to present familiar, stereotypical images of black womanhood. If they went beyond the stereotypes or criticized the stereotypes, they risked being indecipherable. The unfamiliar created confusion and discomfort. Both black and white audiences could easily shut down, unable to make sense of the new vision and unwilling to engage with it.[65]

Singer and songwriter Gloria Jones had worked with Davis when the two women did background vocal work on a session for Hugh Masekela in the 1960s, and she followed Davis's career in the 1970s with interest. Jones, another black American woman with a foot in the rock scene, *did* seem to understand and appreciate what Davis was doing. Commenting on Davis's music in 2012, Jones observed, "It was pure, it was honest. . . . And her sound was a gritty sound, raw. It was a mixture of rock and sort of [what I'd now call] a Lady Gaga sound. . . . It wasn't really something that you were used to hearing, but she was so in the pocket. I would say she was rock."[66] The people responsible for selling Davis's music had a more difficult time than Jones addressing the question of genre.

Breaking the Rules

Betty Davis liberated herself from the rules of respectability that both black and white women were expected to follow, but her brand of black female independence created challenges for the recording industry professionals charged with selling her music. One problem was assigning Davis to a music genre. "Black rock," which is sometimes used interchangeably with funk, was one term for the kind of music that Betty Davis and others in her cohort such as Funkadelic, the Ohio Players, Mandrill, War, and Labelle were producing. They engaged the vocal, instrumental, and performance practices associated with African American music-making, but also incorporated musical and performance practices that were associated with rock music—particularly the centering of the electric guitar, the use of distortion and high volume, exaggerated costuming, raucous expression of sexuality, and social and political commentaries (although these could also be found in black popular music). The genre-blending that these kinds of creative moves involved gave the artists a betwixt-and-between status as they insisted on producing music that was neither definitively "rock" nor exclusively "black."

The people marketing Davis's music responded to their understanding of the racial politics of music by booking concerts in cities with large black fan bases such as Philadelphia, Washington, DC, Detroit, and New York. *Rolling Stone* reviewed Davis's albums, but did not do any features on her. Like the other black rock acts of the era, Davis was not marketed to rock audiences. This racially dictated restriction is lamentable because some rock fans might have appreciated Davis's unusual vocal style and hard-driving music. Commenting on the challenges of promoting Davis's work in this context, Gregg Errico, who produced her first album, noted, "[Betty] had a hard time getting the business people who could make stuff happen to really understand what to do with her and how to do it. It was pretty aggressive stuff. There weren't really radio formats for heavy funk like that. It was just difficult in those days."[67] Funk historian Rickey Vincent has observed that some funk bands sweetened their sound and muted the guitar—in effect tempering the "aggressiveness" or the "rock-ness"—in order to receive airplay on black radio stations.[68] Davis did not take this path, insisting instead on pursuing sonic, lyrical, and performance practices that were not considered appropriate for her race and gender.

These elements stirred controversy, but did not generate record sales. Her label, Island Records, struggled to create a suitable image for her. Vivien Goldman, who was an Island staff member at the time, recalls that Davis's manager insisted that the label destroy publicity stills of a smiling Davis: the photos made her look "too nice," and he believed she had "to look mean" to sell records; it is a situation that suggests Davis's team and her label disagreed about her image.[69] Davis has said that label executives implored her to cover her legs and wear dresses, fearing—accurately it seems—that her sexy displays were turnoffs to mainstream audiences.[70] Still, it is worth remembering that other black musicians were successfully circulating sexy material during this period. Marvin Gaye released *Let's Get It On* in 1973, the same year that *Betty Davis* came out. Whatever outcry there was about the sexual overtones of Gaye's album, its singles received airplay, and the album went to number two on the *Billboard* pop chart.[71] This could be because the sexual self-expression of black men was not policed in the same way as that

of black women and because Gaye's sound was rooted in the familiar musical and lyrical tropes of the R&B loverman. Similarly, vocalist Millie Jackson,
who emerged at roughly the same time as Davis and became known for her
X-rated songs and raps, developed a following in black communities and
saw her singles appear on *Billboard*'s R&B charts from the early 1970s to the
late 1980s.[72] Although lyrically adventurous, her music and vocals fit into the
prevailing R&B style; furthermore, crossover to white audiences was not a
priority. Chaka Khan, the lead vocalist for the band Rufus, also launched her
career in 1973, and like Davis, she created a "wild" visual style and an alluring,
sexually charged stage persona. Khan's affiliation with Rufus, an interracial
rock-funk band in which she was the only female member, put her in the
betwixt-and-between position that black rock and rollers occupy. Like Davis,
Khan had not grown up singing in the black church, but her voice, with its
use of melisma and powerful high notes, had the range and power associated with black women vocalists, and this facilitated success with African
American audiences.[73] Another example is "Lady Marmalade" by the black
female trio Labelle, which I discussed in the previous chapter. This musical
celebration of the sexual magnetism of a Creole prostitute went to number
one on *Billboard*'s pop and R&B charts in 1974, propelled by the gospel-rooted
vocal sound that black women were expected to produce.[74] In contrast to
these examples, Davis's experiments diverged too much from the familiar,
and, by the end of 1976, in the wake of the lackluster sales of *Nasty Gal*, Island had dropped Davis from her contract.[75] Not long after, the label went
on to have a successful run with Grace Jones, another ex-model and *provoc-
ateuse*. They mined and exaggerated Jones's racialized and sexualized difference, which took an androgynous form distinct from Davis's, and placed her
dispassionate alto vocals against discotheque-friendly backing tracks. Jones
perfected a disco–new wave fusion on singles such as "Pull Up to the Bumper" (1981) and "Slave to the Rhythm" (1985), cultivating an underground
audience and outsized reputation in the 1980s.

All of these artists were taking advantage of the fact that popular music
has long been a site for delving into taboo subjects. In blues, R&B, rock, funk,
and rap, black women, most of them from working-class backgrounds, have
produced public discourses that include frank commentary about sexuality.[76] They have sung lyrics that describe romantic and sexual relationships
and comment on their appetites, prowess, fears, and desires. Such musical
performances—whether in the 1920s or the 1970s—transgress black and white
middle-class norms that silence women's speech about sex. In a 1976 interview,

Davis assessed the impact of breaking these silences and reflected on the significance of her style and identity:

> There are many reasons why I turn audiences off. Number one, I'm a woman. And a black woman. . . . I look one way and people think I should be sounding another way. I work like a man. I don't really work like a woman. [Judy] Garland used her hands expressively, for example. Well, I use my body to create similar effects. I don't write about anything people don't do or think about doing. . . . I've had guys get up and walk out while I'm performing. I get more hostility from white males than I do from black males. It's that sexual thing all over again. . . . You put me in New York with a predominantly white male audience and I get a weird reaction.[77]

Davis's creative vision carried her outside the boundaries of proper black and proper female self-presentation and beyond mainstream comfort zones. Indeed, it is telling that she made these comments and received favorable coverage in *High Society,* a pornographic magazine that featured photographs of nude women alongside articles about sex and popular culture. (Davis was stylishly and fully dressed in the photos accompanying the article.) Davis was an innovative woman, but her characterization of her performance practices as being "like a man" and not really "like a woman" reveals just how deeply entrenched notions of gender-appropriate behavior are, even for the individuals who consciously work to challenge them.

In a comment that helps explain the audience responses that Davis describes and that speaks to the radical quality of her performance, feminist historian and cultural critic Tricia Rose notes that black women's sexual agency "displaces masculine privilege—black, white, and beyond—drawing energy away from a male-empowered sexual space toward a female centered and empowered one."[78] This could be the reason that some men walked out of her shows. Rose goes on to delineate an additional challenge that the centering of black women's sexual subjectivity presents: it "de-objectifies black female sexuality without repressing it, which, again, troubles the entrenched notion that explicit female desire is itself vulgar."[79]

Music critic Vernon Gibbs, who wrote favorably about Davis during the height of her visibility, bears out Rose's claims and corroborates Davis's comments when he documents the response Davis was getting in New York City. Writing in *Crawdaddy* in 1975, he observes that Davis "is a phenomenon in places like Washington, Baltimore and especially Philadelphia," but that "none of the radio stations in New York play her records with any consistency, and in her hometown Betty Davis . . . is almost unknown."[80] Chiding New York audiences and critics for being culturally conservative, he states that "the wormy Apple is not ready for a Black Woman's brand of steaming, crotch-grabbing aggression," and notes, "Davis left them too shocked to speak."[81] He also describes a scene at the Bottom Line that supports his contention:

> The hip New York press sat in horror as a *real* woman spread her legs in the ecstasy of the music and admitted that "I used to whip him with a turquoise chain." . . . The horror was universal. The women were all jealous and the men felt emasculated. Davis' group, one of the best post-Sly [Stone] curdling rhythm bands, was fingered as incompetent; her act was called "disgusting," and critics whose job it is to recognize novelty where it exists could only come up with lame lines like, "Well at least we know Miles Davis is a leg man."[82]

Gibbs's commentary pinpoints the ways Davis flummoxed audiences—including New York tastemakers—who were apparently more invested in the status quo than they realized. They might have also been responding to the fact that "young black female sexual agency also displaces the white female subject (and object) in a racist culture that reveres white female sexuality (as much as any female-narrated sexuality is openly revered) at the direct expense of public affirmation of black female sexuality."[83] For Davis, staying true to her artistic vision meant affirming black womanhood in all of its complexity and articulating a black woman's sexual subjectivity. That Davis was expressing this distinctive black woman's perspective through musical and performance tropes might have added to the general discomfort of some audience members—black and white, male and female—who heard rock as the province of white men. Davis upset deeply entrenched rules of race, gender, and genre, making creative choices that drew adventurous fans but alienated listeners who were not yet ready for this degree of liberated black femininity.

Greener Pastures

Worn out by a career marked by limited radio exposure, disappointing sales, censorship, and struggles with record label executives, Betty Davis retreated from the music business and opted to lead a quiet life in Pennsylvania. As a lone African American woman on a singular artistic mission, she deserved the respite. Her contemporaries Labelle had certain advantages over Davis—a more traditional vocal sound, a track record of hits from the girl group era, and access to major labels. Furthermore, as the trio's primary songwriter Nona Hendryx observed, "We had a strong black following, from the Apollo; Labelle had a community. Betty didn't, because she came right out of the box, fully formed."[84] But maybe Labelle's most significant advantage was that they had each other. Discussing her group in 1976, Hendryx told a reporter, "We love each other very much. . . . When you travel on the road like we have for fifteen years, live in the same room, eat hot dogs, you learn all the things that make you respect the other person's values, the things you like about them, and the things you love about them. You cry together, and go through all these things together."[85] In contrast, Davis went through everything alone; she had no supportive sisterhood as she went out on a creative limb.

Davis got further than the majority of performers who try to launch careers in the notoriously competitive and unpredictable recording industry. Although she did not achieve the commercial success she might have hoped for during the 1970s, by the beginning of the new millennium, a confluence of signs indicated that her risk-taking resonated. There was a reissue of the albums she recorded in the 1970s and the release of *Is It Love or Desire* and *Betty Davis: The Columbia Years, 1968–1969*, the long withheld collection of tracks she recorded when she was married to Miles Davis, in 2016. These releases made her music, which had been out of print, widely available to audiences. Related coverage in the music press and the 2017 release of the documentary *Betty: They Say I'm Different* circulated the story of her career. Feminist academics such as Nikki Greene and Cheryl Keyes singled her out as a groundbreaking figure whose music and career merit scholarly analysis.[86] Musicians have taken inspiration from her work. Rappers Ice Cube and Talib Kweli have rhymed over her beats, and rockers Lenny Kravitz, Skin, Joi, and Iggy Pop have covered her songs. Prince seems to have lifted some of his vocal squeals and visual style from Betty Davis. The raincoat and G-string ensemble of his *Dirty Mind* period echo the raincoat and slip Davis wore during her *Nasty Gal* tour; and Vanity 6, the female trio Prince produced in the early eighties, was like Betty Davis in triplicate, right down to the lingerie and a song called "Nasty Girl," released in 1982.[87] Rick James, who started his funk-rock career in the wake of Betty Davis, was an enthusiastic fan; he noted, "[She] was the only woman who was totally cutting edge. I mean, she was what funk was. . . . She was funking! Rock and rolling. Doing it all. . . . And she was doing it in the early '70s. [But] she was too much for people to understand."[88] Davis's liberated black femininity has a special resonance for contemporary black women rock musicians. Tamar-kali Brown, a singer, songwriter, and guitarist, sometimes covers Davis's music in concert. She made the following observation:

> Appearances like hers are rare in this male dominated, sexist, even misogynist industry. She was a fully embodied woman, all parts included. You saw her beauty, smelled her sex, recognized her power and respected, maybe even feared, her. These days . . . the trend for the black female artist is to become more like the video girl in her aesthetic presentation. In that regard, sex is used to trap women, treating them as accessories to their own music. Where is the ownership of one's self?[89]

In 2011, Tamar-kali was the musical director of "They Say She's Different: A Betty Davis Retrospective," a tribute show organized by the Black Rock Coalition and performed in New York at the Schomburg Center for Research in Black Culture. Several years earlier, when poet and activist Jessica Care Moore launched her Black Women Rock! project in 2004 at the National Black Arts Festival in Atlanta, Georgia, she created a ninety-minute multi-artist concert that celebrated Betty Davis.[90] Since then, Moore's Black Women Rock! events have taken place in Detroit, Moore's hometown, and have featured performances by black women singers and instrumentalists whose music presses beyond the boundaries of R&B and rap.

Davis has taken credit for opening the doors for other rebellious black women musicians. In a 1975 interview, she claimed, "I made it easy for a lotta those ladies out there cos I was out there first. I'm glad they've all made it, especially Labelle cos they were out there a long time and they deserve anything they get, any of the riches. But like I'm the one that paid the dues."[91] Davis reaped limited rewards in terms of fame and fortune, but she accomplished a great deal as a performer, songwriter, arranger, and producer, who created on her own terms in an era when women in her field were simply expected to sing well, look good, and listen to the men who were in charge. Still, her trajectory serves as a reminder of the challenges black women musicians face as they struggle to maintain "ownership," as Tamar-kali puts it, over their professional and personal selves.

Davis was a trailblazing artist who worked from a cultural script that marked her as being "ahead of her time"; in other words, she arrived before audiences and critics were prepared to deal with her. She is a sonic and spiritual precursor to artists such as Madonna, Lady Gaga, and Beyoncé, who continue the work of asserting female autonomy, both in their onstage presentation of sexuality and in the management of their careers. The albums Davis released in the 1970s document the efforts of a progressive black woman artist to free herself from constraining aesthetic, social, and cultural rules. Her reward for introducing a vision of liberated black femininity is cult status among aficionados but general obscurity in the realm of popular music. Betty Davis is barely in the funk books, not in the rock books, and absent from the books about soulful divas.[92] There is a chapter devoted to her in journalist Kandia Crazy Horse's edited volume on black rock, but she does not receive a mention in feminist histories of women in rock.[93] Davis struggled to get beyond the margins of the black music circuit and was the wrong gender and race to penetrate the boundaries of rock. Black middle-class arbiters of propriety tried to silence her. Most non-African American music listeners probably never heard her music because of segregated marketing. Reflecting on her career in a 2005 interview, Davis was matter-of-fact about her body of work: "I don't think I was ahead of my time," she said. "I think I was just testing the time."[94] Davis's rejection of the "ahead of her time" rhetoric suggests that she views her daring musical experiment as being very much of its time—a period when sexual, gender, and racial liberation and musical experimentation were central preoccupations. As writer and musician Vivien Goldman put it, Davis was "a free-spirited female, born in 1945, riding high out of the 1960s decade of the Pill and free love, into the infinite possibilities of the 1970s."[95] The musical sound, lyrical content, and visual imagery at the heart of Davis's "test" challenged the ways race, gender, and genre defined expectations for black women's musical performance and offered an image of black womanhood that embraced the pleasures and contradictions of sexual desire and independence.

EIGHT / Tina Turner's Turn to Rock

Finally, when I was thirty-five, I left. I figured I had a
good fifteen years or so ahead of me, and I was gonna
take a chance and see what I could do. / **TINA TURNER**

Tina Turner is the only artist I am writing about with a high degree of name recognition among people who are not popular music aficionados. In the 1980s, her recordings topped the charts and received industry awards, her videos were in regular rotation on MTV, her concerts filled arenas, she had a starring role in the blockbuster action movie *Mad Max: Beyond Thunderdome*, and her autobiography was an international bestseller. By the end of the decade, she had become the indisputable Queen of Rock and Roll. She did not arrive at this position by accident. Turner achieved superstar status through musical and cultural strategies that heightened her proximity to rock. Starting with her 1966 solo project with producer Phil Spector and continuing into the 1970s with her group the Ike and Tina Turner Revue, Turner began to incorporate rock music into her repertoire. This process continued when she set out on her solo career in the late 1970s. With the 1984 release of *Private Dancer,* she established herself as a top-tier entertainer. Maybe the most astonishing fact is that she made her ascent at the age of forty-five, well past the usual sell-by date in the youth-oriented world of rock and roll.[1] In this final chapter, I examine the process through which Turner, the best-known African American woman in rock and roll, wended her way into the mainstream of rock through a skillful navigation of the race, gender, and genre boundaries that governed American popular music at the end of the twentieth century.

Turner secured her position by incorporating rock sound and energy into her electric performances of rhythm and blues music and by allying herself with the white male rock musicians and producers who were among her most devoted fans. On "River Deep, Mountain High," the 1966 single produced by Phil Spector, and in her covers of the hard rock hits of the late sixties, Turner maintained the signature rough, raspy vocal quality and full-throttle attack that she had perfected on the rhythm and blues circuit, but used them on new material to signal a connection to the rock scene. A response to the fraught position black women occupy in relation to rock and roll, Turner's embrace of rock reached its pinnacle in the 1980s as she distanced herself from the rhythm and blues sound that had propelled her early career and positioned herself, instead, as a rocker. This was a deliberate move. From rock and roll's beginnings in the 1950s, African American women provided musical models for artists who went on to establish careers in rock and roll, but, as I have shown in my discussions of Big Mama Thornton, LaVern Baker, the Shirelles, Labelle, and Betty Davis, they struggled to hold their ground in the genre. Turner's insistent affiliation with rock allowed her to avoid relegation to the black music category that she, as an African American woman, would have been expected to work within, particularly given her long-standing professional link to rhythm and blues. The resulting liberation from the racialized music genre enabled her to achieve mainstream visibility and commercial success.

Turner's escape from the limits of the black music category relied on her ability to develop a sound and image that appealed to the predominantly white rock audience. On stage, she paired her passionate vocals with a physicality that functioned as a delivery system for the sexuality that had long animated rock and roll. Tina and her backing vocalists, the Ikettes, dressed in revealing stage costumes and performed an almost continuous flurry of hip-shaking, go-go–style dance steps. Wigs gave them swinging, shoulder-length tresses that accentuated their explosive movements. An editor's comment in the second issue of *Rolling Stone*, which featured Turner on the cover (see figure 8.1), indicates how rock fans were being invited to understand her two years before she started to address them through her covers of rock songs:

Tina Turner is an incredible chick. She comes in this very short miniskirt, way above her knees, with zillions of silver sequins and sparklers pasted on it. Her dancing is completely unrestrained. Unlike the polite handclapping Motown groups, she and the Ikettes scream, wail and do some fantastic boogaloo. No matter what you may think of the music, Tina Turner is worth sitting down and paying close attention to.[2]

FIGURE 8.1 Tina Turner at the hungry i, San Francisco, October 1967. This photo ran on the cover of the second issue of *Rolling Stone* in November 1967. © BARON WOLMAN.

The exciting live show brought a crucial element of the rock and roll aesthetic to life. Clad in a short dress, her face and body gleaming with perspiration after an onslaught of energetic dancing, Turner bristled with a forthright sexual energy that fit the era's ethos to "let it all hang out."

Like Jimi Hendrix, the era's leading African American rock figure, Turner's exaggerated sexuality in performance drew the fascinated attention of white audiences as she mobilized stereotypes of blackness.[3] Musicologist Susan Fast posits that some African American studies scholars have been reluctant to engage with Turner because they view her as performing "minstrelsy barely disguised, a kind of caricature of black sexuality."[4] For example, writing several years after her solo conquest of the airwaves, black feminist critic bell hooks stated, "Tina Turner's singing career has been based on the construction of an image of black female sexuality that is made synonymous with wild animal-istic lust."[5] She goes on to argue that in her 1984 hit song "What's Love Got to Do with It," Turner "evokes images of the strong bitchified black woman who is on the make."[6] Primarily concerned with image, hooks does not dis-cuss Turner's vocal style; she simply compares her, unfavorably, with Aretha Franklin and Anita Baker, African American women vocalists whose singing voices and onstage presentation hooks prefers. More recently, other African American academics have read Turner's forthright sexuality as a positive in-tervention. Cultural critic Madison Moore celebrates her "transgressive over-performance of the self through aesthetics."[7] This "fierceness," he argues, is "a disruptive strategy of performance" that is able to "push back against limiting identity categories."[8] Working from a similar perspective, cultural critic Fran-cesca Royster uses hooks's concept of "oppositional imagination" in a favorable consideration of Turner's performance, which she views as "a strategy very much aware of the tastes and limited social space for black female performers."[9] Like Moore and Royster, I am interested in Turner precisely because she developed strategies that addressed the race, gender, and genre restrictions confront-ing African American women and because she refused to stay in the musical space respectable black women are expected to occupy. My emphasis, how-ever, is not on the visual component of her performance (enticing as it may be), but rather on her vocal sound and sonic strategies.

Before moving into my discussion I offer two caveats. First, my focus here is on Tina's professional relationship with Ike Turner; I refrain from discuss-ing their marriage, a union made in the early sixties. Their domestic situation has been chronicled in Turner's bestselling autobiography, *I, Tina*. Published in 1986, the book detailed the particulars of Ike's physical and emotional abuse of Tina and her struggle to start over professionally after leaving her marriage and the Revue in 1976; it was the source material for the 1993 biopic *What's Love Got to Do with It*, a box office hit that, together with the book, helped establish Turner as an inspirational icon of women's resilience.[10] Ike told his side of the story in his memoir *Takin' Back My Name: The Confessions of Ike Turner*.[11] I consulted the memoirs, music press articles, and Tina Turner's re-cordings to trace her sonic path.

My second caveat is to acknowledge that I come to this chapter with my own biases. When I was a kid watching Tina Turner on TV, she overwhelmed me with her screams, sweat, and an energy I did not quite comprehend. Her stage show was unlike those of the other artists whose televised appearances occupied my attention in the early seventies. She was miles away from the demure elegance of the Supremes and different from the jubilance of the freaky men and women of Sly and the Family Stone, whose incorporation of the sing-song melodies of childhood in their hit "Everyday People" made me feel welcome. And then there was the Jackson Five. I was mesmerized by the group's dancing and the kid singing lead vocals. These artists managed their blackness in performance, making it an accessible consumable for crossover to white audiences (and black suburban me). Turner operated on a different plane. There was nothing kid-friendly about her erotically charged performances, and her throaty vocals, grimaces, perspiration, and physicality unsettled me when I was in elementary school. Turner's mid-1980s ascent coincided with my college years, and at this point, her sound wasn't a match for me for different reasons. Her hits "What's Love Got to Do with It," "Better Be Good to Me," and "We Don't Need Another Hero" sounded too mainstream to my post-punk/alternative rock–saturated ears. The overall feel was more glossy than edgy and rooted in the classic rock tradition that the music I identified with was self-consciously rejecting. Turner's videos were programmed alongside those of new wave women like quirky Cyndi Lauper and gender-blurring Annie Lennox of the Eurythmics, whose sound, style, and oddness resonated more. As much as I enjoyed Turner's video for "What's Love Got to Do with It," I did not purchase *Private Dancer* or consider attending Turner's concerts (but I did like her enough to snag some of the advertising postcards issued when she was promoting Hanes pantyhose in a mid-1990s campaign that capitalized on her famously beautiful legs). Tastes change. Over the course of researching this book, Turner's vocal power and her masterful singing have won me over, but as I trace her rock ascendancy in this chapter, I am mindful of an irony for me as a researcher and music fan: the features of her performance that put me off as a child in the seventies and a college student in the eighties are the features that enabled her to navigate the sonic, performance, and industry terrain she faced as an African American woman. Indeed, the musical and cultural associations she made with classic rock allowed her to address and circumvent the racial and gender expectations of sound in rock and roll.

Inventing Tina

Tina Turner was born Anna Mae Bullock on November 26, 1939, in Brownsville, Tennessee, and grew up in nearby Nutbush, a rural community that she referred to as "a little old town" in the song she wrote in its honor.[12] Her father was the resident overseer of a white-owned farm; her mother, "a black Indian of high spirits," according to Turner's autobiography.[13] Both parents left the farm to work in the defense industries near Knoxville, leaving three-year-old Anna Mae behind with family in Nutbush.[14] As a child, Anna Mae sang the songs she heard on the radio—everything from the mainstream pop of the McGuire Sisters to country music to rhythm and blues. In her autobiography, she recalled learning to sing "Tweedlee Dee," LaVern Baker's hit, "because it was fast. I always liked the fast ones, liked that energy, even then."[15] Sacred music was also an influence. She sang in the sanctified church she sometimes attended, and Sister Rosetta Tharpe, the gospel guitarist and vocalist who crossed and blurred the boundary between sacred and secular music, was Anna Mae's earliest musical inspiration.[16] When she was sixteen, she moved to St. Louis, Missouri, where her mother and older sister were living.[17] There, in 1957, she met Ike Turner (1932–2007), a Clarksdale, Mississippi–born guitarist, bandleader, and local celebrity. He had worked for Modern Records as a songwriter and talent scout, bringing Bobby Bland and Little Walter to the label.[18] He also played piano on B. B. King's first recording, "Three O'Clock Blues," and on early tracks by rhythm and blues idol Johnny Ace and bluesman Howlin' Wolf. Turner's Kings of Rhythm had enjoyed R&B chart success with "Rocket 88," a 1951 release that many rock historians identify as the first rock and roll record. By the late fifties, Turner was a well-known figure on the St. Louis music scene, playing regular gigs at both black and white clubs. Ike and Anna Mae met during an intermission at one of his shows. She recalled, "[I] told him I wanted to sing and he let me try while he played the organ for me. That kind of settled it right there and I went to work for Ike and his Kings of Rhythm as the girl singer."[19] Having a "girl singer" was a risky choice, because, as Ike pointed out, "back in those days, people were not that crazy about women singers."[20] Still, her voice was a compelling, raspy alto with powerful volume and a blast of charisma, and audiences seemed to like her. Ike decided to let her sing with the group, which already featured a male vocalist.[21]

At the time, she was known as Little Ann, but she eventually took the new name, Tina, that Ike chose for her.[22] Although the scanty costumes and provocative dance moves were a few years off, the name *Tina* was linked to a potent sexuality in Ike's mind. "Tina" evoked white jungle women characters with names like Sheena, Queen of the Jungle, and Nyoka (Tarzan's companion), who were portrayed by long-haired actresses wearing skimpy outfits while swinging through the trees in the Hollywood film serials that he had watched when growing up in Mississippi.[23] Attaching his surname to the new first name established a connection between the two, a concern for Ike who had been frustrated by singers who had quit his band just when the group was on the brink of success. "I patented the name [Tina]," Ike explained in his autobiography, "so that if Raymond Hill [Anna Mae's boyfriend] ran off with Little Ann I could find myself another Tina and keep on going."[24] The transformation of Anna Mae Bullock to Tina Turner precipitated another name change: The Kings of Rhythm became the Ike and Tina Turner Revue. "He wanted his name there," Tina explained years later, "because he'd always produced people, only to have them get record deals and leave."[25] In Anna Mae Bullock he had found a good singer, and he wanted to hold onto her. Further boosting the Revue's vocal sound and the show's visual appeal were the Ikettes, a female backing group. Named by and for Ike in the tradition of the Raelettes who backed Ray Charles, they supported Tina in both movement and song. Over the years, numerous women were Ikettes, including P. P. Arnold, Venetta Fields, and Claudia Lennear.[26] A smart, self-reliant man, Ike kept an iron grip on all aspects of his artistic and business affairs; he played guitar and piano, wrote and arranged material, produced recordings, and booked his band's gigs.

Ike brought Anna Mae Bullock into his band on the strength of her distinctive singing voice, one that departed from typical "feminine" sound. In her autobiography, Tina offers the following gendered reading of her voice: "Now, when I say I can sing, I know that I don't have a 'pretty' voice. My voice is not the voice of a woman, so to speak. That's why when I choose my music, I think of men. I can relate to their delivery. I'm attracted to it."[27] She also attributes her sound to her male-centered environment: "When I first started working with Ike, it was all men and just me, and I had to sort of keep up. So I had to take a lot of my training and my patterns of singing from the guys. It wasn't about girls and beauty and femininity."[28] Here, Turner distances her sound from what she views as standard women's vocals. Ike made a similar point: "She doesn't sing like a woman," he said of Tina. "She sings like a man."[29] Perhaps it was fitting that when doing her impromptu audition for Ike back in St. Louis, she sang a B. B. King song. "Most girls in those days sang like girls. But I never did," she told a reporter in 1972. "I always used to sing along with men singers, so I didn't really sound like a girl."[30] Not surprisingly, the influences she claimed were male. "I always did like Ray Charles," she said. "He was my only influence, because I always liked to sing more or less like men sing, and sound like they sound. Like he and Sam Cooke were my influences."[31]

Turner's forceful, raspy vocals and her willingness to forgo a pretty or clean vocal sound are what render her voice as not typically feminine. Describing the qualities of Turner's voice that align her with rock and roll, musicologist Susan Fast pinpoints the very features that contribute to the gender ambiguity of her vocals: "There is a particular bigness . . . and a distinctively hard edge: her voice is raw, assertive, aggressive, shouting, demanding."[32] The resulting in-your-face vocal style, her signature rough and raw vocal sound, are central to her appeal.

Turner is a masterful singer. She accessed the throaty rasps that signaled passion or sang with a full chest voice, but she could also sound quiet and sweet; she seemed comfortable departing from the lower registers to hit high notes and deliver cascading screams. Both "nice and rough," as she described her style in the spoken prelude to the 1971 hit "Proud Mary," Turner is able to strain and scream without sounding forced. Still, the volume and physicality of her vocals make the listener aware of her effort as she pushes out the sound, lending texture to her vocals. Unconcerned with sounding pretty, she embraced grit and heat, her voice sometimes breaking at its low end. Although she might have been categorized as a "girl singer," she sounded like a grown woman. Even when singing rapidly, Turner's excellent diction ensured that her lyrics were mostly comprehensible, a rarity in rock. Her phrasing, in which the words come spilling out of her mouth quickly and then stop suddenly, indexes excitement and energy. The roughness of her voice indicates emotion and earthiness, in other words, the authenticity that black people carried. Turner was a sonic kaleidoscope, her voice conveying sexiness, availability, vulnerability, toughness, resignation, or determination.

Turner tapped into these features on her first recording, a session with the Kings of Rhythm. She was filling in for Art Lassiter, the vocalist originally scheduled to sing "A Fool in Love."[33] Ike had booked and paid for the studio time and, determined to get something out of his investment when Lassiter didn't show, he decided to record the song as a demo with Tina on lead; she had been attending rehearsals and knew the song. She worked within the existing arrangement, and Lassiter's female trio backed her up. "The reason she was hollering so loud, straining, on the record," Ike explained, "is because the song is not in a woman's key. It's in a man's key, for a man to sing."[34] Throughout the song, Turner leans in to her alto, alternating between a sweet, almost girlish tone in the verses and a powerful chest voice as she moves into the chorus. She returns several times to a wordless roar—I'm not sure what vowels and consonants to write down to represent it—that expresses the ill-fated condition of being in love with an uncaring man. Here, as with so many of her performances, Turner sounds like she is giving her vocal all to the song. Sue Records owner Henry "Juggy" Murray heard the demo and urged Ike to release it as a single.[35] The part of the song, penned by Ike, that captured his attention was Tina's voice. The record-buying public agreed. "A Fool in Love" became the duo's first hit, peaking at number two on the R&B charts in the summer of 1960.[36]

The singularity of Turner's vocal sound launched her career in the United States, and she became a favorite singer of white British artists connected to the 1960s blues revival. It is a rock history commonplace that Rolling Stones lead singer Mick Jagger borrowed Tina Turner's dancing and onstage style, but he also studied her vocal attack. Ike and Tina's 1961 hit "It's Gonna Work Out Fine" was one of the first songs Jagger practiced when he was developing his capacity as a blues singer.[37] Steve Marriott, lead singer of Small Faces in the 1960s and Humble Pie in the 1970s, was so enamored of Tina's sound that he patterned his phrasing and inflection after hers and hired a former Ikette, Venetta Fields, to sing background with his band in the early 1970s. When Small Faces reformed as Faces in 1969 after Marriott's departure, they brought in Rod Stewart, a lead singer who also relied heavily on Turner as a vocal model. To use the words of cultural critic Daphne Brooks, recognizing these kinds of cross-racial and cross-gender influences allows us to tell "more nuanced, heterogeneous tales of racial and gender collaborations" in pop music.[38] White male rockers borrowed from Turner, and, as I will explain shortly, she borrowed from them.

"River Deep, Mountain High"

Tina Turner made her first solo steps into rock and roll in 1966, when she recorded "River Deep, Mountain High" with producer Phil Spector. At the point when Spector went to Ike Turner with the proposal to record Tina, his run of hits with African American girl groups had stalled, and his relationship with the Righteous Brothers, the blue-eyed soul duo whose 1965 single "You've Lost That Loving Feeling" had given him his biggest hit, had just ended. Spector was seeking other ways to stay on the American pop charts. Turner's performance during *The Big TNT Show*, a rock and roll concert film he had produced, sparked the idea that he should work with her. He believed that he could make a number one record that would help the Turners cross over from

FIGURE 8.2 This 1966 photo of Ike and Tina Turner with Phil Spector at Gold Star Studios, Hollywood, California, gives the impression that the three were working together on a record, but Ike did not participate in the rehearsals and recording sessions that produced "River Deep, Mountain High," a single that was credited to Ike and Tina Turner. In pursuit of a crossover hit for the duo, Spector directed Tina to apply the emotional power of her rhythm and blues vocals to a pop song arrangement. For Tina, Spector's insistence that she adhere to the song's written melody and his prohibition against the improvised vocals that she performed with Ike were revelations of the musical possibilities beyond rhythm and blues and important first steps on her path to rock. COURTESY RUDY CALVO COLLECTION/ CACHE AGENCY.

R&B to the rock and roll mainstream, giving them well-deserved visibility while recharging his own career. According to his biographer, Spector loved the "carnality, hurt, passion, [and] power" present in Tina's singing voice.[39] Spector made an arrangement with Ike that would allow him to produce a couple of sides with Tina without Ike's involvement or presence in the studio; this was Tina's first experience working professionally without Ike (see figure 8.2).[40] Spector rehearsed Tina for two weeks, an eternity in an era of quick turnaround pop music writing and recording, and she acclimated herself to his demands, including his stipulation that she not "vary his lines."[41] When it came time to record, she did numerous takes of "River Deep, Mountain High," the single that Spector had chosen for the project.[42] Cowritten by Spector and Brill Building songwriting team Jeff Barry and Ellie Greenwich, the song was intended to be more mature than the teen-themed girl group hits "Chapel of Love," "Da Doo Run Run," and "Leader of the Pack" that had helped Barry and Greenwich establish their careers. True, there are references to a girl, a boy, a rag doll, and a puppy, but the song comes from an adult point of view with the narrator assuring her partner that she will love him with the same innocent devotion that she showered on her childhood loves.

The song stitches together sonic tropes of pop and R&B, the two realms that Spector wanted Turner to reach. This is evident in Turner's vocals, which Spector had carefully, even obsessively, directed. Turner begins the song at the low end of her range, and then the melody ascends as the tempo increases. She sings with passion, heightening the promise of the lyrics. Her vocal volume and intensity build over the course of the song's three and a half minutes. In the verses, Turner delivers clean and controlled vocals perfect for the pop market. At first there is little of her familiar rasp, but as she leads up to the chorus, her voice roughens to signal the passion referenced in the lyrics. By the time she reaches the chorus, she is singing full throttle with a throaty physicality. At the bridge, she launches into uncut cries of passion in a way that was not done in the pop world of 1966. She moves from a soulful "yeah, yeah, yeah" to a repeated "baby, baby, baby" before dispensing with words altogether and letting loose with an elongated "owwwww." Here, Turner abandons a pop singing style for emotive vocal territory that would have been recognizable to listeners steeped in African American gospel or James Brown's music, but alien and potentially alienating to those who had only experienced a steady diet of pop. Spector, a fan of African American gospel vocal style, had not delved into this sound on the records he made with the Ronettes, the Crystals, or Darlene Love, but he encouraged Turner to offer up this excess of vocal blackness. Her high-powered vocals are a match for the thick musical backdrop: the track's twenty-one musicians and twenty background singers provided Spector's signature wall of sound through an overload of thunderous drums, soaring strings, pumping brass, and echoing vocals.[43] Reflecting on "River Deep, Mountain High," Turner said, "I loved that song. Because for the first time in my life, it wasn't just R and B—it had structure, it had a melody. You see, Ike would always have me screaming and shouting on his songs—selling them, you know? Because there wasn't really much to them: I'd always have to improvise and ad-lib."[44] Turner offers this assessment in her autobiography, written at the height of her rock star ascendancy, and she was well aware of the musical specificity of the genres she was straddling. Although rhythm and blues songs, even the ones she sang with Ike, did have structure and melody, Turner experienced "River Deep" as being more structured and tuneful in part because Spector demanded that she stick to the written melody, a directive that likely drew her attention to the fact that she did not do this when working with Ike. She liked the different sound and feel of the song and viewed the prohibition against improvised "screaming and shouting" as a sign of superiority to "just R and B," the musical realm she had inhabited up to that point.

Spector was pleased with the track and anticipated a hit when he released the record in May 1966, but the song received little airplay in the United States, and disappeared after only getting as far as number 88 on the pop charts.[45] The fate of "River Deep" might have been the result of "Phil Spector Fatigue" among US disc jockeys, music press writers, and other industry tastemakers who, weary of Spector's arrogance, decided not to push his latest record, but another possibility is problems with the record itself.[46] Cowriter Jeff Barry's assessment was that "the mix of 'River Deep' is terrible. [Spector] buried the lead."[47] To some ears, "River Deep" sounded like "two quite separate songs that seemed to have been plucked from opposite corners of the room and forced to dance together—although the stop-start tempo made dancing almost an impossibility."[48] The larger problem might have been that the sonic experiment that Spector and Turner attempted in "River Deep, Mountain High" made the song an imperfect fit for either the pop or R&B markets. The Turners seized on the relationship between race and music genre to account for the single's poor stateside showing. According to Ike, "The black stations said it was too white, the white stations said it was too black, so the record had no home here."[49] Tina's assessment was similar: "That record just never found a home," she said in her autobiography. "It was too black for the pop stations, and too pop for the black stations. Nobody gave it a chance."[50] Tina's vocals are too raw, too soulful, "too black," for pop radio, but the record's orchestral sound was "too pop" for R&B radio. The genre marriage that animated the crossover plan that Spector and Turner had embarked on resulted in a song with a confusing sonic and racial hybridity. Still, in spite of its weak performance on the US charts, Tina Turner was proud of the record, viewing it as a personal breakthrough. "'River Deep' proved I was capable of doing something other than what Ike had me doing," she stated in her autobiography.[51]

American audiences did not appreciate "River Deep," but rock and roll fans on the other side of the Atlantic did. The bold mix of musical blackness and musical whiteness that stymied the record in the United States was all the rage in England where the blues revival was well underway. British blues–based bands such as the Animals and the Yardbirds were experimenting with the kinds of "black sounds" that Tina's voice conveyed. "River Deep" sailed up the British charts, peaking at number three in July 1966.[52] The song caught the attention of the Rolling Stones, one of the groups at the forefront of the London blues scene and already fans of the duo; the band invited the Ike and Tina Turner Revue onto their autumn 1966 tour. On the road in England, Scotland, and Wales with the Stones, the Yardbirds, and Long John Baldry, the Turners connected to the British blues revival.[53] A caption for a photo of Tina that ran with *Melody Maker*'s coverage of what it called "the wildest tour to ever hit Britain" indicates the impact she had across the pond: "She sings with tremendous feeling and dances a wild routine with the Ikettes. She sends the whole show wild."[54] Wild, wild, and wildest, Tina Turner's high-energy, highly visual performance had unleashed something intoxicating onto the British cultural landscape. The 1966 tour gave the Turners visibility in the United Kingdom and started a long-lasting alliance between Tina, British rock musicians, and the British record-buying public. Acknowledging the personal and professional significance of going abroad, Turner said, "England was the beginning of everything for me—the beginning of my escape from Ike Turner, I guess you could say, and the beginning of me seeing a new way of life."[55] Her time in England was also the beginning of her journey into rock.

Covering Rock

The Ike and Tina Turner Revue offered a musical and live performance model for the artists associated with the blues-based rock and roll scene that blossomed in England in the 1960s. (I cannot prove it, but I have an inkling that black female background vocal groups became the rage among British rockers in part because they wanted to replicate the effect of Tina and the Ikettes.)[56] In return, by 1969 Tina was borrowing the hard rock sound, covering songs originated by rock artists who were drawing on African American musical style. Without abandoning the rhythm and blues and gospel aesthetics in which her vocal and onstage performance style were rooted, Turner added rock songs to the Revue's material, aligning herself with the rock scene that she had begun to access through her work with Spector and the Stones. Music fans who have read about Ike's dominant position in the couple's relationship might assume that he was responsible for all of the duo's creative choices, so it is important to point out that the inclusion of rock material in the Revue's repertoire was Tina's idea.

By the late sixties, rhythm and blues and the rock that had grown out of it represented two distinct realms aesthetically, temporally, and racially. Rock, a growing moneymaker, was consumed by youthful white audiences; rhythm and blues, the black popular music of the previous decade, was being supplanted by soul, the ascendant black music of the 1960s. Rhythm and blues was out of date in comparison to rock and soul, but rhythm and blues was where Ike Turner's musical head was. Tina saw the value in expanding the Revue's repertoire to include rock, and Ike agreed. This addition of rock covers was a way to address the frustrating situation that African American musicians were facing in the wake of the British Invasion and the rise of the counterculture in the late 1960s. The African American–derived sound of rock and roll, launched in the 1950s and landing African Americans such as Fats Domino, Little Richard, Chuck Berry, LaVern Baker, the Drifters, and the Shirelles onto the pop charts, had been appropriated by white artists who began to move to the center of the genre in the mid-1960s. By the early 1970s, African American vocalists were relegated to the black genres of rhythm and blues or soul, black rock bands were classified with the moniker "funk" that distinguished them from white rock bands, and African Americans with contracts at major labels were placed in black music departments that separated them from pop and rock. The Turners, with their rock covers and a touring schedule that included both white and black venues, were responding to this racialized terrain and working to claim space in a scene that relied on black sound, but seemed resistant to the presence of actual black people.

In addition to being a wise marketing move, delving into rock covers was a way for Tina to exercise some creative autonomy from Ike, who was the Revue's principal songwriter. For one thing, covering songs first recorded by male rock bands gave Tina a respite from voicing the state of mind of the brokenhearted, done-wrong female characters Ike kept writing for her. After "A Fool in Love" had topped the R&B chart in 1960, Ike returned to the fool theme numerous times, following the industry practice of recycling the lyrics and melodies of successful songs in an effort to achieve another hit. As Tina's biographer Mark Bego notes, "In a whole string of songs [Ike] had Tina record, she would publicly call herself a 'fool' while the object of her affection was God's gift to women. After 'A Fool in Love' came 'Poor Fool,' 'A Fool for a Fool,' 'A Fool for You,' 'Poor Little Fool,' 'Foolish,' and 'Such a Fool for You.'"[57] The rock covers freed Tina from this demeaning position and gave her access to another set of personae, subject matter, and attitudes, while infusing the Revue's repertoire with material that had already proved successful on the charts. The rock covers also served an important symbolic purpose. Covering a song, musicologist Susan Fast points out, "is a way to bring the familiar into a live performance, which in the best of circumstances has the effect of electrifying a crowd. It also works to *associate* the performers with the artist who made the original recording."[58] The Turners' renditions of rock hits helped the duo establish links to well-known rock artists, while introducing themselves to rock audiences.

Turner has said that her foray into covers grew out of an emerging interest in rock. During her first decade working with Ike, she did not pay much attention to the music on the radio, but in 1969, right before being invited to tour the States with the Rolling Stones, she began to tune in.[59] Describing her initial encounter with the first rock song the duo recorded, she recalled:

> We were in Seattle one day, and [Ike] took me into this record shop, and that's where I first heard "Come Together." I said, "Oh, what's that?" The guy in the store said it was the Beatles. I truly don't think I had ever really heard them before. But I loved that song. I said to Ike, "Please, *please* let me do that song onstage." I was begging him. Then I heard "Honky Tonk Women," and I just had to do that, too. Well, we had always done covers anyway, so Ike said all right.[60]

The important difference was that this new material took them beyond the R&B milieu. Among the songs the Turners covered were four tracks that had been hits on the US pop charts for their white originators in 1969. "Come Together" by the Beatles and "Honky Tonk Women" by the Rolling Stones had both gone to number one.[61] "Whole Lotta Love" by Led Zeppelin had reached number four, and "Proud Mary" by Creedence Clearwater Revival made it to number two.[62] Recording these songs enabled Turner to traverse the race, gender, and genre boundaries that were increasingly barring African American women from rock. She also played with the representations of masculinity animating songs like "Honky Tonk Women" and "Whole Lotta Love," putting a black woman's spin on these "randy affirmations of male sexual identity."[63] Turner appropriated the sexual autonomy these songs articulated for her own purposes and connected herself to the rock ethos of self-expression. Commenting on the Revue's turn to rock covers in 1971, Tina noted, "We give the people a little bit of us and a little bit of what they hear on the radio every day."[64] The resulting mix—rock hits done Ike and Tina Turner style—facilitated the Turners' crossover to the rock audience as they directly engaged the sonic priorities of the scene.

With "Come Together" the Turners projected themselves into rock territory and performed a song whose lyrics departed from typical rhythm and blues subject matter.[65] John Lennon had started writing the song at the request of Timothy Leary, the former Harvard psychology professor whose championing of psychedelic drugs made him a counterculture hero. Using the title that Leary had provided, Lennon developed what one commentator has called "a sly self-portrait in clipped, obtuse images."[66] Turner did not have to be aware of this background to take pleasure in the song's eerie sound, staccato vocal lines, surreal imagery, and odd verbal juxtapositions. She might have simply enjoyed the novelty of singing about something other than a love relationship. In the Turners' cover, the band uses a musical arrangement that is consistent with that of the original, right down to the song's tempo and guitar solo. The notable difference is the bracing vocal presence of Turner and the Ikettes. They sing with a healthy measure of audible blackness, their vocals providing the textured vocal sound that so many white rock artists, inspired by blues and rhythm and blues singing, imitated on their recordings. The response to the track was positive. Writing in *Rolling Stone*, Ben Fong-Torres noted, "What finally carried Ike and Tina through was the 1969 Rolling Stones tour, where the Revue broke out with 'Come Together,' in its own raw style, Tina snake-snapping across the stage, punching out the John Lennon lyric. Raves everywhere, and the mass magazines were stung to attention."[67] The Turners released their "Come Together" in 1970 and used the song to title the album on which it appeared, further aligning themselves with the rock scene. *Come Together* also includes covers of "Honky Tonk Women" and "I Want to Take You Higher" by Sly and the Family Stone. "That was the beginning of me liking rock music," Tina recalled of this phase of her career. "It wasn't like we planned it—'Now we're gonna start doing white rock 'n' roll songs.' But those groups were *interpreting* black music to begin with. They touched on R and B, in a way, but it wasn't obvious. I mean, it wasn't the old thing. It was 'Honky Tonk Women'—wow! I could relate to that."[68] Hearing the familiar but also what was different in hard rock, Turner recognized a way to access a space that was segregated by race and gender. She exploited her gifts as a seasoned rhythm and blues singer as she explored this different musical territory.

As with "Come Together," the Turners' "Honky Tonk Women" follows the original musical arrangement.[69] A loping, syncopated rhythm and up-front, blues-infused guitar lines propel both versions of the song, but the two renditions convey different ideas. In the Stones' version, Jagger laments that in spite of partying and casual sex, he "just can't seem to drink you off my mind." Rather than providing an escape, "the honky tonk women gimme, gimme, gimme the honky tonk blues." In a telling contrast, Turner's version is *not* a woman's meditation on the limits of liquor and sex as tools to mend a broken heart, and *not* a song about honky tonk men giving *her* the blues. Instead, to preserve the original title (since part of the reason for covering a song is to capitalize on its already established name recognition), Turner takes on the persona of a honky tonk woman. She becomes one of the habituées of the bar scene, a woman who revels in drinking and having a good time. In her chorus, she declares, "I'm a honky tonk woman/Gimme gimme gimme a honky tonk man." The activities described in the verses of the original and the cover are similar: Jagger recalls that he met "a gin-soaked barroom queen in Memphis" and "laid a divorcée in New York City"; Turner encountered a "gin-soaked barroom man in Memphis" and "laid a VIP in New York City." Their reflections on their actions, however, differ. Jagger uses the word *blues* and is singing about emotional turmoil; Turner avoids lyrics that describe a depressed mood, deleting both the word *blues* and any inkling of a blues lament from the song. Choosing not to engage the tension that is the point of the song—the emptiness that comes from trying to work through the loss of the lover you really want with not-quite-right substitutes—Turner instead conjures a celebration of recreational sex that I imagine she imagined meshed with the rock scene's libidinous leanings. The chorus becomes an assertive statement of identity and desire. Whether or not the listener is paying attention to the shift in lyrical meaning, the sonic difference is hard to miss. Unlike a lot of rock tracks where overdriven instruments muffle the vocals, Turner's voice bursts out in the front of the mix, drawing the listener's attention to the passion, energy, and cool, confident attitude conveyed through her distinctive vocal timbre. Turner sings with gusto, punctuating the ends of some lines with an emphatic "yeah." A female backing vocalist harmonizes with her at key points to emphasize lyrics and fill out the vocal sound, helping Turner to communicate the pleasure she takes in the experiences and state of mind she describes. In just over three minutes, Turner's version of "Honky Tonk Women" creates a sexy and self-possessed character who can keep up with the guys when it comes to sexual appetite and introduces a singer who can more than keep up with the rock guys when it comes to music-making.[70]

Led Zeppelin's "Whole Lotta Love" is one of rock's supreme statements of heterosexual masculine sexual identity, but in Turner's hands, it becomes a woman's proclamation of sexual prowess and desire.[71] The Zeppelin version runs at an upbeat tempo, and the vocals begin after a few measures of guitar, bass, and drum instrumentals. Zeppelin's lead vocalist Robert Plant sings at an urgent clip, running down the situation—"You need coolin', baby, I'm not foolin'"—and building to a climax where the instruments drop out as he declares, "Way down inside, woman, you need love." Turner dumps this part of the song and excises the original's conclusion, where Plant borrows a phrase from the bluesmen he so admired: "Shake for me, girl / I wanna be your back door man." Turner's arrangement, recorded in 1975, departs from the original in other significant ways. In fact, purist Led Zeppelin fans were probably horrified by the presence of synthesized strings and the keyboard vamp that occupies the first minute and a half of the song before Turner's voice cuts through the mid-seventies funk vibe. I've always heard Zeppelin's version of the song as a man's effort to convince a woman to have sex with him. Turner's rendition sounds less like a proposition to a potential partner than a woman urging a lover on in the midst of a steamy sexual encounter. As if created with Isaac Hayes's 1971 "Theme from *Shaft*" in mind and a perfect sonic fit for a red velvet–laden boudoir, the Turners' "Whole Lotta Love" flows at a slower tempo than the original. Turner mixes whispered sweet talk with full-volume, urgent wails, a contrast to the original's rapid-fire come ons. Describing the benefits of giving in to desire and, through a dexterous modulation of rising and falling vocals, Turner depicts a woman in the throes of passion. Following the second chorus, she stops singing and whispers, *"Give it to me one more time"* in a breathy voice, then issues a delighted "Mmmmm." As the song fades out, she repeats Plant's, "I'm gonna give you my love, every inch of my love, oh, oh, oh" promise, but the difference between the two versions—that of the quick-to-the-point man and the taking-her-time woman—imply a commentary from Turner about ideals of good loving and the particulars of female sexuality.

Both Turner and Plant sing with a hoarse strain, drawing from the well of African American vocal stylistics. That raspy quality is also shared by John Fogerty, lead vocalist of Creedence Clearwater Revival and the writer of "Proud Mary," the song that became the Turners' most commercially successful rock cover.[72] Creedence Clearwater Revival's "Proud Mary" has a moderate tempo that evokes the steady motion of the riverboat referenced in the chorus. Fogerty's faintly southern vocal inflections, twangy guitar leads, and lyrical references to Memphis, New Orleans, and a river that has to be the Mississippi give the song a down-home country feel. The Ike and Tina Turner cover gets down in a different way. The Turners built their "Proud Mary," not on the Creedence original (which Ike did not like), but on an upbeat version that Phil Spector produced for an integrated R&B band called the Checkmates in 1969.[73] Ironically, it was the Phil Spector–inspired, Ike Turner–produced version of "Proud Mary" that gave Ike and Tina the crossover hit that Spector had tried to achieve with "River Deep, Mountain High."

The opening moments of the Turners' version features a spoken word introduction by Tina that imparts a sense of immediacy to the recording. As if addressing an audience at a concert, she says:

> You know, every now and then I think you might like to hear something from us nice and easy. But there's just one thing. You see, we never ever do nothing nice and easy. We always do it nice and rough. But we're gonna take the beginning of this song and do it easy. But then we're going to do the finish rough. The way we do "Proud Mary."

As she speaks, Ike sings the first verse. At the conclusion of her remarks, she joins Ike on the last words of the chorus: "Rolling, rolling on the river." She speaks again, the preacher addressing her flock: "Listen to the story, now," and then moves into the verse of the "easy" version. She and Ike sing it together, his baritone rolling beneath her alto as they are joined by the harmonizing Ikettes. The three vocal strands give the song depth as they alternate singing together, calling and responding to one another, harmonizing, and singing in unison. They proceed this way through the first two verses, winding down at the end of the second chorus. As the final notes and voices fade away, a downbeat introduces drums, bass, guitar, and horns, and launches the up-tempo, "rough" version as a furious drum roll precedes Tina's return to the verse. Ike's vocals drop out, and the song becomes a Tina and Ikettes number with the latter singing harmonized responses to Tina's calls. They share the singing of some rapid-fire "do do do do dos" not present in the original, inserting their lines between blasts from the horn section. At this point, the song loosens up with Tina's improvised-feeling exclamations: "All right, now!," "Oh, yeah!," and "Go ahead, now!" before finally arriving at the third verse. As the final chorus fades out, you can hear Tina calling to her band, "Give me one more time now," leaving the Creedence version behind in their R&B revue dust. In moving from slow to fast, adding horns, and layering the vocals, the Turners reimagine John Fogerty's composition with an arrangement that offers satisfying surprises at every turn. The song was the duo's most successful single;

it reached number five on the R&B chart and number four on the pop chart in February 1971 and won that year's Grammy for Best R&B Vocal Performance by a Group.[74] "Proud Mary" gave the Turners the mainstream hit they had been chasing for years. With a song in the Top 40, they were sought after for television appearances. Performing their hit on network variety shows augmented their visibility, and the arresting stage costumes and dancing of Tina and the Ikettes left a mark on American pop culture.

The Turners were trying to fit into a realm that was sending a message that African Americans and women did not belong. They believed that they did, and the rock covers they performed sent a countermessage intended to make the group legible to the rock audience. To take another example from this period, the Turners' 1970 cover of Sly and the Family Stone's "I Want to Take You Higher" might have been intended to signal that they wanted to be embraced by the rock audience that Sly and the Family Stone was reaching. That band, led by the black and charismatic Sly Stone and comprising both black and white men and women, had a presence on the pop and R&B charts that the Turners hoped for. It was not unreasonable for the Turners to try to access the rock audience. Ike Turner was a pioneering musician who had cut what is arguably the first rock and roll record four years before people started using the new genre term. Together, the Turners had crossed over to the pop charts prior to the British Invasion with "A Fool in Love," in 1960, and "It's Gonna Work Out Fine," in 1961. It made sense for them to insist that there was a place for them in late sixties hard rock, a genre for which they had helped lay the groundwork. The Turners made their point by covering songs by the biggest stars in the rock scene and managed to get on both the R&B and pop charts in the process.[75]

Incorporating the hard rock sound into their act was a way to keep up with the changing musical times, but it is also possible to hear the Turners' covers as a response to a call that white rockers might not have been aware they were making. It was obvious to the Turners that these musicians were borrowing the rhythm and blues tradition and taking it in a new direction. The Who, for example, flagged this link by declaring their musical output "Maximum R&B," and the Rolling Stones launched their career as a blues cover act, with Mick Jagger self-consciously patterning his vocals after those of African American singers including Tina Turner. Her equally self-conscious response was to cover the work of artists who were, in effect, covering her. In the rock covers, we can hear Turner showing the young, white newcomers to rhythm and blues—the style of musical production in which she was an expert—how it was done. Thinking of the Turners' covers as an act of musical one-upmanship may help account for the critical response to this work. (And the absence of a feminine form of "one-upmanship" is indicative of how far beyond the bounds of acceptable female behavior a woman engaging in the practice is going.) Some rock critics took Turner to task for leaving the terrain they believed she ought to have occupied. In a 1972 review for *Crawdaddy*, Wayne Robins argued, "Watching the growing success of Ike and Tina Turner hasn't always been pleasant these last few years. What was once the consummate rhythm 'n' blues show became 'Proud Mary'ed, Beatle'd, Joe Cocker'ed and 'Honky Tonk Woman'ed into overexposure."[76] Striking a similar tone, Dave Marsh used his *Rolling Stone* review of Tina Turner's 1975 solo album *Acid Queen* to outline the problems he saw in her departure from her accustomed genre. Calling the material "ill-chosen," he wrote:

> Tina Turner's attempt to re-create the excitement of five rock classics by the Rolling Stones, the Who and Led Zeppelin never really had a chance. She sings at least one of them, "Let's Spend the Night Together," as well as anyone this side of Aretha Franklin, even though she ruins a couple of the others ("Under My Thumb" and Pete Townshend's title song) with the sheer shrieking bombast that has characterized too much of her recent work.[77]

Performing these covers, Marsh asserts, leaves "this once-great singer pushing herself through a series of songs without either desire or understanding."[78] His preference was for her to work within "an idiom [she] comprehends."[79] In other words, Tina, stick to rhythm and blues.

Both men want Turner to stay in what they understand to be her musical place. What these critics failed to acknowledge and what Turner knew was that she was, in fact, in her musical place and that it was the white musicians who were the interlopers, appropriating African American musical sound and attitude. Robins seems to resent her visibility in the rock scene, and Marsh claims that she did not understand what was, at bottom, her own music. Perhaps they responded to Turner in this way because her presence in the rock arena was an implicit challenge to the authenticity of the white rockers in whom they were so invested. Turner was arguably the genuine article, someone who had the vocal sound that white rock vocalists from Mick Jagger to Janis Joplin to Robert Plant to John Fogerty were trying to achieve. She had the wrenching strain, the effortless rasp, the wails, volume, and passion, as well as the ability to somehow sound both hot and cool. In taking her versions of rock songs to the rock stage, Turner was encroaching on territory that these rock critics wanted to protect. It was as if they wanted to suppress the source of inspiration so the white musicians could emerge as the authentic, artistic originators.[80]

The Turners' musical choices in the late sixties and early seventies suggest that they were trying to find an effective sonic formula, something that could take them beyond the circuit of black clubs that were the bedrock of their touring. Along with the rock covers there were the blues songs "I Smell Trouble" and "You Got Me Running" on *The Hunter* (1969); the nod to soul in "Bold Soul Sister" (1969) and their cover of Otis Redding's "I've Been Loving You Too Long" (1969); and the funk of "Sexy Ida (Part 1)" (1974) and "Whole Lotta Love" (1975). Turner's first solo album, *Tina Turns the Country On* (1974), was a collection of country songs that included Dolly Parton's "There'll Always Be Music" and "If You Love Me (Let Me Know)," a hit for Olivia Newton-John earlier that year. Several tracks featured backing vocals by Merry Clayton and Clydie King, who had contributed their gospel-infused voices to numerous rock recordings.[81] Leaving aside the close musical connections between these genres and the frequent borrowings across them, by the early 1970s country, blues, rhythm and blues, and rock were perceived as distinct genre categories. It is notable that the Turners were laying claim to all of them. Refusing a model of authenticity that would limit them to a single genre, they operated as entertainers seeking out the music that would most entice audiences.

Turner's rock covers reversed a long-standing process that helped produce rock and roll: that of white artists covering the songs of black artists and appropriating black musical style. Turner, a black American, did her version of their version of black American music.[82] "Re-commandeering blue-eyed soul from mostly white male rockers," as Francesca Royster describes it, Turner magnified rock sound and ethos in her performances.[83] Turner's voice made sense in the late sixties rock context, even though her black female body might not have, since at that point, black Americans were on the periphery of the rock scene—Jimi Hendrix, Sly Stone, Arthur Lee of Love, and the indispensable black women backup singers notwithstanding. In contrast to the background vocalists and like the male black rockers, Turner was at center stage. From her place in the spotlight, she performed a repertoire that allowed her to transform herself from a rhythm and blues shouter into a rock singer. Although Turner's vocal style did not change radically when she started working with rock material, the genre category that she could claim did.[84] Turner was elbowing her way into the rock and roll boys' club, fitting herself into what was becoming a more and more homogenous white and male space. Her sonic presence issued a challenge to the race and gender status quo and created a new sense of self: "I felt that I had *become* all the songs that I was covering," Turner declares in her autobiography, "that I had become rock 'n' roll."[85]

Negotiating the R&B and Rock Divide

Because of the role Ike Turner played as the Revue's bandleader, songwriter, producer and manager, he is often represented as being in complete control of the band and his wife. Over the years, Tina shored up this image. A 1971 *Rolling Stone* article quoted her saying, "My whole thing is the fact that I am to Ike—I'm going to use the term 'doll' that you sort of mold. . . . In other words, he put me through a lot of changes. My whole thing is Ike's ideas. I'll come up with a few of them, but not half as creative as Ike."[86] In her autobiography, she similarly credits Ike with being the driving creative force behind the group. It is important, however, not to lose sight of the fact that Tina Turner had creative agency in her own right: a gifted vocalist, dancer, and entertainer, whose talent and charisma propelled the Revue. Her involvement with her professional destiny was evident during her years with the Revue and continued to successful effect when she went solo. She drew on her experience in the recording industry and an understanding of the race and gender expectations that operated there to stage one of popular music's most celebrated comebacks.

As much as both Turners might have wanted onlookers to believe otherwise, Tina was a participant in the shaping of the group's sound. It was, as I have noted, Tina's idea to add rock songs to the Revue's repertoire. These were the songs that put the duo on the pop charts in the 1970s. She also co-produced the 1968 album *Outta Season* with Bob Krasnow and wrote some of the songs the duo recorded.[87] Two of her compositions, "Nutbush City Limits" (1973) and "Sexy Ida (Part 1)" (1974), made it onto the Top 30 of the R&B chart, and "Nutbush" went to number twenty-two on the pop chart, outpacing the success of the songs Ike authored during this period.[88] Her in-studio improvisations filled out the tracks Ike had written with ad-libbed lyrics and vocalizing and were a form of in-the-moment composition. More than "just a girl singer," then, Turner was a songwriter. Although she barely mentions this detail in her autobiography, BMI's online database lists seventy-one Tina Turner–authored or co-authored songs.[89] A profile published in *Crawdaddy* in 1972 highlighted her work as a writer. "I record when Ike cuts the tracks," she told the reporter. "I write the lyrics and then I go in and knock it out."[90] The duo recorded her composition "Bold Soul Sister" in 1970, and she wrote material for the albums *Outta Season* (1968), *Nuff Said* (1971), and *Feel Good* (1972).[91] Ike was willing to share credit and to reflect the collaborative conditions under which the duo's music was created, even if he did not give her a fair share of the couple's earnings.[92] When she needed money after the couple's breakup, she was able to secure an advance from BMI for royalties on songs for which she held songwriting credit.[93]

As journalists reporting on the group in the early 1970s indicate, Tina was an active partner in the operation of the Revue. Discussing the Ikettes, *Jet* magazine stated, "They are all chosen by Ike but are groomed by Tina, who sets the standards for dress, grooming and behavior on the road."[94] Similarly, *Rolling Stone*'s Ben Fong-Torres noted, "What Tina likes, and what she aims for when she choreographs the Ikettes—is *action*."[95] She says little about the role she played developing the visual and choreographic aspects of the Revue in her autobiography or in 1980s era interviews, and it is an interesting omission. Still, in spite of her tendency to downplay her agency, what becomes obvious when reading the coverage of the Revue is that by the late sixties Tina had become the group's de facto spokesperson, partly as a result of Ike's awareness of his limitations. "He had a complex about how he spoke," she told a reporter years after her divorce. "A lot of his fight came because he was embarrassed about his manners and not being educated."[96] When it was time to launch her solo career, she was accustomed to representing herself to the press, and, having watched her husband manage the Revue's career for more than a decade, she had insight into the business side of the industry.

When she went out on her own in 1976, Turner used her reputation and professional experience to get and hold onto gigs. Discussing her situation in a BBC television documentary about her career, she said, "It is common knowledge that Ike took everything. But he didn't. I learned how to survive with Ike. I learned how to perform. I learned how to cover songs and work without a record. This is what I learned. That's what I left him with: knowing I could always work and that's bottom line for me now."[97] She used this knowledge to establish herself as a solo artist. Confronting financial pressures—including the need to pay off large debts owed because she was held liable for the Revue's failure to appear for contracted shows in the months after she left her marriage—Turner needed to earn money quickly and accepted bookings at hotel lounges and on television shows like the *Hollywood Squares*.[98]

She turned to her friends, the singers Cher and Ann-Margaret, for help and was soon following their Vegas lounge style, even borrowing their glitzy Bob Mackie–designed sequined gowns. Turner staged shows with female backup singers, male dancers, and a tuxedo-wearing band. In this decidedly un-rock and roll guise, Turner performed the Revue's rock covers and contemporary Top 40 fare. She secured a recording contract, but her first post-Ike album releases, *Rough* (1978) and *Love Explosion* (1979), were critical and commercial disappointments. She was in debt to her record label and had been dropped from her contract when she met Roger Davies, an Australian music industry professional who had helped manage pop singer Olivia Newton-John. He was interested in working with Turner, but he recognized that she needed to refocus her sound and image to play on the strengths that had attracted him and other fans to her during her years with the Revue.

Together, Davies and Turner charted a path based on an understanding of the operation of race, gender, and genre in the recording industry. They decided to take her career outside of "black music," the category to which she was destined to be assigned because of her race, and set their sights on rock, the more financially lucrative genre. At Davies's behest, Turner dispensed with the Las Vegas–style stage costumes and lounge act choreography; she fired the band, backing singers, and dancers, and hired rock-rooted musicians. She developed a new look—a black leather miniskirt, high-heeled pumps, and a shimmering mane of tousled, blondish hair—that communicated tough, cool, and, above all, rock. Completing the turn to rock that she had started in 1966, Turner embraced the rhetoric of the rock scene that constructed the music as a liberating space of self-expression and traded on her image as one of the handful of women artists associated with it. Soon she was projecting a new attitude: "My stage performance is basically rock 'n' roll," she told *Billboard* in 1984. "I'm more comfortable with it; the energy is good and I like the words. I don't really want to do R&B right now. I can't say that I won't go back to it, because it's my roots. I just like to sing uptempo things. I'm very optimistic now."[99] A *Village Voice* review of a 1981 performance at New York's Ritz noted the change: "What was once at least hip-deep . . . gritty soul, crackling like flames under a mess of ribs, is now blistering rock, powered by Turner's shredded passion."[100] This critic judged her "the finest female rock singer today" and the gender qualifier was, arguably, superfluous.[101]

In 1981, Davies landed Turner high-profile slots as an opening act for Rod Stewart and for the Rolling Stones; she dueted with Stewart on "Hot Legs" and

"Get Back" and with Mick Jagger on "Honky Tonk Women."[102] Working with these well-established rock stars signaled Turner's connection to rock, as did the ways these artists mirrored one another. Turner seemed to have borrowed Stewart's cropped blond hairstyle, and Jagger had been borrowing Turner's dance moves for years. The excitement that these live performances generated, however, could not override what one reporter called the "sexist ageism" that contributed to label executives' skepticism about Turner's ability to sell records as a solo artist.[103] Working to rebuild a career in a youth-oriented field and seeking a record deal as she crept into her forties, she was unable to be as selective as she might have liked about the recording opportunities that came her way. Thus, she found herself covering the Temptations' "Ball of Confusion" as part of *Music of Quality and Distinction, Vol. 1*, a production project by Ian Craig Marsh and Martyn Ware of the British new wave group Heaven 17. Turner was initially dismayed because singing an old Motown hit felt like returning to the Ike-identified R&B world that she was trying to put behind her. Still, the song did well on the European charts and reminded record executives of her powerful vocal presence. Things finally came together in the spring of 1983, when the deal Davies had been struggling to make with Capitol Records, an American company owned by the English label EMI, was sealed with the help of David Bowie. A longtime Tina Turner fan, he brought EMI executives with him to her show at the Ritz in Manhattan.[104] Turner's performance was impressive enough to convince the executives to approve the Capitol contract.

The recording of the album *Private Dancer* came together quickly—a necessity as the label wanted to take advantage of positive buzz over her cover of Al Green's "Let's Stay Together," which had charted as a single in early 1984.[105] Davies selected and Turner approved a mix of covers and new material, including "What's Love Got to Do with It" and "Show Some Respect." Turner initially disliked the songs because their pop sound did not fit the rock and roll style she was now attached to; only after songwriter Terry Britten made them "rough enough" did she commit to recording them.[106] In a new iteration of the transatlantic exchanges between black American and white British artists that had propelled rock in the 1960s, Davies took the project to England and worked with British musicians to get the distinctive sound he wanted, and also, he explained, because "the writers and producers and musicians who most loved her, who respected her talent, were all based there."[107] Complementing the involvement of the Rolling Stones, Bowie, Stewart, Marsh, and Ware, who helped get Turner's comeback underway, were the white male rockers

FIGURE 8.3 On a day off from her 1984 *Private Dancer* tour, Tina Turner filmed the music video for "Better Be Good to Me" at the Beverly Theatre in Beverly Hills, California. Jamie West-Oram (seen in background) and Cy Curnin of the British new wave band the Fixx played on the track. Turner went on to win a Grammy for Best Rock Vocal Performance, Female, for her rendition of the song. PHOTO BY NANCY CLENDANIEL, WWW.NANCY CLENADANIEL.COM.

who contributed to *Private Dancer*. Mark Knopfler, the vocalist and guitarist of the British rock band Dire Straits, wrote the album's title track, and he facilitated the recording of the album by arranging for his band to join Turner in the studio. Scheduling conflicts prevented Knopfler from playing on the sessions, so guitar virtuoso Jeff Beck, best known for his work with the Yardbirds and the Jeff Beck Group, sat in on the moody title track and the up-tempo rocker "Steel Claw." American rock band Spider was the source for "Better Be Good to Me," the second single from the album; Jamie West-Oram and Cy Curnin of the Fixx, a British new wave band enjoying pop chart success at the time, played on the track (see figure 8.3). Covers of "I Can't Stand the Rain," a 1973 soul hit by Ann Peebles, Bowie's "1984," and "Let's Stay Together" filled out the album.

Released in the United States in May 1984, *Private Dancer* featured synthesizers, keyboards, and saxophones alongside hard rock–style electric guitars and smooth background vocalists who accompanied Turner on most of the songs.[108] The album gleamed with the slick, somewhat thin and trebly sound that was the hallmark of much eighties pop. Out in front of the mix was Turner's R&B and gospel-infused voice, reverberating with the fiery texture for which she was known on songs that covered a wide sonic and generic palette: there was the danceable soul of "Let's Stay Together," the in-your-face hard rock of "Steel Claw," and the grown-up pop of "What's Love Got to Do with It" with its world-weary declaration that romantic love was nothing "but a second-hand emotion." "Private Dancer," at more than seven minutes long, provided an opportunity for Turner to display vulnerability and introspection as she voiced the dreams and regrets of a woman musing about the life choices she had made. Across the album's nine tracks, Turner was still recognizably Tina Turner, still that singer who gave her all in every performance, but the screams that were her signature in the sixties and seventies were mostly absent. Turner sang with a hard edge and emotional openness that rock fans might have associated with male rock singers such as Rod Stewart, Mick Jagger, and Robert Plant, vocalists who had, of course, patterned themselves on African American artists, including Turner herself. At the same time, her shift away from R&B shouting tempered the vocal rawness that might have alienated her from an audience accustomed to a smoother pop sound.

The clean musical production and Turner's strong vocals resulted in an album with broad-based appeal. *Private Dancer* received positive reviews in the rock press. *Creem* called it "a must album" and went on to state, "The material is top-notch, expertly fit for Tina, and whether synths are the thing, or a 'real' instruments rock band, the various producers leave her all the room she needs to get to the songs' emotional cores."[109] The *Rolling Stone* review declared, "Tina Turner makes a powerful comeback on *Private Dancer*. Turner throws herself into the material here, her voice rasping but strong, physical and impossibly sensual. There isn't a single dud among the songs, and they're given modern rock settings that are neither detached nor very fussy."[110] The record-buying public agreed with the critical assessments, and the album's commercial success was extraordinary; it sold ten million copies and remained in the *Billboard* Top 100 for more than two years. The first single, "What's Love Got to Do with It," written by British songwriting team Terry Britten and Graham Lyle, gave Turner her first number one pop record in her twenty-four-year recording career; it stayed in the number one spot for three weeks and won the 1984 Grammy for Record of the Year.[111] The effectiveness of Turner's pop-rock mix was borne out by the two other Grammys she won that year: Best Pop Vocal Performance, Female, for "What's Love Got to Do with It" and Best Rock Vocal Performance, Female, for "Better Be Good to Me." Although they did not surpass *Private Dancer*, her subsequent albums earned platinum-level sales and garnered Grammy nominations and awards. Turner's solo tours put her on a par with the era's top musical acts with concerts that broke ticket sales records in South America and Europe.[112] The first black woman stadium rock star, she set a Guinness World Record for drawing the largest audience to see a single performer, when 188,000 paying fans attended her concert at the Maracana Stadium in Rio de Janeiro, Brazil, in January 1988.[113] Her success as a recording artist propelled her to a starring role in the 1985 film *Mad Max beyond Thunderdome*, and she scored a hit with another Britten and Lyle composition, "We Don't Need Another Hero," a song from the movie's soundtrack.

Private Dancer arrived at a time when rock music, a hybrid developed through the creativity of black and white artists, was generally viewed as music performed by and for white people. The overwhelming presence of white artists and fans muted rock's black roots and the innovations of black artists that were essential to its development. Turner was able to traverse the race, gender, and genre boundaries that stymied other black women, in part because of her professional associations with white male rockers who authorized her presence in their scene. These cross-racial collaborations and connections were typical of the experiences of black women in rock and roll, and, as this book makes clear, Turner was not the only African American woman to work with white management, producers, songwriters, and musicians. What makes her trajectory notable beyond the high level of success she achieved is the high profile of the rock luminaries who helped her stage her comeback. A story she recounts in her autobiography about staying up late with Keith Richards and David Bowie in New York's Plaza Hotel, drinking champagne and listening to old R&B records after one of her concerts at the Ritz, signals her insider status.[114]

The alliances with white rockers that launched Turner's solo star turn continued in the ensuing years. She recorded duets with Bowie (the title track of his 1984 release *Tonight*), Eric Clapton ("Tearing Us Apart" in 1987 on his album *August* and "What You Get Is What You See" on her 1986 release *Break Every Rule*), Canadian rocker Bryan Adams ("It's Only Love" for his 1985 album *Reckless*), and Rod Stewart ("It Takes Two" for his 1991 album *Vagabond Heart*).

Intended to sell records while giving mutually adoring artists an opportunity to work together, these productions were also exchanges of symbolic capital. Turner's presence conferred on her white collaborators a measure of African American musical authenticity, while each performance added to her rock bona fides. Other black artists had tapped into this type of symbolism. For African Americans striving for success in rock post-1964, visible association with white fellow musicians seems to be a necessity. From Jimi Hendrix, Sly Stone, and Arthur Lee in the sixties to Prince and Lenny Kravitz in the eighties and nineties, right on through to TV on the Radio and the Alabama Shakes in the twenty-first century, the presence of white bandmates smooths the path for black rockers. Beyond their specific musical contributions, white collaborators mediate the connection between black artists and what is perceived as a white artform and indicate the black artists' openness to white people, reassuring information for potential white fans. Living Colour, the rare all-black rock band that succeeded with the white rock audience, received crucial, path-smoothing assistance from Mick Jagger in the eighties.[115] Black and female, Turner certainly stood out in the mostly white, mostly male mid-eighties rock milieu, but she always seemed right at home with her white collaborators; she appeared with them on stage and in photos, smiling, leaning into or against them as they sang together. My favorite visual representation of her professional positioning at this point is the photograph of the participants in the 1988 Prince's Trust Concert: among the eighteen musicians, there are only two women, both of them black. British singer-songwriter and guitarist Joan Armatrading is characteristically dressed down in denim; she stands among two generations of male rockers, including Bryan Adams, Eric Clapton, Elton John, and Mark Knopfler. Front and center, sitting in a gold chair wearing a crisp white jacket, beige dress, and a broad smile, is Tina Turner. Rod Stewart, Paul McCartney, Phil Collins, and Howard Jones kneel on either side of her.[116] Her placement in the photo emphasizes her centrality to the sound of rock, while also suggesting a queen surrounded by admiring subjects.

Turner's desire to align herself with rock was connected to her belief that maintaining ties to rhythm and blues made neither emotional nor aesthetic sense. She heard significant differences between the two forms. "Rhythm and blues is rhythm and it's blues," she told *Rolling Stone* in 1984, "and blues is blues—people kinda crooning about the hardships of life. Rock & roll is very up music."[117] Whatever the historical connections between the two forms, Turner focused on questions of attitude and audience, the same ones that drove marketing decisions, and she viewed rock as a more favorable expressive arena. In a 1991 BBC documentary, Turner discussed the difference in stark terms, relying on stereotyped notions of race and generation to make her point:

> Can you imagine me standing out and singing about cheating on your wife or your husband to those kids? Those kids can't relate to that. They're naughty. They want to hear some fun things. Rock and roll is fun. It's full of energy, it's laughter. It's naughty. To me, a lot of rhythm and blues songs are depressing. They are, because it's a culture you're writing about and a way of life. Rock and roll is white, basically, 'cause white people haven't had that much of a problem so they write about much lighter things and funnier things.[118]

For Turner, rock and roll offered a respite from the hard facts of life that she associated with blackness and R&B. Youthful white rock was a site of pleasurable and problem-free good times. Focused on the upbeat aspects of rock, she ignored the social critiques and expressions of despair that white rock artists sometimes incorporated into their music during the sixties and seventies and that were a prominent feature of much eighties post-punk and new wave. With Davies, she made a decisive move to a musical place that she viewed as lighter, in terms of both the lyrical content of the music and the skin color of its fans. Rock was also, and not coincidentally, the more economically lucrative field.

Turner's longtime presence as a front woman smoothed her solo path. She made the most of her high degree of name recognition, capacity for riveting performances, and seventies chart hits, as she navigated the race, gender, and genre realities of the recording industry. She understood that to succeed in the field of rock, she had to connect with a sound and scene that by the early 1980s had eschewed visible blackness, while continuing to rely on black musical sound. She capitalized on the authorizing participation of white men and symbolic distancing from blackness to facilitate her success, aligning herself with a white manager and the white supporters I have discussed in this chapter. When speaking to the press, she espoused a pro-rock discourse that celebrated the genre as a repository of expressive freedom and a respite from the woeful realism of black R&B.[119] Sonically, though, Turner's repertoire maintained a connection to blackness indexed through blues-based roots, gospel-inspired vocals, and the polished energy of a rhythm and blues revue. Other African American women such as Nona Hendryx and Joyce Kennedy, who were working in the rock idiom at roughly the same time as Turner's solo rise, were not able to achieve anything close to the kind of career traction that Turner enjoyed. Following the breakup of her group Labelle, Hendryx released a string of solo albums whose musical eclecticism made her inscrutable—to use cultural critic Sonnet Retman's apt term—to audiences and critics who had no trouble making sense of the genre-crossing, culture-blending travels of white male artists such as Peter Gabriel, Sting, and David Byrne.[120] Meanwhile, as front woman for Mother's Finest, an Atlanta-based hard rock band founded in 1972, Kennedy toured on the rock circuit, opening for rock acts such as the Who, Aerosmith, and AC/DC. Their funk metal won some success on the American charts in the mid-1970s, but the band's fan base in the United States was small compared with the committed followers they played to in Europe, particularly in Germany, where the group established a regular presence in the heavy metal and hard rock scenes. In contrast to Hendryx and Kennedy, Turner was able to exploit the rock connections she had forged over the years to convey herself into the center of rock's mainstream. When she slowed down touring and recording in the early 2000s, she had half a dozen Grammys and had been inducted into the Rock and Roll Hall of Fame in 1992 as part of the Ike and Tina Turner Revue.

In the eyes of some onlookers, Turner's professional engagement with white rock and the involvement of white men in her comeback called her blackness into question. Take, as one prominent example, Little Richard, who said, "Tina got what she wanted, but she lost what she had."[121] In the introduction to his friend Ike Turner's autobiography, he stated, "I have nothing against her, but don't forget where you come from."[122] A different reading is one that frames Turner's choices not as forgetting where she came from or who she was, but as reimagining what a black woman vocalist could be. Pushing beyond the boundaries of what counted as authentic black musical behavior, Turner embraced a repertoire that spoke to her creative ideals and that offered her greater professional mobility and earning power. She resisted the expectation that she would limit herself to "black music." Instead, she maintained a broad vision of the music she would perform, extending understandings of what black women could do musically. Turner's expansive blackness confronted the rigid black/white binary that governed decision-making in the segregated popular music industry and rejected the limited vision of black authenticity that dominated the era. Turner's connection to rock made her a racially ambiguous figure. She trafficked in both black and white sounds, drew on both black R&B and white rock repertoire and performance tropes. In this regard, she was doing what the white male rockers who idolized her had been doing for years. The organizational structure and everyday decision-making practices of the US recording industry, however, did not permit African American women the same degree of genre mobility and access as white men. An anomaly, Tina Turner was able to leverage her alliances and reputation in ways that allowed her to project herself into the privileged territory of rock.

There are reasons to celebrate Turner's professional success, well deserved in light of her extraordinary talent. But I want to stress that I do not intend the narrative I have just recounted to read as a story of the transcendence of race and gender. On the contrary, I view Tina Turner's turn to rock as being a result of her direct engagement with the ways race, gender, power, and access worked in the recording industry. Turner was conscious of the limits and possibilities of her professional terrain and was well aware of the place she was expected to occupy as a black woman. Rich with the knowledge and cultural capital she had amassed over the years, she went in a different direction, deploying musical repertoire, rock and roll discourse, personal connections, and her arresting voice in strategic ways that took her all the way to the top.

Epilogue

All my life, I've been strugglin'. I'm still strugglin'. But I'm gonna make it some day. / **BIG MAMA THORNTON**

In July 2016, I went to Brownsville, Tennessee, a town an hour north of Memphis, to visit the Tina Turner Museum at Flagg Grove School. Established in 2014 in the one-room schoolhouse where Anna Mae Bullock had attended school as a child, the museum houses memorabilia from Turner's solo career in one section and re-creates her childhood schoolroom in the other. The compact wooden building had been moved from its original location near Nutbush (Turner's hometown) to Brownsville and restored, with dark brown interior walls and floors and an immaculate white exterior. The first thing visitors encounter once inside are four glass cases displaying mannequins wearing Turner's sequined stage costumes; each outfit is labeled with its designer's name, the song Turner sang while wearing it, and the relevant tour. A television monitor in one of the cases plays concert footage from her solo tours. Also on view are Turner's gold records from the United States, Switzerland, South Africa, and New Zealand; official tour calendars; publicity photographs; and a hardback copy of her autobiography. There is a photo of teenage Turner and her Carver High School basketball teammates posing in uniform. Nearby, her high school yearbook lies open to the page with her senior class picture; she is identified by her name, Ann Bullock, and her stated professional goal, Entertainer. A typed letter from the United Kingdom's Prince Charles thanking Turner for participating in the 1986 Prince's Trust Concert reminds visitors of the exalted circles in which she has traveled; his handwritten note adds, "It was a *great* pleasure to meet you after the concert + I enclose a photograph of the children! Most sincerely Charles."[1]

A few more steps into the building and the focus shifts from ephemera representing Turner as a rock star to materials that provide visitors with a sense of how the school looked when it served the area's black kindergarten through eighth grade children. There are rough-hewn wooden desks and benches, a potbelly stove, and a green chalkboard. The building has no indoor plumbing and the wall text explains that when the school was operating, "There were separate outhouses for boys and girls." The school was founded in 1889 when Benjamin Flagg, who had been born into slavery, acted on his concern that African American children in his community lacked educational opportunities; he sold an acre of land to the trustees who built the school.[2] In an arrangement that was typical for both black and white rural schools, as many as sixty children, ages five to thirteen, attended Flagg Grove School at the same time and were taught by one teacher.[3] A video running on a monitor features comments from Flagg's descendants and interviews with women who were Anna Mae Bullock's schoolmates. They remember her as having a lot of energy, singing all the time, and being something of "a tomboy girl." The short film concludes with an on-camera appearance by Turner talking about her memories of the school. She makes a statement about the importance of education, shares a wish for the success of the museum, and thanks the people who made the museum possible.

Located just off Interstate 40 (a.k.a., Music Highway) between Memphis and Nashville, the museum is part of the West Tennessee Delta Heritage Center, a visitor's center with an array of small museums erected by the city of Brownsville to encourage tourism to western Tennessee.[4] Although at this writing Turner has not visited the museum, she was involved in its creation. According to a 2014 Heritage Center press release, she provided both "a generous monetary donation towards the restoration of the school" and "all the memorabilia, display cases, gold record awards and stage costumes from her long career."[5] The hope is that a museum related to Tina Turner, an internationally known star, will draw tourists to the area. On the day I went to the museum, visitors from Memphis, Ohio, Connecticut, Wales (United Kingdom), France, New Zealand, and South Korea had signed the center's guest book.

The Flagg Grove School museum provides a sensory experience of being in a rural southern school, information about education for African Americans in the pre–civil rights south, and a selective representation of Turner's career. I saw no wall text references to Ike Turner, no photos of the Ike and Tina Turner Revue, no comments about their tireless touring or their electric stage show, and not a single fringed mini dress. Instead, the museum chronicles Turner's time at the schoolhouse in the 1940s and her solo career in the 1980s and beyond. The 1960s and 1970s when she paved the way to her rock and roll ascendancy are absent. You have to know that part of her story going in. Hers, however, is not the easiest story to find in the standard histories of rock and roll. Turner has had commercial success, is a Grammy-winning Rock and Roll Hall of Fame inductee, and is known as the Queen of Rock and Roll, but she is still on the periphery of rock in mainstream representations of the music's history. Musicologist Susan Fast suggests that this might be because "Ike and Tina seem to have been everything that serious popular music posterity reviles: a commercially driven enterprise, not too terribly innovative, not political in the way that some black performers of the 1960s were, with an intriguing but dangerously 'other' woman fronting the organization."[6] The textbooks I have consulted when teaching my rock and roll history course discuss Ike Turner because of his involvement with "Rocket 88," an important early rock and roll record, but they mention Tina and the Ike and Tina Turner Revue only in passing, if at all.[7] *Rolling Stone* magazine declared Tina "nothing short of amazing" in its earliest coverage of her, but in *The Rolling Stone Illustrated History of Rock and Roll*, her solo career warrants only a one-sentence description in a chapter called "Women in Revolt"; her name also appears in lists of artists who worked with producer Phil Spector and performers who participated in the 1985 Live Aid concert.[8]

From time to time, Turner's image is used to represent rock and roll. Her photo graced the front cover of *Who Shot Rock & Roll: A Photographic History, 1955 to the Present*, the catalogue for a museum exhibition about the history of rock photography; the same image, a close-up of Turner's perspiration sprinkled face, appeared on promotional streetlight banners in Brooklyn when the show was on view at the Brooklyn Museum in 2009.[9] It is far less common, though, to encounter commentary about Turner as a vocalist and the extent to which she influenced rock's vocal sound. Only the histories of women in rock, work that contests rock's male-centered master narrative, take her musical contributions seriously.[10] In one such text, music historian Lucy O'Brien addresses the question of Turner's image: "Though she is happy with the raunchy projects, it is also a stereotype that defines her. . . . Male artists talk about her respectfully, yet Turner is still never seen as a serious rock star. She symbolizes fun, parody, a whacking great voice and a potent sexuality."[11] Turner prevailed commercially, but full inclusion in the canon of rock and roll has been elusive. I thought about this simultaneous absence and presence and about the rules of gender, race, and genre that marginalize African American women—even Tina Turner—from rock during my visit to Flagg Grove School. When I finished at the museum, I drove north from Brownsville to Turner's hometown on "Highway number 19," as Turner refers to the road in the song "Nutbush City Limits." Along the way I passed the sign that designated the stretch of road I was on as "Tina Turner Highway." Before setting off I had purchased a refrigerator magnet replica of the sign at the Heritage Center gift shop. It was a portable reminder of the fact that, at least in some quarters, in some ways, Tina Turner was getting her due.

In May 1984, Tina Turner released *Private Dancer*, the album that launched her stratospheric solo success. Two months later, one of the women who helped to launch rock and roll died. Willie Mae "Big Mama" Thornton succumbed to a heart attack on July 25, 1984, at the age of fifty-seven. Years of hard living had taken their toll, and the body that had inspired her nickname had become a thin, drawn shell. Obituaries reported that she died alone in a Los Angeles boarding house, but her half-sister Mattie Fields told a different story, describing a sudden death while playing cards with friends and sipping gin and milk, her favorite drink.[12] Roughly two hundred people attended her "simple but poignant funeral" at a mortuary in central Los Angeles.[13] Many of the mourners made donations to help with the costs of the service and burial, and plans were in place for a benefit concert.[14] Thornton's health had been on the downswing in the last years of her life, but blues singer Jimmy Witherspoon insisted that right up to the end "her voice was still so powerful it made me weak to listen."[15] Musicians who had been her sidemen over the years were among the pallbearers, and her old friend Johnny Otis, who by the 1980s was a minister of his own church, presided over the service. In his eulogy he admonished those in attendance, "Don't waste your sorrow on Big Mama. She's free. Don't feel sorry for Big Mama. There's no more illness. No more pain. No more suffering in a society where the color of skin was more important than the quality of your talent."[16] Big Mama Thornton is buried in Inglewood Park Cemetery. On a visit to Los Angeles in 2010, I went to pay my respects. Her final resting place is at the westernmost edge of the grounds, busy Prairie Avenue just on the other side of the fence. Big Mama Thornton is buried in a grave marked by a simple marble block bearing her surname and the surnames of the other two people who share her burial plot. Neither her first name nor nickname appear on the headstone, and there is no indication that she was one of the greatest blues singers who had ever lived or that she originated songs that helped propel the rock and roll revolution. You have to know her story going in.

While Turner's story concludes with fame, wealth, rock and roll super-stardom, and a small museum honoring her legacy, Thornton's fits the blues singer myth: dead of too little success and buried in the most modest of graves. But Thornton has not been forgotten. The Blues Foundation inducted her into its Blues Hall of Fame in 1984, and she is one of the artists celebrated in the Blues Hall of Fame Museum in Memphis, where, through memorabilia and interactive digital media kiosks, visitors can access background infor-mation about her career, listen to full-length versions of half a dozen of her songs, and see an original 78 record of "Hound Dog" with the red Peacock Records label. There is also a living memorial to her: the Willie Mae Rock Camp for Girls. Since 2004, this Brooklyn-based nonprofit organization has offered girls from ages eight to eighteen musical mentoring. During two one-week day camp sessions each summer, girls learn to play musical in-struments, write lyrics and music for songs, and perform a concert at a local rock club. (I have been a volunteer at the camp and my daughter has been a camper.) Founded by activist feminist musicians, rock camp's goal is to em-power girls, women, and gender nonbinary youth through participation in music-making and conversations about social justice. The founders named their enterprise after a woman who represents the ideals of creativity and self-expression that they value.

The sonic legacy of Thornton, Turner, and the other women whose careers I have chronicled in Black Diamond Queens also reverberates in the music that artists are producing in the twenty-first century. This came into focus the night after I visited the Tina Turner Museum. Still in Tennessee, I went to the Mud Island Amphitheater in Memphis to see the Alabama Shakes featuring Brit-tany Howard on vocals and guitar (see figure E.1). Born in Athens, Alabama, in 1988 to an African American father and a European American mother, Howard has fashioned a career in rock. Ignoring the rules that put women of African descent in the R&B or pop vocalist box, Howard plays electric guitar and sings in a band that traffics in high-volume, blues rock. Fusing southern rock, alternative rock, and southern soul, Howard creates a majestic, guitar-centered sound and deploys her powerful alto voice in unexpected ways, holding notes a *loooong* time for emphasis, reaching down into its depths or spiraling up into a fragile head voice to deliver a pained and haunted howl. Working her voice this way and that, Howard is "by turns ferocious or angelic, sometimes in the same song," as the *New York Times Magazine* put it in a 2015 profile.[17] In "Hold On," the band's debut single, Howard exhorts herself to get back up, to keep on trying, to hoooold on. The song's expression of passionate

FIGURE E.1 Brittany Howard of the Alabama Shakes in concert in 2014, carrying on the spirit of Black Diamond Queens in the twenty-first century. PHOTO BY JANET MACOSKA.

determination was compelling to a critical mass of listeners whose support set the band on a path to success.

At Mud Island, a five-thousand-seat house, Howard captivated the sold-out crowd. We greeted her arrival with an extended round of applause and she bowed in response, then got down to the business of playing material from her band's two albums, *Boys and Girls* (2012) and *Sound and Color* (2015). Early in the set she made a geographically specific comment: "It's good to be back in the South after being overseas. It's good to be eating biscuits. Biscuits!" At random points during the set, audience members cried out, "We love you, Brittany!" Each time, cheers followed the declaration. With her heavy-framed eyeglasses and cropped hair, her body draped in a short-sleeved maxi dress with a floral print, Howard did not present a typical image of female star eye candy. Her long dress and blue electric guitar recalled gospel guitar great Sister Rosetta Tharpe, but her ankle-high, low-heeled boots made me think of the sartorial maneuvers of Big Mama Thornton, who, according to Johnny Otis, wore cowboy boots with a gown when she appeared at the Apollo in the 1950s.[18] As Howard moved through her band's set, I thought beyond Thornton and sought connections between Howard and the other Black Diamond Queens, hearing Howard's sound and style as an archive and extension of the women I have discussed in this book.[19] Consciously or not, she walks on the musical path that they paved.

There are obvious surface parallels between Howard and Thornton: their shared Alabama birthplace and commanding physical presence. Tall and large-framed like Thornton, Howard is, also like Thornton, a woman with a big voice and attitude to burn. Listening to Howard's "huge, gritty voice" and the blues-rock musical settings, one might hear echoes of Janis Joplin, a woman rocker known for a full-tilt vocal attack, who borrowed from Thornton's vocal style.[20] Howard and her band played to the integrated but predominantly white audiences that gathered at events such as Farm Aid, Sun Fest, and the Panorama Festival, and at the concerts that the band headlined. In this regard, she walked the same path as the early rock and roll queens LaVern Baker and the Shirelles, who attracted a generation of white youth with their catchy vocal sounds and tuneful melodies. Howard was the only band member who spoke during the set, so she came across as the leader of a band that consists of Heath Fogg on guitar, Zac Cockrell on bass, Steve Johnson on drums, plus touring keyboard players Ben Tanner and Paul Horton. Also onstage was a trio of background vocalists, two black women and a black man, who provided a gospel sound to support Howard's vocals. Their presence added vocal variety and power against the swirl of instrumental distortion and high volume rave-ups. The trio helped Howard come forward as the star of the show, fulfilling the role black women background vocalists played in their work with white male singers decades ago. The crucial difference here was that a rocking black woman was center stage. The African American background vocalists provided one of the sonic trappings of the classic rock era that the Alabama Shakes draw on to create their twenty-first-century rock sound. As it was with white rock artists in the 1960s and 1970s, the presence of gospel-infused background vocals allowed Howard's band to signal a connection to rock and soul, tapping into sonic features of African American musical traditions while staying connected to rock. The black vocal trio Labelle strived to strike this balance in the 1970s, embracing sounds and performance practices that were coded as either black or white, soul or rock. Labelle's expressive openness won them a fan base notable for its racial and ethnic diversity and for the visible presence of gay men and lesbians. Some of this mix was in evidence at Mud Island; a substantial number of those in attendance sported hair styles, clothing, and body decorations that demonstrated a high degree of comfort rejecting the heteronormative.

Howard's songwriting and her position as a woman creating an artistic vision on stage and behind the scenes linked her to the women of Labelle and to Betty Davis. Her lyrics include unfiltered expressions of longing and desire. She admits devotion and tells her love interest (whose gender is not specified) that she is present, available, and entirely worth it. Howard's exploration of the farthest reaches of her vocal range and her play with sound remind me of the singing experiments of Betty Davis and Marsha Hunt. But Howard's approach to her stage show diverged from that of the 1970s Black Diamond Queens. She was not displaying her body in form-fitting costumes and she did not dance; instead, she restricted her movement to emphatic strides back and forth across the stage. During the set she exhibited the magnetic stage presence that journalists have celebrated. Writing in the *New York Times Magazine*, Joe Rhodes stated that "when she hits that first big unrestrained note—her face contorted as if possessed—or a thundering chord on her Gibson, stomping and quaking, preaching and confessing, her jaw jutting out like an angry, pouting child's, everything changes. It becomes impossible to look anywhere else."[21] To my eye, Howard's onstage style suggested she had spent more time studying the self-presentation of male guitarists than of female singers. She has, however, found ways to expand her range. Thunderbitch, a raucous rock side project that released its debut album in the fall of 2015, gave her an opportunity to take on an alter ego and dress up. For a show at a New York City club, she appeared on-stage "astride a motorcycle, costumed in white face paint, dark shades, and a black leather jacket."[22] Commenting on the spectacle, Howard observed, "It's bringing back the performance side of rock and roll—what used to be the industry standard."[23] Howard's appreciation for David Bowie, with his vari-ous performance personae and highly evolved sense of the theatrical, has made him an obvious reference point for journalists covering her career, but Howard's venture into high performance also recalls Labelle's silver space costumes and aerial arrivals on stage.

In interviews, Howard has named Alice Coltrane, Björk, Led Zeppelin, Prince, and Bowie as sources of inspiration.[24] She has also discussed the Queen of Rock and Roll. "I love singers like Tina Turner," Howard told *Spin* magazine. "She taught me that you don't have to be worried about sounding pretty."[25] This refusal to conform to proper femininity is part of what aligns both Turner and Howard with rock; beyond this commonality, both women fashioned clear sonic and symbolic connections to rock. In the case of Howard, the guitar-centric arrangements of her band's songs and musical references to the pantheon of black and white rock musicians who preceded her establish her rock credentials. The *Rolling Stone* review of Thunderbitch's eponymous album mentions innovative rock and roll guitarist Link Wray, the New York Dolls, and the Velvet Underground as sonic forebears. Howard's race, gender performance, and vocal sound may be ambiguous, but her commitment to rock is clear, even overstated in Thunderbitch song titles like "Wild Child" and "I Just Wanna Rock 'n' Roll." Her membership in a band with three white men further indexes her affinity with rock. As with the Jimi Hendrix Experience, Love, Sly and the Family Stone, and Prince and the Revolution, participation in an in-tegrated band can facilitate the crossover of African-descent musicians to white audiences by telegraphing an attitude of racial inclusiveness. How-ard's success as a rock musician comes, as it did with Turner, through a self-conscious insistence on expanding ideas of the kinds of musical and vocal sounds a woman of African descent could engage and whom she could collaborate with to create them.

Howard is not the only woman of color pushing these sonic expectations, but in the genre of rock in recent years, she is the one who has managed to do so with the most substantial critical and commercial success, achieving a level of visibility that recalls Turner's during her 1980s ascent. The Alabama

Shakes' 2012 debut release *Boys & Girls* received two Grammy nominations, and *Rolling Stone* declared its single "Hold On" the song of the year.[26] *Sound and Color*, their 2015 sophomore effort, went to number one on *Billboard*'s album chart and garnered Grammy awards for best alternative music album, best rock performance, and best rock song (the latter two for "Don't Wanna Fight"), making Howard the first black woman to win a Grammy in a rock category since Tracy Chapman did so in the late 1990s.[27] Since stepping onto the national stage, the Alabama Shakes have enjoyed widespread media coverage and high-profile bookings, including guest appearances on *Saturday Night Live* and at the White House. Rock luminaries welcomed Howard into their fold. In 2015 Paul McCartney invited her to sing "Get Back" with him at Lollapalooza music festival, and Prince summoned her to his Paisley Park production complex for a jam session.[28] Embraced as a rocker, Howard had avoided the R&B label that ensnared the eclectic African American musician Santi White, whose struggles with race, gender, and genre I referenced at the beginning of this book.

"God bless, you," Howard told the Mud Island audience as she took her last bow of the evening. "Until we meet again. Thank you!" For me, the concert had been a total pleasure. Leaving the venue, my ears still buzzing from the wash of loud guitars, I considered a final connection between Howard and all of the women I have discussed: unconventionality. In his *New York Times Magazine* profile, Joe Rhodes catalogued the elements of Howard's difference that marked her as an outcast growing up in her small town and continued to set her apart in her rock star adulthood: "She was too big, too tall, a girl with thick horn-rimmed glasses and a taste for vintage clothes, a daughter of a black father and a white mother and, because of a retinoblastoma treatment that scarred her retina when she was a newborn, nearly blind—noticeably so—in one eye."[29] Howard's acceptance of this difference fuels her refusal to allow mainstream expectations of musical sound, lyrical content, performance style, and standards of dress to confine her. "I have to be myself," she said in an interview with *Rolling Stone*.[30] This attitude is the hallmark of the Black Diamond Queens, maverick women who went their own way, doing their best to sustain careers in a professional entertainment industry that relied on their creative labor and musical contributions, but displaced them and rewarded others who took on key elements of their sound. If we listen beyond racialized musical categories and recording industry common sense, if we pay attention to connections and collaborations that are not foregrounded in the dominant narratives of rock history, we can better hear the voices of these

African American women in rock and roll. All of the women I have discussed in this book pushed the limits of race, gender, and genre expectations to make their music. All of us, fans and musicians, can learn, from these sounds and stories, about the continued reality and rigidity of social and musical boundaries, about valiant efforts to circumvent them, and about the ways Black Diamond Queens keep on stepping.

NOTES

Introduction

1 Santogold, *Santogold* (Atlantic Records/Downtown Records, 2008). White's album was originally released with the artist name and album title Santogold; after an artist named Santo Gold filed a lawsuit against her for using his name, White retitled the album and herself Santigold in 2009. Tom Breihan, "Santogold Is Now Santigold," *Pitchfork*, February 11, 2009, https://pitchfork.com/news/34595-santogold-is-now -santigold/.

2 Santi White quoted in "Santogold Dubs 'Hip-Hop' Comparisons Racist," *Melody Maker*, May 19, 2008, accessed May 17, 2019, https://www.nme.com/news/music /santogold-13-1324234.

3 Susan C. Cook and Judy S. Tsou, "Introduction: 'Bright Cecilia,'" in *Cecilia Reclaimed: Feminist Perspectives on Gender and Music*, ed. Susan C. Cook and Judy S. Tsou (Urbana: University of Illinois Press, 1994), 2. Some representative examples of this work in ethnomusicology and musicology include Elaine Barkin and Lydia Hamessley, eds., *Audible Traces: Gender, Identity, and Music* (Zurich: Carciofoli Verlagshaus, 1999); Jane Bowers and Judith Tick, eds., *Women Making Music: The Western Art Tradition, 1150–1920* (Urbana: University of Illinois Press, 1986); Suzanne G. Cusick, *Francesca Caccini at the Medici Court: Music and the Circulation of Power* (Chicago: University of Chicago Press, 2009); Ellen Koskoff, ed., *Women and Music in Cross-Cultural Perspective* (New York: Greenwood Press, 1987); Ruth A. Solie, ed., *Musicology and Difference: Gender and Sexuality in Music Scholarship* (Berkeley: University of California Press, 1993); and Jane C. Sugarman, *Engendering Song: Singing and Subjectivity at Prespa Albanian Weddings* (Chicago: University of Chicago Press, 1997). Some representative examples of this work in writing about rock music include Mavis Bayton, *Frock Rock: Women Performing Popular Music* (New York: Oxford University Press, 1998); Lori Burns and Mélisse Lafrance, *Disruptive Divas: Feminism, Identity and Popular Music* (New York: Routledge, 2002); Mina Carson, Tisa Lewis, and Susan M. Shaw, *Girls Rock! Fifty Years of Women Making Music* (Lexington: University Press of Kentucky, 2004); Gillian Gaar, *She's a Rebel: The History of Women in Rock and Roll*, 2nd ed. (Seattle: Seal Press, 1992); Gerri Hirshey, *We Gotta Get Out of This Place: The True, Tough Story of Women in Rock* (New York: Atlantic Monthly Press, 2001); Michelle Habell-Pallán, *Loca Motion: The Travels of Chicana and Latina*

Popular Culture (New York: New York University Press, 2005); Evelyn McDonnell and Ann Powers, eds., *Rock She Wrote: Women Write about Rock, Pop, and Rap* (New York: Delta, 1995); Lucy O'Brien, *She Bop: The Definitive History of Women in Rock, Pop and Soul* (New York: Penguin, 1995); Barbara O'Dair, ed., *Trouble Girls: The Rolling Stone Book of Women in Rock* (New York: Random House, 1997);Annie J. Randall, *Dusty, Queen of the Postmods* (New York: Oxford University Press, 2009); Jacqueline Warwick, *Girl Groups, Girl Culture: Popular Music and Identity in the 1960s* (New York: Routledge, 2007); and Sheila Whiteley, *Women and Popular Music: Sexuality, Identity, and Subjectivity* (London: Routledge, 2000).

4 Some representative examples include Daphne A. Brooks, "Nina Simone's Triple Play," *Callaloo* 34, no. 1 (2011): 176–97; Hazel V. Carby, "The Sexual Politics of Women's Blues," in *Cultures in Babylon: Black Britain and African America*, ed. Hazel V. Carby, 7–21 (London: Verso, 1999); Angela Y. Davis, *Blues Legacies and Black Feminism: Gertrude "Ma" Rainey, Bessie Smith, and Billie Holiday* (New York: Pantheon, 1998); Laina Dawes, *What Are You Doing Here? Black Women in Metal, Hardcore and Punk* (Brooklyn, NY: Bazillion Points Books, 2012); Kyra Gaunt, *The Games Black Girls Play: Learning the Ropes from Double-Dutch to Hip-Hop* (New York: New York University Press, 2006); Farah Jasmine Griffin, *If You Can't Be Free, Be a Mystery: In Search of Billie Holiday* (New York: Free Press, 2001); Daphne Duval Harrison, *Black Pearls: Blues Queens of the 1920s* (New Brunswick, NJ: Rutgers University Press, 1988); Eileen M. Hayes, *Songs in Black and Lavender: Race, Sexual Politics, and Women's Music* (Urbana: University of Illinois Press, 2010); Tammy L. Kernodle, *Soul on Soul: The Life and Music of Mary Lou Williams* (Boston: Northeastern University Press, 2004); Gwendolyn Pough, *Check It While I Wreck It: Black Womanhood, Hip-Hop Culture, and the Public Sphere* (Lebanon, NH: Northeastern University Press, 2004); Sonnet Retman, "Between Rock and a Hard Place: Narrating Nona Hendryx's Inscrutable Career," *Women and Performance: A Journal of Feminist Theory* 16, no. 1 (2006): 107–18; Tricia Rose, "Two Inches or a Yard: Silencing Black Women's Sexual Expression," in *Talking Visions: Multicultural Feminism in a Transnational Age*, ed. Ella Shohat (Cambridge, MA: MIT Press, 1998), 315–24; and Sherrie Tucker, *Swing Shift: "All-Girl" Bands of the 1940s* (Durham, NC: Duke University Press, 2000).

5 Brooks, "Nina Simone's Triple Play," 193.

6 Warwick uses the term *rock ideology* for this line of thought. Warwick, *Girl Groups, Girl Culture*, 90.

7 Warwick, *Girl Groups, Girl Culture*, 95.

8 Warwick, *Girl Groups, Girl Culture*, 95. For an analysis of the racial dimensions of this viewpoint, see Jack Hamilton, *Just around Midnight: Rock and Roll and the Racial Imagination* (Cambridge, MA: Harvard University Press, 2016).

9 Laurie Stras, "Introduction: She's So Fine, or Why Girl Singers (Still) Matter," in *She's So Fine: Reflections on Whiteness, Femininity, Adolescence and Class in 1960s Music*, ed. Laurie Stras (Burlington, VT: Ashgate, 2010), 2.

10 Travis A. Jackson, "Interpreting Jazz," in *African American Music: An Introduction*, ed. Mellonee V. Burnim and Portia K. Maultsby (New York: Routledge, 2006), 169.

11 Jackson, "Interpreting Jazz," 169.

12 Jackson, "Interpreting Jazz," 169. For a perceptive discussion of a jazz vocalist engaging in this type of decision-making, see Griffin, *If You Can't Be Free, Be a Mystery*, 84–95.

13 Warwick, *Girl Groups, Girl Culture*, 131.

14 Simon Frith, *Performing Rites: On the Value of Popular Music* (Cambridge, MA: Harvard University Press, 1996), 201.

15 In some streams of rock, the voice in question may be that of the soloing lead guitarist, as with a virtuoso such as Jimi Hendrix or Jimmy Page or notable stylists such as Chuck Berry and Keith Richards. In these cases, the singing voice and lead guitar "voice" take turns being in the foreground of the song.

16 I thank my colleague Martin Daughtry for his assistance in helping me identify and sift through voice studies literature. For research on voice in music that resonates with this study, see Suzanne Cusick, "On Musical Performances of Gender and Sex," in *Audible Traces: Gender, Identity, and Music*, ed. Elaine Barkin and Lydia Hamessley (Zurich: Carciofoli Verlagshaus, 1999), 25–48; Nina Sun Eidsheim, "Marian Anderson and 'Sonic Blackness' in American Opera," *American Quarterly* 63, no. 3 (September 2011): 641–71; Ellie M. Hisama, "Voice, Race, and Sexuality in the Music of Joan Armatrading," in *Audible Traces*, ed. Barkin and Hamessley, 115–32; Laurie Stras, "White Face, Black Voice: Race, Gender, and Region in the Music of the Boswell Sisters," *Journal of the Society for American Music* 1, no. 2 (2007): 207–55. For discussions that historicize the construction of "black music," see Karl Hagstrom Miller, *Segregating Sound: Inventing Folk and Pop Music in the Age of Jim Crow* (Durham, NC: Duke University Press, 2010), and Ronald Radano, *Lying Up a Nation: Race and Black Music* (Chicago: University of Chicago Press, 2003).

17 A volume on women vocalists in global contexts takes a similar approach: "We offer narratives that invoke the interface of the literal singing voice and the metaphorical voice, exploring relationships between a singing voice and voice as agency and examining how a singing voice enables voice as power to be enacted." Ruth Hellier, *Women Singers in Global Contexts: Music, Biography, Identity* (Urbana: University of Illinois Press, 2013), 5.

18 Guthrie P. Ramsey Jr., *The Amazing Bud Powell: Black Genius, Jazz History, and the Challenge of Bebop* (Berkeley: University of California Press, 2013), 8.

19 Some examples of this type of work include David Ake, Charles Hiroshi Garrett, and Daniel Goldmark, eds., *Jazz/Not Jazz: The Music and Its Boundaries* (Berkeley: University of California Press, 2012); David Brackett, *Categorizing Sound: Genre and Twentieth Century Popular Music* (Oakland: University of California Press, 2016); Franco Fabbri, "A Theory of Musical Genres: Two Applications," in *Popular Music: Critical Concepts in Media and Cultural Studies*, vol. 3, ed. Simon Frith (New York: Routledge, 2003), 7–35; Kevin Fellezs, *Birds of Fire: Jazz, Rock, Funk, and the Creation*

of Fusion (Durham, NC: Duke University Press, 2011); Frith, *Performing Rites*; Fabian
Holt, *Genre in Popular Music* (Chicago: University of Chicago Press, 2007); Miller,
Segregating Sound; Keith Negus, *Music Genres and Corporate Cultures* (London:
Routledge, 1999); Richard A. Peterson and Bruce A. Beal, "Alternative Country:
Origins, Music, World-view, Fans, and Taste in Genre Formation," *Popular Music and
Society* 25, no. 1–2 (2001): 233–49; and Steve Waksman, *This Ain't the Summer of Love:
Conflict and Crossover in Heavy Metal and Punk* (Berkeley: University of California
Press, 2009).

20 Holt, *Genre in Popular Music*, 19.

21 Elijah Wald, *How the Beatles Destroyed Rock 'n' Roll: An Alternative History of American Popular Music* (New York: Oxford University Press, 2009), 223.

22 Frith, *Performing Rites*, 76.

23 Simon Frith, "Towards an Aesthetic of Popular Music," in *Music and Society: The
Politics of Composition, Performance, and Reception*, ed. Richard Leppert and Susan
McClary (New York: Cambridge University Press, 1987), 147.

24 For a discussion of how this process operates outside of commercial popular music,
see George Lewis, "Experimental Music in Black and White: The AACM in New York,
1970–1985," in *Uptown Conversation: The New Jazz Studies*, ed. Robert O'Meally,
Brent Hayes Edwards, and Farah Jasmine Griffin (New York: Columbia University
Press, 2004), 50–101.

25 Warwick, *Girl Groups, Girl Culture*, 6. Also see Jacqueline Warwick, "Midnight
Ramblers and Material Girls: Gender and Stardom in Rock and Pop," in *The SAGE
Handbook of Popular Music*, ed. Andy Bennett and Steve Waksman (Los Angeles:
SAGE, 2015), 332–45.

26 Miles Parks Grier, "The Only Black Man at the Party: Joni Mitchell Enters the Rock
Canon," *Genders* 56 (fall 2012), web, [paragraph 5].

27 Retman, "Between Rock and a Hard Place, 114.

28 Frith, *Performing Rites*, 93.

29 Reebee Garofalo, "Culture versus Commerce: The Marketing of Black Popular
Music," *Public Culture* 7, no. 1 (1994): 276.

30 Portia K. Maultsby, "Africanisms in African-American Music" in *Africanisms in
American Culture*, ed. Joseph E. Holloway (Bloomington: Indiana University Press,
1991), 186. For other discussions of African American musical aesthetics and their
relationship to West African musical practices, see Mellonee V. Burnim, "The Black
Gospel Music Tradition: A Complex of Ideology, Aesthetic, and Behavior," in *More
Than Dancing: Essays on Afro-American Music and Musicians*, ed. Irene V. Jackson
(Westport, CT: Greenwood Press, 1985), 147–67; Samuel A. Floyd Jr., *The Power
of Black Music: Interpreting Its History from Africa to the United States* (New York:
Oxford University Press, 1997); LeRoi Jones [Amiri Baraka], *Blues People: Negro
Music in White America* (New York: Perennial, [1963] 2002) and Olly Wilson, "The
Significance of the Relationship between Afro-American Music and West African
Music," *The Black Perspective in Music* 2, no. 1 (1974): 3–22.

31 Maultsby, "Africanisms in African-American Music," 186.

32 In her discussion and analysis of these features, Maultsby highlights "three areas of aesthetic significance in the black music tradition: delivery style, sound quality, and mechanics of delivery," 188. Here, she is drawing on ethnomusicologist Mellonee Burnim's article, "The Black Gospel Music Tradition."

33 John A. Jackson, *Big Beat Heat: Alan Freed and the Early Years of Rock and Roll* (New York: Schirmer Books, 1991), 41.

34 Garofalo, "Culture versus Commerce," 277.

35 A survey of the charts demonstrates the shift: while in 1962 black artists contributed 42 percent of the pop singles, by 1966, only 22 percent of the acts that charted on the pop charts were African American. Garofalo, "Culture versus Commerce," 277.

36 Hamilton, *Just around Midnight*, 10–11.

37 Garofalo, "Culture versus Commerce," 277.

38 David Sanjek, "Tell Me Something I Don't Already Know: The Harvard Report on Soul Music Revisited," in *Rhythm and Business: The Political Economy of Black Music*, ed. Norman Kelley (New York: Akashic, 2002), 59–76.

39 Francesca T. Royster, *Sounding Like a No-No: Queer Sounds and Eccentric Acts in the Post-Soul Era* (Ann Arbor: University of Michigan Press, 2013), 8.

40 Jayna Brown, *Babylon Girls: Black Women Performers and the Shaping of the Modern* (Durham, NC: Duke University Press, 2008).

41 Gayle F. Wald, "From Spirituals to Swing: Sister Rosetta Tharpe and Gospel Cross-over," *American Quarterly* 55, no. 3 (September 2003): 391.

42 Gaunt, *The Games Black Girls Play*.

43 Daphne A. Brooks, "The Write to Rock: Racial Mythologies, Feminist Theory, and the Pleasures of Rock Music Criticism," *Women and Music: A Journal of Gender and Culture* 12 (2008): 57.

44 Brooks, "The Write to Rock," 58.

45 Brooks, "The Write to Rock," 55.

46 Stras, "Introduction: She's So Fine," 7.

47 Stras, "Introduction: She's So Fine," 7.

48 Tucker, *Swing Shift*, 7.

49 Tucker, *Swing Shift*, 13.

50 Res, *How I Do*, MCA Records 088 112 310-2, 2001, CD.

51 Stiffed, *Sex Sells*, Cool Hunter CHCD0003, 2003, CD; Stiffed, *Burned Again*, Outlook Music, OMC-1004, 2005, CD.

52 Maureen Mahon, *Right to Rock: The Black Rock Coalition and the Cultural Politics of Race* (Durham, NC: Duke University Press, 2004).

53 For my early attempt at a historical account of African American women in rock, see Maureen Mahon, "Women in African American Music: Rock," in *African American Music: An Introduction*, ed. Mellonee Burnim and Portia K. Maultsby (New York: Routledge, 2006), 558–77; for an ethnographically grounded account of independent African American women musicians, see Maureen Mahon, "The 'Daughters of Soul'

Tour and the Politics and Possibilities of Black Music," in *Ethnographies of Neoliberalism*, ed. Carol J. Greenhouse (Philadelphia: University of Pennsylvania Press, 2010), 207–20.

54 This practice theory approach is attentive to the dialectical relationship between structure and agency and facilitates the examination of the limits and possibilities of human action. Key texts on practice theory include Pierre Bourdieu, *The Logic of Practice*, trans. Richard Nice (Stanford, CA: Stanford University Press, 1990); Anthony Giddens, *Central Problems in Social Theory: Action, Structure, and Contradiction in Social Analysis* (Berkeley: University of California Press, 1979); and Sherry B. Ortner, *Anthropology and Social Theory: Culture, Power, and the Acting Subject* (Durham, NC: Duke University Press, 2006). For a discussion of practice theory in relation to African American women in rock and roll, see Maureen Mahon, "Musicality, Sexuality, and Power: A Practice Theory Approach," Colloquy on Music and Sexuality, *Journal of the American Musicological Society* 66, no. 3 (fall 2013): 844–48.

55 My impulse echoes a motivation that black feminist author Alice Walker has described: "In my own work I write not only what I want to read—understanding fully and indelibly that if I don't do it no one else is so vitally interested, or capable of doing it to my satisfaction—I write all the things *I should have been able to read*." Alice Walker quoted in Patricia Hill Collins, *Black Feminist Thought: Knowledge, Consciousness, and the Politics of Empowerment* (New York: Routledge, 1991), 13, original emphasis.

56 Recognition of these connections and intersections has been a part of black women's scholarship for decades. See, for example, Collins, *Black Feminist Thought*; Combahee River Collective, "A Black Feminist Statement," in *This Bridge Called My Back: Writings by Radical Women of Color*, ed. Cherríe Moraga and Gloria Anzaldúa (New York: Kitchen Table, Women of Color Press, 1983); Kimberlé Crenshaw, "Mapping the Margins: Intersectionality, Identity Politics, and Violence against Women of Color," in *Critical Race Theory: The Key Writings That Formed the Movement*, ed. Kimberlé Crenshaw, Neil Gotanda, Gary Peller, and Kendall Thomas (New York: New Press, 1995), 357–83; Paula Giddings, *When and Where I Enter: The Impact of Black Women on Race and Sex in America* (New York: Morrow, 1984); and Beverly Guy-Sheftall, ed., *Words of Fire: An Anthology of African-American Feminist Thought* (New York: New Press, 1995).

57 Deborah Willis and Carla Williams, *The Black Female Body: A Photographic History* (Philadelphia: Temple University Press, 2002), 54.

58 Collins, *Black Feminist Thought*. For a twenty-first-century take on the impact of stereotyped images of African American women, see Melissa V. Harris-Perry, *Sister Citizen: Shame, Stereotypes, and Black Women in America* (New Haven, CT: Yale University Press, 2011).

59 Although recorded in 1969, the single's release was delayed until 1971 due to a contract dispute. In the United States, it was released in May 1971 and spent two weeks at number one and stayed on the Top 40 for twelve weeks. In Great Britain, "Brown

Sugar" was released in April 1971; its highest chart position was number two and it remained on the charts for thirteen weeks. Martin Elliott, *The Rolling Stones Complete Recording Sessions, 1963–1989* (London: Blandford, 1990), 102; Joel Whitburn, *The Billboard Book of Top 40 Hits*, 9th ed. (New York: Billboard Books, 2010).

60 The Rolling Stones, "Brown Sugar," *Sticky Fingers*, Universal Music, 80012799-02, 2009, CD. Originally released in 1971.

61 For example, see Angela Y. Davis, *Women, Race, and Class* (New York: Vintage, 1983), and Deborah Gray White, *Ar'n't I a Woman? Female Slaves in the Plantation South* (New York: W. W. Norton, 1999).

62 White, *Ar'n't I a Woman*, 68.

63 White, *Ar'n't I a Woman*, 95.

64 Darlene Clark Hine and Kathleen Thompson, *A Shining Thread of Hope: The History of Black Women in America* (New York: Broadway Books, 1998), 93–94.

65 For example, see Collins, *Black Feminist Thought*; Davis, *Women, Race, and Class*; bell hooks, *Ain't I a Woman: Black Women and Feminism* (Boston: South End Press, 1981); and White, *Ar'n't I a Woman*.

66 Evelynn Hammonds, "Black (W)holes and the Geometry of Black Female Sexuality," *Differences: A Journal of Feminist Cultural Studies* 6, no. 2–3 (1994): 132.

67 Lorraine O'Grady, "Olympia's Maid: Reclaiming Black Female Subjectivity," in *New Feminist Criticism: Art, Identity, Action*, ed. Joanna Frueh, Cassandra Langer, and Arlene Raven (New York: Icon Editions, 1994), 152.

68 Carson, Lewis, and Shaw, *Girls Rock*, 41.

69 Willis and Williams, *The Black Female Body*, 54.

70 Carson, Lewis, and Shaw, *Girls Rock*, 41.

71 An early musical example of this use of the term *rock and roll* is in blues singer Trixie Smith's 1922 song "My Man Rocks Me," which featured the lyric, "My man rocks me with one steady roll."

72 Greg Tate, ed., *Everything but the Burden: What White People Are Taking from Black Culture* (New York: Broadway Books, 2003). For a discussion of this tendency in twentieth-century popular music, see Simon Frith, "Rhythm: Race, Sex, and the Body," in *Performing Rites*, 123–44.

73 Ingrid Monson, "The Problem with White Hipness: Race, Gender, and Cultural Conceptions in Jazz Historical Discourse," *Journal of the American Musicological Society* 48, no. 3 (1995): 396–422.

74 For discussions of some of these dynamics, see Daphne A. Brooks, "'This Voice Which Is Not One': Amy Winehouse Sings the Ballad of Sonic Blue(s)face Culture," *Women and Performance: A Journal of Feminist Theory* 20, no. 1 (2010): 37–60; and Randall, *Dusty, Queen of the Postmods*, especially the chapter on Springfield's collaborations with African American vocalist Madeline Bell.

75 For a detailed history of African American women and work, see Jacqueline Jones, *Labor of Love, Labor of Sorrow: Black Women, Work, and the Family from Slavery to the Present* (New York: Basic Books, 1985).

76 For example, see Collins, *Black Feminist Thought*; Paula Giddings, "The Last Taboo," in *Words of Fire: An Anthology of African-American Feminist Thought*, ed. Beverly Guy-Sheftall (New York: New Press, 1995), 414–28; Paula Giddings, *When and Where I Enter*; Hammonds, "Black (W)holes," 126–45; and Darlene Clark Hine, "Rape and the Inner Lives of Black Women in the Middle West: Preliminary Thoughts on the Culture of Dissemblance," *Signs* 14, no. 4 (1989): 912–20.

77 Hine, "Rape and the Inner Lives of Black Women in the Middle West," 918.

78 Hine, "Rape and the Inner Lives of Black Women in the Middle West," 918.

79 For discussion of the politics of respectability, see Evelyn Brooks Higginbotham, *Righteous Discontent: The Women's Movement in the Black Baptist Church, 1880–1920* (Cambridge, MA: Harvard University Press, 1993). For discussion of the culture of dissemblance, see Hine, "Rape and the Inner Lives of Black Women in the Middle West," 912–20.

80 Hammonds, "Black (W)holes," 133.

81 Audre Lorde, "Uses of the Erotic: The Erotic as Power," in *Sister Outsider: Essays and Speeches* (Trumansburg, NY: Crossing Press, 1984), 53.

82 For an oral history project that examines and seeks to break this silence, see Tricia Rose, *Longing to Tell: Black Women Talk about Sexuality and Intimacy* (New York: Farrar, Straus and Giroux, 2003).

83 Carby, "The Sexual Politics of Women's Blues," 8.

84 For other studies of black women's blues, see Harrison, *Black Pearls*, and Davis, *Blues Legacies and Black Feminism*.

85 Eileen M. Hayes, "New Perspectives in Studies of Black Women and Music," in *Black Women and Music: More Than the Blues*, ed. Eileen M. Hayes and Linda F. Williams (Urbana: University of Illinois Press, 2007), 7–8.

86 Hayes, "New Perspectives in Studies of Black Women and Music," 11.

87 *Fridays* was an early 1980s late-night sketch comedy show on ABC. I don't recall that the sketches were especially funny, but they booked great musical guests.

Chapter One: Rocking and Rolling with Big Mama Thornton

Epigraph: Big Mama Thornton quoted in Arnold Shaw, *The World of Soul: Black America's Contribution to the Pop Music Scene* (New York: Cowles, 1970), 108.

1 Ben Windham, "Big Mama Thornton," *Alabama Heritage* (fall 1987): 31.

2 Research on early twentieth-century black blues women written from black feminist perspectives brings the music and lives of these artists into relief and accentuates the critical consciousness articulated through their lyrics. Hazel V. Carby, "The Sexual Politics of Women's Blues," in *Cultures in Babylon: Black Britain and African America* (London: Verso, 1999), 7–21; Angela Y. Davis, *Blues Legacies and Black Feminism:*

Gertrude "Ma" Rainey, Bessie Smith, and Billie Holiday (New York: Pantheon, 1998); and Daphne Duval Harrison, *Black Pearls: Blues Queens of the 1920s* (New Brunswick, NJ: Rutgers University Press, 1990).

3 Attentive to the significance of these choices, music historian Tyina Steptoe has examined "the racial *and* queer roots of rock 'n' roll" through a queer of color reading of the ways Thornton and her contemporary Little Richard "visually and sonically blurred the line between masculine and feminine." Tyina Steptoe, "Big Mama Thornton, Little Richard, and the Queer Roots of Rock 'n' Roll," *American Quarterly* 70, no. 1 (March 2018): 55, original emphasis. For another queer reading of Thornton, see Judith Halberstam, "Queer Voices and Musical Genders," in *Oh Boy!: Masculinities and Popular Music*, ed. Freya Jarman-Ivens (New York: Routledge, 2007), 183–95.

4 "Big Mama Talks with Chris Strachwitz," track 17 on *Big Mama in Europe*, Arhoolie, CD 9056, 2005, CD. Originally released in 1965, my transcription.

5 Thornton's birthplace is usually identified as Montgomery, but her birth certificate lists Ariton. She might have named Montgomery because it would have been more recognizable to people outside of Alabama than Ariton, or because it was the only place she recalled living in as a child. I thank David Johnson at the Alabama Music Hall of Fame for sharing a copy of Thornton's birth certificate with me. Personal communication, October 20, 2009. For details of Thornton's life and career, see Windham, "Big Mama Thornton," 30–43, and Michael Spörke, *Big Mama Thornton: The Life and Music* (Jefferson City, NC: MacFarland, 2014).

6 "Big Mama Talks with Chris Strachwitz."

7 "Big Mama Talks with Chris Strachwitz."

8 Big Mama Thornton quoted in Anthony Connor and Robert Neff, *The Blues: In Images and Interviews* (New York: Cooper Square Press, 1999), 50.

9 Galen Gart and Roy C. Ames, *Duke/Peacock Records: An Illustrated History with Discography* (Milford, NH: Big Nickel Publications, 1990), 17.

10 "Big Mama Talks with Chris Strachwitz."

11 Gart and Ames, *Duke/Peacock Records*, 17.

12 James M. Salem, *The Late Great Johnny Ace and the Transition from R&B to Rock 'n' Roll* (Urbana: University of Illinois Press, 1999), 78.

13 Big Mama Thornton quoted in Connor and Neff, *The Blues: In Images and Interviews*, 50.

14 Big Mama Thornton quoted in Connor and Neff, *The Blues: In Images and Interviews*, 51.

15 Gart and Ames, *Duke/Peacock Records*, 63.

16 Big Mama Thornton quoted in Connor and Neff, *The Blues: In Images and Interviews*, 113.

17 For an example of one such story about Thornton and physical fights, see Johnny Otis, *Upside Your Head! Rhythm and Blues on Central Avenue* (Hanover, NH: Wesleyan University Press, 1993), 133–34.

18 For a gender-sensitive critique of white fascination with African American musical culture, see Ingrid Monson, "The Problem with White Hipness: Race, Gender, and

Cultural Conceptions in Jazz Historical Discourse," *Journal of the American Musico-logical Society* 48, no. 3 (1995): 396–422.

19 Ralph J. Gleason, "Big Mama Sings the Blues She Likes" [Liner Notes], *Big Mama Thornton and the Chicago Blues Band*, Arhoolie Records, F 1032, 1967, 33⅓ RPM.

20 Big Mama Thornton quoted in Gleason, "Big Mama Sings the Blues She Likes."

21 Big Mama Thornton quoted in Gleason, "Big Mama Sings the Blues She Likes."

22 Kat Dyson, telephone interview with author, October 19, 2012.

23 Kat Dyson, telephone interview with author, October 19, 2012.

24 Terry DeRouen, telephone interview with author, December 17, 2009.

25 "Big Mama Talks with Chris Strachwitz."

26 "Big Mama Talks with Chris Strachwitz"; *Saved*, Pentagram PE 10,005, 1971, 33⅓ RPM.

27 Kat Dyson, telephone interview with author, October 19, 2012; Terry DeRouen, tele-phone interview with author, December 17, 2009.

28 Carol McGraw, "Goodby Blues: Big Mama Thornton—Rich in Voice, Friends—Laid to Rest," *Los Angeles Times*, August 1, 1984, part 2, 2; Kat Dyson, telephone interview with author, October 19, 2012.

29 Salem, *The Late Great Johnny Ace*, 82.

30 George Lipsitz, *Midnight at the Barrelhouse: The Johnny Otis Story* (Minneapolis: University of Minnesota Press, 2010); Otis, *Upside Your Head!*

31 Jerry Leiber and Mike Stoller with David Ritz, *Hound Dog: The Leiber and Stoller Autobiography* (New York: Simon and Schuster, 2009), 39–43.

32 Gart and Ames, *Duke/Peacock Records*, 53.

33 Big Mama Thornton quoted in Gleason, "Big Mama Sings the Blues She Likes."

34 Bill Carpenter, "Big Mama Thornton: Two Hundred Pounds of Boogaloo," *Living Blues* (November/December 1992): 28.

35 "Big Mama Talks with Chris Strachwitz."

36 Nat Dove, telephone interview with author, February 9, 2010.

37 *Billboard* quoted in Salem, *The Late Great Johnny Ace*, 83.

38 *Cash Box* quoted in George A. Moonoogian, "The Puppydom of a Rock 'n' Roll Clas-sic," in *Whiskey, Women, and . . .* (June 1984), 6, original ellipsis.

39 Salem, *The Late Great Johnny Ace*, 82.

40 Big Mama Thornton, "Hound Dog," and Ray Topping, *Big Mama Thornton: The Original Hound Dog* [Liner Notes], Ace Records CDCHD 940, 1990, CD.

41 Moonoogian, "The Puppydom of a Rock 'n' Roll Classic," 10.

42 Alan Govenar, *The Early Years of Rhythm and Blues: Focus on Houston* (Houston: Rice University Press, 1990), 8–9.

43 Big Mama Thornton quoted in Gleason, "Big Mama Sings the Blues She Likes."

44 Leiber and Stoller with Ritz, *Hound Dog*, 94.

45 Elvis Presley, "Hound Dog," *The All Time Greatest Hits*, BMG Music, ND 90100 BMG, 1987, CD; Joel Whitburn, *The Billboard Book of Top 40 R&B and Hip Hop Hits* (New York: Billboard Books, 2006), 463.

46 Big Mama Thornton quoted in Tam Fiofori, "The Blues," *Melody Maker,* April 29, 1972, 44.

47 Halberstam offers a similar interpretation of this quote in "Queer Voices and Musical Genders," 189.

48 For a detailed overview of these musical and performance practices, see Portia K. Maultsby, "Africanisms in African-American Music," in *Africanisms in American Culture,* ed. Joseph E. Holloway (Bloomington: Indiana University Press, 1991), 185–210.

49 John A. Jackson, *Big Beat Heat: Alan Freed and the Early Years of Rock and Roll* (New York: Schirmer Books, 1991), 69.

50 In her short story, "Nineteen Fifty-Five," Alice Walker imagines a meeting between Thornton and Presley, using fictional characters who stand in for the two artists and address issues of appropriation, fame, and knowledge of the meaning of the blues through their encounter. Alice Walker, *You Can't Keep a Good Woman Down: Stories* (New York: Harcourt Brace Jovanovich, 1981), 3–20.

51 Peter Guralnick, *Last Train to Memphis: The Rise of Elvis Presley* (Boston: Little, Brown, 1994), 195.

52 Halberstam, "Queer Voices and Musical Genders," 189.

53 Halberstam, "Queer Voices and Musical Genders," 186.

54 The record was Presley's first single, "That's All Right, Mama" (1954). Arnold Shaw, *Honkers and Shouters: The Golden Years of Rhythm and Blues* (New York: Collier Books, 1978), 502–3.

55 Elvis Presley quoted in Kays Gary, "Elvis Defends Low-Down Style," in *The Rock History Reader,* 2nd ed., ed. Theo Cateforis (New York: Routledge, 2013), 16.

56 Michael Burlingame, *Gunsmoke Blues* (Santa Monica, CA: Hip-O Records, 2004), DVD.

57 Kat Dyson, telephone interview with author, October 19, 2012.

58 Terry DeRouen, telephone interview with author, December 17, 2009.

59 Big Mama Thornton, "Hound Dog," *Ball 'n' Chain.* Arhoolie CD 305, 1985, CD.

60 Gart and Ames, *Duke/Peacock Records,* 69.

61 Salem, *The Late Great Johnny Ace,* 103.

62 Details about the events surrounding Johnny Ace's death are from Gart and Ames, *Duke/Peacock Records,* 71–72; and Salem, *The Late Great Johnny Ace,* 128–40.

63 Big Mama Thornton quoted in Connor and Neff, *The Blues: In Images and Interviews,* 51, original emphasis.

64 Carpenter, "Big Mama Thornton: Two Hundred Pounds of Boogaloo," 29.

65 Big Mama Thornton quoted in Shaw, *Honkers and Shouters,* 482.

66 Salem, *The Late Great Johnny Ace,* 81.

67 Jimmy McCracklin, telephone interview with author, October 29, 2009.

68 Jimmy McCracklin, telephone interview with author, October 29, 2009.

69 Jimmy McCracklin, telephone interview with author, October 29, 2009.

70 Jimmy McCracklin, telephone interview with author, October 29, 2009.

71 Chris Strachwitz, telephone interview with author, August 13, 2009.

72 Jimmy McCracklin, telephone interview with author, October 29, 2009.

73 In the late sixties, Joplin helped to purchase a tombstone for Smith's unmarked grave. Alice Echols, *Scars of Sweet Paradise: The Life and Times of Janis Joplin* (New York: Henry Holt, 1999), 236–37.

74 Connor and Neff, *The Blues: In Images and Interviews*, 51.

75 Joel Selvin, *Summer of Love: The Inside Story of LSD, Rock and Roll, Free Love and High Times in the Wild West* (New York: Dutton, 1994), 104.

76 Big Brother and the Holding Company, "Ball and Chain," *Cheap Thrills*, Sony Music CK 65784, 1999, CD. Originally released in 1968.

77 Peter Albin quoted in Echols, *Scars of Sweet Paradise*, 151, original emphasis.

78 Robert Christgau quoted in Echols, *Scars of Sweet Paradise*, 169.

79 Ellen Willis, "Janis Joplin," in *The Rolling Stone Illustrated History of Rock and Roll*, ed. Anthony DeCurtis and James Henke with Holly George-Warren (New York: Random House, 1992), 385.

80 Echols, *Scars of Sweet Paradise*, 135.

81 Echols, *Scars of Sweet Paradise*, 48.

82 Topping, *Big Mama Thornton* [Liner Notes].

83 Terry DeRouen, telephone interview with author, December 17, 2009.

84 Big Mama Thornton quoted in Fiofori, "The Blues," 44.

85 Big Mama Thornton, "Ball and Chain," *The Rising Sun Collection*, Just a Memory Records, RSCD 0002, 1994, CD. Originally released in 1977.

86 Chris Strachwitz, telephone interview with author, August 13, 2009.

87 Lowell Richards, "Blues Outclasses Rock at Sky River Festival," *DownBeat*, October 31, 1968, 11.

88 Prior to this, blues artists played folk and jazz festivals. Dan Morgenstern, "The Blues Comes to Ann Arbor," *DownBeat*, October 2, 1969, 14.

89 Morgenstern, "The Blues Comes to Ann Arbor," 14.

90 Burlingame, *Gunsmoke Blues*.

91 Kat Dyson, telephone interview with author, October 19, 2012.

92 Big Mama Thornton quoted in Gleason, "Big Mama Sings the Blues She Likes."

93 Ulrich Adelt, "Germany Gets the Blues: Negotiations of 'Race' and Nation at the American Folk Blues Festival," *American Quarterly* 60, no. 4 (2008): 961.

94 Echols, *Scars of Sweet Paradise*, xvi.

95 For a close reading of Joplin's influence on Robert Plant, see Tracy McMullen, "'Bring It on Home': Robert Plant, Janis Joplin, and the Myth of Origin," *Journal of Popular Music Studies* 26, no. 2–3 (2014): 368–96.

96 Leiber and Stoller with Ritz, *Hound Dog*, 62–63.

97 Dick Waterman, *Between Midnight and Day: The Last Unpublished Blues Archive* (New York: Thunder's Mouth Press, 2003).

98 Ian Whitcomb, "Legends of Rhythm and Blues," in *Repercussions: A Celebration of African-American Music*, ed. Geoffrey Haydon and Dennis Marks (London: Century Publishing, 1985), 65.

99 Selvin, *Summer of Love*, 104.

100 Terry DeRouen, telephone interview with author, December 17, 2009.

101 Terry DeRouen, telephone interview with author, December 17, 2009.

102 Kat Dyson, telephone interview with author, October 19, 2012.

103 Burlingame, *Gunsmoke Blues*.

104 James Moore, telephone interview with author, October 12, 2009.

105 Big Mama Thornton quoted in Roy Greenberg, "Big Mama Thornton Follows the Light and Keeps on Going," *Aquarian*, February 25–March 4, 1981, 55.

106 Big Mama Thornton quoted in Greenberg, "Big Mama Thornton Follows the Light," 55.

107 Big Mama Thornton quoted in Greenberg, "Big Mama Thornton Follows the Light," 55.

108 "Big Mama Talks with Chris Strachwitz."

109 "Big Mama Talks with Chris Strachwitz."

Chapter Two: LaVern Baker, the Incredible Disappearing Queen of Rock and Roll

Epigraph: In early press reports, misspellings of Baker's name as Lavern or LaVerne instead of LaVern were common, and over the years the title of her first hit single has been written as both "Tweedle Dee" and "Tweedlee Dee." I have regularized these spellings to "LaVern" and "Tweedle Dee" in the body of the chapter. Geoffrey Himes, "Baker: Still Up with the Blues," *Washington Post*, January 19, 1996, n.p. LaVern Baker clipping file, Rutgers University Institute of Jazz Studies.

1 "Tweedle Dee Girl," *Ebony*, April 1956, 106–10. LaVern Baker clipping file, Rutgers University Institute of Jazz Studies.

2 "Tweedle Dee Girl," *Ebony*, 106.

3 "Tweedle Dee Girl," *Ebony*, 106.

4 "Tweedle Dee Girl," *Ebony*, 106.

5 Mamie Molloy, "Titles by the Dozen," *Rock 'n' Roll Jamboree*, fall 1956, 11, Michael Ochs Collection, Library and Archives, Rock and Roll Hall of Fame.

6 The segment was hosted by Tommy "Dr. Jive" Smalls, an African American disc jockey on New York's WWRL. John A. Jackson, *Big Beat Heat: Alan Freed and the Early Years of Rock and Roll* (New York: Schirmer Books, 1991), 69.

7 "'DownBeat' Institutes Annual Awards in Rhythm, Blues Field," *DownBeat*, May 18, 1955, 5.

8 "Tweedlee-Dee Girl: Youthful Singer Is Credited with 'Putting Rhythm in the Blues,'" *Our World*, June 1955, n.p. LaVern Baker clipping file, Rutgers University Institute of Jazz Studies.

9 Molloy, "Titles by the Dozen," 10.

10 Reebee Garofalo, *Rockin' Out: Popular Music in the USA*, 5th ed. (Englewood Cliffs, NJ: Prentice Hall, 2011), 83; John Covach and Andrew Flory, *What's That Sound? An Introduction to Rock and Its History*, 4th ed. (New York: W. W. Norton, 2014).

11 Joseph G. Schloss, Larry Starr, and Christopher Waterman, *Rock: Music, Culture and Business* (New York: Oxford University Press, 2012), 73, original emphasis.

12 Maureen Mahon, "Women in African American Music: Rock," in *African American Music: An Introduction*, ed. Mellonee Burnim and Portia K. Maultsby (New York: Routledge, 2006), 558–77. I corrected my omission in an updated version of the article for a revised and expanded edition of the volume: "African American Women and the Dynamics of Gender, Race, and Genre in Rock 'n' Roll," in *Issues in African American Music: Power, Gender, Race, Representation*, ed. Mellonee Burnim and Portia K. Maultsby (New York: Routledge, 2016), 287–305.

13 See, for example, Charlie Gillett, *The Sound of the City: The Rise of Rock and Roll*, revised and expanded ed. (New York: Pantheon, 1983), and Arnold Shaw, *Honkers and Shouters: The Golden Years of Rhythm and Blues* (New York: Collier Books, 1978).

14 Rick Coleman, *Blue Monday: Fats Domino and the Lost Dawn of Rock 'n' Roll* (Cambridge, MA: Da Capo Press, 2006), xvii–xviii, original emphasis.

15 Lucy O'Brien, *She Bop: The Definitive History of Women in Rock, Pop, and Soul* (New York: Penguin, 1995), 88.

16 Barbara O'Dair, ed., *Trouble Girls: The Rolling Stone Book of Women in Rock* (New York: Random House, 1997), xxvi.

17 Anthony DeCurtis and James Henke with Holly George-Warren, eds., *The Rolling Stone Illustrated History of Rock and Roll* (New York: Random House, 1992), 14, 104; Robert Christgau, "Chuck Berry," in *The Rolling Stone Illustrated History of Rock and Roll*, ed. DeCurtis and Henke with George-Warren, 64.

18 Ruth Brown with Andrew Yule, *Miss Rhythm: The Autobiography of Ruth Brown, Rhythm and Blues Legend* (New York: Donald Fine Books, 1996); Etta James and David Ritz, *Rage to Survive* (New York: Da Capo Press, 1998).

19 Lee Cotten, *Shake, Rattle, and Roll: The Golden Age of American Rock 'n' Roll, 1952–1955*, vol. 1 (Ann Arbor, MI: Popular Culture Ink, 1989), 189.

20 Cotten, *Shake, Rattle, and Roll*, 237; Lee Cotten, *Reelin' and Rockin': The Golden Age of American Rock 'n' Roll, 1956–1959*, vol. 2 (Ann Arbor, MI: Popular Culture Ink, 1995), 38.

21 For chart positions, I consulted Joel Whitburn, *The Billboard Book of Top 40 Hits*, 9th ed. (New York: Billboard Books, 2010). Little Richard and Elvis Presley made their first appearances on the pop charts in 1956.

22 Jackson, *Big Beat Heat*, 89.

23 Jeffrey Kallberg, *Chopin at the Boundaries: Sex, History, and Musical Genre* (Cambridge, MA: Harvard University Press, 1996), 6.

24 Coleman, *Blue Monday*, xv, original emphasis.

25 Bernard Gendron, *Between Montmartre and the Mudd Club: Popular Music and the Avant-Garde* (Chicago: University of Chicago Press, 2002), 220.

26 Norma Coates, "Teenyboppers, Groupies, and Other Grotesques: Girls and Women and Rock Culture in the 1960s and Early 1970s," *Journal of Popular Music Studies* 15, no. 1 (June 2003): 77–78.

27 Gendron, *Between Montmartre and the Mudd Club*, 220–21.

28 Gendron, *Between Montmartre and the Mudd Club*, 221.

29 Coates, "Teenyboppers, Groupies, and Other Grotesques," 78.

30 Coates, "Teenyboppers, Groupies, and Other Grotesques," 67.

31 Coates, "Teenyboppers, Groupies, and Other Grotesques," 67.

32 Coates, "Teenyboppers, Groupies, and Other Grotesques," 70.

33 Baker is sometimes identified as Delores Williams in reference works, but in a 1991 interview, she told music writer Dennis Garvey that Williams was the surname of her first husband, whom she had married before her career took off. Dennis Garvey, "LaVern Baker: The 'Tweedlee-Dee' Girl Is Back," *Goldmine*, July 12, 1991, 11; Chip Deffaa, *Blue Rhythms: Six Lives in Rhythm and Blues* (Urbana: University of Illinois Press, 1996), 174–75. For overviews of Baker's career, see Deffaa, *Blue Rhythms*, 174–216; Garvey, "LaVern Baker: The 'Tweedlee-Dee' Girl Is Back," 11–15, 19, 151; and Bob Gulla, *Icons of R&B and Soul: An Encyclopedia of the Artists Who Revolutionized Rhythm*, vol. 1 (Westport, CT: Greenwood, 2008), 91–106. A thorough discography accompanies the *Goldmine* article. I am grateful to Dennis Garvey, who sent me a copy of his published profile of Baker and encouraged me to draw on it in my book.

34 Gulla, *Icons of R&B and Soul*, 93; Himes, "Baker: Still Up with the Blues," n.p.

35 Deffaa, *Blue Rhythms*, 175.

36 Deffaa, *Blue Rhythms*, 175.

37 LaVern Baker press material. LaVern Baker clipping file, Rutgers University Institute of Jazz Studies.

38 Deffaa, *Blue Rhythms*, 176.

39 Little Miss Cornshucks (born Mildred Cummings) precedes the black women rock and rollers by nearly a decade, but she influenced them and a host of African American rhythm and blues and soul artists. For a discussion of her life and legacy, see Barry Mazor, "A Soul Forgotten," *No Depression*, May–June 2003, 80–95.

40 LaVern Baker quoted in Garvey, "LaVern Baker: The 'Tweedlee-Dee' Girl Is Back," 11.

41 Deffaa, *Blue Rhythms*, 176–78.

42 Garvey, "LaVern Baker: The 'Tweedlee-Dee' Girl Is Back," 11; Lars Bjorn with Jim Gallert, *Before Motown: A History of Jazz in Detroit, 1920–1960* (Ann Arbor: University of Michigan Press, 2001), 20.

43 Deffaa, *Blue Rhythms*, 178.

44 *The Biggest Show of Stars for '57* [concert program], n.p., Jeff Gold Collection, Library and Archives, Rock and Roll Hall of Fame; Johnnie Ray, "Famous 'Cry' Crooner Tells What Blues Taught Him," *Ebony*, March 1953, 48–56.

45 Gulla, *Icons of R&B and Soul*, 94.

46 Ahmet Ertegun and Perry Richardson, eds., *"What'd I Say": The Atlantic Story. 50 Years of Music* (New York: Welcome Rain Publishers, 2001), 15.

47 Ertegun and Richardson, *"What'd I Say,"* 4.

48 Mazor, "A Soul Forgotten," 90.

49 Ertegun and Richardson, *"What'd I Say,"* 61.

50 Brown with Yule, *Miss Rhythm*, 255.

51 LaVern Baker quoted in Garvey, "LaVern Baker: The 'Tweedlee-Dee' Girl Is Back," 11.

52 Deffaa, *Blue Rhythms*, 181; LaVern Baker, "Soul on Fire," *Soul on Fire: The Best of LaVern Baker*, Atlantic Records Corp. 7 82311-2, 1991, CD. For information about Baker's recordings prior to signing to Atlantic, see Gulla, *Icons of R&B and Soul*, 94; Deffaa, *Blue Rhythms*, 177.

53 LaVern Baker, "Tweedlee Dee," *Soul on Fire*.

54 Deffaa, *Blue Rhythms*, 181.

55 Deffaa, *Blue Rhythms*, 181.

56 Gillett, *The Sound of the City*, 71.

57 Jim Dawson and Steve Propes, *What Was the First Rock 'n' Roll Record?* (Boston: Faber and Faber, 1992), 165.

58 Dawson and Propes, *What Was the First Rock 'n' Roll Record?*, 165.

59 Dawson and Propes, *What Was the First Rock 'n' Roll Record?*, 166.

60 LaVern Baker quoted in Garvey, "LaVern Baker: The 'Tweedlee-Dee' Girl Is Back," 12.

61 Gillett, *The Sound of the City*, 37–38; Dawson and Propes, *What Was the First Rock 'n' Roll Record?*, 166.

62 Whitburn, *The Billboard Book of Top 40 Hits*, 46.

63 Gulla, *Icons of R&B and Soul*, 96.

64 Brown with Yule, *Miss Rhythm*, 85; Deffaa, *Blue Rhythms*, 182.

65 "Tweedlee-Dee Girl," *Our World*, June 1955, n.p.

66 "Pop Disk Men Eyeing R&B as Cover Tunes Proliferate," *Billboard* in *First Pressings: The History of Rhythm and Blues*, vol. 5, comp. and ed. Galen Gart (Milford, NH: Big Nickel Publications, 1990), March 1955, 27.

67 LaVern Baker's "Tweedlee Dee" debuted on the charts on January 15, 1955; the Georgia Gibbs version arrived on the charts on January 29, 1955. It was the first chart hit for Georgia Gibbs. Whitburn, *The Billboard Book of Top 40 Hits*, 48, 266.

68 Whitburn, *The Billboard Book of Top 40 Hits*, 266.

69 LaVern Baker quoted in Himes, "Baker: Still Up with the Blues," n.p.

70 LaVern Baker quoted in "LaVern Baker Smiles over Tune's Success while Defying 'Lifts,'" *Chicago Defender*, February 19, 1955, 6.

71 Deffaa, *Blue Rhythms*, 182.

72 Brown with Yule, *Miss Rhythm*, 110.

73 Fats Domino, the top-selling African American artist of the period, ranked fifth. Whitburn, *The Billboard Book of Top 40 Hits*, 873.

74 "Coast Girl Asks $10,000 for 'Dance with Henry,'" *Chicago Defender*, June 4, 1955, 19.

75 Etta James and David Ritz, *Rage to Survive* (New York: Da Capo Press, 1998), 49–50.

76 James and Ritz, *Rage to Survive*, 49–50.

77 Brown with Yule, *Miss Rhythm*, 76.

78 Little Richard quoted in "Creators—Little Richard, et al.," in Taylor Hackford, *Hail! Hail! Rock 'n' Roll* (Santa Monica, CA: Universal Music, 2006), DVD. Originally released in 1987. Not all of the covers were on major labels—Boone recorded for the independent Dot label—and not all cover artists were white. Dinah Washington, who dominated the R&B charts from the end of the 1940s until her death in 1963, covered the Drifters song "Such a Night," presumably in an effort to keep current with the popular sounds of the day.

79 Wayne Robins, *A Brief History of Rock, Off the Record* (New York: Routledge, 2008), 25.

80 Georgia Gibbs quoted in Robins, *A Brief History of Rock*, 25.

81 "'Covers vs. Copies' Sparking New Hubbub in Rhythm and Blues Field" [March 1955], in Gart, *First Pressings*, 27.

82 "'Covers vs. Copies' Sparking New Hubbub," 27, 30.

83 "Lavern Baker Seeks Bill to Halt Arrangements 'Thefts,'" *Billboard*, March 5, 1955, 13, original ellipsis.

84 Joe "Ziggy" Johnson, "Zig and Zag," *Chicago Defender*, January 12, 1957, 15.

85 Johnson, "Zig and Zag," 15.

86 Ertegun and Richardson, *"What'd I Say,"* 93

87 Bill Simon, "Rhythm and Blues Notes," *Billboard*, March 12, 1955, 24.

88 Deffaa, *Blue Rhythms*, 183.

89 Dawson and Propes, *What Was the First Rock 'n' Roll Record?*, 169; Whitburn, *The Billboard Book of Top 40 Hits*, 48.

90 "Tweedle Dee Girl," *Ebony*, 109.

91 "Tweedle Dee Girl," *Ebony*, 108.

92 "Tweedle Dee Girl," *Ebony*, 108.

93 "Tweedle Dee Girl," *Ebony*, 108.

94 Jackson, *Big Beat Heat*, 89–92.

95 Deffaa, *Blue Rhythms*, 179; Garvey, "LaVern Baker: The 'Tweedlee-Dee' Girl Is Back," 11–12.

96 Coleman, *Blue Monday*, 149, 166; John Goldrosen and John Beecher, *Remembering Buddy: The Definitive Biography of Buddy Holly* (New York: Penguin, 1987), 72. According to Rick Coleman, "Feld also promoted black performers to an even greater degree than Alan Freed. After several tours in 1956 headlined by Bill Haley or Carl Perkins over black stars, the first 1957 Big Show was all black." Coleman, *Blue Monday*, 148.

97 "The Biggest Show of Stars Fall 1957 Program," Rick Kollins Concert Program Collection, Library and Archives, Rock and Roll Hall of Fame Museum; Coleman, *Blue Monday*, 166; Goldrosen and Beecher, *Remembering Buddy*, 72.

98 Peter Guralnick, *Dream Boogie: The Triumph of Sam Cooke* (New York: Little, Brown, 2005), 231.

99 Phil Everly quoted in Richard Spence, *The Real Buddy Holly Story* (West Long Branch, NJ: White Star, 2004), DVD.

100 Beverly Lee quoted in Garvey, "LaVern Baker: The 'Tweedlee-Dee' Girl Is Back," 14.

101 Arlene Smith quoted in Garvey, "LaVern Baker: The 'Tweedlee-Dee' Girl Is Back," 13–14, original ellipsis.

102 Ertegun and Richardson, *"What'd I Say,"* 73.

103 LaVern Baker quoted in Garvey, "LaVern Baker: The 'Tweedlee-Dee' Girl Is Back," 13.

104 LaVern Baker quoted in Garvey, "LaVern Baker: The 'Tweedlee-Dee' Girl Is Back," 13.

105 Garvey, "LaVern Baker: The 'Tweedlee-Dee' Girl Is Back," 13.

106 Goldrosen and Beecher, *Remembering Buddy*, 74.

107 Goldrosen and Beecher, *Remembering Buddy*, 74.

108 Coleman, *Blue Monday*, 174; Garvey, "LaVern Baker: The 'Tweedlee-Dee' Girl Is Back," 13.

109 Citizens' Council of Greater New Orleans, Broadside [Help Save the Youth of America], Citizens' Council Collection, Archives and Special Collections, University of Mississippi Libraries, University of Mississippi Digital Libraries, n.d., accessed April 19, 2019, http: //clio.lib.olemiss.edu/cdm/ref/collection/citizens/id/1631.

110 Asa Carter, c. 1956, quoted in David Espar, *Rock and Roll: Renegades*, part 1 (South Burlington, VT: WGBH Video, 1995), VHS.

111 Goldrosen and Beecher, *Remembering Buddy*, 75.

112 LaVern Baker quoted in Garvey, "LaVern Baker: The 'Tweedlee-Dee' Girl Is Back," 13.

113 Jackson, *Big Beat Heat*, 148.

114 "Tweedle Dee Girl," *Ebony*, 107.

115 Jackson, *Big Beat Heat*, 142.

116 "Tweedle Dee Girl," *Ebony*, 106.

117 "'DownBeat' Institutes Annual Awards," 5.

118 "Tweedle Dee Girl," *Ebony*, 106.

119 "Tweedle Dee Girl," *Ebony*, 106.

120 François Positif, "New York in Jazz Time, Part II," *Jazz Hot*, December 1960, 27. My translation. *Au milieu de "Jim Dandy," un type très bien habillé, très dandy, vient danser sur la scène d'une façon enthousiasmante pendant quelques minutes, et lorsque LaVern vient danser avec lui, c'est un délire sauvage qui s'empare de la foule: tout le monde crie, hurle, gesticule.*

121 "I Cried a Tear" was a noncertified million seller. Baker's "Tweedlee Dee" and "Jim Dandy" also achieved this status. The Recording Industry Association of America (RIAA) began certifying record sales in 1958; Baker's sales are based on reports in *Billboard* and other recording industry trade publications. Joel Whitburn, *Hot R&B Songs, 1942–2010*, 6th ed. (Menomonee Falls, WI: Record Research, 2010), 12, 42; Whitburn, *The Billboard Book of Top 40 Hits*, 48.

122 LaVern Baker quoted in Garvey, "LaVern Baker: The 'Tweedlee-Dee' Girl Is Back," 14.

123 Whitburn, *Hot R&B Songs,* 42; Whitburn, *The Billboard Book of Top 40 Hits,* 48.

124 Whitburn, *The Billboard Book of Top 40 Hits,* 48.

125 Deffaa, *Blue Rhythms,* 199.

126 LaVern Baker quoted in Garvey, "LaVern Baker: The 'Tweedlee-Dee' Girl Is Back," 14.

127 LaVern Baker quoted in Garvey, "LaVern Baker: The 'Tweedlee-Dee' Girl Is Back," 14, original bracketed material.

128 Deffaa, *Blue Rhythms,* 202.

129 Deffaa, *Blue Rhythms,* 203.

130 Elysa Gardner, "Hall of Famer Returns to Spotlight," *New York Times,* August 26, 1995, F1, LaVern Baker clipping file, Rutgers University Institute of Jazz Studies; Garvey, "LaVern Baker: The 'Tweedlee-Dee' Girl Is Back," 14.

131 LaVern Baker quoted in Garvey, "LaVern Baker: The 'Tweedlee-Dee' Girl Is Back," 14.

132 In her autobiography, Brown recounts taking up work as a domestic when her career hit a rough patch. Brown with Yule, *Miss Rhythm,* 163–65.

133 LaVern Baker quoted in Garvey, "LaVern Baker: The 'Tweedlee-Dee' Girl Is Back," 14–15.

134 LaVern Baker quoted in Gardner, "Hall of Famer Returns to Spotlight," F1.

135 LaVern Baker quoted in Sheryl Hunter, "R&B Legend Does More Than Endure," *Daily Hampshire Gazette,* January 19, 1996, 28, LaVern Baker clipping file, Rutgers University Institute of Jazz Studies.

136 Hunter, "R&B Legend Does More Than Endure," 26; Gardner, "Hall of Famer Returns to Spotlight," F1.

137 LaVern Baker quoted in Gardner, "Hall of Famer Returns to Spotlight," F1.

138 Brown with Yule, *Miss Rhythm*; James and Ritz, *Rage to Survive*; Darlene Love with Rob Hoerburger, *My Name Is Love: The Darlene Love Story* (New York: William Morrow, 1998); Ronnie Spector and Vince Waldron, *Be My Baby: How I Survived Mascara, Mini Skirts, and Madness, or My Life as a Fabulous Ronette* (New York: Harmony Books, 1990); Tina Turner with Kurt Loder, *I, Tina* (New York: William Morrow, 1986); and Mary Wilson, *Dreamgirl and Supreme Faith: My Life as a Supreme* (New York: Cooper Square Press, 1999).

139 LaVern Baker quoted in Garvey, "LaVern Baker: The 'Tweedlee-Dee' Girl Is Back," 19.

140 Steve Morse, "Soulful Baker Turns Up Wattage," *Boston Globe,* n.d. (c. 1995), n.p., LaVern Baker clipping file, Rutgers University Institute of Jazz Studies.

141 Gillett, *The Sound of the City,* 51.

Chapter Three: Remembering the Shirelles

Epigraphs: Shirley Alston Reeves quoted in Joseph A. Tortelli, "Shirelles' Lead Shirley Reeves Recalls Girl Group Sound: A Pop Music Trend Cut Short by British Invasion,"

Record Collector Monthly, December 1987–January 1988, 1; Beverly Lee, telephone interview with author, August 7, 2012.

1   *Baby It's You!* [Broadway musical], promotional mailer, author's collection, original ellipsis.

2   Gail Collins, *When Everything Changed: The Amazing Journey of American Women from 1960 to the Present* (New York: Little, Brown, 2009), 22.

3   Alan Betrock, *Girl Groups: The Story of a Sound* (New York: Delilah Books, 1982), 16.

4   For a critical analysis of girl group music and its place in pop music history, see Jacqueline Warwick, *Girl Groups, Girl Culture: Popular Music and Identity in the 1960s* (New York: Routledge, 2007).

5   Betrock, *Girl Groups: The Story of a Sound*; John Clemente, *Girl Groups: Fabulous Females That Rocked the World* (Iola, WI: Krause, 2000); Charlotte Greig, *Will You Still Love Me Tomorrow? Girl Groups from the 50s On . . .* (London: Virago, 1989).

6   Gillian G. Gaar, *She's a Rebel: The History of Women in Rock and Roll*, 2nd ed. (New York: Seal Press, 2002); Lucy O'Brien, *She Bop: The Definitive History of Women in Rock, Pop and Soul* (New York: Penguin, 1995); Barbara O'Dair, ed., *Trouble Girls: The Rolling Stone Book of Women in Rock* (New York: Random House, 1997).

7   Gaar, *She's a Rebel*, 32.

8   Greil Marcus, "Girl Groups," in *The Rolling Stone Illustrated History of Rock and Roll*, ed. Anthony DeCurtis and James Henke with Holly George-Warren (New York: Random House, 1992), 189–91.

9   Charles Isherwood, "Girl Group Tale Is Reharmonized," *New York Times*, April 27, 2011, C1.

10 Isherwood, "Girl Group Tale Is Reharmonized," C1.

11 Donna Gaines, "A Ballad of Codependency," in *Trouble Girls*, ed. O'Dair, 106.

12 Beverly Lee, telephone interview with author, August 7, 2012. For background on the Shirelles, see Betrock, *Girl Groups: The Story of a Sound*, 13–20; Clemente, *Girl Groups: Fabulous Females*, 200–205; and Gaar, *She's a Rebel*, 31–36.

13 Beverly Lee, telephone interview with author, August 7, 2012.

14 Beverly Lee, telephone interview with author, August 7, 2012.

15 Beverly Lee, telephone interview with author, August 7, 2012.

16 Beverly Lee, telephone interview with author, August 7, 2012.

17 Florence Greenberg quoted in Diana Reid Haig, "An Interview with Florence Greenberg" [Liner Notes], *The Scepter Records Story*, Capricorn Records 9 42003-2, 1992, CD, 7.

18 Warwick, *Girl Groups, Girl Culture*, 100.

19 Beverly Lee, telephone interview with author, August 7, 2012.

20 Beverly Lee, telephone interview with author, August 7, 2012.

21 Clemente, *Girl Groups: Fabulous Females*, 200; Betrock, *Girl Groups: The Story of a Sound*, 13.

22 Beverly Lee, telephone interview with author, August 7, 2012.

23 Lee Cotton, *Reelin' and Rockin': The Golden Age of American Rock 'n' Roll, Volume II: 1956–1959* (Ann Arbor, MI: Popular Culture Ink, 1995), 240, 252, 389, 417.

24 Clemente, *Girl Groups: Fabulous Females*, 200.

25 Clemente, *Girl Groups: Fabulous Females*, 200–201.

26 Florence Greenberg quoted in Haig, "An Interview with Florence Greenberg," 7.

27 Diana Reid Haig, "The Scepter Records Story" [Liner Notes], *The Scepter Records Story*, 12.

28 Betrock, *Girl Groups: The Story of a Sound*, 13; Clemente, *Girl Groups: Fabulous Females*, 201.

29 Betrock, *Girl Groups: The Story of a Sound*, 13; Clemente, *Girl Groups: Fabulous Females*, 201.

30 Betrock, *Girl Groups: The Story of a Sound*, 13; Haig, "The Scepter Records Story," 12.

31 Betrock, *Girl Groups: The Story of a Sound*, 13.

32 Beverly Lee, telephone interview with author, August 7, 2012.

33 Beverly Lee, telephone interview with author, August 7, 2012.

34 Betrock, *Girl Groups: The Story of a Sound*, 13.

35 Betrock, *Girl Groups: The Story of a Sound*, 13–14.

36 The Shirelles, "Will You Love Me Tomorrow," *The Best of the Shirelles*, Ace Records CDCHD 356, 1992, CD.

37 Beverly Lee, telephone interview with author, August 7, 2012.

38 Beverly Lee quoted in Sheila Weller, *Girls Like Us: Carole King, Joni Mitchell, and Carly Simon and the Journey of a Generation* (New York: Atria Books, 2008), 55, original emphasis.

39 Weller, *Girls Like Us*, 55.

40 In choosing a "twangy" song, Dixon might have had in mind the success of Chuck Berry, whose mix of country and rhythm and blues crossed over to white audiences in the 1950s.

41 Beverly Lee, telephone interview with author, August 7, 2012.

42 Beverly Lee, telephone interview with author, August 7, 2012.

43 Weller, *Girls Like Us*, 55

44 Beverly Lee, telephone interview with author, August 7, 2012.

45 Clemente, *Girl Groups: Fabulous Females*, 201.

46 Betrock, *Girl Groups: The Story of a Sound*, 14; Joel Whitburn, *The Billboard Book of Top 40 Hits*, 9th ed. (New York: Billboard Books, 2010), 589; Joel Whitburn, *Hot R&B Songs, 1942–2010*, 6th ed. (Menomonee Falls, WI: Record Research, 2010), 591.

47 Clemente, *Girl Groups: Fabulous Females*, 201.

48 Warwick, *Girl Groups, Girl Culture*, 116.

49 Beverly Lee, telephone interview with author, August 7, 2012.

50 Whitburn, *The Billboard Book of Top 40 Hits*, 589. "Will You Love Me Tomorrow" went to number four in England and number six in Australia. Jay Warner, *American*

Singing Groups: A History from 1940 to Today (Milwaukee, WI: Hal Leonard, 2006), 450.

51 Mike Hill, "The Shirelles," *The Rock and Roll Hall of Fame Eleventh Annual Induction Dinner* [program], 1996, Library and Archives, Rock and Roll Hall of Fame.

52 Betrock, *Girl Groups: The Story of a Sound*, 16; Whitburn, *The Billboard Book of Top 40 Hits*, 588.

53 "The Shirelles 'Love Me' Disc on Hit Parade," *Chicago Defender*, January 21, 1961, 19.

54 "Shirelles Quartet Top Moneymakers in '61," *Chicago Defender*, January 27, 1962, 10.

55 "Shirelles Quartet Top Moneymakers in '61," 10.

56 Luther Dixon is credited under the name Barney Williams. Whitburn, *Hot R&B Songs*, 591; Whitburn, *The Billboard Book of Top 40 Hits*, 589.

57 Whitburn, *The Billboard Book of Top 40 Hits*, 589.

58 A gold record represented sales of 500,000 units. "Shirelles Come Up with Another Hit in "Lover" [*sic*], *Chicago Defender*, December 4, 1962, 17.

59 Clemente, *Girl Groups: Fabulous Females*, 201.

60 Betrock, *Girl Groups: The Story of a Sound*, 8.

61 The new sound was also a response to the 1959 payola scandal, during which the US Congress held hearings about the practice of radio disc jockeys accepting money and gifts from record labels in exchange for giving airtime to the records. "This was not a crime," as Clemente points out, "but it fueled the extremist view that this was the only way rock 'n' roll could get on the radio." Clemente, *Girl Groups: Fabulous Females*, 201. For a discussion of payola, see John A. Jackson, *Big Beat Heat: Alan Freed and the Early Years of Rock and Roll* (New York: Schirmer Books, 1991).

62 Spector and Bennett married in the mid-sixties; Bennett took her husband's surname and kept it after their divorce. Ronnie Spector with Vince Waldron, *Be My Baby: How I Survived Mascara, Miniskirts, and Madness, or My Life as a Fabulous Ronette* (New York: Harmony Books, 1990), 42.

63 Beverly Lee, telephone interview with author, August 7, 2012.

64 I attended a performance in 2011 during the show's Broadway run. It premiered in Los Angeles in 2009.

65 Dennis Garvey, telephone interview with author, September 27, 2010.

66 Dennis Garvey, telephone interview with author, September 27, 2010.

67 I am grateful to the late Dennis Garvey and his wife Linda Garvey for putting me in touch with Beverly Lee and for other help with this research.

68 Beverly Lee, telephone interview with author, August 7, 2012.

69 Beverly Lee, telephone interview with author, August 7, 2012.

70 Beverly Lee, telephone interview with author, August 7, 2012.

71 Dick Clark and Richard Robinson, *Rock, Roll, and Remember* (New York: Thomas Y. Crowell, 1976), 230.

72 Clark and Robinson, *Rock, Roll, and Remember*, 231–32.

73 Nadine Cohodas, *Princesse Noire: The Tumultuous Reign of Nina Simone* (New York: Pantheon, 2010), 139; Brian Ward, *Just My Soul Responding: Rhythm and Blues, Black Consciousness, and Race Relations* (Berkeley: University of California Press, 1998), 298.

74 Betrock, *Girl Groups: The Story of a Sound*, 16.

75 Betrock, *Girl Groups: The Story of a Sound*, 16.

76 Beverly Lee, telephone interview with author, August 7, 2012.

77 Cotton, *Reelin' and Rockin'*, 249.

78 Beverly Lee, telephone interview with author, August 7, 2012.

79 Beverly Lee, telephone interview with author, August 7, 2012.

80 Shirley Reeves quoted in Tortelli, "Shirelles' Lead Shirley Reeves," 4.

81 Tortelli, "Shirelles' Lead Shirley Reeves," 4.

82 Beverly Lee, telephone interview with author, August 7, 2012.

83 Warwick points out that uniformity in clothing and bodily poses is a signal element of girl group culture that echoes the preference of many teenage girls to dress like their closest friends. Beyond indicating the cohesiveness of the group, this uniformity helps "to project a notion of inclusiveness to girl listeners," who could imagine themselves becoming a part of the group by adopting its appearance. Warwick, *Girl Groups, Girl Culture*, 79; Cynthia J. Cyrus, "Selling an Image: Girl Groups of the 1960s," *Popular Music* 22, no. 2 (2003): 173–93.

84 Beverly Lee, telephone interview with author, August 7, 2012.

85 Beverly Lee, telephone interview with author, August 7, 2012.

86 Cholly Atkins and Jacqui Malone, *Class Act: The Jazz Life of Choreographer Cholly Atkins* (New York: Columbia University Press, 2001), 131.

87 Ellie Greenwich, "Foreword," in *Girl Groups: Fabulous Females*, ed. Clemente, 5, original ellipsis.

88 For a discussion of Atkins's work with girl groups, see Warwick, *Girl Groups, Girl Culture*, 53–58.

89 Susan J. Douglas, *Where the Girls Are: Growing Up Female with the Mass Media* (New York: Times Books, 1994), 95.

90 Laurie Stras, "Introduction: She's So Fine, or Why Girl Singers (Still) Matter," in *She's So Fine: Reflections on Whiteness, Femininity, Adolescence and Class in 1960s Music*, ed. Laurie Stras (Burlington, VT: Ashgate, 2010), 21.

91 Spector and Waldron, *Be My Baby*, 35.

92 Stras, "Introduction: She's So Fine," 8.

93 Douglas, *Where the Girls Are*, 93.

94 Douglas, *Where the Girls Are*, 97.

95 Joe Dziemianowicz, "*Baby It's You* Sued by Members of The Shirelles: Singers Claim Musical Is Using Their Likeness," *New York Daily News*, April 27, 2011, accessed July 22, 2016, http://www.nydailynews.com/entertainment/music-arts/baby-sued-members-shirelles-singers-claim-musical-likeness-article-1.113105.

96   Reeves was slated to perform at shows running from July 19 to July 22, 2011. Kenneth Jones, "Original 'Shirelle' Shirley Alston Reeves to Perform with *Baby It's You!* in Post-Show Concerts," *Playbill*, June 15, 2011, accessed July 22, 2016, http://www.playbill.com/article/original-shirelle-shirley-alston-reeves-to-perform-with-baby-its-you-in-post-show-concerts-com-180135.

97   Kenneth Jones, "*Baby It's You!* Producers Being Sued by Beverly Lee of the Shirelles, Dionne Warwick and Others," *Playbill*, April 27, 2011, accessed July 22, 2016, http://www.playbill.com/article/baby-its-you-producers-being-sued-by-beverly-lee-of-the-shirelles-dionne-warwick-and-others-com-178629.

98   Betrock, *Girl Groups: The Story of a Sound*, 17.

99   Jones, "*Baby It's You!* Producers Being Sued."

100 Betrock, *Girl Groups: The Story of a Sound*, 20.

101 Neither the details of what happened to the royalties nor information about the settlement was made public. Clemente, *Girl Groups: Fabulous Females*, 203; Stan Soocher, *They Fought the Law: Rock Music Goes to Court* (New York: Schirmer Books, 1999), 67.

102 Shirley Alston Reeves quoted in Betrock, *Girl Groups: The Story of a Sound*, 20.

103 Clemente, *Girl Groups: Fabulous Females*, 203; Betrock, *Girl Groups: The Story of a Sound*, 20. The Shirelles were far from the only artists not to receive all of the royalties they had earned. The practice of exploiting the early rock and rollers, black and white, was deeply embedded in recording industry practices with unscrupulous producers, managers, and label owners withholding money and information. One limitation the Shirelles and their families had was their lack of knowledge about the legal and financial workings of the record business. "Our parents knew nothing about show business and we didn't," Lee told me. "The contract was taken to lawyers and the lawyers, actually, they weren't entertainment lawyers." Beverly Lee, telephone interview with author, August 7, 2012.

104 Betrock, *Girl Groups: The Story of a Sound*, 20.

105 Dixon continued producing after his departure from Scepter but did not again achieve the chart success he enjoyed with the Shirelles. This, coupled with the short memory of pop culture, contributes to his relative obscurity. Haig, "The Scepter Records Story," 20.

106 Haig, "The Scepter Records Story," 20.

107 Warner, *American Singing Groups*, 450.

108 Warner, *American Singing Groups*, 451.

109 Warner, *American Singing Groups*, 451.

110 Music historian Elijah Wald refutes this commonsense premise in *How the Beatles Destroyed Rock 'n' Roll: An Alternative History of American Popular Music* (New York: Oxford University Press, 2009).

111 Beverly Lee, telephone interview with author, August 7, 2012.

112 Beverly Lee, telephone interview with author, August 7, 2012.

113 Mark Lewisohn, *Tune In: The Beatles: All These Years*, vol. 1 (New York: Crown Archetype, 2013), 407, 564.

114 Lewisohn, *Tune In*, 408, 459.

115 Lewisohn, *Tune In*, 459.

116 Paul McCartney quoted in Lewisohn, *Tune In*, 706.

117 John Lennon quoted in David Sheff, *All We Are Saying: The Last Major Interview with John Lennon and Yoko Ono* (New York: St. Martin's, 2000), 168.

118 Steven D. Stark, *Meet the Beatles: A Cultural History of the Band That Shook Youth, Gender, and the World* (New York: HarperCollins, 2005), 129.

119 *Please Please Me* also featured the Beatles' cover of another girl group hit, "Chains," originated by the Cookies, and a cover of another Luther Dixon production, "Twist and Shout," by the Isley Brothers.

120 On their early albums, the Beatles covered songs by Chuck Berry, Buddy Holly, the Isley Brothers, and Motown artists.

121 Bruce Spizer, *The Beatles Are Coming! The Birth of Beatlemania in America* (New Orleans: 498 Productions, 2003), 175.

122 Shirley Reeves quoted in Tortelli, "Shirelles' Lead Shirley Reeves," 5.

123 Keith Richards with James Fox, *Life* (New York: Little, Brown, 2010), 151.

124 I am grateful to Dennis Garvey for pointing out this parallel. Telephone interview with author, October 4, 2010.

125 Whitburn, *The Billboard Book of Top 40 Hits*, 557; Martin Elliott, *The Rolling Stones: Complete Recording Sessions, 1963–1989* (London: Blandford Press, 1990), 20.

126 Jann S. Wenner, "Mick Jagger," in *The Rolling Stone Interviews*, ed. Jann S. Wenner and Joe Levy (New York: Back Bay Books, 2007), 365.

127 Mick Jagger quoted in Wenner, "Mick Jagger," 366.

128 For additional examples of girl group influence on British Invasion bands, see Warwick, *Girl Groups, Girl Culture*, 144–45.

129 Warwick, *Girl Groups, Girl Culture*, 145.

130 Beverly Lee, telephone interview with author, August 7, 2012.

131 Shirley Reeves quoted in Tortelli, "Shirelles' Lead Shirley Reeves Recalls Girl Group Sound," 5.

132 Beverly Lee, telephone interview with author, August 7, 2012.

133 Eriq Gardner "Warner Bros. Settles 'Baby It's You' Lawsuit," *The Hollywood Reporter*, December 16, 2011, accessed April 22, 2019, https://www.hollywoodreporter.com/thr -esq/shirelles-baby-its-you-lawsuit-274744.

134 The street was dedicated in 2008. Amy Ellis Nutt, "Passaic Dedicates Street to the Shirelles," *The Star Ledger*, September 21, 2008, accessed March 24, 2014, http://www .nj.com/news/index.ssf/2008/09/passaic_dedicates_street_to_t; Beverly Lee, telephone interview with author, August 7, 2012.

135 Rhythm and Blues Foundation website, accessed December 15, 2015, http://www .rhythmblues.org/awards.php.

136 Rock and Roll Hall of Fame, "Induction Process," accessed March 24, 2014, http://
www.rockhall.com/inductees/induction-process/.

137 A number of artists have not attended the ceremony due to scheduling conflicts or
lingering contentious relations within the group; few, however, have expressed the
vitriol toward the institution that the Sex Pistols did in 2006. Andy Greene, "A History of Rock and Roll Hall of Fame No-Shows," *Rolling Stone,* April 12, 2012, accessed
March 24, 2014, http://www.rollingstone.com/music/news/a-history-of-rock-and-roll
-hall-of-fame-no-shows-20120412.

138 Artists become eligible for induction twenty-five years after the release of their first
record. Rock and Roll Hall of Fame, "Induction Process." The Shirelles released their
first single, "Met Him on a Sunday" in 1958 and had their first number one pop hit in
1960.

139 David Hinckley, "The Kids in the Hall from Gladys Knight to David Bowie,
Rock and Roll Museum Comes of Age with Lesser Stars Making the Honor
Roll In '96," *New York Daily News,* January 17, 1996, accessed March 24, 2014,
http://www.nydailynews.com/archives/nydn-features/kids-hall-gladys-knight
-david-bowie-rock-roll-museum-age-lesser-stars-making-honor-roll-96-article-1
.715967#ixzz2zisto A17.

140 *The 1996 Annual Induction Ceremony,* Rock and Roll Hall of Fame Foundation Records, Library and Archives, Rock and Roll Hall of Fame. Archival Videotape.

141 *The 1996 Annual Induction Ceremony.*

142 Rock and Roll Hall of Fame, "Induction Process."

143 Rock and Roll Hall of Fame, "Induction Process."

144 Stras, "Introduction: She's So Fine," 10.

145 For an exchange about the flaws of the induction process, see John Covach, "Why No
Yes in the Rock Hall?" in *The Rock History Reader,* 2nd ed., ed. Theo Cateforis (New
York: Routledge, 2013), 367–68, and Lauren Onkey, "A Response to 'Why No Yes in
the Rock Hall,'" in *The Rock History Reader,* ed. Cateforis, 369–71.

146 Beverly Lee, telephone interview with author, August 7, 2012.

147 Beverly Lee, telephone interview with author, August 7, 2012.

148 David Hinckley, "Rock Hall's Identity Crisis Museum Seems to Be Avoiding Genre's
More Commercial Acts," *New York Daily News,* October 5, 1995, accessed March 24,
2014, http://www.nydailynews.com/archives/nydn-features/rock-hall-identity-crisis
-museum-avoiding-genre-commercial-acts-article-1.692455#ixzz2ziuOust.

149 Wald, *How the Beatles Destroyed Rock 'n' Roll,* 223. For a related discussion of the
application of high art values to popular music, see Bernard Gendron, *Between Montmartre and the Mudd Club: Popular Music and the Avant-Garde* (Chicago: University
of Chicago Press, 2002).

150 Warner, *American Singing Groups,* 450; Whitburn, *The Billboard Book of Top 40 Hits,*
588–89; Whitburn, *Hot R&B Songs,* 591.

151 An exception is Ward, *Just My Soul Responding.* Ward devotes sustained attention to
the Shirelles and other girl groups.

152 Doris Coley and Shirley Alston Reeves quoted in David Espar, *Rock and Roll: In the Groove*, part 2 (South Burlington, VT: WGBH Video, 1995), VHS.

153 Greenwich, "Foreword," in *Girl Groups: Fabulous Females*, 5.

154 Mary Wilson, *Dreamgirl and Supreme Faith: My Life as a Supreme* (New York: Cooper Square Press, 1999), 25, 81.

155 Sarah Dash, telephone interview with author, March 4, 2014.

Chapter Four: Call and Response

Epigraph: Gloria Jones, telephone interview with the author, March 13, 2012.

1 Morgan Neville, *Twenty Feet from Stardom* (Beverly Hills, CA: Anchor Bay Entertainment, 2014), DVD; *Fresh Air*, June 12, 2013, National Public Radio; Christian John Wikane, "Keeping Great Company: An Interview with Claudia Lennear," June 12, 2013, accessed July 9, 2013, http://www.popmatters.com/pm/feature/172563-performer-spotlight-the-women-of-20-feet-from-stardom-claudia-lennea/; Ben Travers, "Watch: '20 Feet from Stardom' Singer Darlene Love Steps to the Front on 'Late Show with David Letterman,'" *IndieWire*, June 14, 2013, accessed May 16, 2019, https://www.indiewire.com/2013/06/watch-20-feet-from-stardom-singer-darlene-love-steps-to-the-front-on-late-show-with-david-letterman-37587/.

2 Gerri Hirshey, *We Gotta Get Out of This Place: The True, Tough Story of Women in Rock* (New York: Atlantic Monthly Press, 2001), 53.

3 Hirshey, *We Gotta Get Out of This Place*, 53.

4 Susan Fast, "Genre, Subjectivity and Back-up Singing in Rock Music," in *The Ashgate Research Companion to Popular Musicology*, ed. Derek B. Scott (Surrey, UK: Ashgate, 2009), 171–87; Annie J. Randall, *Dusty, Queen of the Postmods* (New York: Oxford University Press, 2009); and Jacqueline Warwick, "'And the Colored Girls Sing . . .': Backup Singers and the Case of the Blossoms," *Musicological Identities: Essays in Honor of Susan McClary*, ed. Steven Baur, Raymond Knapp, and Jacqueline Warwick (Hampshire, UK: Ashgate, 2008), 63–75. I discuss background vocalists in my overview article of African American women in rock, "Women in African American Music: Rock," in *African American Music: An Introduction*, ed. Mellonee Burnim and Portia K. Maultsby (New York: Routledge, 2006), 558–77.

5 Warwick, "'And the Colored Girls Sing,'" 64.

6 Fast, "Genre, Subjectivity," 186.

7 Fast, "Genre, Subjectivity," 172. Here, Fast is building on Susan McClary's work on convention in musical form: *Conventional Wisdom: The Content of Music Form* (Berkeley: University of California Press, 2000).

8 Warwick, "'And the Colored Girls Sing,'"75.

9 Venetta Fields quoted in Kandia Crazy Horse, "Interview with Venetta Fields," in *Rip It Up: The Black Experience in Rock 'n' Roll*, ed. Kandia Crazy Horse (New York: Palgrave, 2004), 62, original emphasis.

10 Charles I. Nero, "Langston Hughes and the Black Female Gospel Voice in the American Musical," in *Black Women and Music: More Than the Blues*, ed. Eileen M. Hayes and Linda F. Williams (Urbana: University of Illinois Press, 2007), 72.

11 For a discussion of Tharpe's life and cross-genre musical influence, see Gayle F. Wald, *Shout, Sister, Shout! The Untold Story of Rock-and-Roll Trailblazer Sister Rosetta Tharpe* (Boston: Beacon Press, 2007).

12 Nero, "Langston Hughes," 79.

13 Nero, "Langston Hughes," 79. For a related discussion of the symbolic work black women's singing voices have done in US social and political contexts, see Farah Jasmine Griffin, "When Malindy Sings: A Meditation on Black Women's Vocality," in *Uptown Conversation: The New Jazz Studies*, ed. Robert O'Meally, Brent Hayes Edwards, and Farah Jasmine Griffin (New York: Columbia University Press, 2004), 102–18.

14 Nero, "Langston Hughes," 79.

15 Nero, "Langston Hughes," 86.

16 Darlene Love with Rob Hoerburger, *My Name Is Love: The Darlene Love Story* (New York: William Morrow, 1998), 33.

17 Warwick, "'And the Colored Girls Sing,'" 64.

18 Merry Clayton, telephone interview with author, October 22, 2009.

19 Merry Clayton, telephone interview with author, October 22, 2009.

20 Warwick, "'And the Colored Girls Sing,'" 64.

21 Love with Hoerburger, *My Name Is Love*, 14–15.

22 Merry Clayton, telephone interview with author, October 22, 2009.

23 Merry Clayton, telephone interview with author, October 22, 2009.

24 Cissy Houston with Jonathan Singer, *How Sweet the Sound: My Life with God and Gospel* (New York: Doubleday, 1998), 148.

25 Crazy Horse, "Interview with Venetta Fields," 60–61.

26 Merry Clayton quoted in Todd Everett, "She Was Born on Christmas Day," *Rolling Stone*, June 25, 1970, 11.

27 Houston with Singer, *How Sweet the Sound*, 155.

28 Everett, "Born on Christmas Day," 11.

29 Merry Clayton, telephone interview with author, October 22, 2009.

30 Merry Clayton, telephone interview with author, October 22, 2009.

31 I am drawing this characterization from Horace Clarence Boyer, "Contemporary Gospel Music," *The Black Perspective in Music* 7, no. 1 (spring 1979): 5–58.

32 Zora Neale Hurston, "Characteristics of Negro Expression," in *The Sanctified Church* (New York: Marlowe, 1981), 50.

33 For overviews of their careers, see Houston with Singer, *How Sweet the Sound*; Love with Hoerburger, *My Name Is Love*; and Warwick, "'And the Colored Girls Sing,'" 63–75.

34 Spector lifted the name from gospel singer Dorothy Love Coates. Love with Hoerburger, *My Name Is Love*, 64–65.

35 Love with Hoerburger, *My Name Is Love*, 35.
36 Warwick, "'And the Colored Girls Sing,'" 67.
37 Fanita James quoted in Warwick, "'And the Colored Girls Sing,'" 66.
38 Love with Hoerburger, *My Name Is Love*, 37.
39 Love with Hoerburger, *My Name Is Love*, 48.
40 Love with Hoerburger, *My Name Is Love*, 51.
41 Love with Hoerburger, *My Name Is Love*, 287–88.
42 Love with Hoerburger, *My Name Is Love*, 110–12.
43 Marc Weingarten, *Station to Station: The History of Rock 'n' Roll on Television* (New York: Pocket Books, 2000), 127. Dick Clark's *American Bandstand* aired on weekday afternoons in the 1950s and Saturday afternoons starting in the 1960s.
44 The Shindogs, the show's house band, played on these tracks. Many of them were part of the "Wrecking Crew," the highly regarded studio band that helped Phil Spector create his wall of sound. Weingarten, *Station to Station*, 128–29.
45 Weingarten, *Station to Station*, 127.
46 Weingarten, *Station to Station*, 129.
47 Weingarten, *Station to Station*, 129.
48 Love with Hoerburger, *My Name Is Love*, 94. For details about Good's career, see Norma Coates, "Excitement Is Made, Not Born: Jack Good, Television, and Rock and Roll," *Journal of Popular Music Studies* 25, no. 3 (2013): 301–25.
49 Weingarten, *Station to Station*, 130.
50 Warwick, "'And the Colored Girls Sing,'" 72.
51 Any vocalists on studio premises could be pressed into background duty in a pinch, as Patti Labelle and the Bluebelles learned when, under contract at Atlantic Records, they were brought in to sing on Wilson Pickett's 1966 hit "634-5789 (Soulsville, U.S.A.)." Jerry Wexler and David Ritz, *Rhythm and the Blues: A Life in American Music* (New York: Alfred A. Knopf, 1993), 176.
52 Wexler and Ritz, *Rhythm and the Blues*, 208.
53 Houston with Singer, *How Sweet the Sound*, 146–47.
54 Bacharach names only one of the three white women singers, Linda November. Burt Bacharach with Robert Greenfield, *Anyone Who Had a Heart: My Life and Music* (New York: HarperCollins, 2013), 84–85.
55 Houston with Singer, *How Sweet the Sound*, 172, 273–74.
56 Cissy Houston continued her background work in the eighties, singing with her daughter Whitney Houston on "How Will I Know" (1986) and "I Wanna Dance with Somebody (Who Loves Me)" (1987). Houston with Singer, *How Sweet the Sound*, 276–78.
57 Houston with Singer, *How Sweet the Sound*, 274.
58 Houston with Singer, *How Sweet the Sound*, 276–78.
59 Houston with Singer, *How Sweet the Sound*, 274, 278.
60 Peter Guralnick, *Careless Love: The Unmaking of Elvis Presley* (Boston: Little, Brown, 1999), 343, original emphasis.

61 Houston left the Sweet Inspirations in 1969, after Presley's run in Vegas ended. Houston with Singer, *How Sweet the Sound*, 274; David Nathan, "The Sweet Inspirations" [Liner Notes], *Two Classic Albums [The Sweet Inspirations and Sweet Sweet Soul]*, Spy Records SPY 46004-2, 2002, CD; Guralnick, *Careless Love*, 639.

62 Robert Christgau, "The Move into Rock," in *"What'd I Say": The Atlantic Story. 50 Years of Music*, ed. Ahmet Ertegun and Perry Richardson (New York: Welcome Rain Publishers, 2001), 290–93; Wexler and Ritz, *Rhythm and the Blues*, 233.

63 Houston with Singer, *How Sweet the Sound*, 191–92.

64 Randall, *Dusty*, 22. For Springfield, the process culminated in *Dusty in Memphis*, the 1969 album that featured none other than Cissy Houston as a backing vocalist on several tracks, including the Top 10 hit "Son of a Preacher Man."

65 Uli Twelker, "Madeline Bell: Interview-May 2012," May 2012, accessed July 12, 2013, http://www.madelinebell.com/Interview.html. For a discussion of Madeline Bell's early career in London and her collaborations with Dusty Springfield, see Randall, *Dusty*, 35–60.

66 Randall, *Dusty*, 47.

67 Randall, *Dusty*, 156. Dusty Springfield, "In the Middle of Nowhere," *The Dusty Springfield Anthology*, Mercury Records 314 553 501-02, 1997, CD.

68 The program was a special episode of *Ready, Steady, Go!*, a weekly show that presented performances by pop music and rock and roll artists. Randall, *Dusty*, 53.

69 Randall, *Dusty*, 49.

70 Randall, *Dusty*, 47–48, original emphasis.

71 Joel Whitburn, *The Billboard Book of Top 40 Hits*, 9th ed. (New York: Billboard Books, 2010), 557.

72 Keith Richards with James Fox, *Life* (New York: Little, Brown, 2010), 84.

73 Philip Norman, *Mick Jagger* (New York: HarperCollins, 2012), 79.

74 "In September 1976, a federal circuit court judge in New York announced that George [Harrison] had 'subconsciously' plagiarized the tune of 'My Sweet Lord' from the sixties hit 'He's So Fine' and ordered him to pay a fine of $500,000." Joshua M. Greene, *Here Comes the Sun: The Spiritual and Musical Journey of George Harrison* (Hoboken, NJ: John Wiley and Sons, 2006), 231.

75 For discussions of cross-racial and cross-gender exchanges in music and of African American women's underacknowledged imprint on popular culture, see Daphne A. Brooks, *Grace* (New York: Continuum Books, 2005); Daphne A. Brooks and Gayle Wald, "Women Do Dylan: The Aesthetics and Politics of Dylan Covers," in *Highway 61 Revisited: Bob Dylan's Road from Minnesota to the World*, ed. Colleen J. Sheehy and Thomas Swiss (Minneapolis: University of Minnesota Press, 2009), 169–85; Jayna Brown, *Babylon Girls: Black Women Performers and the Shaping of the Modern* (Durham, NC: Duke University Press, 2008); and Kyra Gaunt, *The Games Black Girls Play: Learning the Ropes from Double-Dutch to Hip-Hop* (New York: New York University Press, 2006).

76 Randall, *Dusty, Queen of the Postmods* (New York: Oxford University Press, 2009), 36–37.

77 Small Faces, "Tin Soldier," *The Singles As and Bs . . . Plus*, See for Miles Records, SEE CD 293, 1990, CD.

78 Neil Warwick, Jon Kutner, and Tony Brown, *The Complete Book of the British Charts: Singles and Albums* (London: Omnibus Press, 2004), 50. Highlights from Arnold's recording career are collected on P. P. Arnold, *The Best of P. P. Arnold*, Repertoire DREP 5152, 2009, CD.

79 Warwick, "'And the Colored Girls Sing,'" 65.

80 Fast, "Genre, Subjectivity," 179.

81 Bramlett was a white Midwesterner, but her vocals conveyed an African American sound, a consequence of the time she spent as a teen learning the musical ropes from black jazz and R&B musicians in the nightclubs of East St. Louis. She has the distinction of having been the only white Ikette. Tina Turner with Kurt Loder, *I, Tina* (New York: William Morrow, 1986), 88–89.

82 Merry Clayton, telephone interview with author, October 22, 2009.

83 Merry Clayton quoted in Everett, "Born on Christmas Day," 11.

84 The Rolling Stones, "Gimme Shelter," *Let It Bleed*, ABKCO Records 90042, 2002, CD. Originally released in 1969.

85 For a reading of the symbolic role Clayton plays in this song, see Fast, "Genre, Subjectivity," 181.

86 Fast, "Genre, Subjectivity," 182.

87 Greil Marcus, "You Get What You Need," *Rolling Stone*, December 27, 1969, 52.

88 Gloria Jones, telephone interview with author, March 13, 2012.

89 The Rolling Stones, *Exile on Main Street*, Universal Music International 2734295, 2010, CD. Originally released in 1972.

90 Highlights from these and other Clayton recordings are collected on Merry Clayton, *The Best of Merry Clayton*, Sony Music Entertainment, 2013, CD.

91 Gerardo Liedo, "Rocks Off: Merry Clayton," accessed April 29, 2019, http://www.rocksoff.org/merry.htm.

92 Merry Clayton, telephone interview with author, October 22, 2009.

93 *Joe Cocker*, A&M Records SP-4368, 2015, CD. Originally released in 1972.

94 Gloria Jones, telephone interview with author, April 20, 2012.

95 Gloria Jones, telephone interview with author, April 20, 2012.

96 Gloria Jones, telephone interview with author, March 13, 2012.

97 Venetta Fields quoted in Crazy Horse, "Interview with Venetta Fields," 62.

98 Crazy Horse, "Interview with Venetta Fields," 66.

99 Jerry Gilbert, "Humble Pie Are Sitting Pretty," *Sounds*, May 19, 1973, 5; Ray Telford, "Sweet Stuff in Pie," *Sounds*, March 31, 1973, 15.

100 Venetta Fields quoted in Crazy Horse, "Interview with Venetta Fields," 62.

101 Jerry Shirley with Tim Cohan, *Best Seat in the House: Drumming in the '70s with Marriott, Frampton, and Humble Pie* (Alma, MI: Rebeats, 2011), 296.

102 Telford, "Sweet Stuff," 15.

103 Venetta Fields quoted in Crazy Horse, "Interview with Venetta Fields," 62.

104 Fast, "Genre, Subjectivity," 177.

105 Venetta Fields quoted in Crazy Horse, "Interview with Venetta Fields," 63.

106 Some of the songs the groups recorded together during this period are included on Humble Pie, *The Definitive Collection*, A&M Records B0006880-02, 2006, CD.

107 Paolo Hewitt and John Hellier, *Steve Marriott: All Too Beautiful* (London: Helter Skelter Publishing, 2004), 207.

108 "Humble Pie and the Blackberries in Concert" [advertisements], *Sounds*, October 20, 1973, 15, and October 27, 1973, 13.

109 Pete Erskine, "Road Report: Pie: As Tight as Rubber Hosiery," *Sounds*, November 3, 1973, 11; see also "Album, UK Tour Pie," *Sounds*, September 22, 1973.

110 Hewitt and Hellier, *Steve Marriott*, 205–6.

111 Shirley with Cohan, *Best Seat*, 262; Hewitt and Hellier, *Steve Marriott*, 207.

112 Jerry Shirley quoted in Hewitt and Hellier, *Steve Marriott*, 207.

113 Shirley with Cohan, *Best Seat*, 214–20.

114 Ava Cherry quoted in Paul Trynka [liner notes], Ava Cherry, *The Astronettes Sessions*, Black Barbarella Records BBarbcd001, 2009, CD.

115 Roy Carr and Charles Shaar Murray, *Bowie: An Illustrated Record* (New York: Avon Books, 1981), 54.

116 Carr and Murray, *Bowie*, 54.

117 Paul Trynka, *David Bowie: Starman* (New York: Little, Brown, 2011), 258–59; Carr and Murray, *Bowie*, 69; David Bowie, *Young Americans*, Rykodisc, 1999, CD. Originally released in 1975.

118 Preston played piano and organ on *Let It Be* (1970) by the Beatles, *All Things Must Pass* (1970) by George Harrison, and *Sticky Fingers* (1971) and *Black and Blue* (1976) by the Rolling Stones.

119 The album also featured background vocals from Patti Austin, Valerie Simpson, and Phoebe Snow.

120 Gloria Jones, telephone interview with author, March 13, 2012. COGIC is the acronym for Church of God in Christ, a sanctified denomination.

121 The British band Soft Cell had an international hit with its 1981 cover of "Tainted Love."

122 Gloria Jones, telephone interview with author, March 13, 2012.

123 Gloria Jones, telephone interview with author, March 13, 2012.

124 Warwick, Kutner, and Brown, *The Complete Book of the British Charts*, 1082–83.

125 Geoff Brown, "Bolan's Cosmic Giggler," *Melody Maker*, March 2, 1974, 17.

126 David Yaffe, *Bob Dylan: Like a Complete Unknown* (New Haven, CT: Yale University Press, 2011), 60.

127 Yaffe, *Bob Dylan*, 66, 75. For another well-considered discussion of Dylan's debt to African American women performers, see Brooks and Wald, "Women Do Dylan," 169–85.

128 Yaffe, *Bob Dylan*, 80.

129 Yaffe, *Bob Dylan*, 66, 75.

130 Yaffe, *Bob Dylan*, 75, 87.

131 Helena Springs also became one of Dylan's songwriting partners, cowriting "a larger number of songs with him than any other collaborator in his career." Michael Gray, *The Bob Dylan Encyclopedia* (New York: Continuum Books, 2006), 23, 632. For a discussion of Dylan's conversion to Christianity, see Howard Sounes, *Down the Highway: The Life of Bob Dylan* (New York: Grove Press, 2001), 323–27.

132 Yaffe, *Bob Dylan*, 82.

133 Selections from these recordings are available on Bob Dylan, *Bob Dylan's Greatest Hits*, vol. 3, Columbia Records CK 66783, 1994, CD.

134 Gray, *Bob Dylan Encyclopedia*, 558.

135 Gray, *Bob Dylan Encyclopedia*, 558.

136 Gray, *Bob Dylan Encyclopedia*, 77, 380, 439.

137 Debi Dye-Gibson quoted in Sounes, *Down the Highway*, 315.

138 Yaffe, *Bob Dylan*, 79.

139 Some artists such as Bob Dylan continued to work with black women background vocalists beyond this time frame. Other examples found in my record collection include the following: guitarist Paul Weller, who left his punk band the Jam in the early 1980s and, starting in 1983, channeled his inner Steve Marriott in the Style Council, an R&B style ensemble that featured the vocals of Dee C. Lee (a London-born black Brit) in the P. P. Arnold background role. Roxy Music featured background vocalist Yanick Étienne on the title track of its 1982 release *Avalon*. In 1995 David Bowie hired Gail Ann Dorsey, an African American bass player who contributed backing vocals on record and in concert and worked with him on and off until his death in 2016. In 2004, Nick Cave cut *Abattoir Blues* with the London Community Gospel Choir backing him with the black American gospel sound on most of the tracks. Since 1989 the Rolling Stones have toured with Lisa Fischer as a backing vocalist.

140 Merry Clayton, telephone interview with author, October 22, 2009.

141 Fast, "Genre, Subjectivity," 179.

142 Mick Jagger quoted in Neville, *Twenty Feet from Stardom*.

143 Venetta Fields quoted in Crazy Horse, "Interview with Venetta Fields," 62.

144 Claudia Lennear quoted in Wikane, "Keeping Great Company."

145 Jerry Wexler quoted in Houston with Singer, *How Sweet the Sound*, 180.

146 Fanita James quoted in Warwick, "'And the Colored Girls Sing,'" 65.

147 Venetta Fields quoted in Telford, "Sweet Stuff," 15.

148 Venetta Fields quoted in Telford, "Sweet Stuff," 15.

149 Venetta Fields quoted in Crazy Horse, "Interview with Venetta Fields," 70.

150 Gloria Jones, telephone interview with author, April 20, 2012.

151 Warwick, "'And the Colored Girls Sing,'" 75.

152 Doris Troy quoted in Mark Plummer, "Doris Troy and the Gospel Truth," *Melody Maker*, December 18, 1971, 12.

153 Lynn Mabry quoted in Neville, *Twenty Feet from Stardom*.

154 Fast, "Genre, Subjectivity," 187.

155 For a history and cultural analysis of minstrelsy, see Eric Lott, *Love and Theft: Blackface Minstrelsy and the American Working Class* (New York: Oxford University Press, 1993).

156 For critical analysis of the relationship between white racial identity and African American music, see Daphne A. Brooks, "This Voice Which Is Not One: Amy Winehouse Sings the Ballad of Sonic Blue(s)face Culture," *Women and Performance: A Journal of Feminist Theory* 20, no. 1 (2010): 37–60; Brown, *Babylon Girls*; Dick Hebdige, *Subculture: The Meaning of Style* (London: Routledge, 1979); Ingrid Monson, "The Problem with White Hipness: Race, Gender, and Cultural Conceptions in Jazz Historical Discourse," *Journal of the American Musicological Society* 48, no. 3 (1995): 396–422; and Greg Tate, *Everything but the Burden: What White People Are Taking from Black Culture* (New York: Broadway Books, 2003).

157 For an analysis of these conditions, see Paul Gilroy, *"There Ain't No Black in the Union Jack": The Cultural Politics of Race and Nation* (Chicago: University of Chicago Press, 1991).

158 Venetta Fields quoted in Crazy Horse, "Interview with Venetta Fields," 66.

159 Fast, "Genre, Subjectivity," 178.

160 Bruce Springsteen quoted in Neville, *Twenty Feet from Stardom*.

161 Claudia Lennear quoted in Wikane, "Keeping Great Company."

162 Merry Clayton, telephone interview with author, October 22, 2009.

163 Gloria Jones, telephone interview with the author, March 13, 2012.

164 Gilbert, "Humble Pie," *Sounds*, May 19, 1973, 5.

165 Gloria Jones, telephone interview with author, March 13, 2012.

166 Gloria Jones, telephone interview with author, March 13, 2012.

167 Fast, "Genre, Subjectivity," 181.

168 Fast, "Genre, Subjectivity," 174.

169 I thank Theo Cateforis for sharing this observation.

170 Venetta Fields quoted in Crazy Horse, "Interview with Venetta Fields," 67.

171 Fast, "Genre, Subjectivity," 186.

172 Lisa Fischer quoted in *Twenty Feet from Stardom*.

173 For a discussion of the mammy role and other controlling stereotypes that affect black women, see Patricia Hill Collins, *Black Feminist Thought: Knowledge, Consciousness, and the Politics of Empowerment* (New York: Routledge, 1991).

174 Randall, *Dusty*, 58–59.

175 Randall, *Dusty*, 58–59.

176 Clayton recordings produced by Lou Adler included songs written by Bob Dylan, Mick Jagger and Keith Richards, Carole King, Robby Krieger, Billy Preston, Leon Russell, Paul Simon, James Taylor, Bill Withers, and Neil Young.

177 Lou Adler quoted in *Twenty Feet from Stardom*.

178 Andy Davis, *Doris Troy* [Liner Notes], EMI Apple Records 5099990824326, 2010, CD. Originally released in 1970.

179 Gloria Jones, *Share My Love*, Reel Music 66748-78007-2, 2009, CD. Originally released in 1973; Claudia Lennear, *Phew!*, Warner Brothers, BS2654, 1973,
33⅓ RPM.

180 Telford, "Sweet Stuff," 15.

181 Hewitt and Hellier, *Steve Marriott*, 209.

182 The project was released decades later as *The Astronettes Sessions*.

183 Venetta Fields quoted in Crazy Horse, "Interview with Venetta Fields," 65.

184 Gloria Jones, telephone interview with author, March 13, 2012.

185 Madeline Bell quoted in Uli Twelker, "Madeline Bell: Interview-May 2012," accessed
July 12, 2013, http://www.madelinebell.com/Interview.html.

186 "Madeline Bell: Interview-May 2012."

187 Venetta Fields quoted in Crazy Horse, "Interview with Venetta Fields," 65.

188 Venetta Fields quoted in Crazy Horse, "Interview with Venetta Fields," 68.

189 Crazy Horse, "Interview with Venetta Fields," 65.

190 P. P. Arnold quoted in Patrick Emery, "First Lady of Soul, P. P. Arnold, Looks Forward to Renewing Our Acquaintance," *I-94 Bar*, April 21, 2018, accessed May 1, 2019,
http://www.i94bar.com/interviews/pp-arnold.

191 Garth Cartwright, "High Tide: P. P. Arnold Interview," *Long Live Vinyl* 14, accessed
May 1, 2019, https://www.longlivevinyl.net/high-tide-arnold-interview/.

192 P. P. Arnold quoted in Cartwright, "High Tide."

193 Hewitt and Hellier, *Steve Marriott*, 198.

194 P. P. Arnold quoted in Henry Yates, "Is P. P. Arnold the Most Overlooked Soul Singer
of All Time?," *Classic Rock*, August 15, 2017, https://www.loudersound.com/features/is
-pp-arnold-the-most-overlooked-soul-singer-of-all-time.

195 P. P. Arnold quoted in Cartwright, "High Tide."

196 P. P. Arnold quoted in Cartwright, "High Tide."

197 Love with Hoerburger, *My Name Is Love*, 115.

198 Love with Hoerburger, *My Name Is Love*, 115.

199 Love with Hoerburger, *My Name Is Love*, 115–16.

200 The marriage was registered in Los Angeles County as a "confidential marriage," and
the press did not pick up the story. Dennis filed for divorce in August 1990. Gray, *Bob
Dylan Encyclopedia*, 174; Sounes, *Down the Highway*, 372.

201 Yaffe, *Bob Dylan*, 83.

202 Gray, *Bob Dylan Encyclopedia*, 174.

203 Sounes, *Down the Highway*, 314–18; Yaffe, *Bob Dylan*, 84.

204 Mavis Staples quoted in Yaffe, *Bob Dylan*, 75. For a discussion of the relationship
between Staples and Dylan, see Greg Kot, *I'll Take You There: Mavis Staples, the
Staple Singers, and the March Up Freedom's Highway* (New York: Scribner, 2014),
81–89.

205 For example, Sounes reports that neither Carolyn Dennis nor Clydie King would
speak with him for the record about their relationships with Dylan. Sounes, *Down
the Highway*, 372, 402. Photos of Dylan and King feature prominently in the liner

notes booklet that accompanies Dylan's CD box set *Biograph*, Columbia Records C3K 38830, 1985, CD.

206 The couple was married in 1968 and divorced in 1974. For details, see Ronnie Spector and Vince Waldron, *Be My Baby: How I Survived Mascara, Mini Skirts, and Madness, or My Life as a Fabulous Ronette* (New York: Harmony Books, 1990).

207 Richards with Fox, *Life*, 144.

208 Spector and Waldron, *Be My Baby*, 69–72.

209 Carr and Murray, *Bowie*, 56; David Allen, "David Bowie's 'Lady Grinning Soul' Claudia Lennear of Pomona Remembers Her Friend," *Daily Bulletin*, February 6, 2016, accessed January 18, 2018, http://www.dailybulletin.com/2016/02/06/david-bowies -lady-grinning-soul-claudia-lennear-of-pomona-remembers-her-friend/.

210 I discuss Hunt and Lennear in chapter 5. Marsha Hunt, *Real Life* (London: Chatto and Windus, 1986); Norman, *Mick Jagger*.

211 Trynka, *David Bowie*, 218, 280–82; Slash with Anthony Bozza, *Slash* (New York: Harper Entertainment, 2007), 10.

Chapter Five: Negotiating "Brown Sugar"

1 Emmaretta Marks, telephone interview with author, July 9, 2014.

2 Marsha Hunt, *Real Life* (London: Chatto and Windus, 1986), 130.

3 For some suggestions about who inspired "Brown Sugar," see Stephen Davis, *Old Gods Almost Dead: The 40-Year Odyssey of the Rolling Stones* (New York: Broadway Books, 2001), 300; Bill Wyman with Richard Havers, *Rolling with the Stones* (New York: DK Publishing, 2002); and Christopher Sandford, *Mick Jagger: Primitive Cool* (New York: St. Martin's, 1993), 172–73.

4 Writings on African American women and rock by Daphne A. Brooks, Kandia Crazy Horse, Laina Dawes, and Sonnet Retman are important exceptions.

5 Eric Clapton quoted in David Henderson, *'Scuse Me While I Kiss the Sky: Jimi Hendrix: Voodoo Child* (New York: Atria Books, 2008), 13.

6 Eric Burdon with J. Marshall Craig, *Don't Let Me Be Misunderstood* (New York: Thunder's Mouth Press, 2001), 47.

7 Burdon with Craig, *Don't Let Me Be Misunderstood*, 121.

8 Burdon with Craig, *Don't Let Me Be Misunderstood*, 115.

9 Eric Burdon, *I Used to Be an Animal, But I'm All Right Now* (London: Faber and Faber, 1986), 32.

10 Burdon, *I Used to Be an Animal*, 136–37.

11 Burdon with Craig, *Don't Let Me Be Misunderstood*, 55.

12 Keith Richards with James Fox, *Life* (New York: Little, Brown, 2010), 161–62, original ellipsis and author's ellipsis.

13 Van Morrison quoted in Peter Mills, *Hymns to the Silence: Inside the Words and Music of Van Morrison* (New York: Continuum Books, 2010), 89. For an analysis of

the ways Irish musicians engaged with African American music and mythologies of blackness, see Lauren Onkey, *Blackness and Transatlantic Irish Identity: Celtic Soul Brothers* (New York: Routledge, 2010).

14 "Alongside 'Gloria,' ['Brown-Eyed Girl'] is probably Van Morrison's best-known song, and it is probably the one with which he is more readily identified." Mills, *Hymns to the Silence*, 89.

15 Roy Carr and Charles Shaar Murray, *Bowie: An Illustrated Record* (New York: Avon Books, 1981), 56; David Allen, "David Bowie's 'Lady Grinning Soul' Claudia Lennear of Pomona Remembers Her Friend," *Daily Bulletin*, February 6, 2016, accessed January 18, 2018, http://www.dailybulletin.com/2016/02/06/david-bowies-lady-grinning -soul-claudia-lennear-of-pomona-remembers-her-friend/.

16 Hunt, *Real Life*, 98.

17 John Mayall, "Brown Sugar," *The Blues Alone*, Dera, 820 535-2, CD, 1988. Originally released in 1967.

18 It seems likely that Jagger was familiar with Mayall's song. He might have also heard "Soul Sister, Brown Sugar," an Isaac Hayes/David Porter composition recorded by Sam and Dave that went to number 15 on the British pop charts in January 1969. Graham Betts, *Complete UK Hit Singles, 1952–2004* (London: Collins, 2004), 675.

19 The Rolling Stones, "Brown Sugar," *Sticky Fingers*, Universal Music 80012799-02, 2009, CD. Originally released in 1971. In keeping with the practice of their song-writing partnership, "Brown Sugar" is credited to Mick Jagger/Keith Richards, but in his autobiography, Richards gives Jagger full credit for the song, stating that it is "all Mick," meaning that he did not play his usual role providing musical ideas: "The musical riff is mostly coming from me. I'm the riff master. The only one I missed and that Mick Jagger got was 'Brown Sugar,' and I'll tip my hat there. . . . I mean, I did tidy it up a bit, but that was his, words and music." Richards with Fox, *Life*, 177–78.

20 Martin Elliott, *The Rolling Stones Complete Recording Sessions, 1963–1989* (London: Blandford Press, 1990), 100–102.

21 Richards with Fox, *Life*, 181.

22 Elliott, *Rolling Stones Complete Recording Sessions*, 102; Sandford, *Mick Jagger: Primitive Cool*, 172–73; Wyman with Havers, *Rolling with the Stones*, 379.

23 Davis, *Old Gods*, 300.

24 Marc Spitz, *Jagger: Rebel, Rock Star, Rambler, Rogue* (New York: Gotham Books, 2011), 145.

25 Davis, *Old Gods*, 315–16. Stones historian Martin Elliott acknowledges suggestions that "Brown Sugar" was a drug song, but dismisses that notion, arguing "critics who claim the song is about brown sugar *a la Mexicocaine* were becoming hooked themselves on too many drug references." Elliott, *Rolling Stones Complete Recording Sessions*, 102.

26 Eugene D. Genovese, *Roll, Jordan, Roll: The World the Slaves Made* (New York: Vintage, 1976), 461–67; Darlene Clark Hine and Kathleen Thompson, *A Shining Thread*

of Hope: The History of Black Women in America (New York: Broadway Books, 1998), 97; Deborah Gray White, *Ar'n't I a Woman? Female Slaves in the Plantation South* (New York: W. W. Norton, [1985] 1999), 37–38.

27 The observations art historians Deborah Willis and Carla Williams make about the image of black women in Western art apply to those embedded in "Brown Sugar": "Ultimately, the image of the black woman was associated with prostitution, pornography, and deviant sexuality. Above all else, her image, and particularly her body, was understood as that which could be dominated and that which could be possessed, especially sexually." Deborah Willis and Carla Williams, *The Black Female Body: A Photographic History* (Philadelphia: Temple University Press, 2002), 3.

28 Elliott, *Rolling Stones Complete Recording Sessions*, 102.

29 The logo design is sometimes erroneously attributed to Andy Warhol, who designed the *Sticky Fingers* album cover. Davis, *Old Gods*, 346.

30 Sandford, *Mick Jagger: Primitive Cool*, 172–73.

31 Davis, *Old Gods*, 345.

32 Davis, *Old Gods*, 345.

33 Wyman with Havers, *Rolling with the Stones*, 379.

34 Wyman with Havers, *Rolling with the Stones*, 379.

35 Richards with Fox, *Life*, 276.

36 Sandford, *Mick Jagger: Primitive Cool*, 172–73.

37 The Rolling Stones, "Some Girls," *Some Girls*, Universal Republic Records, 2011, CD. Originally released in 1978.

38 Richards with Fox, *Life*, 401.

39 The Rolling Stones were not alone in linking sex and ethnic/racial stereotypes. For an assessment of the ways white male musicians have fetishized Asian and Asian American women in song, see Ellie M. Hisama, "Postcolonialism on the Make: The Music of John Mellencamp, David Bowie, and John Zorn," *Popular Music* 12, no. 2 (May 1993): 91–104.

40 Martin Scorsese, *Shine a Light* (Hollywood, CA: Paramount Home Entertainment, 2008), DVD.

41 Charles Shaar Murray, *Crosstown Traffic: Jimi Hendrix and the Rock 'n' Roll Revolution* (New York: St. Martin's, 1989), 70.

42 Lisa L. Rhodes, *Electric Ladyland: Women and Rock Culture* (Philadelphia: University of Pennsylvania Press, 2005), 138.

43 For feminist perspectives on groupies, see Norma Coates, "Teenyboppers, Groupies, and Other Grotesques: Girls and Women and Rock Culture in the 1960s and Early 1970s," *Journal of Popular Music Studies* 15, no. 1 (2003): 65–93; Ann Powers, "The Love You Make: Fans and Groupies," in *Trouble Girls: The Rolling Stone Book of Women in Rock*, ed. Barbara O'Dair (New York: Random House, 1997), 181–89; and Rhodes, *Electric Ladyland*. For an insider's view of life as a groupie in the late

1960s and 1970s, see Pamela Des Barres, *I'm with the Band: Confessions of a Groupie* (Chicago: Chicago Review Press, 2005).

Rhodes, *Electric Ladyland*, 146.

45 Lillian Roxon quoted in Rhodes, *Electric Ladyland*, 202.

46 Jimi Hendrix quoted in John Burks, Jerry Hopkins, and Paul Nelson, "The Groupies and Other Girls," *Rolling Stone*, February 15, 1969, 22.

47 Powers, "The Love You Make," 185.

48 Jimmy Page quoted in Burks, Hopkins, and Nelson, "The Groupies," 11.

49 Juma Sultan, telephone interview with author, July 3, 2014.

50 Pat Hartley quoted in Marion Fudger, "Anything That's Been a Horror in Your Life Sounds Like a Funny Story When You Tell It," *Spare Rib*, August 1973, 8.

51 Pat Hartley quoted in Fudger, "Anything That's Been a Horror," 9.

52 Powers, "The Love You Make," 184.

53 Rhodes, *Electric Ladyland*, xii.

54 Charles R. Cross, *Room Full of Mirrors: A Biography of Jimi Hendrix* (New York: Hyperion, 2005), 197.

55 Cross, *Room Full of Mirrors*, 197.

56 Henderson, *'Scuse Me While I Kiss the Sky*, 221.

57 Henderson, *'Scuse Me While I Kiss the Sky*, 221; Quincy Jones, Q: *The Autobiography of Quincy Jones* (New York: Harlem Moon, 2001), 160.

58 Henderson, *'Scuse Me While I Kiss the Sky*, 175.

59 Cross, *Room Full of Mirrors*, 197.

60 John McDermott with Eddie Kramer, *Hendrix: Setting the Record Straight* (New York: Warner Books, 1992), 199.

61 Emmaretta Marks, telephone interview with author, July 9, 2014.

62 Henderson, *'Scuse Me While I Kiss the Sky*, 175.

63 Cross, *Room Full of Mirrors*, 197.

64 Juma Sultan, telephone interview with author, July 3, 2014.

65 Curtis Knight quoted in Johnny Black, *Jimi Hendrix: The Ultimate Experience* (New York: Thunder's Mouth Press, 1999), 39.

66 Arthur Lee quoted in Black, *Jimi Hendrix*, 223.

67 Al Aronowitz quoted in Black, *Jimi Hendrix*, 39.

68 Alvenia Bridges quoted in Black, *Jimi Hendrix*, 39.

69 Cross, *Room Full of Mirrors*, 250.

70 Pat Hartley quoted in Fudger, "Anything That's Been a Horror," 9.

71 Cross, *Room Full of Mirrors*, 249.

72 McDermott with Kramer, *Hendrix: Setting the Record Straight*, 200–201.

73 Devon Wilson quoted in Black, *Jimi Hendrix*, 39.

74 Devon Wilson quoted in Black, *Jimi Hendrix*, 39.

75 Cross, *Room Full of Mirrors*, 249.

76 Jim Marron quoted in Black, *Jimi Hendrix*, 231.

77 Juma Sultan, telephone interview with author, July 3, 2014.

78 McDermott with Kramer, *Hendrix: Setting the Record Straight*, 200.

79 Henderson, *'Scuse Me While I Kiss the Sky*, 220.

80 Emmaretta Marks, telephone interview with author, July 9, 2014.

81 Henderson, *'Scuse Me While I Kiss the Sky*, 220.

82 Cross, *Room Full of Mirrors*, 249; Juma Sultan, telephone interview with author, July 3, 2014.

83 Henderson, *'Scuse Me While I Kiss the Sky*, 410.

84 Henderson, *'Scuse Me While I Kiss the Sky*, 329.

85 Devon Wilson quoted in Daphne Davis, "The Cop of the Year," *Rags*, no. 1 (June 1970): 46.

86 Devon Wilson quoted in Davis, "The Cop of the Year," 46, original emphasis.

87 Devon Wilson quoted in Davis, "The Cop of the Year," 46.

88 Devon Wilson quoted in Davis, "The Cop of the Year," 46, original emphasis.

89 Devon Wilson quoted in Davis, "The Cop of the Year," 46, original italics in lyrics quotation.

90 Devon Wilson quoted in Davis, "The Cop of the Year," 46, original ellipsis.

91 Murray, *Crosstown Traffic*, 71.

92 Henderson, *'Scuse Me While I Kiss the Sky*, 364; Jimi Hendrix, "Dolly Dagger," *First Rays of the New Rising Sun*, MCA Records MCAD-11599, 1997, CD.

93 Cross, *Room Full of Mirrors*, 278.

94 Betty Davis, "Steppin in Her I. Miller Shoes," *Betty Davis*, Light in the Attic Records LITA 026, 2007, CD. Originally released in 1973.

95 Pat Hartley quoted in Fudger, "Anything That's Been a Horror," 9.

96 Emmaretta Marks, telephone interview with author, July 9, 2014.

97 Cross, *Room Full of Mirrors*, 249; McDermott with Kramer, *Hendrix: Setting the Record Straight*, 200–201.

98 Stephen Davis, *Jim Morrison: Life, Death, Legend* (New York: Gotham Books, 2004), 146; Henderson, *'Scuse Me While I Kiss the Sky*, 241–42.

99 Emmaretta Marks, telephone interview with author, July 9, 2014.

100 Cross, *Room Full of Mirrors*, 314.

101 McDermott with Kramer, *Hendrix: Setting the Record Straight*, 292.

102 Cross, *Room Full of Mirrors*, 341–42.

103 Cross, *Room Full of Mirrors*, 341–42; Henderson, *'Scuse Me While I Kiss the Sky*, 19.

104 Emmaretta Marks, telephone interview with author, July 9, 2014.

105 Information for this biographical sketch comes from Hunt, *Real Life*, and Marsha Hunt, *Undefeated* (Vancouver, BC: Greystone Books, 2005).

106 Hunt, *Real Life*, 93.

107 Hunt, *Undefeated*, 17, original emphasis.

108 Hunt, *Undefeated*, 18.

109 For discussions of race and racism in Britain, see Houston A. Baker, Manthia Diawara, and Ruth H. Lindeborg, *Black British Cultural Studies: A Reader* (Chicago:

University of Chicago Press, 1996); Hazel Carby, *Cultures in Babylon: Black Britain and African America* (London: Verso, 1999); and Paul Gilroy, "*There Ain't No Black in the Union Jack*": *The Cultural Politics of Race and Nation* (Chicago: University of Chicago Press, 1991).

110 Hunt, *Real Life*, 140.

111 Hunt, *Real Life*, 90.

112 Hunt, *Real Life*, 106.

113 Hunt, *Real Life*, 103.

114 Graham Bennett, *Soft Machine: Out-Bloody-Rageous* (London: SAF Publishing, 2005), 86.

115 Hunt, *Real Life*, 107.

116 Hunt, *Undefeated*, 18.

117 Hunt, *Real Life*, 139.

118 Hunt, *Undefeated*, 17.

119 Robert Partridge, "Dialogue: *Melody Maker* Special on Women in Rock," *Melody Maker*, November 10, 1973, 36.

120 Hunt, *Real Life*, 114.

121 Patrick Lichfield, *The Most Beautiful Women* (London: Elm Tree Books, 1981), 35.

122 "Beauty Bulletin: The Natural—Marsha Hunt," *Vogue* [US], January 1, 1969, 134, 178; "Marsha Hunt and the Luxury of Going as Far as You Dare," *Vogue* [UK], December 1968, 112–15.

123 The photo was prominently featured in the retrospective "Lichfield: The Early Years" at England's National Portrait Gallery in 2003, and was one of the images for which a souvenir postcard was issued, accessed April 30, 2019, http://www.npg.org.uk /whatson/exhibitions/2003/lichfield-the-early-years.php; Patrick Lichfield, *Lichfield in Retrospect* (London: Weidenfeld and Nicolson, 1988), 17.

124 Hunt, *Real Life*, 122.

125 Hunt, *Undefeated*, 19–20.

126 For discussions of the black female nude in the West and the discourses of eroticism and exoticism that attend these images, see Lisa Collins, *The Art of History: African American Women Artists Engage the Past* (New Brunswick, NJ: Rutgers University Press, 2002), and Willis and Williams, *The Black Female Body*.

127 Tony Visconti, *Tony Visconti: Bowie, Bolan and the Brooklyn Boy: The Autobiography* (New York: HarperCollins, 2007), 175.

128 Hunt, *Real Life*, 122.

129 Visconti, *Tony Visconti*, 135.

130 Hunt, *Real Life*, 122–23.

131 Hunt, *Real Life*, 123.

132 Hunt, *Real Life*, 123.

133 Hunt, *Real Life*, 125.

134 Hunt, *Real Life*, 128.

135 Hunt, *Real Life*, 120.

136 Hunt, *Real Life*, 124.

137 Hunt, *Real Life*, 125.

138 Hunt, *Real Life*, 125.

139 Hunt, *Real Life*, 125.

140 Hunt, *Real Life*, 126.

141 Hunt, *Real Life*, 139.

142 Hunt, *Real Life*, 130.

143 Hunt, *Real Life*, 130.

144 Hunt, *Real Life*, 132.

145 Hunt, *Real Life*, 130.

146 Hunt, *Real Life*, 131.

147 Hunt, *Real Life*, 132.

148 Hunt, *Real Life*, 132.

149 Marsha Hunt quoted in Partridge, "Dialogue," 37.

150 Marsha Hunt quoted in Partridge, "Dialogue," 37.

151 Robin Mackie, "Marsha: Raising the Chat-Show from the Dead," *Sounds*, March 23, 1974, 7.

152 Visconti, *Tony Visconti*, 176–77.

153 Marsha Hunt quoted in Partridge, "Dialogue," 36.

154 This was the second of three Isle of Wight festivals; the third, held in August 1970, featured Jimi Hendrix in his last public performance.

155 Hunt, *Real Life*, 134.

156 Hunt, *Real Life*, 134.

157 Hunt, *Real Life*, 135.

158 Although Hunt doesn't mention it, this occurred around the time Lambert signed Labelle, a black American female vocal group with a more traditional black vocal sound, to Track Records. I discuss Labelle in chapter 6. Hunt, *Real Life*, 144, 162.

159 Mackie, "Marsha: Raising the Chat-Show," 7.

160 Penny Valentine, "Album Reviews" [Review of *Woman Child* by Marsha Hunt], *Sounds*, December 11, 1971, 23.

161 Marsha Hunt, *Woman Child*, Track Records 2410 101, 1971, 33⅓ RPM.

162 Pauline Black, *Black by Design: A 2-Tone Memoir* (London: Serpent's Tail, 2011), 212.

163 I discuss Betty Davis's career in chapter 7.

164 Mackie, "Marsha: Raising the Chat-Show," 7.

165 "Girl Says Mick Jagger Is Child's Father," *The Times* [London], June 20, 1973, 4, col. E.

166 It may be worth noting that in late 1968, Marianne Faithfull, pregnant by Jagger, had miscarried in the seventh month of her pregnancy. Jagger began seeing Hunt a few months later. Davis, *Old Gods*, 272.

167 Hunt, *Real Life*, 141. Hunt recounts the events leading up to the legal suit in detail in her memoir.

168 Hunt, *Real Life*, 141.

169 Hunt, *Real Life*, 141.

170 Hunt, *Real Life*, 147.

171 Tony Sanchez, *Up and Down with the Rolling Stones* (New York: William Morrow, 1979), 210.

172 Hunt, *Real Life*, 168; "Girl Says Mick Jagger Is Child's Father," 4, col. E.

173 Mick Jagger quoted in Sanchez, *Up and Down*, 210–11.

174 Hunt, *Real Life*, 169–70

175 Hunt, *Real Life*, 191.

176 Mick Jagger quoted in Regina Jones, as told to Leonard Pitts Jr., "Papa Was a Rolling Stone?," *Soul*, October 16, 1978, 13.

177 "Mick Jagger Settles Coast Paternity Suit," *Variety*, January 31, 1979, 84. The details of the agreement were not disclosed at the time, but according to Rolling Stones historian Mark Paytress, Jagger was "ordered to pay $1,500 per week towards the upkeep of his daughter." Mark Paytress, *The Rolling Stones: Off the Record* (London: Omnibus Press, 2003), 290. The *Washington Post* reported that the amount was $1,500 a month. In her autobiography, Hunt does not specify the amount of child support she received from Jagger, but says, "It was enough to keep Karis in school at the time," Hunt, *Real Life*, 204. Hunt was represented by Marvin Mitchelson, the lawyer who also handled Bianca Jagger's divorce proceedings, which began in February of 1979, as well as a number of high-profile celebrity divorce and palimony cases. Jura Koncius, "Personalities," *Washington Post*, February 6, 1979, B2.

178 Sandford, *Mick Jagger: Primitive Cool*, 167.

179 Hunt, *Undefeated*, 56.

180 "Marsha Hunt: I'm Glad Mick Didn't Help Raise Our Girl," *Daily Mail Online*, September 27, 2008, accessed June 4, 2013, http://www.dailymail.co.uk/femail/article -1062630/Marsha-Hunt-Im-glad-Mick-didnt-help-raise-girl.html.

181 Hunt, *Undefeated*, 67.

182 Marsha Hunt titles include the novels *Free* (New York: Plume, 1992), *Like Venus Fading* (London: Flamingo, 1999), and *The Punching Man: A Novel in Two Parts* (Dublin: Hag's Head, 2008); the family history *Repossessing Ernestine: A Grand-daughter Uncovers the Secret History of Her Family* (New York: HarperCollins, 1996); and the memoirs *Real Life* and *Undefeated*.

183 Hunt, *Real Life*, 130; Matilda Battersby, "Mick Jagger's Love Letters Reveal 'Secret History' of the Rolling Stone," *Independent*, November 12, 2012, accessed November 14, 2012, http://www.independent.co.uk/arts-entertainment/music/news/mick-jaggers -love-letters-to-marsha-hunt-reveal-secret-history-of-the-rolling-stone-8306604.html.

184 Auctioned by Sotheby's, the letters sold for 187,250 British pounds on December 12, 2012, accessed April 19, 2019, http://www.sothebys.com/en/auctions/ecatalogue/2012 /english-literature-history-l12408/lot.146.esthl.html.

185 Hunt, *Real Life*, 127.

186 "Claudia Lennear, Phew" [press release], n.d., Claudia Lennear clipping file, New York Public Library for the Performing Arts.

187 For background on Lennear, see Katherine Orloff, *Rock 'n' Roll Woman* (Los Angeles: Nash Publishing, 1974), and Christian John Wikane, "Keeping Great Company: An Interview with Claudia Lennear," *Popmatters*, June 19, 2013, accessed July 9, 2013, http://www.popmatters.com/PM/feature/172563-performer-spotlight-the-women-of -20-feet-from-stardom-claudia-lennea/.

188 Ben Fong-Torres, "Claudia in the Afternoon: A Transistor Sister's Blues," *Rolling Stone*, April 12, 1973, 16.

189 Orloff, *Rock 'n' Roll Woman*, 80.

190 Claudia Lennear quoted in Fong-Torres, "Claudia in the Afternoon," 16.

191 Orloff, *Rock 'n' Roll Woman*, 80.

192 Orloff, *Rock 'n' Roll Woman*, 80.

193 Wikane, "Keeping Great Company"; Fong-Torres, "Claudia in the Afternoon," 16; Orloff, *Rock 'n' Roll Woman*, 81.

194 Wikane, "Keeping Great Company."

195 Claudia Lennear, *Phew!* Warner Brothers BS2654, 1973, 33⅓ RPM.

196 Fong-Torres, "Claudia in the Afternoon," 16.

197 Claudia Lennear, "Sister Angela," *Phew!*

198 Toussaint's work on Lennear's album was something of a trial run of the soul-rock fusion for black women that he perfected a year later when he produced *Nightbirds* for the trio Labelle. I discuss this collaboration in chapter 6.

199 For one set of examples, see my discussion of the presence of African American women background vocalists on rock recordings in chapter 4.

200 "Claudia Lennear, Phew."

201 Claudia Lennear quoted in Orloff, *Rock 'n' Roll Woman*, 84.

202 Stephen Holden, "Records," [review of *Phew!*], *Rolling Stone*, March 1, 1973, 68.

203 Holden, "Records," 68.

204 Orloff, *Rock 'n' Roll Woman*, 81.

205 Claudia Lennear quoted in Orloff, *Rock 'n' Roll Woman*, 84.

206 Claudia Lennear quoted in Wikane, "Keeping Great Company," original emphasis.

207 "New Acts: Claudia Lennear," *Variety*, April 18, 1973, 69.

208 "New Acts: Claudia Lennear," 69.

209 Phil Gelormine, "Talent in Action: Rick Nelson, Claudia Lennear, Carnegie Hall, New York," *Billboard*, April 28, 1973, 21.

210 Sam Sutherland, "Talent in Action: Blue Oyster Cult, Claudia Lennear with Bump City," *Billboard*, August 18, 1973, 18.

211 "Claudia Lennear, Phew."

212 "Brown Sugar," *Playboy*, August 1974, 71.

213 "Brown Sugar," 71.

214 "Brown Sugar," 154.

215 "Brown Sugar," 154.

216 Wikane, "Keeping Great Company."

217 Wikane, "Keeping Great Company."

218 Morgan Neville, *Twenty Feet from Stardom* (Beverly Hills, CA: Anchor Bay Entertainment, 2014), DVD.

219 Wikane, "Keeping Great Company."

220 Marsha Hunt quoted in Partridge, "Dialogue," 37.

Chapter Six: The Revolutionary Sisterhood of Labelle

Epigraphs: Sarah Dash quoted in Jean Williams, "Trio Labelle: Patti, Sarah and Nona Favor Revolutionary Songs, Attire," *Billboard*, March 29, 1975, 33. Nona Hendryx quoted in Herschel Johnson, "From Bluebells [*sic*] to Labelle of New York," *Rolling Stone*, October 24, 1974, 17. Patti LaBelle quoted in Johnson, "From Bluebells [*sic*] to Labelle," 18, original emphasis.

1 Johnny Stewart, *In Concert: Labelle*, Take 2. BBC, March 8, 1975. British Film Institute collection, VHS.

2 The musicians were Bud Ellison, keyboards; Rev Batts, guitar; Hector Seda, bass; Jeffrey Shannon, drums; and Chuggy Carter, percussion.

3 Johnson, "From Bluebells [*sic*] to Labelle," 18.

4 Patti LaBelle with Laura B. Randolph, *Don't Block the Blessings: Revelations of a Lifetime* (New York: Riverhead Books, 1996), 88; Sarah Dash, telephone interview with author, March 4, 2014.

5 Sarah Dash, telephone interview with author, March 4, 2014.

6 Michael Watts, "Dinner and Cards with Reggie," *Melody Maker*, November 9, 1974, 23.

7 LaBelle with Randolph, *Don't Block the Blessings*, 173.

8 Henry Edwards, "The Street People Have Taken over the Discotheques!" *High Fidelity*, July 1975, 57.

9 LaBelle with Randolph, *Don't Block the Blessings*, 173.

10 Chris Charlesworth, "American Music Scene: Foxy Ladies," *Melody Maker*, November 22, 1975, 21.

11 Robert Smith, "Labelle: Lively Up Yourself!" *Crawdaddy*, January 1975, 56, original emphasis.

12 Michael Watts, "Caught in the Act: Labelle: Ladies of Pleasure," *Melody Maker*, March 15, 1975, 59.

13 "Labelle: Metamorphosis of the 'Sweethearts of the Apollo,'" *Encore American and Worldwide News*, January 6, 1975, n.p., Rolling Stone Records, Labelle, 1971–1982 file, Library and Archives, Rock and Roll Hall of Fame.

14 LaBelle with Randolph, *Don't Block the Blessings*, 150.

15 Alice Echols, *Hot Stuff: Disco and the Remaking of American Culture* (New York: W. W. Norton, 2010), 97.

16 For overviews of Labelle's career see Echols, *Hot Stuff*, 71–120; LaBelle with Randolph, *Don't Block the Blessings*; and Francesca T. Royster, "Labelle: Funk, Feminism, and the Politics of Flight and Fight," *American Studies* 52, no. 4 (2013): 77–98.

17 Sarah Dash, telephone interview with author, March 4, 2014.

18 LaBelle with Randolph, *Don't Block the Blessings*, 93.

19 LaBelle with Randolph, *Don't Block the Blessings*, 114.

20 LaBelle with Randolph, *Don't Block the Blessings*, 100–26.

21 LaBelle with Randolph, *Don't Block the Blessings*, 127.

22 Robin Katz, "Wear Something Silver," *Sounds*, February 15, 1975, 14.

23 LaBelle with Randolph, *Don't Block the Blessings*, 148.

24 LaBelle with Randolph, *Don't Block the Blessings*, 148.

25 Katz, "Wear Something Silver," 14.

26 Sarah Dash, telephone interview with author, March 4, 2014.

27 LaBelle with Randolph, *Don't Block the Blessings*, 148.

28 Art Harris, "Oh, Baby, It's So Good, It's Labelle," *Rolling Stone*, July 3, 1975, 46.

29 LaBelle with Randolph, *Don't Block the Blessings*, 154.

30 LaBelle with Randolph, *Don't Block the Blessings*, 150–51.

31 Sarah Dash, telephone interview with author, June 3, 2014.

32 Sarah Dash, telephone interview with author, March 4, 2014.

33 Williams, "Trio Labelle," *Billboard*, March 29, 1975, 33.

34 Patti LaBelle quoted in Johnson, "From Bluebells [*sic*] to Labelle," 17.

35 Nona Hendryx quoted in Loraine Alterman, "Rock and Roll Women," *Melody Maker*, October 14, 1972, 51.

36 LaBelle with Randolph, *Don't Block the Blessings*, 152.

37 Alterman, "Rock and Roll Women," 51.

38 Sarah Dash, telephone interview with author, March 4, 2014.

39 David Nathan, *The Soulful Divas* (New York: Billboard Books, 1999), 231. For a discussion of *Gonna Take a Miracle*, see Mark Anthony Neal, "Bellbottoms, Bluebelles, and the Funky-Ass White Girl," in *Songs in the Key of Black Life: A Rhythm and Blues Nation* (New York: Routledge), 79–99. Labelle's close professional collaboration with a white woman, Vicki Wickham, was also notable although her identity as an English woman might have offset some of the tension that emerged between black American and white American women during this period. For a discussion of racialized gender dynamics in political organizations, see Kimberly Springer, *Living for the Revolution: Black Feminist Organizations, 1968–1980* (Durham, NC: Duke University Press, 2005).

40 Steve Lake, "Labelle-Wow!" *Melody Maker*, March 1, 1975, 23.

41 Echols, *Hot Stuff*, 101. For more on black feminism and black nationalist views of feminism, see Springer, *Living for the Revolution*.

42 Smith, "Lively Up Yourself," 56.

43 Frank Rose, *Chameleon* [album review], *Rolling Stone*, October 7, 1976, 70.

44 Mark Vining, "*Pressure Cookin'*" [album review], *Rolling Stone*, November 8, 1973, 75.

45 Jon Landau, "*Nightbirds* by Labelle" [album review], *Rolling Stone*, May 22, 1975, 64.

46 Clayton Riley, "Pop: Labelle Has the Sound and the Power," *New York Times,* February 17, 1974, 35.

47 Nona Hendryx quoted in "Metamorphosis," n.p.

48 Labelle, "Sunday's News," *Something Silver,* Warner Archives 9 46359-2, 1997, CD.

49 Labelle, "What Can I Do for You," *Nightbirds.* Audio Fidelity AFZ5 196, 2015, CD. Originally released in 1974.

50 Nona Hendryx quoted in Watts, "Dinner and Cards with Reggie," 23.

51 Nona Hendryx quoted in Herschel Johnson, "From Bluebells [*sic*] to Labelle," 17.

52 Patti LaBelle quoted in Harris, "Oh, Baby, It's So Good," 45.

53 Ian Doye, "Talent in Action: The Who, Labelle," *Billboard,* August 14, 1971, 18; Russell Gersten, "*Moonshadow*" [by Labelle, album review] *Rolling Stone,* October 12, 1972, 70.

54 Lake, "Labelle-Wow," 23.

55 Vince Aletti, "Records" [review of *Labelle*], *Rolling Stone,* October 14, 1971, 52.

56 Alterman, "Rock and Roll Women," 51.

57 Edwards, "The Street People," 57.

58 Tsuyoko Sako and Timothy White, "For Whom Labelle Tolls: Glitter-Weary Chameleons Moving On," *Crawdaddy,* August 1976, 18.

59 Chris Charlesworth, "Caught in the Act: Labelle: Glitter and Gospel," *Melody Maker,* November 15, 1975, 48.

60 Tom Vickers, "Climax Lacks at Glittering Labelle Premiere," *Rolling Stone,* November 6, 1975, 102.

61 "Making Waves: Labelle," *Melody Maker,* October 23, 1976, 34.

62 Robert Adels, "Labelle Lights Up the Met," *Record World,* October 19, 1974, n.p., Rolling Stone Records, Labelle, 1971–1982 file, Library and Archives, Rock and Roll Hall of Fame.

63 For perceptive discussions of gender and vocal production in rock, see Suzanne Cusick, "On Musical Performances of Gender and Sex," in *Audible Traces: Gender, Identity, and Music,* ed. Elaine Barkin and Lydia Hamessley (Zurich: Carciofoli Verlagshaus, 1999), 25–48; and Jacqueline Warwick, "Singing Style and White Masculinity," in *The Ashgate Research Companion to Popular Musicology,* ed. Derek B. Scott (Surrey, UK: Ashgate, 2009), 349–64.

64 Sarah Dash, telephone interview with author, March 4, 2014.

65 Aletti, "Records" [review of *Labelle*], 52.

66 Riley, "Labelle Has the Sound," 35.

67 Riley, "Labelle Has the Sound," 35.

68 Commenting on the high vocal range of Arlene Smith, lead singer of the Chantels, Jacqueline Warwick observes that in the 1950s, adult pop artists like Rosemary Clooney and Debbie Reynolds and their R&B counterpart Ruth Brown "sang most effectively in a low middle range and with the chest voice, not significantly higher than light baritone/tenor male singers like Bing Crosby or Frank Sinatra." The high-range vocals of Smith and Patti LaBelle were out of step with this practice. Jacqueline Warwick, *Girl Groups, Girl Culture: Popular Music and Identity in the 1960s* (New York: Routledge, 2007), 26–27, 39–40.

69 Smith, "Lively up Yourself," 55; Bonnie Marranca, "*Pressure Cookin'*" [album review], *Crawdaddy*, December 1973, 73.

70 Riley, "Labelle Has the Sound," 35, original emphasis.

71 "Making Waves," 34.

72 Georgia Christgau, "Labelle: Three Notes," *Village Voice*, November 28, 1977, 64; Landau, "*Nightbirds* by Labelle," 64.

73 I thank Guthrie Ramsey and Marti Newland for sharing their insights about Patti LaBelle's vocal style.

74 Aletti, "Records" [review of *Labelle*], 52.

75 James Wolcott, "Labelle: Louder, Funnier and Sexier," *Rolling Stone*, October 23, 1975, 65.

76 Gersten, "*Moonshadow*" [by Labelle, album review], 70.

77 Gersten, "*Moonshadow*" [by Labelle, album review], 70.

78 Gersten, "*Moonshadow*" [by Labelle, album review], 70.

79 Nona Hendryx quoted in David Milton, "Labelle Cookin'," *Melody Maker*, November 17, 1973, 52.

80 Nona Hendryx quoted in Milton, "Labelle Cookin'," 52, original ellipsis.

81 Watts, "Ladies of Pleasure," 59.

82 LaBelle with Randolph, *Don't Block the Blessings*, 150–51.

83 Williams, "Trio Labelle," 33.

84 Charlesworth, "American Music Scene," 21.

85 "Labelle Fax Sheet," n.d. [c. 1976], Labelle folder, Mo Ostin Collection, Library and Archives, Rock and Roll Hall of Fame.

86 Harris, "Oh, Baby, It's So Good," 46.

87 Sarah Dash, telephone interview with author, March 4, 2014.

88 Lake, "Labelle-Wow," 23.

89 LaBelle with Randolph, *Don't Block the Blessings*, 167–68.

90 For a discussion of gender performance in glam rock, see Philip Auslander, *Performing Glam Rock: Gender and Theatricality in Popular Music* (Ann Arbor: University of Michigan Press, 2006).

91 Gillian G. Gaar, *She's a Rebel: The History of Women in Rock and Roll*, 2nd ed. (New York: Seal Press, 2002), 164.

92 Gaar, *She's a Rebel*, 164.

93 Edwards, "The Street People," 57; Vickers, "Climax Lacks," 102; Robin Katz, "Magnetic Space Women Take Earth by Storm," *Sounds*, March 15, 1975, 14.

94 Loraine Alterman, "Labelle" [concert review], *Melody Maker*, June 9, 1973, 52.

95 Johnson, "From Bluebells [*sic*] to Labelle," 18.

96 Auslander, *Performing Glam Rock*, 13–14.

97 Katz, "Wear Something Silver," 14.

98 Vickers, "Climax Lacks," 102; Charlesworth, "Glitter and Gospel," 48.

99 Sarah Dash quoted in Williams, "Trio Labelle," 33.

100 Ken Emerson, "Why Can't America Love New York City's Pop Favorites?," *New York Times*, September 28, 1975, sec. 12, 1.

101 Echols, *Hot Stuff*, 102.

102 For example: "Nona is another extreme altogether, implying all manner of s/M weirdnesses: whips, chains . . . and as an AC/DC figurehead she acts the part far more convincingly than does Bowie." Lake, "Labelle-Wow," 23.

103 Harris, "Oh, Baby, It's So Good," 43.

104 I thank Judith Casselberry for sharing her insights on the significance of Labelle to black lesbians.

105 Nona Hendryx quoted in Harris, "Oh, Baby, It's So Good," 45; *In Concert: Labelle*.

106 Audre Lorde, "Uses of the Erotic: The Erotic as Power," in *Sister Outsider; Essays and Speeches* (Trumansburg, NY: Crossing Press, 1984), 53–59.

107 Sarah Dash quoted in Harris, "Oh, Baby, It's So Good," 42.

108 Emerson, "Why Can't America Love," 1.

109 Johnson, "From Bluebells [*sic*] to Labelle," 18.

110 Watts, "Dinner and Cards with Reggie," 23.

111 Harris, "Oh, Baby, It's So Good," 42.

112 Harris, "Oh, Baby, It's So Good," 45.

113 Sarah Dash, telephone interview with author, March 4, 2014.

114 Sarah Dash, telephone interview with author, March 4, 2014.

115 Sarah Dash quoted in Charlesworth, "American Music Scene," 21.

116 Patti LaBelle quoted in Edwards, "The Street People," 57.

117 Nathan, *Soulful Divas*, 232.

118 John Rockwell, "The Pop Life: Labelle at Met: Sequins, Regions and Acoustics," *New York Times*, October 11, 1974, 25.

119 Charlesworth, "Glitter and Gospel," 48.

120 Vickers, "Climax Lacks," 102.

121 Echols, *Hot Stuff*, 43–44.

122 Vining, "*Pressure Cookin'*" [album review], *Rolling Stone*, November 8, 1973, 75; Marranca, "*Pressure Cookin'*" [album review], *Crawdaddy*, December 1973, 73.

123 Emerson, "Why Can't America," 1; Johnson, "From Bluebells [*sic*] to Labelle," 18; Smith, "Lively Up Yourself," 56.

124 Smith, "Lively Up Yourself," 56; Patti LaBelle quoted in "Making Waves," 34.

125 Ray Townley, "A Marmalade Lady Rings Labelle," *Rolling Stone*, March 13, 1975, 16.

126 Smith, "Lively Up Yourself," 56, original emphasis.

127 Harris, "Oh, Baby, It's So Good," 44.

128 Patti LaBelle quoted in Townley, "A Marmalade Lady," 16.

129 Labelle, "Lady Marmalade," *Nightbirds*.

130 Nona Hendryx quoted in Townley, "A Marmalade Lady," 16.

131 This trajectory differed from traditional crossover in which a song by a black artist broke first on black radio and then got picked up by pop radio. Edwards, "The Street People," 57.

132 Landau, "*Nightbirds* by Labelle," 63.

133 Echols, *Hot Stuff*, 100.

134 Sarah Dash, telephone interview with author, March 4, 2014.

135 Echols, *Hot Stuff*, 96.

136 Patti LaBelle quoted in Harris, "Oh, Baby, It's So Good," 46, original emphasis and ellipsis.

137 Nona Hendryx quoted in Harris, "Oh, Baby, It's So Good," 46.

138 Nona Hendryx quoted in Harris, "Oh, Baby, It's So Good," 46.

139 Penny Valentine, ". . . How the West Was Won—Nearly," *Sounds*, April 26, 1975, 20.

140 Patti LaBelle quoted in Katz, "Magnetic Space Women," 14.

141 Tina Turner appeared on the magazine's cover alone on November 23, 1967, and November 1, 1969, and with Ike Turner on October 14, 1971; Diana Ross appeared on the February 1, 1973, cover, and the women of Sly and the Family Stone appeared on the March 19, 1970, cover as part of a band shot. Holly George-Warren, ed., *Rolling Stone: The Complete Covers, 1967–1997* (New York: Harry N. Abrams, 1998).

142 Cover, *Rolling Stone*, July 3, 1975.

143 Harris, "Oh, Baby, It's So Good," 42–43.

144 Vince Aletti, "Labelle," *Andy Warhol's Interview*, August 1973, 29, 43.

145 Patti LaBelle quoted in Harris, "Oh, Baby, It's So Good," 45.

146 Patti LaBelle quoted in Harris, "Oh, Baby, It's So Good," 42.

147 Sarah Dash quoted in Harris, "Oh, Baby, It's So Good," 42, original ellipsis.

148 Nona Hendryx quoted in Harris, "Oh, Baby, It's So Good," 42–43.

149 Nona Hendryx quoted in Harris, "Oh, Baby, It's So Good," 46.

150 For discussions of this aspect of African American women's blues, see Hazel Carby, "The Sexual Politics of Women's Blues," in *Cultures in Babylon: Black Britain and African America* (London: Verso, 1999), 7–21; Angela Davis, *Blues Legacies and Black Feminism: Gertrude "Ma" Rainey, Bessie Smith, and Billie Holiday* (New York: Pantheon, 1998); and Daphne Duval Harrison, *Black Pearls: Blues Queens of the 1920s* (New Brunswick, NJ: Rutgers University Press, 1988).

151 Royster, "Labelle: Funk, Feminism," 88.

152 Nathan, *Soulful Divas*, 232.

153 Smith, "Lively Up Yourself," 55–56.

154 Harris, "Oh, Baby, It's So Good," 46.

155 See Evelyn Brooks Higginbotham, *Righteous Discontent: The Women's Movement in the Black Baptist Church, 1880–1920* (Cambridge, MA: Harvard University Press, 1993), and Paula Giddings, *When and Where I Enter: The Impact of Black Women on Race and Sex in America* (New York: Morrow, 1984).

156 Charlesworth, "American Music Scene," 21, original ellipsis.

157 Royster, "Labelle: Funk, Feminism," 87. For a thoughtful discussion of the race, gender, and sexuality dynamics of disco, including an analysis of the anti-disco backlash that emerged during the late 1970s, see Echols, *Hot Stuff*.

158 Sarah Dash, telephone interview with author, March 4, 2014.

159 Sonnet Retman, "Between Rock and a Hard Place: Narrating Nona Hendryx's Inscrutable Career," *Women and Performance: A Journal of Feminist Theory* 16, no. 1 (2006): 107.

160 Vicki Wickham quoted in Harris, "Oh, Baby, It's So Good," 46.

161 Labelle tour schedules, November 1971, Labelle folder, Mo Ostin Collection, Library and Archives, Rock and Roll Hall of Fame.

162 Letter from Vicki Wickham to Mo Ostin, September 15, 1971, Labelle folder, Mo Ostin Collection, Library and Archives, Rock and Roll Hall of Fame.

163 Letter from Vicki Wickham to Clyde Bakkemo, August 6, 1971, Labelle folder, Mo Ostin Collection, Library and Archives, Rock and Roll Hall of Fame.

164 Letter from Vicki Wickham to Mo Ostin, September 15, 1971.

165 Letter from Vicki Wickham to Mo Ostin, August 12, 1971.

166 Sarah Dash, telephone interview with author, March 4, 2014.

167 LaBelle with Randolph, *Don't Block the Blessings*, 154–55.

168 Sarah Dash quoted in Johnson, "From Bluebells [*sic*] to Labelle," 18. The women had also struggled with their record labels in their incarnation as a girl group. Nona Hendryx recalled that when they were at Atlantic Records in the 1960s, "We were going from producer to producer and there was never anybody who was constantly there to see what we were about and take us musically in any direction." Hendryx quoted in Alterman, "Rock and Roll Women," 51. Concurring with the substance of this critique, Atlantic Records producer and vice president Jerry Wexler admitted that he and his associates mishandled Patti LaBelle and her group when they were signed to the label: "We didn't find her the right material and, even worse, made the ghastly mistake of trying to turn her Bluebelles into the Supremes," he said years after the fact. Jerry Wexler and David Ritz, *Rhythm and the Blues: A Life in American Music* (New York: Alfred A. Knopf, 1993), 176.

169 Nona Hendryx quoted in Aletti, "Labelle," 29, 43, original emphasis.

170 Vince Aletti, "Labelle: Flowing over the Met," *Village Voice*, October 17, 1974, n.p., Rolling Stone Records, Labelle, 1971–1982 file, Library and Archives, Rock and Roll Hall of Fame.

171 Katz, "Wear Something Silver," 14.

172 Riley, "Labelle Has the Sound," 35.

173 "Labelle" [press release], Patti LaBelle folder, Michael Ochs Collection, Library and Archives, Rock and Roll Hall of Fame.

174 Patti LaBelle quoted in Williams, "Trio Labelle," 33.

175 Patti LaBelle quoted in Smith, "Lively Up Yourself," 56.

176 Sarah Dash, telephone interview with author, March 4, 2014.

177 Nona Hendryx quoted in Watts, "Dinner and Cards with Reggie," 23.

178 Feminist political scientist Melissa V. Harris-Perry observes that this image of black women as "unassailable, tough, and independent is nurtured within black communities" as a positive alternative to stereotypes that debased black women. "African American

women do not define themselves as Jezebels, Mammies, or Sapphires," she explains, "instead they call themselves strong and proudly drape the mantle of self-denying independence across their shoulders." However, she argues, this type is also limiting: "What begins as empowering self-definition can quickly become a prison. By adopting and reproducing the icon of the strong black woman, African American women help craft an expectation that they should be autonomously responsible and self-denying caregivers in their homes and communities." *Sister Citizen: Shame, Stereotypes, and Black Women in America* (New Haven, CT: Yale University Press, 2011), 184–85.

179 Riley, "Labelle Has the Sound," 35.
180 Riley, "Labelle Has the Sound," 35.
181 Smith, "Lively Up Yourself," 55–56, original emphasis.
182 Valentine, ". . . How the West Was Won," 20.
183 Aletti, "Flowing over the Met."
184 Sako and White, "For Whom Labelle Tolls," 18.
185 "Making Waves," 34.
186 Nona Hendryx quoted in Sako and White, "For Whom Labelle Tolls," 18.
187 Joel Whitburn, *Hot R&B Songs, 1942–2010*, 6th ed. (Menomonee Falls, WI: Record Research, 2010), 376.
188 Echols, *Hot Stuff*, 104.
189 Patti LaBelle quoted in "Patti La Belle" [MCA Records bio], n.d., Patti LaBelle folder, Michael Ochs Collection, Library and Archives, Rock and Roll Hall of Fame.
190 Joel Whitburn, *Joel Whitburn's Hot Dance/Disco, 1974–2003* (Menomonee Falls, WI: Record Research, 2004), 70.
191 Whitburn, *Joel Whitburn's Hot Dance/Disco*, 120.
192 Nathan, *Soulful Divas*, 241.
193 Nathan, *Soulful Divas*, 240.
194 "Patti La Belle" [MCA Records bio].
195 Echols, *Hot Stuff*, 106.
196 Combahee River Collective, "A Black Feminist Statement" in *This Bridge Called My Back: Writings by Radical Women of Color*, ed. Cherríe Moraga and Gloria Anzaldúa (New York: Kitchen Table, Women of Color Press, 1983), 212.
197 Patti LaBelle quoted in "Metamorphosis," original ellipsis.
198 Sarah Dash, telephone interview with author, March 4, 2014.

Chapter Seven: The Fearless Funk of Betty Davis

Epigraph: Betty Davis quoted in James Maycock, "She's Gotta Have It," *Mojo*, February 2005, 51.

1 Matt Sullivan, interview with author, July 6, 2007. This reclusiveness abated somewhat with her involvement in the 2017 documentary about her career, *Betty: They Say I'm Different* (Phil Cox, director).

2   For a discussion of these stereotypes and their impact, see Patricia Hill Collins, *Black Feminist Thought: Knowledge, Consciousness, and the Politics of Empowerment* (New York: Routledge, 1990), 67–90, and Melissa V. Harris-Perry, *Sister Citizen: Shame, Stereotypes, and Black Women in America* (New Haven, CT: Yale University Press, 2011).

3   For example, see Angela Y. Davis, *Women, Race, and Class* (New York: Vintage, 1983); Paula Giddings, "The Last Taboo," in *Words of Fire: An Anthology of African-American Feminist Thought*, ed. Beverly Guy-Sheftall (New York: New Press, 1995), 414–28; Evelynn Hammonds, "Black (W)holes and the Geometry of Black Female Sexuality," *Differences: A Journal of Feminist Cultural Studies* 6, no. 2–3 (1994): 126–45; Darlene Clark Hine, "Rape and the Inner Lives of Black Women in the Middle West: Preliminary Thoughts on the Culture of Dissemblance," *Signs* 14, no. 4 (1989): 912–20; and Tricia Rose, *Longing to Tell: Black Women Talk about Sexuality and Intimacy* (New York: Farrar, Straus and Giroux, 2003).

4   For overviews of Davis's career, see John Balloon, "Liberated Sister," *Waxpoetics*, April/May 2007, 112–24; Maycock, "She's Gotta Have It," 48–51; Oliver Wang, *Betty Davis* [Liner Notes], Light in the Attic Records LITA 026, 2007, CD. Originally released in 1973.

5   Betty Davis, telephone interview with author, June 27, 2007.

6   John Szwed, *So What: The Life of Miles Davis* (New York: Simon and Schuster, 2002), 268.

7   "Week's Best Pictures," *Jet*, May 9, 1968, 34–35.

8   Balloon, "Liberated Sister," 118.

9   Betty Davis, telephone interview with author, June 27, 2007.

10 The Chambers Brothers, *The Time Has Come*, Columbia/Legacy, 2000, CD. Originally released in 1966.

11 Balloon, "Liberated Sister," 114.

12 "Miles Davis Takes New Bride of Many Talents," *DownBeat*, November 14, 1968, 10, 13.

13 Paul Tingen, *Miles Beyond: The Electric Explorations of Miles Davis, 1967–1991* (New York: Billboard Books, 2001), 63.

14 Szwed, *So What*, 287.

15 Miles Davis with Quincy Troupe, *Miles: The Autobiography* (New York: Simon and Schuster, 1989), 290.

16 Szwed, *So What*, 271.

17 Szwed, *So What*, 294.

18 Balloon, "Liberated Sister," 114.

19 Maycock, "She's Gotta Have It," 48, 50.

20 Betty Davis quoted in Balloon, "Liberated Sister," 114.

21 Davis with Troupe, *Miles*, 304.

22 Betty Davis, telephone interview with author, June 27, 2007.

23 Maycock, "She's Gotta Have It," 50.

24 Betty Davis, telephone interview with author, June 27, 2007.

25 Balloon, "Liberated Sister," 118.

26 At the time I interviewed Davis, I was not aware of Marsha Hunt, the London-based African American model, actress, and singer. In retrospect, I wonder whether Davis crossed paths with Hunt or heard her music during her time in London. There are compelling sonic parallels between the two women, both of whom departed from the vocal and musical parameters within which African American women typically worked. Both Hunt and Davis had what onlookers and the women themselves characterized as an "aggressive" performance style. I discuss Hunt's career in chapter 5.

27 Betty Davis, telephone interview with author, June 27, 2007.

28 Balloon, "Liberated Sister," 118.

29 Gregg Errico quoted in Maycock, "She's Gotta Have It," 50.

30 Betty Davis, telephone interview with author, June 27, 2007.

31 Geoff Brown, "Betty, First Lady of Funk," *Melody Maker*, September 27, 1975, 47.

32 Maycock, "She's Gotta Have It," 51.

33 Betty Davis, "Anti-Love Song," *Betty Davis*.

34 Betty Davis quoted in Vernon Gibbs, "Entertainers: Betty Davis: Singin' to the Max," *Essence*, July 1974, 30.

35 Betty Davis, telephone interview with author, June 27, 2007.

36 Betty Davis quoted in Brown, "Betty, First Lady of Funk," 47.

37 Vivien Goldman, "Blues for Betty Davis's Smile: The Betty Davis Lacuna," in *Rip It Up: The Black Experience in Rock 'n' Roll*, ed. Kandia Crazy Horse (New York: Palgrave Macmillan, 2004), 57.

38 Davis, "Game Is My Middle Name," *Betty Davis*.

39 I thank Tamar-kali Brown for sharing her insights on the arrangement of "Game Is My Middle Name." Email to author, July 21, 2010.

40 Guthrie P. Ramsey Jr., personal communication, September 30, 2008; Jeffrey Kallberg, *Chopin at the Boundaries: Sex, History, and Musical Genre* (Cambridge, MA: Harvard University Press, 1996), 6.

41 Betty Davis, telephone interview with author, June 27, 2007.

42 Betty Davis, "They Say I'm Different," *They Say I'm Different*, Light in the Attic Records LITA 027, 2007, CD. Originally released in 1974.

43 I have not been able to locate commentaries on Davis written by black women. A favorable article that appeared in *Essence*, a magazine for black women, was written by a man, as was nearly all of the coverage of her career. Gibbs, "Singin' to the Max," 30.

44 Les Ledbetter, "The Pop Life: Mood Isn't Candlelight in Betty Davis's Songs," *New York Times*, June 21, 1974, 28.

45 Max Jones, "Caught in the Act: Betty Davis," *Melody Maker*, October 25, 1975, 34.

46 Robert Ford Jr., "Talent in Action," *Billboard*, January 17, 1976, 40.

47 Matt Sullivan, telephone interview with author, July 6, 2007.

48 Sarah Dash, telephone interview with author, March 4, 2014.

49 This quote appeared in a full-page ad that ran in *Waxpoetics*, April 2007, 125.

50 Sherman Fleming, telephone interview with author, April 7, 2007.

51 Sherman Fleming, telephone interview with author, April 7, 2007.

52 Michael Hill, telephone interview with author, May 3, 2007.

53 Michael Hill, telephone interview with author, May 3, 2007.

54 Betty Davis quoted in Balloon, "Liberated Sister," 122.

55 Betty Davis quoted in Sue Richards and Bob Weinstein, "Betty Davis: Bawdy Bombshell," *High Society*, October 1976, 93.

56 I thank the students who attended my seminar, "The Construction and Performance of Race and Gender in Music" at the Summer 2015 Schomburg-Mellon Humanities Institute on African-American and African Diasporan Studies, for pointing out this connection.

57 Tricia Rose, "Two Inches or a Yard: Silencing Black Women's Sexual Expression," in *Talking Visions: Multicultural Feminism in a Transnational Age*, ed. Ella Shohat (Cambridge, MA: MIT Press, 1998), 318.

58 Brown, "Betty, First Lady of Funk," 47.

59 For discussions of the politics of respectability and racial uplift, see Kevin K. Gaines, *Uplifting the Race: Black Leadership, Politics, and Culture in the Twentieth Century* (Chapel Hill: University of North Carolina Press, 1996), and Evelyn Brooks Higginbotham, *Righteous Discontent: The Women's Movement in the Black Baptist Church, 1880–1920* (Cambridge, MA: Harvard University Press, 1993).

60 Balloon, "Liberated Sister," 122.

61 Betty Davis quoted in Richards and Weinstein, "Bawdy Bombshell," 93.

62 Mark Anthony Neal, *What the Music Said: Black Popular Music and Black Public Culture* (New York: Routledge, 1999), 73.

63 Betty Davis, "Dedicated to the Press," *Nasty Gal*, Light in the Attic Records LITA 046, 2009, CD. Originally released in 1975.

64 Goldman, "Blues for Betty," 57–58.

65 For an overview and assessment of this dilemma, see Harris-Perry, *Sister Citizen*.

66 Gloria Jones, telephone interview with author, April 20, 2012.

67 Gregg Errico quoted in Balloon, "Liberated Sister," 124.

68 Rickey Vincent, *Funk: The Music, the People, and the Rhythm of the One* (New York: St. Martin's Griffin, 1996), 119.

69 Goldman, "Blues for Betty," 55.

70 Richards and Weinstein, "Bawdy Bombshell," 94.

71 I thank Mark Anthony Neal for sharing this observation. The song "Let's Get It On" was number one on the *Billboard* R&B chart for six weeks and number one on the Top 40 chart for two weeks. For chart positions, see Joel Whitburn, *The Billboard Book of Top 40 Hits*, 9th ed. (New York: Billboard Books, 2010), 262, and Joel Whitburn, *Top Pop Albums*, 7th ed. (Menomonee Falls, WI: Record Research, 2010), 305.

72 Joel Whitburn, *The Billboard Book of Top 40 R&B and Hip Hop Hits* (New York: Billboard Books, 2006), 277.

73 Chaka Khan with Tonya Bolden, *Chaka! through the Fire* (New York: Rodale, 2003), 144. For an insightful discussion of Khan's proto-feminist music, see Alice Echols, *Hot Stuff: Disco and the Remaking of American Culture* (New York: W. W. Norton, 2010), 87–95.

74 Whitburn, *The Billboard Book of Top 40 Hits*, 368; Whitburn, *The Billboard Book of Top 40 R&B and Hip Hop Hits*, 376.

75 Balloon, "Liberated Sister," 124.

76 For example, see Hazel Carby, "The Sexual Politics of Black Women's Blues," in *Cultures in Babylon: Black Britain and African America* (London: Verso, 1999), 7–21; Angela Y. Davis, *Blues Legacies and Black Feminism: Gertrude "Ma" Rainey, Bessie Smith, and Billie Holiday* (New York: Pantheon, 1998); Daphne Duval Harrison, *Black Pearls: Blues Queens of the 1920s* (New Brunswick, NJ: Rutgers University Press, 1990); Gwendolyn Pough, *Check It While I Wreck It: Black Womanhood, Hip-Hop Culture, and the Public Sphere* (Lebanon, NH: Northeastern University Press, 2004); and Rose, "Two Inches," 315–24.

77 Betty Davis quoted in Richards and Weinstein, "Bawdy Bombshell," 93.

78 Rose, "Two Inches," 320.

79 Rose, "Two Inches," 320.

80 Vernon Gibbs, "Soul, Man," *Crawdaddy*, September 1975, 16.

81 Gibbs, "Soul, Man," 16.

82 The show he describes was probably part of the run Michael Hill saw and discussed with me, although not necessarily the same performance. Gibbs, "Soul, Man," 16, original emphasis.

83 Rose, "Two Inches," 320.

84 Nona Hendryx quoted in Goldman, "Blues for Betty," 57.

85 Nona Hendryx quoted in Tsuyoko Sako and Timothy White, "For Whom Labelle Tolls: Glitter-Weary Chameleons Moving On," *Crawdaddy*, August 1976, 20.

86 Nikki A. Greene, "The Feminist Funk Power of Betty Davis and Renee Stout," *American Studies* 52, no. 4 (2013): 57–76; Cheryl L. Keyes, "'She Was Too Black for Rock and Too Hard for Soul': (Re)discovering the Musical Career of Betty Mabry Davis," *American Studies* 52, no. 4 (2013): 35–55.

87 I thank Michael Hill for this observation. Email to author, May 8, 2007.

88 Rick James quoted in Balloon, "Liberated Sister," 122.

89 Tamar-kali Brown, email to author, June 7, 2007.

90 Black Women Rock, "About," accessed July 20, 2016, https://blackwomenrock.com/our-mission/.

91 Betty Davis quoted in Brown, "Betty, First Lady of Funk," 47.

92 For example, Davis is mentioned briefly in Vincent, *Funk*, 192, and receives no entry or index listing in Dave Thompson, *Funk* (San Francisco: Backbeat Books, 2001), or in David Nathan, *The Soulful Divas* (New York: Billboard Books, 1999).

93 Goldman, "Blues for Betty," 53–58. For feminist histories of women and rock, see Gillian Gaar, *She's a Rebel: The History of Women in Rock and Roll*, 2nd ed. (Seattle: Seal Press, 1992); Gerri Hirshey, *We Gotta Get Out of This Place: The True, Tough Story of Women in Rock* (New York: Atlantic Monthly Press, 2001); Lucy O'Brien, *She Bop: The Definitive History of Women in Rock, Pop and Soul* (New York: Penguin, 1995); and Barbara O'Dair, ed., *Trouble Girls: The Rolling Stone Book of Women in Rock* (New York: Random House, 1997).

94 Betty Davis quoted in Maycock, "She's Gotta Have It," 51.

95 Goldman, "Blues for Betty," 56.

Chapter Eight: Tina Turner's Turn to Rock

Epigraph: Tina Turner quoted in Brant Mewborn, "Tina Turner: Raunchy, Rollin' and Back in the Rock of It," *Rolling Stone*, July 9, 1981, 48.

1 For overview discussions of Turner's career, see Gillian G. Gaar, *She's a Rebel: The History of Women in Rock and Roll*, 2nd ed. (New York: Seal Press, 1992), 81–83, 286–88; Lucy O'Brien, *She Bop: The Definitive History of Women in Rock, Pop and Soul* (New York: Penguin, 1995), 122–26; and Christian Wright, "Tina Turner," in *Trouble Girls: The Rolling Stone Book of Women in Rock*, ed. Barbara O'Dair (New York: Random House, 1997), 167–69.

2 "Ike and Tina Turner," *Rolling Stone*, November 23, 1967, 2.

3 During his days as an R&B sideman in the early 1960s, Hendrix played with the Ike and Tina Turner Revue. What did he learn from Tina Turner about stage presence? For discussions of the sexualization of Hendrix's image, see Charles Shaar Murray, *Crosstown Traffic: Jimi Hendrix and the Rock 'n' Roll Revolution* (New York: St. Martin's, 1989); and Steve Waksman, "Black Sound, Black Body: Jimi Hendrix, the Electric Guitar, and the Meanings of Blackness," in *Instruments of Desire: The Electric Guitar and the Shaping of Musical Experience* (Cambridge, MA: Harvard University Press, 1999), 167–206.

4 Susan Fast, "Bold Soul Trickster: The 60s Tina Signifies," in *She's So Fine: Reflections on Whiteness, Femininity, Adolescence and Class in 1960s Music*, ed. Laurie Stras (Burlington, VT: Ashgate, 2010), 233.

5 bell hooks, *Black Looks: Race and Representation* (Boston: South End Press, 1992), 67.

6 hooks, *Black Looks*, 69.

7 Madison Moore, "Tina Theory: Notes on Fierceness," *Journal of Popular Music Studies* 24, no. 1 (2012), 72.

8 Moore, "Tina Theory," 72.

9 Francesca T. Royster, "Nice and Rough: The Promise of Privacy in Tina Turner's 'What's Love Got to Do with It' and *I, Tina*," *Performance Research* 12, no. 3 (2007): 104.

10 Turner's memoir, coauthored with *Rolling Stone* writer Kurt Loder, comprises interviews with the Turners and others in their circle. Tina Turner with Kurt Loder, *I, Tina* (New York: William Morrow, 1986).

11 Ike Turner with Nigel Cawthorne, *Takin' Back My Name: The Confessions of Ike Turner* (London: Virgin Books, 1999).

12 I am referring to the 1973 single, "Nutbush City Limits."

13 Turner with Loder, *I, Tina*, 12.

14 Turner with Loder, *I, Tina*, 18.

15 Turner with Loder, *I, Tina*, 36.

16 Ben Fong-Torres, "The World's Greatest Heartbreaker," *Rolling Stone*, October 16, 1971, 40; Gerri Hirshey, *We Gotta Get Out of This Place: The True, Tough Story of Women in Rock* (New York: Atlantic Monthly Press, 2001), 140.

17 Turner with Loder, *I, Tina*, 44.

18 Turner with Cawthorne, *Takin' Back My Name*, 51.

19 Tina Turner quoted in Ken Grevatt, "Ike and Tina—and the Spirit of St. Louis," *Melody Maker*, July 9, 1966, 8.

20 Turner with Cawthorne, *Takin' Back My Name*, 72.

21 Turner with Cawthorne, *Takin' Back My Name*, 72.

22 Grevatt, "Ike and Tina," 8.

23 Turner with Loder, *I, Tina*, 75; Turner with Cawthorne, *Takin' Back My Name*, 35.

24 Turner with Cawthorne, *Takin' Back My Name*, 75.

25 Tina Turner quoted in Nancy Collins, "The *Rolling Stone* Interview: Tina Turner," *Rolling Stone*, October 23, 1986, 52.

26 These women are among the background vocalists I discuss in chapter 4.

27 Turner with Loder, *I, Tina*, 188.

28 Turner with Loder, *I, Tina*, 188.

29 Turner with Cawthorne, *Takin' Back My Name*, 74.

30 Tina Turner quoted in Salli Stevenson, "Tina Turner: 'Ike Only Loved Stallions,'" *Crawdaddy*, October 1972, 47.

31 Tina Turner quoted in Fong-Torres, "World's Greatest," 40.

32 Fast, "Bold Soul Trickster," 216.

33 Ike and Tina Turner, "A Fool in Love," *Tina Turner: The Collected Recordings Sixties to Nineties*. Capitol Records CDP 7243 8 29724 2 6, 1994, CD.

34 Turner with Cawthorne, *Takin' Back My Name*, 74.

35 Turner with Loder, *I, Tina*, 66.

36 Joel Whitburn, *Hot R&B Songs, 1942–2010*, 6th ed. (Menomonee Falls, WI: Record Research, 2010), 674.

37 Philip Norman, *Symphony for the Devil: The Rolling Stones Story* (New York: Simon and Schuster, 1984), 47.

38 Daphne A. Brooks, "The Write to Rock: Racial Mythologies, Feminist Theory, and the Pleasures of Rock Music Criticism," *Women and Music: A Journal of Gender and Culture* 12 (2008), 55.

39 Mick Brown, *Tearing Down the Wall of Sound: The Rise and Fall of Phil Spector* (New York: Knopf, 2007), 200.

40 Spector paid Ike for the privilege of working with Tina; in return, Ike agreed to stay away from the sessions. The song is credited to Ike and Tina Turner, but only Tina is on the record. *Rolling Stone* reported that the deal cost Spector $20,000. Fong-Torres, "World's Greatest," 37.

41 Brown, *Tearing Down the Wall of Sound*, 202.

42 Ike and Tina Turner, "River Deep, Mountain High," *Tina Turner: The Collected Recording*.

43 Brown, *Tearing Down the Wall of Sound*, 203.

44 Turner with Loder, *I, Tina*, 106.

45 The chart failure of the costly single precipitated Spector's three-year retreat from record producing. He reemerged to work with the Checkmates on their cover of "Proud Mary" in 1969 and to piece together the Beatles' swansong, *Let It Be* (1970). From there he produced solo work by John Lennon and George Harrison in the early 1970s and an album by the wall of sound-loving New York punks the Ramones in 1980. With the exception of a single he produced for his then-wife Ronnie Bennett in 1971, Spector did not work with black women after "River Deep." Brown, *Tearing Down the Wall of Sound*, 203.

46 Brown, *Tearing Down the Wall of Sound*, 203.

47 Brown, *Tearing Down the Wall of Sound*, 204.

48 Brown, *Tearing Down the Wall of Sound*, 202.

49 Turner with Cawthorne, *Takin' Back My Name*, 114.

50 Turner with Loder, *I, Tina*, 110.

51 Turner with Loder, *I, Tina*, 110.

52 Neil Warwick, Jon Kutner, and Tony Brown, *The Complete Book of the British Charts: Singles and Albums* (London: Omnibus Press, 2004), 1127.

53 James Karnbach and Carol Bernson, *It's Only Rock 'n' Roll: The Ultimate Guide to the Rolling Stones* (New York: Facts on File, 1997), 125.

54 Alan Walsh, "Wow! Pandemonium! The Stones Roll Out Again—and It's the Wildest Tour Ever to Hit Britain," *Melody Maker*, October 1, 1966, 8–9.

55 Turner with Loder, *I, Tina*, 115–16.

56 This is most clear in Humble Pie's work with the Blackberries, led by former Ikette Venetta Fields during the 1970s. See my discussion of background vocalists in chapter 4. Ray Charles and his black female backing vocalists the Raelettes also made a lasting impression on British artists.

57 Mark Bego, *Tina Turner: Break Every Rule* (Lanham, MD: Taylor Trade Publishing, 2005), 103.

58 Fast, "Bold Soul Trickster," original emphasis.

59 Turner with Loder, *I, Tina*, 139.

60 Turner with Loder, *I, Tina*, 139, original emphasis.

61 Chart positions in Joel Whitburn, *The Billboard Book of Top 40 Hits*, 9th ed. (New York: Billboard Books, 2010), 56, 557.

62 Chart positions in Whitburn, *The Billboard Book of Top 40 Hits*, 159, 374.

63 Liner notes, *Tina Turner: The Collected Recordings*. For a discussion of the Turners' covers of R&B songs during the 1960s, see Fast, "Bold Soul Trickster," 203–34.

64 Tina Turner quoted in Fong-Torres, "World's Greatest," 38.

65 Ike and Tina Turner, "Come Together," *Tina Turner: The Collected Recordings*; The Beatles, "Come Together," *Abbey Road*, EMI Records CDP 7 464462, 1987, CD. Originally released in 1969.

66 For example, "He got walrus gumboot" refers to one of Lennon's best-known songs, "I Am the Walrus," and "He got Ono sideboard" refers to his wife Yoko Ono. Peter Doggett, *Let It Be/Abbey Road: The Beatles* (New York: Schirmer Books, 1998), 99.

67 Fong-Torres, "World's Greatest," 38.

68 Turner with Loder, *I, Tina*, 139, original emphasis.

69 Ike and Tina Turner, "Honky Tonk Women," *Tina Turner: The Collected Recordings*; The Rolling Stones, "Honky Tonk Women," *Hot Rocks, 1964–1971*, ABKCO Records, 66672, 1986, CD. Originally released in 1971.

70 For a discussion of Tina Turner as offering a parodic performance of the "rock chick" figure, see Fast, "Bold Soul Trickster," 226–34, and O'Brien, *She Bop*, 123.

71 Ike and Tina Turner, "Whole Lotta Love," *Tina Turner: The Collected Recordings*; Led Zeppelin, "Whole Lotta Love," *Led Zeppelin II*, Atlantic Records 8236, 1994, CD. Originally released in 1969.

72 Ike and Tina Turner, "Proud Mary," *Tina Turner: The Collected Recordings*; Creedence Clearwater Revival, "Proud Mary," *Bayou Country*, Fantasy Records FCD-4513-2, 1989, CD. Originally released in 1969.

73 Turner with Loder, *I, Tina*, 139; Mark Ribowsky, *He's a Rebel: Phil Spector, Rock and Roll's Legendary Producer* (New York: Da Capo Press, 2006), 241.

74 Whitburn, *Hot R&B Songs*, 574, and Whitburn, *The Billboard Book of Top 40 Hits*, 671; accessed April 24, 2019, https://www.grammy.com/grammys/artists/ike-tina-turner.

75 In 1970, the Turners' "I Want to Take You Higher" went to number 34 on the Pop chart and number 25 on the R&B chart, while "Come Together" was number 21 on the R&B chart; the next year, "Proud Mary" was in the Top 5 of both charts. Whitburn, *The Billboard Book of Top 40 Hits*, 671; Whitburn, *Hot R&B Songs*, 674.

76 Wayne Robins, "Records: *Feel Good*: Ike and Tina Turner" [album review], *Crawdaddy*, November 1972, 80.

77 Dave Marsh, "*Acid Queen*: Tina Turner" [album review], *Rolling Stone*, November 6, 1975, 68.

78 Marsh, "*Acid Queen*," 68.

79 Marsh, "*Acid Queen*," 68.

80 I thank the Women Who Rock collective members Ana Gabriel Cano a.k.a. Black Mama, Michelle Habell-Pallán, Roshanak Khesti, Angelica Macklin, Jade Power-Sotomayor, Sonnet Retman, and Deborah Wong for the stimulating conversation and comments about Turner's covers that raised these points during our March 2018 session. For discussions of this dynamic of appropriation and suppression in rock,

see Jack Hamilton, *Just around Midnight: Rock and Roll and the Racial Imagination* (Cambridge, MA: Harvard University Press, 2016), and specifically in relation to Jimi Hendrix, Charles Shaar Murray, *Crosstown Traffic: Jimi Hendrix and the Rock 'n' Roll Revolution* (New York: St. Martin's, 1989). For a discussion of the ways the late sixties rock press policed the race and gender boundaries of rock, see Norma Coates, "Teenyboppers, Groupies, and Other Grotesques: Girls and Women and Rock Culture in the 1960s and Early 1970s," *Journal of Popular Music Studies* 15, no. 1 (June 2003): 65–93, and Bernard Gendron, *Between Montmartre and the Mudd Club: Popular Music and the Avant-Garde* (Chicago: University of Chicago Press, 2002).

81 Tina Turner, *Tina Turns the Country On.* United Artists Records UA-LA200-G, 1974, 33⅓ RPM.

82 Susan Fast sees this playful reversal as emblematic of the kind of parody and signifying that Tina Turner enacted during her time working with the Revue. Fast, "Bold Soul Trickster," 203–34.

83 Royster, "Nice and Rough," 104.

84 Fast, "Bold Soul Trickster," 218.

85 Turner with Loder, *I, Tina*, 216, original emphasis.

86 Tina Turner quoted in Fong-Torres, "World's Greatest," 37, original ellipsis.

87 Turner with Loder, *I, Tina*, 138.

88 Whitburn, *Hot R&B Songs*, 674, and Whitburn, *The Billboard Book of Top 40 Hits*, 671.

89 BMI is a performance rights organization that collects license fees on behalf of music composers, accessed July 5, 2011, http://www.bmi.com.

90 Tina Turner quoted in Stevenson, "'Ike Only Loved Stallions,'" 46.

91 Stevenson, "'Ike Only Loved Stallions,'" 46.

92 According to Tina Turner's biographer, Ike did not pay her or give her a share of the duo's professional monies. Bego, *Break Every Rule*, 109.

93 Turner with Loder, *I, Tina*, 188.

94 M. Cordell Thompson, "Trouble Trails Tina Turner," *Jet*, April 15, 1976, 58.

95 Fong-Torres, "World's Greatest," 40, original emphasis.

96 Tina Turner quoted in Collins, "*Rolling Stone* Interview," 52.

97 Tina Turner quoted in Chris Cowey, *The Girl from Nutbush*, A Picture Music International Production, EMI Records, 1991, British Film Institute collection, VHS.

98 For discussion of this phase, see Turner with Loder, *I, Tina*, 175–218.

99 Tina Turner quoted in Paul Green, "With 'Let's Stay Together' Tina Turner Rocks Back into Top 40," *Billboard*, February 25, 1984, 41.

100 Jim Feldman, "Tina's Turn," *Village Voice*, October 7, 1981, 82.

101 Feldman, "Tina's Turn," 82.

102 John Gray, *Rod Stewart, The Visual Documentary* (London: Omnibus Press, 1992), 59; and Dora Loewenstein and Philip Dodd, eds., *According to the Rolling Stones* (San Francisco: Chronicle Books, 2003), 232.

103 Feldman, "Tina's Turn," 82.

104 Turner with Loder, *I, Tina*, 209.

105 "Let's Stay Together" reached number six in the United Kingdom, the US Top 30 pop and R&B charts, and was a number one Dance/Disco chart single in early 1984. Whitburn, *The Billboard Book of Top 40 Hits*, 671; Whitburn, *Hot R&B Songs*, 674; and Joel Whitburn, *Joel Whitburn's Hot Dance/Disco, 1974–2003* (Menomonee Falls, WI: Record Research, 2004), 265.

106 Turner with Loder, *I, Tina*, 216.

107 Roger Davies quoted in Turner with Loder, *I, Tina*, 215.

108 Tina Turner, *Private Dancer*. Capitol Records, 7243 8 55833 2 2, 1997, CD. Originally released in 1984.

109 Jim Feldman, "Tina Turner: *Private Dancer*" [album review], *Creem*, November 1984, 53.

110 Debby Miller, "*Private Dancer*: Tina Turner" [album review], *Rolling Stone*, July 5, 1984, 44.

111 Whitburn, *The Billboard Book of Top 40 Hits*, 671, www.grammys.com.

112 Marshall Arts Ltd., advertisement, *Billboard Advertising Supplement*, August 15, 1987, T-2. Bego, *Break Every Rule*, 193.

113 O'Brien, *She Bop*, 124.

114 Turner with Loder, *I, Tina*, 210–11.

115 I discuss Living Colour's career trajectory in *Right to Rock: The Black Rock Coalition and the Cultural Politics of Race* (Durham, NC: Duke University Press, 2004), 142–75.

116 The photo is included in the booklet accompanying *Tina Turner: The Collected Recordings*.

117 Tina Turner quoted in Christopher Connelly, "Random Notes: Tina Turner: Still Sexy," *Rolling Stone*, March 29, 1984, 46.

118 Tina Turner quoted in Cowey, *The Girl from Nutbush*.

119 Susan Fast traces instances in which Turner's distancing from blackness occurs in her autobiography through comments in which she makes unfavorable comparisons between black culture and white culture. Fast, "Bold Soul Trickster," 218–19.

120 Sonnet Retman, "Between Rock and a Hard Place: Narrating Nona Hendryx's Inscrutable Career," *Women and Performance: A Journal of Feminist Theory* 16, no. 1 (March 2006), 107–18.

121 Little Richard, "Introduction," Turner with Cawthorne, *Takin' Back My Name*, xii.

122 Little Richard, "Introduction," Turner with Cawthorne, *Takin' Back My Name*, xiii.

Epilogue

Epigraph: Big Mama Thornton quoted in Jack Jones, "Blues' Big Mama Thornton Dies," *Los Angeles Times*, July 28, 1984, part 3, 15.

1 Original emphasis.

2 "Flagg Grove School Moves to Delta Heritage Center," June 2, 2012, accessed July 11, 2016, www.westheritage.com/flagggrove.html.

3 Wall text at the Tina Turner Museum at Flagg Grove School, Brownsville, TN.

4 "Brownsville Aldermen Vote to Preserve Historic Flagg Grove School," April 10, 2012, accessed July 11, 2016, www.westheritage.com/flagggrove.html.

5 "Tina Turner Contributes to Flagg Grove School Project," January 31, 2014, accessed July 11, 2016, www.westheritage.com/flagggrove.html.

6 Susan Fast, "Bold Soul Trickster: The 60s Tina Signifies," in *She's So Fine: Reflections on Whiteness, Femininity, Adolescence and Class in 1960s Music*, ed. Laurie Stras (Burlington, VT: Ashgate, 2010), 208.

7 "Rocket '88," released in 1951, is credited to Jackie Brenston and His Delta Cats, but it was Ike Turner's band, the Kings of Rhythm, who played on the track; Brenston sang lead vocals. John Covach and Andrew Flory, *What's That Sound? An Introduction to Rock and Its History*, 4th ed. (New York: W. W. Norton, 2014); Reebee Garofalo, *Rockin' Out: Popular Music in the USA*, 5th ed. (Boston: Prentice Hall, 2011); Joseph G. Schloss, Larry Starr, and Christopher Waterman, *Rock: Music, Culture and Business* (New York: Oxford University Press, 2012).

8 "Ike and Tina Turner," *Rolling Stone*, November 23, 1967, 2; Anthony DeCurtis and James Henke with Holly George-Warren, eds., *The Rolling Stone Illustrated History of Rock and Roll* (New York: Random House, 1992), 178, 182, 477, 615.

9 Gail Buckland, *Who Shot Rock and Roll: A Photographic History, 1955 to the Present* (New York: Random House, 2009).

10 The following texts discuss Turner's career: Gillian G. Gaar, *She's a Rebel: The History of Women in Rock and Roll*, 2nd ed. (New York: Seal Press, 1992), 81–83, 286–88; Lucy O'Brien, *She Bop: The Definitive History of Women in Rock, Pop and Soul* (New York: Penguin, 1995), 122–26; Christian Wright, "Tina Turner," in *Trouble Girls: The Rolling Stone Book of Women in Rock*, ed. Barbara O'Dair (New York: Random House, 1997), 167–69.

11 O'Brien, *She Bop*, 126.

12 Pianist Jeannie Cheatham reports that Fields told her this story. *Meet Me with Your Black Drawers On: My Life in Music* (Austin: University of Texas Press, 2006), 310.

13 Carol McGraw, "Goodby Blues: Big Mama Thornton—Rich in Voice, Friends—Laid to Rest," *Los Angeles Times*, August 1, 1984, part 2, 1.

14 McGraw, "Goodby Blues," part 2, 2.

15 Jimmy Witherspoon quoted in McGraw, "Goodby Blues," part 2, 2.

16 Johnny Otis quoted in McGraw, "Goodby Blues," part 2, 1.

17 Joe Rhodes, "Alabama Shakes' Soul-Stirring, Shape-Shifting New Sound," *New York Times Magazine*, March 18, 2015, accessed July 27, 2016, http://www.nytimes.com/2015/03/22/magazine/alabama-shakess-soul-stirring-shape-shifting-new-sound.html.

18 McGraw, "Goodby Blues," part 2, 1.

19 I thank Daphne Brooks for suggesting that I consider the ways vocalists carry embodied archives of musical sound and performance practices. She develops this approach in *Liner Notes for the Revolution: The Intellectual Life of Black Feminist Sound* (Cambridge, MA: Harvard University Press, forthcoming).

20 David Marchese, "Breaking Out: Alabama Shakes," *Spin*, February 22, 2012, accessed July 27, 2016, http://www.spin.com/2012/02/breaking-out-alabama-shakes/.

21 Rhodes, "Alabama Shakes' Soul-Stirring, Shape-Shifting New Sound."

22 Simon Vozick-Levinson, "Alabama Shakes' Brittany Howard on Jamming with Prince, Her Secret Identity," *Rolling Stone*, December 1, 2015, accessed July 27, 2016, http://www.rollingstone.com/music/features/alabama-shakes-brittany-howard-on-jamming-with-prince-her-secret-identity-20151201.

23 Brittany Howard quoted in Vozick-Levinson, "Alabama Shakes' Brittany Howard."

24 Vozick-Levinson, "Alabama Shakes' Brittany Howard."

25 Brittany Howard quoted in Marchese, "Breaking Out."

26 Rhodes, "Alabama Shakes' Soul-Stirring, Shape-Shifting Sound."

27 Brittany Spanos, "How Beyoncé's *Lemonade* Reclaims Rock's Black Female Legacy," *Rolling Stone*, April 26, 2016, accessed March 24, 2018, http://www.rollingstone.com/music/news/how-beyonces-lemonade-reclaims-rocks-black-female-legacy-20160426. Chapman won the 1996 Grammy for Best Rock Song for her composition "Give Me One Reason."

28 Vozick-Levinson, "Alabama Shakes' Brittany Howard."

29 Rhodes, "Alabama Shakes' Soul-Stirring, Shape-Shifting New Sound."

30 Brittany Howard quoted in Vozick-Levinson, "Alabama Shakes' Brittany Howard."

BIBLIOGRAPHY

Books, Articles, and Archival Materials

Adels, Robert. "Labelle Lights Up the Met." *Record World*, October 19, 1974, n.p. Rolling Stone Records, Labelle, 1971–1982 file. Library and Archives, Rock and Roll Hall of Fame.

Adelt, Ulrich. "Germany Gets the Blues: Negotiations of 'Race' and Nation at the American Folk Blues Festival." *American Quarterly* 6, no. 4 (2008): 951–74.

Ake, David, Charles Hiroshi Garrett, and Daniel Goldmark, eds. *Jazz/Not Jazz: The Music and Its Boundaries*. Berkeley: University of California Press, 2012.

"Album, UK Tour Pie." *Sounds*, September 22, 1973, 1.

Aletti, Vince. "Labelle." *Andy Warhol's Interview*, August 1973, 29, 43.

Aletti, Vince. "Labelle: Flowing over the Met." *Village Voice*, October 17, 1974, n.p. Rolling Stone Records, Labelle, 1971–1982 file. Library and Archives, Rock and Roll Hall of Fame.

Aletti, Vince. Liner Notes, *Something Silver* (Warner Archives 9 46359-2, 1997), CD.

Aletti, Vince. "Records" [review of *Labelle*]. *Rolling Stone*, October 14, 1971, 52.

Allen, David. "David Bowie's 'Lady Grinning Soul' Claudia Lennear of Pomona Remembers Her Friend." *Daily Bulletin*, February 6, 2016. Accessed January 18, 2018. http://www.dailybulletin.com/2016/02/06/david-bowies-lady-grinning-soul-claudia -lennear-of-pomona-remembers-her-friend/.

Alterman, Loraine. "Labelle" [concert review]. *Melody Maker*, June 9, 1973, 52.

Alterman, Loraine. "Rock and Roll Women." *Melody Maker*, October 14, 1972, 51.

Atkins, Cholly, and Jacqui Malone. *Class Act: The Jazz Life of Choreographer Cholly Atkins*. New York: Columbia University Press, 2001.

Auslander, Philip. *Performing Glam Rock: Gender and Theatricality in Popular Music*. Ann Arbor: University of Michigan Press, 2006.

Baby It's You! [Broadway musical]. Promotional mailer. Author's collection.

Bacharach, Burt, with Robert Greenfield. *Anyone Who Had a Heart: My Life and Music*. New York: HarperCollins, 2013.

Balloon, John. "Liberated Sister." *Waxpoetics*, April/May 2007, 112–24.

Barkin, Elaine, and Lydia Hamessley, eds. *Audible Traces: Gender, Identity, and Music*. Zurich: Carciofoli Verlagshaus, 1999.

Battersby, Matilda. "Mick Jagger's Love Letters Reveal 'Secret History' of the Rolling Stone." *Independent*, November 12, 2012. Accessed November 14, 2012. http://www .independent.co.uk/arts-entertainment/music/news/mick-jaggers-love-letters-to -marsha-hunt-reveal-secret-history-of-the-rolling-stone-8306604. html.

Bayton, Mavis. *Frock Rock: Women Performing Popular Music*. New York: Oxford University Press, 1998.

"Beauty Bulletin: The Natural—Marsha Hunt." *Vogue* [US], January 1969, 134, 178.

Bego, Mark. *Tina Turner: Break Every Rule*. Lanham, MD: Taylor Trade Publishing, 2005.

Bennett, Graham. *Soft Machine: Out-Bloody-Rageous*. London: SAF Publishing, 2005.

Betrock, Alan. *Girl Groups: The Story of a Sound*. New York: Delilah Books, 1982.

Betts, Graham. *Complete UK Hit Singles, 1952–2004*. London: Collins, 2004.

The Biggest Show of Stars for '57 [concert program]. Jeff Gold Collection. Library and Archives, Rock and Roll Hall of Fame.

Bjorn, Lars, with Jim Gallert. *Before Motown: A History of Jazz in Detroit, 1920–1960*. Ann Arbor: University of Michigan Press, 2001.

Black, Johnny. *Jimi Hendrix: The Ultimate Experience*. New York: Thunder's Mouth Press, 1999.

Black, Pauline. *Black by Design: A 2-Tone Memoir*. London: Serpent's Tail, 2011.

Black Women Rock, "About." Accessed July 20, 2016. https://blackwomenrock.com/our -mission/.

Bourdieu, Pierre. *The Logic of Practice*. Translated by Richard Nice. Stanford, CA: Stanford University Press, 1990.

Bowers, Jane, and Judith Tick, eds. *Women Making Music: The Western Art Tradition, 1150–1920*. Urbana: University of Illinois Press, 1986.

Boyer, Horace Clarence. "Contemporary Gospel Music." *The Black Perspective in Music* 7, no. 1 (spring 1979): 5–58.

Brackett, David. *Categorizing Sound: Genre and Twentieth Century Popular Music*. Oakland: University of California Press, 2016.

Breihan, Tom. "Santogold Is Now Santigold." *Pitchfork*, February 11, 2009. https://pitchfork .com/news/34595-santogold-is-now-santigold/.

Brooks, Daphne A. *Jeff Buckley's Grace*. New York: Continuum Books, 2005.

Brooks, Daphne A. *Liner Notes for the Revolution: The Intellectual Life of Black Feminist Sound*. Cambridge, MA: Harvard University Press, forthcoming.

Brooks, Daphne A. "Nina Simone's Triple Play." *Callaloo* 34, no. 1 (2011): 176–97.

Brooks, Daphne A. "'This Voice Which Is Not One': Amy Winehouse Sings the Ballad of Sonic Blue(s)face Culture." *Women and Performance: A Journal of Feminist Theory* 20, no. 1 (2010): 37–60.

Brooks, Daphne A. "The Write to Rock: Racial Mythologies, Feminist Theory, and the Pleasures of Rock Music Criticism." *Women and Music: A Journal of Gender and Culture* 12 (2008): 54–62.

Brooks, Daphne A., and Gayle Wald. "Women Do Dylan: The Aesthetics and Politics of Dylan Covers." In *Highway 61 Revisited: Bob Dylan's Road from Minnesota to the*

World, edited by Colleen J. Sheehy and Thomas Swiss, 169–85. Minneapolis: University of Minnesota Press, 2009.

Brown, Geoff. "Betty, First Lady of Funk." *Melody Maker*, September 27, 1975, 47.

Brown, Geoff. "Bolan's Cosmic Giggler." *Melody Maker*, March 2, 1974, 17.

Brown, Jayna. *Babylon Girls: Black Women Performers and the Shaping of the Modern*. Durham, NC: Duke University Press, 2008.

Brown, Mick. *Tearing Down the Wall of Sound: The Rise and Fall of Phil Spector*. New York: Knopf, 2007.

Brown, Ruth, with Andrew Yule. *Miss Rhythm: The Autobiography of Ruth Brown, Rhythm and Blues Legend*. New York: Donald Fine Books, 1996.

"Brown Sugar." *Playboy*, August 1974, 70–72, 154.

"Brownsville Aldermen Vote to Preserve Historic Flagg Grove School," April 10, 2012. Accessed July 11, 2016. www.westheritage.com/flagggrove.html.

Buckland, Gail. *Who Shot Rock and Roll: A Photographic History, 1955 to the Present*. New York: Random House, 2009.

Burdon, Eric. *I Used to Be an Animal, but I'm All Right Now*. London: Faber and Faber, 1986.

Burdon, Eric, with J. Marshall Craig. *Don't Let Me Be Misunderstood*. New York: Thunder's Mouth Press, 2001.

Burks, John, Jerry Hopkins, and Paul Nelson. "The Groupies and Other Girls." *Rolling Stone*, February 15, 1969, 11–24.

Burnim, Mellonee V. "The Black Gospel Music Tradition: A Complex of Ideology, Aesthetic, and Behavior." In *More Than Dancing: Essays on Afro-American Music and Musicians*, edited by Irene V. Jackson, 147–67. Westport, CT: Greenwood Press, 1985.

Burns, Lori, and Mélisse Lafrance. *Disruptive Divas: Feminism, Identity and Popular Music*. New York: Routledge, 2002.

Carby, Hazel V. "The Sexual Politics of Black Women's Blues." In *Cultures in Babylon: Black Britain and African America*, 7–21. London: Verso, 1999.

Carpenter, Bill. "Big Mama Thornton: Two Hundred Pounds of Boogaloo." *Living Blues*, November/December 1992, 26–32.

Carr, Roy, and Charles Shaar Murray. *Bowie: An Illustrated Record*. New York: Avon Books, 1981.

Carson, Mina, Tisa Lewis, and Susan M. Shaw. *Girls Rock! Fifty Years of Women Making Music*. Lexington: University Press of Kentucky, 2004.

Cartwright, Garth. "High Tide: P. P. Arnold Interview." *Long Live Vinyl* no. 14. Accessed May 1, 2019. https://www.longlivevinyl.net/high-tide-arnold-interview/.

Charlesworth, Chris. "American Music Scene: Foxy Ladies." *Melody Maker*, November 22, 1975, 21.

Charlesworth, Chris. "Caught in the Act: Labelle: Glitter and Gospel." *Melody Maker*, November 15, 1975, 48.

Charlesworth, Chris. "Labelle" [concert review]. *Melody Maker*, May 24, 1975, 34.

Cheatham, Jeannie. *Meet Me with Your Black Drawers On: My Life in Music*. Austin: University of Texas Press, 2006.

Christgau, Georgia. "Labelle: Three Notes." *Village Voice*, November 28, 1977, 64.

Christgau, Robert. "Chuck Berry." In *The Rolling Stone Illustrated History of Rock and Roll*, edited by Anthony DeCurtis and James Henke with Holly George-Warren, 60–66. New York: Random House, 1992.

Christgau, Robert. "The Move into Rock." In *"What'd I Say": The Atlantic Story. 50 Years of Music*, edited by Ahmet Ertegun and Perry Richardson, 290–93. New York: Welcome Rain Publishers, 2001.

Citizens' Council of Greater New Orleans. Broadside [Help Save the Youth of America]. Citizens' Council Collection, Archives and Special Collections, University of Mississippi Libraries, University of Mississippi Digital Libraries, n.d. Accessed April 19, 2019. http://clio.lib.olemiss.edu/cdm/ref/collection/citizens/id/1631.

Clark, Dick, and Richard Robinson. *Rock, Roll, and Remember*. New York: Thomas Y. Crowell, 1976.

"Claudia Lennear: Phew" [press release]. n.d. Claudia Lennear clipping file. New York Public Library for the Performing Arts.

Clemente, John. *Girl Groups: Fabulous Females That Rocked the World*. Iola, WI: Krause Publications, 2000.

"Coast Girl Asks $10,000 for 'Dance with Henry.'" *Chicago Defender*, June 4, 1955, 19.

Coates, Norma. "Excitement Is Made, Not Born: Jack Good, Television, and Rock and Roll." *Journal of Popular Music Studies* 25, no. 3 (2013): 301–25.

Coates, Norma. "Teenyboppers, Groupies, and Other Grotesques: Girls and Women and Rock Culture in the 1960s and Early 1970s." *Journal of Popular Music Studies* 15, no. 1 (2003): 65–93.

Cohodas, Nadine. *Princesse Noire: The Tumultuous Reign of Nina Simone*. New York: Pantheon, 2010.

Coleman, Rick. *Blue Monday: Fats Domino and the Lost Dawn of Rock 'n' Roll*. Cambridge, MA: Da Capo Press, 2006.

Collins, Gail. *When Everything Changed: The Amazing Journey of American Women from 1960 to the Present*. New York: Little, Brown, 2009.

Collins, Lisa. *The Art of History: African American Women Artists Engage the Past*. New Brunswick, NJ: Rutgers University Press, 2002.

Collins, Nancy. "The *Rolling Stone* Interview: Tina Turner." *Rolling Stone*, October 23, 1986, 46–49, 52, 106, 108.

Collins, Patricia Hill. *Black Feminist Thought: Knowledge, Consciousness, and the Politics of Empowerment*. New York: Routledge, 1991.

Combahee River Collective. "A Black Feminist Statement." In *This Bridge Called My Back: Writings by Radical Women of Color*, edited by Cherríe Moraga and Gloria Anzaldúa, 210–18. New York: Kitchen Table, Women of Color Press, 1983.

Connelly, Christopher. "Random Notes: Tina Turner: Still Sexy." *Rolling Stone*, March 29, 1984, 46.

Connor, Anthony, and Robert Neff. *The Blues: In Images and Interviews*. New York: Cooper Square, 1999.

Cook, Susan C., and Judy S. Tsou, eds. *Cecilia Reclaimed: Feminist Perspectives on Gender and Music*. Urbana: University of Illinois Press, 1994.

Cotten, Lee. *Shake, Rattle, and Roll: The Golden Age of American Rock 'n' Roll*. Vol. 1. Ann Arbor, MI: Popular Culture Ink, 1989.

Cotten, Lee. *Reelin' and Rockin': The Golden Age of American Rock 'n' Roll, 1956–1959*. Vol. 2. Ann Arbor, MI: Popular Culture Ink, 1995.

Covach, John. "Why No Yes in the Rock Hall?" In *The Rock History Reader*. 2nd ed., edited by Theo Cateforis, 367–68. New York: Routledge, 2013.

Covach, John, and Andrew Flory. *What's That Sound? An Introduction to Rock and Its History*. 4th ed. New York: W. W. Norton, 2014.

Crazy Horse, Kandia. "Interview with Venetta Fields." In *Rip It Up: The Black Experience in Rock 'n' Roll*, edited by Kandia Crazy Horse, 59–70. New York: Palgrave, 2004.

Crenshaw, Kimberlé. "Mapping the Margins: Intersectionality, Identity Politics, and Violence against Women of Color." In *Critical Race Theory: The Key Writings That Formed the Movement*, edited by Kimberlé Crenshaw, Neil Gotanda, Gary Peller, and Kendall Thomas. New York: The New Press, 1995.

Cross, Charles R. *Room Full of Mirrors: A Biography of Jimi Hendrix*. New York: Hyperion, 2005.

Cusick, Suzanne G. *Francesca Caccini at the Medici Court: Music and the Circulation of Power*. Chicago: University of Chicago Press, 2009.

Cusick, Suzanne G. "On Musical Performances of Gender and Sex." In *Audible Traces: Gender, Identity, and Music*, edited by Elaine Barkin and Lydia Hamessley, 25–48. Zurich: Carciofoli Verlagshaus, 1999.

Cyrus, Cynthia J. "Selling an Image: Girl Groups of the 1960s." *Popular Music* 22, no. 2 (2003): 173–93.

Davis, Andy. Liner Notes, *Doris Troy* (EMI Apple Records, 2010) 5099990824326, CD.

Davis, Angela Y. *Blues Legacies and Black Feminism: Gertrude "Ma" Rainey, Bessie Smith, and Billie Holiday*. New York: Pantheon, 1998.

Davis, Angela Y. *Women, Race, and Class*. New York: Vintage, 1983.

Davis, Daphne. "The Cop of the Year." *Rags*, no. 1 (June 1970): 46.

Davis, Miles, with Quincy Troupe. *Miles: The Autobiography*. New York: Simon and Schuster, 1989.

Davis, Stephen. *Jim Morrison: Life, Death, Legend*. New York: Gotham Books, 2004.

Davis, Stephen. *Old Gods Almost Dead: The 40-Year Odyssey of the Rolling Stones*. New York: Broadway Books, 2001.

Dawes, Laina. *What Are You Doing Here? Black Women in Metal, Hardcore and Punk*. Brooklyn, NY: Bazillion Points Books, 2012.

Dawson, Jim, and Steve Propes. *What Was the First Rock 'n' Roll Record?* Boston: Faber and Faber, 1992.

DeCurtis, Anthony, and James Henke with Holly George-Warren, eds. *The Rolling Stone Illustrated History of Rock and Roll.* New York: Random House, 1992.

Deffaa, Chip. *Blue Rhythms: Six Lives in Rhythm and Blues.* Urbana: University of Illinois Press, 1996.

Des Barres, Pamela. *I'm with the Band: Confessions of a Groupie.* Chicago: Chicago Review Press, 2005.

Doggett, Peter. *Let It Be/Abbey Road: The Beatles.* New York: Schirmer Books, 1998.

Douglas, Susan J. *Where the Girls Are: Growing Up Female with the Mass Media.* New York: Tines Books, 1994.

"'DownBeat' Institutes Annual Awards in Rhythm, Blues Field." *DownBeat*, May 18, 1955, 5.

Doye, Ian. "Talent in Action: The Who, Labelle." *Billboard*, August 14, 1971, 18.

Dziemianowicz, Joe. "*Baby It's You* Sued by Members of the Shirelles: Singers Claim Musical Is Using Their Likeness." *New York Daily News*, April 27, 2011. Accessed July 22, 2016. http://www.nydailynews.com/entertainment/music-arts/baby-sued-members -shirelles-singers-claim-musical-likeness-article-1.113105.

Echols, Alice. *Hot Stuff: Disco and the Remaking of American Culture.* New York: W. W. Norton, 2010.

Echols, Alice. *Scars of Sweet Paradise: The Life and Times of Janis Joplin.* New York: Henry Holt, 1999.

Edwards, Henry. "The Street People Have Taken over the Discotheques!" *High Fidelity*, July 1975, 56–58.

Eidsheim, Nina Sun. "Marian Anderson and 'Sonic Blackness' in American Opera." *American Quarterly* 63, no. 3 (2011): 641–71.

Elliott, Martin. *The Rolling Stones: Complete Recording Sessions, 1963–1989.* London: Blandford, 1990.

Emerson, Ken. "Why Can't America Love New York City's Pop Favorites?" *New York Times*, September 28, 1975, sec. 12, 1.

Emery, Patrick. "First Lady of Soul, P. P. Arnold, Looks Forward to Renewing Our Acquaintance." *I-94 Bar*, April 21, 2018. Accessed May 1, 2019. http://www.i94bar.com /interviews/pp-arnold.

Erskine, Pete. "Road Report: Pie: As Tight as Rubber Hosiery." *Sounds*, November 3, 1973, 11.

Ertegun, Ahmet, and Perry Richardson, eds. *"What'd I Say": The Atlantic Story. 50 Years of Music.* New York: Welcome Rain Publishers, 2001.

Everett, Todd. "She Was Born on Christmas Day." *Rolling Stone*, June 25, 1970, 11.

Fabbri, Franco. "A Theory of Musical Genres: Two Applications." In *Popular Music: Critical Concepts in Media and Cultural Studies.* Vol. 3, edited by Simon Frith, 7–35. New York: Routledge, 2003.

Fast, Susan. "Bold Soul Trickster: The 60s Tina Signifies." In *She's So Fine: Reflections on Whiteness, Femininity, Adolescence and Class in 1960s Music*, edited by Laurie Stras, 203–34. Burlington, VT: Ashgate, 2010.

Fast, Susan. "Genre, Subjectivity and Back-up Signing in Rock Music." In *The Ashgate Research Companion to Popular Musicology*, edited by Derek B. Scott, 171–87. Surrey, UK: Ashgate, 2009.

Feldman, Jim. "Tina's Turn." *Village Voice*, October 7, 1981, 82.

Feldman, Jim. "Tina Turner: *Private Dancer*" [album review]. *Creem*, November 1984, 53–54.

Fellezs, Kevin. *Birds of Fire: Jazz, Rock, Funk, and the Creation of Fusion*. Durham, NC: Duke University Press, 2011.

Fiofori, Tam. "The Blues." *Melody Maker*, April 29, 1972, 44.

"Flagg Grove School Moves to Delta Heritage Center," June 2, 2012. Accessed July 11, 2016. www.westheritage.com/flagggrove.html.

Floyd, Samuel A., Jr. *The Power of Black Music: Interpreting Its History from Africa to the United States*. New York: Oxford University Press, 1997.

Fong-Torres, Ben. "Claudia in the Afternoon: A Transistor Sister's Blues." *Rolling Stone*, April 12, 1973, 16.

Fong-Torres, Ben. "The World's Greatest Heartbreaker: Tales of Ike and Tina Turner, God Knows How Many Ikettes, and the Closed Circuit TV." *Rolling Stone*, October 16, 1971, 36–40.

Ford, Robert, Jr. "Talent in Action." *Billboard*, January 17, 1976, 40.

Frith, Simon. *Performing Rites: On the Value of Popular Music*. Cambridge, MA: Harvard University Press, 1996.

Frith, Simon. "Towards an Aesthetic of Popular Music." *Music and Society: The Politics of Composition, Performance, and Reception*, edited by Richard Leppert and Susan McClary, 133–49. New York: Cambridge University Press, 1987.

Fudger, Marion. "Anything That's Been a Horror in Your Life Sounds Like a Funny Story When You Tell It." *Spare Rib*, August 1973, 6–9.

Gaar, Gillian G. *She's a Rebel: The History of Women in Rock and Roll*. 2nd ed. New York: Seal Press, 2002.

Gaines, Donna. "A Ballad of Codependency." In *Trouble Girls: The Rolling Stone Book of Women in Rock*, edited by Barbara O'Dair, 103–15. New York: Random House, 1997.

Gaines, Kevin K. *Uplifting the Race: Black Leadership, Politics, and Culture in the Twentieth Century*. Chapel Hill: University of North Carolina Press, 1996.

Gardner, Elysa. "Hall of Famer Returns to Spotlight." *New York Times*, August 26, 1995, F1. LaVern Baker clipping file. Rutgers University Institute of Jazz Studies.

Gardner, Eriq. "Warner Bros. Settles 'Baby It's You' Lawsuit." *Hollywood Reporter*, December 16, 2011. Accessed April 22, 2019. https://www.hollywoodreporter.com/thr-esq/shirelles-baby-its-you-lawsuit-274744.

Garofalo, Reebee. "Culture versus Commerce: The Marketing of Black Popular Music." *Public Culture* 7, no. 1 (1994): 275–87.

Garofalo, Reebee. *Rockin' Out: Popular Music in the USA*. 5th ed. Boston: Prentice Hall, 2011.

Gart, Galen, ed. *First Pressings: The History of Rhythm and Blues*. Vol. 5. Milford, NH: Big Nickel Publications, 1990.

Gart, Galen, and Roy C. Ames. *Duke/Peacock Records: An Illustrated History with Discography*. Milford, NH: Big Nickel Publications, 1990.

Garvey, Dennis. "LaVern Baker: The 'Tweedlee-Dee' Girl Is Back." *Goldmine*, July 12, 1991, 11–15, 19, 151.

Gary, Kays. "Elvis Defends Low-Down Style." In *The Rock History Reader*. 2nd ed., edited by Theo Cateforis, 15–16. New York: Routledge, 2013.

Gaunt, Kyra. *The Games Black Girls Play: Learning the Ropes from Double-Dutch to Hip-Hop*. New York: New York University Press, 2006.

Gelormine, Phil. "Talent in Action: Rick Nelson, Claudia Lennear, Carnegie Hall, New York." *Billboard*, April 28, 1973, 21.

Gendron, Bernard. *Between Montmartre and the Mudd Club: Popular Music and the Avant-Garde*. Chicago: University of Chicago Press, 2002.

Genovese, Eugene D. *Roll, Jordan, Roll: The World the Slaves Made*. New York: Vintage, 1976.

George-Warren, Holly, ed. *Rolling Stone: The Complete Covers, 1967–1997*. New York: Harry N. Abrams, 1998.

Gersten, Russell. "*Moonshadow*" [by Labelle, album review]. *Rolling Stone*, October 12, 1972, 70.

Gibbs, Vernon. "Entertainers: Betty Davis: Singin' to the Max." *Essence*, July 1974, 30.

Gibbs, Vernon. "Soul, Man." *Crawdaddy*, September 1975, 16.

Giddens, Anthony. *Central Problems in Social Theory: Action, Structure, and Contradiction in Social Analysis*. Berkeley: University of California Press, 1979.

Giddings, Paula. "The Last Taboo." In *Words of Fire: An Anthology of African-American Feminist Thought*, edited by Beverly Guy Sheftall, 414–28. New York: The New Press, 1995.

Giddings, Paula. *When and Where I Enter: The Impact of Black Women on Race and Sex in America*. New York: William Morrow, 1984.

Gilbert, Jerry. "Humble Pie Are Sitting Pretty." *Sounds*, May 19, 1973, 5.

Gillett, Charlie. *The Sound of the City: The Rise of Rock and Roll*. Revised and expanded edition. New York: Pantheon, 1983.

Gilroy, Paul. *"There Ain't No Black in the Union Jack": The Cultural Politics of Race and Nation*. Chicago: University of Chicago Press, 1991.

"Girl Says Mick Jagger Is Child's Father." *The Times* [London], June 20, 1973, 4, col. E.

Gleason, Ralph J. "Big Mama Sings the Blues She Likes." Liner Notes, *Big Mama Thornton and the Chicago Blues Band*. Arhoolie Records, F 1032, 1967, LP.

Goldman, Vivien. "Blues for Betty Davis's Smile: The Betty Davis Lacuna." In *Rip It Up: The Black Experience in Rock 'n' Roll*, edited by Kandia Crazy Horse, 53–58. New York: Palgrave Macmillan, 2004.

Goldrosen, John, and John Beecher. *Remembering Buddy: The Definitive Biography of Buddy Holly*. New York: Penguin, 1987.

Govenar, Alan. *The Early Years of Rhythm and Blues: Focus on Houston*. Houston: Rice University Press, 1990.

Gray, John. *Rod Stewart: The Visual Documentary*. London: Omnibus Press, 1992.

Gray, Michael. *The Bob Dylan Encyclopedia*. New York: Continuum Books, 2006.

Green, Paul. "With 'Let's Stay Together' Tina Turner Rocks Back into Top 40." *Billboard*, February 25, 1984, 41.

Greenberg, Roy. "Big Mama Thornton Follows the Light and Keeps on Going." *Aquarian*, February 25–March 4, 1981, 54–55.

Greene, Andy. "A History of Rock and Roll Hall of Fame No-Shows." *Rolling Stone*, April 12, 2012. Accessed March 24, 2014. http://www.rollingstone.com/music/news/a -history-of-rock-and-roll-hall-of-fame-no-shows-20120412.

Greene, Joshua M. *Here Comes the Sun: The Spiritual and Musical Journey of George Harrison*. Hoboken, NJ: John Wiley and Sons, 2006.

Greene, Nikki A. "The Feminist Funk Power of Betty Davis and Renee Stout." *American Studies* 52, no. 4 (2013): 57–76.

Greenwich, Ellie. "Foreword." In John Clemente, *Girl Groups: Fabulous Females That Rocked the World*, 5–6. Iola, WI: Krause Publications, 2000.

Greig, Charlotte. *Will You Still Love Me Tomorrow? Girl Groups from the 50s On*. London: Virago, 1989.

Grevatt, Ken. "Ike and Tina—and the Spirit of St. Louis." *Melody Maker*, July 9, 1966, 8.

Grier, Miles Parks. "The Only Black Man at the Party: Joni Mitchell Enters the Rock Canon." *Genders* 56 (fall 2012). https://www.colorado.edu/gendersarchive1998-2013 /archive/author/grier.

Griffin, Farah Jasmine. *If You Can't Be Free, Be a Mystery: In Search of Billie Holiday*. New York: The Free Press, 2001.

Griffin, Farah Jasmine. "When Malindy Sings: A Meditation on Black Women's Vocality." In *Uptown Conversation: The New Jazz Studies*, edited by Robert O'Meally, Brent Hayes Edwards, and Farah Jasmine Griffin, 102–18. New York: Columbia University Press, 2004.

Gulla, Bob. *Icons of R&B and Soul: An Encyclopedia of the Artists Who Revolutionized Rhythm*. Vol. 1. Westport, CT: Greenwood Press, 2008.

Guralnick, Peter. *Careless Love: The Unmaking of Elvis Presley*. Boston: Little, Brown, 1999.

Guralnick, Peter. *Dream Boogie: The Triumph of Sam Cooke*. New York: Little, Brown, 2005.

Guralnick, Peter. *Last Train to Memphis: The Rise of Elvis Presley*. Boston: Little, Brown, 1994.

Guy-Sheftall, Beverly, ed. *Words of Fire: An Anthology of African-American Feminist Thought*. New York: The New Press, 1995.

Habell-Pallán, Michelle. *Loca Motion: The Travels of Chicana and Latina Popular Culture*. New York: New York University Press, 2005.

Haig, Diana Reid. "An Interview with Florence Greenberg" [Liner Notes], *The Scepter Records Story*. Nashville, TN: Capricorn Records, 1992.

Haig, Diana Reid. "The Scepter Records Story" [Liner Notes], *The Scepter Records Story*. Nashville, TN: Capricorn Records, 1992.

Halberstam, Judith. "Queer Voices and Musical Genders." In *Oh Boy!: Masculinities and Popular Music*, edited by Freya Jarman-Ivens, 183–95. New York: Routledge, 2007.

Hamilton, Jack, *Just around Midnight: Rock and Roll and the Racial Imagination*. Cambridge, MA: Harvard University Press, 2016.

Hammonds, Evelynn. "Black (W)holes and the Geometry of Black Female Sexuality." *Differences: A Journal of Feminist Cultural Studies* 6, no. 2–3 (1994): 126–45.

Harris, Art. "Oh, Baby, It's So Good, It's Labelle." *Rolling Stone*, July 3, 1975, 42–46.

Harrison, Daphne Duval. *Black Pearls: Blues Queens of the 1920s*. New Brunswick, NJ: Rutgers University Press, 1990.

Harris-Perry, Melissa V. *Sister Citizen: Shame, Stereotypes, and Black Women in America*. New Haven, CT: Yale University Press, 2011.

Hayes, Eileen M. "New Perspectives in Studies of Black Women and Music." In *Black Women and Music: More Than the Blues*, edited by Eileen M. Hayes and Linda F. Williams, 1–20. Urbana: University of Illinois Press, 2007.

Hayes, Eileen M. *Songs in Black and Lavender: Race, Sexual Politics, and Women's Music*. Urbana: University of Illinois Press, 2010.

Hebdige, Dick. *Subculture: The Meaning of Style*. London: Routledge, 1979.

Hellier, Ruth. *Women Singers in Global Contexts: Music, Biography, Identity*. Urbana: University of Illinois Press, 2013.

Henderson, David. *'Scuse Me While I Kiss the Sky: Jimi Hendrix: Voodoo Child*. New York: Atria Books, 2008.

Hewitt, Paolo, and John Hellier. *Steve Marriott: All Too Beautiful*. London: Helter Skelter Publishing, 2004.

Higginbotham, Evelyn Brooks. *Righteous Discontent: The Women's Movement in the Black Baptist Church, 1880–1920*. Cambridge, MA: Harvard University Press, 1993.

Hill, Mike. "The Shirelles." *The Rock and Roll Hall of Fame Eleventh Annual Induction Dinner* [program], 1996. Library and Archives, Rock and Roll Hall of Fame.

Himes, Geoffrey. "Baker: Still Up with the Blues." *Washington Post*, January 19, 1996, n.p. LaVern Baker clipping file. Rutgers University Institute of Jazz Studies.

Hinckley, David. "The Kids in the Hall from Gladys Knight to David Bowie, Rock and Roll Museum Comes of Age with Lesser Stars Making the Honor Roll in '96." *New York Daily News*, January 17, 1996. Accessed March 24, 2014. http://www.nydailynews.com/archives/nydn-features/kids-hall-gladys-knight-david-bowie-rock-roll-museum-age-lesser-stars-making-honor-roll-96-article-1.715967#ixzz2zist0A17.

Hinckley, David. "Rock Hall's Identity Crisis Museum Seems to Be Avoiding Genre's More Commercial Acts." *New York Daily News*, October 5, 1995. Accessed March 24, 2014. http://www.nydailynews.com/archives/nydn-features/rock-hall-identity-crisis-museum-avoiding-genre-commercial-acts-article-1.692455#ixzz2ziuOust.

Hine, Darlene Clark. "Rape and the Inner Lives of Black Women in the Middle West: Preliminary Thoughts on the Culture of Dissemblance." *Signs* 14, no. 4 (1989): 912–20.

Hine, Darlene Clark, and Kathleen Thompson. *A Shining Thread of Hope: The History of Black Women in America.* New York: Broadway Books, 1998.

Hirshey, Gerri. *We Gotta Get Out of This Place: The True, Tough Story of Women in Rock.* New York: Atlantic Monthly Press, 2001.

Hisama, Ellie M. "Postcolonialism on the Make: The Music of John Mellencamp, David Bowie, and John Zorn." *Popular Music* 12, no. 2 (May 1993): 91–104.

Hisama, Ellie M. "Voice, Race, and Sexuality in the Music of Joan Armatrading." In *Audible Traces: Gender, Identity, and Music,* edited by Elaine Barkin and Lydia Hamessley, 115–32. Zurich: Carciofoli Verlagshaus, 1999.

Holden, Stephen. "Records" [review of *Phew!* by Claudia Lennear]. *Rolling Stone,* March 1, 1973, 68.

Holt, Fabian. *Genre in Popular Music.* Chicago: University of Chicago Press, 2007.

hooks, bell. *Ain't I a Woman: Black Women and Feminism.* Boston: South End Press, 1981.

hooks, bell. *Black Looks: Race and Representation.* Boston: South End Press, 1992.

Houston, Cissy, with Jonathan Singer. *How Sweet the Sound: My Life with God and Gospel.* New York: Doubleday, 1998.

"Humble Pie and Blackberries in Concert" [advertisements]. *Sounds,* October 20, 1973, 15, and October 27, 1973, 13.

Hunt, Marsha. *Like Venus Fading.* London: Flamingo, 1999.

Hunt, Marsha. *The Punching Man: A Novel in Two Parts.* Dublin: Hag's Head, 2008.

Hunt, Marsha. *Real Life.* London: Chatto and Windus, 1986.

Hunt, Marsha. *Repossessing Ernestine: A Granddaughter Uncovers the Secret History of Her Family.* New York: HarperCollins, 1996.

Hunt, Marsha. *Undefeated.* Vancouver, BC: Greystone Books, 2005.

Hunter, Sheryl. "R&B Legend Does More Than Endure." *Daily Hampshire Gazette,* January 19, 1996, 28. LaVern Baker clipping file. Rutgers University Institute of Jazz Studies.

Hurston, Zora Neale. "Characteristics of Negro Expression." In *The Sanctified Church,* 49–68. New York: Marlowe, 1981.

"Ike and Tina Turner." *Rolling Stone,* November 23, 1967, 2.

Isherwood, Charles. "Girl Group Tale Is Reharmonized." *New York Times,* April 27, 2011, C1.

Jackson, John A. *Big Beat Heat: Alan Freed and the Early Years of Rock and Roll.* New York: Schirmer Books, 1991.

Jackson, Travis A. "Interpreting Jazz." In *African American Music: An Introduction,* edited by Mellonee V. Burnim and Portia K. Maultsby, 167–83. New York: Routledge, 2006.

James, Etta, and David Ritz. *Rage to Survive.* New York: Da Capo Press, 1998.

Johnson, Herschel. "From Bluebells [*sic*] to Labelle of New York." *Rolling Stone,* October 24, 1974, 17.

Johnson, Joe "Ziggy." "Zig and Zag." *Chicago Defender*, January 12, 1957, 15.

Jones, Jack. "Blues' Big Mama Thornton Dies." *Los Angeles Times*, July 28, 1984, part 3, 15.

Jones, Jacqueline. *Labor of Love, Labor of Sorrow: Black Women, Work, and the Family from Slavery to the Present*. New York: Basic Books, 1985.

Jones, Kenneth. "*Baby It's You!* Producers Being Sued by Beverly Lee of the Shirelles, Dionne Warwick and Others." *Playbill*, April 27, 2011. Accessed July 22, 2016. http://www.playbill.com/article/baby-its-you-producers-being-sued-by-beverly-lee-of-the-shirelles-dionne-warwick-and-others-com-178629.

Jones, Kenneth. "Original 'Shirelle' Shirley Alston Reeves to Perform with *Baby It's You!* in Post-Show Concerts." *Playbill*, June 15, 2011. Accessed July 22, 2016. http://www.playbill.com/article/original-shirelle-shirley-alston-reeves-to-perform-with-baby-its-you-in-post-show-concerts-com-180135.

Jones, LeRoi (Amiri Baraka). *Blues People: Negro Music in White America*. New York: Perennial, 2002.

Jones, Quincy. *Q: The Autobiography of Quincy Jones*. New York: Harlem Moon, 2001.

Jones, Regina, as told to Leonard Pitts Jr. "Papa Was a Rolling Stone?" *Soul*, October 16, 1978, 12–13, 16.

Kallberg, Jeffrey. *Chopin at the Boundaries: Sex, History, and Musical Genre*. Cambridge, MA: Harvard University Press, 1996.

Karnbach, James, and Carol Bernson. *It's Only Rock 'n' Roll: The Ultimate Guide to the Rolling Stones*. New York: Facts on File, 1997.

Katz, Robin. "Magnetic Space Women Take Earth by Storm." *Sounds*, March 15, 1975, 14.

Katz, Robin. "Wear Something Silver." *Sounds,* February 15, 1975, 14.

Kernodle, Tammy L. Soul on Soul: The Life and Music of Mary Lou Williams. Boston: Northeastern University Press, 2004.

Keyes, Cheryl L. "'She Was Too Black for Rock and Too Hard for Soul': (Re)discovering the Musical Career of Betty Mabry Davis." *American Studies* 52, no. 4 (2013): 35–55.

Khan, Chaka, with Tonya Bolden. *Chaka! Through the Fire*. New York: Rodale, 2003.

Koncius, Jura. "Personalities." *Washington Post*, February 6, 1979, B2.

Koskoff, Ellen, ed. *Women and Music in Cross-Cultural Perspective*. New York: Greenwood Press, 1987.

Kot, Greg. *I'll Take You There: Mavis Staples, the Staple Singers, and the March Up Freedom's Highway*. New York: Scribner, 2014.

LaBelle, Patti, with Laura B. Randolph. *Don't Block the Blessings: Revelations of a Lifetime*. New York: Riverhead Books, 1996.

"Labelle" [press release]. Patti LaBelle folder, Michael Ochs Collection. Library and Archives, Rock and Roll Hall of Fame.

"Labelle Fax Sheet," n.d. [c. 1976]. Labelle folder, Mo Ostin Collection. Library and Archives, Rock and Roll Hall of Fame.

"Labelle: Metamorphosis of the 'Sweethearts of the Apollo.'" *Encore American and Worldwide News*, January 6, 1975, n.p. Rolling Stone Records, Labelle, 1971–1982 file. Library and Archives, Rock and Roll Hall of Fame.

Labelle tour schedules, November 1971. Labelle folder, Mo Ostin Collection. Library and Archives, Rock and Roll Hall of Fame.

Lake, Steve. "Labelle-Wow!" *Melody Maker*, March 1, 1975, 23.

Landau, Jon. "*Nightbirds* by Labelle" [album review]. *Rolling Stone*, May 22, 1975, 64.

LaVern Baker press material. LaVern Baker clipping file. Rutgers University Institute of Jazz Studies.

"LaVern Baker Seeks Bill to Halt Arrangements 'Thefts.'" *Billboard*, March 5, 1955, 13.

"LaVern Baker Smiles over Tune's Success While Defying 'Lifts.'" *Chicago Defender*, February 19, 1955, 6.

Ledbetter, Les. "The Pop Life: Mood Isn't Candlelight in Betty Davis's Songs." *New York Times*, June 21, 1974, 28.

Leiber, Jerry, and Mike Stoller, with David Ritz. *Hound Dog: The Leiber and Stoller Autobiography*. New York: Simon and Schuster, 2009.

Letter from Vicki Wickham to Clyde Bakkemo, August 6, 1971. Labelle folder, Mo Ostin Collection. Library and Archives, Rock and Roll Hall of Fame.

Letter from Vicki Wickham to Mo Ostin, September 15, 1971. Labelle folder, Mo Ostin Collection. Library and Archives, Rock and Roll Hall of Fame.

Lewis, George. "Experimental Music in Black and White: The AACM in New York, 1970–1985." In *Uptown Conversation: The New Jazz Studies*, edited by Robert O'Meally, Brent Hayes Edwards, and Farah Jasmine Griffin, 50–101. New York: Columbia University Press, 2004.

Lewisohn, Mark. *Tune In: The Beatles: All These Years, Vol. 1*. New York: Crown Archetype, 2013.

Lichfield, Patrick. *Lichfield in Retrospect*. London: Weidenfeld and Nicolson, 1988.

Lichfield, Patrick. *The Most Beautiful Women*. London: Elm Tree Books, 1981.

Liedo, Gerardo. "Rocks Off: Merry Clayton." Accessed April 29, 2019. http://www.rocksoff.org/merry.htm.

Lipsitz, George. *Midnight at the Barrelhouse: The Johnny Otis Story*. Minneapolis: University of Minnesota Press, 2010.

Loewenstein, Dora, and Philip Dodd, eds. *According to the Rolling Stones*. San Francisco: Chronicle Books, 2003.

Lorde, Audre. "Uses of the Erotic: The Erotic as Power." In *Sister Outsider: Essays and Speeches*, 53–59. Trumansburg, NY: Crossing Press, 1984.

Lott, Eric. *Love and Theft: Blackface Minstrelsy and the American Working Class*. New York: Oxford University Press, 1993.

Love, Darlene, with Rob Hoerburger. *My Name Is Love: The Darlene Love Story*. New York: William Morrow, 1998.

Mackie, Robin. "Marsha: Raising the Chat-Show from the Dead." *Sounds*, March 23, 1974, 7.

Mahon, Maureen. "African American Women and the Dynamics of Gender, Race, and Genre in Rock 'n' Roll." In *Issues in African American Music: Power, Gender, Race Representation*, edited by Mellonee V. Burnim and Portia K. Maultsby, 287–305. New York: Routledge, 2016.

Mahon, Maureen. "The 'Daughters of Soul' Tour and the Politics and Possibilities of Black Music." In *Ethnographies of Neoliberalism*, edited by Carol J. Greenhouse, 207–20. Philadelphia: University of Pennsylvania Press, 2010.

Mahon, Maureen. "Listening for Willie Mae 'Big Mama' Thornton's Voice: The Sound of Race and Gender Transgressions in Rock and Roll." *Women and Music: A Journal of Gender and Culture* 15 (2011): 1–17.

Mahon, Maureen. "Musicality, Sexuality, and Power: A Practice Theory Approach." Colloquy on Music and Sexuality. *Journal of the American Musicological Society* 66, no. 3 (fall 2013): 844–48.

Mahon, Maureen. *Right to Rock: The Black Rock Coalition and the Cultural Politics of Race.* Durham, NC: Duke University Press, 2004.

Mahon, Maureen. "They Say She's Different: Race, Gender, Genre and the Liberated Black Femininity of Betty Davis." *Journal of Popular Music Studies* 23, no. 2 (2011): 146–65.

Mahon, Maureen "Women in African American Music: Rock." In *African American Music: An Introduction*, edited by Mellonee V. Burnim and Portia K. Maultsby, 558–77. New York: Routledge, 2006.

"Making Waves: Labelle." *Melody Maker*, October 23, 1976, 34.

Marchese, David. "Breaking Out: Alabama Shakes." *Spin*, February 22, 2012. Accessed July 27, 2016. http://www.spin.com/2012/02/breaking-out-alabama-shakes/.

Marcus, Greil. "Girl Groups." In *The Rolling Stone Illustrated History of Rock and Roll*, edited by Anthony DeCurtis and James Henke with Holly George-Warren, 189–91. New York: Random House, 1992.

Marranca, Bonnie. "*Pressure Cookin'*" [album review]. *Crawdaddy*, December 1973, 73.

Marsh, Dave. "*Acid Queen:* Tina Turner" [album review]. *Rolling Stone*, November 6, 1975, 68.

"Marsha Hunt: I'm Glad Mick Didn't Help Raise Our Girl." *Daily Mail Online*, September 27, 2008. Accessed June 4, 2013. http://www.dailymail.co.uk/femail/article-1062630/Marsha-Hunt-Im-glad-Mick-didnt-help-raise-girl.html.

"Marsha Hunt and the Luxury of Going as Far as You Dare." *Vogue* [UK], December 1968, 112–15.

Marshall Arts Ltd., advertisement, *Billboard Advertising Supplement*, August 15, 1987, T-2.

Maultsby, Portia K. "Africanisms in African-American Music." In *Africanisms in American Culture*, edited by Joseph E. Holloway, 185–210. Bloomington: Indiana University Press, 1991.

Maycock, James. "She's Gotta Have It." *Mojo*, February 2005, 48–51.

Mazor, Barry. "A Soul Forgotten." *No Depression*, May–June 2003, 80–95.

McClary, Susan. *Conventional Wisdom: The Content of Music Form.* Berkeley: University of California Press, 2000.

McClary, Susan. *Feminine Endings: Music, Gender, and Sexuality.* Minneapolis: University of Minnesota Press, 1991.

McDermott, John, with Eddie Kramer. *Hendrix: Setting the Record Straight.* New York: Warner Books, 1992.

McDonnell, Evelyn, and Ann Powers, eds. *Rock She Wrote: Women Write about Rock, Pop, and Rap*. New York: Delta, 1995.

McGraw, Carol. "Goodby Blues: Big Mama Thornton—Rich in Voice, Friends—Laid to Rest." *Los Angeles Times*, August 1, 1984, part 2, 1–2.

McMullen, Tracy. "'Bring It on Home': Robert Plant, Janis Joplin, and the Myth of Origin." *Journal of Popular Music Studies* 26, no. 2–3 (2014): 368–96.

Mewborn, Brant. "Tina Turner: Raunchy, Rollin' and Back in the Rock of It." *Rolling Stone*, July 9, 1981, 48.

"Mick Jagger Settles Coast Paternity Suit." *Variety*, January 31, 1979, 84.

"Miles Davis Takes New Bride of Many Talents." *DownBeat*, November 14, 1968, 10, 13.

Miller, Debby. "*Private Dancer*: Tina Turner" [album review]. *Rolling Stone*, July 5, 1984, 44.

Miller, Karl Hagstrom. *Segregating Sound: Inventing Folk and Pop Music in the Age of Jim Crow*. Durham, NC: Duke University Press, 2010.

Mills, Peter. *Hymns to the Silence: Inside the Words and Music of Van Morrison*. New York: Continuum Books, 2010.

Molloy, Mamie. "Titles by the Dozen." *Rock 'n' Roll Jamboree*, fall 1956, 11. Michael Ochs Collection. Library and Archives, Rock and Roll Hall of Fame.

Monson, Ingrid. "The Problem with White Hipness: Race, Gender, and Cultural Conceptions in Jazz Historical Discourse." *Journal of the American Musicological Society* 48, no. 3 (1995): 396–422.

Moonoogian, George A. "The Puppydom of a Rock 'n' Roll Classic." *Whiskey, Women, and . . .* , June 1984, 4–10.

Moore, Madison. "Tina Theory: Notes on Fierceness." *Journal of Popular Music Studies* 24, no. 1 (2012): 71–86.

Morgenstern, Dan. "The Blues Comes to Ann Arbor." *DownBeat*, October 2, 1969, 14–15, 29.

Murray, Charles Shaar. *Crosstown Traffic: Jimi Hendrix and the Rock 'n' Roll Revolution*. New York: St. Martin's, 1989.

Nathan, David. Liner Notes, "The Sweet Inspirations." *Two Classic Albums* (Spy Records SPY 46004–2, 2002), CD.

Nathan, David. *The Soulful Divas*. New York: Billboard Books, 1999.

Neal, Mark Anthony. "Bellbottoms, Bluebelles, and the Funky-Ass White Girl." In *Songs in the Key of Black Life: A Rhythm and Blues Nation*, 79–99. New York: Routledge.

Neal, Mark Anthony. *What the Music Said: Black Popular Music and Black Public Culture*. New York: Routledge, 1999.

Negus, Keith. *Music Genres and Corporate Cultures*. London: Routledge, 1999.

Nero, Charles I. "Langston Hughes and the Black Female Gospel Voice in the American Musical." In *Black Women and Music: More Than the Blues*, edited by Eileen M. Hayes and Linda F. Williams, 72–89. Urbana: University of Illinois Press, 2007.

"New Acts: Claudia Lennear." *Variety*, April 18, 1973, 69.

Norman, Philip. *Mick Jagger*. New York: HarperCollins, 2012.

Norman, Philip. *Symphony for the Devil: The Rolling Stones Story*. New York: Simon and Schuster, 1984.

Nutt, Amy Ellis. "Passaic Dedicates Street to the Shirelles." *The Star Ledger*, September 21, 2008. Accessed March 24, 2014. https://www.nj.com/news/2008/09/passaic_dedicates _street_to_th.html.

O'Brien, Lucy. *She Bop: The Definitive History of Women in Rock, Pop, and Soul*. New York: Penguin, 1995.

O'Dair, Barbara, ed. *Trouble Girls: The Rolling Stone Book of Women in Rock*. New York: Random House, 1997.

O'Grady, Lorraine. "Olympia's Maid: Reclaiming Black Female Subjectivity." In *New Feminist Criticism: Art, Identity, Action*, edited by Joanna Frueh, Cassandra Langer, and Arlene Raven, 152–70. New York: Icon Editions, 1994.

Onkey, Lauren. *Blackness and Transatlantic Irish Identity: Celtic Soul Brothers*. New York: Routledge, 2010.

Onkey, Lauren. "A Response to 'Why No Yes in the Rock Hall.'" In *The Rock History Reader*, 2nd ed., edited by Theo Cateforis, 369–71. New York: Routledge, 2013.

Orloff, Katherine. *Rock 'n' Roll Woman*. Los Angeles: Nash Publishing, 1974.

Ortner, Sherry B. *Anthropology and Social Theory: Culture, Power, and the Acting Subject*. Durham, NC: Duke University Press, 2006.

Otis, Johnny. *Upside Your Head! Rhythm and Blues on Central Avenue*. Hanover, NH: Wesleyan University Press, 1993.

Partridge, Robert. "Dialogue: Melody Maker Special on Women in Rock." *Melody Maker*, November 10, 1973, 36.

"Patti LaBelle" [MCA Records bio]. n.d. Patti LaBelle folder, Michael Ochs Collection. Library and Archives, Rock and Roll Hall of Fame.

Paytress, Mark. *The Rolling Stones: Off the Record*. London: Omnibus Press, 2003.

Peterson, Richard A., and Bruce A. Beal. "Alternative Country: Origins, Music, Worldview, Fans, and Taste in Genre Formation." *Popular Music and Society* 25, no. 1–2 (2001): 233–49.

Plummer, Mark. "Doris Troy and the Gospel Truth." *Melody Maker*, December 18, 1971, 12.

Positif, François. "New York in Jazz Time, Part II." *Jazz Hot*, December 1960, 27.

Pough, Gwendolyn. *Check It While I Wreck It: Black Womanhood, Hip-Hop Culture, and the Public Sphere*. Lebanon, NH: Northeastern University Press, 2004.

Powers, Ann. "The Love You Make: Fans and Groupies." In *Trouble Girls: The Rolling Stone Book of Women in Rock*, edited by Barbara O'Dair, 181–89. New York: Random House, 1997.

Radano, Ronald. *Lying Up a Nation: Race and Black Music*. Chicago: University of Chicago Press, 2003.

Ramsey, Guthrie P., Jr. *The Amazing Bud Powell: Black Genius, Jazz History, and the Challenge of Bebop*. Berkeley: University of California Press, 2013.

Randall, Annie J. *Dusty, Queen of the Postmods*. New York: Oxford University Press, 2009.

Ray, Johnnie. "Famous 'Cry' Crooner Tells What Blues Taught Him." *Ebony*, March 1953, 48–56.

Retman, Sonnet. "Between Rock and a Hard Place: Narrating Nona Hendryx's Inscrutable Career." *Women and Performance: A Journal of Feminist Theory* 16, no. 1 (2006): 107–18.

Rhodes, Joe. "Alabama Shakes's Soul-Stirring, Shape-Shifting New Sound." *New York Times Magazine*, March 18, 2015. Accessed July 27, 2016. http://www.nytimes.com/2015/03/22/magazine/alabama-shakess-soul-stirring-shape-shifting-new-sound.html.

Rhodes, Lisa L. *Electric Ladyland: Women and Rock Culture*. Philadelphia: University of Pennsylvania Press, 2005.

Ribowsky, Mark. *He's a Rebel: Phil Spector, Rock and Roll's Legendary Producer*. New York: Da Capo Press, 2006.

Richards, Keith, with James Fox, *Life*. New York: Little, Brown, 2010.

Richards, Lowell. "Blues Outclasses Rock at Sky River Festival." *DownBeat*, October 31, 1968, 11.

Richards, Sue, and Bob Weinstein, "Betty Davis: Bawdy Bombshell." *High Society*, October 1976, 56–58, 93.

Riley, Clayton. "Pop: Labelle Has the Sound and the Power." *New York Times*, February 17, 1974, 35.

Robins, Wayne. *A Brief History of Rock, Off the Record*. New York: Routledge, 2008.

Robins, Wayne. "Records: *Feel Good*: Ike and Tina Turner" [album review]. *Crawdaddy*, November 1972, 80.

Rock and Roll Hall of Fame. "Induction Process." Accessed March 24, 2014. http://www.rockhall.com/inductees/induction-process/.

Rockwell, John. "The Pop Life: Labelle at Met: Sequins, Regions and Acoustics." *New York Times*, October 11, 1974, 25.

Rose, Frank. "*Chameleon*" [review of album by Labelle]. *Rolling Stone*, October 7, 1976, 70.

Rose, Tricia. *Longing to Tell: Black Women Talk about Sexuality and Intimacy*. New York: Farrar, Straus and Giroux, 2003.

Rose, Tricia. "Two Inches or a Yard: Silencing Black Women's Sexual Expression." In *Talking Visions: Multicultural Feminism in a Transnational Age*, edited by Ella Shohat, 315–24. Cambridge, MA: MIT Press, 1998.

Royster, Francesca T. "Labelle: Funk, Feminism, and the Politics of Flight and Fight." *American Studies* 52, no. 4 (2013): 77–98.

Royster, Francesca T. "Nice and Rough: The Promise of Privacy in Tina Turner's 'What's Love Got to Do with It' and *I, Tina*." *Performance Research* 12, no. 3 (2007): 103–13.

Royster, Francesca T. *Sounding Like a No-No: Queer Sounds and Eccentric Acts in the Post-Soul Era*. Ann Arbor: University of Michigan Press, 2013.

Sako, Tsuyoko, and Timothy White. "For Whom Labelle Tolls: Glitter-Weary Chameleons Moving On." *Crawdaddy*, August 1976, 18, 20.

Salem, James M. *The Late Great Johnny Ace and the Transition from R&B to Rock 'n' Roll*. Urbana: University of Illinois Press, 1999.

Sanchez, Tony. *Up and Down with the Rolling Stones*. New York: William Morrow, 1979.

Sandford, Christopher. *Mick Jagger: Primitive Cool*. New York: St. Martin's, 1993.

Sanjek, David. "Tell Me Something I Don't Already Know: The Harvard Report on Soul Music Revisited." In *Rhythm and Business: The Political Economy of Black Music*, edited by Norman Kelley, 59–76. New York: Akashic, 2002.

"Santogold Dubs 'Hip-Hop' Comparisons Racist." *Melody Maker*, May 19, 2008. Accessed May 17, 2019. https://www.nme.com/news/music/santogold-13-1324234.

Schloss, Joseph G., Larry Starr, and Christopher Waterman. *Rock: Music, Culture and Business*. New York: Oxford University Press, 2012.

Selvin, Joel. *Summer of Love: The Inside Story of LSD, Rock and Roll, Free Love and High Times in the Wild West*. New York: Dutton Books, 1994.

Shaw, Arnold. *Honkers and Shouters: The Golden Years of Rhythm and Blues*. New York: Collier Books, 1978.

Shaw, Arnold. *The World of Soul: Black America's Contribution to the Pop Music Scene*. New York: Cowles, 1970.

Sheff, David. *All We Are Saying: The Last Major Interview with John Lennon and Yoko Ono*. New York: St. Martin's, 2000.

"Shirelles Come Up with Another Hit in 'Lover.'" *Chicago Defender*, December 4, 1962, 17.

"The Shirelles 'Love Me' Disc on Hit Parade." *Chicago Defender*, January 21, 1961, 19.

"Shirelles Quartet Top Moneymakers in '61." *Chicago Defender*, January 27, 1962, 10.

Shirley, Jerry, with Tim Cohan. *Best Seat in the House: Drumming in the '70s with Marriott, Frampton, and Humble Pie*. Alma, MI: Rebeats, 2011.

Simon, Bill. "Rhythm and Blues Notes." *Billboard*, March 12, 1955, 24.

Simone, Michael. "An Interview with P. P. Arnold." Accessed July 17, 2013. http://www.rogerwaters.org/interviews-new/pparnoldint.html.

Slash, with Anthony Bozza. *Slash*. New York: Harper Entertainment, 2007.

Smith, Robert. "Labelle: Lively Up Yourself!" *Crawdaddy*, January 1975, 54–56.

Solie, Ruth A., ed. *Musicology and Difference: Gender and Sexuality in Music Scholarship*. Berkeley: University of California Press, 1993.

Soocher, Stan. *They Fought the Law: Rock Music Goes to Court*. New York: Schirmer Books, 1999.

Sounes, Howard. *Down the Highway: The Life of Bob Dylan*. New York: Grove Press, 2001.

Spanos, Brittany. "How Beyoncé's *Lemonade* Reclaims Rock's Black Female Legacy." *Rolling Stone*, April 26, 2016. Accessed March 24, 2018. http://www.rollingstone.com/music/news/how-beyonces-lemonade-reclaims-rocks-black-female-legacy-20160426.

Spector, Ronnie, and Vince Waldron. *Be My Baby: How I Survived Mascara, Mini Skirts, and Madness, or My Life as a Fabulous Ronette*. New York: Harmony, 1990.

Spitz, Marc. *Jagger: Rebel, Rock Star, Rambler, Rogue*. New York: Gotham Books, 2011.

Spizer, Bruce. *The Beatles Are Coming! The Birth of Beatlemania in America* (New Orleans: 498 Productions, 2003).

Spörke, Michael. *Big Mama Thornton: The Life and Music*. Jefferson City, NC: MacFarland, 2014.

Springer, Kimberly. *Living for the Revolution: Black Feminist Organizations, 1968–1980*. Durham, NC: Duke University Press, 2005.

Stark, Steven D. *Meet the Beatles: A Cultural History of the Band That Shook Youth, Gender, and the World*. New York: HarperCollins, 2005.

Steptoe, Tyina. "Big Mama Thornton, Little Richard, and the Queer Roots of Rock 'n' Roll." *American Quarterly* 70, no. 1 (March 2018): 55–77.

Stevenson, Salli. "Tina Turner: 'Ike Only Loved Stallions.'" *Crawdaddy*, October 1972, 45–50.

Stras, Laurie. "Introduction: She's So Fine, or Why Girl Singers (Still) Matter." In *She's So Fine: Reflections on Whiteness, Femininity, Adolescence and Class in 1960s Music*, edited by Laurie Stras, 1–29. Burlington, VT: Ashgate, 2010.

Stras, Laurie. "White Face, Black Voice: Race, Gender, and Region in the Music of the Boswell Sisters." *Journal of the Society for American Music* 1, no. 2 (2007): 207–55.

Sugarman, Jane C. *Engendering Song: Singing and Subjectivity at Prespa Albanian Weddings*. Chicago: University of Chicago Press, 1997.

Sutherland, Sam. "Talent in Action: Blue Oyster Cult, Claudia Lennear with Bump City." *Billboard*, August 18, 1973, 18.

Szwed, John. *So What: The Life of Miles Davis*. New York: Simon and Schuster, 2002.

Tate, Greg, ed. *Everything but the Burden: What White People Are Taking from Black Culture*. New York: Broadway Books, 2003.

Telford, Ray. "Sweet Stuff in Pie." *Sounds*, March 31, 1973, 15.

Thompson, Dave. *Funk*. San Francisco: Backbeat Books, 2001.

Thompson, M. Cordell. "Trouble Trails Tina Turner." *Jet*, April 15, 1976, 58.

"Tina Turner Contributes to Flagg Grove School Project," January 31, 2014. www .westheritage.com/flagggrove.html.

Tingen, Paul. *Miles Beyond: The Electric Explorations of Miles Davis, 1967–1991*. New York: Billboard Books, 2001.

Topping, Ray. Liner Notes, *Big Mama Thornton: The Original Hound Dog*. Ace Records, CDCHD 940, 1990, CD.

Tortelli, Joseph A. "Shirelles' Lead Shirley Reeves Recalls Girl Group Sound: A Pop Music Trend Cut Short by British Invasion." *Record Collector Monthly*, December 1987–January 1988, 1, 4–5.

Townley, Ray. "A Marmalade Lady Rings Labelle." *Rolling Stone*, March 13, 1975, 16.

Travers, Ben. "Watch: '20 Feet from Stardom' Singer Darlene Love Steps to the Front on 'Late Show with David Letterman.'" *IndieWire*, June 14, 2013. Accessed May 16, 2019. https://www.indiewire.com/2013/06/watch-20-feet-from-stardom-singer-darlene -love-steps-to-the-front-on-late-show-with-david-letterman-37587/.

Trynka, Paul. *David Bowie: Starman*. New York: Little, Brown, 2011.

Trynka, Paul. Liner Notes, *The Astronettes Sessions*. Black Barbarella Records. BBarbcd001, 2009, CD.

Tucker, Sherrie. *Swing Shift: "All-Girl" Bands of the 1940s*. Durham, NC: Duke University Press, 2000.

Turner, Ike, with Nigel Cawthorne. *Takin' Back My Name: The Confessions of Ike Turner*. London: Virgin Books, 1999.

Turner, Tina, with Kurt Loder. *I, Tina*. New York: William Morrow, 1986.

"Tweedle Dee Girl." *Ebony*, April 1956, 106–10. LaVern Baker clipping file. Rutgers University Institute of Jazz Studies.

"Tweedlee-Dee Girl: Youthful Singer Is Credited with 'Putting Rhythm in the Blues,'" *Our World*, June 1955, n.p. LaVern Baker clipping file. Rutgers University Institute of Jazz Studies.

Twelker, Uli. "Madeline Bell: Interview-May 2012." May 2012. Accessed July 12, 2013. http://www.madelinebell.com/Interview.html.

Valentine, Penny. "Album Reviews" [review of *Woman Child* by Marsha Hunt]. *Sounds*, December 11, 1971, 23.

Valentine, Penny. ". . . How the West Was Won—Nearly." *Sounds*, April 26, 1975, 20.

Vickers, Tom. "Climax Lacks at Glittering Labelle Premiere." *Rolling Stone*, November 6, 1975, 102.

Vincent, Rickey. *Funk: The Music, the People, and the Rhythm of the One*. New York: St. Martin's Griffin, 1996.

Vining, Mark. "*Pressure Cookin'*" [album review]. *Rolling Stone*, November 8, 1973, 75.

Visconti, Tony. *Tony Visconti: Bowie, Bolan and the Brooklyn Boy: The Autobiography*. New York: HarperCollins, 2007.

Vozick-Levinson, Simon. "Alabama Shakes' Brittany Howard on Jamming with Prince, Her Secret Identity." *Rolling Stone,* December 1, 2015. Accessed July 27, 2016. http://www.rollingstone.com/music/features/alabama-shakes-brittany-howard-on-jamming-with-prince-her-secret-identity-20151201.

Waksman, Steve. "Black Sound, Black Body: Jimi Hendrix, the Electric Guitar, and the Meanings of Blackness." In *Instruments of Desire: The Electric Guitar and the Shaping of Musical Experience*, 167–206. Cambridge, MA: Harvard University Press, 1999.

Waksman, Steve. *This Ain't the Summer of Love: Conflict and Crossover in Heavy Metal and Punk*. Berkeley: University of California Press, 2009.

Wald, Elijah. *How the Beatles Destroyed Rock 'n' Roll: An Alternative History of American Popular Music*. New York: Oxford University Press, 2009.

Wald, Gayle F. "From Spirituals to Swing: Sister Rosetta Tharpe and Gospel Crossover." *American Quarterly* 55, no. 3 (2003): 387–416.

Wald, Gayle F. *Shout, Sister, Shout! The Untold Story of Rock-and-Roll Trailblazer Sister Rosetta Tharpe*. Boston: Beacon Press, 2007.

Walker, Alice. "Nineteen Fifty-Five." In *You Can't Keep a Good Woman Down: Stories*, 3–20. New York: Harcourt Brace Jovanovich, 1981.

Walsh, Alan. "Wow! Pandemonium! The Stones Roll Out Again—and It's the Wildest Tour Ever to Hit Britain." *Melody Maker*, October 1, 1966, 8–9.

Wang, Oliver. Liner Notes, *Betty Davis*. Light in the Attic Records LITA 026, 2007, CD.

Ward, Brian. *Just My Soul Responding: Rhythm and Blues, Black Consciousness, and Race Relations*. Berkeley: University of California Press, 1998.

Warner, Jay. *American Singing Groups: A History from 1940 to Today*. Milwaukee, WI: Hal Leonard, 2006.

Warwick, Jacqueline. "'And the Colored Girls Sing . . .': Backup Singers and the Case of the Blossoms." In *Musicological Identities: Essays in Honor of Susan McClary*, edited by Steven Baur, Raymond Knapp, and Jacqueline Warwick, 63–75. Hampshire, UK: Ashgate, 2008.

Warwick, Jacqueline. *Girl Groups, Girl Culture: Popular Music and Identity in the 1960s*. New York: Routledge, 2007.

Warwick, Jacqueline. "Midnight Ramblers and Material Girls: Gender and Stardom in Rock and Pop." In *The SAGE Handbook of Popular Music*, edited by Andy Bennett and Steve Waksman, 332–45. Los Angeles: SAGE, 2015.

Warwick, Jacqueline. "Singing Style and White Masculinity." In *The Ashgate Research Companion to Popular Musicology*, edited by Derek B. Scott, 349–64. Surrey, UK: Ashgate, 2009.

Warwick, Neil, Jon Kutner, and Tony Brown. *The Complete Book of the British Charts: Singles and Albums*. London: Omnibus Press, 2004.

Waterman, Dick. *Between Midnight and Day: The Last Unpublished Blues Archive*. New York: Thunder's Mouth, 2003.

Watts, Michael. "Caught in the Act: Labelle: Ladies of Pleasure." *Melody Maker*, March 15, 1975, 59.

Watts, Michael. "Dinner and Cards with Reggie." *Melody Maker*, November 9, 1974, 22–23.

"Week's Best Pictures." *Jet*, May 9, 1968, 34–35.

Weingarten, Marc. *Station to Station: The History of Rock 'n' Roll on Television*. New York: Pocket Books, 2000.

Weller, Sheila. *Girls Like Us: Carole King, Joni Mitchell, and Carly Simon and the Journey of a Generation*. New York: Atria Books, 2008.

Wenner, Jann S. "Mick Jagger." In *The Rolling Stone Interviews*, edited by Jann S. Wenner and Joe Levy, 362–76. New York: Back Bay Books, 2007.

Wexler, Jerry, and David Ritz. *Rhythm and the Blues: A Life in American Music*. New York: Alfred A. Knopf, 1993.

Whitburn, Joel. *The Billboard Book of Top 40 Hits*. 9th ed. New York: Billboard Books, 2010.

Whitburn, Joel. *The Billboard Book of Top 40 R&B and Hip Hop Hits*. New York: Billboard Books, 2006.

Whitburn, Joel. *Joel Whitburn's Hot Dance/Disco, 1974–2003*. Menomonee Falls, WI: Record Research, 2004.

Whitburn, Joel. Hot R&B Songs, 1942–2010, 6th ed. Menomonee Falls, WI: Record Research, 2010.

Whitburn, Joel. *Top Pop Albums*. 7th ed. Menomonee Falls, WI: Record Research, 2010.

Whitcomb, Ian. "Legends of Rhythm and Blues." In *Repercussions: A Celebration of African-American Music*, edited by Geoffrey Haydon and Dennis Marks, 54–79. London: Century Publishing, 1985.

White, Deborah Gray. *Ar'n't I a Woman? Female Slaves in the Plantation South*. New York: W. W. Norton, 1999.

Whiteley, Sheila. *Women and Popular Music: Sexuality, Identity, and Subjectivity*. London: Routledge, 2000.

Wikane, Christian John. "Keeping Great Company: An Interview with Claudia Lennear." *Pop Matters*, June 19, 2013. Accessed July 9, 2013. http://www.popmatters.com/pm /feature/172563-performer-spotlight-the-women-of-20-feet-from-stardom-claudia -lennea/.

Williams, Jean. "Trio Labelle: Patti, Sarah and Nona Favor Revolutionary Songs, Attire." *Billboard*, March 29, 1975, 33.

Willis, Deborah, and Carla Williams. *The Black Female Body: A Photographic History*. Philadelphia: Temple University Press, 2002.

Willis, Ellen. "Janis Joplin." In *The Rolling Stone Illustrated History of Rock and Roll*, edited by Anthony DeCurtis and James Henke with Holly George-Warren, 382–87. New York: Random House, 1992.

Wilson, Mary. *Dreamgirl and Supreme Faith: My Life as a Supreme*. New York: Cooper Square, 1999.

Wilson, Olly. "The Significance of the Relationship between Afro-American Music and West African Music." *The Black Perspective in Music* 2, no. 1 (1974): 3–22.

Windham, Ben. "Big Mama Thornton." *Alabama Heritage*, fall 1987, 30–43.

Wolcott, James. "Labelle: Louder, Funnier and Sexier." *Rolling Stone*, October 23, 1975, 65.

Wright, Christian. "Tina Turner." In *Trouble Girls: The Rolling Stone Book of Women in Rock*, edited by Barbara O'Dair, 167–69. New York: Random House, 1997.

Wyman, Bill, with Richard Havers. *Rolling with the Stones*. New York: DK Publishing, 2002.

Yaffe, David. *Bob Dylan: Like a Complete Unknown*. New Haven, CT: Yale University Press, 2011.

Yates, Henry. "Is P. P. Arnold the Most Overlooked Soul Singer of All Time?" *Classic Rock*, August 15, 2017. https://www.loudersound.com/features/is-pp-arnold-the-most -overlooked-soul-singer-of-all-time.

Interviews

Merry Clayton, telephone interview with author, October 22, 2009.

Sarah Dash, telephone interview with author, March 4, 2014, and June 3, 2014.

Betty Davis, telephone interview with author, June 27, 2007.

Terry DeRouen, telephone interview with author, December 17, 2009.

Nat Dove, telephone interview with author, February 9, 2010.

Kat Dyson, telephone interview with author, October 19, 2012.

Sherman Fleming, telephone interview with author, April 7, 2007.

Dennis Garvey, telephone interview with author, September 27, 2010, and October 4, 2010.

Michael Hill, telephone interview with author, May 3, 2007.

Gloria Jones, telephone interview with author, March 13, 2012, and April 20, 2012.

Beverly Lee, telephone interview with author, August 7, 2012.

Emmaretta Marks, telephone interview with author, July 9, 2014.

Jimmy McCracklin, telephone interview with author, October 29, 2009.

Chris Strachwitz, telephone interview with author, August 13, 2009.

Matt Sullivan, telephone interview with author, July 6, 2007.

Juma Sultan, telephone interview with author, July 3, 2014.

Audio Recordings

Alabama Shakes. *Boys and Girls*, New York, ATO Records ATO0142, 2012, CD.

Alabama Shakes. *Sound and Color*. ATO Records ATO0269, 2015, CD.

Arnold, P. P. *The Best of P. P. Arnold*. Repertoire REP 5152, 2009, CD.

Baker, LaVern. *Soul on Fire: The Best of LaVern Baker*. Atlantic Records 7 82311-2, 1991, CD.

The Beatles. *Abbey Road*. EMI Records CDP 7 464462, 1987, CD. Originally released in 1969.

Big Brother and the Holding Company. *Cheap Thrills*. Sony Music CK 65784, 1999, CD.
    Originally released in 1968.

Bowie, David. *Young Americans*. Rykodisc RCD 10140, 1999, CD. Originally released in 1975.

The Chambers Brothers. *The Time Has Come*. Columbia/Legacy CK 63984, 2000, CD.
    Originally released in 1966.

Cherry, Ava. *The Astronettes Sessions*. Black Barbarella Records BBarbcd001, 2009, CD.

Clayton, Merry. *The Best of Merry Clayton*. Sony Music Entertainment 88883739602, 2013,
    CD.

Cocker, Joe. *Joe Cocker*. A&M Records SP-4368, 2015, CD. Originally released in 1972.

Cocker, Joe. *With a Little Help from My Friends*. A&M Records 069 490 419-2, 1999, CD.
    Originally released in 1969.

Creedence Clearwater Revival. *Bayou Country*. Fantasy Records FCD-4513-2, 1989, CD.
    Originally released in 1969.

Davis, Betty. *Betty Davis*. Light in the Attic Records LITA 026, 2007, CD. Originally released
    in 1973.

Davis, Betty. *The Columbia Years, 1968–1969*. Light in the Attic Records LITA 135, 2016, CD.

Davis, Betty. *Is It Love or Desire*. Light in the Attic Records LITA 047, 2009, CD. Originally
    recorded in 1976.

Davis, Betty. *Nasty Gal*. Light in the Attic Records LITA 046, 2009, CD. Originally released
    in 1975.

Davis, Betty. *They Say I'm Different*. Light in the Attic Records LITA 027, 2007, CD. Origi-
    nally released in 1974.

Dylan, Bob. *Biograph*. Columbia Records C3K 38830, 1985, CD.

Dylan, Bob. *Bob Dylan's Greatest Hits*. Vol. 3. Columbia Records CK 66783, 1994, CD.

Hendrix, Jimi. *First Rays of the New Rising Sun*. MCA Records MCAD-11599, 1997, CD.

Humble Pie. *The Definitive Collection*. A&M Records B0006880-02, 2006, CD.

Hunt, Marsha. *Woman Child*. Track Records 2410 101, 1971, 33⅓.

Jones, Gloria. *Share My Love*. Reel Music 66748-78007-2, 2009, CD. Originally released in 1973.

Labelle. *Back to Now*. Verve Music Group N0011511-02, 2008, CD.

Labelle. *Nightbirds*. Audio Fidelity AFZ5 196, 2015, CD. Originally released in 1974.

Labelle. *Pressure Cookin'*. Reel Music 66748-780289-2, 2010, CD. Originally released in 1973.

Labelle. *Something Silver*. Warner Archives 9 46359-2, 1997, CD.

Led Zeppelin. *Led Zeppelin II*. Atlantic Records 8236, 1994, CD. Originally released in 1969.

Lennear, Claudia. *Phew!* Warner Brothers BS2654, 1973, 33⅓.

Mayall, John. *The Blues Alone*. Dera 820 535-2, 1988, CD. Originally released in 1967.

Nyro, Laura, and Labelle. *Gonna Take a Miracle*. Columbia Legacy, CK 85762, 2002, CD. Originally released in 1971.

Presley, Elvis. *The All Time Greatest Hits*. BMG Music, ND 90100 BMG, 1987, CD.

Res. *How I Do*. MCA Records 088 112 310-2, 2001, CD.

The Rolling Stones. *Exile on Main Street*. Universal Music International 2734295, 2010, CD. Originally released in 1972.

The Rolling Stones. *Hot Rocks, 1964–1971*. ABKCO Records. 66672, 1986, CD. Originally released in 1971.

The Rolling Stones. *Let It Bleed*. ABKCO Records 90042, 2002, CD. Originally released in 1969.

The Rolling Stones. *Some Girls*. Universal Republic Records B0016235-02, 2011, CD. Originally released in 1978.

The Rolling Stones. *Sticky Fingers*. Universal Music. 80012799-02, 2009, CD. Originally released in 1971.

Santogold. *Santogold*. Downtown Records DWT70034, 2012, CD.

The Scepter Records Story. Capricorn Records 9 42003-2, 1992, CD.

The Shirelles. *The Best of the Shirelles*. Ace Records CDCHD 356, 1992, CD.

Small Faces. *The Singles As & Bs . . . Plus*. See for Miles Records. SEE CD 293, 1990, CD.

Springfield, Dusty. *The Dusty Springfield Anthology*. Mercury Records 314 553 501-502, 1997, CD.

Stiffed. *Burned Again*. Outlook Music. OMC-1004, 2005, CD.

Stiffed. *Sex Sells*. Cool Hunter CHCD0003, 2003, CD.

The Sweet Inspirations. *Two Classic Albums [The Sweet Inspirations and Sweet Sweet Soul]*. Spy Records SPY 46004-2, 2002, CD.

Thornton, Big Mama. *Ball 'n' Chain*. Arhoolie CD 305, 1985, CD.

Thornton, Big Mama. *Big Mama in Europe*. Arhoolie, CD 9056, 2005, CD. Originally released in 1965.

Thornton, Big Mama. *Big Mama Thornton: The Original Hound Dog*. Ace Records CDCHD 940, 1990, CD.

Thornton, Big Mama. *Big Mama Thornton and the Chicago Blues Band*. Arhoolie Records, F 1032, 1967, 33⅓.

Thornton, Big Mama. *The Rising Sun Collection*. Just a Memory Records, RSCD 0002, 1994, CD. Originally released in 1977.

Thornton, Big Mama. *Saved*. Pentagram PE 10,005, 1971, 33⅓.

T. Rex. *Zinc Alloy and the Hidden Riders of Tomorrow*. Rhino R2 73219, 2002, CD. Originally released in 1974.

T. Rex. *Dandy in the Underworld*. Rhino R2 73220, 2002, CD. Originally released in 1977.

Troy, Doris. *Doris Troy*. EMI Apple Records 5099990824326, 2010, CD. Originally released in 1970.

Turner, Tina. *Private Dancer*. Capitol Records. 7243 8 55833 2 2, 1997, CD. Originally released in 1984.

Turner, Tina. *Tina Turner: The Collected Recordings Sixties to Nineties*. Capitol Records CDP 7243 8 29724 2 6, 1994, CD.

Turner, Tina. *Tina Turns the Country On*. United Artists Records UA-LA200-G, 1974, 33⅓.

Films

Burlingame, Michael, dir. *Gunsmoke Blues*. Santa Monica, CA: Hip-O Records, 2004. DVD.

Cowey, Chris, dir. *The Girl from Nutbush*. A Picture Music International Production, EMI Records, 1991. British Film Institute collection. VHS.

Dubin, Charles, dir. *Mr. Rock and Roll*. New York: Video Beat, 1994. DVD. Originally released in 1957.

Espar, David, prod. *Rock & Roll: In the Groove*, Part 2. South Burlington, VT: WGBH Video, 1995. VHS.

Espar, David, prod. *Rock & Roll: Renegades*, Part 1. South Burlington, VT: WGBH Video, 1995. VHS.

Hackford, Taylor, dir. *Hail! Hail! Rock 'n' Roll*. Santa Monica, CA: Universal Music, 2006. DVD. Originally released in 1987.

Neville, Morgan, dir. *Twenty Feet from Stardom*. Beverly Hills, CA: Anchor Bay Entertainment, 2014. DVD.

The 1996 Annual Induction Ceremony, Rock and Roll Hall of Fame Foundation Records. Library and Archives, Rock and Roll Hall of Fame. Archival Videotape.

Price, Will, dir. *Rock, Rock, Rock!* United States: H&H Music Ltd., 2017. DVD. Originally released in 1956.

Scorsese, Martin, dir. *Shine a Light*. Hollywood, CA: Paramount Home Entertainment, 2008. DVD.

Spence, Richard, dir. *The Real Buddy Holly Story*. West Long Branch, NJ: White Star, 2004. DVD.

Stewart, Johnny, prod. *In Concert: Labelle*, Take 2. BBC, March 8, 1975. British Film Institute collection. VHS.

INDEX

Page numbers followed by f indicate illustrations.

Abramson, Herb, 58–59
Ace, Johnny, 42–43
Adams. Bryan, 268
Adelt, Ulrich, 47
Adler, Lou, 135
African diaspora, 9
Ain't I a Woman: Black Women and Feminism (hooks), 27
Alabama Shakes, 27, 277–82, *278; Songs and Albums: Boys and Girls,* 279, 282; "Hold On," 277–79, 282; *Sound and Color,* 279
Albin, Peter, 45
album-oriented rock (AOR) radio, 13
albums as artistic works, 102, 191, 205
Aletti, Vince, 193, 207, 210
Allen, Hoss, 10
Alomar, Carlos, 126
American Bandstand, 89, 90, 112, 185
American Folk Blues Festival, 1965, 33, 44
A&M Records, 121, 125f, 135
"Angel of the Morning" (Arnold), 119
Angels, 78
Animals, 98, 117, 144–45
Ann Arbor Blues Festival, 1969, 46
Apollo Theater (Harlem), 32, 88, 187, 198
Apple Records, 135
Armatrading, Joan, 26, 269
Arnold, P. P., 108, 119, 138, 246
Aronowitz, Al, 154
Artes, Mary Alice, 128
Atkins, Cholly, 92
Atlanta Feminist Lesbian Alliance, 197

Atlantic Records, 54, 58–59, 187, 335n168; backup vocalists for, 114–16; fortieth anniversary, 73
audible blackness, 2, 11, 13, 84–85, 104–8, 113f, 114–17, 123–24, 131–32, 173, 255
authenticity: artistry as requirement for, 102, 191, 205; attributed to black musicians, 132; symbolic labor of background vocalists, 131–36; of visible blackness, 117, 124, 126
autobiographies and memoirs, 74, 105
Ayers, Virginia, 121

"Baby, It's You" (Beatles), 97
Baby It's You! (Broadway musical), 76–78, 90, 104; critiques of, 78
Bacharach, Burt, 114–15
background vocalists, 5, 13, 104, 105–40; for Alabama Shakes, 279–280; audibility and invisibility of, 106–8; as audible property, 123–24; beginnings of, 110–16; Blackberries, 123–25, 125f, 133, 135, 343n56; "black sound," 112–17, 124, 132; black voices sought out, 107; Blossoms, 109, 111–14, 113f, 130, 131; call-and-response form, 108, 117, 119, 126; creative labor of, 129–31; cross-racial collaborations and, 116–29; dynamics of race, gender, and genre and, 107; gospel music and, 106, 108–11; as helpmates, 134; ideological work of, 106–7; male, 126, 279; multiple styles mastered by, 111–12; romantic relationships, 136–40; session work, 110, 111–12, 131, 136; singing "in the world,"

background vocalists (cont.)
109–10; solo career attempts, 134–135;
Sweet Inspirations, 41, 111, 114–15; symbolic
labor of, 131–36; *Twenty Feet from Stardom*
(documentary), 105, 133, 134, 180; white
male sexual fantasies and hegemonic
power structures, 133–34; white vocal
sound performed by, 111

Bad Brains, 16

Baker, LaVern, 5, 52–75, 279; awards received,
53, 70; categorization of, 55; covers of,
60–64; as Delores Williams, 299n33; disappearance from rock and roll genre, 71–75;
double exclusion from rock and roll, 56;
film appearances, 67–71; as first Queen
of Rock and Roll, 75; health, 72, 73–74;
humor of, 63; as Little Miss Sharecropper,
57–58; mentoring by, 64–65, 74–75; not
given attention in histories of rock and
roll, 53–55; as novelty act, 57–60; overseas
work and life, 72–74; photographs of, 68f,
70f; on the road, 64–67; visual presentation of, 67–71; *Songs and Albums:* "I
Cried a Tear," 71, 302n121; "Jim Dandy,"
59, 63–64, 71, 302n121; *LaVern Baker Sings
Bessie Smith*, 71; "Love Me in the Morning," 69; "Saved," 72; "See See Rider," 72;
"Soul on Fire," 59; "Think Twice," 72; "Tra
La La," 59, 61, 67, 69; "Tweedlee Dee," 52,
59–60, 70, 245, 302n121

Baldry, Long John, 162

"Ball and Chain" (Joplin), 29, 33, 42–47

"Ball and Chain" (Thornton), 30, 45–47

Balloon, John, 219–20

bands: integrated, 46, 268–72, 281; self-
contained, 12, 13, 78–79. *See also* British
Invasion bands; individual bands

Bangladesh, 173–74

Banks, Bessie, 117

Barnum, Billie, 123, 124, 125f

Barry, Jeff, 250, 251

Bay Area blues scene, 33, 43–44

Baytone Records, 45

"Bear Cat" (Thomas), 38

Beatlemania, 88

Beatles, 5, 11, 79, 140; covers of black artists,
117; Murray the K and, 89–90; Shirelles'
influence on, 96–97; Supremes as only
chart rival to, 87; *Songs and Albums:* "Baby,
It's You," 97; "Boys," 97; "Come Together,"
254, 255, 344n66; "Please Please Me," 96;
Please Please Me, 97; "P.S. I Love You," 96

Beck, Jeff, 98, 266

Bego, Mark, 253

Bell, Madeline, 108, 116–17, 120, 136; with Blue
Mink, 134–35; *Comin' Atcha*, 136

"Be My Baby" (Ronettes), 87

Bennett, Estelle, 139–40

Bennett, Veronica "Ronnie" (Spector), 87, 93,
139–40, 306n62, 320n206

Berry, Chuck, 12, 54, 305n40

Betrock, Alan, 90

Beyoncé, 27

Big Beat, 10, 52, 74

Big Brother and the Holding Company,
45–46

Biggest Rhythm & Blues Revue, 1954, 55

Biggest Rock 'n' Roll Show of 1956, 55

Biggest Show of Stars, 1956, 1957, and 1958,
58, 64–65

"Big Midnite Blues Special" (Danville
Armory), 65

Big TNT Show, The (concert film), 248

Billboard magazine, 11, 13, 33, 71; on Baker,
62–63; Betty Davis, review of, 224; Davis
and, 233–34; "Hound Dog" (Thornton)
and, 37; Labelle's hit on, 234; on Lennear,
178; Turner's interview with, 264

Bill Haley and His Comets, 10, 55

binaries, race-based, 4, 14, 19, 131–32, 135, 207

Birdsong, Cindy, 185, 186f, 188

Black, Pauline, 26–27, 170

Black and Blue (Broadway musical revue),
54, 73

Blackberries, 123–25, 125f, 133, 135, 343n56

black consciousness, 12–13

Black Diamond Queens, black women in rock as, 278f, 279–83; Baker as first Queen of Rock and Roll, 75; Turner, Tina as Queen of Rock and Roll, 2, 240, 275, 281

black feminism, 184, 189–90, 208–9, 212, 214–15, 216, 231

black feminist scholars, 17, 19, 21, 22, 27

"Black is Beautiful," 142, 163

blackness: hiding of due to racism, 87–88; presence of in rock and roll, 10–13, 26, 44–45, 69; stereotypes of black women, 16–18, 140–41, 143, 162–63. *See also* background vocalists

Black Rock Coalition, 16, 238

"black sound," 13, 20, 40, 178, 193, 252–53; background vocalists, 112–17, 124, 132

Blackwell, Chris, 221

black women: sexual objectification of, 17–18, 140–41, 147–48; as tough and independent, 209, 335–36n178

Black Women Rock! project, 238

Blakley, Dorian, 196

Blossoms, 109, 111–14, 113f, 130, 131

Bluebelle Records Company, 185

Blue Mink, 134–35

blues, 203, 222; as cultural production of working-class black women, 22; improvisatory spirit of, 35; revival of 1950s and 1960s, 33, 47, 146, 252; sound, feel, energy, and attitude of, 35, 39; white audience for, 33, 39–40, 46–47. *See also* "Hound Dog" (Thornton)

Bluesbreakers, 146

Blues Foundation, 36, 277

Blues Hall of Fame (Memphis), 36, 277

Bluesology, 162

BMI (performing rights organization), 262, 263

Bobbettes, 79

body, devalued as source of music, 3–4, 47

Bolan, Marc, 126–27, 140, 162, 165, 220

Bolan, Rolan, 140

Boone, Pat, 62

Bowie, David, 26, 125–26, 135, 140, 164, 195, 268, 281; Turner and, 265; *Songs and Albums: Aladdin Sane,* 126, 146; "Lady Grinning Soul," 140, 146; "Panic in Detroit," 126; *Station to Station,* 140; "Suffragette City," 152; *Young Americans,* 126, 140

Bramlett, Bonnie, 119, 120, 315n81

Bridges, Alvenia, 144, 154

Britain: black Americans in, 161; black residents, 132, 161; Turner, response to, 251–52

British artists, 11, 23; black women, 26–27, 269; blues, 146–47, 162; Northern Soul scene, 126

British Invasion bands, 79, 90, 96, 142; authenticity of visible blackness, 117, 124, 126; background vocalists, 117–21; covers of black artists, 96–98, 117–18

Britten, Terry, 265, 267

Brooklyn Fox (theater), 88

Brooklyn Paramount Theater, 71, 88, 89

Brooks, Daphne, 3, 15, 248, 347n19

Brown, James, 12, 13, 126, 187

Brown, Jayna, 14

Brown, Ruth, 54, 331n68; domestic employment, 73; *Songs:* "Mama, He Treats Your Daughter Mean," 60; "Oh, What a Dream," 61, 62; "So Long," 58

Brown, Tamar-kali, 16, 238

"Brown-Eyed Girl" (Van Morrison), 115, 146, 321n14

"Brown Sugar," as concept, 179–81, 204

"brown sugar," as name for heroin, 148, 321n25

"Brown Sugar" (Mayall), 146–47, 151, 321n18

"Brown Sugar" (Rolling Stones), 17–19, 21, 23, 140, 143, 146–51, 290–91n59, 321n19; bad boy identity of Rolling Stones and, 148–50; Hunt and, 141; lyrics, 142, 148–50, 321n25; New Orleans setting of, 148

Brown v. Board of Education, 66

Brunswick Records, 72

Bullock, Anna Mae. *See* Turner, Tina

Burdon, Eric, 144–46, 154

Burned Again (Stiffed), 16
Burrows, Stephen, 217

call-and-response form, 108, 117, 119, 126, 197, 258
Capital Radio, 170
Capitol Records, 265
Caravan of Stars summer tours, 89
Carby, Hazel, 22
Cash Box magazine, 37, 60, 86
Chambers Brothers, 217–18
Change of Habit (film), 112
Chantels, 74, 79, 331n68
Chapman, Tracy, 282
Charles, Ray, 108, 114, 121, 246
charts (music popularity): gender differences in length of stay on, 72; segregated, 11; Shirelles on, 78–82, 84–89, 95–96, 98, 102–3
Cheap Thrills (Big Brother and the Holding Company), 46
Checkmates, 258
Cherry, Ava, 125, 135, 140
Chicago Defender, 43, 61, 63, 86
Chicago nightspots, 57
Chiffons, 118, 314n74
Chitlin Circuit, 89, 183
choreography, 92
Christgau, Robert, 54, 58
"Christmas, Baby, Please Come Home" (Love), 105–6
"Cissy and the girls," 115
civil rights movement, 7, 10, 66, 132, 138
Clapton, Eric, 47, 98, 116, 143, 219–20, 268
Clark, Dick, 89, 90
Clark, Robin, 126
"classic rock era," 5
Clayton, Merry, 5, 101, 105, 108, 109–10, 122f, 129, 133, 261, 318n176; on "Gimme Shelter," 119–20; influences on, 109; with the Rolling Stones, 119–21; solo career, 135
Clemente, John, 87, 306n61
Clinton, George, 196

Coates, Norma, 56
Cocker, Joe, 121, 173
Cole, Clay, 89
Coleman, Rick, 54, 55
Coley, Doris (Jackson), 76, 77, 80–81, 83f, 91f, 103; as lead singer, 84–85; at Rock and Roll Hall of Fame induction ceremony, 101. *See also* Shirelles
Collins, Patricia Hill, 17
Combahee River Collective, 212
comedians, 89
"Come Together" (Beatles), 254, 255, 344n66
"Come Together" (Ike and Tina Turner Revue), 254, 255
commoditization, 8
Commodores, 219, 220
Concert for Bangladesh (film), 173–74
Connery, Sean, 144
"controlling images," 17
Cooke, Sam, 108, 110, 246
Copyright Act of 1909, 62–63
copyright system, 62–63
Cousin Brucie (Bruce Morrow), 90
Covach, John, 53
covers, 11–12, 60–64, 301n78; audience turn toward originals, 63–64, 190; British, of black artists, 96–98, 117–18; of Davis, 237–38; Labelle and, 189; of rock, by Turner, 252–62; of Thornton, by Joplin, 45–46; of Thornton, by Presley, 38–42
Cox, Ida, 22
Crawdaddy, 12, 56; Davis, review of, 235–36; on Ike and Tina Turner, 260; on Labelle, 200; on Turner's songs, 262–63
Crazy Horse, Kandia, 107, 136–37, 139, 239
Creedence Clearwater Revival, 254, 257–58
Creem, 267
Crewe, Bob, 200
Cross, Charles, 153, 154, 156, 159
crossover music, 6–7, 11, 67, 243–44; Shirelles and, 80, 83–88, 91f, 103
cross-racial borrowing, 14, 20, 40–42, 58, 132, 248

cross-racial collaborations, 7, 46–47, 130–32; background vocalists and, 116–29; Fields on, 132–33, 136–37; Turner and, 264–69; white alliances authorize black performers, 268–72

cross-racial interactions, Jim Crow segregation and, 65–66, 75

"Cry" (Ray), 58

Crystals, 92

Cues (Atlantic's house background group), 59

cultural capital, 56, 172, 272

cultural memory, 102

cultural Others, 23; background vocalists as, 134, 135; fascination with, 137; women in rock as, 56

cultural work of genre categories, 7–8

Curnin, Cy, 266, 266f

Darin, Bobby, 110

Dark Side of the Moon (Pink Floyd), 124, 134

Darren, James, 111

Dash, Sarah, 104, 182, 183, 186f, 196f; Davis, opinion of, 224; early career, 185–87; on innovation of Labelle, 212; on sexuality, 203; solo career, 211; on women's movement, 208–9; work with Keith Richards, 211. *See also* Labelle; Patti LaBelle and the Bluebelles

Davies, Roger, 264–65, 270

Davis, Angela, 174–75

Davis, Betty, 5, 6, 13, 170, 213–39, 280, 338n26; artistic autonomy of, 230–32; *Betty: They Say I'm Different* (documentary), 237; confidence of, 217–18; covers of, 237–38; gender and class analysis, 231; genre-bending, 216; influence of, 237; interviews, 213–14, 217–18, 219–20, 229–30, 238; marriage to Miles Davis, 218–19, 230; as model, 217; musical lineage of, 223; in performance, 224–27, 225f; photographs of, 215f, 225f; politics of sexuality in lyrics of, 214–16, 221, 227, 230–32; protests against, 231–32, 239; reissue of albums, 213–14, 224, 226,

237; retirement from music industry, 236–39; as rule-breaker, 232–36; as songwriter, 216, 217–21; sound and vision of, 227–30; vocal style, 216, 222–23; on Wilson, 158–59; *Songs and Albums:* "Anti-Love Song," 221; *Betty Davis,* 213, 220–21, 233; *Betty Davis: The Columbia Years, 1968–1969,* 237; *Crashin' from Passion,* 221; "Dedicated to the Press," 231–32; "Game Is My Middle Name," 222–23; "Get Ready for Betty," 217; "If I'm in Luck I Might Get Picked Up," 231; *Is It Love or Desire,* 237; "Live, Love, Learn" / "It's My Life," 217; *Nasty Gal,* 221, 225f, 226–27, 237; "Steppin in Her I. Miller Shoes," 6, 158–60; *They Say I'm Different,* 213, 221; "They Say I'm Different," 223; "Uptown to Harlem" (Chambers Brothers recording), 217

Davis, Miles, 218–21, 223, 230, 236; *Songs and Albums: Bitches Brew,* 218; *Filles de Kilimanjaro,* 219; "Mademoiselle Mabry," 219

Dean, Jenni, 160

Decca Records, 82

"Dedicated to the One I Love" (Shirelles), 82, 85, 86

Deffaa, Chip, 59, 63

Del Capris, 185

Dennis, Carolyn, 139, 319n205

Dennis-Dylan, Desiree Gabrielle, 139

DeRouen, Terry, 35, 42, 48

desegregation/integration, 7, 24, 231; musical miscegenation, 10–11, 139; sexuality and, 137–38; southern opposition to, 11, 65–66, 114. *See also* cross-racial collaborations; segregation

Diggs, Charles, Jr., 62–63

Dire Straits, 266

disco, 205, 211–12

disco–new wave fusion, 234

dissemblance, culture of, 21–22

Dixie Hummingbirds, 126

Dixon, Luther, 78, 79, 82–87, 95, 103, 305n40, 308n105

Domino, Fats, 54, 55, 64

"Don't Make Me Over" (Warwick), 115

doo-wop music, 80–81, 185

Douglas, Susan, 93

Dowd, Tom, 61

DownBeat, 46, 53, 70, 218

Drifters, 65, 84

Dr. John, 164

Duncan, Lesley, 116–17

Dye-Gibson, Debi, 128

Dylan, Bob, 5, 12, 127–29, 317n131; secrecy about relationships, 139, 319–20n205

Dyson, Kat, 35, 42, 48

Earth, Wind & Fire, 13, 25

Easter, Eric, 213

Eat It (Humble Pie), 123, 125f

Ebony magazine, Baker featured in, 52, 58, 60, 64, 69–71; *EbonyJet.com*, 213

Echols, Alice, 45, 185, 189, 197–98, 210, 211–12

Ed Sullivan Show, The, 62, 90, 97

Eldorado Club (Houston), 32

Electric Lady Studios, 156, 158

Eleventh Hour, 200

Emerson, Ken, 197

EMI, 265

Epic Records, 200, 207

Epstein, Brian, 188

erasure, 40, 100; of background vocalists, 106; of black women from rock and roll, 12–13, 21, 27, 53, 67, 275–76; of Willie Mae Thornton, 39–42

erotic, the, 22, 198

Errico, Gregg, 220, 233

Erskine, Pete, 124

Ertegun, Ahmet, 58–59, 100

Escott, Colin, 76–77

Estey, Chris, 213

Etchingham, Kathy, 154

Everly, Phil, 65

Exciters, 116, 117

Exile on Main Street (Rolling Stones), 136

Faithfull, Marianne, 101, 165, 326n166

Fast, Susan, 106–7, 120, 129, 133–34; on Turner, 242–43, 247, 254, 275

Feld, Irvin, 64–65, 301n96

femininity, 90–94; black women as inadequately feminine, 17, 21, 44, 148, 166–67; soft rock and, 228–29; unconventional forms of, 30–31; visual presentation and, 68f, 90–92, 91f; white standards of, 19, 21–22; Wilson's flagrant violations of, 157–60. *See also* gender

Fields, Mattie, 276

Fields, Venetta, 5, 107, 110, 120–21, 124, 125f, 130–31, 343n56; on cross-racial collaborations, 132–33, 136–37; as Ikette, 110, 123, 138, 246, 248

"First Cut Is the Deepest, The" (Arnold), 119

Fischer, Lisa, 134

"5" Royales, 82

Fixx, the, 266, 266f

Flagg, Benjamin, 274

Flagg Grove School, 273–76

Flame Show Bar (Detroit), 57–58

Fleetwood, Mick, 146, 162

Fleming, Sherman, 226

Flory, Andrew, 53

Fogerty, John, 257

Fong-Torres, Ben, 174, 255, 263

For Your Love (Yardbirds), 98

Four Tops, 24

Franklin, Aretha, 12, 54, 72, 73, 109, 125, 135, 193, 194

Freddie Bell and the Bellboys, 38

Free at Last, 162

Freed, Alan, 10, 55, 64, 89

Free Speech movement, 161

Fresh Air, 105

Frith, Simon, 4

funk, 13, 220, 222–24; as black rock, 232–33; "generic contract" of, 222–23

Funkadelic, 13, 152

Gaar, Gillian, 54, 77

Gaines, Donna, 78

Gamble, Kenny, 126

Gardner, Beverly, 121

Gari, Brian, 105

Garofalo, Reebee, 53

Garvey, Dennis, 57, 88–89

Gaunt, Kyra, 15

gay and lesbian fans, 190, 195, 197–200

Gaye, Marvin, 13, 126, 136, 188, 190, 205; *Let's Get It On*, 233–34

gender: as field in which power is articulated, 16; "hard" vs. "soft" sounds, 167; Howard's expression of, 281; Thornton's expression of, 30, 32–33, 38, 40, 48, 293n3. *See also* femininity; sexuality

Gendron, Bernard, 56

genre: betwixt-and-between positions, 7, 103, 174, 205–9, 232–34, 250–51, 260–61; interpretation based on "current precepts," 55–56; as mechanism for policing race, gender, and sexuality, 5; new narratives, 14–16; racialized, 6, 9–13, 21, 114–15, 175–78, 207, 216, 223–24, 227–28, 232–33, 241, 253, 282–83; synthesis of styles, 191–92; unstable definitions in, 55–56

genre-blending music, 1, 6, 9

genre cultures, 6–9

genre histories, 9–13

Gersten, Russell, 193–94

Gibbs, Georgia, 61–62, 63, 300n67

Gibbs, Vernon, 235–36

Gilmour, Dave, 123

girl groups, 3, 74–75, 185, 186f; accessibility of, 85; audibility and visibility problems, 77; cultural significance of, 93; as interchangeable, 77–78; matching clothing, 91f, 92, 307n83; Shirelles' influence on, 103–4; "talent" assumed to lie in producers, 77–78; white, 78. *See also* Patti LaBelle and the Bluebelles; Ronettes; Shirelles

glam rock, 126, 195–97

Gleason, Ralph, 33, 35, 36

Gliders (session quintet), 59

Goffin, Gerry, 5, 84, 86

"golden oldies" tours, 74, 96, 187, 191

Goldman, Vivien, 222, 231–32, 233, 239

Gonna Take a Miracle (Nyro/Labelle), 104, 189, 208

Good, Jack, 114

Gordon, Bill, 10

Gordy, Berry, 11, 87, 103

Gospelaires, 114

gospel music, 12, 14–15, 35–36, 108–11, 245; background vocalists' training in, 106, 184–85; Baptist and Pentecostal choirs, 109; features of, 109–10; feeling of, 133; singing "in the world," 109–10; sound of in British music, 117, 121

Graham, Larry, 220

Grammy Awards, 259, 268, 282

Green, Al, 211, 265

Greenberg, Florence, 77, 78, 79, 94, 99, 101

Greenberg, Mary Jane, 81, 101

Greene, Nikki, 237

Greenwich, Ellie, 92, 104, 250

Grier, Miles Parks, 8

Gross, Terry, 105

groupies, 142, 151–54; abuse suffered by, 159. *See also* Wilson, Devon

guitar-centered style, 47–48, 55–56, 79, 100, 287n15

Guns N' Roses, 140

Guralnick, Peter, 40

Gurley, James, 45

Hair (musical), 108, 140, 142, 162; "Let the Sunshine In," 169

Halberstam, Judith, 40

Haley, Bill, 55, 64

Hamilton, Jack, 12

Hammonds, Evelynn, 22

Hancock, Hunter, 10

handclap and jump rope games, 15

Harding, Carol, 114

harmonizing, 77, 80–82, 104, 119, 198, 258

Harris, Addie "Micki" (Jackson), 77, 80–81, 83f, 91f, 94. *See also* Shirelles

Harris, Art, 203

Harrison, George, 118, 135, 140, 314n74

Harris-Perry, Melissa V., 335n178

Hartley, Pat, 152, 154, 159

Hayes, Eileen, 22

Heaven 17, 265

Henderson, David, 153, 156

Hendrix, Jimi, 13, 47, 138, 142–43, 223, 242;
Betty Davis's friendship with, 216, 218–19;
death of, 159; on groupies, 152; with Ike
and Tina Turner Revue, 341n3; Wilson
and, 153–56; *Songs and Albums:* "Dolly
Dagger," 158; "The Wind Cries Mary," 219

Hendryx, Nona, 9, 182, 183, 186f, 196f, 270–71,
333n102; on Davis, 237; early career, 185–87;
on gendered race challenges, 209; on
sexuality, 203; solo career, 211; songwriting, 190–91; stage ensemble, 197. *See also*
Labelle; Patti LaBelle and the Bluebelles

"He's So Fine" (Chiffons), 118, 314n74

High Society, 235

Hill, Michael, 226–27

Hinckley, David, 100, 102

Hine, Darlene Clark, 18, 21

Hirshey, Gerri, 106

Holden, Stephen, 177

"Hold On" (Alabama Shakes), 277–79

Holly, Buddy, 64, 66

Holte, Patsy, 185. *See also* LaBelle, Patti

"Honky Tonk Women" (Ike and Tina Turner
Revue), 254–56

"Honky Tonk Women" (Rolling Stones), 120,
164, 254–56

hooks, bell, 27, 242–43

Hot Harlem Revue (Sammy Green), 32

"Hound Dog" (Presley), 10, 29, 33, 38–41;
nonsensical lyrics, 39

"Hound Dog" (Thornton), 2, 29, 36–42, 277;
differences from standard rhythm and
blues, 37; instrumentation of, 37–38; lyrics,
39–40

Houston, Cissy, 5, 110, 111, 115, 130, 314n64

Houston, John, 114

Houston, Whitney, 114

Howard, Brittany, 27, 277–82, 278f

Howard Theater (Washington, DC), 82, 89

How I Do (Res), 16

Hudson, Ola, 140

Huff, Leon, 126

Humble Pie, 123–25, 125f, 130, 133, 135, 248,
343n56; *Rock On,* 138

Hunt, Karis, 140, 150–51, 170–72, 327n177

Hunt, Marsha, 5, 160–72, 280, 338n26; at
Capital Radio, 170; careers, 172; drugs refused by, 165–66; *Hair,* 140, 142, 162; Jagger
and, 140–42, 151, 162–65, 170–72; Mayall
and, 146–47, 151; paternity case, 170–71,
327n177; photograph of, 168f; *Real Life*
(memoir), 141, 160, 162–63, 172, 326n158;
stage persona, 166–67; *Songs and Albums:*
"Walk on Gilded Splinters," 164; *Woman
Child,* 167–70

Hurston, Zora Neale, 111

I, Tina (Tina Turner), 243, 342n10

"I Cried a Tear" (Baker), 71, 302n121

"(If You Think You're) Groovy" (Arnold), 119

Ike and Tina Turner Revue, 110, 123, 246,
275; covers of rock, 252–62; Lennear with,
172, 174; visual and choreographic aspects,
263; *Songs and Albums:* "Bold Soul Sister,"
263; *Come Together,* 255; "Come Together,"
254, 255; "A Fool in Love," 247–48, 253,
259; "Honky Tonk Women," 254–56; *The
Hunter,* 261; "It's Gonna Work Out Fine,"
248, 259; "I Want to Take You Higher," 127,
255, 259; "Proud Mary," 127, 254, 257–59;
"River Deep, Mountain High," 241, 249–52,
343n40; "Whole Lotta Love," 254, 257.
See also Turner, Ike; Turner, Tina

Ikettes, 110, 118, 123, 127, 173, 242, 246; creative
labor of, 130; on "Proud Mary," 258; Tina's
choreography of, 263

"I Met Him on a Sunday" (Poquellos/Shire-
lles), 81–82, 104

Immediate Records, 119

instrumentalists: guitar-centered style, 47–48, 55–56, 79, 100, 287n15; valued over vocalists, 3–4, 47; women, 16

intersection of race, gender, and genre, 16, 17, 74, 290n56; Labelle and, 183, 207; Lennear and, 177–80

Isherwood, Charles, 78

Island Records, 221, 233, 234

Isle of Wight Festival, 167

"I Want You Back" (Jackson Five), 24

Jackson, Chuck, 94

Jackson, Michael, 24

Jackson, Millie, 234

Jackson, Travis, 4

Jackson Five, 24, 244

Jagger, Jade, 172

Jagger, Mick, 18, 97, 118, 119–20, 138; on background vocals, 129; black bands, assistance to, 269; black culture, interest in, 157–58; Hunt and, 140–42, 151, 162–65, 170–72; Lennear and, 172–73, 174; paternity case, 170–71, 327n177; Turner's onstage style borrowed by, 248; Wilson and, 156–58

James, Etta, 54, 61–62

James, Fanita, 111, 113f, 130

James, Rick, 237

jazz, 4, 20, 23

Jeff Beck Group, 266

Jenifer, Darryl, 16

Jessy Dixon Singers, 126

Jesus Christ Superstar (musical), 108

Jet magazine, 217, 227, 263; EbonyJet.com, 213

Jim Crow segregation, 65–66

"Jim Dandy" (Baker), 59, 63–64, 71, 302n121

Jimi Hendrix Experience, 161

Johnson, Merline, 57

Jones, Brian, 157

Jones, Gloria, 5, 105, 108, 109, 120, 121, 131, 133, 140; Bolan and, 126–27; Davis, view of, 232; at Motown, 126–27; solo releases, 135; Songs: "Heartbeat," 126; "Tainted Love," 126

Jones, Grace: "Pull Up to the Bumper," 234; "Slave to the Rhythm," 234

Jones, John Paul, 136

Jones, Quincy, 153, 156

Joplin, Janis, 5, 13, 29, 44–46, 279; "Ball and Chain," 29, 33; vocal style, 45

"Just One Look" (Troy), 117, 135

Just Sunshine Records, 220–21

Kallberg, Jeffrey, 55

Kennedy, Joyce, 270–71

Keyes, Cheryl, 237

Keys, Bobby, 18

Khan, Chaka, 234

Kincaid, Jamaica, 195

King, Carole, 5, 84, 86, 104, 228

King, Clydie, 120, 123, 125f, 139, 261, 319–20n205

King, Freddie, 226, 227

King, Jean, 112, 113f

Kings of Rhythm, 128, 245, 247–48

Kiss, 196

Knight, Curtis, 153

Knight, Gladys, 109

Knopfler, Mark, 266

Korner, Alexis, 162

Krasnow, Bob, 262

Labelle, 5, 6, 13, 104, 182–212, 236–37, 280, 326n158; autonomy of, 185, 208–10, 212; black feminism of, 184, 189–90, 208–9; on the border of rock and soul, 191–94, 205–10; clothing choices, 187, 188–89, 195–200; departure from expectations, 194; dressing-up tradition, 183–84; formation of, 187–88; gay and lesbian fans, 190, 195, 197–200; genre labels, synthesis of, 191, 205; as individuals, 192; lyrics, 190; marketing challenges, 205–10; at Metropolitan Opera, 183–84, 197; photograph of, 196f; reunion, 211; reviews of, 193–94, 196–97, 199–201, 209–10; sex-positivity of, 190, 197; socially relevant subjects in lyrics,

Labelle (cont.)
187, 189–91, 205, 207, 212; solo careers, 211; stagecraft, 184; theatricality of, 195–97; as "the power," 209, 210; vocal range, 192–193; as white British/black American alliance, 188; *Songs and Albums: Back to Now,* 211; *Chameleon,* 207, 210; *Gonna Take a Miracle* (with Nyro), 104, 189, 208; "(Can I Speak to You before You Go to) Hollywood," 182, 191; "Lady Marmalade," 182–83, 200–202, 203–4, 205, 234; *Moon Shadow,* 190, 193, 207; *Nightbirds,* 182–83, 200, 207; "Nightbirds," 191; *Phoenix,* 207, 210; *Pressure Cookin',* 200, 207; "Sunday's News," 191, 201; "The Revolution Will Not Be Televised," 189, 201; "What Can I Do for You," 191, 210

LaBelle, Patti, 109, 182, 183, 186f, 196f; early career, 185–87; on gendered race and genre challenges, 208; on sexuality, 203; vocal range, 192, 331n68; *Songs and Albums: Burnin',* 211; "On My Own," 211; "Release Yourself," 211; *The Winner in You,* 211. *See also* Labelle; Patti LaBelle and the Bluebelles

labor exploitation, 94–95

"Lady Grinning Soul" (Bowie), 140, 146

"Lady Marmalade" (Labelle), 182–83, 200–202, 203–4, 205, 234

Lambert, Kit, 164, 165–66, 167, 207, 326n158

Lang, Michael, 220

Lassiter, Art, 247

"Leader of The Pack" (Shangri-Las), 78

"Lean on Me," 105

Leary, Timothy, 255

Led Zeppelin, 136, 152; "Whole Lotta Love," 254, 257

Lee, Arthur, 153–54, 269

Lee, Beverly, 65, 76–77, 80–81, 83, 83f, 86, 89–90, 91f; at Rock and Roll Hall of Fame induction ceremony, 101, 102. *See also* Shirelles

Lee, Brenda, 74

LeGaspi, Larry, 195–96, 196f

Leiber, Jerry, 5, 33, 36, 41, 48, 115

Lennear, Claudia, 5, 105, 133, 246; as background vocalist, 173–74, 179–80; Bowie and, 140, 142, 146; "Brown Sugar" and, 172–73; as Ikette, 130; Jagger and, 140, 141, 142, 172–73, 174; performances, 178–79; racial genre divide and, 175–78; solo releases, 135, 174–77; *Stellar Gypsy* nickname, 173; Warner Brothers contract, 174; *Songs and Albums:* "Not At All," 174; *Phew!,* 174–77, 175f; "Sister Angela," 174–75

Lennon, John, 97, 101, 140

Let's Get It On (Gaye), 233–34

Letterman, David, 105–6

Lewis, Linda, 126

Lewis, Pete, 38

Lewisohn, Mark, 96

Lichfield, Patrick, 163

Light in the Attic Records, 213–14, 224

Little Esther (Phillips), 32, 36, 58

Little Miss Cornshucks (Mildred Cummings), 57–58, 299n39

Little Richard, 62, 271

Live Aid concert (1985), 275

Living Colour, 269

London Bach Choir, 120

London Symphony Orchestra and Chamber Choir, 120

Lorde, Audre, 22, 198

Love (band), 153–54

Love, Darlene, 5, 101, 105–6, 109–10, 111–12, 113f, 114, 139

Lyle, Graham, 267

Mabry, Elizabeth (Betty). *See* Davis, Betty

Mabry, Lynn, 131

Mad Dogs and Englishmen (Cocker), 121, 173

Mad Max: Beyond Thunderdome (movie), 240, 268

"Mama, He Treats Your Daughter Mean" (Brown), 60

mammy role, 134

Mandrill, 13, 232

Manfred Mann, 98, 99, 117

March on Washington, 1963, 89

Marcus, Greil, 77–78, 120

Marks, Emmaretta, 141, 153, 156, 159–60, 217

Marriott, Steve, 119, 123, 124, 125f, 130, 135, 138, 248

Marron, Jim, 156

Marsh, Dave, 260

Marsh, Ian Craig, 265

Martin, George, 97

Marvelettes, 88, 117

masculinity, 40, 205, 254; appropriation and projection across racial and class boundaries, 20–21; background vocalists contribution to white males', 134; Davis as threat to, 235–36; girl groups' influence on, 98; guitar-centered style and, 47–48; hypermasculinity attributed to black men, 145; naturalization of in rock, 8, 56; Turner as threat to, 261

Masekela, Hugh, 217

Matthews, Sherlie, 121

Maultsby, Portia, 9–10

Mayall, John, 146–47, 162, 321n18

"Maybe" (Chantels), 79

Mayfield, Curtis, 13, 190, 205, 206

McCartney, Paul, 96, 269, 282

McCracklin, Jimmy, 43–44

McDermott, John, 153, 154

McDonald, Michael, 211

McVie, John, 146

Meibach, Ina, 208

Melody Maker, 127, 193, 198, 199, 224

Memphis Minnie (nee Lizzie Douglas), 57

Mercury Records, 46, 61

Meters, 200

Metropolitan Opera, 183–84, 197

middle class, black, 204, 231, 239

Mike Douglas Show, 203–4

minstrelsy, 132

miscegenation, musical, 10–11, 139

Mitchell, Joni, 8–9, 228

Modern Records, 245

Monáe, Janelle, 27

Monson, Ingrid, 20

Monterey Jazz Festival, 1964, 33, 44

Monterey Pop festival, 1967, 12, 153

Montgomery, Robbie, 127

Moore, James, 50

Moore, Jessica Care, 238

Moore, Madison, 243

moral panic, 11

motherhood, language of, 134

Mother's Finest, 271

Motown, 11, 24, 87, 96, 103, 117, 126, 230; girl groups and, 79

"Mr. Lee" (Bobbettes), 79

Mr. Rock and Roll (film), 67–69

Mud Island Amphitheater (Memphis), 277, 279

Murray, Charles Shaar, 151, 158

Murray, Henry "Juggy," 248

Murray the K, 89–90

Muscle Shoals Sound Studios, 147

Music of Quality and Distinction, Vol. 1, 265

Mutrux, Floyd, 76–77

"My Boyfriend's Back" (Angels), 78

My Name Is Love (Love), 105

"My Sweet Lord" (Harrison), 118, 314n74

Nasty Gal (Davis), 221, 225f, 226–27, 237

Nathan, David, 199

National Association for the Advancement of Colored People (NAACP), 231

National Association of Colored Women (NACW), 21

National Black Arts Festival, 238

naturalization of singing, 130

Neal, Bob, 39–40

Neal, Mark Anthony, 231

Ned Kelly (film), 172

Nero, Charles, 108–9

Neville, Morgan, 105

Newman, Nanette, 120

new wave music, 234, 244, 265, 266, 266f, 270

New York Age Defender, 42
New York Daily News, 100
New York Times, 78, 192, 199, 209
New York Times Magazine, 277
Nightbirds (Labelle), 182–83, 200
Nolan, Kenny, 200
Northern Soul scene, 126
novelty songs, 57–60
Nyro, Laura, 104, 189, 208, 228

O'Brien, Lucy, 54, 275
Odetta, 44, 127
O'Grady, Lorraine, 19
"Oh, What a Dream" (Brown), 61, 62
Ohio Players, 13
Oldham, Andrew Loog, 119, 188
O'Neill, Jimmy, 112
Ordettes, 185
Orloff, Katherine, 177
Otis, Johnny, 32, 36–37, 276, 279
Our World magazine, 53, 60
Outta Season (Turner and Krasnow), 262, 263
Owens, Shirley. *See* Reeves, Shirley Alston (Owens)

Page, Jimmy, 98, 152
Page, Patti, 61, 62
Parker, "Colonel Tom," 39–40, 41
Parks, Rosa, 66
Parliament-Funkadelic, 196
Pashe, John, 149
Patti LaBelle and the Bluebelles, 104, 117, 185–87, 195, 198, 313n51; "I Sold My Heart to the Junkman," 185, 187; photograph of, 186f. *See also* Labelle
Peacock Records label, 32, 36, 37, 41, 43, 277
Peccinotti, Harry, 163
Peete, Darlene (nee Wright). *See* Love, Darlene
Perez Morena de Macias. Bianca (Jagger), 171, 327n177
performance practices, 14–15
Phew! (Lennear), 174–77, 175f

Phillips, Dewey, 10
Phillips, Sam, 10, 40, 116
Philly soul sound, 126
Pink Floyd, 123–24, 131, 134
Plant, Robert, 257
"plastic soul," 126
Playboy, 174, 179
"Please Mr. Postman" (Marvelettes), 88
Pointer Sisters, 220, 222
Poly Styrene, 27
Poquellos, 81
Portrait of Bobby (Sherman), 24
post–World War II era, 6–7
Powers, Ann, 152
Presley, Elvis, 5, 69, 139, 295n50; backup vocals for, 112; comeback performances, 115; covers of Baker, 74; *Songs:* "Don't Be Cruel," 41; "Hound Dog," 10, 29, 33, 38–41; "Suspicious Minds," 115
Preston, Billy, 126
Prince, 237, 282
Prince's Trust Concert, 269, 273
Private Dancer (Turner), 240, 244, 265–68, 266f, 276
"Proud Mary" (Creedence Clearwater Revival), 257–58
"Proud Mary" (Turner), 257–59
publishers, 60–61, 82
punk rock, 16, 100, 222

Queens of Rhythm, 128

"race records," 9
radio, 10, 25, 89–90, 306n61; segregated, 61; Top 40 format, 87
Radio Recorders studio (Los Angeles), 36
Raelettes, 114, 118, 123, 246, 343n56
Rags magazine, 155f, 157, 159
Rainey, Ma, 22
Ramsey, Guthrie, 7
Randall, Annie, 21, 116, 117, 118
Ratledge, Michael, 162
Rauch, Doug, 220

Ray, Johnnie, 58, 64
RCA label, 110, 207
Ready, Steady, Go (pop music program), 187
Reagon, Toshi, 16, 27
Real Life (Hunt), 141, 160, 162–63, 172
Redding, Otis, 12
Reed, Lou, 129
Reeves, Shirley Alston (Owens), 76, 77, 78,
    80–81, 83f, 90, 91f, 94, 104; on Beatles, 97;
    on British Invasion, 98–99; as inspiration
    for other artists, 87, 97, 104; as lead singer,
    84–85; at Rock and Roll Hall of Fame
    induction ceremony, 101. *See also* Shirelles
Res (vocalist), 16
respectability politics, 21–22, 142, 186f; avoid-
    ance of sexuality as topic, 215; background
    vocalists and, 137–38; backlash against
    Labelle, 204; Shirelles and, 90–93, 91f
Retman, Sonnet, 9, 205, 271
Rhodes, Joe, 280, 282
Rhodes, Todd, 58
rhythm and blues, 11; adult topics, 59; aes-
    thetics of, 173; Big Beat, 10, 52, 74; subject
    matter, 269–70; as genre label, 9
Richards, Keith, 18, 97, 118–19, 139–40, 268,
    321n19; on black women in U.S., 145–46,
    147–48; on "Brown Sugar" lyrics, 150;
    Dash's work with, 211; *Main Offender,* 211;
    Talk Is Cheap, 211
Richie, Lionel, 219
Righteous Brothers, 139, 248
Riley, Clayton, 192, 209
"riots" at rock shows, 66
"River Deep, Mountain High" (Ike and Tina
    Turner Revue), 241, 248–52, 249f, 343n40
Robey, Don, 32, 36, 41, 43
Robins, Wayne, 260
Rock, Rock, Rock (film), 67–69
rock and roll: associated with violence and
    juvenile delinquency, 69; black artists and
    women pushed to margins, 55–56; as black
    cultural form, 10–11; blackness present in,
    26, 47–48; changing aesthetics, 12, 40, 47,

78–79, 96; erasure of black women from,
    12–13, 21, 27, 53, 67, 275–76; gospel music
    and, 108–11; guitar-centered style, 47–48,
    55–56, 79, 100, 287n15; as hybrid of rhythm
    and blues, country, blues, pop, and Latin
    music, 10; mainstream histories of, 2;
    moral panic response, 11; sexuality as part
    of ethos, 20–21; shift to "rock," 73; as slang
    term for sex, 20; teenagers, topics for, 59;
    as term, 10, 291n71; unstable definition of,
    55–56
Rock and Roll Hall of Fame, 53, 73, 310n137;
    Shirelles and, 99–102
"Rock Around The Clock" (Bill Haley and
    His Comets), 10, 55, 64
"Rocket 88" (Kings of Rhythm), 245, 275
Rockin' Out (Garofalo), 53
Rock: Music, Culture, and Business (Schloss,
    Starr, and Waterman), 53
rock musicals, 108–9
"rock mythologies," 15
Rock 'n' Roll Easter Jubilee, 1955, 55, 64
Rock 'N' Roll Jamboree, 53
Rock 'n' Roll Woman (Orloff), 177
Rolling Stone magazine, 12, 56, 152; Davis,
    reviews of, 233; Labelle, reviews and pro-
    files of, 191, 193–94, 197–200, 202–3, 206;
    Lennear, reviews and profiles of, 174, 175f,
    177; Turner, reviews and profiles of, 241,
    242f, 255, 263, 267, 275, 334n141
*Rolling Stone Illustrated History of Rock 'n'
    Roll,* 54, 275; on girl groups, 77–78
Rolling Stones, 6, 13; *25 × 5* (video retro-
    spective), 172; Atlantic Records and, 116;
    backup vocalists for, 118, 119; Ike and
    Tina Turner Revue and, 252; *Shine a Light*
    (documentary), 150; Shirelles' influence
    on, 97–98; tongue logo, 149; Turner as
    opening act for, 264–65; Turner's influ-
    ence on, 248, 259; *Songs and Albums:*
    "Brown Sugar," 17–19, 21, 23, 140, 141–81,
    290–91n59, 321n19; *Exile on Main Street,*
    120, 136; "Gimme Shelter," 119–20; "Honky

Rolling Stones (cont.)
    Tonk Women," 120, 164, 254–56; *Let It
    Bleed,* 120; "Some Girls," 150; "Star, Star,"
    152; *Steel Wheels,* 211; *Sticky Fingers,* 149;
    "Tell Me," 97; "Time Is on My Side," 118;
    "Tumbling Dice," 120; "You Can't Always
    Get What You Want," 120
Rolling Stones Records, 116, 149
Ronettes, 90, 93, 139–40; "Be My Baby," 87
Rose, Tricia, 235
Ross, Diana, 87, 187
Roxon, Lillian, 152
royalties, 82, 95; covers and, 61–64
Royster, Francesca, 14, 243, 261
Rufus, 234

Salem, James, 37, 43
"Salute to Freedom '63" fundraiser, 89
Samwell, Ian, 174
Sanctified Sisters, 121
Santana, Carlos, 220
Santogold (White), 1, 16
Santogold label, 1
Scepter Records, 76–77, 79, 82; built on
    Shirelles' fame, 94–95
Schiffman, Frank, 32
Schloss, Joseph, 53
scholarship on black women in rock, 237;
    Baker not given attention, 53–55; black
    feminist, 292n2; instrumentalists priori-
    tized, 3; practice theory approach, 290n54
Schon, Neal, 220
Scorsese, Martin, 150
Scott-Heron, Gil, 189
segregation, 6–7, 65; British bands and, 125;
    challenges to, 138; covers and, 62–63;
    cross-racial interactions and, 65–66, 75;
    marginalization of black artists as, 67;
    racial information withheld, 87–88. *See
    also* desegregation/integration
Selecter, 27, 170
Selvin, Joel, 48
Sex Pistols, 100

Sex Sells (Stiffed), 16, 20
sexuality, 5; black women and rock and
    roll, 19–22; expression of denied to black
    women, 21–22; hypersexuality attributed
    to black women, 21, 202, 204–5; in Labelle's
    lyrics, 216; likened to music, 203; as part
    of rock and roll ethos, 20–21; politics of in
    Davis's lyrics, 214–16; prostitution linked
    to black women, 204–5; racialized, 147;
    stereotypes of black women, 17–18, 140–41,
    143, 162–63, 322n39; transgressive/uncon-
    ventional, 30–31; Turner's performance of,
    241–43, 254–57, 275; white men's virility in
    relation to black women, 145–46
sexual violence: against enslaved women,
    18–19, 148, 322n27; rape, 18–19, 21
"Sha La La" (Shirelles), 98, 99
Shangri-Las, 78, 93
Shaw, Arnold, 40
She Bop (O'Brien), 54
Shemwell, Sylvia, 114
Sherman, Bobby, 24
She's a Rebel (Gaar), 54
Shindig! (television program), 112–14, 113f
Shine a Light (documentary about Rolling
    Stones), 150
Shirelles, 5, 65, 72, 74–75, 76–104, 279; acces-
    sibility of, 88–89; nightclubs, move toward,
    98; *Baby It's You!* (Broadway musical),
    76–78, 90, 94, 99, 104; covers of, 96–99,
    117; crossover sound, 83–88; early years,
    80–81; earnings, 86, 95; honoring, 99–104;
    marginalization of, 99; multiracial fan
    base, 77; onstage, 90–94; photographs of,
    83f, 91f; as pivotal group, 80; racial infor-
    mation about withheld, 87–88; racially
    ambiguous sound of, 84–85; shifts in
    rock and roll and, 103; *Songs and Albums:*
    "Baby, It's You," 86; *Baby It's You,* 98;
    "Boys," 97; "Dedicated to the One I Love,"
    82, 85, 86; "Don't Say Goodnight and Mean
    Goodbye," 95; "Foolish Little Girl," 95; "I
    Met Him on a Sunday," 81–82, 104; "I Saw

a Tear," 85; "Mama Said," 86, 96; "Putty in
Your Hands," 98; "Sha La La," 98, 99; "Sol-
dier Boy," 86–87, 90; "The Things I Want to
Hear," 97; *Tonight's the Night*, 88; "Tonight's
the Night," 84, 85, 90; "Will You Love Me
Tomorrow," 79, 83–86, 91f
Shirley, Jerry, 123, 125, 125f
Shirley and the Shirelles, 96
Sigma Sound studio, 126
silence, politics of, 22
Silk and Soul (Simone), 23–24
Simon, Paul, 126
Simone, Nina, 23–24, 117, 189, 211
"Sixteen Candles" (Crests), 82
Sky River Rock Festival, 1968, 46
Slash (Saul Hudson), 140
Sly and the Family Stone, 13, 220, 244; "I
Want to Take You Higher," 255, 259
Small Faces, 119, 123, 138, 248
Smalls, Tommy (Dr. Jive), 80
Smith, Arlene, 65, 331n68
Smith, Bessie, 22, 32, 44
Smith, Myrna, 114, 115
Soft Machine, 162
soft rock, 228–29
songwriters: background vocalists, uncred-
ited labor of, 130; Davis as, 216, 217–21;
Hendryx as, 190–91; Leiber and Stoller as,
5, 33, 36, 41, 48; supplanted by bands, 12;
Turner as, 262–63; valorization of, 3
soul music, 12–13
"Soul on Fire" (Baker), 59
Sounds magazine, 124, 133, 167, 209
Sounds of Motown (television special), 117
southern black circuit, 32
Spector, Phil, 78, 79, 87, 111, 139, 249f, 306n62;
Ike and Tina Turner Revue and, 248–52,
258, 343n40; "Phil Spector Fatigue," 251
Spector, Ronnie Bennett. See Bennett, Ve-
ronica "Ronnie" (Spector)
Spider, 266
Spin magazine, 281
Spitz, Marc, 148

Spivey, Victoria, 22, 127
Springfield, Dusty, 116–17, 314n64; "In the
Middle of Nowhere," 116–17; "Son of a
Preacher Man," 115
Springs, Helena, 128, 317n131
Springsteen, Bruce, 133
Stamp, Chris, 165–66
Staples, Mavis, 123, 127, 139
Staple Singers, 110, 127
Starr, Larry, 53
"Steppin in Her I. Miller Shoes" (Davis), 6,
158–60
Stewart, Ian, 18
Stewart, Rod, 248, 264–65, 268, 269
Stiffed, 16
St. John, Barry, 124
Stoller, Mike, 5, 33, 36, 41, 48, 115
Stone, Sly, 223, 259
Strachwitz, Chris, 31, 32, 36, 43, 46, 51
Stras, Laurie, 4, 15, 93, 102
Strike, Liza, 124
string sound, 83–84, 87
Sullivan, Ed, 39, 53, 90
Sullivan, Matt, 214, 224
Sultan, Juma, 152, 153, 156
Sun Records, 77, 116
Superbs, 173
Supreme Court, 66, 199
Supremes, 78, 79, 92, 187; on *Ed Sullivan
Show*, 90; on "golden oldies" circuit, 191;
Shirelles' influence on, 104; "Where Did
Our Love Go," 87
Sweet Inspirations, 41, 111, 114, 115
swing band musicians, women, 16
Sylvester, 220, 222
symbolic capital, 134, 269
Szwed, John, 219

*Takin' Back My Name: The Confessions of Ike
Turner* (Ike Turner), 243
Talking Heads, 131, 211
Talley, Nedra, 140
Tapestry (King), 104

"teen idols," 71

"Tell Him" (Exciters), 116

Tharpe, Sister Rosetta, 14–15, 108, 245, 279

"They Say She's Different: A Betty Davis Retrospective" (tribute show), 238

Thomas, Irma, 118

Thomas, Rufus, 38

Thompson, Kathleen, 18

Thornton, Willie Mae "Big Mama," 2, 5, 29–51, 273, 279, 295n50; analytical voice of, 30; blues revival and, 47; as bridge figure, 29–30; clothing worn onstage, 30, 33, 44, 279; death of, 36, 276–77; differences from standard rhythm and blues, 37; early life, 31–32, 293n5; expressive capacity, 33–35; gender presentation, 30, 32–33, 38, 40, 48, 293n3; gospel music, 35–36; humor of, 31, 42; instruments played by, 32, 36, 43; interviews, 29, 30, 31, 49–50; Joplin influenced by, 44–45; nonmusical reputation, 32–33; photograph of, 34f; presence and obscurity in story of, 29; Presley influenced by, 39–40; readings of as dangerous, 48–51; sonic space claimed by, 38; as taskmaster, 48; vocal power of, 30, 33, 45; *Songs:* "Ball and Chain," 29, 30, 33, 45–46; "Hound Dog," 2, 29, 36–42; "Yes, Baby" (with Ace), 42

Thunderbitch, 280–81

Thunder Thighs, 129

Tiara Records, 81–82

Tina Turner Museum (Flagg Grove School), 273–76, 277

Toast of the Town (television show), 39, 53

Tommy (The Who), 120, 123

Tonight's the Night (Shirelles), 88

"Tonight's the Night" (Shirelles), 84, 85, 90

Top 40 radio format, 87

Top of the Pops (television program), 164

Torry, Clare,124

touring: Jim Crow segregation and, 65–66; mentoring, 64–65; "rock and roll highway," 64–67; rock and roll package shows, 64, 89

Toussaint, Allen, 174, 175–76, 200, 328n198

Track Records, 164, 165–66, 187, 188

"Tra La La" (Baker), 59, 61, 67, 69

T. Rex, 126–27, 164, 195; *Dandy in the Underworld,* 127; *Zinc Alloy and the Hidden Riders of Tomorrow,* 127

Trouble Girls: The Rolling Stone Book of Women in Rock, 54

Troy, Doris, 120, 124, 131; *Doris Troy,* 135; "Just One Look," 117, 135

Tucker, Sherrie, 16

Turner, Big Joe, 40–41, 49

Turner, Ike, 128, 130, 243, 245–46, 249f, 252–53, 262, 275

Turner, Tina, 5, 6, 17, 54, 123, 240–72; audience for white rock and, 241–42; autobiography, 240, 243, 342n10; black academic response to, 242–43; covers of rock, 252–62; creative agency of, 262; early years, 244–46; financial pressures on, 263–64; influence of on white musicians, 248, 259–60; marketing strategy, 240–41; negotiating R&B and rock divide, 262–72; photographs of, 242f, 249f, 266f; as Queen of Rock and Roll, 2, 240, 275, 281; rock, link with, 240–41; sexist ageism in industry and, 265; sexuality portrayed on stage, 241–43, 254–57, 275; as songwriter, 262–63; sonic features, 247; as stadium rock star, 267; videos, 244; vocal style, 246–47; white male/black female collaboration, 135, 264–69; *Songs and Albums: Acid Queen,* 260; "Ball of Confusion" cover, 265; "Better Be Good to Me," 266, 266f; "Let's Stay Together," 265, 267; *Love Explosion,* 264; "Nutbush City Limits," 262, 276; *Private Dancer,* 240, 244, 265–68, 266f, 276; "Private Dancer," 267; "Proud Mary," 247, 257–59; "River Deep, Mountain High," 241, 248–52; *Rough,* 264; "Sexy Ida (Part 1)," 262; "Show Some Respect," 265; "Steel Claw," 266, 267; *Tina Turns the Country On,* 261; "We Don't Need Another Hero," 244, 268; "What's Love Got To Do with It,"

27, 243, 244, 265, 267–68. *See also* Ike and
    Tina Turner Revue
"Turning Point, The," (Simone), 24
"Tweedlee Dee" (Baker), 52, 59–60, 70, 245,
    302n121
Twenty Feet from Stardom (Neville), 105, 133,
    134, 180

uc-Berkeley, 161

Valentine, Penny, 167, 169–170, 209–10
Vandross, Luther, 126
Vanity 6, 237
Van Morrison, 115, 146, 321n14
Variety magazine, 42, 71, 178
Vaughan, Sarah, 53
Village Gate, 198
Village Voice, 264
Vincent, Rickey, 233
Visconti, Tony, 164, 165, 166–67
visual presentation: of Baker, 67–71, 68f, 71f;
    of Davis, 228; femininity and, 90–92, 91f;
    racial information withheld, 87–88; "safe,"
    69, 92; Shirelles, 90–94
Vogue magazine, 163
voice, 4–5, 287n16, 287n17

Wald, Elijah, 8, 102
Wald, Gayle, 14–15
Walker, Alice, 290n55, 295n50
"Walk on the Wild Side" (Reed), 129
"wall of sound," 24, 87, 250, 313n44
Wang, Oliver, 213
War, 13, 144, 232
Ware, Martyn, 265
Warhol, Andy, 149, 322n29
Warner Brothers, 173, 176, 194, 206–7
Warshavsky, Oren, 94–95
Warwick, Dee Dee, 114, 115
Warwick, Dionne, 94, 95, 114–15
Warwick, Jacqueline, 3–4, 8, 98, 107, 111, 131,
    307n83, 331n68
Washington, Dinah, 58, 110, 301n78

Waterman, Christopher, 53
Waterman, Dick, 48
Wenner, Jann, 97, 100
West African aesthetics, 9
West-Oram, Jamie, 266, 266f
West Tennessee Delta Heritage Center,
    274, 276
Wexler, Jerry, 114, 130, 335n168
What's Love Got to Do with It (biopic), 243
"What's Love Got to Do with It" (Turner),
    27, 243, 244, 265, 267–68
*What's That Sound? An Introduction to Rock
    and Its History* (Covach and Flory), 53
"Where Did Our Love Go" (Supremes), 87
White, Deborah Gray, 18
White, Santi, 1–2, 8, 16, 20, 282, 285n1
White Trash, 167
*Who Shot Rock & Roll: A Photographic His-
    tory, 1955 to the Present*, 275
Who, the, 120, 123, 161, 165, 167, 259; Labelle
    concerts with, 183, 205, 206
Wickham, Vicki, 183–84, 187–88, 200, 205–6,
    330n39
Williams, Carlena, 124
Williams, Delores. *See* Baker, LaVern
Williams, Winona, 217
Willie Mae Rock Camp for Girls, 277
Willis, Ellen, 45
Wills, Viola, 121
"Will You Love Me Tomorrow" (Shirelles),
    79, 83–86, 91f
Wilson, Devon, 5, 6, 151–60, 165, 217; death
    of, 159–60; flagrant violations of feminine
    behavior, 157–60; Hendrix and, 153–56;
    Jagger and, 141, 155f, 156–57
Wilson, Ida Mae. *See* Wilson, Devon
Wilson, Jackie, 72
Wilson, Mary, 104
wins radio, 89–90
With a Little Help from My Friends (Cocker),
    121
Witherspoon, Jimmy, 276
Wolcott, James, 193

Woman Child (Hunt), 167–70

Wonder, Stevie, 13, 25, 188, 189, 190, 205

Woodstock festival, 12, 46

Wright, Billy, 32

Wright, Edna, 121

Wyman, Bill, 150

Yaffe, David, 127–28

Yardbirds, 98, 266

Your Arms Too Short to Box with God (musical), 211

"You've Lost That Loving Feeling" (Righteous Brothers), 248